STUDY GUIDE / SOLUTIONS MANUAL
to accompany
General
Chemistry

CAROLE H. McQUARRIE

DONALD A. McQUARRIE
University of California, Davis

PETER A. ROCK
University of California, Davis

W. H. FREEMAN AND COMPANY
New York

ISBN 0-1573-2

Printed in the United States of America

2 3 4 5 6 7 8 9 0   SL   2 1 0 8 9 8 7 6 5 4

Table of Atomic Masses *

	Symbol	Atomic Number	Atomic Mass
Actinium	Ac	89	(227)†
Aluminum	Al	13	26.98
Americium	Am	95	(243)
Antimony	Sb	51	121.8
Argon	Ar	18	39.95
Arsenic	As	33	74.92
Astatine	At	85	(210)
Barium	Ba	56	137.3
Berkelium	Bk	97	(247)
Beryllium	Be	4	9.012
Bismuth	Bi	83	209.0
Boron	B	5	10.81
Bromine	Br	35	79.90
Cadmium	Cd	48	112.4
Calcium	Ca	20	40.08
Californium	Cf	98	(251)
Carbon	C	6	12.01
Cerium	Ce	58	140.1
Cesium	Cs	55	132.9
Chlorine	Cl	17	35.45
Chromium	Cr	24	52.00
Cobalt	Co	27	58.93
Copper	Cu	29	63.55
Curium	Cm	96	(247)
Dysprosium	Dy	66	162.5
Einsteinium	Es	99	(252)
Erbium	Er	68	167.3
Europium	Eu	63	152.0
Fermium	Fm	100	(257)
Fluorine	F	9	19.00
Francium	Fr	87	(223)
Gadolinium	Gd	64	157.3
Gallium	Ga	31	69.72
Germanium	Ge	32	72.59
Gold	Au	79	197.0
Hafnium	Hf	72	178.5
Helium	He	2	4.003
Holmium	Ho	67	164.9
Hydrogen	H	1	1.008
Indium	In	49	114.8
Iodine	I	53	126.9
Iridium	Ir	77	192.2
Iron	Fe	26	55.85
Krypton	Kr	36	83.80
Lanthanum	La	57	138.9
Lawrencium	Lr	103	(260)
Lead	Pb	82	207.2
Lithium	Li	3	6.941
Lutetium	Lu	71	175.0
Magnesium	Mg	12	24.31
Manganese	Mn	25	54.94
Mendelevium	Md	101	(258)
Mercury	Hg	80	200.6
Molybdenum	Mo	42	95.94
Neodymium	Nd	60	144.2
Neon	Ne	10	20.18
Neptunium	Np	93	(237)
Nickel	Ni	28	58.70
Niobium	Nb	41	92.91
Nitrogen	N	7	14.01
Nobelium	No	102	(259)
Osmium	Os	76	190.2
Oxygen	O	8	16.00
Palladium	Pd	46	106.4
Phosphorus	P	15	30.97
Platinum	Pt	78	195.1
Plutonium	Pu	94	(244)
Polonium	Po	84	(209)
Potassium	K	19	39.10
Praseodymium	Pr	59	140.9
Promethium	Pm	61	(145)
Protactinium	Pa	91	(231)
Radium	Ra	88	226.0
Radon	Rn	86	(222)
Rhenium	Re	75	186.2
Rhodium	Rh	45	102.9
Rubidium	Rb	37	85.47
Ruthenium	Ru	44	101.1
Samarium	Sm	62	150.4
Scandium	Sc	21	44.96
Selenium	Se	34	78.96
Silicon	Si	14	28.09
Silver	Ag	47	107.9
Sodium	Na	11	22.99
Strontium	Sr	38	87.62
Sulfur	S	16	32.06
Tantalum	Ta	73	180.9
Technetium	Tc	43	(98)
Tellurium	Te	52	127.6
Terbium	Tb	65	158.9
Thallium	Tl	81	204.4
Thorium	Th	90	232.0
Thulium	Tm	69	168.9
Tin	Sn	50	118.7
Titanium	Ti	22	47.90
Tungsten	W	74	183.9
Uranium	U	92	238.0
Vanadium	V	23	50.94
Xenon	Xe	54	131.3
Ytterbium	Yb	70	173.0
Yttrium	Y	39	88.91
Zinc	Zn	30	65.38
Zirconium	Zr	40	91.22

*The values given here are to four significant figures. A table of more accurate atomic masses is given in Appendix F of the text.

†A value given in parentheses denotes the mass of the longest-lived isotope.

STUDY GUIDE / SOLUTIONS MANUAL
to accompany

General
Chemistry

Contents

Acknowledgments

We would like to thank Dr. Joseph Ledbetter for checking the answers and solutions to all the problems and for reading the entire manuscript. His contribution far exceeds any recognition that we can give him here. We would also like to thank Heather Wiley of W. H. Freeman and Company for overseeing the production of this Manual in a most professional way and Elaine Rock for the excellent typing of the manuscript.

To the Student

This Study Guide/Solutions Manual accompanies the text *General Chemistry,* by Donald A. McQuarrie and Peter A. Rock. For each chapter in the text, this Manual has sections entitled

- **A** Outline of the Chapter
- **B** Self-Test
- **C** Calculations You Should Know How to Do
- **D** Solutions to the Odd-Numbered Problems
- **E** Answers to the Even-Numbered Problems
- **F** Answers to the Self-Test

There is also a Glossary that is cross-referenced to the text.

The Outline (Section A) of each chapter lists the headings for each section of the text, together with a few concise sentences that describe the key contents of each section.

The Self-Test (Section B) consists of about 40 short questions such as true/false or fill-in-the-blank questions. The Self-Test questions will give you a good indication of your understanding of the material in each chapter of the text, and we recommend that you answer these questions before you go on to do the numerical problems. The Answers to the Self-Test questions are given in Section F.

Section C, Calculations You Should Know How to Do, outlines each type of calculation that is presented in the chapter. It tells you what calculations you are expected to be able to do and keys these calculations to the worked Examples in the chapter and to the Problems at the end of the chapter. If you understand each type of calculation outlined in this section, then you are ready to go on to the Problems.

Occasionally, Section C also contains a detailed review of mathematical topics that appear in the chapter. For example, Chapter 1 requires a knowledge of exponents and writing numbers in scientific notation. Consequently, we treat these topics in this manual and include a number of worked examples and practice Exercises (with Answers). Other mathematical topics that are discussed are the equation of a straight line and its use to plot data (Chapter 5), the quadratic equation (Chapter 15), logarithms (Chapter 16), and logarithms and antilogarithms (Chapter 17).

We feel that Section D, Solutions to the Odd-Numbered Problems, is an especially valuable part of this manual. Most general chemistry courses tend to emphasize numerical problems, and so we have included detailed solutions to all the odd-numbered problems. There is definitely a correct way and an incorrect way to use these problem solutions. When you are assigned a specific odd-numbered problem, you should do that problem first and compare your answer with the answer given in Appendix G of the text. If you are unable to get the correct answer, then you should refer to the detailed solution presented here in order to *understand* how to do the problem. Once you truly understand how to do the problem, you should do the following even-numbered problem and check your answer with the answer given in Section E of this manual. Note that the problems in the text have been arranged such that every odd-numbered problem and the even-numbered problem next to it constitute a pair of similar problems. Furthermore, the problems in the text have been grouped and labeled according to topic, and so if you have difficulty with a particular topic, you should work on additional problems, using this manual as an aid. It is of little or no value for you to refer to the solutions given here before you make an honest, thoughtful attempt to do the problems yourself. Only by using the solutions as an aid to your understanding of how to do the problems will the solutions be of real value.

The final two sections of each chapter (Sections E and F) list the answers to the Even-Numbered Problems in the text and the Answers to the Self-Test in the manual. Between the text and this manual, you have the answers to all the problems in the text and the detailed solutions to the odd-numbered problems.

CAROLE H. McQUARRIE
DONALD A. McQUARRIE
PETER A. ROCK

June 1984

1 / Atoms and Molecules

A   OUTLINE OF CHAPTER 1

1-1   Why should you study chemistry?

1-2   Elements are the simplest substances.

An element is a substance that consists of identical atoms.

A compound is a substance that can be broken down into simpler substances.

1-3   About three fourths of the elements are metals.

The elements are classified into metals and nonmetals.

Chemical symbols of some common metals and nonmetals are given in Tables 1-3 through 1-5.

Some nonmetals exist as diatomic molecules (Figure 1-1).

1-4   Antoine Lavoisier was the founder of modern chemistry.

A quantitative measurement is one in which the result is expressed as a number.

A qualitative observation is a notation of a particular characteristic such as color or taste.

The law of conservation of mass: In an ordinary chemical reaction, the total mass of the reacting substances is equal to the total mass of the products formed.

1-5   The relative amount of each element in a compound is always the same.

The law of constant composition is based on the chemical analysis of compounds.

The mass percentage composition of a compound can be calculated from the chemical analysis of the compound (Example 1-1).

1-6   Dalton's atomic theory explains the law of constant composition.

The postulates of Dalton's atomic theory are given on page 7 of the text.

Atoms are the small, indivisible particles of which matter is composed.

A molecule is the particle that results when two or more atoms are joined together.

Atomic mass is the mass of one atom relative to that of another atom.

Atomic mass unit (amu) is a unit assigned to atomic masses.

1-7 Molecules are groups of atoms joined together.

A molecular picture of chemical reactions is introduced.

1-8 The assignment of names to compounds is called chemical nomenclature.

If a compound is composed of a metal and a nonmetal, the metal is named first and then the nonmetal with the ending changed to -ide (Table 1-6).

Subscripts in a chemical formula of a compound indicate the number of each kind of atom in the compound.

If a compound is composed of two nonmetals, then the number of each element is indicated in the name by Greek prefixes (Table 1-7).

1-9 Molecular mass is the sum of the masses of the atoms in a molecule.

The molecular masses of compounds can be calculated from the chemical formulas.

Mass percentage compositions are calculated using atomic masses and molecular masses (Example 1-4).

1-10 The law of multiple proportions is explained by the atomic theory.

If two elements combine in more than one way, then the mass of one element that combines with a fixed mass of the other element will always be in the ratio of small, whole numbers.

Calculations illustrating the law of multiple proportions are presented (Example 1-5).

1-11 The discovery of subatomic particles changed our view of the atom.

The electron was discovered in 1897 by Joseph J. Thomson.

The electron is a negatively charged particle with a mass $\frac{1}{1837}$ that of a hydrogen atom.

The proton was discovered in the early 1900's by Ernest Rutherford.

The proton is a positively charged particle with a mass almost the same as the mass of the hydrogen atom.

1-12 Most of the mass of an atom is concentrated in the nucleus.

Radioactivity is the process in which certain nuclei spontaneously break apart.

Alpha particles, β-particles and γ-rays are products of radioactive disintegrations (Table 1-8).

The nucleus was discovered by Rutherford from the scattering of α-particles by a thin gold foil (Figure 1-7).

1-13 Atoms consist of protons, neutrons, and electrons.

The neutron was postulated to account for the mass of a nucleus and was discovered by James Chadwick in 1932.

The neutron is an uncharged particle with essentially the same mass as the proton.

Atomic number is the number of protons in an atom and is denoted by Z.

Mass number is the total number of protons and neutrons in an atom and is denoted by A.

1-14 Isotopes contain the same number of protons but different numbers of neutrons.

An isotope is denoted by $_Z^A X$.

The natural abundance of isotopes of an element can be measured (Table 1-9).

Calculations involving isotopic abundances and the atomic mass of an element are illustrated.

1-15 Isotopes can be separated by a mass spectrometer.

Ions are atoms that have either more or less electrons than the neutral atom.

1-16 There are uncertainties associated with measured quantities.

The accuracy of measured quantities is indicated by the number of significant figures used to express the result.

1-17 Calculated numbers should show the correct number of significant figures.

The result of multiplication and division can be no more accurate than the quantity with the fewest significant figures.

The result of addition and subtraction can be expressed to no more digits after the decimal point than the quantity with the fewest digits after the decimal point.

1-18 The value of a physical quantity depends on the units.

A physical quantity is converted from one unit to another by using a unit conversion factor.

Many physical quantities are expressed in compound units.

B   SELF-TEST

1   An element is a substance that consists of only one kind of _____.

2   A pure substance that can be decomposed into simpler substances is called a _____.

3   Three properties of a metal are (a) _____, (b) _____, and (c) _____.

4   Most metals are solids at room temperature. *True/False*

5   Nonmetals are usually good conductors of electricity. *True/False*

6   Give the chemical symbol for the following metals: aluminum ____, calcium ____, potassium ____, and zinc ____.

7 Name the elements whose symbol are Ba _____, Cu _____, Fe _____, and Na _____.

8 All nonmetals are gases at room temperature. *True/False*

9 Two examples of elements that exist as diatomic molecules are _____ and _____.

10 A quantitative measurement is one in which the result is expressed as _____.

11 Explain how a qualitative result and a quantitative result differ.

12 In an ordinary chemical reaction, the total mass of the reacting substances is equal to _____.

13 The mass percentage of each element in a compound depends on how the compound is prepared. *True/False*

14 The law of constant composition states that the mass percentages of each element in a compound are equal. *True/False*

15 Chemical analysis of a compound is a determination of the _____ _____.

16 State in your own words the postulates of Dalton's atomic theory.
(a)

(b)

(c)

(d)

(e)

17 Explain the meaning of the scale of atomic masses.

18 The unit of the atomic mass scale is called _____.

19 The atomic mass of an element is the mass in grams of one atom of the element. *True/False*

20 Explain the law of constant composition in terms of Dalton's atomic theory.

21 In a chemical reaction, the atoms of the reacting compounds are _____ to form the products.

22 The rule for naming binary compounds composed of a metal and a nonmetal is
(a)

(b)

23 The name of the compound CaS is _____.

24 The name of the compound CO_2 is _____.

25 The molecular mass of a compound is the _____
_____.

26 Explain the law of multiple proportions in terms of Dalton's atomic theory.

27   A beam of electrons passing between a voltage applied across electrodes will be deflected toward the _____ charged electrode.

28   A beam of protons passing between the same voltage as in Question 27 will be deflected in the same direction as the beam of electrons. *True/False*

29   A beam of protons passing between a voltage will be deflected to the (*same, greater, lesser*) extent than a beam of electrons.

30   Compare the relative charges and masses of a proton, a neutron, and an electron.

31   A neutron has the same mass as an electron. *True/False*

32   Explain why some α-particles will be deflected through large angles when a beam of α-particles is directed at a thin gold foil.

33   Compare the mass of an atom to the mass of its nucleus.

34   The atomic number of an atom indicates the number of neutrons in the atom. *True/False*

35   An element can be identified by its mass number. *True/False*

36   All isotopes of an element have the same atomic number. *True/False*

37   Isotopes of an element contain the same number of _____ but different numbers of _____.

38   The notation for one isotope of oxygen is $^{16}_{8}O$. The superscript designates the _____ of the isotope and the subscript designates the _____.

39   The isotopes chlorine-35 and chlorine-37 differ by _____.

40   Deuterium is a naturally occurring isotope of which element?

_____.

41   Why does naturally occurring chlorine have an atomic mass that is not close to a whole number?

_____.

42   Isotopes of an element can be separated in a mass spectrometer on the basis of their differences in (*mass, charge, chemical behavior*).

43 A positively charged ion is an atom that has _____.

44 A negatively charged ion is an atom that has _____.

45 The result of a measurement expressed as 251.43 g may have an uncertainty in the digit _____ .

46 All the digits in 251.43 g are significant figures. *True/False*

47 The zeros in the result 0.0289 m are significant figures. *True/False*

48 The result of the calculation 8.436 × 2.09 should be expressed to _____ significant figures.

49 The result of the calculation 8.436 + 2.09 should be expressed to _____ digits after the decimal point.

50 The statement that the mass of a substance is 0.0289 is meaningless. *True/False*

51 A physical quantity is converted from one unit to another by the use of a _____ .

52 The preferred system of units in scientific work are the _____ units, which are part of the _____ system.

C CALCULATIONS YOU SHOULD KNOW HOW TO DO

1 Use the results of a quantitative chemical analysis to calculate the mass percentage of each element in a compound. See Example 1-1 and Problems 1-5 through 1-10.

2 Use a table of atomic masses to calculate the molecular mass of a compound. See page 13 and Problems 1-17 through 1-20.

3 Use a table of atomic masses to calculate the mass percentage of each element in a compound. See Example 1-4 and Problems 1-21 through 1-28.

4 Use mass percentages of elements in compounds to illustrate the law of multiple proportions. See Example 1-5 and Problems 1-29 through 1-34.

5 Calculate the observed atomic mass of an element, given the masses of its isotopes and their percent abundances. See Example 1-8 and Problems 1-43 through 1-52.

6 Use unit conversion factors to convert a quantity from one unit to another. See Example 1-12 and Problems 1-69 through 1-74.

Scientific Notation and Calculations Using Exponents
The numbers encountered in chemistry are often extremely large (such as Avogadro's number) or extremely small (such as the mass of an electron in kilograms). To work with such numbers it is convenient to express them in scientific notation, whereby the number is written as a number between one and ten multiplied by 10 raised to the appropriate power. For example, the number 2831 is 2.831×1000, which is written 2.831×10^3 in scientific notation. Some other

examples are

$$42500 = 4.25 \times 10^4$$

$$293100 = 2.931 \times 10^5$$

The zeros in these numbers are not regarded as significant figures and are dropped. Notice that in each case the power of 10 is the number of places that the decimal point is moved to the left.

$$4\,2500 \qquad 2\,93100$$

4 places   5 places

When numbers less than one are expressed in scientific notation, 10 is raised to a negative power. For example, 0.529 becomes 5.29×10^{-1}. Recall that a negative exponent is governed by the relation

$$10^{-n} = \frac{1}{10^n}$$

Some other examples are

$$0.006 = 6 \times 10^{-3}$$

$$0.000000742 = 7.42 \times 10^{-7}$$

Notice that the power of 10 in each case is the number of places that the decimal point is moved to the right.

$$0.006 \qquad 0.000000742$$

3 places   7 places

Example 1 Express the following numbers in scientific notation.
(a) 0.000126   (b) 7380000000

Solution (a) We move the decimal point four places to the right to obtain 1.26×10^{-4}.

(b) We move the decimal point nine places to the left to obtain 7.38×10^9. Note that we do not retain the zeros following 8 because they are not significant figures.

It is necessary to be able to work with numbers in scientific notation. To add or subtract two or more numbers expressed in scientific notation, the power of 10 must be the same in each number. For example, consider the sum

$$1.711 \times 10^3 + 9.056 \times 10^2$$

We rewrite the first number to the power of 10^2:

$$1.711 \times 10^3 = 17.11 \times 10^2$$

Note that in having changed the 10^3 factor to 10^2, we have made the factor in front of 10^2 one power of 10 larger. Thus we have

$$1.711 \times 10^3 + 9.056 \times 10^2 = (17.11 + 9.056) \times 10^2$$
$$= 26.17 \times 10^2$$
$$= 2.617 \times 10^3$$

Similarly, we have

$$(6.287 \times 10^{-6}) - (1.562 \times 10^{-7}) = (6.287 - 0.1562) \times 10^{-6} = 6.131 \times 10^{-6}$$

When multiplying two numbers, we add the powers of 10 because of the relation

$$(10^x)(10^y) = 10^{x+y}$$

For example,

$$(2.00 \times 10^7)(6.00 \times 10^3) = (2.00)(6.00) \times 10^{10}$$
$$= 12.0 \times 10^{10}$$
$$= 1.20 \times 10^{11}$$

and

$$(5.014 \times 10^4)(7.143 \times 10^{-6}) = (5.014)(7.143) \times 10^{-2}$$
$$= 35.82 \times 10^{-2}$$
$$= 3.582 \times 10^{-1}$$

To divide, we subtract the power of 10 of the number in the denominator from the power of 10 of the number in the numerator because of the relation

$$\frac{10^x}{10^y} = 10^{x-y}$$

For example,

$$\frac{3.0 \times 10^{10}}{6.0 \times 10^{23}} = \left(\frac{3.0}{6.0}\right) \times 10^{10-23}$$
$$= 0.50 \times 10^{-13}$$
$$= 5.0 \times 10^{-14}$$

and

$$\frac{3.56 \times 10^{-6}}{8.73 \times 10^{-12}} = \left(\frac{3.56}{8.73}\right) \times 10^{-6+12}$$
$$= 0.408 \times 10^6$$
$$= 4.08 \times 10^5$$

Example 2 Evaluate

$$x = \frac{(3.076 \times 10^{-4})(1.38 \times 10^{12})}{(6.67 \times 10^{-32})(7.110 \times 10^{21})}.$$

Solution We rewrite x as

$$x = \frac{(3.076)(1.38)}{(6.67)(7.110)} \times 10^{-4+12+32-21}$$
$$= 0.0895 \times 10^{19}$$
$$= 8.95 \times 10^{17}$$

Note that we express our answer to three significant figures.

To raise a number to a power, we use the relation

$$(10^x)^n = 10^{nx}$$

For example,

$$(3.141 \times 10^4)^3 = (3.141)^3 \times 10^{12}$$
$$= 30.99 \times 10^{12}$$
$$= 3.099 \times 10^{13}$$

To take a root of a number, we use the relation

$$\sqrt[n]{10^x} = (10^x)^{1/n} = 10^{x/n}$$

Thus the power of 10 must be written so that it is divisible by the root. For example, the cube root of 6.40×10^7 is

$$\sqrt[3]{6.40 \times 10^7} = (6.40 \times 10^7)^{1/3} = (64.0 \times 10^6)^{1/3}$$
$$= (64.0)^{1/3} \times 10^2 = 4.00 \times 10^2$$

$$\sqrt{4.60 \times 10^5} = (4.60 \times 10^5)^{1/2} = (46.0 \times 10^4)^{1/2}$$
$$= (46.0)^{1/2} \times 10^2 = 6.78 \times 10^2$$

Example 3 Evaluate

$$x = \left(\frac{4.16 \times 10^{-3}}{9.723 \times 10^{12}} \right)^{1/3}$$

Solution

$$x = \left(\frac{4.16}{9.723} \times 10^{-15} \right)^{1/3} = (0.428 \times 10^{-15})^{1/3}$$

$$= (428 \times 10^{-18})^{1/3}$$

$$= (428)^{1/3} \times 10^{-6}$$

$$= 7.54 \times 10^{-6}$$

You should realize that you can carry out all these calculations directly on your hand calculator. You can enter numbers in exponential notation, multiply and divide them, take roots and powers, and so on. It is well worth the effort to learn how to do this on your own hand calculator. Use your calculator to do the following exercises.

Exercises

Evaluate

1 $(4.164 \times 10^{-16})(9.275 \times 10^{12})$

2 $\dfrac{1.00 \times 10^4}{7.25 \times 10^8}$

3 $(6.176 \times 10^7)^{1/2}$

4 $(5.60 \times 10^{-3})^5$

5 $\dfrac{(2.14 \times 10^6)(7.813 \times 10^{-12})}{(8.89 \times 10^{16})}$

6 $\dfrac{(0.0929)(1728)}{(6.626 \times 10^{14})}$

7 $\left[\dfrac{(4.49 \times 10^5)(7.071 \times 10^{29})}{(1.019 \times 10^{-6})(6.88 \times 10^8)} \right]^{1/4}$

8 $\left[\dfrac{(5.716 \times 10^{-6})(4.28)}{(14.67 \times 10^2)} \right]^{1/3}$

Answers

1 3.862×10^{-3}

2 1.38×10^{-5}

3 7.859×10^3

4 5.51×10^{-12}

5 1.88×10^{-22}

6 2.42×10^{-13}

7 1.46×10^8

8 2.55×10^{-3}

D   SOLUTIONS TO THE ODD-NUMBERED PROBLEMS

1-1   (a) Cd   (f) Xe
      (b) In   (g) Cu
      (c) Pb   (h) K
      (d) Sn   (i) U
      (e) Hg   (j) P

See the alphabetical list of the elements in the inside front cover.

1-3   (a) selenium   (f) hydrogen
      (b) gold   (g) silicon
      (c) silver   (h) vanadium
      (d) palladium   (i) plutonium
      (e) lithium   (j) helium

See the alphabetical list of the elements in the inside front cover.

1-5   The mass percentage of potassium is given by

$$\text{mass \% of K} = \frac{\text{mass of K}}{\text{mass of compound}} \times 100 = \frac{0.229\,\text{g}}{0.436\,\text{g}} \times 100 = 52.5\%$$

The mass percentage of chlorine is given by

$$\text{mass \% of Cl} = \frac{\text{mass of Cl}}{\text{mass of compound}} \times 100 = \frac{0.207\,\text{g}}{0.436\,\text{g}} \times 100 = 47.5\%$$

1-7   The mass percentage of calcium in the sample of calcium oxide is

$$\text{mass \% of Ca} = \frac{\text{mass of Ca}}{\text{mass of CaO}} \times 100 = \frac{1.28\,\text{g}}{1.79\,\text{g}} \times 100 = 71.5\%$$

The mass of oxygen in the sample of calcium oxide is

$$\text{mass of O} = \text{mass of CaO} - \text{mass of Ca}$$
$$= 1.79\,\text{g} - 1.28\,\text{g} = 0.51\,\text{g}$$

The mass percentage of oxygen in the sample of calcium oxide is

$$\text{mass \% of O} = \frac{\text{mass of O}}{\text{mass of CaO}} \times 100 = \frac{0.51\,\text{g}}{1.79\,\text{g}} \times 100 = 28\%$$

Note that the mass percentage of O is expressed as two significant figures because the mass of O is known to only two significant figures.

1-9   The respective mass percentages are

$$\text{mass \% of K} = \frac{\text{mass of K}}{\text{mass of KCN}} \times 100 = \frac{7.58\,\text{mg}}{12.63\,\text{mg}} \times 100 = 60.0\%$$

$$\text{mass \% of C} = \frac{\text{mass of C}}{\text{mass of KCN}} \times 100 = \frac{2.33 \text{ mg}}{12.63 \text{ mg}} \times 100 = 18.4\%$$

$$\text{mass \% of N} = \frac{\text{mass of N}}{\text{mass of KCN}} \times 100 = \frac{2.72 \text{ mg}}{12.63 \text{ mg}} \times 100 = 21.5\%$$

Note that the mass percentage of O is expressed as two significant figures because the mass of O is known to only two significant figures.

Using Table 1-6 and the list of the elements in the inside front cover, we have

1-11   (a) lithium chloride   (d) sodium phosphide
        (b) magnesium oxide   (e) potassium iodide
        (c) aluminum fluoride

1-13   (a) calcium carbide   (d) potassium oxide
        (b) gallium arsenide   (e) strontium fluoride
        (c) beryllium nitride

1-15   (a) iodine trifluoride and iodine pentafluoride
        (b) iodine monochloride and iodine trichloride
        (c) nitrogen dioxide and dinitrogen tetraoxide
        (d) arsenic trifluoride and arsenic pentafluoride
        (e) chlorine monoxide and chlorine dioxide

1-17   Refer to the inside front cover for the atomic masses.

(a) The molecular mass of CH_4 is

$$\text{molecular mass} = (\text{atomic mass of C}) + (4 \times \text{atomic mass of H})$$
$$= (12.01) + (4 \times 1.008)$$
$$= 16.04$$

(b) The molecular mass of C_3H_8 is

$$\text{molecular mass} = (3 \times \text{atomic mass of C}) + (8 \times \text{atomic mass of H})$$
$$= (3 \times 12.01) + (8 \times 1.008)$$
$$= 44.09$$

(c) The molecular mass of C_4H_{10} is

$$\text{molecular mass} = (4 \times \text{atomic mass of C}) + (10 \times \text{atomic mass of H})$$
$$= (4 \times 12.01) + (10 \times 1.008)$$
$$= 58.12$$

(d) The molecular mass of C_8H_{18} is

$$\text{molecular mass} = (8 \times \text{atomic mass of C}) + (18 \times \text{atomic mass of H})$$
$$= (8 \times 12.01) + (18 \times 1.008)$$
$$= 114.22$$

1-19   (a)   molecular mass of $CaWO_4$ = (atomic mass of Ca) + (atomic mass of W)

$$+ (4 \times \text{atomic mass of O})$$
$$= (40.08) + (183.9) + (4 \times 16.00)$$
$$= 288.0$$

(b)   molecular mass of Fe_3O_4 = $(3 \times \text{atomic mass of Fe})$

$$+ (4 \times \text{atomic mass of O})$$
$$= (3 \times 55.85) + (4 \times 16.00)$$
$$= 231.55$$

(c)   molecular mass of Na_3AlF_6 = $(3 \times \text{atomic mass of Na})$ + (atomic mass of Al)

$$+ (6 \times \text{atomic mass of F})$$
$$= (3 \times 22.99) + (26.98) + (6 \times 19.00)$$
$$= 209.95$$

(d)   molecular mass of $Be_3Al_2Si_6O_{18}$ = $(3 \times \text{atomic mass of Be}) +$

$$(2 \times \text{atomic mass of Al})$$
$$+ (6 \times \text{atomic mass of Si})$$
$$+ (18 \times \text{atomic mass of O})$$
$$= (3 \times 9.012) + (2 \times 26.98) + (6 \times 28.09)$$
$$+ (18 \times 16.00)$$
$$= 537.54$$

(e)   molecular mass of Zn_2SiO_4 = $(2 \times \text{atomic mass of Zn})$ + (atomic mass of Si)

$$+ (4 \times \text{atomic mass of O})$$
$$= (2 \times 65.38) + (28.09) + (4 \times 16.00)$$
$$= 222.85$$

1-21   formula mass of ZnS = 65.38 + 32.06 = 97.44

$$\text{mass \% of Zn} = \frac{\text{atomic mass of Zn}}{\text{formula mass of ZnS}} \times 100 = \frac{65.38}{97.44} \times 100 = 67.10\%$$

$$\text{mass \% of S} = \frac{\text{atomic mass of S}}{\text{formula mass of ZnS}} \times 100 = \frac{32.06}{97.44} \times 100 = 32.90\%$$

1-23   molecular mass of CH_4 = (12.01) + (4×1.008) = 16.04

$$\text{mass \% of C} = \frac{\text{atomic mass of C}}{\text{molecular mass of CH}_4} \times 100 = \frac{12.01}{16.04} \times 100 = 74.88\%$$

$$\text{mass \% of H} = \frac{4 \times \text{atomic mass of H}}{\text{molecular mass of CH}_4} \times 100 = \frac{4.032}{16.04} \times 100 = 25.14\%$$

1-25   molecular mass of $C_{12}H_{22}O_{11}$ = 342.30

$$\text{mass \% of C} = \frac{12 \times \text{atomic mass of C}}{\text{molecular mass of } C_{12}H_{22}O_{11}} \times 100$$

$$= \frac{12 \times 12.01}{342.30} \times 100 = 42.10\%$$

$$\text{mass \% of H} = \frac{22 \times \text{atomic mass of H}}{\text{molecular mass of } C_{12}H_{22}O_{11}} \times 100$$

$$= \frac{22 \times 1.008}{342.30} \times 100 = 6.479\%$$

$$\text{mass \% of O} = \frac{11 \times \text{atomic mass of O}}{\text{molecular mass of } C_{12}H_{22}O_{11}} \times 100$$

$$= \frac{11 \times 16.00}{342.30} \times 100 = 51.42\%$$

1-27   (a) mass % of N in N_2O_3 = $\dfrac{2 \times 14.01}{(2 \times 14.01) + (3 \times 16.00)} \times 100 = 36.86\%$

   (b) mass % of N in HNO_3 = $\dfrac{14.01}{(1.008) + (14.01) + (3 \times 16.00)} \times 100 = 22.23\%$

   (c) mass % of N in NH_3 = $\dfrac{14.01}{(14.01) + (3 \times 1.008)} \times 100 = 82.27\%$

   (d) mass % of N in NH_4Cl = $\dfrac{14.01}{(14.01) + (4 \times 1.008) + (35.45)} \times 100 = 26.19\%$

   (e) mass % of N in PbN_6 = $\dfrac{6 \times 14.01}{(207.2) + (6 \times 14.01)} \times 100 = 28.86\%$

Ammonia (NH_3) has the highest mass percentage of nitrogen.

1-29   When working with mass percentages, it is convenient to take a 100-gram sample. For compound I,

$$\frac{\text{mass of F}}{\text{mass of Xe}} = \frac{22.44 \text{ g F}}{77.56 \text{ g Xe}} = \frac{0.2893 \text{ g F}}{1.000 \text{ g Xe}}$$

For compound II,

$$\frac{\text{mass of F}}{\text{mass of Xe}} = \frac{36.66 \text{ g F}}{63.34 \text{ g Xe}} = \frac{0.5788 \text{ g F}}{1.000 \text{ g Xe}}$$

The ratio of the mass of F per gram of Xe in compound II to compound I is

$$\text{ratio} = \frac{(0.5788 \text{ g F}/1.000 \text{ g Xe})}{(0.2893 \text{ g F}/1.000 \text{ g Xe})} = 2.001 = 2$$

which is a small, whole number. Compound II has twice as many fluorine atoms per xenon atom as does compound I. The two compounds are XeF_2 and XeF_4.

1-31   Using a 100 g sample, we can write

$$\text{compound I:} \quad \frac{\text{mass of H}}{\text{mass of O}} = \frac{11.2 \text{ g H}}{88.8 \text{ g O}} = \frac{0.126 \text{ g H}}{1.000 \text{ g O}}$$

$$\text{compound II:} \quad \frac{\text{mass of H}}{\text{mass of O}} = \frac{5.94 \text{ g H}}{94.1 \text{ g O}} = \frac{0.0631 \text{ g H}}{1.000 \text{ g O}}$$

The ratio of the mass of H per gram of O in compound I to compound II is

$$\text{ratio} = \frac{(0.126 \text{ g H}/1.000 \text{ g O})}{(0.0631 \text{ g H}/1.000 \text{ g O})} = 2.00 = 2$$

which is a small, whole number. Compound I has twice as many hydrogen atoms per oxygen atom as does compound II. The two compounds are H_2O and H_2O_2.

1-33   For compound I, the masses of Cu and O are 6.35 g Cu and 7.95 g − 6.35 g = 1.60 g O. For compound II, we have 6.35 g Cu and 7.15 g − 6.35 g = 0.80 g O.

$$\text{compound I:} \quad \frac{\text{mass of O}}{\text{mass of Cu}} = \frac{1.60 \text{ g O}}{6.35 \text{ g Cu}} = \frac{0.252 \text{ g O}}{1.00 \text{ g Cu}}$$

$$\text{compound II:} \quad \frac{\text{mass of O}}{\text{mass of Cu}} = \frac{0.80 \text{ g O}}{6.35 \text{ g Cu}} = \frac{0.126 \text{ g O}}{1.00 \text{ g Cu}}$$

The ratio of the mass of O per gram of Cu in compound I to compound II is

$$\text{ratio} = \frac{(0.252 \text{ g O}/1.00 \text{ g Cu})}{(0.126 \text{ g O}/1.00 \text{ g Cu})} = 2.00 = 2$$

which is a small, whole number. Compound I contains twice as many oxygen atoms per copper atom as does compound II. The compounds are CuO and Cu_2O.

1-35   For $^{131}_{53}I$ there are 53 protons and $131 − 53 = 78$ neutrons. In a neutral atom the number of electrons is equal to the number of protons, and so there are 53 electrons. For $^{125}_{53}I$, there are 53 protons, 53 electrons, and $125 − 53 = 72$ neutrons.

1-37   From the atomic numbers, we find that

	Protons	*Electrons*	*Neutrons*
(a) plutonium-239	94	94	239 − 94 = 145
(b) cobalt-60	27	27	60 − 27 = 33
(c) potassium-43	19	19	43 − 19 = 24
(d) uranium-235	92	92	235 − 92 = 143

The atomic number determines the element. The mass number is the sum of the atomic number and the number of neutrons.

1-39

Symbol	Atomic number	Number of neutrons	Mass number
$^{12}_{6}C$	6	6	12
$^{32}_{16}S$	16	16	32
$^{196}_{79}Au$	79	117	196
$^{20}_{10}Ne$	10	10	20

1-41

Symbol	Atomic number	Number of neutrons	Mass number
$^{23}_{11}Na$	11	12	23
$^{202}_{80}Hg$	80	122	202
$^{239}_{94}Pu$	94	145	239
$^{249}_{98}Cf$	98	151	249

Using the data in Table 1-9, we have

1-43   atomic mass of O = $(15.9949)\left(\dfrac{99.758}{100}\right) + (16.9991)\left(\dfrac{0.038}{100}\right) + (17.9992)\left(\dfrac{0.204}{100}\right)$

$$= 15.956 + 0.0065 + 0.0367$$

$$= 15.999$$

1-45   atomic mass of C = $(12.0000)\left(\dfrac{98.89}{100}\right) + (13.0034)\left(\dfrac{1.11}{100}\right)$

$$= 11.87 + 0.144$$

$$= 12.01$$

1-47   Let x be the percentage of bromine-79 in naturally occurring bromine. The percentage of bromine-81 must be $100 - x$. Now set up the equation

$$\text{atomic mass of Br} = 79.904 = (78.9183)\left(\frac{x}{100}\right) + (80.9163)\left(\frac{100 - x}{100}\right)$$

Multiply this equation through by 100 and collect terms to obtain

$$7990.4 = 78.9183x + 8091.63 - 80.9163x$$

Collecting terms, we get

$$1.9980x = 101.2$$

or

$$x = 50.65\% = \% \text{ of bromine-79}$$

The percentage of bromine-81 is

$$\% \text{ bromine-81} = 100 - x = 49.35\%$$

1-49 Let x be the percentage of nitrogen-15 in naturally occurring nitrogen. The percentage of nitrogen-14 must be $100 - x$. Now set up the equation

$$\text{atomic mass of N} = 14.0067 = (14.0031)\left(\frac{100 - x}{100}\right) + (15.0001)\left(\frac{x}{100}\right)$$

Multiply through by 100 to obtain

$$1400.67 = 1400.31 - 14.0031x + 15.0001x$$

Collecting terms, we get

$$0.9970x = 0.36$$

or

$$x = 0.36\% = \% \text{ of nitrogen-15}$$

1-51 Let x be the percentage of silicon-29 in naturally occurring silicon. The percentages of silicon-29 and silicon-30 must be equal to

$$\% \text{ of silicon-29} + \% \text{ of silicon-30} = \text{total } \% - \% \text{ of silicon-28}$$
$$= 100.00 - 92.23$$
$$= 7.77$$

Because x is the percentage of silicon-29, the percentage of silicon-30 is

$$\% \text{ of silicon-30} = 7.77 - x$$

Now set up the equation

$$\text{atomic mass of Si} = 28.0855 = (27.9769)\left(\frac{92.23}{100}\right)$$
$$+ (28.9765)\left(\frac{x}{100}\right) + (29.9738)\left(\frac{7.77 - x}{100}\right)$$

Multiply through by 100 and collect terms to get

$$x = 4.67\% = \% \text{ of silicon-29}$$

The percentage of silicon-30 is

$$\% \text{ of silicon-30} = 7.77 - 4.67 = 3.10\%$$

1-53 The number of moles in 1 metric ton of H_2O is

$$\text{moles of } H_2O = (1000 \text{ kg})\left(\frac{1000 \text{ g}}{1 \text{ kg}}\right)\left(\frac{1 \text{ mol}}{18.02 \text{ g}}\right) = 5.55 \times 10^4 \text{ mol}$$

We now calculate the number of moles of oxygen and hydrogen in 1 metric ton of H_2O

$$\text{moles of H} = (5.55 \times 10^4 \text{ mol } H_2O)\left(\frac{2 \text{ mol H}}{1 \text{ mol } H_2O}\right) = 1.11 \times 10^5 \text{ mol}$$

$$\text{moles of O} = (5.55 \times 10^4 \text{ mol } H_2O)\left(\frac{1 \text{ mol O}}{1 \text{ mol } H_2O}\right) = 5.55 \times 10^4 \text{ mol}$$

We now calculate the number of moles of ^2_1H, $^{17}_8O$, and $^{18}_8O$ in 1 metric ton of H_2O using the natural abundances for each given in Table 1-9.

$$\text{moles of } ^2_1H = (1.11 \times 10^5 \text{ mol})\left(\frac{0.015}{100}\right) = 16.65 \text{ mol}$$

$$\text{moles of } ^{17}_8O = (5.55 \times 10^4 \text{ mol})\left(\frac{0.038}{100}\right) = 21.1 \text{ mol}$$

$$\text{moles of } ^{18}_8O = (5.55 \times 10^4 \text{ mol})\left(\frac{0.204}{100}\right) = 113.2 \text{ mol}$$

The masses of ^2_1H, $^{17}_8O$, and $^{18}_8O$ are calculated using the isotopic masses of each given in Table 1-9. Thus we have

$$\text{mass of } ^2_1H = (16.65 \text{ mol})\left(\frac{2.0141 \text{ g}}{1 \text{ mol}}\right) = 34 \text{ g}$$

$$\text{mass of } ^{17}_8O = (21.1 \text{ mol})\left(\frac{16.9991 \text{ g}}{1 \text{ mol}}\right) = 360 \text{ g}$$

$$\text{mass of } ^{18}_8O = (113.2 \text{ mol})\left(\frac{17.9992 \text{ g}}{1 \text{ mol}}\right) = 2040 \text{ g}$$

1-55   The number of electrons = atomic number − ionic charge.

   (a) 18   (d) 18
   (b) 18   (e) 10
   (c) 18

1-57   (a) 38   (d) 36
   (b) 89   (e) 18
   (c) 47

1-59   (a) Mg^{2+}, Al^{3+}, F^-, O^{2-}
   (b) Cl^-, K^+, Ca^{2+}, S^{2-}
   (c) I^-, Cs^+, Ba^{2+}, Te^{2-}
   (d) B^-, N^+, O^{2+}
   (e) P^{3-}, S^{2-}, K^+, Ca^{2+}

1-61

Atom	Atomic radius/10^{-12} m	Nuclear radius/10^{-15} m	Ratio
C-12	77	3.0	2.6×10^4
Ar-40	94	4.4	2.1×10^4
Ag-108	144	6.2	2.3×10^4
Ra-226	220	7.9	2.8×10^4

1-63 (a) 7.510 has four significant figures: 7, 5, 1, 0.
(b) 0.00797 has three significant figures: 7, 9, 7.
(c) 3.65×10^{-5} has three significant figures: 3, 6, 5.
(d) 226,000,000 has three significant figures: 2, 2, 6. The word about implies that the zeros serve only to position the decimal point.
(e) The integer 2 is an exact number; there is no uncertainty associated with an integer.

1-65 (a) The molecular mass of H_2O = $(2 \times 1.0079) + (15.9994) = 18.0152$.
(b) The molecular mass of PbO_2 = $(207.2) + (2 \times 15.9994) = 239.2$.
(c) The molecular mass of $AlCl_3$ = $(26.98154) + (3 \times 35.453) = 133.341$.
(d) The molecular mas of $TcBr_2$ = $(98) + (2 \times 79.904) = 258$.

1-67 (a) 56.77 (The result cannot be more accurate than two digits past the decimal point.)
(b) 219.499
(c) 19.12 (The calculated result cannot be expressed to more than four significant figures.)
(d) 0.3598 if 19 is the number 19, and 0.36 if 19 is a measured quantity
(e) 7.6

1-69 (a) To convert from quarts to liters, we use the unit conversion factor of 0.94633 L/qt and compute

$$(1.00 \text{ qt})\left(\frac{0.94633 \text{ L}}{\text{qt}}\right) = 0.946 \text{ L}$$

(b) There are 1000 m in a kilometer; thus

$$(3.00 \times 10^8 \text{ m} \cdot \text{s}^{-1})\left(\frac{1 \text{ km}}{1000 \text{ m}}\right) = 3.00 \times 10^5 \text{ km} \cdot \text{s}^{-1}$$

To convert to miles, we use the conversion factor 1.6093 km/1 mile

$$(3.00 \times 10^5 \text{ km} \cdot \text{s}^{-1})\left(\frac{1 \text{ mile}}{1.6093 \text{ km}}\right) = 1.86 \times 10^5 \text{ miles} \cdot \text{s}^{-1}$$

To convert to hours, we use the conversion factors 60 s/min and 60 min/h

$$\left(1.86 \times 10^5 \frac{\text{miles}}{\text{s}}\right)\left(\frac{60 \text{ s}}{\text{min}}\right)\left(\frac{60 \text{ min}}{1 \text{ h}}\right) = 6.71 \times 10^8 \text{ miles} \cdot \text{h}^{-1}$$

(c) To convert from calories to joules, we use the conversion factor 4.184 J/1 cal

$$(1.9872 \text{ cal} \cdot \text{K}^{-1} \cdot \text{mol}^{-1})\left(\frac{4.184 \text{ J}}{1 \text{ cal}}\right) = 8.314 \text{ J} \cdot \text{K}^{-1} \cdot \text{mol}^{-1}$$

1-71   The distance is given by

distance = speed × time

$$= (3.00 \times 10^8 \text{ m} \cdot \text{s}^{-1})(1 \text{ yr})\left(\frac{365 \text{ d}}{1 \text{ yr}}\right)\left(\frac{24 \text{ h}}{1 \text{ d}}\right)\left(\frac{60 \text{ min}}{1 \text{ h}}\right)\left(\frac{60 \text{ s}}{1 \text{ min}}\right)$$

$$= 9.46 \times 10^{15} \text{ m}$$

The distance in miles is

$$\text{distance} = (9.46 \times 10^{15} \text{ m})\left(\frac{1 \text{ km}}{10^3 \text{ m}}\right)\left(\frac{1 \text{ mile}}{1.6093 \text{ km}}\right)$$

$$= 5.88 \times 10^{12} \text{ miles}$$

1-73   The total volume of soda in an eight-pack is

volume = (8)(16 oz) = 128 oz

The volume in milliliters is

$$\text{volume} = (128 \text{ oz})\left(\frac{0.94633 \text{ L}}{32 \text{ oz}}\right)\left(\frac{10^3 \text{ mL}}{1 \text{ L}}\right) = 3785 \text{ mL}$$

The cost per mL of soda in the eight-pack is

$$\text{cost per mL} = \left(\frac{3 \text{ dollars}}{3785 \text{ mL}}\right)\left(\frac{100 \text{ cents}}{1 \text{ dollar}}\right)$$

$$= 0.0793 \text{ cents per mL}$$

The cost per mL of soda in the 750-mL bottle is

$$\text{cost per mL} = \frac{67 \text{ cents}}{750 \text{ mL}} = 0.089 \text{ cents per mL}$$

The eight-pack is the better buy.

E   ANSWERS TO THE EVEN-NUMBERED PROBLEMS

1-2   (a) V   (d) Mg
      (b) Au   (e) Fe
      (c) Zn   (f) Cs

(g) Br   (i) Sb
(h) Kr   (j) As

1-4   (a) platinum   (f) chromium
          (b) strontium   (g) nickel
          (c) lead   (h) tin
          (d) tungsten   (i) sulfur
          (e) calcium   (j) carbon

1-6   mass % of La = 85.4%; mass % of O = 14.6%

1-8   mass % of Sn = 75.74%; mass % of F = 24.3% (Note that the mass percentage of F is given to three significant figures.)

1-10 mass % of C = 52.2%; mass % of H = 13%; mass % of O = 34.6% (Note that the mass percentage of H is given to two significant figures.)

1-12 (a) barium fluoride   (d) cesium chloride
          (b) magnesium nitride   (e) calcium sulfide
          (c) rubidium bromide

1-14 (a) aluminum oxide   (d) magnesium selenide
          (b) magnesium fluoride   (e) lithium phosphide
          (c) aluminum nitride

1-16 (a) antimony trichloride and antimony pentachloride
          (b) iodine trichloride and iodine pentachloride
          (c) krypton difluoride and kyrpton tetrafluoride
          (d) selenium dioxide and selenium trioxide
          (e) carbon monosulfide and carbon disulfide

1-18 (a) 102.13   (c) 116.16
          (b) 144.21   (d) 158.23

1-20 (a) 286.44   (d) 793.26
          (b) 300.81   (e) 176.12
          (c) 376.37

1-22 mass % of N = 46.68%; mass % of O = 53.32%

1-24 mass % of Si = 46.75%; mass % of O = 53.25%

1-26 mass % of Na = 32.85%; mass % of Al = 12.85%; mass % of F = 54.30%

1-28 mass % of Li in Li_2CO_3 = 18.79%
          mass % of Li in $LiC_2H_3O_2$ = 10.52%
          mass % of Li in $Li_3C_6H_5O_7$ = 9.92%
          mass % of Li in Li_2SO_4 = 12.63%

1-30 The ratio of the mass of fluorine per gram of bromine in compound II to compound I is 1.666, or $\frac{5}{3}$. Compound I is BrF_3 and compound II is BrF_5.

1-32 The ratio of the mass of chlorine per gram of tin in compound II to compound I is 2.000. Compound II has twice as many chlorine atoms per tin atom as does compound I. The two compounds are $SnCl_2$ and $SnCl_4$.

1-34 The ratio of the mass of chlorine per gram of iron in compound II to compound I is 1.50, or $\frac{3}{2}$. The two compounds are $FeCl_2$ and $FeCl_3$.

1-36

	Electrons	Protons	Neutrons
C-14	6	6	8
Pb-206	82	82	124

1-38

	Electrons	Protons	Neutrons
(a) P-30	15	15	15
(b) Tc-97	43	43	54
(c) Fe-55	26	26	29
(d) Am-240	95	95	145

1-40

Symbol	Atomic number	Number of neutrons	Mass number
$^{48}_{20}Ca$	20	28	48
$^{90}_{40}Zr$	40	50	90
$^{131}_{53}I$	53	78	131
$^{99}_{42}Mo$	42	57	99

1-42

Symbol	Atomic number	Number of neutrons	Mass number
$^{39}_{19}K$	19	20	39
$^{56}_{26}Fe$	26	30	56
$^{84}_{36}Kr$	36	48	84
$^{120}_{50}Sn$	50	70	120

1-44 24.31

1-46 28.09

1-48 19.9% (B-10) and 80.1% (B-11)

1-50 48% (Eu-151) and 52% (Eu-153)

1-52 (a) 6.942
     (b) 1.6%

1-54 5060 g

1-56 (a) 36   (d) 46
     (b) 18   (e) 78
     (c) 28

1-58 (a) 54   (d) 78
     (b) 54   (e) 74
     (c) 54

1-60 (a) N^{2-}, O^-, Ne^+ (d) N^{3-}, O^{2-}, F^-, Na^+, Mg^{2+}, Al^{3+}
     (b) Li^-, B^+, C^{2+} (e) C^-, O^+, F^{2+}
     (c) La^+, Ce^{2+}, Cs^-

1-62 300 m

1-64 (a) three significant figures
     (b) three significant figures

(c) an exact number with no uncertainty
(d) two significant figures
(e) one significant figure and one significant figure

1-66 (a) 16.043   (c) 189.71
       (b) 78.08   (d) 349

1-68 (a) 33209   (d) 1.43883×10^{-2}
       (b) 254   (e) -1.25×10^{-13}
       (c) 3.4×10^{22}

1-70 (a) 99.1 m
       (b) 154 pm; 0.154 nm
       (c) 79.4 kg

1-72 7.44×10^3 cm^3; 7.44 L

1-74 40 m $\cdot$ s^{-1}; 0.46 s

F   ANSWERS TO THE SELF-TEST

1 atom

2 compound

3 luster, malleability, conductivity of heat and electricity

4 true

5 false

6 Al, Ca, K, Zn

7 barium, copper, iron, sodium

8 false

9 H_2, N_2, O_2, F_2, Cl_2, Br_2, I_2

10 a number

11 Consult Section 1-4 of the text.

12 the total mass of the products (law of conservation of mass)

13 false

14 false

15 mass percentage of each element in the compound

16 Consult Section 1-6 of the text.

17 Consult Section 1-6 of the text.

18 atomic mass unit, amu

19 false

20 Consult Section 1-6 of the text.

21 rearranged

22 Consult Section 1-8 of the text.

23 calcium sulfide

24 carbon dioxide

25 sum of the atomic masses of the elements corresponding to all the atoms in the molecule

26 Consult Section 1-10 of the text.

27 positively

28 false

29 lesser

30

	Relative mass	Relative charge
proton	1	+1
neutron	1	0
electron	$\frac{1}{1837}$	−1

31 false

32 Consult Section 1-12 of the text.

33 The protons and neutrons are located in the nucleus and the electrons are located outside the nucleus. Consequently, the mass of an atom is essentially equal to the mass of its nucleus.

34	false	43	lost one or more electrons
35	false	44	gained one or more electrons
36	true	45	3
37	protons, neutrons	46	true
38	mass number, atomic number	47	false
39	two neutrons	48	three
40	hydrogen	49	two
41	Naturally occurring chlorine is composed of more than one isotope.	50	true; no units are given
		51	unit conversion factor
42	mass and charge	52	SI, metric

2 / The Chemical Elements and the Periodic Table

A   OUTLINE OF CHAPTER 2

2-1   New substances are formed in chemical reactions.

2-2   Chemical reactions are represented by chemical equations.

 The reactants are the substances that react with each other.

 The products are the substances formed in the reaction.

 The symbols (*s*), (*l*), and (*g*) denote that a substance is a solid, liquid, or gas, respectively.

2-3   A chemical equation must be balanced.

 The conservation of atoms in chemical reactions means that individual atoms of various types are neither created nor destroyed.

 Chemical equations are balanced by using balancing coefficients.

 The method of balancing chemical equations by inspection is discussed.

2-4   Some elements have similar chemical properties.

 Representative reactions of the alkali metals (Group 1) are presented in Table 2-1.

 Representative reactions of the alkaline earth metals (Group 2) are presented in Table 2-2.

 Representative reactions of the halogens (Group 7) are presented in Table 2-3.

 The prediction of reaction products can be made using representative reactions.

2-5   The elements show a periodic pattern when listed in order of increasing atomic number.

The chemical properties of the elements exhibit periodic behavior (Mendeleev).

In a modern periodic table of the elements the elements are ordered according to increasing atomic number (Figure 2-9).

2-6 Elements in the same column in the periodic table have similar chemical properties.

Groups or families of elements appear in the same column of the periodic table.

The extreme right-hand column contains the group of unreactive elements called the noble gases (Group 8).

The prediction of reaction products can be made using the periodic table.

2-7 Mendeleev predicted the existence and properties of elements not yet discovered.

Mendeleev used periodicity to predict chemical and physical properties of undiscovered elements.

2-8 The periodic table organizes our study of the elements.

The more common version of the table has the lanthanide series and the actinide series placed at the bottom of the table (Figure 2-12).

2-9 Elements are arranged as main-group elements, transition metals, and inner transition metals.

The periodic table organizes the elements into

groups (columns)

periods (rows)

semimetals

metals

nonmetals

main-group elements

transition metals

inner transition metals, the lanthanides ($Z = 57$ to $Z = 70$) and the actinides ($Z = 89$ to $Z = 102$)

Elements can be classified based on their positions in the periodic table (Figures 2-13 and 2-16).

2-10 The periodic table contains some irregularities.

Hydrogen does not fit readily into any group.

The first member of a group often reacts somewhat differently than the other members of the group.

2-11 Many atoms form ions that have a noble-gas electron arrangement.

The nuclear model of the atom is reviewed.

Noble-gas electron arrangements are unusually stable.

Ions are formed by loss or gain of electrons.

The charge on an ion is designated by a superscript following the symbol for the atom that has lost or gained electrons.

2-12 Ionic charges can be used to write chemical formulas.

Metal atoms lose electrons and form positive ions.

Ionic charges are positive or negative numbers assigned to elements and can be used to write correct chemical formulas.

An ionic compound has no net charge—the total positive charge equals the total negative charge.

The prediction of chemical formulas of ionic compounds is made using ionic charges:

Group	Ionic charge
1	+1
2	+2
3	+3
6	−2
7	−1

2-13 Oxidation-reduction reactions involve a transfer of electrons.

An atom is oxidized when it loses electrons (the charge on the atom becomes more positive).

An atom is reduced when it gains electrons (the charge on the atom becomes more negative).

A reaction in which electrons are transferred from one element to another is an oxidation-reduction reaction.

B   SELF-TEST

1 Substances formed in chemical reactions have a combination of the properties of the substances from which they are produced. *True/False*

2 Sodium chloride has similar properties to those of sodium and chlorine. *True/False*

3 $H_2(g) + O_2(g) \rightarrow H_2O(l)$. The chemical equation is balanced as written. *True/False*

4 Balancing coefficients are placed _____ of the chemical formulas of the reactants and products of a chemical equation.

5 The number of each kind of atom in the reactants must _____ in the products of a balanced chemical equation.

6 The chemical formulas of the products of a chemical reaction can be changed to balance the equation. *True/False*

7 The chemical properties of lithium are similar to those of _____ and _____ .

8 Complete and balance the equations
(a) $Li(s) + Cl_2(g) \longrightarrow$
(b) $K(s) + H_2(g) \longrightarrow$
(c) $Na(s) + H_2O(l) \longrightarrow$

9 The chemical properties of magnesium are similar to those of _____ , _____ , and _____ .

10 Complete and balance the equations
(a) $Mg(s) + O_2(g) \longrightarrow$
(b) $Mg(s) + H_2O(g) \longrightarrow$
(c) $Ca(s) + Cl_2(g) \longrightarrow$
(d) $Ca(s) + H_2(g) \longrightarrow$

11 The halogens consist of the elements _____ , _____ , _____ , _____ , and _____ .

12 Complete and balance the equations
(a) $Na(s) + F_2(g) \longrightarrow$
(b) $Ca(s) + I_2(s) \longrightarrow$
(c) $H_2(g) + Br_2(l) \longrightarrow$
(d) $Sr(s) + Cl_2(g) \longrightarrow$

13 Mendeleev arranged the elements in order of increasing _____ .

14 The elements that appear in the same column of the periodic table have _____ properties.

15 Elements with similar chemical properties appear in the same row of the periodic table. *True/False*

16 In the modern periodic table, the elements are arranged in order of increasing _____ .

17 Elements that have similar chemical properties are placed in the same column of the periodic table. *True/False*

18 Group 1 metals are also called _____ .

19 Group 2 metals are also called _____ .

20 The halogens appear in column _____ of the periodic table.

21 The noble gases occur in column _____ of the periodic table.

22 The noble gases used to be called _____ .

23 Silicon is a nonmetal. *True/False*

24 Some properties of semimetals are _____, _____, and _____.

25 There are almost as many nonmetals as metals. *True/False*

26 Where are the main-group elements located in the periodic table? _____.

27 The main group elements have many chemical properties in common. *True/False*

28 The transition metals are more similar in their properties than the main-group elements. *True/False*

29 The transition metals occur between _____ and _____ in the periodic table.

30 The inner transition metals occur in the series that begin with _____ and with _____.

31 The lanthanide series is also called _____.

32 Members of the lanthanide series have very similar chemical properties. *True/False*

33 One of the properties that the elements in the actinide series have in common is that they are _____.

34 Explain why the inner transition metal series are placed at the bottom of many versions of the periodic table.

35 Hydrogen is sometimes placed in Group 1 because it is an alkali metal. *True/False*

36 The first member of a main-group family is typical of the group and behaves identically to the other members. *True/False*

37 The electron arrangements of the noble gases seem to be exceptionally stable. *True/False*

38 The noble gases are reactive nonmetals. *True/False*

39 An element in Group 1 loses one electron to attain the electron arrangement of _____.

40 An element in Group 7 gains one electron to attain the electron arrangement of _____.

41 An oxygen atom gains _____ electrons to form the oxide ion.

42 An ionic compound consists of _____ and _____.

43 The net charge on an ionic compound is _____.

44 The charge of a magnesium ion is _____; the charge of a bromide ion is _____. The chemical formula of magnesium bromide is _____.

45 An element is oxidized when the charge on its atoms _____.

46 An oxidation-reduction reaction involves _____.

47 In an oxidation-reduction reaction, the number of electrons lost by the element that is oxidized is equal to _____

_____.

C   CALCULATIONS YOU SHOULD KNOW HOW TO DO

1 Balance chemical reactions by inspection. See Examples 2-1 and 2-2 and Problems 2-1 through 2-10.

2 Predict the products of chemical reactions using the representative reactions given in Tables 2-1, 2-2, and 2-3. See Examples 2-3 through 2-6 and Problems 2-11 through 2-16.

3 Use the periodic table to predict physical and chemical properties. See Table 2-5 and Problems 2-17 through 2-20 and 2-25 through 2-28.

4 Classify elements into metals and nonmetals and into main group elements, transition metals and inner transition metals. See Example 2-7 and Problems 2-21 through 2-26.

5 Predict ionic charges using the attainment of noble-gas electron arrangements in ions. See Examples 2-8 and 2-9 and Problems 2-29 through 2-34.

6 Use ionic charges to predict chemical formulas. See Examples 2-10 through 2-12 and Problems 2-35 through 2-40.

7 Write formulas from names and then predict reaction products. See Problems 2-41 through 2-44 (combine methods in 2, 5, and 6 given above).

8 Determine which element is oxidized and which element is reduced in an oxidation-reduction reaction. See Example 2-13 and Problems 2-45 through 2-48.

D   SOLUTIONS TO THE ODD-NUMBERED PROBLEMS

2-1 (a) The procedure for balancing equations of the type considered in this chapter is the balancing by inspection method outlined in Section 2-3. For example, in this problem we want to balance the equation

$$AgClO_3(aq) + CaBr_2(aq) \longrightarrow AgBr(s) + Ca(ClO_3)_2(aq)$$

The designation (aq) denotes a substance dissolved in water; aq comes from aqua, the Latin name for water. We first note that there are two Br atoms on the left and only one on the right; thus we insert a 2 in front of AgBr(s) to balance the Br

$$AgClO_3(aq) + CaBr_2(aq) \longrightarrow 2AgBr(s) + Ca(ClO_3)_2(aq)$$

There are now two Ag on the right and only one Ag on the left; thus we insert a 2 in front of AgClO$_3$(aq)

$$2AgClO_3(aq) + CaBr_2(aq) \longrightarrow 2AgBr(s) + Ca(ClO_3)_2(aq)$$

The placement of a 2 in front of AgClO$_3$(aq) balances the Ag and also the ClO$_3^-$ unit. The atoms of each type are now the same on both sides of the arrow and, therefore, the equation is balanced. The solutions to parts (b), (c), (d), and (e) are obtained in a strictly analogous manner.

(b) $Ba(s) + 2HNO_3(aq) \longrightarrow Ba(NO_3)_2(aq) + H_2(g)$
(c) $H_2SO_4(aq) + 2KOH(aq) \longrightarrow K_2SO_4(aq) + 2H_2O(l)$
(d) $2C_3H_8(g) + 7O_2(g) \longrightarrow 6CO(g) + 8H_2O(g)$
(e) $CaH_2(s) + 2H_2O(l) \longrightarrow Ca(OH)_2(aq) + 2H_2(g)$

2-3 (a) $2NO(g) + Br_2(g) \longrightarrow 2NOBr(g)$
     (b) $2Na(s) + O_2(g) \longrightarrow Na_2O_2(s)$
     (c) $2P(s) + 3Br_2(l) \longrightarrow 2PBr_3(l)$
     (d) $3H_2(g) + N_2(g) \longrightarrow 2NH_3(g)$
     (e) $MgO(s) + SiO_2(s) \longrightarrow MgSiO_3(s)$

2-5 (a) $CH_4(g) + 2O_2(g) \longrightarrow CO_2(g) + 2H_2O(l)$
     (b) $2CO(g) + O_2(g) \longrightarrow 2CO_2(g)$
     (c) $C_3H_8(g) + 5O_2(g) \longrightarrow 3CO_2(g) + 4H_2O(l)$
     (d) $C_6H_{12}O_6(s) + 6O_2(g) \longrightarrow 6CO_2(g) + 6H_2O(l)$
     (e) $2Sr(s) + O_2(g) \longrightarrow 2SrO(s)$

2-7 (a) $6Li(s) + N_2(g) \longrightarrow 2Li_3N(s)$
     (b) $4Li(s) + O_2(g) \longrightarrow 2Li_2O(s)$
     (c) $2Li(s) + 2H_2O(l) \longrightarrow 2LiOH(s) + H_2(g)$
     (d) $2Li(s) + H_2(g) \longrightarrow 2LiH(s)$
     (e) $2Li(s) + 2CO_2(g) + 2H_2O(g) \longrightarrow 2LiHCO_3(s) + H_2(g)$

2-9 This problem differs from Problems 2-1 through 2-8 in that we also are asked to give the names of the reactant(s) and product(s). Recall that in naming a compound composed of a metal and a nonmetal, we first name the metal and then the nonmetal, using an -ide ending for the nonmetal. Compounds composed of two nonmetals are named in a similar manner, with the second listed element given the -ide ending and prefixes (mono-, di-, tri-, tetra-, penta-, and hexa-) used to distinguish cases where more than one compound is possible between the two elements.

(a) $2Al(s)\ +\ 3Cl_2(g) \longrightarrow\quad 2AlCl_3(s)$
    aluminum   chlorine   aluminum chloride

(b) $4Al(s)\ +\ 3O_2(g) \longrightarrow\quad 2Al_2O_3(s)$
    aluminum   oxygen   aluminum oxide

(c) $COCl_2(g) + 2Na(s) \longrightarrow\quad CO(g)\ +\ 2NaCl(s)$
    phosgene   sodium   carbon   sodium
                              monoxide   chloride

(d) $2Be(s)\ +\ O_2(g) \longrightarrow\quad 2BeO(s)$
    beryllium   oxygen   beryllium oxide

(e) $2K(s)\ +\ S(l) \longrightarrow\quad K_2S(s)$
    sodium   sulfur   sodium sulfide

2-11 In order to predict the reaction products in problems of this type, we consult the representative reactions of the various groups of elements given in Tables 2-1 and 2-2. Thus, to complete the reaction

$$K(s) + H_2O(l) \longrightarrow$$

we find in Table 2-1 that the alkali metals react with water to produce hydrogen gas and the alkali metal hydroxide

$$K(s) + H_2O(l) \longrightarrow KOH(s) + H_2(g) \qquad \text{(not balanced)}$$

Once we have set down the formulas for the reaction products, we next balance the equation, using the same procedure as in Problems 2-1 through 2-10. Your instructor may require you to memorize the reactions in Tables 2-1 and 2-2.

(a) $2K(s) + 2H_2O(l) \longrightarrow 2KOH(s) + H_2(g)$
(b) $3Mg(s) + N_2(g) \longrightarrow Mg_3N_2(s)$
(c) $2Ca(s) + O_2(g) \longrightarrow 2CaO(s)$
(d) $2Na(s) + I_2(s) \longrightarrow 2NaI(s)$
(e) $Sr(s) + 2HCl(g) \longrightarrow SrCl_2(s) + H_2(g)$

2-13 Consult Table 2-2 for the analogous representative reactions.

(a) $Mg(s) + Br_2(l) \longrightarrow MgBr_2(s)$
(b) $2Ba(s) + O_2(g) \longrightarrow 2BaO(s)$
(c) $Ba(s) + S(s) \longrightarrow BaS(s)$
(d) $Mg(s) + 2HCl(g) \longrightarrow MgCl_2(s) + H_2(g)$
(e) $Sr(s) + H_2(g) \longrightarrow SrH_2(s)$

2-15 Consult Tables 2-1 and 2-2 for the analogous representative reactions.

(a) $2Na(s) + H_2(g) \longrightarrow 2NaH(s)$
(b) $Ba(s) + H_2(g) \longrightarrow BaH_2(s)$
(c) $2K(s) + F_2(g) \longrightarrow 2KF(s)$
(d) $Ba(s) + Br_2(l) \longrightarrow BaBr_2(s)$
(e) $3Ca(s) + N_2(g) \longrightarrow Ca_3N_2(s)$

2-17 Problems 2-17 through 2-20 are worked using the knowledge that elements of the same group in the periodic table have similar properties. Iodine has chemical properties similar to those of F_2, Cl_2, and Br_2; therefore, I_2 belongs to the halogen family.

2-19 By analogy with the properties of the other halogens, we predict the following:

(a) solid   (d) At_2
(b) NaAt   (e) black
(c) white

2-21 In, a main-group (3) metal; Er, an inner transition metal; Ar, a main-group (8) nonmetal; Y, a transition metal; Rh, a transition metal; Cf, an inner transition metal; Be, a main-group (2) metal.

2-23 See the periodic table.

2-25   Antimony, Sb, is a Group 5 element. The reaction of Sb with oxygen is predicted by analogy with the reactions of P and As with O_2 that are described in Example 2-6.

$$4Sb(s) + 3O_2(g) \longrightarrow Sb_4O_6(s)$$

2-27   Radium is a Group 2 metal, and thus we use Table 2-2 to predict the reactions of Ra by analogy with the other Group 2 metals.
   (a) $2Ra(s) + O_2(g) \longrightarrow 2RaO(s)$
   (b) $Ra(s) + Cl_2(g) \longrightarrow RaCl_2(s)$
   (c) $Ra(s) + 2HCl(g) \longrightarrow RaCl_2(s) + H_2(g)$
   (d) $Ra(s) + H_2(g) \longrightarrow RaH_2(s)$
   (e) $Ra(s) + S(s) \longrightarrow RaS(s)$

2-29   For positive atomic ions, the number of electrons is equal to the atomic number Z minus the charge. Thus for Fe^{2+} ($Z = 26$) we have $26 - 2 = 24$ electrons. For negative atomic ions, the number of electrons is equal to the atomic number plus the charge. Thus for Se^{2-} ($Z = 34$) we have $34 + 2 = 36$ electrons.
   (a) 24   (d) 18
   (b) 36   (e) 10
   (c) 10

2-31   We first determine the number of electrons in the ion, as in Problem 2-29, and then compare the result with the Z values for the noble gases. For example, for K^+ we have 18 ($19 - 1$) electrons and $Z = 18$ for argon; thus K^+ has a noble-gas electron arrangement.
   (a) yes (Ar)   (d) yes (Ne)
   (b) no   (e) yes (Ne)
   (c) no   (f) yes (Xe)

2-33   We determine the charges on the atomic ions in ionic compounds using Figure 2-18. For example, for K_2S we note that potassium is a Group 1 metal and thus has an ionic charge of $+1$. There are two K^+ for each sulfur atom, and thus sulfur must have an ionic charge of -2 because the ionic compound K_2S has no net charge.
   (a) K^+ S^{2-} (d) Cs^+ I^-
   (b) Al^{3+} N^{3-} (e) Mg^{2+} Se^{2-}
   (c) Al^{3+} F^-

2-35   To determine the chemical formula of an ionic compound, we use the procedure outlined in Example 2-12. For example, consider gallium oxide. Gallium is a Group 3 metal; therefore, a gallium ion has a charge of $+3$. Oxygen is a Group 6 nonmetal and the oxide ion has a charge of -2; thus we have

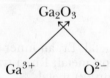

that is, Ga_2O_3 is the formula for gallium oxide.

Consider strontium iodide. (Part e.) Strontium belongs to Group 2 and iodine belongs to Group 7. Thus we have

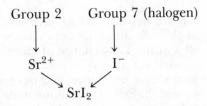

The other compounds are

(a) Ga_2O_3
(b) $AlCl_3$
(c) Li_2O

(d) HBr
(e) SrI_2

2-37 See Problem 2-35.

(a) Li_3N
(b) RbI
(c) Ga_2S_3

(d) BaO
(e) MgI_2

2-39 To determine the chemical formula of an ionic compound formed from a positive ion and a negative ion, we use the fact that the compound does not have any net charge. Thus, to balance the charges for the pair of ions Ga^{3+} and O^{2-}, we have to use two Ga^{3+} ions and three O^{2-} ions.

$$Ga_2O_3 \qquad 2 \times (+3) + 3 \times (-2) = 0$$

(a) Ga_2O_3
(b) ZnI_2
(c) FeS

(d) $RuCl_3$
(e) Ag_2S

2-41 To work a problem like this, you have to know how to write chemical formulas from names (see Problems 2-35 through 2-38). Once we have written down the formulas for the reactants and the products, then we proceed to balance the equation (see, for example, Problem 2-1). Thus,

$$\text{potassium} + \text{water} \longrightarrow \text{potassium hydroxide} + \text{hydrogen}$$

$$K(s) \quad + H_2O(l) \longrightarrow \qquad KOH(s) \qquad + \quad H_2(g)$$

and balancing the equation yields

(a) $2K(s) + 2H_2O(l) \longrightarrow 2KOH(s) + H_2(g)$
(b) $KH(s) + H_2O(l) \longrightarrow KOH(s) + H_2(g)$
(c) $SiO_2(s) + 3C(s) \longrightarrow SiC(s) + 2CO(g)$
(d) $SiO_2(s) + 4HF(g) \longrightarrow SiF_4(g) + 2H_2O(l)$
(e) $2P(s) + 3Cl_2(g) \longrightarrow 2PCl_3(l)$

2-43 See Problem 2-41.

(a) $2Na(s) + H_2(g) \longrightarrow 2NaH(s)$
(b) $2Al(s) + 3S(s) \longrightarrow Al_2S_3(s)$

(c) $H_2O(g) + C(s) \longrightarrow CO(g) + H_2(g)$
(d) $C(s) + 2H_2(g) \longrightarrow CH_4(g)$
(e) $PCl_3(l) + Cl_2(g) \longrightarrow PCl_5(s)$

2-45 (a) Calcium atoms are neutral and so have no charge. A chlorine molecule is neutral; each chlorine atom has zero charge. In $CaCl_2$ the ionic charge of calcium is $+2$ and the ionic charge of chlorine is -1. Thus calcium is oxidized and chlorine is reduced.
   (b) Aluminum atoms have no charge, and oxygen atoms in O_2 have no charge. In Al_2O_3 the ionic charges of aluminum and oxygen are $+3$ and -2, respectively. Thus aluminum is oxidized and oxygen is reduced.
   (c) Rubidium is oxidized and bromine is reduced.
   (d) Sodium is oxidized and sulfur is reduced.

2-47 (a) Each calcium atom loses two electrons, and each of the two chlorine atoms gains one electron. Thus a total of two electrons is transferred.
   (b) Each aluminum atom loses three electrons, and each oxygen atom gains two electrons. Because the formula unit of the product Al_2O_3 involves two aluminum atoms, a total of 2×3 or 6 electrons is transferred per formula unit of product. The overall balanced equation shows that two formula units $(2Al_2O_3)$ are produced.
   (c) One electron. However, two formula units are produced.
   (d) Two electrons.

E   ANSWERS TO THE EVEN-NUMBERED PROBLEMS

2-2 (a) $Li_3N(s) + 3H_2O(l) \longrightarrow 3LiOH(s) + NH_3(g)$
   (b) $Al_4C_3(s) + 12HCl(aq) \longrightarrow 4AlCl_3(aq) + 3CH_4(g)$
   (c) $H_2S(g) + 2NaOH(aq) \longrightarrow Na_2S(aq) + 2H_2O(l)$
   (d) $2HCl(aq) + CaCO_3(s) \longrightarrow CaCl_2(aq) + CO_2(g) + H_2O(l)$
   (e) $4CoO(s) + O_2(g) \longrightarrow 2Co_2O_3(s)$

2-4 (a) $3N_2H_4(g) \longrightarrow 4NH_3(g) + N_2(g)$
   (b) $2GeO_2(s) \longrightarrow 2GeO(g) + O_2(g)$
   (c) $2KHF_2(s) \longrightarrow 2KF(s) + H_2(g) + F_2(g)$
   (d) $2H_2O_2(l) \longrightarrow 2H_2O(l) + O_2(g)$
   (e) $2N_2O(g) \longrightarrow 2N_2(g) + O_2(g)$

2-6 (a) $2AgNO_3(aq) + Cu(s) \longrightarrow Cu(NO_3)_2(aq) + 2Ag(s)$
   (b) $Zn(s) + 2HCl(aq) \longrightarrow ZnCl_2(aq) + H_2(g)$
   (c) $2KI(aq) + Br_2(l) \longrightarrow 2KBr(aq) + I_2(s)$
   (d) $2ZnS(s) + 3O_2(g) \longrightarrow 2ZnO(s) + 2SO_2(g)$
   (e) $2GaBr_3(aq) + 3Cl_2(g) \longrightarrow 2GaCl_3(aq) + 3Br_2(l)$

2-8 (a) $Ca(s) + H_2(g) \longrightarrow CaH_2(s)$
   (b) $2S(s) + 3O_2(g) \longrightarrow 2SO_3(g)$
   (c) $PCl_5(s) + 4H_2O(l) \longrightarrow H_3PO_4(l) + 5HCl(g)$
   (d) $P_4O_{10}(s) + 6H_2O(l) \longrightarrow 4H_3PO_4(l)$
   (e) $2Sb(s) + 3Cl_2(g) \longrightarrow 2SbCl_3(s)$

2-10 (a) $NaH(s) + H_2O(l) \longrightarrow NaOH(s) + H_2(g)$

sodium   water   sodium   hydrogen
hydride   hydroxide

(b) $Li_3N(s) + 3D_2O(l) \longrightarrow 3LiOD(s) + ND_3(g)$

lithium   deuterium   lithium   nitrogen
nitride   oxide   deuteroxide   trideuteride

(c) $2NaN_3(s) \longrightarrow 2Na(s) + 3N_2(g)$

sodium   sodium   nitrogen
azide

(d) $LiD(s) + D_2O(l) \longrightarrow LiOD(s) + D_2(g)$

lithium   deuterium   lithium   deuterium
deuteride   oxide   deuteroxide

(e) $LiOH(s) + HCl(g) \longrightarrow LiCl(s) + H_2O(g)$

lithium   hydrogen   lithium   water
hydroxide   chloride   chloride

2-12 (a) $2K(s) + Cl_2(g) \longrightarrow 2KCl(s)$
(b) $Sr(s) + S(s) \longrightarrow SrS(s)$
(c) $Ba(s) + H_2O(g) \longrightarrow BaO(s) + H_2(g)$
(d) $2Li(s) + H_2(g) \longrightarrow 2LiH(s)$
(e) $2Na(s) + Br_2(l) \longrightarrow 2NaBr(s)$

2-14 (a) $2Li(s) + I_2(s) \longrightarrow 2LiI(s)$
(b) $2Na(s) + S(s) \longrightarrow Na_2S(s)$
(c) $2K(s) + H_2(g) \longrightarrow 2KH(s)$
(d) $2Li(s) + F_2(g) \longrightarrow 2LiF(s)$
(e) $2K(s) + Br_2(l) \longrightarrow 2KBr(s)$

2-16 (a) $2P(s) + 3Cl_2(g) \longrightarrow 2PCl_3(l)$
(b) $H_2(g) + F_2(g) \longrightarrow 2HF(g)$
(c) $2Sb(s) + 3Cl_2(g) \longrightarrow 2SbCl_3(s)$
(d) $2As(s) + 3Br_2(l) \longrightarrow 2AsBr_3(s)$
(e) $2P(s) + 3I_2(s) \longrightarrow 2PI_3(s)$

2-18 Argon is a noble gas; potassium is an alkali metal.

2-20 (a) colorless   (c) Ra
(b) odorless   (d) no reaction

2-22 Te is a main group (6) nonmetal; P is a main group (5) nonmetal; Mn is a transition metal; Kr is a main group (8) nonmetal; W is a transition metal; Pb is a main group (4) metal; Ga is a main group (3) metal.

2-24 Sodium is a main group (1) metal; carbon is a main group (4) nonmetal; helium is a main group (8) nonmetal; iron is a transition metal; copper is a transition metal; zinc is a transition metal.

2-26 Noble gas (Group 8).

2-28 Strontium has similar chemical properties to calcium, which is an important element of the human body (for example, bones and teeth).

2-30 (a) 23   (d) 54
(b) 18   (e) 54
(c) 54

2-32 (a) yes (Xe)   (d) yes (Ar)
     (b) no   (e) yes (Kr)
     (c) yes (Kr)   (f) no

2-34 (a) Li^+ O^{2-} (d) Al^{3+} S^{2-}
     (b) Ca^{2+} S^{2-} (e) K^+ I^-
     (c) Mg^{2+} N^{3-}

2-36 (a) Al_2S_3 (d) BaF_2
     (b) Na_2O (e) KI
     (c) $GaBr_3$

2-38 (a) Cs_2O (d) Li_2S
     (b) Na_2Se (e) CaI_2
     (c) SrS

2-40 (a) PtF_4 (d) $BaAt_2$
     (b) Au_2O_3 (e) Zn_3N_2
     (c) Fe_2Se_3

2-42 (a) $2Na(s) + S(s) \longrightarrow Na_2S(s)$
     (b) $Ca(s) + Br_2(l) \longrightarrow CaBr_2(s)$
     (c) $2Ba(s) + O_2(g) \longrightarrow 2BaO(s)$
     (d) $2SO_2(g) + O_2(g) \longrightarrow 2SO_3(g)$
     (e) $3Mg(s) + N_2(g) \longrightarrow Mg_3N_2(s)$

2-44 (a) $2CO(g) + O_2(g) \longrightarrow 2CO_2(g)$
     (b) $2Cs(s) + Br_2(l) \longrightarrow 2CsBr(s)$
     (c) $2NO(g) + O_2(g) \longrightarrow 2NO_2(g)$
     (d) $4NH_3(g) + 5O_2(g) \longrightarrow 4NO(g) + 6H_2O(l)$
     (e) $Ga(s) + As(s) \longrightarrow GaAs(s)$

2-46 (a) Lithium is oxidized and selenium is reduced.
     (b) Scandium is oxidized and iodine is reduced.
     (c) Gallium is oxidized and phosphorus is reduced.
     (d) Potassium is oxidized and fluorine is reduced.

2-48 (a) Two electrons.
     (b) Three electrons.
     (c) Three electrons.
     (d) One electron.

F   ANSWERS TO THE SELF-TEST

1 false

2 false

3 false

4 in front

5 be the same as

6 false

7 sodium, potassium (or other Group 1 metals)

8 (a) $2Li(s) + Cl_2(g) \longrightarrow 2LiCl(s)$
   (b) $2K(s) + H_2(g) \longrightarrow 2KH(s)$
   (c) $2Na(s) + 2H_2O(l) \longrightarrow$
       $\qquad\qquad 2NaOH(s) + H_2(g)$

9 calcium, strontium, barium

10 (a) $2Mg(s) + O_2(g) \longrightarrow 2MgO(s)$

(b) $Mg(s) + H_2O(g) \xrightarrow{\text{high T}}$
$MgO(s) + H_2(g)$

(c) $Ca(s) + Cl_2(g) \longrightarrow CaCl_2(s)$

(d) $Ca(s) + H_2(g) \longrightarrow CaH_2(s)$

11 fluorine, chlorine, bromine, iodine, and astatine

12 (a) $2Na(s) + F_2(g) \longrightarrow 2NaF(s)$
(b) $Ca(s) + I_2(s) \longrightarrow CaI_2(s)$
(c) $H_2(g) + Br_2(l) \longrightarrow 2HBr(g)$
(d) $Sr(s) + Cl_2(g) \longrightarrow SrCl_2(s)$

13 atomic mass

14 similar

15 false

16 atomic number

17 true

18 alkali metals

19 alkaline earth metals

20 7

21 8

22 the inert gases

23 false (Si is a semimetal.)

24 semiconducting, brittle, dull, nonductile

25 false

26 in groups that are headed by numbers

27 false

28 true

29 Group 2 and Group 3

30 lanthanum, actinium

31 the rare earths

32 true

33 radioactive

34 The members of each series have such similar chemical properties that they can be placed in one position in the periodic table. Also, this version of the periodic table is more compact.

35 false

36 false (The properties of the first member are not as typical as those of the other members.)

37 true

38 false

39 a noble gas

40 a noble gas

41 two

42 positive ions and negative ions

43 zero

44 +2, −1, $MgBr_2$

45 increases

46 a transfer of electrons

47 the number of electrons gained by the element that is reduced

3 / Chemical Calculations

OUTLINE OF CHAPTER 3

3-1   The quantity of a substance that is equal to its formula mass in grams is called a mole.

Formula mass is the mass of the formula unit of a substance on the atomic mass scale.

The number of moles in a given mass of a substance is calculated, using the unit conversion factor

$$1 = \frac{1 \text{ mol}}{\text{formula mass in grams}}$$

3-2   One mole of any substance contains Avogadro's number of formula units.

Avogadro's number, 6.022×10^{23} is the number of formula units in one mole of a substance.

The formula unit is the group of atoms or ions represented by the chemical formula of a substance (see Table 3-1).

The mass of a formula unit is calculated by dividing the formula mass by Avogadro's number.

The number of atoms and molecules in a given mass of a substance is found, using Avogadro's number and the formula mass of the substance.

3-3   Simplest formulas can be determined by chemical analysis.

Stoichiometry is the calculation of the quantities of elements or compounds involved in chemical equations.

The simplest chemical formula of a substance is given as the number of atoms of each type in the substance expressed as smallest whole numbers.

The empirical formula is the simplest chemical formula of a substance.

3-4   The determination of atomic mass requires a knowledge of empirical formulas.

The atomic mass of an element can be determined from the empirical formula of one of its compounds.

3-5   An empirical formula along with the molecular mass determines the molecular formula.

The molecular formula of a substance is found from the empirical formula and the molecular mass of the substance.

3-6   The coefficients in chemical equations can be interpreted as numbers of moles.

The balancing coefficients in a chemical equation are the relative numbers of moles of each reactant and product in the balanced equation.

The various interpretations of chemical reactions in terms of molecules, moles, and grams are summarized in Table 3-2.

Some calculations involving chemical reactions are discussed.

3-7   Calculations involving chemical reactions are carried out in terms of moles.

The procedure for calculations involving chemical reactions is given in Figure 3-1.

3-8   When two or more substances react, the quantity of product is determined by the limiting reactant.

The limiting reactant is the reactant that is consumed completely in a chemical reaction.

The excess reactant is the reactant that is not consumed completely in a chemical reaction.

When the quantities of two or more reactants are given, it is necessary to determine which is the limiting reactant.

3-9   Many reactions take place in solution.

A solution is a mixture of two or more substances that is uniform at the molecular level.

The solute is the substance that is dissolved.

The solvent is the liquid in which the solute is dissolved.

The process of dissolving a substance in water can be represented by a chemical equation.

3-10   The concentration of a solution can be expressed in terms of molarity.

Molarity is defined as the number of moles of solute per liter of solution: as an equation,

$$\text{molarity} = \frac{\text{moles of solute}}{\text{liters of solution}} \tag{3-5}$$

or in symbols,

$$M = \frac{n}{V} \tag{3-6}$$

The molarity of a solution can be calculated from the mass of solute in a given volume of solution.

The procedure for preparing a solution of known molarity is described.

Calculations involving reactions in solution are discussed.

B   SELF-TEST

1   The atomic mass of an element is the mass of an atom relative to
   _____ .

2   The atomic mass of helium is 4.003 g. *True/False*

3   The formula mass of a substance is the _____ .

4   One mole of a substance is the quantity of the substance that is _____
   _____ .

5   Two moles of Be has a mass of _____ grams.

6   The question, "Two moles of nitrogen has a mass of _____ grams," is ambiguous. Why?

7   The number of moles in 36 g of carbon is _____ .

8   The number of moles in 36 g of water, H_2O, is _____ .

9   One mole of ammonia, NH_3, has the same mass as one mole of nitrogen dioxide, NO_2. *True/False*

10 The value of Avogadro's number is _____ .

11 _____ of any substance contains Avogadro's number of formula units.

12 Two moles of hydrogen chloride, HCl, contain _____ molecules.

13 One mole of carbon dioxide, CO_2, contains the same number of molecules as one mole of carbon monoxide, CO. *True/False*

14 One mole of CO_2 contains Avogadro's number of oxygen atoms. *True/False*

15 Two moles of NaCl contain _____ chloride ions.

16 Two moles of $CaCl_2$ contain _____ chloride ions.

17 The simplest chemical formula of a compound in which two atoms of Cu combine with one atom of O is _____ .

18 Chemical analysis of a compound provides us with the number of each kind of atom in the compound. *True/False*

19 The expression 88.82 g Cu ⇌ 11.18 g O means that _____
   _____ .

20 The number of moles of Cu and O that combine can be found from the data in Question 19 by _____ .

21 The simplest chemical formula of the compound of Cu and O given in Question 19 is Cu_4O_2. *True/False*

22 The empirical formula of a compound is always the actual molecular formula of the compound. *True/False*

23 The molecular formula of a compound can be determined from the empirical formula and _____.

24 A substance has the empirical formula CH_2 and its molecular mass is 42. The molecular formula is _____.

25 A hydrocarbon is a compound that consists of the elements _____ and _____.

26 The balancing coefficients in a chemical equation can be interpreted as _____.

Questions 27 through 30 refer to the balanced chemical equation

$$2C_2H_6(g) + 7O_2(g) \longrightarrow 4CO_2(g) + 6H_2O(l)$$

27 How many moles of C_2H_6 react with 14 mol of O_2?

28 In order to calculate the number of grams of CO_2 produced from 14 mol of O_2, we first must calculate the _____ of CO_2 produced.

29 We can calculate the mass of CO_2 produced from 14 mol of O_2 by _____ _____.

30 The procedure to calculate the mass of O_2 that is necessary for the complete combustion of a given mass of C_2H_6 is
(1) _____
(2) _____
(3) _____

31 In a reaction between 10 g of hydrogen, H_2, and 32 g of oxygen, O_2, 6 g of hydrogen remains after the consumption of all the oxygen. The limiting reactant is _____ and the excess reactant is _____.

32 A solution is prepared by dissolving 1.0 g of sodium chloride in 100 mL of water. The solute is _____ and the solvent is _____.

33 Molarity is defined as _____ _____.

34 The molarity of a solution in which 0.50 mol of sodium chloride is dissolved in 500 mL of solution is _____.

35 A 1.0 M solution of sodium chloride is prepared by dissolving 1.0 mol of sodium chloride in 1.0 L of water. *True/False*

36 The procedure to prepare 500 mL of a 0.50 M solution of sodium chloride is as follows: _____

_____ .

37 There are _____ moles of sodium chloride in 10 mL of a 1.0 M solution of sodium chloride.

C   CALCULATIONS YOU SHOULD KNOW HOW TO DO

Chapter 3 contains many different types of calculations. You should learn how all the calculations presented are unified by the concept of a mole. The procedure for any calculation involving chemical reactions is summarized in Figure 3-2. You should be able to do the following types of calculations.

1 Calculate the number of moles in a given mass of a substance. You must know the formula of the substance to be able to do this. See Example 3-1 and Problems 3-3 through 3-6.

2 Calculate the mass of one molecule of a substance. See Example 3-2 and Problems 3-11 through 3-14.

3 Calculate the number of molecules in a given mass of a substance. See Examples 3-3 and 3-4 and Problems 3-15 through 3-18.

4 Determine the simplest formula from chemical analysis. See Examples 3-5 and 3-6 and Problems 3-19 through 3-26.

5 Determine the atomic mass from the empirical formula. See Example 3-7 and Problems 3-27 through 3-30.

6 Determine the molecular formula from the simplest formula and the molecular mass. See Example 3-8 and Problems 3-31 through 3-34.

7 Calculate the quantities of reactants and products that are involved in chemical reactions. See Examples 3-9 and 3-10 and Problems 3-35 through 3-46.

8 Calculate quantities involving limiting reactants. See Examples 3-12 and 3-13 and Problems 3-47 through 3-52.

9 Calculate the molarity of a solution. See Section 3-10 and Problems 3-53 through 3-56.

10 Calculate quantities in order to prepare solutions of a given molarity. See Example 3-14 and Problems 3-57 and 3-58.

11 Calculate quantities of reactants and products of reactions that take place in solution. See Example 3-15 and Problems 3-59 through 3-68.

D   SOLUTIONS TO THE ODD-NUMBERED PROBLEMS

3-1 (a) formula mass of H_2O = (2 × atomic mass of H) + (atomic mass of O)

$$= (2 \times 1.008) + 16.00$$

$$= 18.02$$

(b) formula mass of $FeSO_4$ = (atomic mass of Fe) + (atomic mass of S)

$$+ (4 \times \text{atomic mass of O})$$

$$= (55.85) + (32.06) + (4 \times 16.00)$$

$$= 151.91$$

(c) formula mass of $BaCl_2$ = (atomic mass of Ba) + (2 × atomic mass of Cl)

$$= (137.3) + (2 \times 35.45)$$

$$= 208.2$$

(d) formula mass of $C_6H_{12}O_6$ = (6 × atomic mass of C)

$$+ (12 \times \text{atomic mass of H}) + (6 \times \text{atomic mass of O})$$

$$= (6 \times 12.01) + (12 \times 1.008) + (6 \times 16.00)$$

$$= 180.16$$

3-3 (a) formula mass of $C_{10}H_{12}O_2$ = 164.20

$$\text{number of moles} = (250 \text{ g})\left(\frac{1 \text{ mol}}{164.20 \text{ g}}\right) = 1.52 \text{ mol}$$

(b) formula mass of $C_{18}H_{14}O_3$ = 278.29

$$\text{number of moles} = (250 \text{ g})\left(\frac{1 \text{ mol}}{278.29 \text{ g}}\right) = 0.898 \text{ mol}$$

(c) formula mass of $C_{10}H_{20}O$ = 156.26

$$\text{number of moles} = (250 \text{ g})\left(\frac{1 \text{ mol}}{156.26 \text{ g}}\right) = 1.60 \text{ mol}$$

3-5 (a) formula mass of H_2O = 18.02

$$\text{number of moles} = (28.0 \text{ g})\left(\frac{1 \text{ mol}}{18.02 \text{ g}}\right) = 1.55 \text{ mol}$$

(b) formula mass of C = 12.01

$$\text{number of moles} = (200 \text{ mg})\left(\frac{1 \text{ g}}{10^3 \text{ mg}}\right)\left(\frac{1 \text{ mol}}{12.01 \text{ g}}\right) = 0.0167 \text{ mol}$$

(c) formula mass of NaCl = 58.44

$$\text{number of moles} = (454 \text{ g})\left(\frac{1 \text{ mol}}{58.44 \text{ g}}\right) = 7.77 \text{ mol}$$

3-7   Mass of Avogadro's number of baseballs = $(142 \text{ g})(6.022 \times 10^{23})$
$$= 8.55 \times 10^{25} \text{ g}$$

The mass of the earth = 5.975×10^{24} kg = 5.975×10^{27} g.

The ratio of the mass of one mol of baseballs to the mass of the earth is

$$\frac{8.55 \times 10^{25} \text{ g}}{5.975 \times 10^{27} \text{ g}} = 1.43 \times 10^{-2}$$

The mass of one mol of baseballs is 1.43×10^{-2} that of the mass of the earth.

3-9   The charge on an electron is given to be 1.602×10^{-19} coulombs $\cdot$ electron^{-1}. The number of electrons in 894 coulombs is

$$\frac{894 \text{ coulombs}}{1.602 \times 10^{-19} \text{ coulombs} \cdot \text{electron}^{-1}} = 5.58 \times 10^{21} \text{ electrons}$$

This number of electrons plates out 1.00 g of Ag, or

$$(1.00 \text{ g})\left(\frac{1 \text{ mol}}{107.9 \text{ g}}\right) = 9.27 \times 10^{-3} \text{ mol Ag}$$

It requires one electron to convert one silver ion to a silver atom $(\text{Ag}^+ + e^- \rightarrow \text{Ag})$, and so 5.58×10^{21} electrons corresponds to 9.27×10^{-3} moles. Therefore, one mole of electrons contains

$$\frac{5.58 \times 10^{21} \text{ electrons}}{9.27 \times 10^{-3} \text{ moles}} = 6.02 \times 10^{23} \text{ electrons} \cdot \text{mol}^{-1}$$

3-11   (a) formula mass of NH_3 = 17.03

$$\text{mass of one } NH_3 \text{ molecule} = \left(\frac{17.03 \text{ g}}{1 \text{ mol}}\right)\left(\frac{1 \text{ mol}}{6.022 \times 10^{23} \text{ molecules}}\right)$$
$$= 2.828 \times 10^{-23} \text{ g}$$

(b) formula mass of $C_6H_{12}O_6$ = 180.16

$$\text{mass of one } C_6H_{12}O_6 \text{ molecule} = \left(\frac{180.16 \text{ g}}{1 \text{ mol}}\right)\left(\frac{1 \text{ mol}}{6.022 \times 10^{23} \text{ molecules}}\right)$$
$$= 2.992 \times 10^{-22} \text{ g}$$

(c) formula mass of Fe = 55.85

$$\text{mass of one Fe atom} = \left(\frac{55.85 \text{ g}}{1 \text{ mol}}\right)\left(\frac{1 \text{ mol}}{6.022 \times 10^{23} \text{ atom}}\right)$$
$$= 9.274 \times 10^{-23} \text{ g}$$

3-13 (a) formula mass of Cu = 63.55

$$\text{mass of 200 Cu atoms} = \left(\frac{63.55\ \text{g}}{1\ \text{mol}}\right)\left(\frac{1\ \text{mol}}{6.022 \times 10^{23}\ \text{atom}}\right)(200\ \text{atom})$$

$$= 2.111 \times 10^{-20}\ \text{g}$$

(b) formula mass of NH_3 = 17.03

mass of 10^{16} NH_3 molecules

$$= \left(\frac{17.03\ \text{g}}{1\ \text{mol}}\right)\left(\frac{1\ \text{mol}}{6.022 \times 10^{23}\ \text{molecule}}\right)(10^{16}\ \text{molecule})$$

$$= 2.828 \times 10^{-7}\ \text{g}$$

(c) formula mass of F = 19.00

$$\text{mass of } 10^6 \text{ F atoms} = \left(\frac{19.00\ \text{g}}{1\ \text{mol}}\right)\left(\frac{1\ \text{mol}}{6.022 \times 10^{23}\ \text{atom}}\right)(10^6\ \text{atom})$$

$$= 3.155 \times 10^{-17}\ \text{g}$$

(d) formula mass of F_2 = 38.00

mass of 10^6 F_2 molecules

$$= \left(\frac{38.00\ \text{g}}{1\ \text{mol}}\right)\left(\frac{1\ \text{mol}}{6.022 \times 10^{23}\ \text{molecule}}\right)(10^6\ \text{molecule})$$

$$= 6.310 \times 10^{-17}\ \text{g}$$

3-15 10.0 g H_2O corresponds to

$$(10.0\ \text{g})\left(\frac{1\ \text{mol}}{18.02\ \text{g}}\right) = 0.555\ \text{mol}$$

The number of H_2O molecules in 0.555 mol is

$$(0.555\ \text{mol})\left(\frac{6.022 \times 10^{23}\ \text{molecule}}{1\ \text{mol}}\right) = 3.34 \times 10^{23}\ \text{molecules}$$

There are three atoms in each molecule, and so the total number of atoms is

$$(3\ \text{atom} \cdot \text{molecule}^{-1})(3.34 \times 10^{23}\ \text{molecule}) = 1.00 \times 10^{24}\ \text{atoms}$$

3-17 The number of molecules is

$$(4.10 \times 10^{-6}\ \text{g})\left(\frac{1\ \text{mol}}{238\ \text{g}}\right)\left(\frac{6.022 \times 10^{23}\ \text{molecule}}{1\ \text{mol}}\right) = 1.04 \times 10^{16}\ \text{molecules}$$

The number of molecules in one cubic centimeter of air is

$$\frac{(1.04 \times 10^{16} \text{ molecules})}{(4.10 \times 10^3 \text{ m}^3)} \left(\frac{1 \text{ m}}{100 \text{ cm}}\right)^3 = 2.54 \times 10^6 \text{ molecules} \cdot \text{cm}^{-3}$$

3-19 Take a 100-g sample and write

$$62.5 \text{ g Ca} \backsimeq 37.5 \text{ g C}$$

Divide each quantity by its corresponding atomic mass to get

$$(62.5 \text{ g})\left(\frac{1 \text{ mol}}{40.08 \text{ g}}\right) = 1.56 \text{ mol Ca} \backsimeq (37.5 \text{ g})\left(\frac{1 \text{ mol}}{12.01 \text{ g}}\right) = 3.12 \text{ mol C}$$

Divide by the smaller quantity (1.56) to obtain

$$1.00 \text{ mol Ca} \backsimeq 2.00 \text{ mol C}$$

The empirical formula is CaC_2.

3-21 The mass percentage of Cu in the compound is

$$\text{mass \% Cu} = \left(\frac{1.23 \text{ g}}{2.61 \text{ g}}\right) \times 100 = 47.1\%$$

Therefore, mass % Cl = 52.9%. Assume a 100-g sample and write

$$47.1 \text{ g Cu} \backsimeq 52.9 \text{ g Cl}$$

Divide each quantity by the corresponding atomic mass to get

$$(47.1 \text{ g})\left(\frac{1 \text{ mol}}{63.55 \text{ g}}\right) = 0.741 \text{ mol Cu} \backsimeq (52.9 \text{ g})\left(\frac{1 \text{ mol}}{35.45 \text{ g}}\right) = 1.49 \text{ mol Cl}$$

Divide both quantities by the smaller number (0.741) to get

$$1.00 \text{ mol Cu} \backsimeq 2.01 \text{ mol Cl}$$

Now recognize that 2.01 is essentially 2 and write the empirical formula as $CuCl_2$.

3-23 The problem states that 2.00 g of bromine react with fluorine to yield 4.37 g of a compound. Therefore; the mass of F in the compound is 4.37 g − 2.00 g = 2.37 g F. Thus we have the stoichiometric correspondence

$$2.00 \text{ g Br} \backsimeq 2.37 \text{ g F}$$

Divide each quantity by its corresponding atomic mass to get

$$0.0250 \text{ mol Br} \backsimeq 0.125 \text{ mol F}$$

or

$$1.00 \text{ mol Br} \backsimeq 5.00 \text{ mol F}$$

The empirical formula is BrF_5.

3-25 Take a 100-g sample and write

$$9.9 \text{ g C} \backsimeq 58.7 \text{ g Cl} \backsimeq 31.4 \text{ g F}$$

Divide each quantity by its corresponding atomic mass to obtain

$$0.82 \text{ mol C} \backsimeq 1.66 \text{ mol Cl} \backsimeq 1.65 \text{ mol F}$$

Divide by the smallest quantity (0.82) to obtain

$$1.0 \text{ mol C} \backsimeq 2.0 \text{ mol Cl} \backsimeq 2.0 \text{ mol F}$$

The empirical formula is CCl_2F_2.

3-27 mass % M $= \left(\dfrac{2.885 \text{ g}}{3.365 \text{ g}} \right) \times 100 = 85.74\%$

Assuming a 100 gram sample, we have

$$85.74 \text{ g M} \backsimeq 100.00 \text{ g} - 85.74 \text{ g} = 14.26 \text{ g O}$$

We do not know the atomic mass of M, but we can divide 14.26 g O by the atomic mass of O(16.00) to obtain

$$85.74 \text{ g M} \backsimeq 0.8913 \text{ mol O}$$

We know from the given empirical formula that

$$2 \text{ mol M} \backsimeq 3 \text{ mol O}$$

Thus we have

$$85.74 \text{ g M} \backsimeq 0.8913 \text{ mol O} \left(\frac{2 \text{ mol M}}{3 \text{ mol O}} \right)$$

or

$$85.74 \text{ g M} \backsimeq 0.5942 \text{ mol M}$$

Divide by 0.5942 to get

$$1.000 \text{ mol M} \approx 144.3 \text{ g M}$$

The atomic mass of M is 144.3, which corresponds to neodynium (Nd).

3-29 $\text{mass \% of } H_2O = \left(\dfrac{0.0949 \text{ g}}{0.642 \text{ g}} \right) \times 100 = 14.8\%$

Therefore, mass % MCl_2 = 85.2%. Assuming a 100-g sample,

$$14.8 \text{ g } H_2O \approx 85.2 \text{ g } MCl_2$$

Divide by the formula mass of H_2O (we do not know the formula mass of MCl_2 because we do not know the atomic mass of M) to obtain

$$0.821 \text{ mol } H_2O \approx 85.2 \text{ g } MCl_2$$

We know from the chemical formula of the compound that

$$2 \text{ mol } H_2O \approx 1 \text{ mol } MCl_2$$

Thus we have

$$0.821 \text{ mol } H_2O \left(\frac{1 \text{ mol } MCl_2}{2 \text{ mol } H_2O} \right) \approx 85.2 \text{ g } MCl_2$$

or

$$0.4105 \text{ mol } MCl_2 \approx 85.2 \text{ g } MCl_2$$

Divide both sides of the correspondence by 0.4105 to get

$$1.00 \text{ mol } MCl_2 \approx 208 \text{ g } MCl_2$$

There are two chlorine atoms in MCl_2, and so the atomic mass of M is

$$\text{atomic mass of M} = 208 - (2 \times 35.45) = 137$$

The metal is barium.

3-31   Take a 100 gram sample and write

$$62.0 \text{ g C} \approx 10.4 \text{ g H} \approx 27.5 \text{ g O}$$

Divide by the corresponding atomic masses to get

$$5.16 \text{ mol C} \approx 10.3 \text{ mol H} \approx 1.72 \text{ mol O}$$

Now divide by the smallest quantity (1.72) to get

$$3.00 \text{ mol C} \backsimeq 5.99 \text{ mol H} \backsimeq 1.00 \text{ mol O}$$

The simplest formula is C_3H_6O whose formula mass is 58.1. Given that the formula mass is 58.1, the molecular formula is C_3H_6O.

3-33   Assume a 100 gram sample and write

$$22.5 \text{ g Na} \backsimeq 30.4 \text{ g P} \backsimeq 47.1 \text{ g O}$$

Divide by the corresponding atomic masses to get

$$0.979 \text{ mol Na} \backsimeq 0.982 \text{ mol P} \backsimeq 2.94 \text{ mol O}$$

Divide through by 0.979 to obtain

$$1.00 \text{ mol Na} \backsimeq 1.00 \text{ mol P} \backsimeq 3.00 \text{ mol O}$$

The empirical formula is $NaPO_3$. The formula mass corresponding to this empirical formula is 102, and this divides into the observed molecular mass (612) six times. Thus the molecular formula is $Na_6P_6O_{18}$.

3-35   The equation is

$$C(s) + H_2O(g) \longrightarrow CO(g) + H_2(g)$$

One metric ton of char $[C(s)]$ corresponds to

$$(1000 \text{ kg})\left(\frac{10^3 \text{ g}}{1 \text{ kg}}\right)\left(\frac{1 \text{ mol}}{12.01 \text{ g}}\right) = 8.33 \times 10^4 \text{ mol C}$$

We see from the reaction that one mole of H_2 results from each mole of C, and

$$\text{mol } H_2 = (8.33 \times 10^4 \text{ mol C})\left(\frac{1 \text{ mol } H_2}{1 \text{ mol C}}\right) = 8.33 \times 10^4 \text{ mol } H_2$$

The mass of H_2 obtained is

$$\text{mass of } H_2 = (8.33 \times 10^4 \text{ mol})\left(\frac{2.016 \text{ g } H_2}{1 \text{ mol } H_2}\right) = 1.68 \times 10^5 \text{ g } H_2$$

$$= 168 \text{ kg} = 0.168 \text{ metric tons } H_2$$

3-37   The reaction is

$$2NaCl(aq) + 2H_2O(l) \xrightarrow{\text{electrolysis}} 2NaOH(aq) + Cl_2(g) + H_2(g)$$

The quantity of pure NaCl involved is

$$\text{mass of NaCl} = (1.00 \text{ kg})(0.95) = 0.95 \text{ kg} = 950 \text{ g}$$

The number of moles of NaCl is

$$\text{mol of NaCl} = (950 \text{ g})\left(\frac{1 \text{ mol}}{58.44 \text{ g}}\right) = 16.26 \text{ mol}$$

According to the equation for the reaction, two moles of NaOH, one mole of H_2, and one mole of Cl_2 are produced from two moles of NaCl. Therefore,

$$\text{mol of NaOH} = (16.26 \text{ mol NaCl})\left(\frac{2 \text{ mol NaOH}}{2 \text{ mol NaCl}}\right) = 16.26 \text{ mol NaOH}$$

$$\text{mol of } Cl_2 = (16.26 \text{ mol NaCl})\left(\frac{1 \text{ mol } Cl_2}{2 \text{ mol NaCl}}\right) = 8.128 \text{ mol } Cl_2$$

$$\text{mol of } H_2 = (16.26 \text{ mol NaCl})\left(\frac{1 \text{ mol } H_2}{2 \text{ mol NaCl}}\right) = 8.128 \text{ mol } H_2$$

The masses produced are

$$\text{mass of NaOH} = (16.26 \text{ mol})\left(\frac{40.00 \text{ g}}{1 \text{ mol}}\right) = 650 \text{ g NaOH} = 0.650 \text{ kg NaOH}$$

$$\text{mass of } Cl_2 = (8.128 \text{ mol})\left(\frac{70.90 \text{ g}}{1 \text{ mol}}\right) = 576 \text{ g } Cl_2 = 0.576 \text{ kg } Cl_2$$

$$\text{mass of } H_2 = (8.128 \text{ mol})\left(\frac{2.016 \text{ g}}{1 \text{ mol}}\right) = 16.4 \text{ g } H_2 = 0.0164 \text{ kg } H_2$$

3-39   The reaction is
$$\text{FeSAs}(s) \longrightarrow \text{FeS}(s) + \text{As}(s)$$

The number of moles of As produced is

$$\text{mol of As} = (10.0 \text{ g})\left(\frac{1 \text{ mol}}{74.92 \text{ g}}\right) = 0.133 \text{ mol (As)}$$

There is a one-to-one correspondence between moles of As and moles of FeSAs, and we see that 0.133 mol of FeSAs are required to produce 10.0 g of As. The mass required is

$$\text{mass of FeSAs} = (0.133 \text{ mol})\left(\frac{162.83 \text{ g}}{1 \text{ mol}}\right) = 21.7 \text{ g FeSAs}$$

3-41   The mass percentage of Pb in $PbSO_4$ is

$$\text{mass \% Pb in } PbSO_4 = \frac{\text{atomic mass of Pb}}{\text{formula mass of } PbSO_4} \times 100 = \frac{207.2}{303.3} \times 100$$
$$= 68.32\%$$

The mass of Pb in the $PbSO_4$ is

$$\text{mass of Pb} = (0.6832)(13.73 \text{ g}) = 9.380 \text{ g Pb}$$

The percentage of lead in the ore is

$$\frac{\text{mass of lead}}{\text{mass of ore}} \times 100 = \left(\frac{9.380 \text{ g}}{53.92 \text{ g}}\right) \times 100 = 17.40\%$$

3-43 Note that one mole of Zn results from each mole of ZnS. The number of moles of ZnS is

$$\text{mol of ZnS} = (2.00 \times 10^5 \text{ kg})\left(\frac{10^3 \text{ g}}{1 \text{ kg}}\right)\left(\frac{1 \text{ mol}}{97.44 \text{ g}}\right) = 2.05 \times 10^6 \text{ mol}$$

This is the number of moles of Zn produced. The mass of Zn produced is

$$\text{mass of Zn} = (2.05 \times 10^6 \text{ mol})\left(\frac{65.38 \text{ g}}{1 \text{ mol}}\right) = 1.34 \times 10^8 \text{ g Zn}$$

$$= 1.34 \times 10^5 \text{ kg Zn}$$

3-45 The number of moles of ammonia, NH_3, is

$$\text{mol of } NH_3 = (6.40 \times 10^4 \text{ kg})\left(\frac{10^3 \text{ g}}{1 \text{ kg}}\right)\left(\frac{1 \text{ mol}}{17.03 \text{ g}}\right) = 3.76 \times 10^6 \text{ mol}$$

From the set of three reactions, we see that

$$1 \text{ mol } NH_3 \longrightarrow 1 \text{ mol NO} \longrightarrow 1 \text{ mol } NO_2 \longrightarrow \tfrac{2}{3} \text{ mol } HNO_3$$

Thus, there are 2 mol of HNO_3 produced from 3 mol of NH_3. The moles of HNO_3 produced are

$$\text{mol of } HNO_3 = (3.76 \times 10^6 \text{ mol } NH_3)\left(\frac{2 \text{ mol } HNO_3}{3 \text{ mol } NH_3}\right)$$

$$= 2.51 \times 10^6 \text{ mol } HNO_3$$

The mass of HNO_3 produced is

$$\text{mass of } HNO_3 = (2.51 \times 10^6 \text{ mol})\left(\frac{63.02 \text{ g}}{1 \text{ mol}}\right)$$

$$= 1.58 \times 10^8 \text{ g } HNO_3 = 1.58 \times 10^5 \text{ kg } HNO_3$$

3-47 Because we are given the quantities of two reactants, we must check to see if one of them acts as a limiting reactant. The number of moles of KCl and HNO_3 are

$$\text{mol of KCl} = (81.6 \text{ kg})\left(\frac{10^3 \text{ g}}{1 \text{ kg}}\right)\left(\frac{1 \text{ mol}}{74.55 \text{ g}}\right) = 1.09 \times 10^3 \text{ mol}$$

$$\text{mol of HNO}_3 = (40.8 \text{ kg})\left(\frac{10^3 \text{ g}}{1 \text{ kg}}\right)\left(\frac{1 \text{ mol}}{63.02 \text{ g}}\right) = 6.474 \times 10^2 \text{ mol}$$

Thus we see that KCl is in great excess and that HNO_3 is the limiting reactant. The mass of KNO_3 produced is

$$\text{mass of KNO}_3 = (6.474 \times 10^2 \text{ mol HNO}_3)\left(\frac{4 \text{ mol KNO}_3}{4 \text{ mol HNO}_3}\right)\left(\frac{101.11 \text{ g KNO}_3}{1 \text{ mol KNO}_3}\right)$$

$$= 6.55 \times 10^4 \text{ g KNO}_3 = 65.5 \text{ kg KNO}_3$$

The mass of Cl_2 produced is

$$\text{mass of Cl}_2 = (6.474 \times 10^2 \text{ mol HNO}_3)\left(\frac{2 \text{ mol Cl}_2}{4 \text{ mol HNO}_3}\right)\left(\frac{70.90 \text{ g Cl}_2}{1 \text{ mol Cl}_2}\right)$$

$$= 2.30 \times 10^4 \text{ g Cl}_2 = 23.0 \text{ kg Cl}_2$$

3-49 We must determine which reactant is the limiting reactant. The number of moles of NaOH and H_3PO_4 are

$$\text{mol of NaOH} = (60.0 \text{ g})\left(\frac{1 \text{ mol}}{40.00 \text{ g}}\right) = 1.50 \text{ mol}$$

$$\text{mol of H}_3\text{PO}_4 = (20.0)\left(\frac{1 \text{ mol}}{97.99 \text{ g}}\right) = 0.204 \text{ mol}$$

Each mole of H_3PO_4 requires three moles of NaOH, and so we see that 0.204 mol of H_3PO_4 requires 0.612 mol of NaOH. Thus, the NaOH is in excess and H_3PO_4 is the limiting reactant. The mass of Na_3PO_4 that will be produced is

$$\text{mass of Na}_3\text{PO}_4 = (0.204 \text{ mol H}_3\text{PO}_4)\left(\frac{1 \text{ mol Na}_3\text{PO}_4}{1 \text{ mol H}_3\text{PO}_4}\right)\left(\frac{163.94 \text{ g Na}_3\text{PO}_4}{1 \text{ mol Na}_3\text{PO}_4}\right)$$

$$= 33.4 \text{ g Na}_3\text{PO}_4$$

3-51 The number of moles of reactants is

$$\text{mol of Fe}_3\text{O}_4 = (2.00 \text{ g})\left(\frac{1 \text{ mol}}{231.55 \text{ g}}\right) = 8.64 \times 10^{-3} \text{ mol}$$

$$\text{mol of O}_2 = (7.50 \text{ g})\left(\frac{1 \text{ mol}}{32.00 \text{ g}}\right) = 0.234 \text{ mol}$$

The O_2 is in great excess and Fe_3O_4 is the limiting reactant. The mass of Fe_2O_3 that will be produced is

$$\text{mass of Fe}_2\text{O}_3 = (8.64 \times 10^{-3} \text{ mol Fe}_3\text{O}_4)\left(\frac{6 \text{ mol Fe}_2\text{O}_3}{4 \text{ mol Fe}_3\text{O}_4}\right)\left(\frac{159.70 \text{ g Fe}_2\text{O}_3}{1 \text{ mol Fe}_2\text{O}_3}\right)$$

$$= 2.07 \text{ g Fe}_2\text{O}_3$$

3-53   The number of moles of $Ca(OH)_2$ is

$$\text{mol of } Ca(OH)_2 = (0.185 \text{ g})\left(\frac{1 \text{ mol}}{74.10 \text{ g}}\right) = 2.50 \times 10^{-3} \text{ mol}$$

The molarity is calculated using Equation (3-6)

$$\text{molarity} = \frac{n}{V} = \left(\frac{2.50 \times 10^{-3} \text{ mol}}{100 \text{ mL}}\right)\left(\frac{1000 \text{ mL}}{1 \text{ L}}\right) = 0.0250 \text{ M}$$

3-55   The number of moles of NaOH is

$$\text{mol of NaOH} = (572 \text{ g})\left(\frac{1 \text{ mol}}{40.00 \text{ g}}\right) = 14.3 \text{ mol}$$

Because the 14.3 moles are dissolved in one liter of solution, the molarity of the solution is 14.3 M.

3-57   Dissolve 0.250 mol of sucrose in about one half a liter of water and then dilute the solution to one liter using a volumetric flask. The mass of sucrose to use is

$$\text{mass of sucrose} = (0.250 \text{ mol})\left(\frac{342.3 \text{ g}}{1 \text{ mol}}\right) = 85.6 \text{ g}$$

3-59   The number of moles of Zn that react is

$$\text{mol of Zn} = (4.33 \text{ g})\left(\frac{1 \text{ mol}}{65.38 \text{ g}}\right) = 6.623 \times 10^{-2} \text{ mol}$$

The number of moles of HCl required is

$$\text{mol of HCl} = (6.623 \times 10^{-2} \text{ mol Zn})\left(\frac{2 \text{ mol HCl}}{1 \text{ mol Zn}}\right) = 1.325 \times 10^{-1} \text{ mol}$$

The volume of a 3.00 M solution to use can be found using Equation (3-6)

$$V = \frac{n}{M} = \frac{1.325 \times 10^{-1} \text{ mol}}{3.00 \text{ mol} \cdot \text{L}^{-1}} = 0.0442 \text{ L} = 44.2 \text{ mL}$$

3-61   We must first determine the number of moles of NaOH. Using Equation (3-6), we have

$$\text{mol of NaOH} = MV = (5.00 \text{ mol} \cdot \text{L}^{-1})(10.0 \text{ L}) = 50.0 \text{ mol}$$

The number of moles of Cl_2 required is

$$\text{mol of } Cl_2 = (50.0 \text{ mol NaOH})\left(\frac{1 \text{ mol } Cl_2}{2 \text{ mol NaOH}}\right) = 25.0 \text{ mol } Cl_2$$

and the mass of Cl_2 is

$$\text{mass of } Cl_2 = (25.0 \text{ mol})\left(\frac{70.90 \text{ g}}{1 \text{ mol}}\right) = 1770 \text{ g } Cl_2$$

3-63   The number of moles of KOH that reacts is

$$\text{mol of KOH} = (15.0 \text{ g})\left(\frac{1 \text{ mol}}{56.11 \text{ g}}\right) = 0.267 \text{ mol}$$

According to the reaction,

$$\text{mol of } HNO_3 = (0.267 \text{ mol KOH})\left(\frac{1 \text{ mol } HNO_3}{1 \text{ mol KOH}}\right) = 0.267 \text{ mol } HNO_3$$

The volume of HNO_3 required can be found by using Equation (3-6)

$$V = \frac{n}{M} = \frac{0.267 \text{ mol}}{1.00 \text{ mol} \cdot L^{-1}} = 0.267 \text{ L} = 267 \text{ mL}$$

3-65   The number of moles of HCl can be found by using Equation (3-6)

$$\text{mol of HCl} = MV = (0.10 \text{ mol} \cdot L^{-1})(47 \text{ mL})\left(\frac{1 \text{ L}}{1000 \text{ mL}}\right)$$

$$= 4.7 \times 10^{-3} \text{ mol}$$

The number of moles of $Mg(OH)_2$ required to react with all the HCl is

$$\text{mol of } Mg(OH)_2 = (4.7 \times 10^{-3} \text{ mol HCl})\left(\frac{1 \text{ mol } Mg(OH)_2}{2 \text{ mol HCl}}\right)$$

$$= 2.4 \times 10^{-3} \text{ mol}$$

and the mass of $Mg(OH)_2$ is

$$\text{mass of } Mg(OH)_2 = (2.4 \times 10^{-3} \text{ mol})\left(\frac{58.33 \text{ g}}{1 \text{ mol}}\right) = 0.14 \text{ g}$$

3-67   The volume of blood in liters is

$$V = (8.0 \text{ pints})\left(\frac{1 \text{ quart}}{2 \text{ pints}}\right)\left(\frac{1 \text{ L}}{1.06 \text{ quarts}}\right) = 3.8 \text{ L}$$

The number of moles of tetrodotoxin is

$$n = MV = (1.0 \times 10^{-8} \text{ mol} \cdot L^{-1})(3.8 \text{ L}) = 3.8 \times 10^{-8} \text{ mol}$$

The mass of tetrodotoxin is

$$\text{mass of tetrodotoxin} = (3.8 \times 10^{-8} \text{ mol})\left(\frac{319 \text{ g}}{1 \text{ mol}}\right)$$
$$= 1.2 \times 10^{-5} \text{ g}$$
$$= 12 \ \mu\text{g (micrograms)}$$

E ANSWERS TO THE EVEN-NUMBERED PROBLEMS

3-2 (a) 180.15   (c) 136.97
(b) 793.26   (d) 165.39

3-4 (a) 3.03 mol   (c) 2.89 mol
(b) 3.43 mol

3-6 (a) 3.4×10^{-4} mol   (c) 4.4×10^{-9} mol
(b) 5.2×10^{-6} mol

3-8 2.62×10^{15} dollars/person (2620 trillion dollars/person)

3-10 See Problems 3-7 and 3-8 for examples.

3-12 (a) 5.314×10^{-23} g   (c) 5.684×10^{-22} g
(b) 2.523×10^{-22} g

3-14 (a) 3.771×10^{-20} g   (c) 1.897×10^{-12} g
(b) 1.886×10^{-18} g   (d) 7.971×10^{-22} g

3-16 (a) 3.76×10^{23} CH_3OH molecules   (c) 3.76×10^{23} C atoms
(b) 1.50×10^{24} H atoms   (d) 3.76×10^{23} O atoms

3-18 The nerve gas is present in less than lethal amounts (0.41 pg $\cdot$ L^{-1}).

3-20 Fe_2O_3

3-22 FeS

3-24 Al_2O_3

3-26 $PbSO_4$

3-28 atomic mass = 47.3; titanium

3-30 atomic mass = 35.4; chlorine

3-32 $C_6H_{12}O_6$

3-34 59,700

3-36 216 g

3-38 472 g

3-40 30 g of O_2; 41 g of CO_2

3-42 11.6%

3-44 2.46×10^3 kg

3-46 358 g

3-48 0.0708 g

3-50 19.4 g

3-52 1280 g Na_2CS_3; 442 g Na_2CO_3; 225 g H_2O

3-54 0.821 M

3-56 6.53×10^{-3} M

3-58 Dissolve 2.50 g of $CuSO_4 \cdot 5H_2O$ in 40 mL of H_2O, and then dilute to 50.0 mL in a volumetric flask.

3-60 320 g of Br_2; 142 g of Cl_2

3-62 0.0322 L

3-64 1.33 M

3-66 440 mL

3-68 4.2 mL

F   ANSWERS TO THE SELF-TEST

1 carbon-12 being assigned a mass of exactly 12

2 false (Atomic masses have no units because they are relative quantities.)

3 mass of the formula unit of the substance on the atomic mass scale

4 equal to its formula mass in grams or contains Avogadro's number of formula units

5 $2 \times 9.012 = 18.024$

6 You must have the formula of the substance in order to calculate number of moles. Nitrogen could mean N or N_2.

7 3.0 mol

8 2.0 mol

9 false

10 6.022×10^{23}

11 one mole

12 $2 \times 6.022 \times 10^{23} = 1.204 \times 10^{24}$

13 true

14 false

15 $2 \times 6.022 \times 10^{23} = 1.204 \times 10^{24}$

16 $4 \times 6.022 \times 10^{23} = 2.408 \times 10^{24}$

17 Cu_2O

18 false (only relative numbers)

19 88.82 g of Cu combines with or is stoichiometrically equivalent to 11.18 g of O.

20 dividing the mass of each by its atomic mass

21 false (The simplest formula is Cu_2O.)

22 false

23 molecular mass

24 C_3H_6

25 carbon and hydrogen

26 See Table 3-2.

27 4 mol

28   number of moles

29   multiplying the number of moles of CO_2 by the unit conversion factor 44.01 g CO_2/1 mol CO_2

30   (1) Calculate the number of moles of C_2H_6.
   (2) Calculate the number of moles of O_2 that is required to react with the number of moles of C_2H_6 in (1).
   (3) Calculate the mass of the number of moles of O_2 in (2).

31 O_2; H_2

32   NaCl; H_2O

33   the number of moles of solute per liter of solution

34   1.0 M

35   false

36   Dissolve 0.50 mol (29.22 g) of NaCl in about 400 mL of H_2O and then dilute to 500 mL.

37   0.010

4 / Chemical Reactions

A OUTLINE OF CHAPTER 4

4-1 The reaction of two substances to form a single product is a combination reaction.

    Combination reactions can involve a metal and a nonmetal or two nonmetals.

    Combustion reactions involve the burning of a compound in oxygen.

    Ionic compounds are composed of ions.

    Molecular compounds are composed of molecules.

4-2 There are many stable polyatomic ions.

    The nomenclature of compounds containing polyatomic ions is similar to that for binary compounds.

    A compound containing a polyatomic ion is named, using Table 4-1.

    The formula of a compound containing a polyatomic ion can be written from its name, using Table 4-1.

    Cations are positively charged ions.

    Anions are negatively charged ions.

4-3 Transition metal ions have more than one possible ionic charge.

    Roman numerals in parentheses are used to denote the charge on transition metal ions (Table 4-2).

4-4 Many oxides combine with water to produce acids or bases.

    Bases yield hydroxide ions in water.

    Basic anhydrides are oxides that yield bases when dissolved in water.

    Water soluble metal oxides are basic anhydrides.

    Acids yield hydrogen ions $H^+(aq)$ in water.

Acidic anhydrides are oxides that yield acids when dissolved in water.

Certain nonmetal oxides are acidic anhydrides.

Some common acids are listed in Tables 4-4 and 4-5.

4-5 In a decomposition reaction, a substance is broken down into two or more simpler substances.

There is usually only one reactant in a decomposition reaction.

Some decomposition reactions involve metal oxides, carbonates, nitrates, and chlorates.

4-6 In a single-replacement reaction, one element in a compound is replaced by another.

One metal may replace another metal in a compound.

A reactive metal replaces hydrogen in a dilute acid to produce hydrogen gas (Figure 4-6).

4-7 Metals can be ordered in terms of relative reactivity.

Some single-replacement reactions involve one metal replacing another in a compound (Figure 4-7).

The metals can be ranked in order of their reactivity in a reactivity series of the metals (Table 4-6).

4-8 Single-replacement reactions do not have to take place in solution.

Thermite reactions involve reactions of aluminum metal and metal oxide that produce heat (Figure 4-9).

The reaction of carbon and a metal oxide is an important type of single replacement reaction.

4-9 The reactivity order of the halogens is $F_2 > Cl_2 > Br_2 > I_2$.

A halogen may replace a less reactive halogen in a compound.

Sources of some of the halogens are discussed.

4-10 A double-replacement reaction is one of the type $AB + CD \rightarrow AD + BC$.

A precipitation reaction involves the formation of an insoluble product.

Precipitate formation is a driving force for chemical reactions that occur in solution.

Net ionic equations are used to describe double-replacement reactions.

Spectator ions are not directly involved in double-replacement reactions.

4-11 Neutralization is the reaction between an acid and a base.

The formation of water is the driving force for neutralization reactions.

A salt is an ionic compound formed in the reaction between an acid and a base.

Some properties of acids and bases are summarized in Table 4-7.

Litmus paper is used to test if a solution is acidic or basic.

4-12 The concentration of an acid or a base can be determined by titration.

A titration is a process in which a given volume of a base (acid) is neutralized by a measured volume of an acid (base) of known concentration (Figure 4-12).

A buret is used to measure the volume of the solution added in a titration.

The end point of a titration is the point at which the base (acid) has been completely neutralized by the added acid (base).

An acid-base indicator is used to signal the endpoint in a titration.

Titration calculations involve the equation $n = MV$.

B   SELF-TEST

1   The reaction $2Rb(s) + Br_2(l) \rightarrow 2RbBr(s)$ is an example of a _____ reaction.

2   The reaction between a metal and a nonmetal usually results in (*ionic/molecular*) compound.

3   The reaction between sulfur and oxygen to produce SO_2 is an example of a _____ reaction.

4   Magnesium sulfate, $MgSO_4$, dissolved in water consists of _____ ions and _____ ions.

5   The carbonate ion is an example of a _____ ion.

6   All transition metals have only one possible ionic charge. *True/False*

7   The name tin(IV) indicates that tin has an ionic charge of _____.

8   All metal oxides are soluble in water. *True/False*

9   Metal oxides that dissolve in water yield _____ ions in solution.

10 A base is a compound that _____ when dissolved in water.

11 The compound NaOH is an example of a _____.

12 The compound $Na_2O(s)$ is an example of a _____ anhydride.

13 An acid is a compound that _____ when dissolved in water.

14 An acidic anhydride yields _____ when dissolved in water.

15 The compound SO_3 is an example of an _____ anhydride.

16 The hydrogen ion exists as H^+ in aqueous solution. *True/False*

17 An example of a sulfur oxyacid is _____.

18 Binary acids contain only two elements. *True/False*

19 Decomposition reactions usually involve (1, 2, 3) reactant(s).

20 Oxygen can be produced in the laboratory by heating _____.

21 Many metal carbonates decompose upon heating to produce _____ and _____ gas.

22 When a reactive metal is added to an aqueous solution of an acid, _____ gas is produced.

23 All metals react with acids producing hydrogen gas. *True/False*

24 The metal copper does not liberate hydrogen from acid solutions. *True/False*

25 A metal will replace a less reactive metal from a compound. *True/False*

26 Gold will replace calcium from the compound calcium nitrate, $Ca(NO_3)_2$. *True/False*

27 The _____ of the metals is an ordering of the metals with respect to their reactivity.

28 Any metal will replace any other metal that lies (*above/below*) it in the reactivity series of the metals.

29 Many metals can be produced from their oxides by heating the metal oxide with _____ .

30 Fluorine, F_2, will replace iodine in the compound sodium iodide, NaI. *True/False*

31 The most reactive halogen is _____ .

32 A precipitate is an _____ product of a reaction that takes place in solution.

33 A double-replacement reaction is a reaction in which _____ _____ .

34 Consider the reaction

$$AgNO_3(aq) + NaCl(aq) \longrightarrow NaNO_3(aq) + AgCl(s)$$

(a) The spectator ions are _____ and _____ .
(b) The precipitate is _____ .
(c) The net ionic equation is _____ .

35 The driving force for the chemical reaction between NaCl(*aq*) and $AgNO_3$(*aq*) is _____ .

36 Consider the reaction

$$HNO_3(aq) + KOH(aq) \longrightarrow KNO_3(aq) + H_2O(l)$$

(a) The spectator ions are _____ and _____ .
(b) The net ionic equation is _____ .

37 The driving force for the chemical reaction between HNO_3(*aq*) and KOH(*aq*) is _____ .

38 The reaction between an acid and a base is called a _____ _____ reaction.

39 An ionic compound formed in the reaction between an acid and a base is called a _____.

40 An acidic solution tastes _____.

41 A basic solution tastes _____.

42 The color of litmus is _____ in an acidic solution and _____ in a basic solution.

43 Ammonia, NH_3, is an acidic anhydride. *True/False*

44 In a titration experiment, an acid solution is added to a given volume of a base solution until _____.

45 When the end point in the titration experiment in Question 44 is reached, the last drop of acid makes the solution (*acidic, basic*).

46 The end point of a titration is signaled by _____.

47 The concentration of a solution of a base can be determined by a titration experiment using a solution of NaOH of known concentration. *True/False*

48 The formula mass of an acid can be determined in a titration experiment. *True/False*

49 Classify the following reactions as to type
   (a) $MgO(s) + CO_2(g) \longrightarrow MgCO_3(s)$
   (b) $2KOH(aq) + Cu(NO_3)_2(aq) \longrightarrow 2KNO_3(aq) + Cu(OH)_2(s)$
   (c) $2KOH(aq) + H_2SO_4(aq) \longrightarrow K_2SO_4(aq) + 2H_2O(l)$
   (d) $MgCO_3(s) \longrightarrow MgO(s) + CO_2(g)$

C   CALCULATIONS YOU SHOULD KNOW HOW TO DO

1 Nomenclature of chemical compounds. See Examples 4-1 and 4-2, Tables 4-1, 4-2, and 4-3, and Problems 4-1 through 4-12.

2 Prediction of reaction products.
   (a) For combination reactions, see Examples 4-3 and 4-4 and Problems 4-13 through 4-16.
   (b) For decomposition reactions, see Example 4-5 and Problems 4-17 and 4-18.
   (c) For single replacement reactions, see Example 4-6, Table 4-6, and Problems 4-19 through 4-22.
   (d) For halogen single replacement reactions, see Examples 4-8 and 4-9.
   (e) For double replacement reactions, see Examples 4-10 and 4-11 and Problems 4-27 through 4-30.

3 Relative reactivities of metals. See Example 4-7, Table 4-6, and Problems 4-23 through 4-26.

4 Writing net ionic equations. See Example 4-10 and Problems 4-27 through 4-30.

5 Acid-base reactions. See Example 4-11 and Problems 4-31 through 4-34 (qualitative).

6 Neutralization and titration calculations. See Examples 4-12 through 4-14 and Problems 4-43 through 4-54.

7 Classification of chemical reactions. See Problems 4-35 through 4-40.

D   SOLUTIONS TO THE ODD-NUMBERED PROBLEMS

4-1 In order to name chemical compounds, it is necessary to know the names and symbols of the elements, as well as the names and symbols of the common polyatomic ions (see Table 4-1). Once you have learned the names and symbols, nomenclature becomes simple. For example, consider the compound RbCN. We first note that this compound contains the Group 1 metal rubidium which has a charge of +1, that is, Rb^+; thus the anion is CN^-, which is the cyanide ion. Therefore, the name of the compound is rubidium cyanide.

    (a) rubidium cyanide   (d) cesium permanganate
    (b) silver perchlorate   (e) aluminum hydroxide
    (c) lanthanum chromate

4-3 (a) sodium nitrate   (d) calcium phosphate
       (b) ammonium sulfate   (e) potassium phosphate
       (c) ammonium phosphate

4-5 In going from the name of an ionic compound to the chemical formula, we first write down the formulas for the cation and anion with appropriate ionic charges, and then we use the fact that an ionic compound has no net charge to determine the relative numbers of cations and anions in the formula unit. For example, sodium thiosulfate contains sodium ions, Na^+, and thiosulfate ions, $S_2O_3^{2-}$. It takes two Na^+ to balance the -2 charge on $S_2O_3^{2-}$; thus the formula is $Na_2S_2O_3$. Polyatomic ions are enclosed in parentheses if there are two or more polyatomic ions in the chemical formula.

    (a) $Na_2S_2O_3$ (d) $CaCO_3$
    (b) $Al(HCO_3)_3$ (e) $Ba(C_2H_3O_2)_2$
    (c) $KClO_4$

4-7 (a) Na_2CrO_4 (d) $LiClO_4$
       (b) K_3PO_4 (e) NH_4NO_3
       (c) RbOH

4-9 Problems 4-9 through 4-12 differ from 4-1 through 4-8 in that these compounds contain transition metal cations which have more than one possible charge. The value of the metal ion charge is indicated by a Roman numeral. For example, consider the compound HgO. This compound is a metal oxide, and thus the charge on oxygen is -2. Therefore, the charge on the mercury ion is $+2$, and the systematic name of the compound is mercury(II) oxide.

(a) mercury(II) oxide
(b) tin(IV) oxide
(c) copper(I) iodide
(d) cobalt(II) bromide
(e) chromium(III) cyanide

4-11 (a) CuO
      (b) $AuCl$
      (c) $Sn_3(PO_4)_2$
      (d) $Fe(C_2H_3O_2)_2$
      (e) $Co_2(SO_4)_3$

4-13 The reactions are combination reactions, and thus only a single reaction product is formed. To determine the reaction product, we have to know the resulting charges on the positively charged metal ion and the negatively charged nonmetal ion. For example, consider the reaction

$$Mg(s) + N_2(g) \longrightarrow$$

Mg is a Group 2 metal and thus has a charge of $+2$ in its compounds. The nonmetal nitrogen is a Group 5 element and forms N^{3-}, the nitride ion. Thus we have

$$3Mg(s) + N_2(g) \longrightarrow [3Mg^{2+} \text{ and } 2N^{3-}] \longrightarrow Mg_3N_2(s)$$

where we have used the fact that the net charge on the compound formed is zero to deduce the relative numbers of Mg^{2+} and N^{3-} in the compound.

(a) $3Mg(s) + N_2(g) \longrightarrow Mg_3N_2(s)$
(b) $H_2(g) + S(s) \longrightarrow H_2S(g)$
(c) $2K(s) + Br_2(l) \longrightarrow 2KBr(s)$
(d) $4Al(s) + 3O_2(g) \longrightarrow 2Al_2O_3(s)$
(e) $MgO(s) + SO_2(g) \longrightarrow MgSO_3(s)$

4-15 Note that in each of the cases (a) through (d) a compound is brought in contact with water acting as a reactant and/or a solvent. The key to predicting the products of the reaction is based on the recognition of the type and corresponding properties of the reactant. Thus we recognize $Li_2O(s)$ as an alkali metal oxide. We learned that alkali metal oxides are basic anhydrides and thus we write

(a) $LiO_2(s) + H_2O(l) \xrightarrow{H_2O(l)} 2LiOH(aq) \xrightarrow{H_2O(l)} 2Li^+(aq) + 2OH^-(aq)$

We recognize $SO_3(g)$ as an acidic anhydride that yields $H^+(aq)$ in water.

(b) $SO_3(g) + H_2O(l) \xrightarrow{H_2O(l)} H_2SO_4(aq) \xrightarrow{H_2O(l)} 2H^+(aq) + SO_4^{2-}(aq)$

Using Tables 4-4 and 4-5, we recognize that H_2SO_4 and HBr are acids.

(c) $H_2SO_4(l) \xrightarrow{H_2O(l)} 2H^+(aq) + SO_4^{2-}(aq)$

(d) $HBr(g) \xrightarrow{H_2O(l)} H^+(aq) + Br^-(aq)$

4-17 Recall that decomposition reactions involve the breakdown of a substance into smaller molecules. We predict the products of the reactions given by analogy with known cases. Thus metal carbonates like $CaCO_3(s)$ give off $CO_2(g)$ on heating to yield the corresponding metal oxide.

(a) $CaCO_3(s) \xrightarrow{\text{high T}} CaO(s) + CO_2(g)$

Hydrogen peroxide, H_2O_2, gives off oxygen gas in the presence of light

(b) $2H_2O_2(aq) \xrightarrow{\text{light}} 2H_2O(l) + O_2(g)$

Heavy metal sulfites give off $SO_2(g)$ when heated

(c) $PbSO_3(s) \xrightarrow{\text{high T}} PbO(s) + SO_2(g)$

The oxides of unreactive metals like silver, gold, and platinum decompose on heating to the metal and oxygen

(d) $2Ag_2O(s) \xrightarrow{\text{high T}} 4Ag(s) + O_2(g)$

4-19 In order for a metal-metal replacement reaction to occur, the free metal must be a more reactive metal than the metal in the compound (see Table 4-6). Also, a more reactive free halogen will replace a less reactive halogen in compounds.

(a) $3Na(l) + AlCl_3(s) \longrightarrow 3NaCl(s) + Al(s)$
(b) $Cu(s) + Fe_2O_3(s) \longrightarrow$ N.R.
(c) $Zn(s) + K_2SO_4(aq) \longrightarrow$ N.R.
(d) $Fe(s) + SnCl_2(aq) \longrightarrow FeCl_2(aq) + Sn(s)$
(e) $Br_2(l) + 2NaI(aq) \longrightarrow 2NaBr(aq) + I_2(s)$

4-21 (a) $Cu(NO_3)_2(aq) + Au(s) \longrightarrow$ N.R.
(b) $NaCl(aq) + I_2(aq) \longrightarrow$ N.R.
(c) $2AgNO_3(aq) + Mg(s) \longrightarrow Mg(NO_3)_2(aq) + 2Ag(s)$
(d) $Ag(s) + HCl(aq) \longrightarrow$ N.R.
(e) $Pb(s) + H_2O(l) \longrightarrow$ N.R.

4-23 See Table 4-6.
Na, Fe, Sn, Au

4-25 $2PbS(s) + 3O_2(g) \longrightarrow 2PbO(s) + 2SO_2(g)$
$2PbO(s) + C(s) \longrightarrow 2Pb(s) + CO_2(g)$
$2Ag_2O(s) + C(s) \longrightarrow 4Ag(s) + CO_2(g)$

or

$2Ag_2O(s) \xrightarrow{\text{high T}} 4Ag(s) + O_2(g)$

4-27 To determine the net ionic equation that corresponds to the complete ionic equation, we determine the precipitate or other favored product formed. The ions that are used to form this species are the reactants in the net ionic equation. Thus for case (a) we have $H_2S(g)$ as the key product, and thus

(a) $2H^+(aq) + S^{2-}(aq) \longrightarrow H_2S(g)$

This procedure is equivalent to discarding the spectator ions.

(b) $Pb^{2+}(aq) + S^{2-}(aq) \longrightarrow PbS(s)$
(c) $H^+(aq) + OH^-(aq) \longrightarrow H_2O(l)$
(d) $OH^-(aq) + H^+(aq) \longrightarrow H_2O(l)$ (Na_2O is a basic anhydride)
(e) $NH_3(aq) + H^+(aq) \longrightarrow NH_4^+(aq)$

4-29 (a) $Fe(NO_3)_2(aq) + 2NaOH(aq) \longrightarrow Fe(OH)_2(s) + 2NaNO_3(aq)$
$Fe^{2+}(aq) + 2OH^-(aq) \longrightarrow Fe(OH)_2(s)$

(b) $Zn(ClO_4)_2(aq) + K_2S(aq) \longrightarrow ZnS(s) + 2KClO_4(aq)$
$Zn^{2+}(aq) + S^{2-}(aq) \longrightarrow ZnS(s)$
(c) $Pb(NO_3)_2(aq) + 2KOH(aq) \longrightarrow Pb(OH)_2(s) + 2KNO_3(aq)$
$Pb^{2+}(aq) + 2OH^-(aq) \longrightarrow Pb(OH)_2(s)$
(d) $Zn(NO_3)_2(aq) + Na_2CO_3(aq) \longrightarrow ZnCO_3(s) + 2NaNO_3(aq)$
$Zn^{2+}(aq) + CO_3^{2-}(aq) \longrightarrow ZnCO_3(s)$
(e) $Cu(ClO_4)_2(aq) + Na_2CO_3(aq) \longrightarrow CuCO_3(s) + 2NaClO_4(aq)$
$Cu^{2+}(aq) + CO_3^{2-}(aq) \longrightarrow CuCO_3(s)$

4-31 (a) acidic
(b) acidic
(c) basic
(d) acidic
(e) basic

4-33 (a) $2HClO_3(aq) + Ba(OH)_2(aq) \longrightarrow Ba(ClO_3)_2(aq) + 2H_2O(l)$
barium chlorate

(b) $HC_2H_3O_2(aq) + KOH(aq) \longrightarrow KC_2H_3O_2(aq) + H_2O(l)$
potassium acetate

(c) $2HI(aq) + Mg(OH)_2(s) \longrightarrow MgI_2(aq) + 2H_2O(l)$
magnesium iodide

(d) $H_2SO_4(aq) + 2RbOH(aq) \longrightarrow Rb_2SO_4(aq) + 2H_2O(l)$
rubidium sulfate

(e) $H_3PO_4(aq) + 3LiOH(aq) \longrightarrow Li_3PO_4(aq) + 3H_2O(l)$
lithium phosphate

4-35 (a) decomposition   (c) single-replacement
(b) combination   (d) double-replacement

4-37 (a) $ZnBr_2(s) + Cl_2(g) \longrightarrow ZnCl_2(s) + Br_2(l)$ single-replacement
(b) $2HCl(aq) + Mg(OH)_2(s) \longrightarrow MgCl_2(aq) + 2H_2O(l)$ double-replacement/
neutralization
(c) $BaO(s) + CO_2(g) \longrightarrow BaCO_3(s)$ combination
(d) $2Ag_2O \xrightarrow{heat} 4Ag(s) + O_2(g)$ decomposition
(e) $2Li(s) + 2H_2O(l) \longrightarrow 2LiOH(aq) + H_2(g)$ single-replacement

4-39 (a) $HCl(aq) + KCN(aq) \longrightarrow HCN(g) + KCl(aq)$
(b) $2K(s) + 2H_2O(l) \longrightarrow H_2(g) + 2KOH(aq)$
(c) $2H_2O_2(aq) \longrightarrow O_2(g) + 2H_2O(l)$
(d) $H_2(g) + Br_2(l) \longrightarrow 2HBr(g)$

4-41 $2Pb(l) + O_2(g) \longrightarrow 2PbO(s)$
$Ag(l) + O_2(g) \longrightarrow$ N.R.

4-43 The number of moles of NaOH required to neutralize the HCl solution is

$$\text{moles of NaOH} = MV = (0.250 \text{ mol} \cdot L^{-1})(0.0173 \text{ L})$$

$$= 0.00433 \text{ mol}$$

We see from the neutralization reaction

$$NaOH(aq) + HCl(aq) \longrightarrow NaCl(aq) + H_2O(l)$$

that it requires one mole of NaOH to neutralize one mole of HCl. Thus we have

$$\text{moles of HCl} = \text{moles of NaOH} = 0.00433 \text{ mol}$$

The concentration of the HCl solution is

$$\text{molarity} = \frac{n}{V} = \frac{0.00433 \text{ mol}}{0.0376 \text{ L}} = 0.115 \text{ M}$$

4-45 (a) The number of moles of $Ca(OH)_2$ that is neutralized is

$$\text{moles of } Ca(OH)_2 = MV = (0.010 \text{ mol} \cdot L^{-1})(15.0 \text{ } \mu L)\left(\frac{1 \text{ L}}{10^6 \text{ } \mu L}\right)$$

$$= 1.5 \times 10^{-7} \text{ mol}$$

We see from the neutralization reaction

$$2HNO_3(aq) + Ca(OH)_2(aq) \longrightarrow Ca(NO_3)_2(aq) + 2H_2O(l)$$

that it requires two moles of HNO_3 to neutralize one mole of $Ca(OH)_2$. Thus we have

$$\text{moles of } HNO_3 = [1.5 \times 10^{-7} \text{ mol } Ca(OH)_2]\left[\frac{2 \text{ mol } HNO_3}{1 \text{ mol } Ca(OH)_2}\right]$$

$$= 3.0 \times 10^{-7} \text{ mol}$$

The volume of HNO_3 required is

$$V = \frac{n}{M} = \frac{3.0 \times 10^{-7} \text{ mol}}{0.250 \text{ mol} \cdot L^{-1}} = 1.2 \times 10^{-6} \text{ L} = 1.2 \text{ } \mu L$$

(b) The number of moles of NaOH that is neutralized is

$$\text{moles of NaOH} = MV = (0.100 \text{ mol} \cdot L^{-1})(0.0250 \text{ L})$$

$$= 0.00250 \text{ mol}$$

From the neutralization reaction

$$2NaOH(aq) + H_2SO_4(aq) \longrightarrow Na_2SO_4(aq) + 2H_2O(l)$$

we have

$$\text{moles of } H_2SO_4 = (0.00250 \text{ mol NaOH})\left(\frac{1 \text{ mol } H_2SO_4}{2 \text{ mol NaOH}}\right)$$

$$= 0.00125 \text{ mol}$$

The volume of the H_2SO_4 solution required is

$$V = \frac{n}{M} = \frac{0.00125 \text{ mol}}{0.300 \text{ mol} \cdot \text{L}^{-1}} = 0.00417 \text{ L} = 4.17 \text{ mL}$$

4-47   The number of moles of OH^- added to the $HCl(aq)$ solution is

$$\text{moles of } OH^- = \text{moles of } KOH(s) = (20.0 \text{ g})\left(\frac{1 \text{ mol}}{56.11 \text{ g}}\right) = 0.356 \text{ mol}$$

The number of moles of $HCl(aq)$ initially present is

$$\text{moles of } HCl = MV = (0.125 \text{ mol} \cdot \text{L}^{-1})(1.00 \text{ L}) = 0.125 \text{ mol}$$

Thus an amount of KOH *in excess* of that required to neutralize all of the HCl was added. The neutralization reaction is

$$HCl(aq) + KOH(aq) \longrightarrow H_2O(l) + KCl(aq)$$

The moles of KCl produced are equal to the moles of HCl initially present, which is 0.125 mol. The molarity of KCl is the number of moles of KCl per liter of solution. The volume of the final solution is

$$\text{final volume} = \text{initial volume} + \text{volume added}$$
$$= 1.00 \text{ L} + 0.20 \text{ L} = 1.20 \text{ L}$$

Thus,

$$\text{molarity of } KCl = \frac{n}{V} = \frac{0.125 \text{ mol}}{1.20 \text{ L}} = 0.104 \text{ M}$$

4-49   The number of moles of NaOH present in the sample is equal to the number of moles of HCl required for neutralization. Thus,

$$\text{moles of } NaOH = (0.0317 \text{ L})(0.150 \text{ M HCl})\left(\frac{1 \text{ mol NaOH}}{1 \text{ mol HCl}}\right)$$
$$= 0.00476 \text{ mol}$$
$$\text{mass of } NaOH = (0.00476 \text{ mol})\left(\frac{40.00 \text{ g}}{1 \text{ mol}}\right)$$
$$= 0.190 \text{ g}$$

The percent NaOH in the mixture equals the mass of NaOH divided by the total mass times 100:

$$\% \text{ NaOH} = \frac{0.190 \text{ g NaOH}}{0.365 \text{ g mixture}} \times 100$$
$$= 52.1\%$$

4-51   The number of moles of base required to neutralize the acid is

$$\text{moles of NaOH} = MV = (0.250 \text{ mol} \cdot \text{L}^{-1})(0.0666 \text{ L}) = 0.01665 \text{ mol}$$

Therefore, the number of moles of acid present in the original 100 mL solution was 0.01665 mol. Thus we have

$$1.00 \text{ g acid} \approx 0.01665 \text{ mol acid}$$

Dividing by 0.01665, we obtain

$$60.1 \text{ g} \approx 1.00 \text{ mol}$$

The formula mass of the acid is 60.1.

4-53   The number of moles of base required to neutralize the acid is

$$\text{moles of NaOH} = MV = (0.250 \text{ mol} \cdot \text{L}^{-1})(0.0888 \text{ L}) = 0.0222 \text{ mol}$$

Because the acid has two acidic protons, it requires two moles of NaOH to neutralize one mole of the acid. Thus,

$$\text{moles of acid} = (0.0222 \text{ mol NaOH})\left(\frac{1 \text{ mol acid}}{2 \text{ mol NaOH}}\right) = 0.0111 \text{ mol}$$

We have

$$1.00 \text{ g acid} \approx 0.0111 \text{ mol acid}$$

$$90.1 \text{ g} \approx 1.00 \text{ mol}$$

The formula mass of the acid is 90.1.

E   ANSWERS TO THE EVEN-NUMBERED PROBLEMS

4-2   (a) sodium acetate
(b) calcium chlorate
(c) ammonium carbonate

(d) potassium hydroxide
(e) barium nitrate

4-4   (a) ammonium thiosulfate
(b) sodium carbonate
(c) sodium sulfite

(d) potassium carbonate
(e) sodium thiosulfate

4-6   (a) $HC_2H_3O_2$
(b) $HClO_3$
(c) H_2CO_3

(d) $HClO_4$
(e) $HMnO_4$

4-8   (a) $NaClO_4$
(b) $KMnO_4$
(c) $AgC_2H_3O_2$

(d) $CaSO_3$
(e) $LiCN$

4-10 (a) chromium(II) sulfate   (d) tin(II) nitrate
      (b) iron(III) oxide   (e) copper(I) carbonate
      (c) cobalt(II) cyanide

4-12 (a) $Hg_2(C_2H_3O_2)_2$ (d) $Fe(HCO_3)_2$
      (b) $Hg(CN)_2$ (e) $CrSO_3$
      (c) $Co(OH)_3$

4-14 (a) $2Na(s) + Cl_2(g) \longrightarrow 2NaCl(s)$
      (b) $K(s) + O_2(g) \longrightarrow KO_2(s)$
      (c) $MgO(s) + CO_2(g) \longrightarrow MgCO_3(s)$
      (d) $2H_2(g) + O_2(g) \longrightarrow 2H_2O(l)$
      (e) $N_2(g) + 3H_2(g) \longrightarrow 2NH_3(g)$

4-16 (a) $SrO(s) + H_2O(l) \xrightarrow{H_2O(l)} Sr^{2+}(aq) + 2OH^-(aq)$

      (b) $HNO_3(l) \xrightarrow{H_2O(l)} H^+(aq) + NO_3^-(aq)$

      (c) $Cs_2O + H_2O(l) \xrightarrow{H_2O(l)} 2Cs^+(aq) + 2OH^-(aq)$

      (d) $HI(g) \xrightarrow{H_2O(l)} H^+(aq) + I^-(aq)$

4-18 (a) $MgCO_3(s) \xrightarrow{high\ T} MgO(s) + CO_2(g)$

      (b) $2NaClO_3(s) \xrightarrow{high\ T} 2NaCl(s) + 3O_2(g)$

      (c) $2NaN_3(s) \xrightarrow{high\ T} 2Na(s) + 3N_2(g)$

      (d) $2Au_2O_3(s) \xrightarrow{high\ T} 4Au(s) + 3O_2(g)$

4-20 (a) $Ba(s) + H_2O(g) \longrightarrow BaO(s) + H_2(g)$
      (b) $Fe(s) + H_2SO_4(aq) \longrightarrow FeSO_4(aq) + H_2(g)$
      (c) $Ca(s) + 2HBr(aq) \longrightarrow CaBr_2(aq) + H_2(g)$
      (d) $Pb(s) + 2HCl(aq) \longrightarrow PbCl_2(aq) + H_2(g)$
      (e) $Zn(s) + CaCl_2(aq) \longrightarrow$ N.R.

4-22 (a) $2Na(l) + NiO(s) \longrightarrow Na_2O(s) + Ni(s)$

      (b) $Ca(s) + PbCl_2(s) \xrightarrow{high\ T} CaCl_2(s) + Pb(s)$

      (c) $4Mg(s) + Fe_3O_4(s) \xrightarrow{high\ T} 4MgO(s) + 3Fe(s)$
      (d) $Cu(s) + Al_2O_3(s) \longrightarrow$ N.R.
      (e) $Ag(s) + Zn(NO_3)_2(s) \longrightarrow$ N.R.

4-24 K, Zn, Ag, Pt

4-26 $2CuO(s) + C(s) \xrightarrow{high\ T} 2Cu(s) + CO_2(g)$

      $SnO_2(s) + C(s) \xrightarrow{high\ T} Sn(s) + CO_2(g)$

      $2Fe_2O_3(s) + 3C(s) \xrightarrow{high\ T} 4Fe(s) + 3CO_2(g)$

4-28 (a) $H^+(aq) + OH^-(aq) \longrightarrow H_2O(l)$
      (b) $Pb^{2+}(aq) + CO_3^{2-}(aq) \longrightarrow PbCO_3(s)$
      (c) $2Ag^+(aq) + SO_4^{2-}(aq) \longrightarrow Ag_2SO_4(s)$
      (d) $S^{2-}(aq) + Zn^{2+}(aq) \longrightarrow ZnS(s)$
      (e) $Hg_2^{2+}(aq) + 2Cl^-(aq) \longrightarrow Hg_2Cl_2(s)$

4-30 (a) $2AgNO_3(aq) + Na_2S(aq) \longrightarrow Ag_2S(s) + 2NaNO_3(aq)$
$2Ag^+(aq) + S^{2-}(aq) \longrightarrow Ag_2S(s)$
(b) $H_2SO_4(aq) + Pb(NO_3)_2(aq) \longrightarrow PbSO_4(s) + 2HNO_3(aq)$
$SO_4^{2-}(aq) + Pb^{2+}(aq) \longrightarrow PbSO_4(s)$
(c) $Hg(NO_3)_2(aq) + 2NaI(aq) \longrightarrow HgI_2(s) + 2NaNO_3(aq)$
$Hg^{2+}(aq) + 2I^-(aq) \longrightarrow HgI_2(s)$
(d) $CdCl_2(aq) + 2AgClO_4(aq) \longrightarrow 2AgCl(s) + Cd(ClO_4)_2(aq)$
$Cl^-(aq) + Ag^+(aq) \longrightarrow AgCl(s)$
(e) $2LiBr(aq) + Pb(ClO_4)_2(aq) \longrightarrow PbBr_2(s) + 2LiClO_4(aq)$
$2Br^-(aq) + Pb^{2+}(aq) \longrightarrow PbBr_2(s)$

4-32 (a) basic   (d) basic
(b) acidic   (e) basic
(c) acidic

4-34 $NH_3(aq) + HCHO_2(aq) \longrightarrow NH_4CHO_2(aq)$

4-36 (a) double-replacement   (c) double-replacement
(b) decomposition   (d) single-replacement

4-38 (a) $SrCO_3(s) \xrightarrow{\text{heat}} SrO(s) + CO_2(g)$ decomposition
(b) $4Li(s) + O_2(g) \longrightarrow 2Li_2O(s)$ combination
(c) $Zn(s) + H_2SO_4(aq) \longrightarrow ZnSO_4(aq) + H_2(g)$ single replacement
(d) $Na_2O(s) + CO_2(g) \longrightarrow Na_2CO_3(s)$ combination

(e) $XeF_4(s) \xrightarrow{\text{heat}} Xe(g) + 2F_2(g)$ decomposition

4-40 (a) $ZnS(s) + 2HCl(aq) \longrightarrow H_2S(g) + ZnCl_2(aq)$
(b) $3CaCl_2(aq) + 2H_3PO_4(aq) \longrightarrow Ca_3(PO_4)_2(s) + 6HCl(aq)$
(c) $2HCl(aq) + Na_2CO_3(s) \longrightarrow CO_2(g) + H_2O(l) + 2NaCl(aq)$
(d) $ZnCl_2(aq) + Na_2S(aq) \longrightarrow ZnS(s) + 2NaCl(aq)$

4-42 $HgS(s) + O_2(g) \xrightarrow{\text{heat}} Hg(g) + SO_2(g)$

$$\downarrow \text{cool}$$

$$Hg(l) + SO_2(g)$$

4-44 0.738 M

4-46 170 mL by $Mg(OH)_2$; 190 mL by $Al(OH)_3$

4-48 conc. HBr = 0; conc. NaOH = 0.11 M; conc. NaBr = 0.0286 M

4-50 92.8% (Assume impurities do not react with HCl.)

4-52 46.1

4-54 118

F   ANSWERS TO THE SELF-TEST

1 combination   **4** $Mg^{2+}(aq)$, $SO_4^{2-}(aq)$

2 an ionic   **5** polyatomic ion

3 a combination (or combustion)   **6** false
reaction   **7** +4

8 false (For example, Al_2O_3 is insoluble in water.)

9 hydroxide, $OH^-(aq)$, ions

10 yields hydroxide ions

11 base

12 basic

13 yields hydrogen ions, $H^+(aq)$, in water

14 an acid

15 acidic

16 false (The hydrogen ion in water is associated with one or more water molecules and is represented as $H^+(aq)$.)

17 sulfuric acid, H_2SO_4

18 true

19 1

20 $KClO_3$, potassium chlorate

21 the metal oxide and carbon dioxide, CO_2

22 hydrogen, H_2

23 false

24 true

25 true

26 false

27 reactivity series

28 below

29 carbon

30 true

31 fluorine

32 insoluble

33 the cations in two different compounds exchange anions

34 (a) $Na^+(aq)$ and $NO_3^-(aq)$
(b) $AgCl(s)$
(c) $Ag^+(aq) + Cl^-(aq) \longrightarrow AgCl(s)$

35 the formation of the precipitate $AgCl(s)$

36 (a) $NO_3^-(aq)$ and $K^+(aq)$
(b) $H^+(aq) + OH^-(aq) \longrightarrow H_2O(l)$

37 the formation of unionized water molecules

38 neutralization

39 salt

40 sour

41 bitter

42 red in acid, blue in base

43 false (NH_3 is a basic anhydride.)

44 the base has just been completely neutralized

45 acidic

46 the change in color of the added indicator (litmus)

47 false (You would use a solution of acid of known concentration.)

48 true

49 (a) combination
(b) double-replacement
(c) double-replacement (neutralization)
(d) decomposition

5 / The Properties of Gases

A OUTLINE OF CHAPTER 5

5-1 The physical states of matter are solid, liquid, and gas.

A solid has a fixed volume and shape.

A liquid has a fixed volume but assumes the shape of its container.

A gas occupies the entire volume of its container.

The molecules of a gas are widely separated.

5-2 The pressure of a gas can support a column of liquid.

Gas molecules are separated widely and are in constant motion.

Pressure is force per unit area.

A manometer is used to measure the pressure exerted by a gas (Figure 5-2).

The pressure of a gas can be expressed as the height of a column of mercury supported by the gas.

The unit torr is a pressure of 1 mmHg.

The height of a column of liquid supported by a gas depends upon the density of the liquid (Figure 5-3).

5-3 The earth's atmosphere exerts a pressure.

A barometer is used to measure the pressure due to the atmosphere (Figure 5-4).

Barometric pressure is the pressure due to the atmosphere.

Barometric pressure decreases with increasing altitude.

One standard atmosphere equals 760 torr.

5-4 Pressure is expressed in various units.

The pascal is the SI unit of pressure.

The various units of pressure are given in Table 5-1.

One standard atmosphere equals 1.013×10^5 Pa.

5-5   At constant temperature, the volume of a gas is inversely proportional to its pressure.

Boyle's law can be expressed as $V \propto 1/P$.

In an equation, Boyle's law is $V = c/P$, where c is a proportionality constant.

Boyle's law can also be written $PV = c$ (Equation 5-1).

5-6   At constant pressure, the volume of a gas is proportional to its absolute temperature.

The equation expressing Charles' law is $V = kT$ (constant pressure). (Equation 5-2).

The absolute temperature scale is related to the Celsius scale by the expression $T/K = t/°C + 273.15$ (Equation 5-3).

The absolute (Kelvin) temperature scale has the units of kelvin, K.

A gas thermometer is based on Charles' law (Figure 5-8).

5-7   Equal volumes of gases at the same pressure and temperature contain equal numbers of molecules.

Gay-Lussac's law of combining volumes states that when all volumes are measured at the same pressure and temperature, the volumes in which gases combine in chemical reactions are related by simple, whole numbers (Figure 5-9).

5-8   Boyle's law, Charles' law, and Avogadro's law can be combined into one equation.

An ideal gas is a gas that obeys the ideal-gas law.

The ideal-gas law is expressed by the ideal-gas equation

$$PV = nRT \qquad (5\text{-}5)$$

One value of the gas constant R is $0.0821 \text{ L} \cdot \text{atm} \cdot \text{K}^{-1} \cdot \text{mol}^{-1}$.

The molar volume of an ideal gas is 22.4 L at 0°C and 1.00 atm.

5-9   The ideal-gas equation can be used to calculate gas densities and molar masses.

The ideal-gas equation expressed in terms of the density of the gas in grams per liter, ρ, is

$$\rho = MP/RT \qquad (5\text{-}8)$$

Gas density increases as gas pressure increases and as gas temperature decreases.

Molar mass is the mass of one mole $(\text{g} \cdot \text{mol}^{-1})$.

The molar mass of a gas can be determined from the density of the gas.

5-10   The total pressure of a mixture of gases is the sum of the partial pressures of all the gases in the mixture.

Dalton's law of partial pressures states that

$$P_{total} = P_1 + P_2 + \cdots \qquad (5\text{-}9)$$

The total pressure of a mixture of gases is determined by the total number of moles of gas in the mixture or

$$P_{total} = n_{total}\left(\frac{RT}{V}\right) \qquad (5\text{-}10)$$

When a gas is collected over water, Dalton's law of partial pressures, $P_{total} = P_{gas} + P_{H_2O}$, is used to find the pressure of the gas.

5-11 The kinetic theory of gases views the molecules of a gas as being in constant motion.

Collisions of gas molecules with the container walls give rise to the gas pressure.

Kinetic energy is the energy associated with the motion of a body.

The kinetic energy of a particle of mass m and speed v is given by $E = \frac{1}{2}mv^2$ (Equation 5-11).

The SI unit of energy is the joule where 1 joule = 1 J = 1 kg $\cdot$ m$^2 \cdot$ s^{-2}.

There is a distribution of molecular speeds in a gas (Figure 5-13).

The average kinetic energy per mole of a gas, $\bar{E}_{av}$, is directly proportional to the absolute temperature of the gas.

$$\bar{E}_{av} = \tfrac{3}{2}RT, \text{ where } R \text{ is the gas constant} \qquad (5\text{-}12)$$

The average speed, v_{av} in m $\cdot$ s^{-1}, of a molecule in a gas is defined by $\bar{E}_{av} \equiv \frac{1}{2}M_{kg}v_{av}^2$, where M_{kg} is the molar mass in kilograms (Equation 5-13).

The average speed is given by

$$v_{av} = \left(\frac{3RT}{M_{kg}}\right)^{1/2} \qquad (5\text{-}14)$$

The average molecular speed increases with increasing temperature and decreases with increasing molar mass at a fixed temperature (Table 5-3).

5-12 The average distance a molecule travels between collisions is the mean free path.

At 0°C and 1 atm a gas molecule undergoes about 10^{10} collisions per second, and travels about 10^5 picometers between collisions.

The mean free path is given by

$$l = (3.1 \times 10^7 \text{ pm}^3 \cdot \text{atm} \cdot \text{K}^{-1})\frac{T}{\sigma^2 P} \qquad (5\text{-}15)$$

where σ is the molecular diameter of the gas molecule (see Table 5-4).

The mean free path increases with increasing temperature and decreasing pressure.

An estimate of the number of collisions a gas molecule undergoes per second is given by $z = v_{av}/l$ (Equation 5-16).

5-13 Different gases leak through a small hole in a container at different rates.

The rate of effusion, the process of leaking through a small hole, is directly proportional to the average speed of the gas molecules.

Graham's law of effusion is given by the relation

$$\frac{\text{rate}_A}{\text{rate}_B} = \left(\frac{M_B}{M_A}\right)^{1/2} \tag{5-17}$$

Effusion can be used to separate gases of different molecular mass.

5-14 The ideal-gas equation is not valid at high pressures.

Deviations from ideal-gas behavior are due to the volume of the gas molecules and the attraction between gas molecules.

The ideal-gas equation is not valid at high pressure (Figure 5-15).

The ratio PV/RT for one mol of gas is less than 1 as the pressure is increased because of the attraction between the gas molecules.

The ratio PV/RT is greater than 1 as the pressure is further increased because of the volume of the gas molecules.

One equation for non-ideal-gas behavior is the van der Waals equation

$$\left(P + \frac{n^2 a}{V^2}\right)(V - nb) = nRT \tag{5-19}$$

where a and b are van der Waals constants, whose values depend upon the particular gas (Table 5-5).

B   SELF-TEST

1   The particles in a solid move throughout the solid. *True/False*

2   The particles in a liquid move throughout the liquid. *True/False*

3   When a solid melts, the liquid has a much lower density. *True/False*

4   When a liquid is vaporized, there is a large increase in (*volume/density*).

5   Most of the volume of a gas is _____.

6   A gas has a large compressibility because _____ _____.

7   A manometer is a device used to measure _____.

8   The height of mercury in a manometer depends upon _____ _____.

9   A barometer is a device used to measure _____.

10 The pressure due to the atmosphere is a constant. *True/False*

11 At sea level atmospheric pressure is always 760 torr. *True/False*

12 The pressure of a gas may be expressed as the height of a column of mercury. *True/False*

13 One standard atmosphere is defined as _____.

14 The pascal is the _____.

15 In meteorology, atmospheric pressure is often reported in the units _____, _____, or _____.

16 Boyle's law states that the volume of a gas is _____ proportional to the _____ at constant _____.

17 A volume of 2.4 L of gas whose pressure is 1.5 atm is compressed to 1.2 L with no change in temperature. The pressure of the gas is now _____ atm.

18 Charles' law states that the volume of a gas is _____ proportional to the _____ at constant _____.

19 A volume of 3.4 L of gas at 100°C is heated to 200°C with no change in pressure. The volume of the gas is now 6.8 L. *True/False*

20 The absolute temperature scale is also called the _____ scale and has the unit _____.

21 A temperature of 20°C is equivalent to _____ K.

22 The lowest possible temperature on the absolute temperature scale is _____; on the Celsius scale it is _____.

23 A constant-pressure gas thermometer measures _____ through its proportionality to the _____ of a gas at _____.

24 At the same temperature and pressure, 3 volumes of hydrogen and 1 volume of nitrogen produce _____ volumes of ammonia.

25 The ideal-gas law can be expressed as _____ = _____.

26 An ideal gas is a gas that _____.

27 One mole of an ideal gas at 0°C and 1 atm occupies a volume of _____.

28 The value of the gas constant depends on the units used. *True/False*

29 Two values of the gas constant are _____ and _____.

30 When $R = 0.0821 \ \text{L} \cdot \text{atm} \cdot \text{mol}^{-1} \cdot \text{K}^{-1}$ is used in the ideal-gas equation, P must be expressed in _____, V in _____, n in _____, and T in _____.

31 The volume of a gas (*increases, decreases*) when the temperature of the gas decreases and the pressure of the gas remains constant.

32 The pressure of a gas (*increases, decreases*) when the temperature of the gas increases and the volume of the gas remains constant.

33 A reaction between a gas and a solid to produce a solid product takes place at constant temperature and volume. After the consumption of part of the gas, the pressure due to the gas (*increases, decreases*).

34 The partial pressure of one gas in a mixture of gases depends on the pressure of the other gases. *True/False*

35 When a gas such as nitrogen is collected over water, the pressure of the nitrogen gas is the total pressure (*plus, minus*) the pressure due to water vapor.

36 The pressure exerted by a gas is caused by _____.

37 All the molecules of a gas travel at the same speed. *True/False*

38 The average kinetic energy of a gas depends only on its _____.

39 The average speed of the molecules in a gas (*increases, decreases*) as the temperature increases.

40 Heavier gas molecules have a (*higher, lower*) average speed than lighter molecules.

41 The average distance travelled between collisions by a molecule in a gas whose pressure is 1 atm is quite small when compared to the distance between the walls of the container. *True/False*

42 The mean free path is the average distance _____.

43 The number of collisions that one gas molecule undergoes in one second is approximately _____ collisions per second at 0°C and 1 atm.

44 The average speed of nitrogen molecules at 20°C is approximately (*50, 500, 5000*) m · s^{-1}.

45 The mean free path of a molecule depends on the _____, _____, and _____.

46 The number of collisions that a gas molecule undergoes in one second can be estimated from the _____ and the _____ of the molecule.

47 All gases effuse at the same rate. *True/False*

48 Propane (C_3H_8) will effuse at a slower rate than methane (CH_4). *True/False*

49 The ideal-gas equation is valid at high pressures and low temperatures. *True/False*

50 The van der Waals equation describes (*ideal, nonideal*) gas behavior.

51 The value of the ratio PV/RT for one mole of gas is less than 1 when

_____ .

C   CALCULATIONS YOU SHOULD KNOW HOW TO DO

1 Convert from one unit of pressure to another (torr $\rightleftharpoons$ pascals $\rightleftharpoons$ atm). See Examples 5-2 and 5-3, Table 5-1, and Problems 5-1 through 5-6.

2 Convert between Kelvin and Celsius temperature scales, $T/K = t/°C + 273.15$.

3 Use Boyle's law in the form $P_iV_i = P_fV_f$. See Problems 5-9 through 5-12.

4 Use Charles' law in the form $V_i/T_i = V_f/T_f$. See Example 5-4 and Problems 5-13 and 5-14.

5 Use Gay-Lussac's law of combining volumes. See Problems 5-15 and 5-16.

6 Use the ideal-gas law, $PV = nRT$. See Examples 5-5 through 5-7, Problems 5-17 through 5-26, and Problems 5-65 through 5-70, in which P is expressed in pascals.

7 Use the ideal-gas law in the form $\rho = MP/RT$ to calculate gas density, ρ, and to determine molar mass. See Examples 5-8 through 5-10 and Problems 5-33 through 5-40.

8 Use the ideal-gas law in stoichiometric calculations. See Example 5-11 and Problems 5-27 through 5-32.

9 Use Dalton's law of partial pressures, $P_{total} = P_1 + P_2 + \cdots$. See Example 5-11 and Problems 5-41 through 5-46.

10 Calculate the average speed of a gas molecule using $v_{av} = (3RT/M_{kg})^{1/2}$. See Example 5-12 and Problems 5-47 through 5-52.

11 Calculate the mean free path of a gas molecule using $l = (3.1 \times 10^7 \text{ pm}^3 \cdot \text{atm} \cdot K^{-1})T/\sigma^2 P$. See Table 5-4 and Problems 5-53 through 5-56.

12 Estimate the number of collisions (collision frequency) that a gas molecule undergoes per second using $z = v_{av}/l$. See Problems 5-57 and 5-58.

13 Use Graham's law of effusion, $\text{rate}_A/\text{rate}_B = t_B/t_A = (M_B/M_A)^{1/2}$. See Example 5-13 and Problems 5-59 through 5-62.

14 Calculate the pressure of a gas using van der Waals equation (Equation 5-20). See Table 5-5 and Problems 5-63 and 5-64.

Plotting Data

It is usually desirable to plot equations or experimental data such that a straight line is obtained. The mathematical equation of a straight line is of the form

$$y = mx + b \tag{1}$$

In this equation, m and b are constants: m is the *slope* of the line and b is its *intercept* with the y axis. The slope of a straight line is a measure of its steepness; it is defined as the ratio of its vertical rise to the corresponding horizontal distance.

Let's plot the two straight lines

$$\text{(I)} \quad y = x + 1$$

and

$$\text{(II)} \quad y = 2x - 2$$

We first make a table of values of x and y

Equation I		Equation II	
x	y	x	y
-3	-2	-3	-8
-2	-1	-2	-6
-1	0	-1	-4
0	1	0	-2
1	2	1	0
2	3	2	2
3	4	3	4
4	5	4	6
5	6	5	8

These results are plotted in Figure 1. Note that curve I intersects the y axis at $y = 1$ ($b = 1$) and has a slope of 1 ($m = 1$). Curve II intersects the y axis at $y = -2$ ($b = -2$) and has a slope of 2 ($m = 2$).

Usually the equation to be plotted will not appear to be of the form of Equation 1 at first. For example, consider Boyle's law

$$V = \frac{c}{P} \quad \text{(constant temperature)} \tag{2}$$

where c is a proportionality constant. The value of the proportionality constant depends upon the temperature for a given sample. For example, for a 0.29 g sample of air at 25°C, $c = 0.244$ L·atm. Some results for such a sample are presented in Table 1. The data in Table 1 are plotted as volume versus pressure in Figure 2.

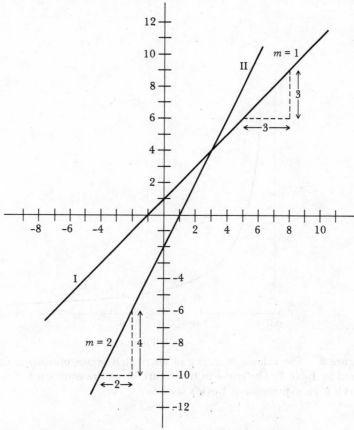

Figure 1. Plot of Equation I: $y = x + 1$ Plot of Equation II: $y = 2x - 2$

Table 1 Pressure-volume data for a sample of 0.29 g of air at 25°C

P/atm	V/L	$\dfrac{1}{P}$/atm^{-1}
0.26	0.938	3.85
0.41	0.595	2.44
0.83	0.294	1.20
1.20	0.203	0.83
2.10	0.116	0.48
2.63	0.093	0.38
3.14	0.078	0.32

It may appear at first sight that Equation 2 is not of the form $y = mx + b$. However, if we let $V = y$ and $1/P = x$, then Equation 2 becomes

$$y = cx$$

which is the equation of a straight line with $m = c$ and $b = 0$. Thus, if we plot V versus $1/P$ instead of P, a straight line will result. The data in Table 1 are plotted as V versus $1/P$ in Figure 3. Note that a straight line is obtained.

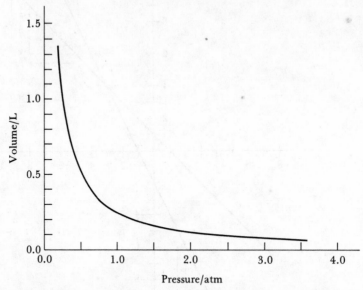

Figure 2. The volume of 0.29 g of air plotted versus pressure at 25°C. The data are given in Table 1. The curve in this figure obeys the equation $V = 0.244 \text{ L} \cdot \text{atm}/P$, which is an expression of Boyle's law.

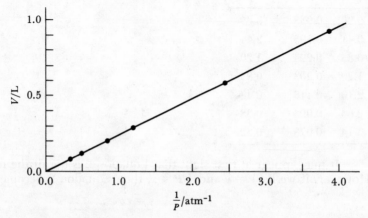

Figure 3. The volume of 0.29 g of air plotted versus the reciprocal of the pressure $(1/P)$ at 25°C. If we compare this curve to that of Figure 2, we see that a straight line results by plotting V versus $1/P$ instead of versus P.

D   SOLUTIONS TO THE ODD-NUMBERED PROBLEMS

5-1   Recall for unit conversions that we multiply by the appropriate conversion factor, that is, the units in the numerator of the conversion factor are the units desired for the result, and the units in the denominator are the units from which we want to change. Thus to convert atm to torr we multiply by (760 torr/1 atm). Note that the relation (Table 5-1)

$$760 \text{ torr} = 1 \text{ atm}$$

is used to form the conversion factor

$$\frac{760 \text{ torr}}{1 \text{ atm}} = 1$$

Thus we have

$$P = (100 \text{ atm})\left(\frac{760 \text{ torr}}{1 \text{ atm}}\right) = 76{,}000 \text{ torr} = 7.60 \times 10^4 \text{ torr}$$

$$P = (100 \text{ atm})\left(\frac{1.013 \text{ bar}}{1 \text{ atm}}\right) = 101 \text{ bar}$$

5-3   The atmospheric pressure in atm is

$$P = (580 \text{ torr})\left(\frac{1 \text{ atm}}{760 \text{ torr}}\right) = 0.76 \text{ atm}$$

The pressure in bars is

$$P = (580 \text{ torr})\left(\frac{1 \text{ atm}}{760 \text{ torr}}\right)\left(\frac{1.013 \text{ bar}}{1 \text{ atm}}\right) = 0.77 \text{ bar}$$

5-5   A torr corresponds to a millimeter of mercury; thus we have to convert the 500 mm height of di-n-butylphthalate to the corresponding height in mercury using the densities of di-n-butyl-phthalate and mercury. Because mercury is denser than di-n-butylphthalate, the height of the corresponding mercury column will be less than the height of the di-n-butylphthalate column. Thus

$$\text{gas pressure} = (500 \text{ mm})\left(\frac{1.043 \text{ g} \cdot \text{mL}^{-1}}{13.6 \text{ g} \cdot \text{mL}^{-1}}\right) = 38.3 \text{ mmHg}$$

$$= 38.3 \text{ torr}$$

5-7

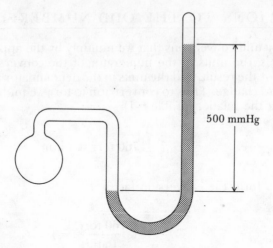

500 mmHg

5-9 Boyle's law problems are worked using Boyle's law in the form

$$P_iV_i = P_fV_f \quad \text{(constant } T\text{)}$$

where i stands for initial and f for final. Thus we have for the volume V_f

$$V_f = \frac{P_iV_i}{P_f} = \frac{(3.46 \text{ atm})(0.650 \text{ mL})}{(1.00 \text{ atm})} = 2.25 \text{ mL}$$

5-11 We use Boyle's law $P_iV_i = P_fV_f$.

Solving for P_f, we have

$$P_f = \frac{P_iV_i}{V_f} = \frac{(0.44 \text{ L})(1.0 \text{ atm})}{(0.073 \text{ L})} = 6.0 \text{ atm}$$

5-13 Charles' law problems are worked using Charles' law in the form

$$\frac{V_i}{T_i} = \frac{V_f}{T_f} \tag{5-4}$$

where T_i and T_f are absolute (Kelvin) temperatures. Celsius temperatures must be converted to Kelvin temperatures before substituting into Charles' law.

$$T_i = 0 + 273 = 273 \text{ K}$$
$$T_f = 100 + 273 = 373 \text{ K}$$

Solving Charles' law for V_f, we have

$$V_f = \frac{T_fV_i}{T_i} = \frac{(373 \text{ K})(14.7 \text{ mL})}{273 \text{ K}} = 20.1 \text{ mL at } 100°\text{C}$$

5-15   We see from Gay-Lussac's law and the reaction stoichiometry that 1.0 L of CH_4 reacts with 2.0 L of O_2. Because air is 20% O_2, the volume V of air needed is

$$(0.20)V = 2.0 \text{ L}$$

$$V = \frac{2.0 \text{ L}}{0.20} = 10 \text{ L air}$$

5-17   The first step in the solution of an ideal-gas problem is to write the ideal-gas law

$$PV = nRT$$

Next we note which quantities are given. In this problem we are given that the gas pressure is 600 torr, the temperature is 37°C and the number of moles of gas is 1.00 mol. We want to calculate the volume V of the gas. We solve the ideal gas equation for V (divide both sides by P) to obtain

$$V = \frac{nRT}{P}$$

Recall that using the gas constant R in the units $0.0821 \text{ L} \cdot \text{atm} \cdot \text{K}^{-1} \cdot \text{mol}^{-1}$ requires P in atm and T in kelvin. We must convert P and T to the proper units:

$$P = (600 \text{ torr})\left(\frac{1 \text{ atm}}{760 \text{ torr}}\right) = 0.789 \text{ atm}$$

$$T = 37 + 273 = 310 \text{ K}$$

Substituting these values into the ideal gas equation yields

$$V = \frac{(1.00 \text{ mol})(0.0821 \text{ L} \cdot \text{atm} \cdot \text{K}^{-1} \cdot \text{mol}^{-1})(310 \text{ K})}{(0.789 \text{ atm})}$$

$$= 32.3 \text{ L}$$

It is a good idea to check the cancellation of units to make sure that the answer is obtained in the desired units and that the right units were used for the various quantities involved in the calculation.

5-19   In order to use the ideal-gas law we must first convert the mass of water to moles of water

$$n = (18 \text{ g})\left(\frac{1 \text{ mol}}{18.02 \text{ g}}\right) = 1.0 \text{ mol}$$

The ideal-gas equation is then used to calculate the gas pressure. Solving for P, we have

$$P = \frac{nRT}{V}$$

Converting the temperature to kelvin,

$$T = 100 + 273 = 373 \text{ K}$$

and substituting the values for n, R, T, and V into the expression for P, we have

$$P = \frac{(1.0 \text{ mol})(0.0821 \text{ L} \cdot \text{atm} \cdot \text{mol}^{-1} \cdot \text{K}^{-1})(373 \text{ K})}{(18 \text{ L})} = 1.7 \text{ atm}$$

The volume of water is calculated from the density of water $d = m/V$ or

$$\text{volume of water} = \frac{m}{d} = \frac{18 \text{ g}}{1.00 \text{ g} \cdot \text{mL}^{-1}} = 18 \text{ mL}$$

5-21 In this problem we first use the ideal gas equation to compute the number of moles, n, of helium. Then we compute the number of molecules by multiplying n by Avogadro's number. The expression for n is

$$n = \frac{PV}{RT}$$

The temperature in kelvin is

$$T = -200 + 273 = 73 \text{ K}$$

Substituting the values for P, V, R, and T into the expression for n, we have

$$n = \frac{(0.0010 \text{ atm})(1.0 \text{ L})}{(0.0821 \text{ L} \cdot \text{atm} \cdot \text{mol}^{-1} \cdot \text{K}^{-1})(73 \text{ K})} = 1.67 \times 10^{-4} \text{ mol}$$

The number of molecules of helium is given by

$$\text{number of molecules} = (1.67 \times 10^{-4} \text{ mol})(6.022 \times 10^{23} \text{ molecules} \cdot \text{mol}^{-1})$$
$$= 1.0 \times 10^{20} \text{ molecules}$$

Recall that at 1.0 atm and 0°C one mole of an ideal gas occupies 22.4 L. Thus the number of moles in 1.0 L at 1.0 atm and 0°C is

$$n = \frac{1.0 \text{ L}}{22.4 \text{ L} \cdot \text{mol}^{-1}} = 4.46 \times 10^{-2} \text{ mol}$$

and thus

$$\text{number of molecules} = (4.46 \times 10^{-2} \text{ mol})(6.022 \times 10^{23} \text{ molecules} \cdot \text{mol}^{-1})$$
$$= 2.7 \times 10^{22} \text{ molecules}$$

We could also have calculated n at 0°C, 1.0 atm and 1.0 L from the ideal gas equation.

5-23   This problem is similar to Problem 5-21. We use the ideal-gas equation to calculate the number of moles of ozone in 1.0 L and then multiply n by Avogadro's number to obtain the number of molecules.

$$n = \frac{PV}{RT}$$

The temperature in kelvin is

$$T = -23 + 273 = 250 \text{ K}$$

Substituting the values for P, V, R, and T into the expression for n, we have

$$n = \frac{(1.4 \times 10^{-7} \text{ atm})(1.0 \text{ L})}{(0.0821 \text{ L} \cdot \text{atm} \cdot \text{mol}^{-1} \cdot \text{K}^{-1})(250 \text{ K})} = 6.8 \times 10^{-9} \text{ mol}$$

$$\text{number of molecules} = (6.8 \times 10^{-9} \text{ mol})(6.022 \times 10^{23} \text{ molecules} \cdot \text{mol}^{-1})$$

$$= 4.1 \times 10^{15} \text{ molecules}$$

5-25   The number of moles of gas n and the volume V of the gas remain constant while the pressure P and temperature T change. Application of the ideal-gas equation to the initial and final conditions yields

$$P_i V = nRT_i \qquad P_f V = nRT_f$$

If we divide the first equation into the second, then we obtain

$$\frac{P_f \cancel{V}}{P_i \cancel{V}} = \frac{\cancel{n}\cancel{R}T_f}{\cancel{n}\cancel{R}T_i}$$

Solving for T_f, the unknown temperature, we have

$$T_f = \frac{T_i P_f}{P_i}$$

Both pressures must be in the same units. Let's convert 800 torr to atm.

$$P_i = (800 \text{ torr})\left(\frac{1 \text{ atm}}{760 \text{ torr}}\right) = 1.05 \text{ atm}$$

Thus

$$T_f = \frac{(273 \text{ K})(3.0 \text{ atm})}{1.05 \text{ atm}} = 780 \text{ K}$$

or

$$t_f = 780 - 273 = 510°C$$

5-27 The solution to a problem involving the application of the ideal gas equation to a chemical reaction proceeds in two stages. One stage involves the use of the reaction stoichiometry to compute the numbers of moles of a reactant consumed and product produced. The other stage involves the use of the ideal-gas equation and is similar to the calculations carried out in Problems 5-17 through 5-26. Let's see how this applies to Problem 5-27. The number of moles of CaC_2 in 100 g is

$$n = (100 \text{ g})\left(\frac{1 \text{ mol}}{64.10 \text{ g}}\right) = 1.56 \text{ mol}$$

From the reaction stoichiometry we note that 1 mol of CaC_2 yields 1 mol of C_2H_2, thus the number of the moles of C_2H_2 produced is

$$n = (1.56 \text{ mol } CaC_2)\left(\frac{1 \text{ mol } C_2H_2}{1 \text{ mol } CaC_2}\right) = 1.56 \text{ mol } C_2H_2$$

We now use the ideal-gas equation to compute the volume V from the known values of n, T, and P:

$$V = \frac{nRT}{P}$$

At 0°C and 1.00 atm, we have

$$V = \frac{(1.56 \text{ mol})(0.0821 \text{ L} \cdot \text{atm} \cdot \text{K}^{-1} \cdot \text{mol}^{-1})(273 \text{ K})}{(1.00 \text{ atm})} = 35.0 \text{ L}$$

At 120°C and 1.00 atm, we have

$$V = \frac{(1.56 \text{ mol})(0.0821 \text{ L} \cdot \text{atm} \cdot \text{K}^{-1} \cdot \text{mol}^{-1})(393 \text{ K})}{(1.00 \text{ atm})} = 50.3 \text{ L}$$

5-29 The number of moles of glucose in 1.00 g is

$$n = (1.00 \text{ g})\left(\frac{1 \text{ mol}}{180.2 \text{ g}}\right) = 0.00555 \text{ mol}$$

From the reaction stoichiometry, the number of moles of CO_2 produced is

$$n = (0.00555 \text{ mol } C_6H_{12}O_6)\left(\frac{6 \text{ mol } CO_2}{1 \text{ mol } C_6H_{12}O_6}\right) = 0.0333 \text{ mol } CO_2$$

We now compute the volume using the ideal gas equation

$$V = \frac{nRT}{P} = \frac{(0.0333 \text{ mol})(0.0821 \text{ L} \cdot \text{atm} \cdot \text{mol}^{-1} \cdot \text{K}^{-1})(310 \text{ K})}{(1.00 \text{ atm})}$$

$$= 0.848 \text{ L} = 848 \text{ mL}$$

5-31 The number of moles of NaCl in 2.50 kg is

$$n = (2.50 \text{ kg})\left(\frac{10^3 \text{ g}}{1 \text{ kg}}\right)\left(\frac{1 \text{ mol}}{58.44 \text{ g}}\right) = 42.8 \text{ mol}$$

The number of moles of H_2 produced is

$$n_{H_2} = (42.8 \text{ mol NaCl})\left(\frac{1 \text{ mol } H_2}{2 \text{ mol NaCl}}\right) = 21.4 \text{ mol}$$

The moles of Cl_2 produced are equal to the moles of H_2 produced. Thus the number of moles of Cl_2 is

$$n_{Cl_2} = 21.4 \text{ mol}$$

The volume of H_2 or Cl_2 at 10.0 atm and 298 K is

$$V = \frac{nRT}{P} = \frac{(21.4 \text{ mol})(0.0821 \text{ L} \cdot \text{atm} \cdot \text{K}^{-1} \cdot \text{mol}^{-1})(298 \text{ K})}{(10.0 \text{ atm})}$$

$$= 52.4 \text{ L}$$

5-33 Problems involving gas density usually involve the ideal gas equation in the form

$$\rho = \frac{MP}{RT}$$

where ρ is the density and M is the molar mass. Thus for $H_2O(g)$ at 100°C and 1.00 atm we compute

$$\rho = \frac{(18.02 \text{ g} \cdot \text{mol}^{-1})(1.00 \text{ atm})}{(0.0821 \text{ L} \cdot \text{atm} \cdot \text{K}^{-1} \cdot \text{mol}^{-1})(373 \text{ K})} = 0.588 \text{ g} \cdot \text{L}^{-1}$$

The density of liquid water at 100°C is $0.958 \text{ g} \cdot \text{mL}^{-1}$ or

$$d = (0.958 \text{ g} \cdot \text{mL}^{-1})\left(\frac{1000 \text{ mL}}{1 \text{ L}}\right) = 958 \text{ g} \cdot \text{L}^{-1}$$

The ratio of the densities of $H_2O(l)$ and $H_2O(g)$ at 100°C is

$$\frac{958 \text{ g} \cdot \text{L}^{-1}}{0.588 \text{ g} \cdot \text{L}^{-1}} = 1630$$

Notice that we use ρ to represent gas densities and d to represent solid or liquid density.

5-35 We can compute the density of ether from the given mass and volume

$$\rho = \frac{1.21 \text{ g}}{0.250 \text{ L}} = 4.84 \text{ g} \cdot \text{L}^{-1}$$

The molar mass is related to the density by the equation

$$\rho = \frac{MP}{RT}$$

Thus,

$$M = \frac{\rho RT}{P} = \frac{(4.84 \text{ g} \cdot \text{L}^{-1})(0.0821 \text{ L} \cdot \text{atm} \cdot \text{K}^{-1} \cdot \text{mol}^{-1})(323 \text{ K})}{(1.73 \text{ atm})}$$

$$= 74.2 \text{ g} \cdot \text{mol}^{-1}$$

5-37 We first determine the empirical formula of the compound. Taking a 100 g sample, we have

$$85.60 \text{ g C} \backsimeq 14.40 \text{ g H}$$

Dividing the mass of each by its atomic mass, we have

$$\frac{85.60}{12.01} \text{ mol C} \backsimeq \frac{14.40}{1.008} \text{ mol H}$$

$$7.127 \text{ mol} \backsimeq 14.29 \text{ mol H}$$

Dividing by 7.127, we have

$$1.00 \text{ mol C} \backsimeq 2.00 \text{ mol H}$$

Thus the empirical formula is CH_2. The molar mass is computed from the gas density at a known temperature and pressure

$$M = \frac{\rho RT}{P}$$

$$M = \frac{(0.9588 \text{ g} \cdot \text{L}^{-1})(0.0821 \text{ L} \cdot \text{atm} \cdot \text{K}^{-1} \cdot \text{mol}^{-1})(298 \text{ K})}{(635 \text{ torr})\left(\dfrac{1 \text{ atm}}{760 \text{ torr}}\right)}$$

$$= 28.1 \text{ g} \cdot \text{mol}^{-1}$$

The formula mass of CH_2 is 14.03. Two CH_2 units, that is, C_2H_4 has a formula mass of $14.03 \times 2 = 28.06$. Thus the molecular formula of ethylene is C_2H_4.

5-39 The method of solution for this problem is basically the same as for Problem 5-37.

$$39.99 \text{ g C} \backsimeq 6.73 \text{ g H} \backsimeq 53.28 \text{ g O}$$

Dividing each by its atomic mass, we have

$$3.33 \text{ mol C} \backsimeq 6.68 \text{ mol H} \backsimeq 3.33 \text{ mol O}$$

$$1.00 \text{ mol C} \backsimeq 2.01 \text{ mol H} \backsimeq 1.00 \text{ mol O}$$

Therefore, the empirical formula is CH_2O. The molar mass is

$$M = \frac{\rho RT}{P} = \frac{\left(\dfrac{0.3338 \text{ g}}{0.300 \text{ L}}\right)(0.0821 \text{ L} \cdot \text{atm} \cdot \text{K}^{-1} \cdot \text{mol}^{-1})(423 \text{ K})}{(326 \text{ torr})\left(\dfrac{1 \text{ atm}}{760 \text{ torr}}\right)}$$

$$= 90.1 \text{ g} \cdot \text{mol}^{-1}$$

The formula mass of CH_2O is 30.03. The molecular mass of 90.1 is three times 30.03, and thus the molecular formula of lactic acid is $C_3H_6O_3$.

5-41 The pressure of nitrogen when the volume is 35.0 mL is

$$P_{N_2} = 740 \text{ torr}$$

If we now increase the volume available to the N_2 from 35.0 mL to 50.0 mL, then the partial pressure of nitrogen decreases. Because T and n_{N_2} are constant we have

$$P_i V_i = P_f V_f$$

and thus

$$P_f \text{ (of } N_2) = \frac{P_i V_i}{V_f} = \frac{(740 \text{ torr})(35.0 \text{ mL})}{(50.0 \text{ mL})}$$

$$= 518 \text{ torr}$$

The mixture of N_2 and O_2 in the 50.0 mL volume has a total pressure of 740 torr:

$$P_{\text{total}} = 740 \text{ torr} = P_{O_2} + P_{N_2}$$

thus

$$P_{O_2} = 740 \text{ torr} - 518 \text{ torr} = 222 \text{ torr}$$

5-43 The reaction stoichiometry is

$$4C_3H_5(NO_3)_3(s) \longrightarrow 12CO_2(g) + 10H_2O(l) + 6N_2(g) + O_2(g)$$

Because the gaseous are collected at 25°C, $H_2O(g)$ will condense to $H_2O(l)$, and so 4 moles of nitroglycerin yield $12 + 6 + 1 = 19$ moles of gas. Thus 10 g of nitroglycerin yields the following number of moles of gas at 25°C:

$$n = (10 \text{ g nitro})\left(\frac{1 \text{ mol nitro}}{227.1 \text{ g nitro}}\right)\left(\frac{19 \text{ mol gas}}{4 \text{ mol nitro}}\right) = 0.209 \text{ mol gas}$$

The volume is calculated from the ideal gas equation

$$V = \frac{nRT}{P} = \frac{(0.209 \text{ mol})(0.0821 \text{ L} \cdot \text{atm} \cdot \text{K}^{-1} \cdot \text{mol}^{-1})(298 \text{ K})}{(1.0 \text{ atm})} = 5.1 \text{ L}$$

The pressure that will be produced when the gases are confined to 0.50 L is

$$P = \frac{nRT}{V} = \frac{(0.209 \text{ mol})(0.0821 \text{ L} \cdot \text{atm} \cdot \text{K}^{-1} \cdot \text{mol}^{-1})(298 \text{ K})}{0.50 \text{ L}} = 10 \text{ atm}$$

5-45 The mixture is 75% CO_2 and 25% H_2O by volume at 200°C. Therefore, we have for the partial pressure of CO_2 at 200°C

$$P_{CO_2} = (0.75)(2.00 \text{ atm}) = 1.50 \text{ atm}$$

Similarly, we have for the partial pressure of H_2O at 200°C

$$P_{H_2O} = (0.25)(2.00 \text{ atm}) = 0.50 \text{ atm}$$

Upon cooling, the volume remains constant and the number of moles of CO_2 in the gas phase also remains constant. Thus we obtain from the ideal-gas equation

$$P_f = \frac{P_i T_f}{T_i} \approx P_{CO_2}$$

Therefore, at 50°C,

$$P_{CO_2} = \frac{(1.50 \text{ atm})(323 \text{ K})}{473 \text{ K}} = 1.02 \text{ atm}$$

5-47 Recall that in working kinetic theory problems we use the value of $R = 8.31 \text{ J} \cdot \text{mol}^{-1} \cdot \text{K}^{-1}$. The average speed in $\text{m} \cdot \text{s}^{-1}$ of a gas molecule is calculated from the equation

$$v_{av} = \left[\frac{3RT}{M_{kg}} \right]^{1/2}$$

where M_{kg} is the molar mass in kilogram-per-mole units. For Cl_2 we have

$$M_{kg} = \frac{70.9 \text{ g} \cdot \text{mol}^{-1}}{1000 \text{ g} \cdot \text{kg}^{-1}} = 0.0709 \text{ kg} \cdot \text{mol}^{-1}$$

Thus at 298 K we have for the average speed of a Cl_2 molecule

$$v_{av} = \left[\frac{(3)(8.31 \text{ J} \cdot \text{mol}^{-1} \cdot \text{K}^{-1})(298 \text{ K})}{(0.0709 \text{ kg} \cdot \text{mol}^{-1})} \right]^{1/2}$$

$$= 324 \text{ m} \cdot \text{s}^{-1}$$

5-49 Application of the equation for the average speed

$$v_{av} = \left[\frac{3RT}{M_{kg}} \right]^{1/2}$$

to the temperatures T_f and T_i yields

$$\frac{v_{av_f}}{v_{av_i}} = \frac{\left[\dfrac{3RT_f}{M_{kg}}\right]^{1/2}}{\left[\dfrac{3RT_i}{M_{kg}}\right]^{1/2}} = \left[\frac{\dfrac{\cancel{3RT_f}}{\cancel{M_{kg}}}}{\dfrac{\cancel{3RT_i}}{\cancel{M_{kg}}}}\right]^{1/2} = \left[\frac{T_f}{T_i}\right]^{1/2}$$

But $T_f = 2T_i$. Thus,

$$\frac{v_{av_f}}{v_{av_i}} = \left(\frac{2T_i}{T_i}\right)^{1/2} = 2^{1/2} = \sqrt{2}$$

Solving for v_{av_f}, we have

$$v_{av_f} = \sqrt{2}\, v_{av_i}$$

The average speed of a molecule is increased by a factor of $\sqrt{2}$ when the temperature T is doubled.

5-51 If we divide the equation for the average speed of gas A by that of gas B, then we have

$$\frac{v_{av_A}}{v_{av_B}} = \frac{\left[\dfrac{3RT}{M_A}\right]^{1/2}}{\left[\dfrac{3RT}{M_B}\right]^{1/2}} = \left[\frac{\dfrac{\cancel{3RT}}{M_A}}{\dfrac{\cancel{3RT}}{M_B}}\right]^{1/2} = \left[\frac{M_B}{M_A}\right]^{1/2}$$

or

$$\frac{v_{av_A}}{v_{av_B}} = \left[\frac{M_B}{M_A}\right]^{1/2}$$

Applying this expression to helium and oxygen, we have

$$\frac{v_{av_{O_2}}}{v_{av_{He}}} = \left[\frac{M_{He}}{M_{O_2}}\right]^{1/2} = \left[\frac{4.003}{32.00}\right]^{1/2} = 0.3537$$

5-53 The mean free path is given by

$$l = (3.1 \times 10^7 \text{ pm}^3 \cdot \text{atm} \cdot \text{K}^{-1})\frac{T}{\sigma^2 P}$$

From Table 5-4 we find that the molecular diameter of H_2 is 280 pm. Thus,

$$l = \frac{(3.1 \times 10^7 \text{ pm}^3 \cdot \text{atm} \cdot \text{K}^{-1})(293 \text{ K})}{(280 \text{ pm})^2(1.0 \text{ atm})} = 1.2 \times 10^5 \text{ pm}$$

$$l = (1.2 \times 10^5 \text{ pm})\left(\frac{1 \text{ m}}{10^{12} \text{ pm}}\right) = 1.2 \times 10^{-7} \text{ m}$$

The collision frequency per molecule, z, is given by

$$z = \frac{v_{av}}{l}$$

Thus,

$$z = \frac{\left[\dfrac{3RT}{M_{kg}}\right]^{1/2}}{l}$$

For H_2 at 293 K we compute for z,

$$z = \frac{[(3)(8.31 \text{ J} \cdot \text{K}^{-1} \cdot \text{mol}^{-1})(293 \text{ K})/2.02 \times 10^{-3} \text{ kg}]^{1/2}}{1.2 \times 10^{-7} \text{ m}}$$

$$= 1.6 \times 10^{10} \text{ collisions} \cdot \text{s}^{-1}$$

5-55   In order to calculate the mean free path using the equation

$$l = (3.1 \times 10^7 \text{ pm}^3 \cdot \text{atm} \cdot \text{K}^{-1})\frac{T}{\sigma^2 P}$$

we need the pressure expressed in atmospheres. We have to compute the pressure corresponding to a density of one atom/m³ at 10 K. From the ideal-gas equation we have

$$P = \left(\frac{n}{V}\right)RT$$

If we convert n/V in atoms/m³ to mol/L, then we can compute P in atm using the above equation

$$\frac{n}{V} = \left(\frac{1 \text{ atom}}{1 \text{ m}^3}\right)\left(\frac{1 \text{ mol}}{6.022 \times 10^{23} \text{ atom}}\right)\left(\frac{1 \text{ m}}{100 \text{ cm}}\right)^3\left(\frac{1000 \text{ cm}^3}{1 \text{ L}}\right)$$

$$= 1.7 \times 10^{-27} \text{ mol} \cdot \text{L}^{-1}$$

Thus,

$$P = (1.7 \times 10^{-27} \text{ mol} \cdot \text{L}^{-1})(0.0821 \text{ L} \cdot \text{atm} \cdot \text{K}^{-1} \cdot \text{mol}^{-1})(10 \text{ K})$$

$$= 1.4 \times 10^{-27} \text{ atm}$$

We can now compute the mean free path:

$$l = \frac{(3.1 \times 10^7 \text{ pm}^3 \cdot \text{atm} \cdot \text{K}^{-1})(10 \text{ K})}{(100 \text{ pm})^2 (1.4 \times 10^{-27} \text{ atm})} = 2.2 \times 10^{31} \text{ pm}$$

$$= (2.2 \times 10^{31} \text{ pm})\left(\frac{1 \text{ m}}{10^{12} \text{ pm}}\right) = 2.2 \times 10^{19} \text{ m}$$

5-57 The number of collisions per second (collision frequency) is given by

$$z = \frac{v_{av}}{l}$$

The average speed of O_2 molecules at 20°C is

$$v_{av} = \left(\frac{3RT}{M_{kg}}\right)^{1/2} = \left[\frac{3(8.31 \text{ kg} \cdot \text{m}^2 \cdot \text{s}^{-2} \cdot \text{K}^{-1} \cdot \text{mol}^{-1})(293 \text{ K})}{(32.0 \times 10^{-3} \text{ kg} \cdot \text{mol}^{-1})}\right]^{1/2}$$

$$= 478 \text{ m} \cdot \text{s}^{-1}$$

The mean free path of O_2 at 20°C and 1.00 atm is ($\sigma_{O_2} = 370$ pm from Table 5-4)

$$l = (3.1 \times 10^7 \text{ pm}^3 \cdot \text{atm} \cdot \text{K}^{-1})\frac{T}{\sigma^2 P}$$

$$= \frac{(3.1 \times 10^7 \text{ pm}^3 \cdot \text{atm} \cdot \text{K}^{-1})(293 \text{ K})}{(370 \text{ pm})^2 (1.00 \text{ atm})} = 6.6 \times 10^4 \text{ pm}$$

$$= (6.6 \times 10^4 \text{ pm})\left(\frac{1 \text{ m}}{10^{12} \text{ pm}}\right) = 6.6 \times 10^{-8} \text{ m}$$

Thus,

$$z = \frac{478 \text{ m} \cdot \text{s}^{-1}}{6.6 \times 10^{-8} \text{ m}} = 7.2 \times 10^9 \text{ collisions} \cdot \text{s}^{-1}$$

5-59 The ratio of the rates of effusion (leaking) of the two gases is given by Graham's law:

$$\frac{\text{rate}_A}{\text{rate}_B} = \left(\frac{M_B}{M_A}\right)^{1/2}$$

If we take A = helium and B = nitrogen, then we have

$$\text{rate}_{He} = (\text{rate}_{N_2})\left(\frac{M_{N_2}}{M_{He}}\right)^{1/2}$$

Substituting in the values for rate_{N_2}, M_{N_2}, and M_{He}, we have

$$\text{rate}_{He} = (75 \text{ mL} \cdot \text{h}^{-1})\left(\frac{28.02}{4.003}\right)^{1/2} = 200 \text{ mL} \cdot \text{h}^{-1}$$

5-61 Graham's law gives

$$\frac{\text{rate}_A}{\text{rate}_B} = \left(\frac{M_B}{M_A}\right)^{1/2}$$

or

$$\frac{M_B}{M_A} = \left(\frac{\text{rate}_A}{\text{rate}_B}\right)^2$$

If we let B = unknown gas and A = nitrogen, then we have

$$M_{unknown} = (M_{N_2})\left(\frac{\text{rate}_{N_2}}{\text{rate}_{unknown}}\right)^2$$

The rate of effusion of N_2 is

$$\text{rate}_{N_2} = \frac{1.00 \text{ mL}}{145 \text{ s}} = 6.90 \times 10^{-3} \text{ mL} \cdot \text{s}^{-1}$$

The rate of effusion of the unknown gas is

$$\text{rate}_{unknown} = \frac{1.00 \text{ mL}}{230 \text{ s}} = 4.35 \times 10^{-3} \text{ mL} \cdot \text{s}^{-1}$$

Thus,

$$M_{unknown} = (28.02)\left(\frac{6.90 \times 10^{-3} \text{ mL} \cdot \text{s}^{-1}}{4.35 \times 10^{-3} \text{ mL} \cdot \text{s}^{-1}}\right)^2$$

$$= 70.5$$

5-63 The van der Waals equation is

$$\left(P + \frac{n^2 a}{V}\right)(V - nb) = nRT$$

Solving for P, we have (Equation (5-20))

$$P = \frac{nRT}{V - nb} - \frac{n^2 a}{V^2}$$

The number of moles of N_2 in 30.0 g is

$$n = (30.0 \text{ g})\left(\frac{1 \text{ mol}}{28.02 \text{ g}}\right) = 1.07 \text{ mol}$$

Using Table 5-5, the values of a and b for N_2 are $a = 1.390 \text{ L}^2 \cdot \text{atm} \cdot \text{mol}^{-2}$ and $b = 0.0391 \text{ L} \cdot \text{mol}^{-1}$. Thus,

$$P = \frac{(1.07 \text{ mol})(0.0821 \text{ L} \cdot \text{atm} \cdot \text{mol}^{-1} \cdot \text{K}^{-1})(400 \text{ K})}{0.155 \text{ L} - (1.07 \text{ mol})(0.0391 \text{ L} \cdot \text{mol}^{-1})}$$

$$- \frac{(1.07 \text{ mol})^2(1.390 \text{ L}^2 \cdot \text{atm} \cdot \text{mol}^{-2})}{(0.155 \text{ L})^2}$$

$$= 310 \text{ atm} - 66.2 \text{ atm}$$

$$= 244 \text{ atm}$$

The ideal-gas law is

$$P = \frac{nRT}{V}$$

$$= \frac{(1.07 \text{ mol})(0.0821 \text{ L} \cdot \text{atm} \cdot \text{mol}^{-1} \cdot \text{K}^{-1})(400 \text{ K})}{0.155 \text{ L}}$$

$$= 227 \text{ atm}$$

5-65 From the ideal-gas equation we have for the number of moles of Cl_2,

$$n = \frac{PV}{RT}$$

Note that $1 \text{ Pa} = 1 \text{ N} \cdot \text{m}^{-2}$ and $1 \text{ J} = 1 \text{ N} \cdot \text{m}$. When we use R in the units $\text{J} \cdot \text{K}^{-1} \cdot \text{mol}^{-1}$, we must express the volume in the units m^3, thus

$$V = (5.00 \text{ mL})\left(\frac{1 \text{ L}}{10^3 \text{ mL}}\right)\left(\frac{10^{-3} \text{ m}^3}{1 \text{ L}}\right) = 5.00 \times 10^{-6} \text{ m}^3$$

$$n = \frac{(2.15 \times 10^4 \text{ N} \cdot \text{m}^{-2})(5.00 \times 10^{-6} \text{ m}^3)}{(8.31 \text{ N} \cdot \text{m} \cdot \text{K}^{-1} \cdot \text{mol}^{-1})(313 \text{ K})} = 4.13 \times 10^{-5} \text{ mol}$$

The number of molecules is obtained by multiplying n by Avogadro's number

$$\text{number of molecules} = (4.13 \times 10^{-5} \text{ mol})(6.022 \times 10^{23} \text{ molecules} \cdot \text{mol}^{-1})$$

$$= 2.49 \times 10^{19} \text{ molecules}$$

5-67 Using the ideal-gas law, we have

$$\frac{P_i V_i}{T_i} = \frac{P_f V_f}{T_f}$$

Solving for the final volume, we have

$$V_f = V_i \left(\frac{T_f}{T_i}\right)\left(\frac{P_i}{P_f}\right)$$

Thus,

$$V_f = (7.12 \ \mu\text{L})\left(\frac{273 \ \text{K}}{295 \ \text{K}}\right)\left(\frac{8.72 \times 10^4 \ \text{Pa}}{1.013 \times 10^5 \ \text{Pa}}\right)$$

$$= 5.67 \ \mu\text{L}$$

The number of moles of radon is

$$n = \frac{PV}{RT}$$

We must first convert the volume to m^3:

$$V = (7.12 \ \mu\text{L})\left(\frac{1 \ \text{mL}}{10^3 \ \mu\text{L}}\right)\left(\frac{1 \ \text{L}}{10^3 \ \text{mL}}\right)\left(\frac{10^{-3} \ \text{m}^3}{1 \ \text{L}}\right) = 7.12 \times 10^{-9} \ \text{m}^3$$

Thus,

$$n = \frac{(8.72 \times 10^4 \ \text{N} \cdot \text{m}^{-2})(7.12 \times 10^{-9} \ \text{m}^3)}{(8.31 \ \text{N} \cdot \text{m} \cdot \text{K}^{-1} \cdot \text{mol}^{-1})(295 \ \text{K})} = 2.53 \times 10^{-7} \ \text{mol}$$

The mass of radon is

$$m = (2.53 \times 10^{-7} \ \text{mol})\left(\frac{222 \ \text{g}}{1 \ \text{mol}}\right) = 5.62 \times 10^{-5} \ \text{g}$$

$$= 56.2 \ \mu\text{g}$$

Note that either set of conditions can be used in the ideal-gas equation to calculate n.

5-69   From the ideal-gas equation we have

$$\rho = \frac{MP}{RT}$$

$$= \frac{(20.06 \ \text{g} \cdot \text{mol}^{-1})(2.00 \times 10^3 \ \text{N} \cdot \text{m}^{-2})}{(8.31 \ \text{N} \cdot \text{m} \cdot \text{K}^{-1} \cdot \text{mol}^{-1})(273 \ \text{K})} = 17.7 \ \text{g} \cdot \text{m}^{-3}$$

E ANSWERS TO THE EVEN-NUMBERED PROBLEMS

5-2   0.032 atm, 32 mbar

5-4   0.977 atm, 743 torr

5-6 1.65×10^3 mm

5-8

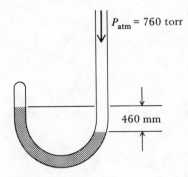

$P_{atm} = 760$ torr

460 mm

5-10   2 cylinders

5-12 2.0×10^4 breaths

5-14   2.82 L

5-16   0.28 L O_2; 0.55 L H_2O

5-18   42 g; first calculate n, the moles of $Cl_2(g)$, then compute the mass corresponding to n

5.9 moles Cl_2 | 70.9 g
 | 1 mole Cl_2 =

5-20   48.8 L

5-22 1.97×10^{24} molecules

5-24 3.3×10^{13} molecules

5-26 1.2×10^4 L

5-28   0.12 g O_2

5-30 8.6×10^3 gal of air

5-32   1.75 g

5-34 5.39 g $\cdot$ L^{-1}

5-36   84.3

5-38 C_6H_6

5-40 $C_4H_8O_2$

5-42 $P_{O_2} = 0.80$ atm; lower percent oxygen to 5.0% in tank to yield $P_{O_2} = 0.20$ atm

5-44 9.9×10^2 L, 56 atm

5-46   0.177 L, 7.90×10^{-3} mol

5-48   607 m $\cdot$ s^{-1}

5-50 The speed of sound is 67% that of N_2 and 71% of O_2.

5-52 11.22

5-54 For He, $l = 1.6 \times 10^8$ pm $= 1.6 \times 10^{-4}$ m at 1.00 torr and 2.1×10^5 pm $= 2.1 \times 10^{-7}$ m at 760 torr; for Kr, $l = 4.1 \times 10^7$ pm $= 4.1 \times 10^{-5}$ m at 1.00 torr and 5.4×10^4 pm $= 5.4 \times 10^{-8}$ m at 760 torr

5-56 0.12 atm, 1.2×10^{-4} atm, 1.2×10^{-7} atm

5-58 1.0×10^4 collisions $\cdot$ s^{-1}

5-60 7.01 mL

5-62 46% CO

5-64 Neglect nb compared to V and n^2a/V^2 compared to RT/V because n/V is small.

5-66 1.92×10^5 Pa

5-68 1.74 g

5-70 Convert L to m^3 and atm to Pa; $R = 8.31$ J $\cdot$ mol^{-1} $\cdot$ K^{-1}.

F   ANSWERS TO THE SELF-TEST

1. false
2. true
3. false (The density usually does not change appreciably.)
4. volume
5. empty space
6. the gas molecules occupy only a small fraction of the available space
7. pressure
8. the difference in pressures on the two mercury surfaces
9. the pressure due to the atmosphere
10. false (It depends on weather conditions and altitude.)
11. false
12. true
13. 760 torr or 1.013×10^5 Pa
14. SI unit of pressure
15. inches of mercury, pascals, millibars
16. inversely . . . pressure . . . temperature
17. 3.0 atm ($P_iV_i = P_fV_f$)
18. directly . . . absolute temperature . . . pressure
19. false (Volume is proportional to the absolute temperature, not the Celsius temperature $V_f = (T_f/T_i)V_i = (473\ K/373\ K)(3.4\ L)$.)
20. Kelvin temperature . . . kelvin, K
21. 293 K
22. 0 K . . . $-273.15°C$
23. temperature . . . volume . . . constant pressure
24. 2
25. $PV = nRT$
26. obeys the ideal gas equation $PV = nRT$
27. 22.4 L
28. true
29. 0.0821 L $\cdot$ atm $\cdot$ K^{-1} $\cdot$ mol^{-1} . . . 8.31 J $\cdot$ K^{-1} $\cdot$ mol^{-1}

30 P in atmospheres, V in liters, n in moles, and T in kelvin

31 decreases

32 increases

33 decreases

34 false

35 minus

36 collisions of the gas molecules with the walls of the container

37 false, there is a distribution of molecular speeds

38 absolute temperature

39 increases

40 lower

41 true

42 traveled by a molecule between collisions

43 10^{10}

44 500

45 temperature, pressure and molecular diameter

46 average speed . . . mean free path

47 false

48 true

49 false

50 nonideal

51 The effect of the attraction between the molecules of the gas becomes important.

6 / Chemical Reactions and Energy

The enthalpy change for a chemical reaction is

$$\Delta H_{rxn} = H_{prod} - H_{react} \qquad (6\text{-}5)$$

For an exothermic reaction, $\Delta H_{rxn} < 0$.

For an endothermic reaction, $\Delta H_{rxn} > 0$ (Figure 6-2).

ΔH°_{rxn} denotes the standard enthalpy change for a reaction, for which the reactants and products are at 1 atm pressure.

6-3 Heats of reaction can be calculated from tabulated heats of formation.

The standard molar enthalpy of formation, $\Delta \bar{H}^{\circ}_f$, is the value of ΔH°_{rxn} of the reaction in which one mole of a substance is formed from the elements that comprise the substance.

The value of $\Delta \bar{H}^{\circ}_f$ is zero for an element in its normal state at 25°C and 1 atm.

For the general chemical equation aA + bB → yY + zZ, the value of ΔH°_{rxn} is given by

$$\Delta H^{\circ}_{rxn} = y\Delta \bar{H}^{\circ}_f [Y] + z\Delta \bar{H}^{\circ}_f [Z] - a\Delta \bar{H}^{\circ}_f [A] - b\Delta \bar{H}^{\circ}_f [B] \qquad (6\text{-}6)$$

Values of $\Delta \bar{H}^{\circ}_f$ of some substances are given in Table 6-1.

6-4 Hess's law says that enthalpy changes for chemical reactions are additive.

Hess's law states that if two or more chemical equations are added together, then the value of ΔH°_{rxn} for the resulting equation is equal to the sum of the ΔH°_{rxn} values for the separate equations.

ΔH°_{rxn} (reverse reaction) = $-\Delta H^{\circ}_{rxn}$ (forward reaction) (Equation 6-8).

6-5 The value of ΔH°_{rxn} is determined primarily by the difference in the bond enthalpies of the reactant and product molecules.

The molar bond enthalpy is the energy required to break Avogadro's number of bonds.

The total enthalpy change for a reaction is approximately given by

$$\Delta H^{\circ}_{rxn} \approx \bar{H}(bond)_R - \bar{H}(bond)_P \qquad (6\text{-}9)$$

where $\bar{H}(bond)_R$ represents the sum of the molar bond enthalpies for all the reactant bonds and $\bar{H}(bond)_P$ represents the sum of the molar bond enthalpies for all the product bonds.

The values of average molar bond enthalpies of some bonds are given in Table 6-2.

6-6 Heat capacity measures the ability of a substance to take up energy as heat.

At constant pressure, the heat capacity is given by

$$C_P = \frac{\Delta H}{\Delta T} \qquad (6\text{-}10)$$

The molar heat capacity, $\bar{C}_P$, is the heat capacity per mole of a substance at constant pressure.

The specific heat, c_{sp}, is the heat capacity per gram of a substance at constant pressure.

The heat capacities per mole and per gram at constant pressure of some substances are given in Table 6-3.

6-7 A calorimeter is a device used to measure the amount of heat evolved or absorbed in a reaction.

For a reaction that takes place in a calorimeter (Figure 6-9)

$$\Delta H_{rxn} = -\Delta H_{calorimeter} \qquad (6\text{-}11)$$

For the reaction

$$\Delta H_{rxn} = -C_{p,\ calorimeter}\Delta T \qquad (6\text{-}13)$$

where ΔT is the measured temperature change.

6-8 Combustion reactions can be used as energy sources.

Combustion reactions that evolve a large quantity of heat per unit mass of the substance burned can be used as energy sources.

In a bomb calorimeter, $\Delta U_{rxn} = q_V$ (Equation 6-2).

In most cases, $\Delta U_{rxn} \approx \Delta H_{rxn}$.

The heat of combustion of a substance can be measured in a bomb calorimeter (Figure 6-10).

The heats of combustion of some fuels are given in Table 6-4.

6-9 Food is fuel.

The popular term calorie is actually a kilocalorie.

The approximate energy values of some common foods are given in Table 6-5.

6-10 Rockets and explosives utilize highly exothermic reactions with gaseous products.

B   SELF TEST

1 The first law of thermodynamics states that _____

_____ .

2 Chemical reactions always evolve energy in the form of heat. *True/False*

3 For a chemical reaction, the energy change, ΔU_{rxn}, is equal to _____ .

4 For a chemical reaction that takes place at constant volume, the energy change is equal to _____ .

5 The thermodynamic function, enthalpy, is defined as H equals
_____.

6 For a chemical reaction that takes place at constant pressure, the enthalpy change, ΔH_{rxn} is equal to _____.

7 When a chemical reaction is run in a reaction vessel open to the atmosphere, the reaction takes place at constant _____.

8 The enthalpy change for a chemical reaction is given by ΔH_{rxn} equals _____
_____.

9 Reactions that give off energy as heat are called _____.

10 Reactions that take up energy as heat are called _____.

11 If the value of ΔH_{rxn} is negative then the reaction is _____ thermic.

12 If the value of ΔH_{rxn} is positive then heat is absorbed by a reaction. *True/False*

13 The value of ΔH_{rxn} is equal to the heat absorbed or evolved by a reaction when the reaction takes place at constant_____.

14 If a reaction takes place at constant volume, then the heat absorbed or evolved by the reaction is equal to _____.

15 The standard molar enthalpy of formation, $\Delta \bar{H}_f^\circ$, of a substance is defined as
_____.

16 The value of $\Delta \bar{H}_f^\circ$ of N_2 at 25°C and 1 atm is _____.

17 For the reaction

$$CH_4(g) + 2O_2(g) \longrightarrow CO_2(g) + 2H_2O(g)$$

the values of $\Delta \bar{H}_f^\circ$ of the reactants and products are known. The value of ΔH_{rxn}° can be found by the relation ΔH_{rxn}° equals _____.

18 If two chemical equations are added together, then the value of ΔH_{rxn}° for the resulting equation equals _____.

19 State Hess's law in your own words.

20 Energy is required to break a bond between two atoms. *True/False*

21 The values of the bond enthalpies in the products and reactants of a reaction can be used to predict the value of ΔH_{rxn}°. *True/False*

22 The amount of heat required to raise the temperature of one mole of a substance by one kelvin is the _____ of the substance.

23 The quantity of heat required to raise the temperature of one gram of a substance by one degree Celsius is called _____.

24 The specific heat of water is $4.18 \text{ J} \cdot \text{K}^{-1} \cdot \text{g}^{-1}$ and the specific heat of sodium is $1.34 \text{ J} \cdot \text{K}^{-1} \cdot \text{g}^{-1}$. It will require (*more/less*) heat to raise the temperature of one gram of water by one degree than one gram of sodium.

25 An input of 100 J of heat will heat 10 g of water to a (*higher/lower*) temperature than 10 g of sodium when both are initially at the same temperature.

26 Suggest a reason why the heat capacity of a substance is given as the specific heat or molar heat capacity instead of simply the heat capacity. _____

_____ .

27 A calorimeter is a device used to measure _____ .

28 Only heats of combustion can be measured in a calorimeter. *True/False*

29 Why is the heat absorbed or given off by a calorimeter equal to the heat of the reaction taking place in the calorimeter? _____

_____ .

30 In a calorimeter, the change in _____ is the physical change measured.

31 The value of ΔH°_{rxn} is determined from the _____ of the calorimeter and the change in _____ .

32 Combustion is an example of an _____ thermic reaction.

33 An apparatus in which ΔU_{rxn} can be measured is called a _____ calorimeter.

34 The enthalpy change for a reaction often is almost equal to the energy change for the reaction. *True/False*

35 Why is the heat of combustion of a substance important in deciding whether a substance can be used as a fuel? _____ .

36 The value of ΔH°_{rxn} for the reaction between glucose and oxygen depends on whether the reaction takes place in a calorimeter or in the body. *True/False*

37 The reaction between hydrogen and oxygen to form water is exothermic. The dissociation of water to form hydrogen and oxygen will be an (*exothermic/endothermic*) reaction.

C   CALCULATIONS YOU SHOULD KNOW HOW TO DO

1 Calculate ΔH°_{rxn} using values of $\Delta \bar{H}^{\circ}_{f}$ (Table 6-1) and calculations involve using Equation (6-6) $\Delta H^{\circ}_{rxn} = y\Delta \bar{H}^{\circ}_{f}[Y] + z\Delta \bar{H}^{\circ}_{f}[Z] - a\Delta \bar{H}^{\circ}_{f}[A] - b\Delta \bar{H}^{\circ}_{f}[B]$. See Examples 6-1 and 6-2, and Problems 6-5 through 6-16.

2   Use Hess's law to calculate ΔH_{rxn}° for a reaction by adding or subtracting ΔH_{rxn}°'s for two or more reactions. See Example 6-3 and Problems 6-17 through 6-26.

3   Use the bond enthalpies in Table 6-2 to calculate ΔH_{rxn}°. See Example 6-5 and Problems 6-29 and 6-30.

4   Calculate bond enthalpies from ΔH_{rxn}° for certain reactions. See Example 6-5 and Problems 6-27, 6-28, and 6-31 through 6-34.

5   Use heat capacity to calculate the heat absorbed or evolved by a temperature change. See Example 6-7, Problems 6-37 and 6-38, and Problems 6-53 through 6-56.

6   Calculate the final temperature when two substances at different temperatures are brought into contact. See Problems 6-39 through 6-42.

7   Calculate ΔH_{rxn}° using data that are obtained from running the reaction in a calorimeter. See Examples 6-8 and 6-9 and Problems 6-43 through 6-52.

D   SOLUTIONS TO THE ODD-NUMBERED PROBLEMS

6-1   We are given the amount of heat evolved (501 kJ) when 10.0 g of methane is burned. The amount of heat that is evolved when one mole (16.04 g) of methane is burned is

$$\left(\frac{501 \text{ kJ}}{10.0 \text{ g}}\right)\left(\frac{16.04 \text{ g}}{1 \text{ mol}}\right) = 804 \text{ kJ} \cdot \text{mol}^{-1}$$

6-3   This problem is similar to Problem 6-1. The reaction is

$$C(s) + 2S(s) \longrightarrow CS_2(l)$$

One mole of CS_2 is formed when one mole of carbon reacts. Therefore,

$$\text{heat evolved per mole } CS_2 = \left(\frac{2.38 \text{ kJ}}{0.320 \text{ g}}\right)\left(\frac{12.01 \text{ g}}{1 \text{ mol}}\right) = 89.3 \text{ kJ} \cdot \text{mol}^{-1}$$

6-5   (a) $\Delta H_{rxn}^\circ = \Delta \bar{H}_f^\circ[C_2H_5OH(l)] - \Delta \bar{H}_f^\circ[C_2H_4(g)] - \Delta \bar{H}_f^\circ[H_2O(l)]$

Using the data from Table 6-1, we have

$\Delta H_{rxn}^\circ = (1 \text{ mol})(-277.7 \text{ kJ} \cdot \text{mol}^{-1}) - (1 \text{ mol})(52.28 \text{ kJ} \cdot \text{mol}^{-1})$

$$- (1 \text{ mol})(-285.8 \text{ kJ} \cdot \text{mol}^{-1})$$

$\quad = -44.2 \text{ kJ} \qquad \text{exothermic}$

(b) $\Delta H_{rxn}^\circ = 2\Delta \bar{H}_f^\circ[CO_2(g)] + 2\Delta \bar{H}_f^\circ[H_2O(g)] - \Delta \bar{H}_f^\circ[C_2H_4(g)] - 3\Delta \bar{H}_f^\circ[O_2(g)]$

$\quad = (2 \text{ mol})(-393.5 \text{ kJ} \cdot \text{mol}^{-1}) + (2 \text{ mol})(-241.8 \text{ kJ} \cdot \text{mol}^{-1})$

$$- (1 \text{ mol})(52.28 \text{ kJ} \cdot \text{mol}^{-1}) - (0)$$

$\quad = -1322.9 \text{ kJ} \qquad \text{exothermic}$

(c) $\Delta H_{rxn}^\circ = \Delta \bar{H}_f^\circ[C_2H_6(g)] - \Delta \bar{H}_f^\circ[C_2H_4(g)] - \Delta \bar{H}_f^\circ[H_2(g)]$

$\quad = (1\ \text{mol})(-84.68\ \text{kJ} \cdot \text{mol}^{-1}) - (1\ \text{mol})(52.28\ \text{kJ} \cdot \text{mol}^{-1}) - (0)$

$\quad = -136.96\ \text{kJ} \qquad \text{exothermic}$

6-7   (a) $\Delta H_{rxn}^\circ = 2\Delta \bar{H}_f^\circ[CO_2(g)] + 3\Delta \bar{H}_f^\circ[H_2O(g)] - \Delta \bar{H}_f^\circ[C_2H_5OH(l)] - 3\Delta \bar{H}_f^\circ[O_2(g)]$

$\quad = (2\ \text{mol})(-393.5\ \text{kJ} \cdot \text{mol}^{-1}) + (3\ \text{mol})(-241.8\ \text{kJ} \cdot \text{mol}^{-1})$

$$- (1\ \text{mol})(-277.7\ \text{kJ} \cdot \text{mol}^{-1}) - (0)$$

$\quad = -1234.7\ \text{kJ}$

The heat of combustion of $C_2H_5OH(l)$ per gram is

$$\left(\frac{-1234.7\ \text{kJ}}{1\ \text{mol}} \right)\left(\frac{1\ \text{mol}}{46.07\ \text{g}} \right) = -26.80\ \text{kJ} \cdot \text{g}^{-1}$$

(b) $\Delta H_{rxn}^\circ = 2\Delta \bar{H}_f^\circ[CO_2(g)] + 3\Delta \bar{H}_f^\circ[H_2O(g)] - \Delta \bar{H}_f^\circ[C_2H_6(g)] - \frac{7}{2}\Delta \bar{H}_f^\circ[O_2(g)]$

$\quad = (2\ \text{mol})(-393.5\ \text{kJ} \cdot \text{mol}^{-1}) + (3\ \text{mol})(-241.8\ \text{kJ} \cdot \text{mol}^{-1})$

$$- (1\ \text{mol})(-84.68\ \text{kJ} \cdot \text{mol}^{-1}) - (0)$$

$\quad = -1427.7\ \text{kJ}$

The heat of combustion of $C_2H_6(g)$ per gram is

$$\left(\frac{-1427.7\ \text{kJ}}{1\ \text{mol}} \right)\left(\frac{1\ \text{mol}}{30.07\ \text{g}} \right) = -47.48\ \text{kJ} \cdot \text{g}^{-1}$$

The combustion of one gram of $C_2H_6(g)$ produces almost twice as much heat per gram as does $C_2H_5OH(l)$.

6-9 $\Delta H_{rxn}^\circ = 6\Delta \bar{H}_f^\circ[CO_2(g)] + 6\Delta \bar{H}_f^\circ[H_2O(l)] - \Delta \bar{H}_f^\circ[C_6H_{12}O_6(s)] - 6\Delta \bar{H}_f^\circ[O_2(g)]$

In this case we are given ΔH_{rxn}° and must determine $\Delta \bar{H}_f^\circ[C_6H_{12}O_6(s)]$. Using the data in Table 6-1, we have

$-2815.8\ \text{kJ} = (6\ \text{mol})(-393.5\ \text{kJ} \cdot \text{mol}^{-1}) + (6\ \text{mol})(-285.8\ \text{kJ} \cdot \text{mol}^{-1})$

$$- (1\ \text{mol})\Delta \bar{H}_f^\circ[C_6H_{12}O_6(s)] - (0)$$

Solving for $\Delta \bar{H}_f^\circ[C_6H_{12}O_6(s)]$

$(1\ \text{mol})\Delta \bar{H}_f^\circ[C_6H_{12}O_6(s)] = (6\ \text{mol})(-393.5\ \text{kJ} \cdot \text{mol}^{-1})$

$$+ (6\ \text{mol})(-285.8\ \text{kJ} \cdot \text{mol}^{-1}) + 2815.8\ \text{kJ}$$

$$\Delta \bar{H}_f^\circ[C_6H_{12}O_6(s)] = -1260.0\ \text{kJ} \cdot \text{mol}^{-1}$$

6-11 $\Delta H_{rxn}^\circ = 2\Delta \bar{H}_f^\circ[O_3(g)] - \Delta \bar{H}_f^\circ[O_2(g)] - \Delta \bar{H}_f^\circ[O(g)]$

$\quad = (2\ \text{mol})(142\ \text{kJ} \cdot \text{mol}^{-1}) - (0) - (1\ \text{mol})(247.5\ \text{kJ} \cdot \text{mol}^{-1})$

$\quad = 37\ \text{kJ}$

6-13 (a) $\Delta H^\circ_{rxn} = 2\Delta\bar{H}^\circ_f[N(g)] - \Delta\bar{H}^\circ_f[N_2(g)]$

$$945.2 \text{ kJ} = (2 \text{ mol})\Delta\bar{H}^\circ_f[N(g)] - (0)$$

or $\qquad\qquad \Delta\bar{H}^\circ_f[N(g)] = \dfrac{945.2 \text{ kJ}}{2 \text{ mol}} = 472.6 \text{ kJ} \cdot \text{mol}^{-1}$

Similarly,

(b) $\Delta\bar{H}^\circ_f[F(g)] = \dfrac{158.0 \text{ kJ}}{2 \text{ mol}} = 79.0 \text{ kJ} \cdot \text{mol}^{-1}$

(c) $\Delta\bar{H}^\circ_f[H(g)] = \dfrac{436.0 \text{ kJ}}{2 \text{ mol}} = 218.0 \text{ kJ} \cdot \text{mol}^{-1}$

(d) $\Delta\bar{H}^\circ_f[Cl(g)] = \dfrac{243.4 \text{ kJ}}{2 \text{ mol}} = 121.7 \text{ kJ} \cdot \text{mol}^{-1}$

The bond strength of each diatomic molecule given is equal to the value of the corresponding ΔH°_{rxn}. Therefore, $N_2(g)$ has the greatest bond strength.

6-15 Iodine is a solid at 25°C and 1 atm and so the reaction is

$$I_2(s) \longrightarrow I_2(g)$$

and the heat required to vaporize one mole of iodine is equal to ΔH°_{rxn}. Thus

$$\text{heat} = \Delta H^\circ_{rxn} = \Delta\bar{H}^\circ_f[I_2(g)] - \Delta\bar{H}^\circ_f[I_2(s)]$$

From Table 6-1,

$$\text{heat} = (1 \text{ mol})(62.4 \text{ kJ} \cdot \text{mol}^{-1}) - (0)$$
$$= 62.4 \text{ kJ}$$

6-17 To obtain the second equation, simply reverse the first equation. Thus,

$$\Delta H^\circ_{rxn}(2) = -\Delta H^\circ_{rxn}(1) = +145.4 \text{ kJ}$$

6-19 To obtain the third equation, reverse the first equation, add it to the second equation, and divide by 2

$2PCl_3(g) \longrightarrow 2P(s) + 3Cl_2(g)$	$\Delta H^\circ_{rxn} = -(-613 \text{ kJ}) = +613 \text{ kJ}$	
$2P(s) + 5Cl_2(g) \longrightarrow 2PCl_5(g)$	$\Delta H^\circ_{rxn} = -790 \text{ kJ}$	

$$\overline{2PCl_3(g) + 2Cl_2(g) \longrightarrow 2PCl_5(g) \qquad \Delta H^\circ_{rxn} = 613 \text{ kJ} - 790 \text{ kJ}}$$
$$= -177 \text{ kJ}$$

or $PCl_3(g) + Cl_2(g) \longrightarrow PCl_5(g)$ $\Delta H^\circ_{rxn} = \dfrac{-177 \text{ kJ}}{2}$

$$= -88.5 \text{ kJ}$$

6-21   The equation that we want can be obtained from the two given equations by reversing the first equation, multiplying it by 3 and then adding it to 2 times the second equation.

$3Fe_2O_3(s) \longrightarrow 6Fe(s) + \frac{9}{2}O_2(g)$ $\Delta H^\circ_{rxn} = -(3)(-823.41 \text{ kJ})$

$$= 2470.23 \text{ kJ}$$

$6Fe(s) + 4O_2(g) \longrightarrow 2Fe_3O_4(s)$ $\Delta H^\circ_{rxn} = (2)(-1120.48 \text{ kJ})$

$$= -2240.96 \text{ kJ}$$

$3Fe_2O_3(s) \longrightarrow 2Fe_3O_4(s) + \frac{1}{2}O_2(g)$ $\Delta H^\circ_{rxn} = 2470.23 \text{ kJ} - 2240.96 \text{ kJ}$

$$= +229.27 \text{ kJ}$$

6-23   The equations that correspond to the combustion reactions are
(1) $C_{12}H_{22}O_{11}(s) + 12O_2(g) \longrightarrow 12CO_2(g) + 11H_2O(l)$
      sucrose

$$\Delta H^\circ_{rxn}(1) = -5646.7 \text{ kJ}$$

(2) $C_6H_{12}O_6(s) + 6O_2(g) \longrightarrow 6CO_2(g) + 6H_2O(l)$
      glucose

$$\Delta H^\circ_{rxn}(2) = -2815.8 \text{ kJ}$$

(3) $C_6H_{12}O_6(s) + 6O_2(g) \longrightarrow 6CO_2(g) + 6H_2O(l)$
      fructose

$$\Delta H^\circ_{rxn}(3) = -2826.7 \text{ kJ}$$

To obtain the desired equation, reverse equations (2) and (3) and add them to equation (1):

$C_{12}H_{22}O_{11}(s) + 12O_2(g) \longrightarrow 12CO_2(g) + 11H_2O(l)$
      sucrose

$$\Delta H^\circ_{rxn} = -5646.7 \text{ kJ}$$

$6CO_2(g) + 6H_2O(l) \longrightarrow C_6H_{12}O_6(s) + 6O_2(g)$
      glucose

$$\Delta H^\circ_{rxn} = +2815.8 \text{ kJ}$$

$6CO_2(g) + 6H_2O(l) \longrightarrow C_6H_{12}O_6(s) + 6O_2(g)$
      fructose

$$\Delta H^\circ_{rxn} = +2826.7 \text{ kJ}$$

(4) $C_{12}H_{22}O_{11}(s) + H_2O(l) \longrightarrow C_6H_{12}O_6(s) + C_6H_{12}O_6(s)$
      sucrose   glucose   fructose

$$\Delta H^\circ_{rxn}(4) = -5646.7 \text{ kJ} + 2815.8 \text{ kJ} + 2826.7 \text{ kJ}$$

$$= -4.2 \text{ kJ}$$

6-25 To calculate $\Delta \bar{H}_f^{\circ}[\text{NO}(g)]$, we need to find ΔH_{rxn}° for the reaction

$$\tfrac{1}{2}\text{N}_2(g) + \tfrac{1}{2}\text{O}_2(g) \longrightarrow \text{NO}(g)$$

To obtain this equation, divide equations (1) and (2) by four, reverse the second equation, and add

$$\text{NH}_3(g) + \tfrac{5}{4}\text{O}_2(g) \longrightarrow \text{NO}(g) + \tfrac{6}{4}\text{H}_2\text{O}(l) \qquad \Delta H_{rxn}^{\circ} = \frac{-1170 \text{ kJ}}{4} = -292.5 \text{ kJ}$$

$$\tfrac{1}{2}\text{N}_2(g) + \tfrac{6}{4}\text{H}_2\text{O}(l) \longrightarrow \text{NH}_3(g) + \tfrac{3}{4}\text{O}_2(g) \qquad \Delta H_{rxn}^{\circ} = \frac{+1530 \text{ kJ}}{4} = +382.5 \text{ kJ}$$

$$\tfrac{1}{2}\text{N}_2(g) + \tfrac{1}{2}\text{O}_2(g) \longrightarrow \text{NO}(g) \qquad \Delta \bar{H}_f^{\circ} = \Delta H_{rxn}^{\circ} = +90.0 \text{ kJ}$$

6-27 The reaction involves breaking three Cl—F bonds; thus

$$\Delta H_{rxn}^{\circ} \approx 3\bar{H}(\text{Cl}—\text{F})$$

Given the value of ΔH_{rxn}°, we can calculate $\bar{H}(\text{Cl}—\text{F})$.

$$514 \text{ kJ} \approx (3 \text{ mol})\bar{H}(\text{Cl}—\text{F})$$

$$\bar{H}(\text{Cl}—\text{F}) \approx \frac{514 \text{ kJ}}{3 \text{ mol}} = 171 \text{ kJ} \cdot \text{mol}^{-1}$$

6-29 There are four C—H bonds in CH_4 and four C—Cl bonds in CCl_4. Therefore,

$$\begin{aligned}
\Delta H_{rxn}^{\circ} &\approx 4\bar{H}(\text{C}—\text{H}) + 4\bar{H}(\text{Cl}—\text{Cl}) - 4\bar{H}(\text{C}—\text{Cl}) - 4\bar{H}(\text{H}—\text{Cl}) \\
&\approx (4 \text{ mol})(414 \text{ kJ} \cdot \text{mol}^{-1}) + (4 \text{ mol})(243 \text{ kJ} \cdot \text{mol}^{-1}) \\
&\qquad - (4 \text{ mol})(331 \text{ kJ} \cdot \text{mol}^{-1}) - (4 \text{ mol})(431 \text{ kJ} \cdot \text{mol}^{-1}) \\
&\approx -420 \text{ kJ}
\end{aligned}$$

6-31 $\Delta H_{rxn}^{\circ} \approx 2\bar{H}(\text{H}—\text{H}) + \bar{H}(\text{O}—\text{O}) - 4\bar{H}(\text{O}—\text{H})$

The value of ΔH_{rxn}° is $\Delta H_{rxn}^{\circ} = 2\Delta \bar{H}_f^{\circ}[\text{H}_2\text{O}(g)] = (2 \text{ mol})(-241.8 \text{ kJ} \cdot \text{mol}^{-1}) = -483.6 \text{ kJ}$

Thus we can write

$$\begin{aligned}
-483.6 \text{ kJ} &\approx 2\bar{H}(\text{H}—\text{H}) + \bar{H}(\text{O}—\text{O}) - 4\bar{H}(\text{O}—\text{H}) \\
&= (2 \text{ mol})(435 \text{ kJ} \cdot \text{mol}^{-1}) + (1 \text{ mol})\bar{H}(\text{O}—\text{O}) \\
&\qquad\qquad\qquad\qquad\qquad\qquad - (4 \text{ mol})(464 \text{ kJ} \cdot \text{mol}^{-1}) \\
&= 870 \text{ kJ} + (1 \text{ mol})\bar{H}(\text{O}—\text{O}) - 1856 \text{ kJ}
\end{aligned}$$

$$\bar{H}(\text{O}—\text{O}) \approx +\frac{502 \text{ kJ}}{1 \text{ mol}} = +502 \text{ kJ} \cdot \text{mol}^{-1}$$

6-33 The relevant reaction is

$$CH_4(g) \longrightarrow C(g) + 4H(g)$$

We have that $\Delta H^\circ_{rxn} \approx 4\bar{H}(C\text{—}H)$

and

$$\Delta H^\circ_{rxn} = \Delta \bar{H}^\circ_f[C(g)] + 4\Delta \bar{H}^\circ_f[H(g)] - \Delta \bar{H}^\circ_f[CH_4(g)]$$
$$= (1 \text{ mol})(709 \text{ kJ} \cdot \text{mol}^{-1}) + (4 \text{ mol})(218 \text{ kJ} \cdot \text{mol}^{-1})$$
$$- (1 \text{ mol})(-74.86 \text{ kJ} \cdot \text{mol}^{-1})$$
$$= 1656 \text{ kJ}$$

Therefore, we have that $4\bar{H}(C\text{—}H) = 1656$ kJ, or

$$\bar{H}(C\text{—}H) = \frac{1656 \text{ kJ}}{4 \text{ mol}} = 414 \text{ kJ} \cdot \text{mol}^{-1}$$

6-35 Use Equation 6-10:

$$C_P = \frac{\Delta H}{\Delta T}$$

In this case, $\Delta H = 2210$ J and $\Delta T = 12.3°C = 12.3$ K. Therefore, the total heat capacity is

$$C_P = \frac{2210 \text{ J}}{12.3 \text{ K}} = 180 \text{ J} \cdot \text{K}^{-1}$$

for the 73.0 gram sample of C_2H_5OH. The specific heat is the heat capacity per gram, or

$$c_{sp} = \frac{180 \text{ J} \cdot \text{K}^{-1}}{73.0 \text{ g}} = 2.47 \text{ J} \cdot \text{K}^{-1} \cdot \text{g}^{-1}$$

The molar heat capacity is

$$\bar{C}_P = (2.47 \text{ J} \cdot \text{K}^{-1} \cdot \text{g}^{-1})\left(\frac{46.07 \text{ g}}{1 \text{ mol}}\right) = 114 \text{ J} \cdot \text{K}^{-1} \cdot \text{mol}^{-1}$$

6-37 For this problem, $\Delta T = (49.7 - 25.0)°C = 24.7°C = 24.7$ K. The heat capacity of the 50 kg of water is

$$C_P = (75.2 \text{ J} \cdot \text{K}^{-1} \cdot \text{mol}^{-1})\left(\frac{1 \text{ mol}}{18.02 \text{ g}}\right)(50 \times 10^3 \text{ g})$$
$$= 2.09 \times 10^5 \text{ J} \cdot \text{K}^{-1}$$

Using Equation 6-10, we have

$$\Delta H = \bar{C}_P \Delta T = (2.09 \times 10^5 \, \text{J} \cdot \text{K}^{-1})(24.7 \, \text{K})$$
$$= 5.2 \times 10^6 \, \text{J}$$

6-39 The sample of copper, being at a lower temperature than the water, will absorb heat from the water and so increase its temperature. As heat is absorbed from the water, it will cool down. This process will continue until the copper and the water are at the same temperature. The key fact here is that the heat absorbed by the copper must be equal to the heat given up by the water. In an equation, we have

$$\Delta H_{\text{Cu}} = \Delta H_{\text{H}_2\text{O}}$$

Using Equation 6-10, this equation becomes

$$\bar{C}_{P,\text{Cu}} \Delta T_{\text{Cu}} = \bar{C}_{P,\text{H}_2\text{O}} \Delta T_{\text{H}_2\text{O}}$$

For the sample of copper

$$\Delta T_{\text{Cu}} = t_f - 25.0°\text{C}$$

and for the water

$$\Delta T_{\text{H}_2\text{O}} = 40.0°\text{C} - t_f$$

where t_f is the final Celsius temperature. The value of $\bar{C}_{P,\text{Cu}}$ is

$$\bar{C}_{P,\text{Cu}} = (0.385 \, \text{J} \cdot \text{K}^{-1} \cdot \text{g}^{-1})(25.0 \, \text{g}) = 9.625 \, \text{J} \cdot \text{K}^{-1} = 9.625 \, \text{J} \cdot °\text{C}^{-1}$$

and the value of $\bar{C}_{P,\text{H}_2\text{O}}$ is

$$\bar{C}_{P,\text{H}_2\text{O}} = (4.18 \, \text{J} \cdot \text{K}^{-1} \cdot \text{g}^{-1})(100.0 \, \text{g}) = 418 \, \text{J} \cdot \text{K}^{-1} = 418 \, \text{J} \cdot °\text{C}^{-1}$$

Substituting in the values of $\bar{C}_{P,\text{Cu}}$ and $\bar{C}_{P,\text{H}_2\text{O}}$ and the expressions for ΔT_{Cu} and $\Delta T_{\text{H}_2\text{O}}$, we have

$$\Delta H_{\text{Cu}} = \Delta H_{\text{H}_2\text{O}}$$

or

$$9.625 \, \text{J} \cdot °\text{C}^{-1}(t_f - 25.0°\text{C}) = (418 \, \text{J} \cdot °\text{C}^{-1})(40.0°\text{C} - t_f)$$
$$427.6 \, t_f = 17000°\text{C}$$
$$t_f = 39.7°\text{C}$$

6-41 As in Problem 6-39, the heat balance equation is

$$\bar{C}_{P,\text{Al}} \Delta T_{\text{Al}} = \bar{C}_{P,\text{Cu}} \Delta T_{\text{Cu}}$$

For the aluminum

$$\bar{C}_{P,\text{Al}} = (24.2 \text{ J} \cdot \text{K}^{-1} \cdot \text{mol}^{-1})(1.00 \text{ kg})\left(\frac{10^3 \text{ g}}{1 \text{ kg}}\right)\left(\frac{1 \text{ mol}}{26.98 \text{ g}}\right)$$

$$= 897 \text{ J} \cdot \text{K}^{-1} = 897 \text{ J} \cdot {}^{\circ}\text{C}^{-1}$$

$$\Delta T_{\text{Al}} = 600{}^{\circ}\text{C} - t_f$$

For the copper

$$\bar{C}_{P,\text{Cu}} = (24.5 \text{ J} \cdot \text{K}^{-1} \cdot \text{mol}^{-1})(1.00 \text{ kg})\left(\frac{10^3 \text{ g}}{1 \text{ kg}}\right)\left(\frac{1 \text{ mol}}{63.55 \text{ g}}\right)$$

$$= 386 \text{ J} \cdot \text{K}^{-1} = 386 \text{ J} \cdot {}^{\circ}\text{C}^{-1}$$

$$\Delta T_{\text{Cu}} = t_f - 100{}^{\circ}\text{C}$$

Putting all this into the heat balance equation gives

$$(897 \text{ J} \cdot {}^{\circ}\text{C}^{-1})(600{}^{\circ}\text{C} - t_f) = (386 \text{ J} \cdot {}^{\circ}\text{C}^{-1})(t_f - 100{}^{\circ}\text{C})$$

or

$$1280 \, t_f = 5.77 \times 10^{5}{}^{\circ}\text{C}$$

or

$$t_f = 450{}^{\circ}\text{C}$$

6-43   The heat evolved by the reaction is given by Equation 6-13:

$$\Delta H_{rxn} = -\bar{C}_{P,calorimeter}\Delta T$$

$$= -(480 \text{ J} \cdot \text{K}^{-1})(1.17 \text{ K}) = -562 \text{ J}$$

This amount of heat is evolved when 0.0500 L of 0.200 M solutions react. The number of moles that react is given by

$$n = MV = (0.200 \text{ mol} \cdot \text{L}^{-1})(0.0500 \text{ L}) = 0.0100 \text{ moles}$$

The heat of reaction for one mole of reactants is

$$\Delta H^{\circ}_{rxn} = \frac{-562 \text{ J}}{0.0100 \text{ mol}} = -56.2 \text{ kJ} \cdot \text{mol}^{-1}$$

6-45   The value of ΔH°_{rxn} is

$$\Delta H^{\circ}_{rxn} = -(4.92 \text{ kJ} \cdot \text{K}^{-1})(3.06 \text{ K}) = -15.06 \text{ kJ}$$

The 2.00 gram sample of NH_4NO_3 is equivalent to

$$(2.00 \text{ g})\left(\frac{1 \text{ mol}}{80.05 \text{ g}}\right) = 0.0250 \text{ mol } NH_4NO_3$$

The heat evolved per mole for the decomposition of NH_4NO_3 is

$$\Delta H^{\circ}_{rxn} = \frac{-15.06 \text{ kJ}}{0.0250 \text{ mol}} = -602 \text{ kJ} \cdot \text{mol}^{-1}$$

6-47 The temperature of the calorimeter *decreases*, and so heat is absorbed in the process of dissolving KCl in water. The heat absorbed is

$$\Delta H^{\circ}_{rxn} = -(4.51 \text{ kJ} \cdot \text{K}^{-1})(-0.256 \text{ K}) = +1.155 \text{ kJ}$$

A 5.00 gram sample of KCl corresponds to

$$(5.00 \text{ g})\left(\frac{1 \text{ mol}}{74.55 \text{ g}}\right) = 0.06707 \text{ mol KCl}$$

The molar heat of solution of KCl in H_2O is

$$\Delta \bar{H}^{\circ}_{soln} = \frac{1.155 \text{ kJ}}{0.06707 \text{ mol}} = 17.2 \text{ kJ} \cdot \text{mol}^{-1}$$

6-49 $\Delta H_{rxn} = -(32.7 \text{ kJ} \cdot \text{K}^{-1})(4.25 \text{ K}) = -139 \text{ kJ}$

$$\Delta H^{\circ}_{comb} = \frac{-139 \text{ kJ}}{3.00 \text{ g}} = -46.3 \text{ kJ} \cdot \text{g}^{-1}$$

$$= (-46.3 \text{ kJ} \cdot \text{g}^{-1})\left(\frac{44.09 \text{ g}}{1 \text{ mol}}\right) = -2040 \text{ kJ} \cdot \text{mol}^{-1}$$

6-51 $\Delta H^{\circ}_{rxn} = -(8.75 \text{ kJ} \cdot \text{K}^{-1})(0.312 \text{ K}) = -2.73 \text{ kJ}$

$$\Delta H^{\circ}_{comb} = \frac{-2.73 \text{ kJ}}{1.00 \text{ g}} = -2.73 \text{ kJ} \cdot \text{g}^{-1}$$

$$= (-2.73 \text{ kJ} \cdot \text{g}^{-1})\left(\frac{90.04 \text{ g}}{1 \text{ mol}}\right) = -246 \text{ kJ} \cdot \text{mol}^{-1}$$

The equation for the combustion of oxalic acid is

$$H_2C_2O_4(s) + \tfrac{1}{2}O_2(g) \longrightarrow 2CO_2(g) + H_2O(l)$$

The value of ΔH°_{rxn} for the combustion of oxalic acid is given by

$$\Delta H^{\circ}_{rxn} = 2\Delta \bar{H}^{\circ}_f[CO_2(g)] + \Delta \bar{H}^{\circ}_f[H_2O(l)] - \Delta \bar{H}^{\circ}_f[H_2C_2O_4(s)] - \tfrac{1}{2}\Delta \bar{H}^{\circ}_f[O_2(g)]$$

Using the above value for ΔH°_{rxn} and the data in Table 6-1, we have

$$-246 \text{ kJ} = (2 \text{ mol})(-393.5 \text{ kJ} \cdot \text{mol}^{-1}) + (1 \text{ mol})(-285.8 \text{ kJ} \cdot \text{mol}^{-1})$$

$$- (1 \text{ mol})\Delta \bar{H}^{\circ}_f[H_2C_2O_4(s)] - (\tfrac{1}{2} \text{ mol})(0)$$

$$= -1072.8 \text{ kJ} - (1 \text{ mol})\Delta \bar{H}^{\circ}_f[H_2C_2O_4(s)]$$

Solving for $\Delta \bar{H}_f^\circ[H_2C_2O_4(s)]$, we get

$$\Delta \bar{H}_f^\circ[H_2C_2O_4(s)] = -827 \text{ kJ} \cdot \text{mol}^{-1}$$

6-53 The heat capacity of 40 gal of water is

$$C_P = (40 \text{ gal})\left(\frac{4 \text{ qt}}{1 \text{ gal}}\right)\left(\frac{1 \text{ L}}{1.057 \text{ qt}}\right)\left(\frac{10^3 \text{ g}}{1 \text{ L}}\right)(4.2 \text{ J} \cdot \text{K}^{-1} \cdot \text{g}^{-1})$$

$$= 6.36 \times 10^5 \text{ J} \cdot \text{K}^{-1}$$

The value of ΔT must be converted to degrees Celsius. Use the formula

$$^\circ C = \tfrac{5}{9}(^\circ F - 32) \qquad\qquad \text{(Inside back cover)}$$

to get

$$t_{final} = \tfrac{5}{9}(135^\circ F - 32) = 57.2^\circ C$$

$$t_{initial} = \tfrac{5}{9}(46^\circ F - 32) = 7.8^\circ C$$

so that

$$\Delta T = 49.4^\circ C = 49.4 \text{ K}$$

The heat required to raise the temperature of the 40 gal of water 49.4 K is

$$\Delta H = C_P \Delta T = (6.36 \times 10^5 \text{ J} \cdot \text{K}^{-1})(49.4 \text{ K})$$

$$= 3.14 \times 10^7 \text{ J} = 3.14 \times 10^4 \text{ kJ}$$

The heat of combustion of methane is given in Table 6-4 as

$$\Delta H_{rxn}^\circ = -802 \text{ kJ} \cdot \text{mol}^{-1}$$

According to the problem, 20 percent of this heat is lost to the surroundings, and so the available heat per mole of methane is

$$(0.80)(802 \text{ kJ} \cdot \text{mol}^{-1}) = 642 \text{ kJ} \cdot \text{mol}^{-1}$$

The number of moles of methane that must be burned is given by

$$\frac{\text{total heat required}}{\text{heat supplied per mole of methane}} = \frac{3.14 \times 10^4 \text{ kJ}}{642 \text{ kJ} \cdot \text{mol}^{-1}} = 49 \text{ mol}$$

6-55 The heat required to raise the temperature of 1.0 L of water by 37°C is

$$\Delta H = (4.18 \text{ J} \cdot \text{K}^{-1} \cdot \text{g}^{-1})(1.0 \text{ L})\left(\frac{1000 \text{ mL}}{1 \text{ L}}\right)\left(\frac{1.0 \text{ g}}{1 \text{ mL}}\right)(37 \text{ K})$$

$$= 150 \text{ kJ}$$

Given that one kilogram of body fat yields 33,000 kJ, we see that

$$\frac{150 \text{ kJ}}{33,000 \text{ kJ} \cdot \text{kg}^{-1}} = 0.0045 \text{ kg}$$

or 4.5 g of body fat will be burned.

6-57 Let's set up the following table for the proposed formula of the compound of thallium and chlorine.

Proposed formula	Value of N in Dulong and Petit's rule	Predicted value of $\overline{C}_P / J \cdot K^{-1} \cdot mol^{-1}$	Observed value of $\overline{C}_P$ from specific heat and proposed formula
TlCl	2	50	$(0.208 \text{ J} \cdot \text{K}^{-1} \cdot \text{g}^{-1})\left(\dfrac{239.9 \text{ g}}{1 \text{ mol}}\right)$ $= 49.9 \text{ J} \cdot \text{K}^{-1} \cdot \text{mol}^{-1}$
TlCl$_2$	3	75	$(0.208 \text{ J} \cdot \text{K}^{-1} \cdot \text{g}^{-1})\left(\dfrac{275.3 \text{ g}}{1 \text{ mol}}\right)$ $= 57.3 \text{ J} \cdot \text{K}^{-1} \cdot \text{mol}^{-1}$
TlCl$_3$	4	100	$(0.208 \text{ J} \cdot \text{K}^{-1} \cdot \text{g}^{-1})\left(\dfrac{310.8 \text{ g}}{1 \text{ mol}}\right)$ $= 64.6 \text{ J} \cdot \text{K}^{-1} \cdot \text{mol}^{-1}$

Because of the agreement between the predicted and observed values of $\overline{C}_P$, we conclude that the formula of the compound is TlCl.

6-59 The molar heat capacity of stilleite, using Dulong and Petit's Rule is

$$\overline{C}_P = (2)(25 \text{ J} \cdot \text{K}^{-1} \cdot \text{mol}^{-1}) = 50 \text{ J} \cdot \text{K}^{-1} \cdot \text{mol}^{-1}$$

if stilleite is ZnSe.

The observed molar heat capacity of stilleite is

$$\overline{C}_P = (0.348 \text{ J} \cdot \text{K}^{-1} \cdot \text{g}^{-1})\left(\frac{144.34 \text{ g}}{1 \text{ mol}}\right) = 50.2 \text{ J} \cdot \text{K}^{-1} \cdot \text{mol}^{-1}$$

if stilleite is ZnSe.

Thus we determine the formula of stilleite to be ZnSe.

E   ANSWERS TO THE EVEN-NUMBERED PROBLEMS

6-2   860 kJ

6-4   601 kJ

6-6   (a) -196.0 kJ, exothermic
          (b) -101 kJ, exothermic
          (c) -904.6 kJ, exothermic

6-8   (a) -638.4 kJ; -19.93 kJ $\cdot$ g^{-1}
          (b) -543.2 kJ; -16.67 kJ $\cdot$ g^{-1}

          The combustion of one gram of CH_3OH produces 1.2 times as much heat per gram as does N_2H_4.

6-10 -2219 kJ $\cdot$ mol^{-1}

6-12 -11.7 kJ

6-14 (a) -542.2 kJ, exothermic   (c) -92.38 kJ, exothermic
          (b) -566.0 kJ, exothermic   (d) -113.04 kJ, exothermic

6-16 44.0 kJ

6-18 0.7594 kJ $\cdot$ g^{-1}

6-20 70 kJ

6-22 -512.8 kJ

6-24 2.9 kJ

6-26 -98 kJ

6-28 184 kJ

6-30 -435 kJ

6-32 943 kJ $\cdot$ mol^{-1}

6-34 331 kJ $\cdot$ mol^{-1}

6-36 $c_{sp} = 2.27$ J $\cdot$ K^{-1} $\cdot$ g^{-1}; $\bar{C}_P = 195$ J $\cdot$ K^{-1} $\cdot$ mol^{-1}

6-38 at least 7.46×10^4 g

6-40 1.81°C

6-42 0.89 J $\cdot$ K^{-1} $\cdot$ g^{-1}

6-44 -26.0 kJ $\cdot$ mol^{-1}

6-46 -66.3 kJ $\cdot$ mol^{-1}

6-48 -33.3 kJ $\cdot$ mol^{-1}

6-50 $\Delta H^{\circ}_{comb} = -15.7$ kJ $\cdot$ g^{-1} $= -2820$ kJ $\cdot$ mol^{-1}; 15.7 kJ

6-52 $\Delta H^{\circ}_{comb} = -1343$ kJ $\cdot$ mol^{-1}; $\Delta \bar{H}^{\circ}_f[C_3H_6O_3(s)] = -695$ kJ $\cdot$ mol^{-1}

6-54 70 miles

6-56   66 g

6-58 RbO_2

6-60   PbFCl

F   ANSWERS TO THE SELF-TEST

1   Energy is neither created nor destroyed but is transformed from one form to another; energy is conserved.

2   false

3   The energy transferred as heat plus the energy transferred as work, $\Delta U_{rxn} = q + w$

4   heat evolved or absorbed, q_V

5 $U + PV$

6   heat evolved or absorbed, q_P

7   pressure

8 $H_{products} - H_{reactants}$; the enthalpy of the products minus the enthalpy of the reactants

9   exothermic

10   endothermic

11   exo-

12   true

13   pressure

14 ΔU_{rxn}

15   the energy that is evolved or absorbed as heat when the substance is formed directly from its elements in their standard form at one atm

16   0

17 $\Delta H_{rxn}^\circ = \Delta \bar{H}_f^\circ[CO_2(g)]$
$+ 2\Delta \bar{H}_f^\circ[H_2O(g)]$
$- \Delta \bar{H}_f^\circ[CH_4(g)] - 2\Delta \bar{H}_f^\circ[O_2(g)]$

18   the sum of the ΔH_{rxn}° values for each reaction

19   See Section 6-4.

20   true

21   true (See Example 6-5.)

22   molar heat capacity

23   specific heat

24   more

25   lower

26   The value of the heat capacity of a substance depends upon its mass.

27   heat evolved or absorbed in a process by measuring ΔT

28   false

29   All the heat that is evolved or absorbed by the reaction is absorbed or supplied by the calorimeter.

30   temperature

31   heat capacity; temperature

32   exo-

33   bomb

34   true

35   The heat of combustion is the quantity of heat that is evolved when the substance burns.

36   false (assuming that the temperatures are equal)

37   endothermic

7 / The Quantum Theory and Atomic Structure

A   OUTLINE OF CHAPTER 7

7-1   First ionization energy is a periodic property.

The ionization energy is the energy required to remove an electron from an atom or ion.

A plot of the first ionization energy I_1 against atomic number (Figure 7-1) displays the periodic nature of I_1.

I_1 generally increases across each row of the periodic table (Figure 7-2).

The electronic structure of the noble gases is relatively stable.

7-2   The values of successive ionization energies suggest a shell structure.

Table 7-1 lists successive ionization energies of the elements hydrogen through argon.

The inner-core electron structure of an atom is that of the preceding noble gas.

A Lewis electron-dot formula (Table 7-2) is a representation of an atom with the noble-gaslike inner electrons represented by the symbol of the atom and the outer electrons represented by dots around the symbol.

The values of the ionization energies of atoms suggest that there exist subshells (Tables 7-1 and 7-3).

7-3   Electromagnetic radiation can be described as waves.

The wavelength, λ, (Figure 7-4) and frequency, ν, of electromagnetic radiation are related by $\lambda\nu = c$ [Equation (7-1)], where c is the speed of light, $3.00 \times 10^8 \text{ m} \cdot \text{s}^{-1}$

The complete range of wavelengths or frequencies of electromagnetic radiation is called the electromagnetic spectrum (Table 7-4).

7-4   The spectra emitted by atoms are line spectra.

A prism is used to separate electromagnetic radiation into its components (Figure 7-5).

The visible region consists of electromagnetic radiation in the range 400 nm to 700 nm.

A continuous spectrum consists of all wavelengths.

A line spectrum consists of only certain wavelengths.

An atomic spectrum is a line spectrum. Each type of atom has a characteristic atomic spectrum (Figure 7-6 and the frontispiece).

Atomic spectra can be used to determine the atomic composition of a substance.

7-5   A study of blackbody radiation led Planck to the first quantum hypothesis, $E = h\nu$

A blackbody is an idealized heated body that is radiating energy.

Plots of the intensity of blackbody radiation versus frequency for several temperatures are given in Figure 7-7.

Planck assumed that radiation could be emitted only in energy packets called quanta. The energy associated with these quanta is related to the frequency by $E = h\nu$ (Equation 7-2).

Planck's constant, h, is equal to $6.626 \times 10^{-34}\,\text{J} \cdot \text{s}$.

The packets of energy of electromagnetic radiation are called photons.

Blackbody radiation is used in astronomy to determine the surface temperature of stars.

7-6   De Broglie postulated that matter has wavelike properties.

The wave-particle duality of light suggested to de Broglie that matter may appear wavelike.

De Broglie proposed that a moving object has a wavelength associated with it.

The wavelength of a particle of mass m and speed v is given by $\lambda = h/mv$ (Equation 7-3).

7-7   De Broglie waves are observed experimentally.

A beam of electrons can behave similarly to a beam of X-rays (Figure 7-9).

The wavelike property of electrons is used in electron microscopes.

7-8   The energy of the electron in a hydrogen atom is quantized.

An energy is quantized when it can have only certain fixed values.

Quantum theory predicts these quantized energies.

The Schrödinger wave equation (not given) is the central equation of quantum theory.

Application of Schrödinger's wave equation to the hydrogen atom gives the allowed, discrete energy states of the electron:

$$E_n = -\frac{2.18 \times 10^{-18}\,\text{J}}{n^2} \qquad n = 1, 2, 3, \cdots \qquad (7\text{-}4)$$

A stationary state is an allowed energy state.

The ground state is the stationary state of lowest energy, $n = 1$.

An excited state is a stationary state of higher energy than the ground state, $n = 2, 3, \ldots$.

The energy states of the electron in a hydrogen atom are shown in Figure 7-12.

7-9 Atoms emit or absorb electromagnetic radiation when they undergo transitions from one stationary state to another.

When an electron goes from a higher energy state to the ground state, the frequency of the emitted radiation is given by $\Delta E = E_n - E_1 = h\nu_{n \to 1}$ or

$$\nu_{n \to 1} = (3.29 \times 10^{15} \text{ s}^{-1})\left(\frac{1}{1^2} - \frac{1}{n^2}\right) \qquad n = 2, 3, 4, \cdots \qquad (7\text{-}8)$$

These frequencies correspond to the series of lines in the hydrogen atom emission spectrum called the Lyman series (Table 7-5).

When an electron goes from a higher energy state to the $n = 2$ state, the frequency of the emitted radiation is given by $\Delta E = E_n - E_2 = h\nu_{n \to 2}$ or

$$\nu_{n \to 2} = (3.29 \times 10^{15} \text{ s}^{-1})\left(\frac{1}{2^2} - \frac{1}{n^2}\right) \qquad n = 3, 4, 5, \cdots \qquad (7\text{-}9)$$

These frequencies correspond to the Balmer series in the hydrogen atom emission spectrum (Figure 7-14).

An emission spectrum occurs when excited atoms return to the ground state.

An absorption spectrum occurs when atoms in the ground state absorb energy and are excited to higher energy states (Figure 7-16).

7-10 A wave function is used to calculate the probability that an electron will be found in some region of space.

The Schrödinger equation also provides an associated set of functions called wave functions (orbitals), ψ.

The value of the square of the wave function is a probability density, $\psi^2(x, y, z)$.

The electron cannot be located precisely, but can be assigned only a probability of being located in a certain region.

The principal quantum number n specifies the energy of the electron in the hydrogen atom.

The quantum numbers n, l, and m_l are needed to specify the wave functions.

The $1s$ orbital is the wave function that describes the ground state of the hydrogen atom (Figure 7-17).

The $1s$ orbital is spherically symmetric.

The 1s orbital can be represented by a stippled diagram, a contour diagram, or a 99% probability sphere as shown in Figure 7-18.

7-11   The azimuthal quantum number determines the shape of an orbital.

The azimuthal quantum number l is restricted to the values $l = 0$, $1, \ldots, n - 1$.

s, p, d, and f orbitals are those for which $l = 0$, 1, 2, and 3, respectively.

Orbitals are usually designated by the values of n and l (Table 7-6).

All s orbitals are spherically symmetric (Figure 7-24).

The 2p orbitals are cylindrically symmetric.

The 2p orbitals can be represented by a stippled diagram, a contour diagram, or a 99% probability surface as shown in Figure 7-25.

A surface on which the probability density is zero is a nodal surface.

7-12   The magnetic quantum number determines the spatial orientation of an orbital.

The magnetic quantum number m_l is restricted to the values $m_l = -l, -l + 1$, $\ldots, -1, 0, 1, 2, \ldots, l$.

The allowed values of the quantum numbers l and m_l for $n = 1$ to $n = 4$ are given in Table 7-7.

The three 2p orbitals are designated p_x, p_y, and p_z; the subscript indicates the axis along which the orbital is directed (Figure 7-27).

7-13   An electron possesses an intrinsic spin.

The spin quantum number m_s is restricted to the values $m_s = +\frac{1}{2}$ or $-\frac{1}{2}$.

The allowed combinations of the four quantum numbers for $n = 1$ to $n = 3$ are given in Table 7-8.

B   SELF-TEST

1   The first-ionization energy of an atom is always greater than the second-ionization energy of that atom. *True/False*

2   The atoms of which group in the periodic table have the largest first-ionization energies for a given row? _____

3   A small first-ionization energy indicates a stable electronic structure. *True/False*

4   The alkali metals have relatively (*small/large*) values of the first-ionization energy.

5   The chemically active electrons that are most responsible for the chemical activity of an atom are located _____.

6   A lithium atom consists of a _____-like inner shell and

_____.

7   A magnesium atom consists of a _____-like inner shell and

_____.

8   The Lewis dot formula of a carbon atom is _____.

9   The Lewis dot formula of a magnesium atom is _____.

10 The wavelength and frequency of electromagnetic radiation are related by the equation _____.

11 The speed of light is denoted by the symbol _____ and has the value _____ $m \cdot s^{-1}$.

12 The spectrum of white light is an example of a (*continuous/line*) spectrum.

13 A line spectrum consists of _____.

14 An atomic spectrum is a (*continuous/line*) spectrum.

15 The atomic spectrum of an element is unique to that element. *True/False*

16 The blue part of the flame in a Bunsen burner is at a higher temperature than the yellow part. *True/False*

17 A blackbody is an ideal body that _____.

18 Planck assumed that radiation from a blackbody could be emitted _____.

19 The energy associated with quanta of electromagnetic radiation is given by the equation $E =$ _____ where _____ _____.

20 Planck's constant is denoted by _____ and is equal to _____.

21 A photon is a quantum of _____.

22 The de Broglie wavelength of a moving particle is given by the expression $\lambda =$ _____ where _____.

23 The de Broglie wavelength of a particle is significant when the mass of the particle is _____.

24 The _____ property of electrons is exploited in electron microscopes.

25 When the Schrödinger equation is solved for a hydrogen atom, the energies that the electron may have are found to be restricted to discrete values. *True/False*

26 The energies of the electron in a hydrogen atom are given by $E_n =$ _____ where _____.

27 The interaction energy between an electron and a proton is zero when _____.

28 A negative energy state is (*more/less*) stable relative to a zero energy state.

29 The ground state of an atom is _____.

30 Excited states of an atom are _____.

31 When an atom undergoes a transition from a higher energy state to a lower energy state, the atom (*emits/absorbs*) electromagnetic radiation.

32 When the electron in a hydrogen atom goes from the $n = 3$ state to the $n = 1$ state, energy is (*emitted/absorbed*) and the value of the energy is given by $\Delta E =$ _____.

33 The atomic absorption spectrum of an element is due to _____ _____.

34 Wave functions are a set of functions that are solutions of _____ _____.

35 The square of a wave function is _____.

36 The principal quantum number n determines the _____ _____ of the electron in a hydrogen atom.

37 The orbital that the electron occupies in the ground state of the hydrogen atom is designated _____.

38 The wave function that describes the ground state of a hydrogen atom depends only upon the _____.

39 The value of ψ_{1s}^2 (*increases/decreases*) with the distance of the electron from the nucleus.

40 The azimuthal quantum number _____ determines _____ _____ of an orbital.

41 The azimuthal quantum number, l, may have the values _____ _____ when $n = 2$.

42 The $2s$ orbital is _____ symmetric.

43 The $2p$ orbital is _____ symmetric.

44 For a $2p$ orbital, n is _____ and l is _____.

45 When $n = 3$ and $l = 2$, the orbital is designated _____.

46 The magnetic quantum number _____ determines _____ _____ of an orbital.

47 The magnetic quantum number may have the values _____ when $n = 2$ and $l = 1$.

48 A $2p$ hydrogen atomic orbital for which $m_l = 0$ and one for which $m_l = 1$ differ in energy. *True/False*

49 The spin quantum number m_s designates _____.

C   CALCULATIONS YOU SHOULD KNOW HOW TO DO

1   Convert between the frequency and wavelength of electromagnetic radiation. The equation is

$$\lambda \nu = c \tag{7-1}$$

where λ is the wavelength (in meters), ν is the frequency (in cycles per second), and c is the speed of light, 3.00×10^8 m · s^{-1}. See Example 7-1 and Problems 7-9 and 7-10.

2   Calculate the energy associated with electromagnetic radiation. The equation to use is

$$E = h\nu \tag{7-2}$$

where ν is the frequency of the radiation (in cycles per second), h is Planck's constant (6.626×10^{-34} J · s), and E is the energy. See Example 7-2.

Often the wavelength instead of the frequency of the electromagnetic radiation will be given. In this case, you must convert wavelength to frequency using Equation (7-1). See Example 7-3.

The energy can be calculated directly in terms of the wavelength λ by solving Equation (7-1) for ν and then substituting the result into Equation (7-2). The result is

$$E = \frac{hc}{\lambda}$$

See Problems 7-11 through 7-16.

3   Calculate the number of photons in a given amount of electromagnetic radiation of a specified frequency or wavelength. To do this type of problem, first calculate the energy of one photon using Equation (7-1) and then divide this result into the energy of the electromagnetic radiation. See Problems 7-17 through 7-20.

4   Calculate the de Broglie wavelengths of moving bodies. The equation is

$$\lambda = \frac{h}{mv} \tag{7-3}$$

where λ is the de Broglie wavelength, h is Planck's constant (6.626×10^{-34} J · s), m is the mass of the body (in kilograms) and v is its speed (in meters per second). See Example 7-4 and Problems 7-25 through 7-30.

5   Calculate the frequencies and wavelengths in the hydrogen atomic spectrum. The starting point for calculations like these is Equation (7-4), which gives the energy states of the electron in a hydrogen atom

$$E_n = -\frac{2.18 \times 10^{-18} \text{ J}}{n^2} \qquad n = 1, 2, 3, \cdots \tag{7-4}$$

Using this equation, the energy and the frequency associated with a transition from state n to state m are obtained using conservation of energy. For a transition from state n to state m, we write

$$\nu_{n \to m} = \frac{E_m - E_n}{h} \qquad m > n \qquad \text{(absorption)}$$

$$\nu_{m \to n} = \frac{E_m - E_n}{h} \qquad m > n \qquad \text{(emission)}$$

See Examples 7-5 and 7-6 and Problems 7-33 through 7-38.

D   SOLUTIONS TO THE ODD-NUMBERED PROBLEMS

7-1 Of the four species listed, Li^+ has the largest ionization energy because it is positively charged. The ionization energies of the remaining three species decrease in the order He, Ne, and Ar because ionization energies decrease with increasing atomic size within a family. The farther away an electron is from the nucleus, the easier it is to remove the electron from the atom. Thus we write Ar, Ne, He, and Li^+.

7-3 Using Table 7-1, we have for a lithium atom

n	$I_n/\text{MJ} \cdot \text{mol}^{-1}$	$\log[I_n/\text{MJ} \cdot \text{mol}^{-1}]$
1	0.52	−0.28
2	7.30	0.86
3	11.81	1.07

If we plot $\log[I_n/\text{MJ} \cdot \text{mol}^{-1}]$ versus n, then we obtain

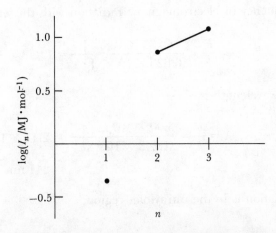

The first electron is relatively easy to remove, suggesting that the electrons in a lithium atom are arranged in two shells. The inner shell is relatively stable.

7-5   The alkali metals are in Group 1 and have one outer electron. The Lewis electron-dot formulas of the alkali metals are

$$\text{Li} \cdot \quad \text{Na} \cdot \quad \text{K} \cdot \quad \text{Rb} \cdot \quad \text{Cs} \cdot \quad \text{Fr} \cdot$$

The halogens are in Group 7 and have seven outer electrons. The electron-dot formulas of the halogen atoms are

$$:\overset{\cdot\cdot}{\underset{\cdot\cdot}{F}}\cdot \quad :\overset{\cdot\cdot}{\underset{\cdot\cdot}{Cl}}\cdot \quad :\overset{\cdot\cdot}{\underset{\cdot\cdot}{Br}}\cdot \quad :\overset{\cdot\cdot}{\underset{\cdot\cdot}{I}}\cdot \quad :\overset{\cdot\cdot}{\underset{\cdot\cdot}{At}}\cdot$$

7-7   Boron (Group 3) has three outer electrons; B^+ has two outer electrons, and so for B^+ we write $\cdot B \cdot {}^+$.

Nitrogen (Group 5) has five outer electrons; N^{3-} has eight outer electrons, and so we write $:\overset{\cdot\cdot}{N}:{}^{3-}$.

Fluorine (Group 7) has seven outer electrons; F^- has eight outer electrons, and so we write $:\overset{\cdot\cdot}{\underset{\cdot\cdot}{F}}:{}^-$.

Both O^{2-} and Na^+ have eight outer electrons, and so we have $:\overset{\cdot\cdot}{\underset{\cdot\cdot}{O}}:{}^{2-}$ and $:\overset{\cdot\cdot}{\underset{\cdot\cdot}{Na}}:{}^+$ or Na^+.

7-9   Solve Equation (7-1) for ν.

$$\nu = \frac{c}{\lambda} = \frac{3.00 \times 10^8 \text{ m} \cdot \text{s}^{-1}}{633 \times 10^{-9} \text{ m}} = 4.74 \times 10^{14} \text{ s}^{-1}$$

7-11   We use Equation (7-2), but we must first convert 495.8 kJ $\cdot$ mol^{-1} to J $\cdot$ atom^{-1} by dividing by Avogadro's number

$$E = \frac{495.8 \times 10^3 \text{ J} \cdot \text{mol}^{-1}}{6.022 \times 10^{23} \text{ atom} \cdot \text{mol}^{-1}} = 8.233 \times 10^{-19} \text{ J} \cdot \text{atom}^{-1}$$

The frequency of electromagnetic radiation with this energy is given by

$$\nu = \frac{E}{h} = \frac{8.233 \times 10^{-19} \text{ J}}{6.626 \times 10^{-34} \text{ J} \cdot \text{s}} = 1.243 \times 10^{15} \text{ s}^{-1}$$

and the wavelength is

$$\lambda = \frac{c}{\nu} = \frac{3.00 \times 10^8 \text{ m} \cdot \text{s}^{-1}}{1.243 \times 10^{15} \text{ s}^{-1}} = 2.41 \times 10^{-7} \text{ m}$$

$$= 241 \text{ nm}$$

This radiation is in the ultraviolet region.

7-13 Substitute Equation (7-1) for ν into Equation (7-2) to obtain

$$E = \frac{hc}{\lambda} = \frac{(6.626 \times 10^{-34}\,\text{J}\cdot\text{s})(3.00 \times 10^{8}\,\text{m}\cdot\text{s}^{-1})}{100 \times 10^{-9}\,\text{m}} = 1.99 \times 10^{-18}\,\text{J}$$

The energy per mole of bonds is

$$E = (1.99 \times 10^{-18}\,\text{J}\cdot\text{bond}^{-1})(6.022 \times 10^{23}\,\text{bonds}\cdot\text{mol}^{-1})$$
$$= 1.20 \times 10^{6}\,\text{J}\cdot\text{mol}^{-1} = 1200\,\text{kJ}\cdot\text{mol}^{-1}$$

7-15 Substitute Equation (7-1) for ν into Equation (7-2) to write

$$E = \frac{hc}{\lambda} = \frac{(6.626 \times 10^{-34}\,\text{J}\cdot\text{s})(3.00 \times 10^{8}\,\text{m}\cdot\text{s}^{-1})}{210 \times 10^{-12}\,\text{m}} = 9.47 \times 10^{-16}\,\text{J}$$

This is the energy of one photon. To obtain the energy of a mole of photons, we multiply by Avogadro's number

$$E = (9.47 \times 10^{-16}\,\text{J}\cdot\text{photon}^{-1})(6.022 \times 10^{23}\,\text{photon}\cdot\text{mol}^{-1})$$
$$= 5.70 \times 10^{8}\,\text{J}\cdot\text{mol}^{-1}$$

7-17 The energy per photon is given by Equations (7-1) and (7-2):

$$E = \frac{hc}{\lambda} = \frac{(6.626 \times 10^{-34}\,\text{J}\cdot\text{s})(3.00 \times 10^{8}\,\text{m}\cdot\text{s}^{-1})}{510 \times 10^{-9}\,\text{m}} = 3.90 \times 10^{-19}\,\text{J}$$

The number of photons striking 1 m^2 per second is

$$\frac{1.0 \times 10^{3}\,\text{J}\cdot\text{s}^{-1}\cdot\text{m}^{-2}}{3.90 \times 10^{-19}\,\text{J}\cdot\text{photon}^{-1}} = 2.6 \times 10^{21}\,\text{photons}\cdot\text{s}^{-1}\cdot\text{m}^{-2}$$

The number of photons striking 1 cm^2 per second is

$$(2.6 \times 10^{21}\,\text{photon}\cdot\text{s}^{-1}\cdot\text{m}^{-2})\left(\frac{1\,\text{m}}{100\,\text{cm}}\right)^2 = 2.6 \times 10^{17}\,\text{photons}\cdot\text{s}^{-1}\cdot\text{cm}^{-2}$$

7-19 The energy of one photon is given by

$$E = \frac{hc}{\lambda} = \frac{(6.626 \times 10^{-34}\,\text{J}\cdot\text{s})(3.00 \times 10^{8}\,\text{m}\cdot\text{s}^{-1})}{337.1 \times 10^{-9}\,\text{m}} = 5.90 \times 10^{-19}\,\text{J}$$

The number of photons in a pulse of 10 mJ is

$$\frac{10 \times 10^{-3}\,\text{J}}{5.90 \times 10^{-19}\,\text{J}\cdot\text{photon}^{-1}} = 1.7 \times 10^{16}\,\text{photons}$$

7-21 According to Figure 7-8, the maximum intensity occurs at a wavelength of around 500 nm. The surface temperature of the sun then is

$$T = \frac{2.89 \times 10^{-3} \text{ m} \cdot \text{K}}{500 \times 10^{-9} \text{ m}} = 6000 \text{ K}$$

7-23 Using the equation that is given in Problem 7-21, we have

$$\lambda_{max} = \frac{2.89 \times 10^{-3} \text{ m} \cdot \text{K}}{1.1 \times 10^4 \text{ K}} = 2.6 \times 10^{-7} \text{ m}$$

$$= 260 \text{ nm}$$

This wavelength lies just outside the visible region in the ultraviolet region; but this is the wavelength at the maximum of the blackbody radiation curve (for example, see Figure 7-7). Much of the radiation will be in the violet to blue region, and so Sirius will appear to be violet-blue.

7-25 We use Equation (7-3)

$$\lambda = \frac{h}{mv}$$

The mass and the speed of the proton are given, and so

$$\lambda = \frac{6.626 \times 10^{-34} \text{ J} \cdot \text{s}}{(1.67 \times 10^{-27} \text{ kg})(1.00 \times 10^5 \text{ m} \cdot \text{s}^{-1})}$$

$$= 3.97 \times 10^{-12} \text{ m} = 3.97 \text{ pm}$$

Don't forget that a joule is equal to a $\text{kg} \cdot \text{m}^2 \cdot \text{s}^{-2}$.

7-27 The mass of a nitrogen molecule is

$$m = \frac{28.02 \text{ g} \cdot \text{mol}^{-1}}{6.022 \times 10^{23} \text{ molecule} \cdot \text{mol}^{-1}} = 4.653 \times 10^{-23} \text{ g}$$

$$= 4.653 \times 10^{-26} \text{ kg}$$

Therefore,

$$\lambda = \frac{h}{mv} = \frac{6.626 \times 10^{-34} \text{ J} \cdot \text{s}}{(4.653 \times 10^{-26} \text{ kg})(500 \text{ m} \cdot \text{s}^{-1})} = 2.85 \times 10^{-11} \text{ m}$$

$$= 28.5 \text{ pm}$$

We have used the fact that a joule is equal to a $\text{kg} \cdot \text{m}^2 \cdot \text{s}^{-2}$.

7-29 Again we use Equation (7-3). In this problem we solve for the speed v. The mass of an electron is given on the inside back cover. Thus,

$$v = \frac{h}{\lambda m} = \frac{6.626 \times 10^{-34}\,\text{J} \cdot \text{s}}{(1.0 \times 10^{-11}\,\text{m})(9.11 \times 10^{-31}\,\text{kg})} = 7.3 \times 10^7\,\text{m} \cdot \text{s}^{-1}$$

We have used that fact that a joule is equal to a $\text{kg} \cdot \text{m}^2 \cdot \text{s}^{-2}$.

7-31 Money: units of one cent and no fractions thereof
People: units of one person in population studies
Any other quantity that you count.

7-33 The energy required for the electron in a hydrogen atom to make a transition from the $n = 2$ state to the $n = 3$ state is given by (see Figure 7-12)

$$\Delta E = E_3 - E_2 = -\frac{2.18 \times 10^{-18}\,\text{J}}{3^2} - \left[-\frac{2.18 \times 10^{-18}\,\text{J}}{2^2} \right]$$

$$= 3.03 \times 10^{-19}\,\text{J}$$

The wavelength of a photon with this energy is obtained from Equations (7-1) and (7-2)

$$\lambda = \frac{hc}{\Delta E} = \frac{(6.626 \times 10^{-34}\,\text{J} \cdot \text{s})(3.00 \times 10^8\,\text{m} \cdot \text{s}^{-1})}{3.03 \times 10^{-19}\,\text{J}} = 6.56 \times 10^{-7}\,\text{m}$$

$$= 656\,\text{nm}$$

7-35 The energy required to ionize a hydrogen atom that is in its ground electronic state is given by (Example 7-6)

$$IE = E_\infty - E_1 = 0 - \left(-\frac{2.18 \times 10^{-18}\,\text{J}}{1^2} \right)$$

$$= 2.18 \times 10^{-19}\,\text{J}$$

The wavelength of a photon that corresponds to this energy is given by

$$\lambda = \frac{hc}{IE} = \frac{(6.626 \times 10^{-34}\,\text{J} \cdot \text{s})(3.00 \times 10^8\,\text{m} \cdot \text{s}^{-1})}{2.18 \times 10^{-18}\,\text{J}} = 9.12 \times 10^{-8}\,\text{m}$$

$$= 91.2\,\text{nm}$$

7-37 To calculate the ionization energies, we let $Z = 2$ for He^+, $Z = 3$ for Li^{2+}, and $Z = 4$ for Be^{3+}. The results are

$$IE(He^+) = E_\infty - E_1 = \frac{(2.18 \times 10^{-18}\,\text{J})2^2}{1^2} = 8.72 \times 10^{-18}\,\text{J}$$

$$IE(Li^{2+}) = \frac{(2.18 \times 10^{-18}\,\text{J})3^2}{1^2} = 1.96 \times 10^{-17}\,\text{J}$$

$$IE(Be^{3+}) = \frac{(2.18 \times 10^{-18}\,\text{J})4^2}{1^2} = 3.49 \times 10^{-17}\,\text{J}$$

The values given in Table 7-1 are per mole, and so we must multiply each of these results by Avogadro's number in order to compare with Table 7-1. The results are

$$IE(He^+) = 5.25 \text{ MJ} \cdot \text{mol}^{-1} = I_2$$
$$IE(Li^{2+}) = 11.8 \text{ MJ} \cdot \text{mol}^{-1} = I_3$$
$$IE(Be^{3+}) = 21.0 \text{ MJ} \cdot \text{mol}^{-1} = I_4$$

in excellent agreement with the values in Table 7-1.

7-39   The density of dots in any region is a measure of the probability of finding an electron in that region.

7-41   When $n = 4$, l may be 0, 1, 2, 3. For each value of l, m_l may be $l, l - 1, \ldots 0, \ldots -l$. Thus we have

l	m_l
0	0
1	1, 0, −1
2	2, 1, 0, −1, −2
3	3, 2, 1, 0, −1, −2, −3

There are one $4s$ orbital, three $4p$ orbitals, five $4d$ orbitals, and seven $4f$ orbitals for a total of 16 orbitals.

7-43   (a) $n = 7$, $l = 0$ (possible)
(b) $n = 1$, $l = 1$ (not possible, $l = n$)
(c) $n = 5$, $l = 2$ (possible)
(d) $n = 2$, $l = 2$ (not possible, $l = n$)
(e) $n = 4$, $l = 3$ (possible)

7-45   For a $4f$ orbital, $n = 4$ and $l = 3$.

n	l	m_l	m_s
4	3	−3	$+\frac{1}{2}, -\frac{1}{2}$
		−2	$+\frac{1}{2}, -\frac{1}{2}$
		−1	$+\frac{1}{2}, -\frac{1}{2}$
		0	$+\frac{1}{2}, -\frac{1}{2}$
		1	$+\frac{1}{2}, -\frac{1}{2}$
		2	$+\frac{1}{2}, -\frac{1}{2}$
		3	$+\frac{1}{2}, -\frac{1}{2}$

Thus there is a total of 14 possible sets of the four quantum numbers for an electron in a $4f$ orbital.

7-47   (a) $2p$ (b) $4s$ (c) $5f$ (d) $3d$

7-49   If $l = 2$, then n must be at least 3 because $l = 0, 1, 2, \ldots, n - 1$.
If $m_l = 3$, then l must be at least 3 because $m_l = -l, -l + 1, \ldots, -1, 0, +1, \ldots, l$.

7-51   (a) Allowed
(b) Not allowed; m_l cannot equal $+1$ if $l = 0$.
(c) Allowed
(d) Not allowed; l cannot equal 1 if $n = 1$.
(e) Not allowed; m_s cannot equal 0.

7-53   We must use Hess's law to do this problem. From Table 7-1, we find that

(a)
$$\text{Li}(g) \longrightarrow \text{Li}^+(g) + e^-(g) \qquad \Delta H^\circ_{rxn} = I_1 = 0.52 \text{ MJ}$$
$$\text{Na}^+(g) + e^-(g) \longrightarrow \text{Na}(g) \qquad \Delta H^\circ_{rxn} = -I_1 = -0.50 \text{ MJ}$$
$$\overline{\text{Li}(g) + \text{Na}^+(g) \longrightarrow \text{Li}^+(g) + \text{Na}(g) \qquad \Delta H^\circ_{rxn} = 0.02 \text{ MJ}}$$
$$= 20 \text{ kJ}$$

(b)
$$\text{Mg}^{2+}(g) + e^-(g) \longrightarrow \text{Mg}^+(g) \qquad \Delta H^\circ_{rxn} = -I_2 = -1.45 \text{ MJ}$$
$$\text{Mg}(g) \longrightarrow \text{Mg}^+(g) + e^-(g) \qquad \Delta H^\circ_{rxn} = I_1 = 0.74 \text{ MJ}$$
$$\overline{\text{Mg}^{2+}(g) + \text{Mg}(g) \longrightarrow 2\text{Mg}^+(g) \qquad \Delta H^\circ_{rxn} = -0.71 \text{ MJ}}$$
$$= -710 \text{ kJ}$$

(c)
$$\text{Al}^{3+}(g) + e^-(g) \longrightarrow \text{Al}^{2+}(g) \qquad \Delta H^\circ_{rxn} = -I_3 = -2.74 \text{ MJ}$$
$$\text{Al}^{2+}(g) + e^-(g) \longrightarrow \text{Al}^+(g) \qquad \Delta H^\circ_{rxn} = -I_2 = -1.82 \text{ MJ}$$
$$\text{Al}^+(g) + e^-(g) \longrightarrow \text{Al}(g) \qquad \Delta H^\circ_{rxn} = -I_1 = -0.58 \text{ MJ}$$
$$\overline{\text{Al}^{3+}(g) + 3e^-(g) \longrightarrow \text{Al}(g) \qquad \Delta H^\circ_{rxn} = -5.14 \text{ MJ}}$$

E   ANSWERS TO THE EVEN-NUMBERED PROBLEMS

7-2   F, Ne, Li^+, Be^{2+}

7-4

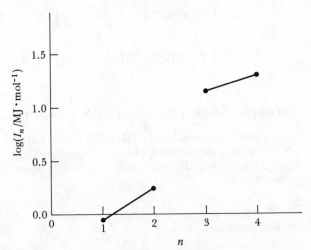

7-6 $\cdot$ He $\cdot$ $:$ Ne $:$ $:$ Ar $:$ $:$ Kr $:$ $:$ Xe $:$ $:$ Rn $:$

The noble gases are in Group 8 and have eight outer electrons, except for He.

7-8 $:$ Ar $:$ $\cdot$ S $\cdot$ $:$ S $:^{2-}$ $:$ Al $:^{3+}$ or Al^{3+} $:$ Cl $:^{-}$

7-10 $5.09 \times 10^{14}\,s^{-1}$

7-12   Yes. E(photon) $= 2.48 \times 10^{-15}\,J$; $IE = 3.45 \times 10^{-18}\,J \cdot atom^{-1}$

7-14   400 bonds

7-16   (a) $1.5 \times 10^{14}\,s^{-1}$; (b) $2.0 \times 10^{-6}\,m$

7-18   6 photons

7-20 $1.88 \times 10^{-20}\,J \cdot pulse^{-1}$; 5×10^{19} photons per pulse

7-22   (a) 3600 K   (b) 4300 K   (c) 4800 K   (d) 5700 K

7-24   4300 K

7-26 $1.2 \times 10^{-34}\,m$

7-28   79.7 pm

7-30 $7.27 \times 10^{6}\,m \cdot s^{-1}$

7-32   Because the lines are due to transitions from one level to another, and the frequency is directly proportional to the difference in energies of the two levels

7-34 $n = 3$

7-36 $5.45 \times 10^{-19}\,J$

7-38   Can derive formulas such as

$$\nu_{n \rightarrow 1} = (1.32 \times 10^{16}\,s^{-1})\left(\frac{1}{1^2} - \frac{1}{n^2}\right) \qquad n = 2, 3, \cdots$$

$$\nu_{n \rightarrow 2} = (1.32 \times 10^{16}\,s^{-1})\left(\frac{1}{2^2} - \frac{1}{n^2}\right) \qquad n = 3, 4, \cdots$$

which gives analogs of the Lyman and Balmer series for atomic hydrogen.

7-40   When the contours are closely spaced, the property that is plotted such as the probability of finding an electron within a region or the elevation of the land is changing rapidly. When the contours are widely separated, the property is changing slowly.

7-42   7 orbitals

7-44   Only (a) is not possible

7-46 $4d$ orbital

n	l	m_l	m_s
4	2	-2	$+\frac{1}{2}$
			$-\frac{1}{2}$
		-1	$+\frac{1}{2}$
			$-\frac{1}{2}$
		0	$+\frac{1}{2}$
			$-\frac{1}{2}$
		1	$+\frac{1}{2}$
			$-\frac{1}{2}$
		2	$+\frac{1}{2}$
			$-\frac{1}{2}$

7-48 (a) $3d$ (b) $3d$ (c) $2p$ (d) $4f$

7-50 $4p$, $3s$, $2p$

7-52 Both (b) and (c) are allowed.

7-54 (a) 6.88 MJ   (b) -1.15 MJ   (c) -4.70 MJ

F   ANSWERS TO THE SELF-TEST

1 false

2 the noble gases

3 false

4 small

5 in the outer shell

6 helium; a lone outer electron

7 neon; two outer electrons

8 $\cdot \overset{\cdot}{C} \cdot$

9 $\cdot Mg \cdot$

10 $\lambda\nu = c$

11 c; 3.00×10^8 m $\cdot$ s^{-1}

12 continuous

13 a set of lines with definite wavelengths

14 line

15 true

16 true

17 absorbs and emits electromagnetic radiation of all frequencies

18 only in quantized packets

19 $E = h\nu$; h is Planck's constant $(6.626 \times 10^{-34}$ J $\cdot$ s$)$ and ν is the frequency

20 h; 6.626×10^{-34} J $\cdot$ s

21 electromagnetic radiation

22 $\lambda = h/mv$ where h is Planck's constant, m is the mass of the particle, and v is its speed.

23 small

24 wavelike

25 true

26 $E_n = -(2.18 \times 10^{-18}$ J$)/n^2$ where $n = 1, 2, 3, \ldots$

27 They are infinitely far apart.

28 more

29 the state of lowest energy

30 states with energies greater than the ground state

31 emits

32 emitted; $\Delta E = E_3 - E_1$

33 electrons making transitions from states of lower energies to states of higher energies

34 the Schrödinger equation

35 a probability density

36 energy

37 $1s$

38 distance of the electron from the nucleus

39 decreases

40 l; the shape

41 0 and 1

42 spherically

43 cylindrically

44 $n = 2$ and $l = 1$

45 $3d$

46 m_l; spatial orientation

47 $+1, 0, -1$

48 false (Energy levels depend upon only n.)

49 m_s; the spin of an electron

8 / Electronic Structure and Periodic Properties of Atoms

A   OUTLINE OF CHAPTER 8

8-1   The energy states of atoms with two or more electrons depend upon both n and l.

Multielectron atoms involve electron-electron interactions.

The relative energies of the orbitals of atoms with two or more electrons are given in Figures 8-2 and 8-3.

8-2   No two electrons in the same atom can have the same set of four quantum numbers.

The Pauli exclusion principle is used to assign electrons to orbitals.

The sets of allowed quantum numbers are given in Table 8-1.

Shells are the levels designated by n.

Subshells are the groups of orbitals designated by l within the shells.

8-3   Electronic configurations are obtained by placing electrons into the available orbitals of lowest energy.

The ground-state electron configurations of atoms and atomic ions are the assignments of electrons to orbitals.

The assignment of electrons to oribitals of lowest energies gives the ground-state electron configuration of an atom or an ion.

The value of the first ionization energy of an atom depends on the electron configuration of the atom.

8-4   Hund's rule is used to predict ground-state electron configurations.

Hund's rule states that for any set of orbitals of the same energy, the ground-state electron configuration is obtained by placing the electrons into different orbitals of this set with parallel spins until each of the orbitals has one electron.

Hund's rule is used to predict the ground-state electron configuration of an atom with a partially filled subshell.

8-5   The second and third rows of the periodic table have similar outer electron configurations.

An excited electronic state is a state in which the elctron configuration corresponds to a higher energy than the ground state.

The electron configuration of atoms is correlated to their positions in the periodic table (Figure 8-5).

8-6   The principal quantum number of the outer *s* electrons is equal to the number of the row in the periodic table.

The alkali metals have the electron configuration [noble gas]ns^1.

The alkaline earth metals have the electron configuration [noble gas]ns^2.

8-7   In the first set of transition metals the five *3d* orbitals are filled sequentially.

The *3d* transition metal series consists of the elements Sc through Zn (Figure 8-6).

The *4d* transition metal series consists of the elements Y through Cd (Figure 8-6).

Half filled and completely filled *d* subshells are relatively stable.

8-8   The lanthanides have similar chemical properties.

Chemical activity is determined by the outer electrons.

The inner transition metals involve the filling of *f* orbitals.

The lanthanides La through Yb involve the filling of the *4f* orbitals (Figure 8-6).

The *5d* transition metals follow the lanthanides and involve the filling of the *5d* orbitals (Figure 8-6).

The actinide series, Ac through No, involve the filling of the *5f* orbitals (Figure 8-6).

The transuranium elements are all radioactive.

8-9   Atomic radius is a periodic property.

Atomic radii determined by X-ray analysis of crystal structures are called crystallographic radii (Figures 8-9 and 8-11).

Atomic radii usually decrease from left to right across the periodic table.

Atomic radii increase going down a column of the periodic table (Figure 8-10).

First ionization energies decrease going down a column of the periodic table.

B   SELF-TEST

1   The electronic energy of the hydrogen atom depends upon the quantum numbers n and l. *True/False*

2   The electronic energy of multielectron atoms depends upon the three quantum numbers, n, l, and m_l. *True/False*

3   The $3p$ orbitals and the $3d$ orbitals of the iron atom have the same energy. *True/False*

4   The Pauli exclusion principle states that _____
    _____.

5   The term spin up refers to electrons with _____.

6   The set of $2p$ orbitals may hold a maximum of _____ electrons.

7   The $1s$ orbital may hold two electrons with parallel spins. *True/False*

8   The L shell can contain a maximum of _____ electrons.

9   The L shell is the level for which n equals _____.

10 The L shell contains _____ subshells.

11 The element _____ has a full outer L shell.

12 The symbol $2p^5$ signifies that _____.

13 The symbol _____ signifies that there are 6 electrons in the $3d$ orbitals.

14 In neutral atoms the $4s$ orbital is of higher energy than the $3d$ orbital. *True/False*

15 The $5d$ orbital is of higher energy than the $4f$ orbital in neutral atoms. *True/False*

16 The ground-state electron configuration of the nitrogen atom ($Z = 7$) is
    _____.

17 The ground-state electron configuration of the vanadium atom ($Z = 23$) is
    _____.

18 Hund's rule states that _____
    _____.

19 The pictorial representation of the electron configuration of the ground state of nitrogen is _____.

20 The outer electron configuration of the ground state of the Group 2 metals is
    _____.

21 The outer electron configuration of the ground state of the halogens is
    _____.

22 The first member of each row of the periodic table is an
    _____ metal.

23 The last member of each row of the periodic table is a _____.

24 Alkali metals lose one electron to attain a _____ electron configuration.

25 The halogens gain one electron to attain a _____ electron configuration.

26 The ground-state electron configuration of Mg^{2+} $(Z = 12)$ is _____.

27 The ground-state electron configuration of O^{2-} $(Z = 8)$ is _____.

28 The transition metals occur because of the sequential filling of the _____ orbitals.

29 A half-filled subshell has an extra stability compared to other partially filled subshells. *True/False*

30 The outer electron configuration of chromium is $4s^2 3d^4$. *True/False*

31 The outer electron configurations of the $3d$ transition metals are _____.

32 The lanthanides occur because of the sequential filling of the _____ orbitals.

33 The rare earths are difficult to separate because _____ _____.

34 The actinide series occurs because of the sequential filling of the _____ orbitals.

35 The actinides are all radioactive. *True/False*

36 Atomic radii can be determined from _____ _____.

37 Atomic radii (*increase/decrease*) in going from left to right across a row in the periodic table.

38 Atomic radii (*increase/decrease*) in going down a column in the periodic table.

39 The Group _____ elements have the largest atomic radius in a row of the periodic table.

40 The first ionization energy decreases as the radius increases because _____.

41 Sodium has a (*larger/smaller*) first ionization energy than potassium.

C   CALCULATIONS YOU SHOULD KNOW HOW TO DO

1   Know the mnemonic for the order of the orbital energies in neutral gas atoms

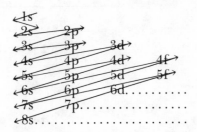

Determine the allowed sets of quantum numbers (n, l, m_l, m_s). See Problems 8-1 through 8-8. Use the Pauli exclusion principle. See Problems 8-9 through 8-12.

2   Assign electrons to orbitals in atoms and write out ground-state electron configurations. See Examples 8-1, 8-2, 8-3, and 8-4, and Problems 8-13 through 8-20.

3   Correlate electron configurations and the periodic table. See Example 8-7 and Problems 8-21 through 8-28.

4   Use Hund's rule to write ground-state electron configurations. See Example 8-5 and Problems 8-29 through 8-32.

5   Write Lewis electron-dot formulas. See Problems 8-33 through 8-36.

6   Write the ground-state electron configurations of ions. See Example 8-5 and Problems 8-37 through 8-44.

7   Write excited-state electron configurations. See Example 8-6 and Problems 8-45 through 8-48.

8   Use the periodic table to predict relative values of atomic and ionic radii. See Problems 8-49 through 8-52.

9   Use the periodic table to predict relative values of first ionization energies. See Problems 8-53 through 8-56.

D   SOLUTIONS TO THE ODD-NUMBERED PROBLEMS

8-1   To work problems of this type you have to know the order of the orbital energies as shown in Figures 8-2 and 8-3.

(a) $4p$ (d) $5p$
(b) $4p$ (e) $4f$
(c) $6s$

8-3   For a $3d$ orbital $n = 3$ and $l = 2$; thus m_l can be -2, -1, 0, 1 or 2. For each value of m_l, m_s can be $+\frac{1}{2}$ or $-\frac{1}{2}$. Therefore, the 10 possible sets of four quantum numbers are

n	l	m_l	m_s
3	2	-2	$+\frac{1}{2}$
			$-\frac{1}{2}$
		-1	$+\frac{1}{2}$
			$-\frac{1}{2}$
		0	$+\frac{1}{2}$
			$-\frac{1}{2}$
		$+1$	$+\frac{1}{2}$
			$-\frac{1}{2}$
		$+2$	$+\frac{1}{2}$
			$-\frac{1}{2}$

8-5 Note that for each value of m_l, m_s can have the values $+\frac{1}{2}$ or $-\frac{1}{2}$. Thus the maximum number of electrons in a subshell is equal to two times the number of possible values of m_l

Maximum number of electrons

s orbital	$l = 0$	$m_l = 0$	$m_s = +\frac{1}{2}, -\frac{1}{2}$	$2 \times 1 = 2$ electrons
p orbital	$l = 1$	$m_l = 1, 0, 1$	$m_s = +\frac{1}{2}, -\frac{1}{2}$	$2 \times 3 = 6$ electrons
d orbital	$l = 2$	$m_l = -2, -1, 0, 1, 2$	$m_s = +\frac{1}{2}, -\frac{1}{2}$	$2 \times 5 = 10$ electrons
f orbital	$l = 3$	$m_l = -3, -2, -1, 0,$ $1, 2, 3$	$m_s = +\frac{1}{2}, -\frac{1}{2}$	$2 \times 7 = 14$ electrons

8-7 In a d-transition series the five d orbitals are being filled. A set of five d orbitals can hold up to 10 electrons.

8-9 (a) Allowed
(b) Ruled out; a $3s$ orbital cannot hold 3 electrons.
(c) Ruled out; the $3d$ orbitals hold only 10 electrons.
(d) Ruled out; the $3p$ orbitals cannot hold 8 electrons.

8-11 Recall that the electrons in a ground-state electron configuration fill the available orbitals with the lowest energy consistent with the Pauli exclusion principle.

(a) ground state   (c) ground state
(b) excited state   (d) ground state

Note that all three $2p$ orbitals are equivalent.

8-13 (a) $1s^2 2s^2 2p^6 3s^2 3p^2$ 14 electrons, silicon
(b) $1s^2 2s^2 2p^6 3s^2 3p^6 4s^1 3d^5$ 24 electrons, chromium
(c) $1s^2 2s^2 2p^6 3s^2 3p^6 4s^2 3d^{10} 4p^2$ 32 electrons, germanium
(d) $1s^2 2s^2 2p^6 3s^2 3p^6 4s^2 3d^{10} 4p^5$ 35 electrons, bromine
(e) $1s^2 2s^2 2p^1$ 5 electrons, boron

8-15 (a) 22 electrons $1s^2 2s^2 2p^6 3s^2 3p^6 4s^2 3d^2$
(b) 42 electrons $1s^2 2s^2 2p^6 3s^2 3p^6 4s^2 3d^{10} 4p^6 5s^1 4d^5$

(c) 29 electrons $1s^22s^22p^63s^23p^64s^13d^{10}$
(d) 30 electrons $1s^22s^22p^63s^23p^64s^23d^{10}$
(e) 47 electrons $1s^22s^22p^63s^23p^64s^23d^{10}4p^65s^14d^{10}$

8-17 (a) 15 electrons $1s^22s^22p^63s^23p^3$
(b) 28 electrons $1s^22s^22p^63s^23p^64s^23d^8$
(c) 53 electrons $1s^22s^22p^63s^23p^64s^23d^{10}4p^65s^24d^{10}5p^5$
(d) 48 electrons $1s^22s^22p^63s^23p^64s^23d^{10}4p^65s^24d^{10}$
(e) 60 electrons $1s^22s^22p^63s^23p^64s^23d^{10}4p^65s^24d^{10}5p^66s^24f^4$

8-19 (a) We see that the $3d$ orbitals are partially occupied, so that the element must be a $3d$ transition metal. There are 8 electrons in the $3d$ orbitals; thus the element is the eighth member of the series. The element is nickel.
(b) The outer electron configuration is $5s^14d^{10}$, which corresponds to that of the ninth member of the $4d$ transition metal series. The element is silver.
(c) The outer electron configuration is $3s^23p^4$, which corresponds to that of the member of group 6 located in the third row of the periodic table. The element is sulfur.
(d) The outer electron configuration is $6s^25d^{10}6p^2$, which corresponds to that of the second element after the $5d$ transition metal series. The element is lead.

8-21 (a) $[Ne]3s^2$ (d) $[Xe]6s^1$
(b) $[Ar]4s^23d^{10}4p^5$ (e) $[Ar]4s^23d^{10}4p^1$
(c) $[Xe]6s^14f^{14}5d^{10}$

8-23 Once we determine the outer electron configuration of the element with $Z = 16$, then we proceed to find the next element with the same outer electron configuration.

(a) The electron configuration corresponding to $Z = 16$ electrons is $1s^22s^22p^63s^23p^4$. The outer electron configuration is $3p^4$. The next element with an np^4 configuration is $[Ar]4s^23d^{10}4p^4$ and $Z = 34$. The next element with np^4 is $[Kr]5s^24d^{10}5p^4$ and $Z = 52$. The next element with np^4 is $[Xe]6s^24f^{14}5d^{10}6p^4$ and $Z = 84$. The first element with np^4 is $[He]2s^22p^4$ and $Z = 8$.
(b) Eleven electrons corresponds to the electron configuration $1s^22s^22p^63s^1$. The succeeding elements with ns^1 outer electron configurations are

$[Ar]4s^1$, $Z = 19$
$[Kr]5s^1$, $Z = 37$
$[Xe]6s^1$, $Z = 55$
$[Rn]7s^1$, $Z = 87$
The first elements are
$[He]2s^1$, $Z = 3$
$1s^1$, $Z = 1$

8-25 (a) Groups 1 and 2   (c) The transition metals
(b) Groups 3, 4, 5,   (d) The lanthanides and the
    6, 7, 8   actinides

8-27 Recall that we show only the outer-shell electrons in the Lewis electron-dot formula. For example, silicon is a Group 4 element, and thus has 4 outer-shell electrons.

(a) $\cdot\overset{\displaystyle\cdot}{\text{Si}}\cdot$ (d) $:\overset{\displaystyle\cdot\cdot}{\text{I}}\cdot$

(b) $\cdot\overset{\displaystyle\cdot\cdot}{\underset{\displaystyle\cdot}{\text{P}}}\cdot$ (e) $\cdot\text{Sr}\cdot$

(c) $\cdot\overset{\displaystyle\cdot\cdot}{\text{Se}}\cdot$

8-29 Recall that Hund's rule says that the ground state has the maximum possible number of parallel unpaired electrons in an incompletely filled subshell.

		$1s$	$2s$		$2p$	
(a)	7 electrons	⇅	⇅	↑	↑	↑
(b)	7 electrons	⇅	⇅	↑	↑	↑
(c)	8 electrons	⇅	⇅	⇅	↑	↑
(d)	6 electrons	⇅	⇅	↑	↑	○
(e)	8 electrons	⇅	⇅	⇅	↑	↑

8-31 We first write the ground-state electron configuration; then using Hund's rule we determine the number of unpaired electrons in the partially filled subshell.

	Ground-state configuration	Number of unpaired electrons
(a)	$[\text{Ne}]3s^23p^2$	2
(b)	$[\text{Ne}]3s^23p^3$	3
(c)	$[\text{Ar}]4s^23d^2$	2
(d)	$[\text{Ar}]4s^23d^{10}3p^4$	2
(e)	$[\text{Kr}]5s^24d^2$	2

8-33 Recall that the Lewis electron-dot formula shows only the outer-shell electrons. For neutral main group elements the number of outer-shell electrons is equal to the group number.

$$\cdot\overset{\cdot\cdot}{\underset{\cdot}{\text{O}}}\cdot \qquad \cdot\overset{\cdot\cdot}{\underset{\cdot}{\text{S}}}\cdot \qquad \cdot\overset{\cdot\cdot}{\text{Se}}\cdot \qquad \cdot\overset{\cdot\cdot}{\text{Te}}\cdot \qquad \cdot\overset{\cdot\cdot}{\text{Po}}\cdot$$

8-35 The number of electrons gained is equal to the number of electrons that must be added to attain the noble-gas configuration at the end of the row in which the element is located in the periodic table.

(a)	1 electron	$\cdot\text{H}\cdot^{-}$	helium
(b)	2 electrons	$:\overset{\cdot\cdot}{\underset{\cdot\cdot}{\text{O}}}:^{2-}$	neon
(c)	4 electrons	$:\overset{\cdot\cdot}{\underset{\cdot\cdot}{\text{C}}}:^{4-}$	neon
(d)	2 electrons	$:\overset{\cdot\cdot}{\underset{\cdot\cdot}{\text{S}}}:^{2-}$	argon
(e)	1 electron	$:\overset{\cdot\cdot}{\underset{\cdot\cdot}{\text{Cl}}}\cdot^{-}$	argon

8-37 First we determine the number of electrons in the ion, and then we write the ground-state electron configuration.

(a) $19 - 1 = 18$ electrons: $1s^2 2s^2 2p^6 3s^2 3p^6$ or [Ar]
(b) $35 + 1 = 36$ electrons: $1s^2 2s^2 2p^6 3s^2 3p^6 4s^2 3d^{10} 4p^6$ or [Kr]
(c) $16 + 2 = 18$ electrons: $1s^2 2s^2 2p^6 3s^2 3p^6$ or [Ar]
(d) $56 - 2 = 54$ electrons: $1s^2 2s^2 2p^6 3s^2 3p^6 4s^2 3d^{10} 4p^6 5s^2 4d^{10} 5p^6$ or [Xe]
(e) $13 - 3 = 10$ electrons: $1s^2 2s^2 2p^6$ or [Ne]

They all have a noble-gas electron configuration.

8-39 We first determine the total number of electrons in the ion, then we figure out the ground-state electron configuration, and finally we count the number of unpaired electrons.

Species	Ground-state configuration	Number of unpaired electrons
(a) F^-	[He]$2s^2 2p^6$ or [Ne]	0
(b) Sn^{2+}	[Kr]$5s^2 4d^{10}$	0
(c) Bi^{3+}	[Xe]$6s^2 4f^{14} 5d^{10}$	0
(d) Ar^+	[Ne]$3s^2 3p^5$	1
(e) S^-	[Ne]$3s^2 3p^5$	1

8-41 Isoelectronic means having the same number of electrons. We thus determine the number of electrons for each species using the atomic number together with the ionic charge.

10 electrons:	F^-, O^{2-}, Na^+
18 electrons:	Sc^{3+}, Ti^{4+}, Ar
2 electrons:	Be^{2+}, B^{3+}, He
36 electrons:	Rb^+, Y^{3+}, Se^{2-}

8-43 In this problem we work out the electronic configurations of the reactants and the products.

(a) $O(g) + 2e^- \longrightarrow O^{2-}(g)$
[He]$2s^2 2p^4 + 2e^- \longrightarrow$ [He]$2s^2 2p^6$ or   [Ne]
(b) $Ca(g) + Sr^{2+}(g) \longrightarrow Sr(g) + Ca^{2+}(g)$
[Ar]$4s^2 +$ [Kr] $\longrightarrow$ [Kr]$5s^2 +$ [Ar]

8-45 First we figure out the electron configuration of the ground state; then we promote one electron from the highest energy subshell that is occupied to the lowest energy subshell that is unoccupied.

(a) The ground state of Na^+ ($11 - 1 = 10$ electrons) is $1s^2 2s^2 2p^6$. The highest energy occupied subshell is the $2p$, and the lowest energy unoccupied subshell is the $3s$; thus the first excited state is obtained by promoting an electron from the $2p$ subshell to the $3s$ subshell to yield $1s^2 2s^2 2p^5 3s^1$.
(b) The ground state of He^+ (1 electron) is $1s^1$. The first excited state is $2s^1$.
(c) The ground state of F^- (10 electrons) is $1s^2 2s^2 2p^6$. The first excited state is $1s^2 2s^2 2p^5 3s^1$.
(d) The ground state of O^+ is $1s^2 2s^2 2p^3$. The first excited state is $1s^2 2s^2 2p^2 3s^1$.

8-47 Count the total number of electrons and then determine the ground-state electron configuration. Compare your result with the configuration given.

(a) excited state   (c) excited state
(b) excited state   (d) excited state

8-49 Recall that atomic radii increase as we move down a column of the periodic table, whereas atomic radii decrease as we move from left to right across a row of the periodic table.

(a) P > N   (c) S > Ar
(b) P > S   (d) Kr > Ar

8-51 (a) Li < Na < Rb < Cs
(b) P < Al < Mg < Na
(c) Ca < Sr < Ba

8-53 The electron configurations of the alkaline earth metals are of the type [noble gas]ns^2. The energy of attraction between the nucleus and the outer electrons is greater the higher the value of the nuclear charge Z and is less the higher the value of n, the principal quantum number. These two effects oppose one another as we move down a group. However, the underlying electrons in the noble-gaslike core partially screen off the nuclear charge, and the farther the electrons from the nucleus (larger n) the lower the ionization energy.

8-57 Cs < K < Br < Cl < F

E   ANSWERS TO THE EVEN-NUMBERED PROBLEMS

8-2 (a) $5d$ (d) $5s$
(b) $4p$ (e) $6p$
(c) $4f$

8-4

n	l	m_l	m_s
4	3	-3	$+\frac{1}{2}$
			$-\frac{1}{2}$
		-2	$+\frac{1}{2}$
			$-\frac{1}{2}$
		-1	$+\frac{1}{2}$
			$-\frac{1}{2}$
		0	$+\frac{1}{2}$
			$-\frac{1}{2}$
		1	$+\frac{1}{2}$
			$-\frac{1}{2}$
		2	$+\frac{1}{2}$
			$-\frac{1}{2}$
		3	$+\frac{1}{2}$
			$-\frac{1}{2}$

8-6   K shell $n = 1$ $l = 0$ $m_l = 0$ $\qquad\qquad$ $m_s = +\frac{1}{2}, -\frac{1}{2}$ (2×1)
$\qquad\qquad\qquad\qquad\qquad\qquad\qquad\qquad\qquad\qquad\qquad\qquad\qquad\qquad\qquad$ = 2 electrons

$\qquad$ L shell $n = 2$ $l = 0$ $m_l = 0$ $\qquad\quad$ $m_s = +\frac{1}{2}, -\frac{1}{2}$
$\qquad\qquad\qquad\qquad$ $l = 1$ $m_l = -1, 0, 1$ $\quad$ $m_s = +\frac{1}{2}, -\frac{1}{2}$ $(2 \times 1) + (2 \times 3)$
$\qquad\qquad\qquad\qquad\qquad\qquad\qquad\qquad\qquad\qquad\qquad\qquad\qquad\qquad\qquad$ = 8 electrons

$\qquad$ M shell $n = 3$ $l = 0$ $m_l = 0$ $\qquad\qquad$ $m_s = +\frac{1}{2}, -\frac{1}{2}$
$\qquad\qquad\qquad\qquad$ $l = 1$ $m_l = 1, 0, 1$ $\qquad$ $m_s = +\frac{1}{2}, -\frac{1}{2}$
$\qquad\qquad\qquad\qquad$ $l = 2$ $m_l = -2, -1, 0, 1, 2$ $\quad$ $m_s = +\frac{1}{2}, -\frac{1}{2}$ $(2 \times 1) + (2 \times 3)$
$\qquad\qquad\qquad\qquad\qquad\qquad\qquad\qquad\qquad\qquad\qquad\qquad\qquad\qquad\qquad$ $+ (2 \times 5)$
$\qquad\qquad\qquad\qquad\qquad\qquad\qquad\qquad\qquad\qquad\qquad\qquad\qquad\qquad\qquad$ = 18 electrons

$\qquad$ N shell $n = 4$ $l = 0$ $m_l = 0$ $\qquad\qquad$ $m_s = +\frac{1}{2}, -\frac{1}{2}$
$\qquad\qquad\qquad\qquad$ $l = 1$ $m_l = 1, 0, 1$ $\qquad$ $m_s = +\frac{1}{2}, -\frac{1}{2}$
$\qquad\qquad\qquad\qquad$ $l = 2$ $m_l = -2, -1, 0, 1, 2$ $\quad$ $m_s = +\frac{1}{2}, -\frac{1}{2}$
$\qquad\qquad\qquad\qquad$ $l = 3$ $m_l = -3, -2, -1, 0,$ $\;$ $m_s = +\frac{1}{2}, -\frac{1}{2}$ $(2 \times 1) + (2 \times 3)$
$\qquad\qquad\qquad\qquad\qquad\qquad\quad$ $1, 2, 3$ $\qquad\qquad\qquad\qquad\qquad\qquad$ $+ (2 \times 5) + (2 \times 7)$
$\qquad\qquad\qquad\qquad\qquad\qquad\qquad\qquad\qquad\qquad\qquad\qquad\qquad\qquad\qquad$ = 32 electrons

8-8   In an f transition series the f orbitals are being filled. A set of seven f orbitals can hold up to 14 electrons.

8-10   (a) and (c) ruled out

8-12   (a) $2s$ can hold a maximum of 2 electrons.
$\qquad$ (b) $3s$ can hold a maximum of 2 electrons.
$\qquad$ (c) $2p$ can hold maximum of 6 electrons.
$\qquad$ (d) $3p$ is filled before higher energy orbitals and $3d$ can hold maximum of 10 electrons

8-14   (a) $1s^2 2s^2 2p^6 3s^2 3p^1$ $\qquad\qquad$ 13 electrons, aluminum
$\qquad$ (b) $1s^2 2s^2 2p^6 3s^2 3p^6 4s^2 3d^3$ $\qquad$ 23 electrons, vanadium
$\qquad$ (c) $1s^2 2s^2 2p^5$ $\qquad\qquad\qquad\qquad$ 9 electrons, fluorine
$\qquad$ (d) $1s^2 2s^2 2p^6 3s^2 3p^6 4s^2 3d^{10} 4p^1$ $\quad$ 31 electrons, gallium
$\qquad$ (e) $1s^2 2s^2 2p^4$ $\qquad\qquad\qquad\qquad$ 8 electrons, oxygen

8-16   (a) 26 electrons $\qquad$ $1s^2 2s^2 2p^6 3s^2 3p^6 4s^2 3d^6$
$\qquad$ (b) 74 electrons $\qquad$ $1s^2 2s^2 2p^6 3s^2 3p^6 4s^2 3d^{10} 4p^6 5s^2 4d^{10} 5p^6 6s^2 4f^{14} 5d^4$
$\qquad$ (c) 33 electrons $\qquad$ $1s^2 2s^2 2p^6 3s^2 3p^6 4s^2 3d^{10} 4p^3$
$\qquad$ (d) 10 electrons $\qquad$ $1s^2 2s^2 2p^6$
$\qquad$ (e) 19 electrons $\qquad$ $1s^2 2s^2 2p^6 3s^2 3p^6 4s^1$

8-18   (a) 34 electrons $\qquad$ $1s^2 2s^2 2p^6 3s^2 3p^6 4s^2 3d^{10} 4p^4$
$\qquad$ (b) 25 electrons $\qquad$ $1s^2 2s^2 2p^6 3s^2 3p^6 4s^2 3d^5$
$\qquad$ (c) 50 electrons $\qquad$ $1s^2 2s^2 2p^6 3s^2 3p^6 4s^2 3d^{10} 4p^6 5s^2 4d^{10} 5p^2$
$\qquad$ (d) 79 electrons $\qquad$ $1s^2 2s^2 2p^6 3s^2 3p^6 4s^2 3d^{10} 4p^6 5s^2 4d^{10} 5p^6 6s^1 4f^{14} 5d^{10}$
$\qquad$ (e) 63 electrons $\qquad$ $1s^2 2s^2 2p^6 3s^2 3p^6 4s^2 3d^{10} 4p^6 5s^2 4d^{10} 5p^6 6s^2 4f^7$

8-20   (a) aluminum
$\qquad$ (b) molybdenum
$\qquad$ (c) iron
$\qquad$ (d) mercury

8-22   (a) N (half-filled p) Group 5; Mn (half-filled d)
$\qquad$ (b) He, Ne, Group 8
$\qquad$ (c) As, Group 5; Mn

8-24 (a) La (Note that this is actually $5d^1$.)   (d) S
      (b) V   (e) Ca
      (c) Cu

8-26 $1s^2 2s^2 2p^6 3s^2 3p^6 4s^2 3d^{10} 4p^6 5s^2 4d^{10} 5p^6 6s^2 4f^{14} 5d^{10} 6p^6 7s^2 5f^{14} 6d^{10} 7p^6 8s^2 5g^{1-18}$

      $Z = 121$ through $Z = 138$, 18 elements in the series

8-28 (a) 1   (d) 3
      (b) 6   (e) 4
      (c) 5

8-30 (c) and (e) are ground states.

8-32 (a) 0   (d) 1
      (b) 3   (e) 2
      (c) 0

8-34 ·Be·   ·Mg·   ·Ca·   ·Sr·   ·Ba·   ·Ra·

8-36 (a) 2 electrons, Ca^{2+}, argon
      (b) 1 electron, Li^+, helium
      (c) 1 electron, Na^+, neon
      (d) 2 electrons, Mg^{2+}, neon
      (e) 3 electrons, Al^{3+}, neon

8-38 (a) $1s^2 2s^2 2p^6 3s^2 3p^6 4s^2 3d^{10} 4p^6$
      (b) $1s^2 2s^1$
      (c) $1s^2 2s^2 2p^6 3s^2 3p^6 4s^2 3d^{10}$
      (d) $[Xe]6s^2 4f^{14} 5d^{10}$
      (e) $1s^2 2s^2 2p^6 3s^2 3p^6$

8-40

Species	Ground-state configuration	Number of unpaired electrons
(a) K^+	[Ar]	0
(b) Sc^{3+}	[Ar]	0
(c) F^+	$[He]2s^2 2p^4$	2
(d) Cl^-	[Ar]	0
(e) O^-	$[He]2s^2 2p^5$	1

8-42 2 electrons: H^-, Li^+, C^{4+}
      10 electrons: Mg^{2+}, Ne, N^{3-}
      18 electrons: K^+, Ca^{2+}, P^{3-}
      36 electrons: Sr^{2+}, Br^-, Kr

8-44 (a) $I(g) + e^- \longrightarrow I^-(g)$
          $[Kr]5s^2 4d^{10} 5p^5 + e^- \longrightarrow [Kr]5s^2 4d^{10} 5p^6$ or [Xe]
      (b) $K(g) + F(g) \longrightarrow K^+(g) + F^-(g)$
          $[Ar]4s^1 + [He]2s^2 2p^5 \longrightarrow [Ar] + [He]2s^2 2p^6$ or [Ne]

8-46 (a) $1s^1 2s^1$
      (b) $1s^2 2s^2 2p^5 3s^1$
      (c) $1s^2 2s^2 2p^5 3s^1$
      (d) $1s^2 2s^2 2p^5 3s^1$

8-48 (b), (c), and (d)

8-50 (a) He < Ne < Ar < Kr
(b) Li < Na < K < Rb
(c) Ne < F < N < B < Be

8-52 For a given nuclear charge, the less the number of electrons the smaller the species. The electrons are drawn closer to the nucleus.

8-54 (a) B < O < F < Ne
(b) Sb < Te < I < Xe
(c) Cs < Rb < K < Ca
(d) Na < Al < S < Ar

8-56 Ba < Sr < Ca < Se < S < O

F   ANSWERS TO THE SELF-TEST

1 false

2 false (only on n and l)

3 false

4 No two electrons can have the same four quantum numbers in the same atom.

5 positive spin or $m_s = +\frac{1}{2}$

6 six

7 false (Spins must be opposed.)

8 eight

9 two

10 two (s and p)

11 Ne

12 There are 5 electrons in the $2p$ orbitals.

13 $3d^6$

14 false

15 true

16 $1s^2 2s^2 2p^3$

17 $1s^2 2s^2 2p^6 3s^2 3p^6 4s^2 3d^3$

18 For any set of orbitals of the same energy, the ground-state electron configuration is obtained by placing the electrons into different orbitals of this set with parallel spins until each of the orbitals has one electron.

19

20 ns^2

21 $ns^2 np^5$

22 alkali

23 noble gas

24 noble gas

25 noble gas

26 $1s^2 2s^2 2p^6$ or [Ne]

27 $1s^2 2s^2 2p^6$ or [Ne]

28 d

29 true

30 false ($4s^1 3d^5$)

31 $4s^2 3d^1$ through $4s^2 3d^{10}$

32 $4f$

33 They have similar chemical properties.

34 $5f$

35 true

36 crystallographic data; X-ray analysis of crystal structure

37 decrease

38 increase

39 1

40 the outer electron is farther from the nucleus

41 larger

9 / Ionic Compounds

A   OUTLINE OF CHAPTER 9

9-1 The electrostatic attraction that binds oppositely charged ions together is called an ionic bond.

Electrostatic attraction binds ions together in an ionic bond.

Certain metals lose electrons and nonmetals gain electrons to attain noble-gas electron configurations.

An ionic compound is composed of cations and anions.

9-2 Reactive metals combine with reactive nonmetals to produce ionic compounds.

Lewis electron-dot formulas can be used to predict the products of reactions between certain metals and nonmetals (Table 9-1).

9-3 Many ions do not have a noble-gas electron configuration.

Some metals (Table 9-2) lose electrons to form ions with a pseudo-noble-gas electron configuration, $ns^2np^6nd^{10}$.

Some metals (Table 9-3) form ions with the outer electron configuration [noble gas]$(n + 1)s^2nd^{10}$.

Many metals do not obey any simple rules for predicting their relatively stable ions (Table 9-4).

In the d transition metal ions, the nd orbital is of lower energy than the $(n + 1)s$ orbital.

9-4 Ionic radii are not the same as atomic radii.

Positive atomic ions are smaller than their parent neutral atoms (Figure 9-8).

Negative atomic ions are larger than their parent neutral atoms (Figure 9-8).

For positive ions in the same row of the periodic table, the higher the positive charge, the smaller the ion.

Isoelectronic species contain the same number of electrons.

The values of some ionic radii are given in Table 9-1.

9-5   Solutions that contain ions conduct an electric current.

Ionic compounds yield ions when they dissolve in water.

Moving charges (ions) constitute an electric current.

Electrolytes in aqueous solution conduct an electric current.

Nonelectrolytes in aqueous solution do not conduct an electric current.

Some guidelines for predicting whether a substance is a strong, weak, or non-electrolyte are given on pages 343 and 344 (Example 9-8).

9-6   Ionic compounds conduct an electric current when they are melted.

Ionic crystals contain three-dimensional ordered arrays of positive and negative ions (Figure 9-12).

When melted, the ions in an ionic compound are free to move throughout the liquid (Figure 9-13).

9-7   Electron affinity is the energy released when an atom gains an electron.

The ionization energy is the energy required to remove an electron from an atom or ion.

The electron affinity (EA) is the energy released in the process

$$\text{atom}(g) + \text{electron} \longrightarrow \text{negative ion}(g) + \text{EA}$$

The values of the electron affinities of some nonmetals are given in Table 9-2.

The distance between the centers of the ions in an ion pair is the sum of the radii of the ions.

9-8   Coulomb's law is used to calculate the energy of an ion pair.

Coulomb's law is given by

$$E = (2.31 \times 10^{-16}\,\text{J} \cdot \text{pm})\frac{Z_1 Z_2}{d} \qquad (9\text{-}2)$$

where d is the sum of the ionic radii.

The energy change for the reaction

$$M(g) + X(g) \longrightarrow M^+X^-(g)$$

equals the sum of the ionization energy of $M(g)$, the electron affinity of $X(g)$, and the Coulombic energy of the ion pair (Figure 9-16).

9-9   The formation of ionic solids from the elements is an exothermic process.

The energy change for the reaction

$$M(s) + \tfrac{1}{2}X_2(s,\, l,\, \text{or } g) \longrightarrow M^+X^-(s)$$

equals the sum of the vaporization energy of $M(s)$, the vaporization energy and dissociation energy of X_2, the ionization energy of $M(g)$, the electron affinity of $X(g)$, and the lattice energy of $M^+X^-(s)$ (see Figure 9-17).

B   SELF-TEST

1   If a sodium atom loses an electron, then the electron configuration of the sodium ion is _____.

2   If a chlorine atom gains an electron, then the electron configuration of the chloride ion is _____.

3   The compound, sodium chloride, consists of _____ and _____.

4   The bonds in NaCl are called _____ bonds.

5   Write the formula of the ionic compound formed in the reaction between barium atoms and chlorine atoms _____.

6   Using Lewis electron-dot formulas, the reaction between barium atoms and chlorine atoms is _____.

7   The Group 2 metals lose _____ electron(s) to attain a _____ configuration.

8   The Group 6 nonmetals gain _____ electron(s) to attain a _____ configuration.

9   The group of transition metals headed by Cu lose _____ electron(s) to attain a _____ configuration.

10   The Group 5 metals lose _____ electron(s) to attain a _____ configuration.

11   The first electrons lost by a transition metal are the outer s electrons. *True/False*

12   The energy of the $3d$ orbitals is lower than the $4s$ orbital in a transition metal ion. *True/False*

13   The radius of an ion is the same as the radius of the atom. *True/False*

14   The radius of a chloride ion is (*larger/smaller*) than the radius of a chlorine atom because _____.

15   The radius of a potassium ion is (*larger/smaller*) than the radius of a potassium atom because _____.

16   Isoelectronic species always have the same size. *True/False*

17   An aqueous solution of sodium chloride contains _____ and _____.

18   A substance that exists as ions when dissolved in water will conduct an electric current. *True/False*

19   All substances that dissolve in water produce solutions that conduct electricity. *True/False*

20 All electrolytes are good conductors of electricity. *True/False*

21 Weak electrolytes are substances that ionize completely in water. *True/False*

22 Hydrochloric acid, HCl(aq), is a _____ electrolyte.

23 Acetic acid, $HC_2H_3O_2$, is a _____ electrolyte.

24 Benzene, C_6H_6, is a _____ electrolyte.

25 Sodium chloride when melted conducts electricity because _____.

26 Gaseous sodium chloride consists of _____.

27 Crystalline sodium chloride consists of _____.

28 Liquid sodium chloride consists of _____.

29 Energy is required to remove an electron from a lithium atom. *True/False*

30 Energy is required to add an electron to a fluorine atom. *True/False*

31 The electron affinity of a chlorine atom has a (*positive/negative*) value.

32 The energy required to bring two ions together in the gas phase is found from _____ law.

33 The energy required to bring a positive ion and a negative ion together is negative. The ion pair is (*more/less*) stable than the separated ions.

34 Coulomb's law states that $E =$ _____ where _____ _____.

35 The Coulombic energy for the process

$$M^+(g) + X^-(g) \longrightarrow MX(g)$$

is greater the (*greater/less*) the separation between the _____ _____.

36 The energies used to calculate the energy evolved in the process

$$Na(g) + Cl(g) \longrightarrow Na^+Cl^-(g)$$

are
(a) _____
(b) _____
(c) _____

37 Energy is (*absorbed/released*) when isolated fluoride ions and isolated lithium ions are brought together to form crystalline lithium fluoride.

38 The lattice energy of an ionic crystal has a (*positive/negative*) value.

39 The reaction between a metal and a nonmetal to form an ionic crystal is an _____ thermic reaction.

40 Write out the five steps used to analyze the energetics of the formation of LiF(s) from Li(s) and F$_2$(g).

(a) _____

(b) _____

(c) _____

(d) _____

(e) _____

41 The sum of the energy terms in the five steps involved in question 40 is equal to the energy change for the reaction _____.

42 The lattice energy of NaCl(s) is equal to the energy released in the process

_____.

C   CALCULATIONS YOU SHOULD KNOW HOW TO DO

1 Use the electron configurations and the Lewis electron-dot formulas to predict reaction products and chemical formulas. See Examples 9-1 through 9-3, and Problems 9-1 through 9-8 (reaction products) and Problems 9-17 through 9-20 (chemical formulas).

2 Determine the electron configurations for transition metal ions. See Examples 9-4 through 9-6, and Problems 9-9 through 9-14.

3 Use electron configurations and the charges on the ions to predict the relative sizes of ions. See Example 9-7 and Problems 9-21 and 9-22.

4 Use the rules given in Section 9-5 to classify electrolytes as strong, weak or non-electrolytes. See Example 9-8 and Problems 9-27 through 9-30.

5 Use the ionization energies and electron affinities to estimate the values of ΔH°_{rxn}. See Example 9-9 and Problems 9-35 through 9-38.

6 Calculate the energy released in the formation of ion pairs, using Coulomb's law. See Example 9-9 and Problems 9-39 through 9-46.

7 Calculate the energy released in the formation of ionic crystals from the elements. See Example 9-10 and Problems 9-47 through 9-52.

D   SOLUTIONS TO THE ODD-NUMBERED PROBLEMS

9-1 In problems of this type we simply write out the ground-state electron configurations of the various species. Recall that the number of electrons in a neutral atomic species is equal to the atomic number Z. For positive ions the number of electrons is equal to Z minus the charge on the ion; for negative ions the number of electrons is equal to Z plus the charge on the ion. In order to emphasize the attainment of noble-gas configurations for ions, we write the electron configurations in terms of noble-gas configurations. Thus [Ar] denotes the configuration $1s^2 2s^2 2p^6 3s^2 3p^6$.

(a) $K([Ar]4s^1) + Cl([Ne]3s^2 3p^5) \longrightarrow K^+([Ar]) + Cl^-([Ar]) \longrightarrow KCl(g)$
(b) $Sr([Kr]5s^2) + 2Br([Ar]4s^2 3d^{10} 4p^5) \longrightarrow Sr^{2+}([Kr]) + 2Br^-([Kr])$
$$\longrightarrow SrBr_2(g)$$
(c) $2Al([Ne]3s^2 3p^1) + 3O([He]2s^2 2p^4) \longrightarrow 2Al^{3+}([Ne]) + 3O^{2-}([Ne])$
$$\longrightarrow Al_2O_3(g)$$

9-3 This problem is similar to Problems 9-1 and 9-2, except that in this case we first have to write down the balanced reaction.

(a) $Ga(g) + 3F(g) \longrightarrow GaF_3(g)$
$Ga([Ar]4s^2 3d^{10} 4p^1) + 3F([He]2s^2 2p^5) \longrightarrow Ga^{3+}([Ar]3d^{10}) + 3F^-([Ne])$
$$\longrightarrow GaF_3(g)$$
(b) $Ca(g) + S(g) \longrightarrow CaS(g)$
$Ca([Ar]4s^2) + S([Ne]3s^2 3p^4) \longrightarrow Ca^{2+}([Ar]) + S^{2-}([Ar]) \longrightarrow CaS(g)$
(c) $3Li(g) + N(g) \longrightarrow Li_3N(g)$
$3Li([He]2s^1) + N([He]2s^2 2p^3) \longrightarrow 3Li^+([He]) + N^{3-}([Ne]) \longrightarrow Li_3N(g)$

9-5 (a) If we write the Lewis electron-dot formulas for Li and N, then the reaction can be written

$$3Li\cdot + \cdot \ddot{N}\cdot \longrightarrow \underbrace{3Li^+ + :\ddot{N}:^{3-}}_{Li_3N}$$

Each lithium atom gives up one outer electron to achieve a noble-gas electron configuration. The nitrogen atom accepts one electron from each of the three lithium atoms to achieve a noble-gas electron configuration.
(b) If we write the Lewis electron-dot formulas for Na and H, then the reaction can be written

$$Na\cdot + H\cdot \longrightarrow \underbrace{Na^+ + H:^-}_{NaH}$$

Sodium gives up one outer-electron to achieve a noble-gas electron configuration. Hydrogen accepts one electron to achieve a noble-gas electron configuration.
(c) If we write the Lewis electron-dot formulas for Al and I, then we can write the reaction as

$$\cdot Al\cdot + 3:\ddot{I}\cdot \longrightarrow \underbrace{Al^{3+} + 3:\ddot{I}:^-}_{AlI_3}$$

Each aluminum atom gives up three outer-electrons to achieve a noble-gas electron configuration. Each iodine atom accepts one of the electrons from an aluminum atom to achieve a noble-gas electron configuration. It takes three iodine atoms to accept the three outer electrons given up by one aluminum atom.

9-7 (a) The Lewis electron-dot formulas for Ca and S are

$$\cdot \text{Ca} \cdot \quad \text{and} \quad \cdot \overset{\cdot \cdot}{\underset{\cdot \cdot}{\text{S}}} \cdot$$

The calcium atom can achieve a noble-gas electron configuration by losing two electrons. The sulfur atom can achieve a noble-gas electron configuration by gaining two electrons. Thus the product will be CaS.

(b) The Lewis electron-dot formulas for Al and Cl are

$$\cdot \text{Al} \cdot \quad \text{and} \quad : \overset{}{\underset{\cdot}{\text{Cl}}} \cdot$$

The aluminum atom can achieve a noble-gas electron configuration by losing three electrons. The chlorine atom can achieve a noble-gas electron configuration by gaining one electron, and so it requires three chlorine atoms for each aluminum atom. The product is $AlCl_3$.

(c) The Lewis electron-dot formulas for Be and O are

$$\cdot \text{Be} \cdot \quad \text{and} \quad \cdot \overset{\cdot \cdot}{\underset{\cdot \cdot}{\text{O}}} \cdot$$

The beryllium atom can achieve a noble-gas electron configuration by losing two electrons. The oxygen atom can achieve a noble-gas electron configuration by gaining two electrons. The product is BeO.

9-9 Recall that for neutral atoms the $(n+1)s$ orbitals are of lower energy than the nd orbitals, for example, $4s < 3d$. For ions, however, the reverse is true, that is, $3d < 4s$. Thus we first determine the number of electrons in the ion, and then we write the electron configuration filling the orbitals in the order $1s, 2s, 2p, 3s, 3p, 3d, 4s$, and so forth. For Cr^{2+} we have $Z - 2 = 24 - 2 = 22$ electrons; thus we have

(a) $Cr^{2+}([Ar]3d^4)$
(b) $Cu^{2+}([Ar]3d^9)$
(c) $Co^{3+}([Ar]3d^6)$
(d) $Mn^{2+}([Ar]3d^5)$
(e) $Ni^{3+}([Ar]3d^7)$

9-11 For $+2$ ions the nth member of a d transition series has nd electrons, because the two $(n+1)s$ electrons have been removed. Thus the sixth member has six d electrons, and so forth.

(a) Fe, Ru, Os
(b) Zn, Cd, Hg
(c) Sc, Y, Lu
(d) Mn, Tc, Re
(e) Ni, Pd, Pt

9-13 (a) For $n = 3$ or 4, a pseudo-noble-gas outer electron configuration is one of the type $ns^2np^6nd^{10}$. For $n = 4$ the corresponding noble gas is Kr (the fourth noble gas); thus for Cd^{2+} we have $Cd^{2+}([Kr]4d^{10})$.

(b) In^{3+}([Kr]$4d^{10}$)

(c) In this case, $n = 5$ and the corresponding pseudo-noble-gas outer electron configuration is of the type $ns^2np^6(n-1)f^{14}nd^{10}$ or $5s^25p^64f^{14}5d^{10}$, thus we have $Tl^{3+}([Xe]4f^{14}5d^{10})$.

(d) $Zn^{2+}([Ar]3d^{10})$

9-15 In this problem we simply determine the number of electrons in the positive ion and in the negative ion. If the numbers are the same, then the ions are isoelectronic

(a) $Li^+(2)$, $F^-(10)$, not isoelectronic
(b) $Na^+(10)$, $F^-(10)$, isoelectronic
(c) $K^+(18)$, $Br^-(36)$, not isoelectronic
(d) KCl, isoelectronic ions, each has 18 electrons
(e) BaI_2, isoelectronic ions, each has 54 electrons
(f) AlF_3, isoelectronic ions, each has 10 electrons

9-17 Figure 9-1 gives the ionic charges of various ions that correspond to noble-gas electron configurations. We use these charges, together with the requirement that the ionic compound must be electrically neutral, to work out the formula.

(a) Y_2S_3 (d) Rb_3N
(b) $LaBr_3$ (e) Al_2Se_3
(c) MgTe

9-19 In this problem the charge on the positive ions is determined by the attainment of a pseudo-noble-gas configuration (see Figure 9-2). The charge on the negative ion is determined by the attainment of a noble-gas configuration (see Figure 9-1).

(a) AgCl   (d) CuBr
(b) CdS   (e) Ga_2O_3
(c) Zn_3N_2

9-21 (a) Cl^- A negative ion is larger than a positive ion with the same number of electrons.

(b) Ag^+ The higher charged ion is smaller because of the larger nuclear attraction for the same number of electrons.

(c) Cu^+ Same reason as (b).
(d) O^{2-} The higher the negative charge for the same number of electrons, the larger is the ion, because the smaller nuclear charge exerts less attraction for the electrons.

(e) P^{3-} Same reason as (d).

9-23 We simply add the appropriate ionic radii given in Table 9-1.

(a) 126 pm + 181 pm = 307 pm
(b) 181 pm + 110 pm = 291 pm   Hg—Cl distance
    291 pm + 291 pm = 582 pm   Cl—Cl distance
(c) 74 pm + 140 pm = 214 pm

9-25 The radius of atomic chlorine is 100 pm (Figure 8-11). The volume of a chlorine atom is

$$V = \tfrac{4}{3}\pi r^3 = (\tfrac{4}{3})(3.14)(100 \text{ pm})^3 = 4.19 \times 10^6 \text{ pm}^3$$

The radius of a chlorine ion is 181 pm (Table 9-1). The volume of a chloride ion is

$$V = \tfrac{4}{3}\pi r^3 = (\tfrac{4}{3})(3.14)(181 \text{ pm})^3 = 2.48 \times 10^7 \text{ pm}^3$$

$$\text{Increase in volume} = 2.48 \times 10^7 \text{ pm}^3 - 0.419 \times 10^7 \text{ pm}^3$$
$$= 2.06 \times 10^7 \text{ pm}^3$$

$$\% \text{ increase in volume} = \frac{2.06 \times 10^7 \text{ pm}^3}{4.19 \times 10^6 \text{ pm}^3} \times 100$$
$$= 492\%$$

There is about a 5-fold increase in volume.

9-27 (a) Na^+ and F^- ions   (d) Sr^{2+} and I^- ions
(b) Zn^{2+} and Cl^- ions   (e) Sc^{3+} and I^- ions
(c) Ag^+ and F^- ions

9-29 To work this problem we use the rules given in Section 9-5.

(a) $CaCl_2$, strong electrolyte − a salt
(b) $PbCl_2$, weak electrolyte − a chloride of a metal with a high atomic number
(c) $HC_2H_3O_2$, weak electrolyte − an organic acid
(d) CH_3COCH_3, nonelectrolyte − an organic compound

9-31 See Table 9-2 for electron affinities. The higher the EA value of an atom, the easier it is to add an electron. The order of the EA values is

$$Cl > Br > I > H$$

9-33 From Table 9-2 we note that the EA values decrease by 25 to 30 $kJ \cdot mol^{-1}$ as we go from Cl to Br to I; thus we estimate that the EA value for At is 25 to 30 $kJ \cdot mol^{-1}$, less than that for I, or $EA \simeq 265$ to $270 \text{ kJ} \cdot mol^{-1}$.

9-35 The value of ΔH°_{rxn} for a reaction in which separated gaseous ions are formed is equal to the sum of the ΔH°_{rxn} of the ionization energy of the metal and the electron affinity of the nonmetal.

(a) $Rb(g) + 403 \text{ kJ} \longrightarrow Rb^+(g) + e^-$
$Br(g) + e^- \longrightarrow Br^-(g) + 324 \text{ kJ}$
If we add these two equations, then we have
$Rb(g) + Br(g) + 79 \text{ kJ} \longrightarrow Rb^+(g) + Br^-(g)$ $\Delta H^\circ_{rxn} = 79 \text{ kJ}$
(b) $Li(g) + 520 \text{ kJ} \longrightarrow Li^+(g) + e^-$
$Cl(g) + e^- \longrightarrow Cl^-(g) + 348 \text{ kJ}$
Adding these two equations, we have
$Li(g) + Cl(g) + 172 \text{ kJ} \longrightarrow Li^+(g) + Cl^-(g)$ $\Delta H^\circ_{rxn} = 172 \text{ kJ}$
(c) $K(g) + 419 \text{ kJ} \longrightarrow K^+(g) + e^-$
$F(g) + e^- \longrightarrow F^-(g) + 333 \text{ kJ}$
Adding these two equations, we have
$K(g) + F(g) + 86 \text{ kJ} \longrightarrow K^+(g) + F^-(g)$ $\Delta H^\circ_{rxn} = 86 \text{ kJ}$

9-37 (a) $Cu(g) + 745 \text{ kJ} \longrightarrow Cu^+(g) + e^-$
$Cl(g) + e^- \longrightarrow Cl^-(g) + 348 \text{ kJ}$

$Cu(g) + Cl(g) + 397 \text{ kJ} \longrightarrow Cu^+(g) + Cl^-(g)$ $\Delta H^\circ_{rxn} = 397 \text{ kJ}$

(b) $Cl(g) + e^- \longrightarrow Cl^-(g) + 348 \text{ kJ}$
$I^-(g) + 295 \text{ kJ} \longrightarrow I(g) + e^-$

$Cl(g) + I^-(g) \longrightarrow Cl^-(g) + I(g) + 53 \text{ kJ}$ $\Delta H^\circ_{rxn} = -53 \text{ kJ}$

(c) $Ag(g) + 731 \text{ kJ} \longrightarrow Ag^+(g) + e^-$
$\underline{F(g) + e^- \longrightarrow F^-(g) + 333 \text{ kJ}}$

$Ag(g) + F(g) + 398 \text{ kJ} \longrightarrow Ag^+(g) + F^-(g) \qquad \Delta H^\circ_{rxn} = 398 \text{ kJ}$

9-39 The radius of $K^+ = 133$ pm.
The radius of $Cl^- = 181$ pm.
The distance between the centers of the ions is

$$133 \text{ pm} + 181 \text{ pm} = 314 \text{ pm}$$

From Coulomb's law we have

$$E = (2.31 \times 10^{-16} \text{ J} \cdot \text{pm})\frac{Z_1 Z_2}{d}$$

where

$$Z_1 = +1 \text{ for } K^+ \qquad \text{and} \qquad Z_2 = -1 \text{ for } Cl^-$$

Thus

$$E = \frac{(2.31 \times 10^{-16} \text{ J} \cdot \text{pm})(+1)(-1)}{314 \text{ pm}}$$

$$= -7.36 \times 10^{-19} \text{ J}$$

9-41 (a) For the ionization of K (Figure 8-12)
$K(g) + 419 \text{ kJ} \longrightarrow K^+(g) + e^-$
(b) For the electron addition to Br (Table 9-2)
$Br(g) + e^- \longrightarrow Br^-(g) + 324 \text{ kJ}$
If we add steps (a) and (b), then we have
$K(g) + Br(g) + 95 \text{ kJ} \longrightarrow K^+(g) + Br^-(g)$
(c) We now bring together K^+ and Br^- to their ion-pair separation. According to Table 9-1, the radius of K^+ is 133 pm and the radius of Br^- is 195 pm. Their separation as an ion pair is 328 pm. We now use Coulomb's law to calculate the energy released by the formation of one ion pair from the ions:
$K^+(g) + Br^-(g) \longrightarrow K^+Br^-(g)$

$$E = (2.31 \times 10^{-16} \text{ J} \cdot \text{pm})\frac{Z_1 Z_2}{d}$$

$$E = \frac{(2.31 \times 10^{-16} \text{ J} \cdot \text{pm})(+1)(-1)}{328 \text{ pm}}$$

$$E = -7.04 \times 10^{-19} \text{ J}$$

For the energy released on the formation of one mole of ion pairs, we multiply this result by Avogadro's number:

$$E = \left(-7.04 \times 10^{-19} \frac{\text{J}}{\text{ion-pair}}\right)\left(6.02 \times 10^{23} \frac{\text{ion-pair}}{\text{mol}}\right)$$

$$E = -424 \text{ kJ} \cdot \text{mol}^{-1}$$

Thus

$$K^+(g) + Br^-(g) \longrightarrow K^+Br^-(g) + 424 \text{ kJ} \qquad (d = 328 \text{ pm})$$

We combine this result with the result

$$K(g) + Br(g) + 95 \text{ kJ} \longrightarrow K^+(g) + Br^-(g)$$

to obtain the final result

$$K(g) + Br(g) \longrightarrow K^+Br^-(g) + 329 \text{ kJ} \qquad (d = 328 \text{ pm})$$

9-43   (a)   For the ionization of Na (Figure 8-12),
        $Na(g) + 496 \text{ kJ} \longrightarrow Na^+(g) + e^-$
     (b)   For the electron addition to H (Table 9-2),
        $H(g) + e^- \longrightarrow H^-(g) + 72 \text{ kJ}$
        Adding steps (a) and (b), we have
        $Na(g) + H(g) + 424 \text{ kJ} \longrightarrow Na^+(g) + H^-(g)$
     (c)   We now bring together the Na^+ and H^- to their ion-pair separation

$$\begin{array}{r} \text{radius of } Na^+ = 95 \text{ pm} \\ \underline{\text{radius of } H^- = 154 \text{ pm}} \\ \text{separation} = 249 \text{ pm} \end{array}$$

We use Coulomb's law to calculate the energy released by the formation of one ion-pair:

$$E = (2.31 \times 10^{-16} \text{ J} \cdot \text{pm})\frac{Z_1 Z_2}{d}$$

$$E = \frac{(2.31 \times 10^{-16} \text{ J} \cdot \text{pm})(+1)(-1)}{249 \text{ pm}}$$

$$E = -9.28 \times 10^{-19} \text{ J}$$

The energy released on formation of one mole of ion-pairs is

$$E = \left(-9.28 \times 10^{-19}\frac{\text{J}}{\text{ion-pair}}\right)\left(6.02 \times 10^{23}\frac{\text{ion-pair}}{\text{mol}}\right)$$

$$E = -558 \text{ kJ} \cdot \text{mol}^{-1}$$

Thus we have for the reaction

$$Na^+(g) + H^-(g) \longrightarrow NaH(g) + 558 \text{ kJ} \qquad (d = 249 \text{ pm})$$

Combining the above result with

$$Na(g) + H(g) + 424 \text{ kJ} \longrightarrow Na^+(g) + H^-(g)$$

we obtain

$$Na(g) + H(g) \longrightarrow NaH(g) + 134 \text{ kJ} \qquad (d = 249 \text{ pm})$$

9-45

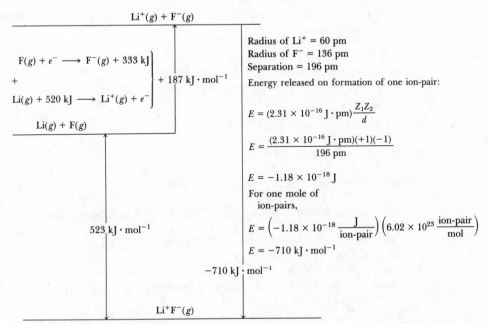

Radius of Li^+ = 60 pm
Radius of F^- = 136 pm
Separation = 196 pm

Energy released on formation of one ion-pair:

$$E = (2.31 \times 10^{-16} \text{ J} \cdot \text{pm})\frac{Z_1 Z_2}{d}$$

$$E = \frac{(2.31 \times 10^{-16} \text{ J} \cdot \text{pm})(+1)(-1)}{196 \text{ pm}}$$

$$E = -1.18 \times 10^{-18} \text{ J}$$

For one mole of
ion-pairs,

$$E = \left(-1.18 \times 10^{-18} \frac{\text{J}}{\text{ion-pair}}\right)\left(6.02 \times 10^{23} \frac{\text{ion-pair}}{\text{mol}}\right)$$

$$E = -710 \text{ kJ} \cdot \text{mol}^{-1}$$

9-47 Following the steps outlined in Section 9-9, we have

(a) Vaporize one mole of sodium metal:
$$Na(s) + 93 \text{ kJ} \longrightarrow Na(g)$$

(b) Dissociate one-half mole of $F_2(g)$:
$$\tfrac{1}{2}F_2(g) + 78 \text{ kJ} \longrightarrow F(g)$$
where 78 kJ = $(\tfrac{1}{2} \text{ mol})(155 \text{ kJ} \cdot \text{mol}^{-1})$

(c) Ionize one mole of $Na(g)$ (Figure 8-12):
$$Na(g) + 496 \text{ kJ} \longrightarrow Na^+(g) + e^-$$

(d) Attach one mole of electrons to one mole of fluorine atoms (Table 9-2):
$$F(g) + e^- \longrightarrow F^-(g) + 333 \text{ kJ}$$

(e) Bring one mole of $Na^+(g)$ and one mole of $F^-(g)$ together to form crystalline $NaF(s)$ (lattice energy):
$$Na^+(g) + F^-(g) \longrightarrow NaF(s) + 919 \text{ kJ}$$

(f) Add the equation in steps (a) through (e) to obtain
$(93 + 78 + 496 - 333 - 919 = -585)$;
$$Na(s) + \tfrac{1}{2}F_2(g) \longrightarrow NaF(s) + 585 \text{ kJ}$$
Thus
$$\Delta H^\circ_{rxn} = -585 \text{ kJ}$$

9-49 (a) Vaporize one mole of sodium metal:
$$Na(s) + 93 \text{ kJ} \longrightarrow Na(g)$$

(b) Sublime and dissociate one-half mole of I_2
$$\tfrac{1}{2}I_2(s) + 107 \text{ kJ} \longrightarrow I(g)$$
where 107 kJ = $(\tfrac{1}{2} \text{ mol})(214 \text{ kJ} \cdot \text{mol}^{-1})$.

(c) Ionize one mole of Na(g) (Figure 8-12):
   Na(g) + 496 kJ $\longrightarrow$ Na$^+$(g) + e^-

(d) Attach one mole of electrons to one mole of I(g) (Table 9-2):
   I(g) + e^- $\longrightarrow$ I$^-$(g) + 295 kJ

(e) Bring one mole of Na$^+$(g) and one mole of I$^-$(g) together to form crystalline NaI (lattice energy):
   Na$^+$(g) + I$^-$(g) $\longrightarrow$ NaI(s) + 704 kJ

(f) Add the equations in steps (a) through (e) to obtain
   (93 + 107 + 496 − 295 − 704 = −303)
   Na(s) + $\frac{1}{2}$I$_2$(s) $\longrightarrow$ NaI(s) + 303 kJ
   $\Delta H^\circ_{rxn} = -303$ kJ

9-51 (a) Vaporize one mole of calcium metal:
   Ca(s) + 179 kJ $\longrightarrow$ Ca(g)

(b) Dissociate one mole of Cl$_2$(g):
   Cl$_2$(g) + 244 kJ $\longrightarrow$ 2Cl(g)

(c) Ionize one mole of Ca(g) to Ca$^+$(g) (Figure 8-12):
   Ca(g) + 590 kJ $\longrightarrow$ Ca$^+$(g) + e^-
   Ionize one mole of Ca$^+$(g) to Ca^{2+}(g) (second ionization energy):
   Ca$^+$(g) + 1140 kJ $\longrightarrow$ Ca^{2+}(g) + e^-
   Thus for the production of Ca^{2+}(g) from Ca(g), we have
   Ca(g) + 1730 kJ $\longrightarrow$ Ca^{2+}(g) + 2e^-
   where 1730 = 590 + 1140.

(d) Attach two moles of electrons to two moles of Cl(g)
   (2 mol)(348 kJ · mol^{-1}) = 696 kJ:
   2Cl(g) + 2e^- $\longrightarrow$ 2Cl$^-$(g) + 696 kJ

(e) Bring one mole of Ca^{2+}(g) and two moles of Cl$^-$ together to form crystalline CaCl$_2$ (lattice energy):
   Ca^{2+}(g) + 2Cl$^-$(g) $\longrightarrow$ CaCl$_2$(s) + 2256 kJ

(f) Add the equations in steps (a) through (e) to obtain
   (179 + 244 + 1730 − 696 − 2256 = −799):
   Ca(s) + Cl$_2$(g) $\longrightarrow$ CaCl$_2$(s) + 799 kJ $\Delta H^\circ_{rxn} = -799$ kJ

E   ANSWERS TO THE EVEN-NUMBERED PROBLEMS

9-2 (a) Ca([Ar]4s^2) + 2F([He]2$s^2$2p^5) $\longrightarrow$ Ca^{2+}([Ar]) + 2F$^-$([Ne]) $\longrightarrow$ CaF$_2$(g)

(b) 2Na([Ne]3s^1) + O([He]2$s^2$2p^4) $\longrightarrow$ 2Na$^+$([Ne]) + O^{2-}([Ne]) $\longrightarrow$ Na$_2$O(g)

(c) Mg([Ne]3s^2) + S([Ne]3$s^2$3p^4) $\longrightarrow$ Mg^{2+}([Ne]) + S^{2-}([Ar]) $\longrightarrow$ MgS(s)

9-4 (a) Ca([Ar]4s^2) + 2Br([Ar]4$s^2$3d^{10}4p^5) $\longrightarrow$ Ca^{2+}([Ar]) + 2Br$^-$([Kr])
   The product is CaBr$_2$.

(b) 3Mg([Ne]3s^2) + 2N([He]2$s^2$2p^3) $\longrightarrow$ 3Mg^{2+}([Ne]) + 2N^{3-}([Ne])
   The product is Mg$_3$N$_2$.

(c) 2Cs([Xe]6s^1) + Se([Ar]4$s^2$3d^{10}4p^4) $\longrightarrow$ 2Cs$^+$([Xe]) + Se^{2-}([Kr])
   The product is Cs$_2$Se.

9-6 (a) K· + :I· $\longrightarrow$ $\underbrace{\text{K}^+ + :\ddot{\text{I}}:^-}_{\text{KI}}$

(b) $\cdot Ba \cdot \; + \; \cdot \overset{\cdot\cdot}{\underset{}{O}} \cdot \; \longrightarrow \; \underbrace{Ba^{2+} \; + \; :\overset{\cdot\cdot}{\underset{\cdot\cdot}{O}}:^{2-}}_{BaO}$

(c) $\cdot Be \cdot \; + \; \cdot \overset{}{\underset{}{Se}} \cdot \; \longrightarrow \; \underbrace{Be^{2+} \; + \; :\overset{\cdot\cdot}{\underset{\cdot\cdot}{Se}}:^{2-}}_{BeSe}$

9-8 (a) $2Na \cdot \; + \; \cdot \overset{\cdot\cdot}{\underset{}{O}} \cdot \; \longrightarrow \; \underbrace{2Na^{+} \; + \; :\overset{\cdot\cdot}{\underset{\cdot\cdot}{O}}:^{2-}}_{Na_2O}$

(b) $\cdot \overset{\cdot}{Sc} \cdot \; + \; 3 :\overset{\cdot\cdot}{\underset{}{Cl}} \cdot \; \longrightarrow \; \underbrace{Sc^{3+} \; + \; 3 :\overset{\cdot\cdot}{\underset{\cdot\cdot}{Cl}}:^{-}}_{ScCl_3}$

(c) $2 \cdot \overset{\cdot}{Al} \cdot \; + \; 3 \cdot \overset{\cdot\cdot}{\underset{}{S}} \cdot \; \longrightarrow \; \underbrace{2Al^{3+} \; + \; 3 :\overset{\cdot\cdot}{\underset{\cdot\cdot}{S}}:^{2-}}_{Al_2S_3}$

9-10 (a) $Ru^{2+}([Kr]4d^{6})$
     (b) $W^{3+}([Xe]4f^{14}5d^{3})$
     (c) $Pd^{2+}([Kr]4d^{8})$
     (d) $Ag^{2+}([Kr]4d^{9})$
     (e) $Ir^{3+}([Xe]4f^{14}5d^{6})$

9-12 (a) 6 d electrons
     (b) 10 d electrons
     (c) 3 d electrons
     (d) 8 d electrons
     (e) 2 d electrons

9-14 (a) $Cu^{+}([Ar]3d^{10})$
     (b) $Ga^{3+}([Ar]3d^{10})$
     (c) $Hg^{2+}([Xe]4f^{14}5d^{10})$
     (d) $Au^{+}([Xe]4f^{14}5d^{10})$

9-16 (a) not isoelectronic   (d) isoelectronic
     (b) isoelectronic   (e) isoelectronic
     (c) not isoelectronic   (f) not isoelectronic

9-18 (a) AlI_3 (d) $BaBr_2$
     (b) NaF (e) K_2S
     (c) CaO

9-20 (a) $PbCl_2$ (d) MoF_3
     (b) Bi_2S_3 (e) Co_2O_3
     (c) FeO

9-22 $Al^{3+} < Mg^{2+} < Na^{+} < F^{-} < O^{2-}$

9-24 (a) 212 pm   Be—Cl distance
         424 pm   Cl—Cl distance
     (b) 218 pm
     (c) 249 pm

9-26 267%

9-28 (a) K^+ and I^- ions
(b) Cd^{2+} and Br^- ions
(c) Ca^{2+} and OH^- ions
(d) Ni^{2+} and Cl^- ions
(e) Li^+ and Br^- ions

9-30 (a) C_3H_7OH, nonelectrolyte
(b) KNO_3, strong electrolyte
(c) $HClO$, weak electrolyte
(d) Na_2SO_3, strong electrolyte

9-32 $K > Na > Li > Ca > Al$ (Calcium and aluminum are very close.)

9-34 Recall that metals lose electrons to form noble-gas or pseudo-noble-gas electron configurations, which are relatively stable electron configurations. Metals cannot form such electron configurations by gaining electrons, and thus all metals have negative electron affinities.

9-36 (a) 71 kJ (b) 201 kJ (c) 196 kJ

9-38 (a) 595 kJ (b) -15 kJ (c) 234 kJ

9-40 -1.00×10^{-18} J

9-42 $70 \, kJ \cdot mol^{-1}$ released

9-44 $4 \, kJ \cdot mol^{-1}$ absorbed

9-46

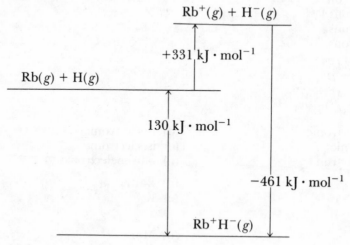

$Rb^+(g) + H^-(g)$

$+331 \, kJ \cdot mol^{-1}$

$Rb(g) + H(g)$

$130 \, kJ \cdot mol^{-1}$

$-461 \, kJ \cdot mol^{-1}$

$Rb^+H^-(g)$

9-48 $\Delta H^\circ_{rxn} = -392$ kJ

9-50 $\Delta H^\circ_{rxn} = -90$ kJ

9-52 $\Delta \bar{H}^\circ_{vap} = 264 \, kJ \cdot mol^{-1}$

F   ANSWERS TO THE SELF-TEST

1 $1s^2 2s^2 2p^6$ or [Ne]

2 $1s^2 2s^2 2p^6 3s^2 3p^6$ or [Ar]

3 Na^+ ions and Cl^- ions

4 ionic

5 $BaCl_2$

6 $Ba\cdot + 2\,:\!\overset{..}{\underset{..}{Cl}}\!\cdot \longrightarrow :\!\overset{..}{\underset{..}{Cl}}\!:^-$
$+ Ba^{2+} + :\!\overset{..}{\underset{..}{Cl}}\!:^- \longrightarrow BaCl_2$

7 two; noble-gas electron

8 two; noble-gas electron

9 one; pseudo-noble-gas electron

10 three; the outer electron configuration $ns^2np^6(n + 1)s^2nd^{10}$

11 true

12 true

13 false (Cations are smaller and anions are larger than the parent atoms.)

14 larger; of the additional electron

15 smaller; of the smaller number of electrons

16 false

17 $Na^+(aq)$ and $Cl^-(aq)$

18 true

19 false

20 false (Weak electrolytes are only weakly conductive.)

21 false (Weak electrolytes are only partially ionized.)

22 strong

23 weak

24 non-

25 the liquid consists of Na^+ and Cl^- ions

26 neutral NaCl ion pairs

27 Na^+ and Cl^- ions in an ordered array

28 Na^+ and Cl^- ions

29 true

30 false (Energy is released in the process $F(g) + e^- \to F^-(g)$.)

31 positive

32 Coulomb's

33 more

34 $E = (2.31 \times 10^{-16}\,\text{J} \cdot \text{pm})\,Z_1Z_2/d$; Z_1 and Z_2 are the ionic chargers and d is the distance between the ion centers in picometers.

35 less; ions

36 (a) the ionization energy of $Na(g)$
   (b) the electron affinity of $Cl(g)$
   (c) the coulombic energy of the Na^+Cl^- ion pair

37 released

38 negative (The lattice is more stable than the gaseous ions.)

39 exothermic

40 (a) the sublimation of $Li(s)$:
       $Li(s) \longrightarrow Li(g)$
   (b) the ionization of $Li(g)$:
       $Li(g) \longrightarrow Li^+(g) + e^-$
   (c) the dissociation of $F_2(g)$:
       $\frac{1}{2}F_2(g) \longrightarrow F(g)$
   (d) the formation of $F^-(g)$ from $F(g)$:
       $F(g) + e^- \longrightarrow F^-(g)$
   (e) the formation of $LiF(s)$:
       $Li^+(g) + F^-(g) \longrightarrow LiF(s)$

41 $Li(s) + \frac{1}{2}F_2(g) \longrightarrow LiF(s)$

42 $Na^+(g) + Cl^-(g) \longrightarrow NaCl(s)$ or bringing the isolated ions into the ionic crystal lattice.

10 / Lewis Formulas

Formal charges are determined by a set of rules and do not necessarily represent the actual charges on the atoms.

The formal charge on an atom is given by Equation (10-1):

$$\begin{pmatrix} \text{formal charge} \\ \text{on an atom in a} \\ \text{Lewis formula} \end{pmatrix} = \begin{pmatrix} \text{total number of} \\ \text{valence electrons} \\ \text{in the free atom} \end{pmatrix} - \begin{pmatrix} \text{total number} \\ \text{of lone pair} \\ \text{electrons} \end{pmatrix} - \frac{1}{2} \begin{pmatrix} \text{total number} \\ \text{of shared} \\ \text{electrons} \end{pmatrix}$$

10-7 Resonance can be used to predict relative bond lengths in molecules.

When it is possible to write two or more satisfactory Lewis formulas *without altering the positions of the nuclei,* the actual formula is viewed as an average or a superposition of the individual formulas.

Each of the individual Lewis formulas is said to be a resonance form and the phenomenon itself is called resonance.

10-8 Formal charge can be used to choose a preferred Lewis formula.

The preferred Lewis formula has the lowest formal charges.

10-9 The octet rule fails for species with an odd number of electrons.

A free radical has one or more unpaired electrons.

An electron-deficient compound does not have enough valence electrons to satisfy the octet rule for each atom.

A coordinate-covalent bond is a covalent bond that is formed when one atom contributes both electrons to the covalent bond.

A donor-acceptor complex results from a coordinate-covalent bond.

10-10 Atoms in the third row of the periodic table can accommodate more than eight electrons in their valence shells.

Some atoms expand their valence shell by using their *d* orbitals.

10-11 Most chemical bonds are intermediate between purely ionic and purely covalent.

Electronegativity is a measure of the force with which an atom attracts the electrons in its covalent bonds.

Figure 10-5 gives the electronegativities of the elements.

Electronegativities tend to decrease going down a column and to increase going across from left to right in a row in the periodic table (Figure 10-6).

If the electronegativities of the two atoms joined by a covalent bond differ, then the electrons in the bond are not shared equally.

A polar bond occurs when the electrons in the covalent bond are attracted to the more electronegative atom.

The electrons in a nonpolar bond are shared equally by the two atoms.

10-12 Lewis formulas do not indicate the shapes of molecules.

The dipole moment of a bond is a measure of the polarity of a bond.

A dipole moment has both magnitude and direction.

CO_2 is a linear molecule and has no dipole moment (Figure 10-7).

H_2O is a bent molecule and has a dipole moment (Figure 10-8).

B   SELF-TEST

1   A covalent bond results when electrons are _____ between two atoms.

2   The covalent bond in a Lewis formula of a molecule is represented as _____.

3   A pair of electrons that is not shared between two atoms is called _____.

4   The Lewis formula is I_2 is _____.

5   The constituent units of a molecular crystal are _____.

6   A molecular crystal has a higher melting point than an ionic crystal. *True/False*

7   The attraction between the molecules of a molecular crystal is stronger than the attraction between the ions in an ionic crystal. *True/False*

8   Bond length is _____.

9   An oxygen atom usually forms _____ covalent bonds.

10   The octet rule states that _____.

11   The octet rule always works for carbon, oxygen, nitrogen, and fluorine. *True/False*

12   The hydrogen atom does not obey the octet rule because _____.

13   A hydrogen atom may form _____ covalent bond(s).

14   A double bond occurs when two atoms share _____ electrons.

15   The Lewis formula for CO_2 is _____.

16   A double bond can occur only when the two atoms are the same. *True/False*

17   A triple bond occurs when two atoms share _____ electrons.

18   A triple bond can occur only when the two atoms are the same. *True/False*

19   The Lewis formula for N_2 is _____.

20   The atoms in a polyatomic ion are joined by ionic bonds. *True/False*

21   The formal charge of an atom is a charge _____.

22   The formal charge of an atom in a polyatomic species represents the actual charge on the atom. *True/False*

23 When it is possible to write two or more Lewis formulas for a molecule or ion without altering the positions of the nuclei, the actual structure is _____ .

24 Each of the individual Lewis formulas in question 23 is said to be a _____ .

25 Due to resonance in the nitrite ion, NO_2^-, the bond lengths of the two N—O bonds are _____ .

26 The N—O bonds in the nitrite ion, NO_2^-, are both single bonds. *True/False*

27 A free radical is a species in which _____ _____ .

28 A free radical must contain an odd number of electrons. *True/False*

29 An electron-deficient compound is a compound that _____ _____ .

30 An atom in a compound may have more than eight electrons in its valence shell. *True/False*

31 The electrons in all covalent bonds are shared equally by the two atoms. *True/False*

32 Electronegativity is a measure of _____ _____ .

33 Electronegativities increase from _____ to _____ across the second and third rows of the periodic table.

34 The most electronegative atom is _____ .

35 The oxygen atom is (*more/less*) electronegative than the carbon atom.

36 The electrons in a covalent bond are shared equally by the two atoms when the _____ .

37 A polar bond occurs when _____ _____ .

38 When the bond between two atoms is a polar bond, one of the atoms has a _____ charge and the other has a _____ charge.

39 The symbol $\delta +$ in the Lewis formula $\overset{\delta+}{H}—\overset{\delta-}{\ddot{C}l}:$ represents _____ _____ .

40 The dipole moment of a bond is a measure of _____ .

41 A dipole moment has both _____ and _____ .

42 A nonpolar molecule has no net dipole moment. *True/False*

C   CALCULATIONS YOU SHOULD KNOW HOW TO DO

There are not many calculations in this chapter. The determination of formal charge by means of Equation 10-1 is the only type of numerical problem in the chapter. See Example 10-9.

D   SOLUTIONS TO THE ODD-NUMBERED PROBLEMS

10-1   The electron-dot formulas of the two fluorine atoms are

$$:\overset{..}{\underset{..}{F}}\cdot \qquad \cdot \overset{..}{\underset{..}{F}}:$$

If we join these two fluorine atoms together by sharing a pair of electrons, then both fluorine atoms will have a noble-gas electron configuration and the Lewis formula of F_2 is

$$:\overset{..}{\underset{..}{F}}:\overset{..}{\underset{..}{F}}:$$

or

$$:\overset{..}{\underset{..}{F}}-\overset{..}{\underset{..}{F}}:$$

The electron-dot formulas of iodine atoms are similar to fluorine atoms, and so we obtain

$$:\overset{..}{\underset{..}{I}}-\overset{..}{\underset{..}{I}}:$$

Note that there are 7 valence electrons in each atom and 7 pairs of electrons in the resulting molecule.

10-3   (a) Because the phosphorus atom is the unique atom in PCl_3, we assume that the phosphorus atom will be a central atom and write

$$:\overset{..}{\underset{..}{Cl}}\cdot \quad \cdot \overset{.}{P}\cdot \quad \cdot \overset{..}{\underset{..}{Cl}}:$$

$$:\overset{.}{\underset{..}{Cl}}:$$

We join the atoms by sharing electron pairs and obtain

$$:\overset{..}{\underset{..}{Cl}}-\overset{..}{P}-\overset{..}{\underset{..}{Cl}}:$$
$$|$$
$$:\overset{..}{Cl}:$$

Note that there are 26 valence electrons in the constituent atoms and 13 electron pairs in the molecule.

(b) Because the silicon atom is unique in SiF_4, we assume that it is a central atom and write

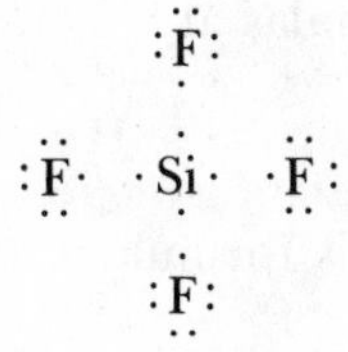

$$:\ddot{F}:$$
$$:\dot{F}\cdot \quad \cdot \dot{Si}\cdot \quad \cdot \dot{F}:$$
$$:\ddot{F}:$$

We join the atoms by sharing electron pairs and write

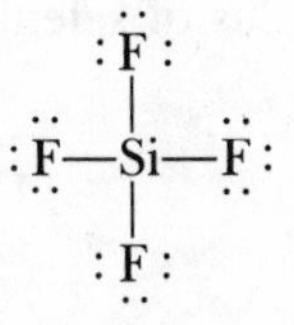

$$:\ddot{F}:$$
$$| \quad$$
$$:\ddot{F}-\ddot{Si}-\ddot{F}:$$
$$|$$
$$:\ddot{F}:$$

Note that there are 32 valence electrons in the constituent atoms and 16 electron pairs in the molecule.

(c) By assuming that the nitrogen is a central atom, we obtain

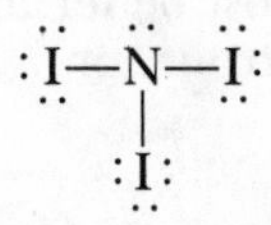

$$:\ddot{I}-N-\ddot{I}:$$
$$|$$
$$:\ddot{I}:$$

There are 26 valence electrons in the constituent atoms and 13 electron pairs in the molecule.

10-5 Because the phosphorus atom is unique in PH_3, we assume that it is a central atom and write

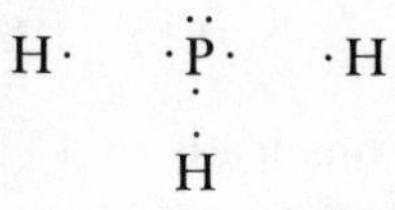

$$H\cdot \quad \cdot \dot{P}\cdot \quad \cdot H$$
$$H$$

Joining the atoms by sharing the electron pair, we get

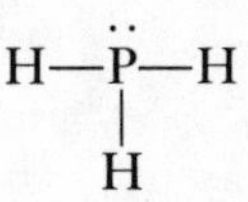

$$H-\ddot{P}-H$$
$$|$$
$$H$$

The electron-dot formulas of arsenic and antimony are similar to that of phosphorus, and so we have

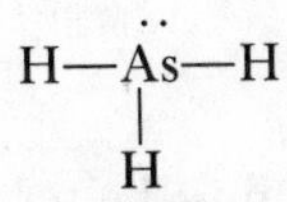

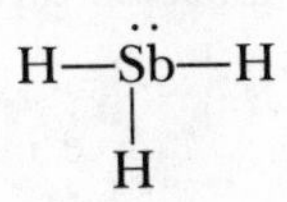

$$H-\ddot{As}-H$$
$$|$$
$$H$$

$$H-\ddot{Sb}-H$$
$$|$$
$$H$$

In each case there are 8 valence electrons in the constituent atoms and 4 electron pairs in the molecule.

10-7   The electron-dot formulas are

$$H\cdot \qquad \cdot \overset{\cdot\cdot}{S}\cdot \qquad \cdot H$$

and the resulting Lewis formula is

$$H-\overset{\cdot\cdot}{\underset{\cdot\cdot}{S}}-H$$

The electron-dot formulas of selenium and tellurium are similar to that of sulfur, and so we have

$$H-\overset{\cdot\cdot}{\underset{\cdot\cdot}{Se}}-H$$

$$H-\overset{\cdot\cdot}{\underset{\cdot\cdot}{Te}}-H$$

In each case there are 8 valence electrons in the constituent atoms and 4 electron pairs in the molecule.

10-9   The hydrogen atoms must be terminal atoms in the Lewis formula. There is a total of 14 valence electrons, or 7 electron pairs, in the molecule. The Lewis formula is

$$H-\overset{\cdot\cdot}{\underset{\cdot\cdot}{O}}-\overset{\cdot\cdot}{\underset{\cdot\cdot}{O}}-H$$

10-11   Assume that the nitrogen atom is central to obtain

$$:\overset{\cdot\cdot}{\underset{\cdot\cdot}{Cl}}-\overset{\cdot\cdot}{N}-\overset{\cdot\cdot}{\underset{\cdot\cdot}{Cl}}:$$
$$\underset{:\overset{}{\underset{\cdot\cdot}{Cl}}:}{|}$$

10-13   (a) Eight valence electrons leads to 4 electron pairs in the molecule

$$\begin{array}{c} H \\ | \\ H-C-H \\ | \\ H \end{array}$$

(b)

$$\begin{array}{c} H \\ | \\ H-C-\overset{\cdot\cdot}{\underset{\cdot\cdot}{F}}: \\ | \\ H \end{array}$$

(c)   The hydrogen atoms must be terminal atoms, and so

$$\begin{array}{c} H \\ | \\ H-C-\overset{\cdot\cdot}{N}-H \\ | \quad\; | \\ H \;\; H \end{array}$$

10-15 The hydrogen atoms must be terminal atoms and so

$$
\begin{array}{c c c}
\text{H} & \text{H} & \text{H} \\
| & | & | \\
\text{H---C---C---C---H} \\
| & | & | \\
\text{H} & \text{H} & \text{H}
\end{array}
\qquad \text{home heating gas}
$$

propane

There are 20 valence electrons, or 10 electron pairs, in C_3H_8. For C_4H_{10} we have

$$
\begin{array}{c c c c}
\text{H} & \text{H} & \text{H} & \text{H} \\
| & | & | & | \\
\text{H---C---C---C---C---H} \\
| & | & | & | \\
\text{H} & \text{H} & \text{H} & \text{H}
\end{array}
\qquad \text{fuel in cigarette lighters}
$$

butane

and for C_8H_{18} we have

$$
\begin{array}{c c c c c c c c}
\text{H} & \text{H} & \text{H} & \text{H} & \text{H} & \text{H} & \text{H} & \text{H} \\
| & | & | & | & | & | & | & | \\
\text{H---C---C---C---C---C---C---C---C---H} \\
| & | & | & | & | & | & | & | \\
\text{H} & \text{H} & \text{H} & \text{H} & \text{H} & \text{H} & \text{H} & \text{H}
\end{array}
\qquad \text{a component of gasoline}
$$

octane

10-17 Line up the carbon and oxygen atoms as they appear in the chemical formula and place the hydrogen atoms on them in terminal positions to get

(a)

$$
\begin{array}{c c}
\text{H} & \text{H} \\
| & | \\
\text{H---C---C---\ddot{O}---H} \\
| & | \\
\text{H} & \text{H}
\end{array}
$$

ethyl alcohol

Note that there are 20 valence electrons in the constituent atoms and 10 electron pairs in CH_3CH_2OH. Similarly, we get

(b)

$$
\begin{array}{c c c}
\text{H} & \text{H} & \text{H} \\
| & | & | \\
\text{H---C---C---C---\ddot{O}---H} \\
| & | & | \\
\text{H} & \text{H} & \text{H}
\end{array}
$$

n-propyl alcohol

and

(c)

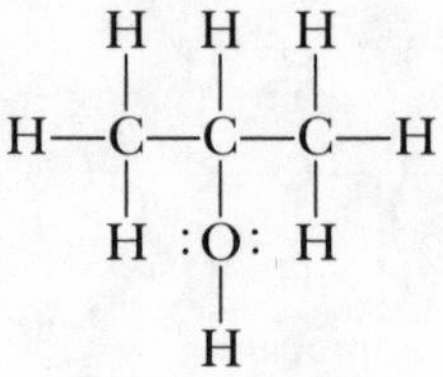

$$H-\overset{\displaystyle H}{\underset{\displaystyle H}{C}}-\overset{\displaystyle H}{\underset{:O:}{C}}-\overset{\displaystyle H}{\underset{\displaystyle H}{C}}-H$$

isopropyl alcohol

10-19 There are only two possibilities. A chlorine atom is bonded to each carbon atom

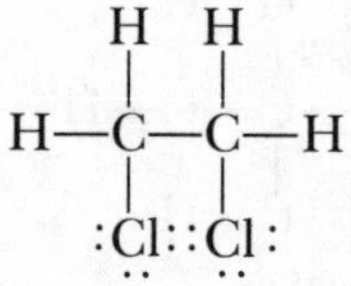

$$H-\overset{\displaystyle H}{\underset{:\ddot{C}l:}{C}}-\overset{\displaystyle H}{\underset{:\ddot{C}l:}{C}}-H$$

or both chlorine atoms are bonded to one carbon atom

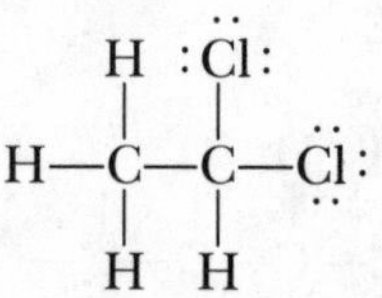

$$H-\overset{\displaystyle H}{\underset{\displaystyle H}{C}}-\overset{:\ddot{C}l:}{\underset{\displaystyle H}{C}}-\ddot{C}l:$$

Two molecules that have the same chemical formula ($C_2H_4Cl_2$) but different structures are called *structural isomers*.

10-21 The Lewis formulas for the compounds are

(a) 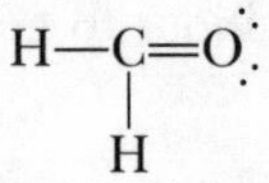 $H-\overset{\displaystyle }{\underset{\displaystyle H}{C}}=\ddot{O}:$

(b) 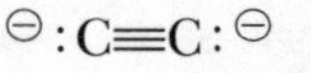 $^{\ominus}:C\equiv C:^{\ominus}$

Therefore, C_2^{2-} has a triple bond.

(c) 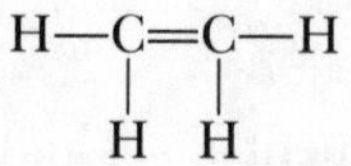 $H-\overset{\displaystyle }{\underset{\displaystyle H}{C}}=\overset{\displaystyle }{\underset{\displaystyle H}{C}}-H$

10-23 (a) Line up the carbon and nitrogen atoms as they appear in the chemical formula, remembering that the hydrogen atoms are terminal. The carbon and nitrogen atoms must satisfy the octet rule. Thus we write

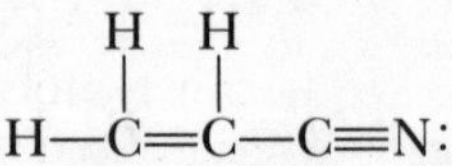

$$H-\overset{\displaystyle H}{\underset{\displaystyle }{C}}=\overset{\displaystyle H}{\underset{\displaystyle }{C}}-C\equiv N:$$

There are 20 valence electrons, or 10 electron pairs, in this molecule.

(b) The nitrogen atom is central, and there are 18 valence electrons. Therefore, we get

$$\ddot{\overset{..}{O}}=\ddot{N}-\ddot{\overset{..}{O}}-H$$

(c) SiO_2 is analogous to CO_2

$$\ddot{\overset{..}{O}}=Si=\ddot{\overset{..}{O}}$$

10-25 There are 18 valence electrons, or 9 electron pairs, in HCOOH. The only way to satisfy the octet rule for the carbon and oxygen atoms using 9 electron pairs is to write

$$H-\overset{\displaystyle \ddot{O}}{\underset{\displaystyle \|}{C}}-\ddot{\overset{..}{O}}-H$$

The —COOH group, which has the Lewis formula

$$-\overset{\displaystyle \ddot{O}}{\underset{\displaystyle \|}{C}}-\ddot{\overset{..}{O}}-H$$

is characteristic of organic acids (see Problem 10-26).

10-27 The chemical formula CH_3COCH_3 implies that each group of three hydrogen atoms is attached to a terminal carbon atom in a CH_3 group. The only way to satisfy the octet rule for carbon and oxygen atoms using 12 electron pairs is to write

$$H-\underset{\displaystyle H}{\overset{\displaystyle H}{C}}-\overset{\displaystyle \ddot{O}}{\underset{\displaystyle \|}{C}}-\underset{\displaystyle H}{\overset{\displaystyle H}{C}}-H$$

10-29 Line up the carbon atoms as they appear in the chemical formula and add the hydrogen atoms. There are 9 electron pairs to distribute, and each carbon atom must satisfy the octet rule. Therefore, we obtain

$$H-\underset{\displaystyle H}{\overset{\displaystyle H}{C}}-\overset{\displaystyle H}{C}=\overset{\displaystyle H}{C}-H$$

10-31 The hydrogen atoms are terminal atoms. There are 12 valence electrons, or 6 electron pairs, in N_2H_2. The nitrogen atoms must satisfy the octet rule, and so

$$H-\ddot{N}=\ddot{N}-H$$

10-33   There are 18 valence electrons, or 9 electron pairs, in $HCOO^-$. Two resonance forms are

$$H-\overset{\overset{\displaystyle \cdot\ddot{O}\cdot}{\|}}{C}-\ddot{\underset{\cdot\cdot}{O}}:^{\ominus} \longleftrightarrow H-\overset{\overset{\displaystyle ^{\ominus}:\ddot{O}:}{|}}{C}=\ddot{\underset{\cdot\cdot}{O}}:$$

The superposition of these two resonance forms gives

$$\left[H-\overset{\overset{\displaystyle \cdot\ddot{O}\cdot}{\|}}{C}\!\!=\!\!\ddot{\underset{\cdot\cdot}{O}}\cdot \right]^{-}$$

The two carbon-oxygen bonds in $HCOO^-$ are equivalent; they have the same bond length and the same bond energy.

10-35   The three resonance forms are

$$^{\ominus}:\ddot{\underset{\cdot\cdot}{O}}-\overset{\overset{\displaystyle \cdot\ddot{O}\cdot}{\|}}{C}-\ddot{\underset{\cdot\cdot}{O}}:^{\ominus} \longleftrightarrow \cdot\ddot{\underset{\cdot\cdot}{O}}=\overset{\overset{\displaystyle :\ddot{O}:^{\ominus}}{|}}{C}-\ddot{\underset{\cdot\cdot}{O}}:^{\ominus} \longleftrightarrow ^{\ominus}:\ddot{\underset{\cdot\cdot}{O}}-\overset{\overset{\displaystyle :\ddot{O}:^{\ominus}}{|}}{C}=\ddot{\underset{\cdot\cdot}{O}}\cdot$$

The superposition of these three resonance forms is

$$\left[:\ddot{\underset{\cdot\cdot}{O}}\!\!=\!\!\overset{\overset{\displaystyle \cdot\ddot{O}\cdot}{\|}}{C}\!\!=\!\!\ddot{\underset{\cdot\cdot}{O}}: \right]^{2-}$$

The three bonds in CO_3^{2-} are equivalent; they have the same bond length and the same bond energy.

10-37   If the nitrogen atoms are adjacent, then we find two resonance forms

$$^{\ominus}\cdot\ddot{N}\!\!=\!\!\overset{\oplus}{N}\!\!=\!\!\ddot{O}\cdot \longleftrightarrow :N\!\!\equiv\!\!\overset{\oplus}{N}\!\!-\!\!\ddot{\underset{\cdot\cdot}{O}}:^{\ominus}$$

If the oxygen atom is central, then we find

$$\ddot{\underset{\cdot\cdot}{N}}\!\!=\!\!\overset{\overset{\displaystyle \ominus}{\underset{\displaystyle}{O}}}{\overset{2+}{O}}\!\!=\!\!\ddot{\underset{\cdot\cdot}{N}}\cdot$$

The formal charges in NON are larger than in NNO, and so we predict that the formula is NNO.

10-39   (a)   The thiocarbonate ion CS_3^{2-} is similar to the carbonate ion (Problem 10-35). Three Lewis formulas are

$$^{\ominus}:\ddot{\underset{\cdot\cdot}{S}}-\overset{\overset{\displaystyle}{|}}{\underset{\underset{\displaystyle \cdot\ddot{S}:^{\ominus}}{|}}{C}}=\ddot{S}\cdot \longleftrightarrow \cdot\ddot{S}=\overset{\overset{\displaystyle}{|}}{\underset{\underset{\displaystyle :\ddot{S}:^{\ominus}}{|}}{C}}-\ddot{\underset{\cdot\cdot}{S}}:^{\ominus} \longleftrightarrow ^{\ominus}:\ddot{\underset{\cdot\cdot}{S}}-\overset{\overset{\displaystyle}{|}}{\underset{\underset{\displaystyle \cdot\ddot{S}\cdot}{\|}}{C}}-\ddot{\underset{\cdot\cdot}{S}}:^{\ominus}$$

and their superposition is

$$\left[\; \ddot{S}=\overset{\overset{\displaystyle \ddot{S}}{|}}{C}=\ddot{S} \; \right]^{2-}$$

(b) $\ddot{O}=\overset{..}{C}-\overset{..}{C}=\ddot{O}$ ⟷ $^{\ominus}:\ddot{O}-\overset{\overset{\displaystyle \ddot{O}\,:\ddot{O}:^{\ominus}}{|}}{C}-\overset{..}{C}=\ddot{O}$ ⟷ $^{\ominus}:\ddot{O}:\;\overset{..}{O}$ $\ddot{O}=\overset{..}{C}-\overset{..}{C}-\ddot{O}:^{\ominus}$ ⟷

$$^{\ominus}:\ddot{O}-\overset{\overset{\displaystyle \ddot{O}}{\|}}{C}-\overset{\overset{\displaystyle \ddot{O}}{\|}}{C}-\ddot{O}:^{\ominus}$$

Their superposition is

$$\left[\; :\ddot{O}=\overset{\overset{\displaystyle \ddot{O}}{\|}}{C}-\overset{\overset{\displaystyle \ddot{O}}{\|}}{C}=\ddot{O}: \; \right]^{2-}$$

10-41 (a) NO_2 contains 23 electrons and 17 valence electrons. Lewis formulas for NO_2 are

$$\cdot\ddot{O}-N=\ddot{O}: \; \longleftrightarrow \; :\ddot{O}=N-\ddot{O}\cdot \qquad \text{odd electron}$$

(b) CO contains 14 electrons and 10 valence electrons. The Lewis formula for CO is

$$:\overset{\ominus}{C}\equiv\overset{\oplus}{O}:$$

(c) O_3^- contains 25 electrons and 19 valence electrons. Lewis formulas for O_3^- are

$$\ddot{O}-\overset{\overset{\displaystyle \ominus}{}}{\ddot{O}}-\ddot{O}: \; \longleftrightarrow \; :\ddot{O}-\overset{\overset{\displaystyle \ominus}{}}{\ddot{O}}-\ddot{O}\cdot \qquad \text{odd electron}$$

(d) O_2^- contains 17 electrons and 13 valence electrons. Lewis formulas for O_2^- are

$$^{\ominus}\cdot\ddot{O}-\ddot{O}\cdot \; \longleftrightarrow \; \cdot\ddot{O}-\ddot{O}:^{\ominus} \qquad \text{odd electron}$$

(e) SO_2 contains 24 electrons and 18 valence electrons. Lewis formulas for SO_2 are

$$:\ddot{O}=\overset{\oplus}{S}-\overset{\ominus}{\ddot{O}}: \; \longleftrightarrow \; ^{\ominus}:\ddot{O}-\overset{\oplus}{S}=\ddot{O}: \; \longleftrightarrow \; :\ddot{O}=S=\ddot{O}:$$

10-43 Write the C, N, N, O atoms in a row as suggested by the chemical formula and add the hydrogen atoms to the carbon atom. There is an odd number of valence electrons (23), and the Lewis formula is

$$H-\overset{\underset{\displaystyle |}{H}}{\underset{\underset{\displaystyle H}{|}}{C}}-\ddot{N}-\ddot{N}=\ddot{O}\cdot$$

Methylnitrosamine is a free radical.

10-45 (a) $H-\overset{\underset{\displaystyle |}{H}}{\underset{\underset{\displaystyle H}{|}}{C}}\cdot + \cdot\overset{\underset{\displaystyle |}{H}}{\underset{\underset{\displaystyle H}{|}}{C}}-H \longrightarrow H-\overset{\underset{\displaystyle |}{H}}{\underset{\underset{\displaystyle H}{|}}{C}}-\overset{\underset{\displaystyle |}{H}}{\underset{\underset{\displaystyle H}{|}}{C}}-H$

(b) $\cdot\ddot{N}\cdot + \cdot\ddot{N}=\ddot{O}\cdot \longrightarrow \cdot\overset{\ominus}{\ddot{N}}=\overset{\oplus}{N}=\ddot{O}\cdot$ (See Problem 10-37)

10-47 (a) There are 48 valence electrons, or 24 electron pairs in PCl_6^-. Putting the phosphorus atom as the central atom, we have

$$\begin{array}{ccc} \ddot{Cl} & & \ddot{Cl} \\ & \overset{\ominus}{} & \\ \ddot{Cl}-P-\ddot{Cl} & & \\ \ddot{Cl} & & \ddot{Cl} \end{array}$$

Notice that phosphorus does not obey the octet rule.

(b) There are 22 valence electrons, or 11 electron pairs, in I_3^-.

$$\overset{\ominus}{\ddot{I}-\ddot{I}-\ddot{I}}$$

(c) There are 24 electron pairs in SiF_6^{2-}. Placing the silicon atom as the central atom, we have

$$\begin{array}{ccc} \ddot{F} & \overset{2-}{} & \ddot{F} \\ \ddot{F}-Si-\ddot{F} & & \\ \ddot{F} & & \ddot{F} \end{array}$$

10-49 There are 22 valence electrons, or 11 electron pairs, in XeF_2. The xenon atom is central, and so

$$\ddot{F}-\ddot{Xe}-\ddot{F}$$

There are 36 valence electrons, or 18 electron pairs, in XeF_4. The xenon atom is central, and so

$$\begin{array}{c} :\ddot{F}: \\ | \\ :\ddot{F}\!-\!\ddot{X}e\!-\!\ddot{F}: \\ | \\ :\ddot{F}: \end{array}$$

There are 50 valence electrons, or 25 electron pairs, in XeF_6. The xenon atom is central, and so

$$\begin{array}{c} \ddot{F}\quad\quad\ddot{F} \\ \diagdown\quad\diagup \\ :\ddot{F}\!-\!\ddot{X}e\!-\!\ddot{F}: \\ \diagup\quad\diagdown \\ \ddot{F}\quad\quad\ddot{F} \end{array}$$

There are 42 valence electrons, or 21 electron pairs, in $XeOF_4$. Placing the xenon atom (the largest atom) at the center gives

$$\begin{array}{c} \ddot{O} \\ \| \\ :\ddot{F}\!-\!\ddot{X}e\!-\!\ddot{F}: \\ \diagup\quad\diagdown \\ \ddot{F}\quad\quad\ddot{F} \end{array}$$

There are 34 valence electrons, or 17 electron pairs, in XeO_2F_2. Placing the xenon atom (the unique atom) central gives

$$\begin{array}{c} \ddot{F}\quad\quad\ddot{F} \\ \diagdown\quad\diagup \\ :\ddot{O}\!=\!\ddot{X}e\!=\!\ddot{O}: \end{array}$$

10-51   (a) 32 valence electrons, 16 electron pairs, nitrogen atom central

$$\begin{array}{c} :\ddot{F}: \\ | \\ :\ddot{F}\!-\!\overset{\oplus}{N}\!-\!\ddot{F}: \\ | \\ :\ddot{F}: \end{array}$$

(b) 34 valence electrons, 17 electron pairs, chlorine atom central

$$\begin{array}{c} \ddot{F}\quad\quad\ddot{F} \\ \diagdown\quad\diagup \\ :\ddot{F}\!-\!Cl\!-\!\ddot{F}: \\ \underset{\oplus}{} \end{array}$$

(c) 8 valence electrons, 4 electron pairs, phosphorus atom central

$$\begin{array}{c} H \\ | \\ H\!-\!\overset{\oplus}{P}\!-\!H \\ | \\ H \end{array}$$

(d) 48 valence electrons, 24 electron pairs, arsenic atom central

(e) 36 valence electrons, 18 electron pairs, bromine atom central

10-53   (a) 26 valence electrons, 13 electron pairs, chlorine atom central

(b) 18 valence electrons, 9 electron pairs, nitrogen atom central

(c) 32 valence electrons, 16 electron pairs, iodine atom central

(d) 20 valence electrons, 10 electron pairs, bromine atom central

(e) 26 valence electrons, 13 electron pairs, sulfur atom central

10-55   (a) 20 valence electrons, 10 electron pairs, sulfur atom central

(b) 34 valence electrons, 17 electron pairs, sulfur atom central

$$:\overset{..}{\underset{..}{Cl}} \diagdown \diagup \overset{..}{\underset{..}{Cl}}:$$
$$:\overset{..}{\underset{..}{Cl}}-S-\overset{..}{Cl}:$$

(c) 48 valence electrons, 24 electron pairs, selenium atom central

$$\overset{..}{\underset{..}{F}} \quad \overset{..}{\underset{..}{F}}$$
$$:\overset{..}{F}-Se-\overset{..}{F}:$$
$$\overset{..}{\underset{..}{F}} \quad \overset{..}{\underset{..}{F}}$$

(d) 40 valence electrons, 20 electron pairs, sulfur atoms central

$$:\overset{..}{F}::\overset{..}{F}:$$
$$| \quad |$$
$$:\overset{..}{F}-S=S-\overset{..}{F}:$$

(e) 26 valence electrons, 13 electron pairs, selenium atoms central

$$:\overset{..}{\underset{..}{Br}}-\overset{..}{Se}-\overset{..}{Se}-\overset{..}{\underset{..}{Br}}:$$

10-57 There are 56 valence electrons, or 28 electron pairs, in $Cr_2O_7^{2-}$. The Lewis formula is

$$\overset{..}{\underset{..}{O}} \qquad \overset{..}{\underset{..}{O}}$$
$$\ominus:\overset{..}{\underset{..}{O}}-\overset{..}{\underset{..}{Cr}}-\overset{..}{\underset{..}{O}}-\overset{..}{\underset{..}{Cr}}-\overset{..}{\underset{..}{O}}:\ominus$$
$$\overset{..}{\underset{..}{O}} \qquad \overset{..}{\underset{..}{O}}$$

plus other resonance forms.

10-59 The Lewis formula of BrCl is

$$:\overset{..}{\underset{..}{Br}}-\overset{..}{\underset{..}{Cl}}:$$

The electronegativity of chlorine is greater than that of bromine, and so we have

$$\overset{\delta+}{:\overset{..}{\underset{..}{Br}}}-\overset{\delta-}{\overset{..}{\underset{..}{Cl}}}:$$

or

$$\xrightarrow{+}$$
$$:\overset{..}{\underset{..}{Br}}-\overset{..}{\underset{..}{Cl}}:$$

10-61 (a) Fluorine is more electronegative than nitrogen, and so we have

$$\overset{\delta+}{}$$
$$\delta-:\overset{..}{\underset{..}{F}}-N-\overset{..}{\underset{..}{F}}:\delta-$$
$$|$$
$$:\overset{..}{\underset{..}{F}}:_{\delta-}$$

(b) Fluorine is more electronegative than oxygen, and so we have

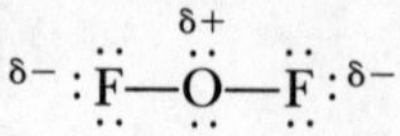

$$\overset{\delta-}{:}\ddot{\text{F}}\overset{..}{\underset{..}{\text{—}}}\overset{\delta+}{\ddot{\text{O}}}\overset{..}{\underset{..}{\text{—}}}\ddot{\text{F}}\overset{\delta-}{:}$$

(c) Oxygen is more electronegative than bromine, and so we have

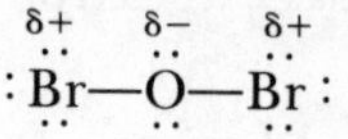

$$\overset{\delta+}{:}\ddot{\text{Br}}\overset{\delta-}{\text{—}}\ddot{\text{O}}\overset{\delta+}{\text{—}}\ddot{\text{Br}}:$$

E   ANSWERS TO THE EVEN-NUMBERED PROBLEMS

10-2 (a) 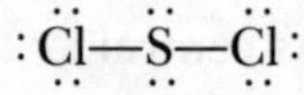 $:\ddot{\text{Cl}}\text{—}\ddot{\text{S}}\text{—}\ddot{\text{Cl}}:$

                 $:\ddot{\text{Cl}}:$

                  $|$

(b) 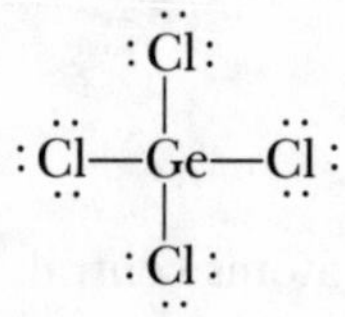 $:\ddot{\text{Cl}}\text{—}\text{Ge}\text{—}\ddot{\text{Cl}}:$

                 $:\ddot{\text{Cl}}:$

(c) 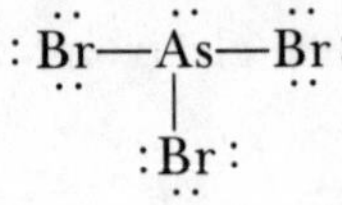 $:\ddot{\text{Br}}\text{—}\ddot{\text{As}}\text{—}\ddot{\text{Br}}:$

                 $:\text{Br}:$

10-4 $:\ddot{\text{F}}\text{—}\ddot{\text{N}}\text{—}\ddot{\text{N}}\text{—}\ddot{\text{F}}:$

with $:\ddot{\text{F}}:$ above each N

10-6 (a) 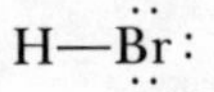 $\text{H}\text{—}\ddot{\text{Br}}:$

(b) 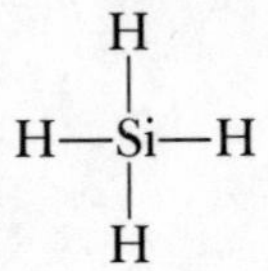 $\text{H}\text{—}\underset{\overset{|}{\text{H}}}{\overset{\text{H}}{\text{Si}}}\text{—}\text{H}$

(c) 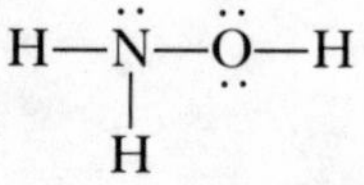 $\text{H}\text{—}\underset{\overset{|}{\text{H}}}{\ddot{\text{N}}}\text{—}\ddot{\text{O}}\text{—}\text{H}$

10-8 $:\ddot{\text{Cl}}\text{—}\ddot{\text{Ti}}\text{—}\ddot{\text{Cl}}:$

with $:\ddot{\text{Cl}}:$ above and below Ti

10-10 $\text{H}\text{—}\overset{\ominus}{\underset{..}{\text{N}}}\text{—}\text{H}$

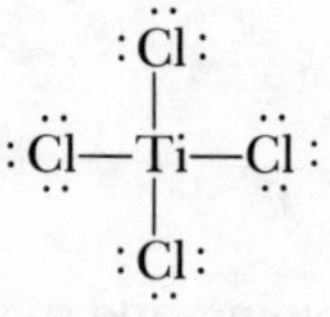

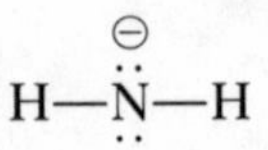

NaNH_2 sodium amide
$\text{Ba(NH}_2)_2$ barium amide

10-12 (S₈ ring structure of sulfur)

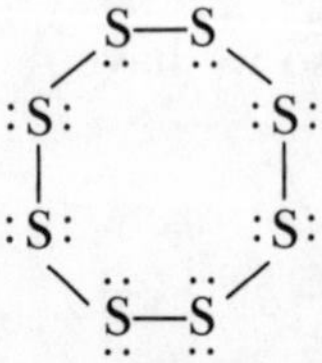

10-14 (a)

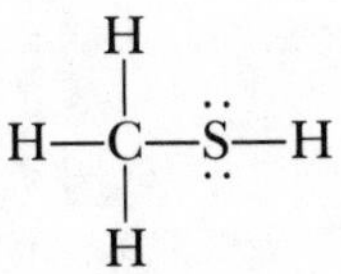

```
        H
        |
   H — C — S̈ — H
        |    ··
        H
```

(b)

```
     H          H
     |          |
H — C — Ö — C — H
     |    ··    |
     H          H
```

(c)

```
   H        H
   |        |
H—C — N̈ — C—H
   |        |
   H        H
   H — C — H
        |
        H
```

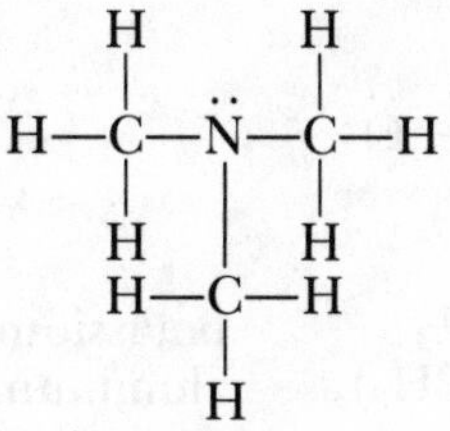

10-16 (a)

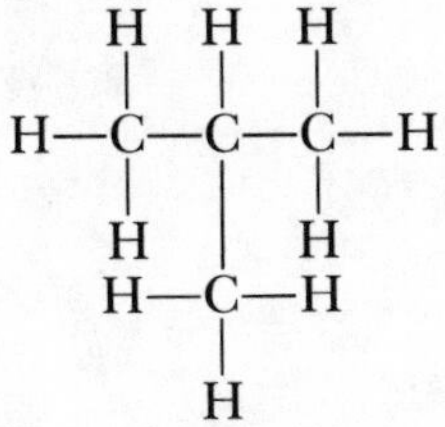

```
   H   H   H
   |   |   |
H—C — C — C—H
   |   |   |
   H   |   H
   H — C — H
        |
        H
```

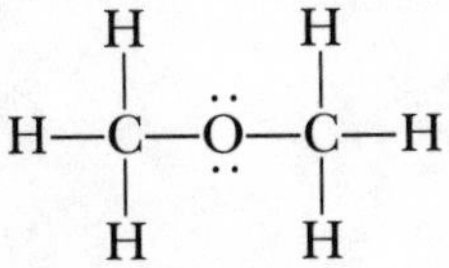

(b)

```
        H
        |
   H — C — H
   H    |   H
   |    |   |
H—C — C — C—H
   |    |   |
   H    |   H
   H — C — H
        |
        H
```

(c)

```
   H   H   H   H
   |   |   |   |
H—C — C — C — C—H
   |   |   |   |
   H   H   |   H
       H — C — H
            |
            H
```

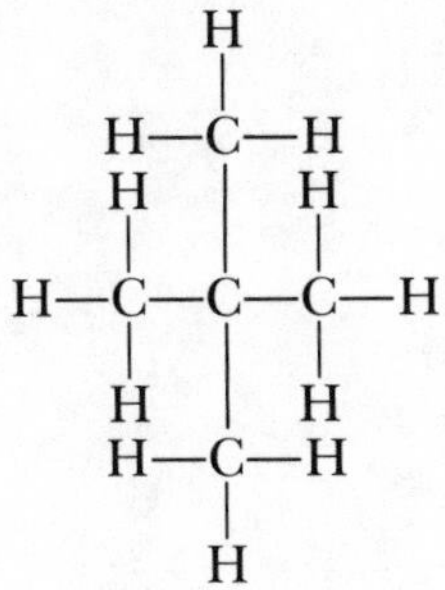

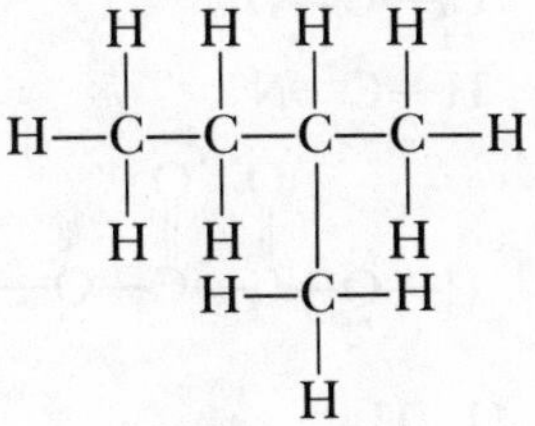

10-18

```
          ··
        :Cl:
         |
   ·· ··
  :Cl—C—Cl:
   ·· |  ··
        :Cl:
          ··
```

```
        H
        |
   ·· ··
  :Cl—C—Cl:
   ·· |  ··
        :Cl:
          ··
```

```
        H
        |
   ·· ··
  :Cl—C—Cl:
   ·· |  ··
        H
```

```
        H
        |
   ·· ··
  H—C—Cl:
        |   ··
        H
```

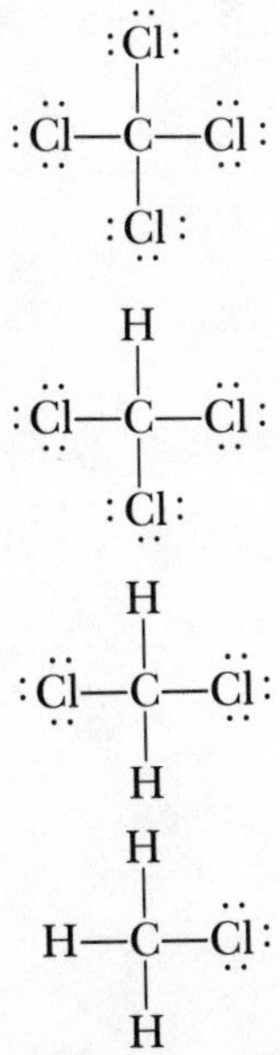

10-20

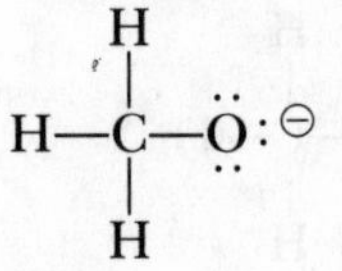

```
      H
      |
H —— C —— O:⁻
      |    ··
      H
```

KOCH₃   potassium methoxide
Al(OCH₃)₃   aluminum methoxide

10-22 (a)

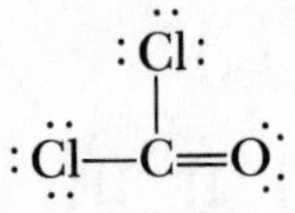

```
         :Cl:
          ··
    ··    |
  :Cl —— C == O:
    ··         ··
```

(b)   H —— C ≡ N:

(c)

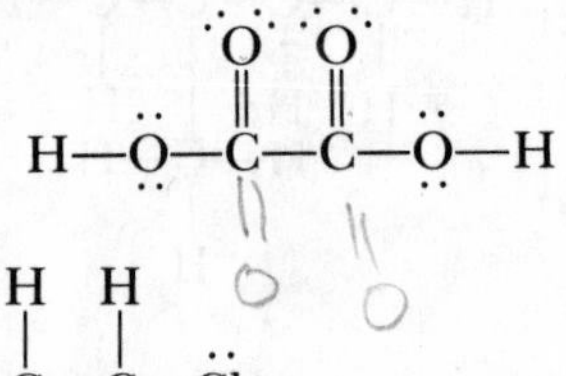

```
          ··  ··
          O   O
          ‖   ‖
  ··      |   |      ··
H—O —— C —— C —— O—H
  ··              ··
```

10-24

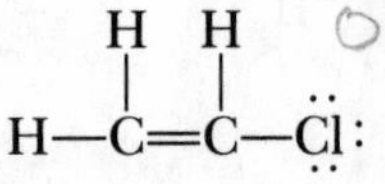

```
  H   H
  |   |    ··
H—C = C—Cl:
          ··
```

10-26

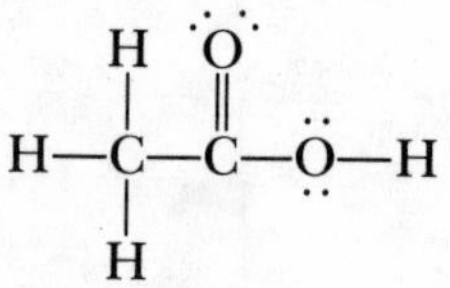

```
  H   ·O·
  |    ‖
H—C —— C —— O—H
  |         ··
  H
```

10-28

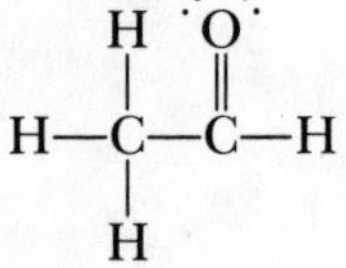

```
  H   ·O·
  |    ‖
H—C —— C —— H
  |
  H
```

10-30

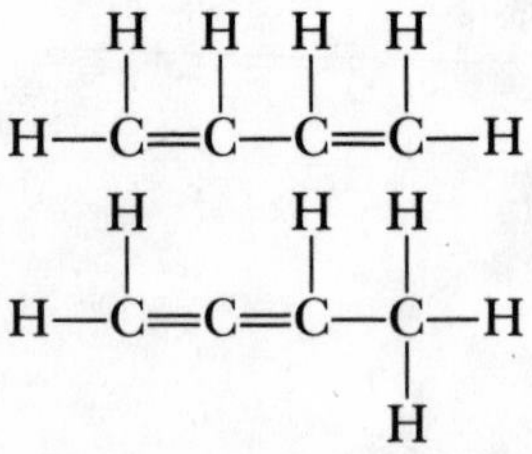

```
  H   H   H   H
  |   |   |   |
H—C = C—C = C—H
```

```
  H   H   H
  |   |   |
H—C = C = C—C—H
              |
              H
```

10-32   :N̈ = N⁺ = N̈—H ; :N̈ = N⁺ = N̈:⁻
        ⊖   ⊕   ⊖   ⊕   ⊖

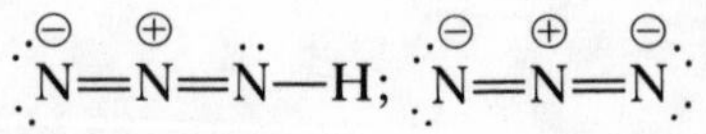

10-34

```
  H  ·O·                   H  :O:⁻
  |   ‖                    |   |
H—C —— C —— O:⁻   ⟷   H—C —— C = O:
  |         ··             |          ··
  H                        H
```

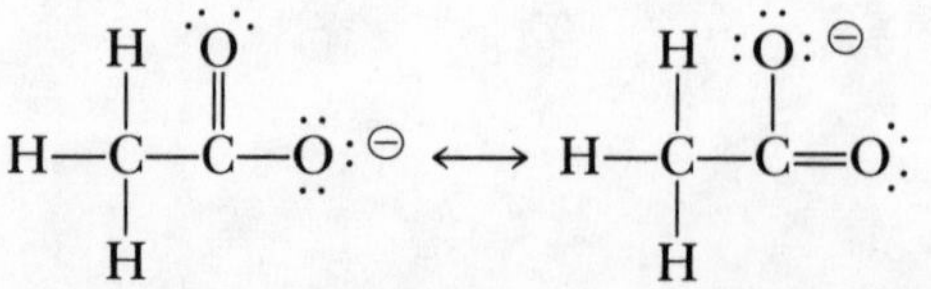

The superposition of these two resonance forms gives

$$\left[\begin{array}{c} \text{H} \quad \ddot{\text{O}}\cdot \\ | \quad\quad || \\ \text{H}-\overset{|}{\underset{|}{\text{C}}}-\text{C}=\ddot{\text{O}}\ddot{} \\ \text{H} \end{array}\right]^{-}$$

The two carbon-oxygen bonds in CH_3COO^- are equivalent; they have the same bond length and the same energy.

10-36 The two resonance forms are

$$\ddot{\text{O}}=\overset{\oplus}{\ddot{\text{O}}}-\ddot{\text{O}}:^{\ominus} \longleftrightarrow {}^{\ominus}:\ddot{\text{O}}-\overset{\oplus}{\ddot{\text{O}}}=\ddot{\text{O}}\ddot{}$$

The superposition of these two resonance forms is

$$\ddot{\text{O}}{=}{=}\ddot{\text{O}}{=}{=}\ddot{\text{O}}\ddot{}$$

The two bonds in O_3 are equivalent; they have the same bond length and the same energy.

10-38 $:\ddot{\text{C}}\text{l}-\ddot{\text{N}}=\ddot{\text{O}}\ddot{}$ or $:\ddot{\text{C}}\text{l}-\overset{\oplus}{\ddot{\text{O}}}=\text{N}\ddot{}^{\ominus}$
(correct formula)

10-40 N_2O $\overset{\ominus}{\ddot{\text{N}}}=\overset{\oplus}{\text{N}}=\ddot{\text{O}}\ddot{} \longleftrightarrow :\text{N}{\equiv}\overset{\oplus}{\text{N}}-\ddot{\text{O}}:^{\ominus}$

NO $\cdot\dot{\text{N}}=\ddot{\text{O}}\ddot{}$

N_2O_3 $\ddot{\text{O}}=\overset{\oplus}{\text{N}}-\ddot{\text{N}}=\ddot{\text{O}}\ddot{} \longleftrightarrow {}^{\ominus}:\ddot{\text{O}}-\overset{\oplus}{\text{N}}-\ddot{\text{N}}=\ddot{\text{O}}\ddot{}$
$\quad\quad\quad :\ddot{\text{O}}:^{\ominus} \quad\quad\quad\quad\quad\quad .\ddot{\text{O}}.$

NO_2 $\cdot\ddot{\text{O}}-\text{N}=\ddot{\text{O}}\ddot{} \longleftrightarrow \ddot{\text{O}}=\text{N}-\ddot{\text{O}}\cdot$

N_2O_4 $\overset{\ominus}{:\ddot{\text{O}}}-\overset{\oplus}{\text{N}}-\overset{\oplus}{\text{N}}-\overset{\ominus}{\ddot{\text{O}}}:$ + other resonance forms
$\quad\quad\quad\quad || \quad\quad ||$
$\quad\quad\quad .\ddot{\text{O}}. \quad .\ddot{\text{O}}.$

N_2O_5 $^{\ominus}:\ddot{\text{O}}-\overset{\oplus}{\text{N}}-\ddot{\text{O}}-\overset{\oplus}{\text{N}}-\ddot{\text{O}}:^{\ominus}$ + other resonance forms
$\quad\quad\quad\quad || \quad\quad\quad ||$
$\quad\quad\quad\quad .\ddot{\text{O}}. \quad\quad .\ddot{\text{O}}.$

10-42 (a) :O=Br=O: + other resonance forms   odd electron
⊕ (on Br)
:O:⊖

(b) :O=S=O: + other resonance forms
⊕ (on S)
:O:⊖

(c) H—N=O:

(d) H—O—O· ⟷ H—O=O: odd electron

(e) :O=S=O: + other resonance forms   odd electron
:O:
⊖:O:

10-44 NO   ·N=O: free radical

NO$_2$ ⊖:O—N=O: ⟷ :O=N—O:⊖   free radical
(⊕ on N)

HO   H—O·   free radical

HNO$_3$:O:⊖ / O=N—O—H ⟷ O / ⊖:O—N—O—H
(⊕ on N)

10-46 (a) H—O· + ·O—H ⟶ H—O—O—H

(b) :Cl· + ·C(H)(H)—H ⟶ :Cl—C(H)(H)—H
    H   H

10-48 (a) Some resonance forms are

:O: :O:⊖ ⟷ :O: :O: ⟷ ⊖:O: :O: ⟷ :O: ⊖:O:
    S   S   S   S
⊖:O: :O: ⟷ ⊖:O: :O:⊖ ⟷ :O: :O:⊖ ⟷ :O: :O:⊖

The superposition of these resonance forms give

$$\left[\begin{array}{c} \ddot{O} \quad \ddot{O} \\ S \\ \ddot{O} \quad \ddot{O} \end{array}\right]^{2-}$$

All four bonds are equivalent; they have the same bond length and the same bond energy.

(b) Some resonance forms are

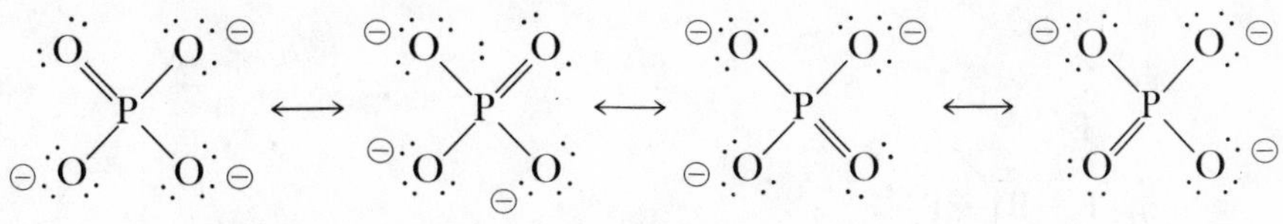

The superposition of these resonance forms is

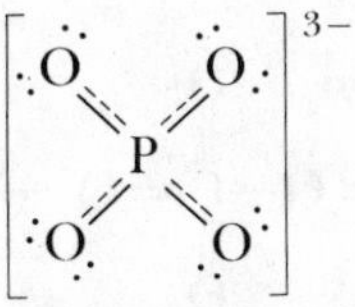

All four bonds are equivalent; they have the same bond length and the same bond energy.

(c) 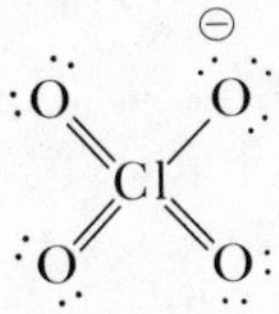   + 3 resonance forms

The superposition formula is

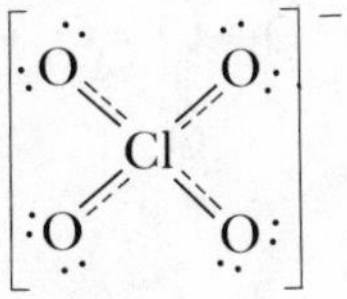

All four bonds are equivalent; they have the same bond length and the same bond energy.

10-50 (a)

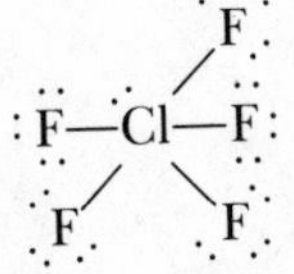

(b)

(c)

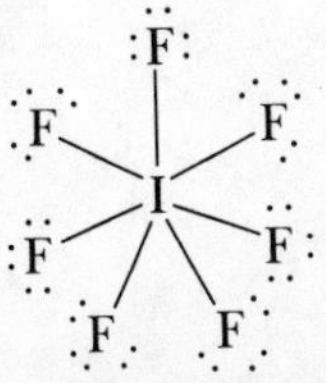

(d) 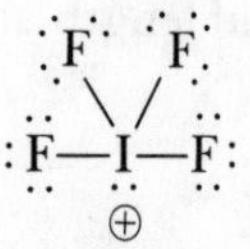
```
     :F̤  :F̤
       \ /
 :F̤—I—F̤:
       ⊕
```

(e) 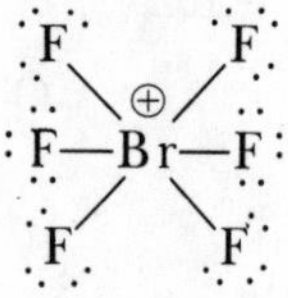
```
   :F̤     :F̤
     \ ⊕ /
 :F̤—Br—F̤:
     /   \
   :F̤     :F̤
```

10-52 (a) 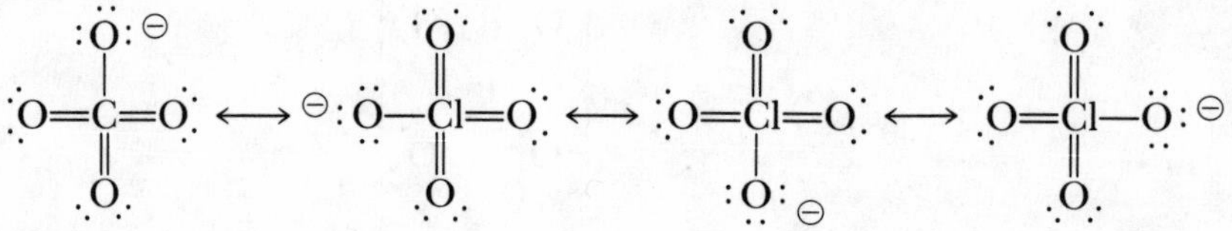
```
     :Ö:⊖              :Ö:              :Ö:              :Ö:
      ‖                 ‖                ‖                ‖
 O̤=C=O̤    ⟷  ⊖:Ö—Cl—Ö̤  ⟷  :O̤=Cl=O̤:  ⟷  :O̤=Cl—Ö:⊖
      |                 |                |                |
     :Ö̤:               :Ö:             :Ö:⊖            :Ö:
                                        
```

or
```
        ⎡      :Ö:      ⎤⁻
        ⎢       ‖       ⎥
        ⎢ :O̤══Cl══O̤:   ⎥
        ⎢       ‖       ⎥
        ⎣      :Ö:      ⎦
```

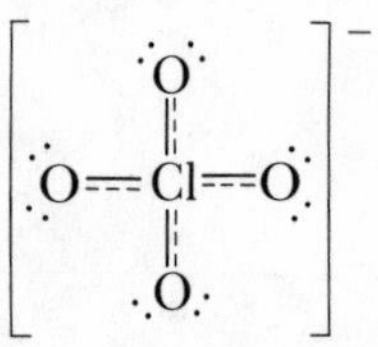

(b) ·C̤l=Ö̤

(c)
```
 :O̤=C̤l=O̤:   ⟷  ⊖:Ö—C̤l=O̤:  ⟷  :O̤=C̤l—Ö:⊖
      |                |               |
   ⊖:Ö:              :Ö̤:             :Ö̤:
```

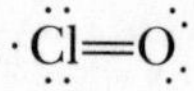

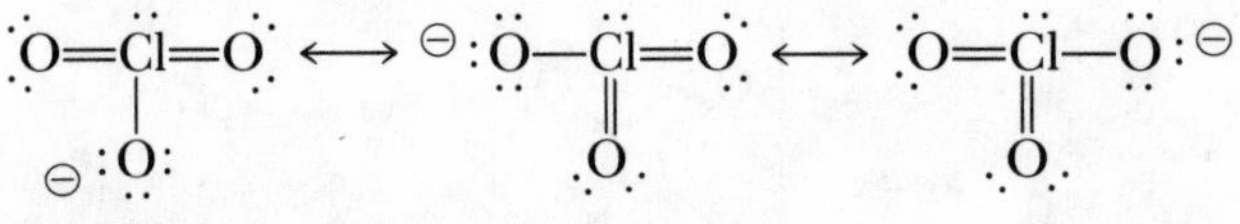

(d) 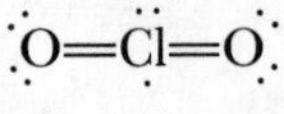 :O̤=C̤l=O̤:

(e) 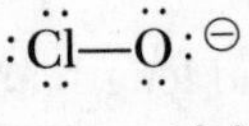 :C̤l—Ö:⊖

10-54 (a) 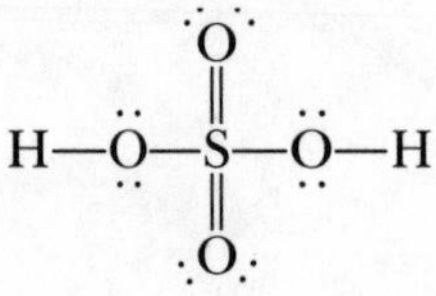
```
       :Ö:
        ‖
 H—Ö—S—Ö—H
        |
       :Ö̤:
```

(b) 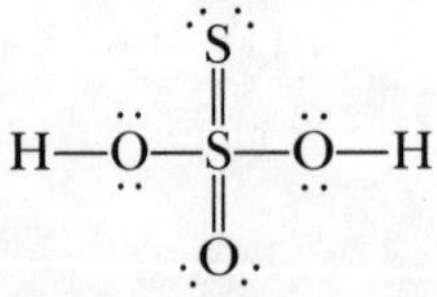
```
       :S̤:
        ‖
 H—Ö—S—Ö—H
        |
       :Ö̤:
```

(c) 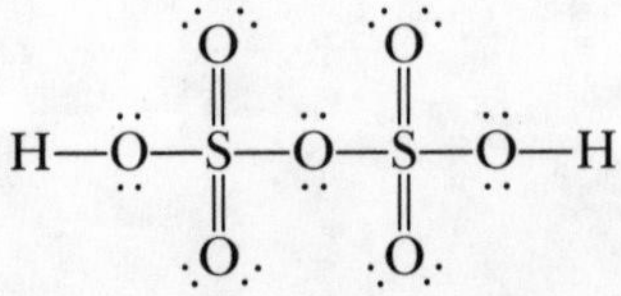
```
       :Ö:       :Ö:
        ‖         ‖
 H—Ö—S—Ö—S—Ö—H
        |         |
       :Ö̤:       :Ö̤:
```

(d) 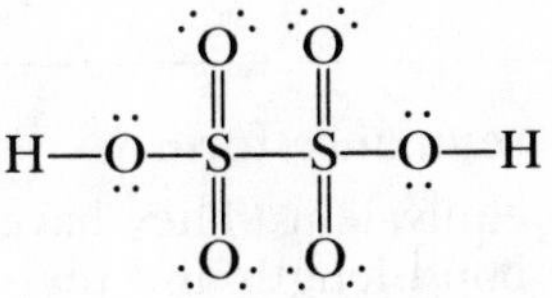

(e) 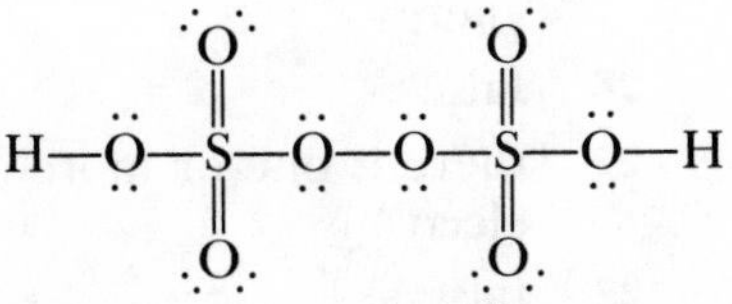

10-56 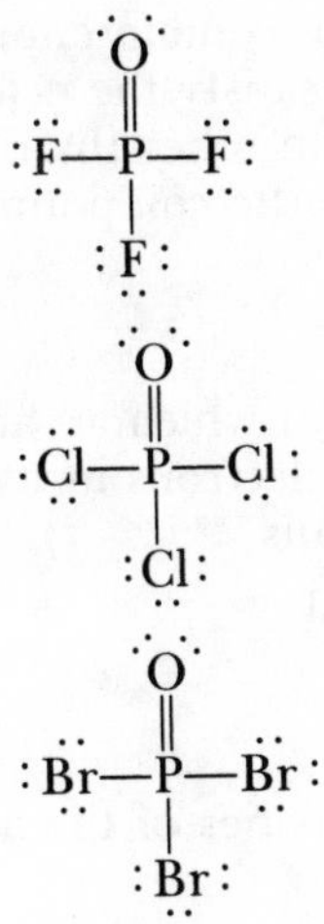

10-58 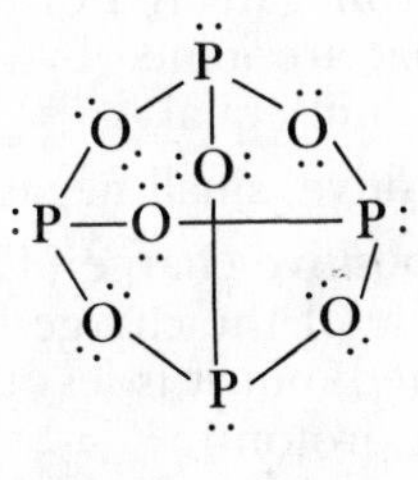

10-60 (a) HI HBr HCl HF
(b) AsH_3 PH_3 NH_3
(c) F_2O Cl_2O H_2O
(d) ClF_3 BrF_3 IF_3
(e) H_2Te H_2Se H_2S H_2O

10-62 (a) 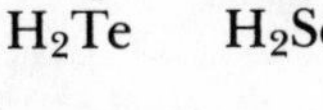
(b) 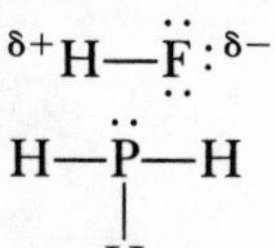
(c) 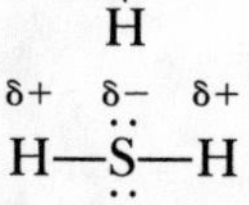

F   ANSWERS TO SELF-TEST

1 shared

2 a line joining the two atoms

3 a lone pair

4 $:\ddot{I}—\ddot{I}:$

5 molecules

6 false

7 false

8 the distance between the nuclei of two atoms that are joined by a bond

9 two

10 many elements form covalent bonds so as to end up with eight electrons in their valence shells

11 true

12 a hydrogen atom can achieve a noble-gas-like electron configuration by having two electrons in its outer shell

13 only one

14 two pairs of, or four

15 $:\ddot{O}{=}C{=}\ddot{O}:$

16 false

17 three pairs of, or six

18 false

19 $:N{\equiv}N:$

20 false

21 that is assigned according to Equation 10-1

22 false

23 a superposition of the various Lewis formulas

24 resonance form

25 equivalent (They have the same bond length and the same energy.)

26 false

27 there is one or more unpaired electrons

28 false

29 that does not contain enough electrons to satisfy the octet rule for each atom other than hydrogen in the compound

30 true

31 false

32 the force with which an atom attracts the electrons in its covalent bonds

33 left (to) right

34 fluorine

35 more

36 electronegativities of the atoms are equal

37 the electronegativities of the atoms that are joined by the bond are not equal

38 small positive, small negative

39 a small positive charge (The magnitude of the charge is unspecified, but it is less than that of a proton.)

40 the polarity of the bond

41 magnitude, direction

42 true

11 / The Shapes of Molecules

A   OUTLINE OF CHAPTER 11

11-1   Lewis formulas do not represent the shapes of molecules.

Geometrical isomers are molecules that have the same chemical formula but different spatial arrangements of their atoms.

A regular tetrahedron has four equivalent vertices and four identical faces, each of which is an equilateral triangle (Figure 11-2).

11-2   All four vertices of a regular tetrahedron are equivalent.

When four atoms are bonded to a carbon atom, they are arranged in a tetrahedral array around the carbon atom which is in the center of the tetrahedron (Figure 11-1).

The regular tetrahedron bond angle is 109.5° (for example, the H—C—H bond angle in CH_4 is 109.5°).

A space-filling model of a molecule represents the angles between bonds and the relative sizes of the atoms (Figure 11-3).

A ball-and-stick model of a molecule represents the angles between bonds (Figure 11-4).

Structural chemistry is the study of the shapes and sizes of molecules.

11-3   Valence-shell electron-pair repulsion theory is used to predict the shapes of molecules.

VSEPR theory postulates that the shape of a molecule is determined by the mutual repulsion of the electron pairs in the valence shell of the central atom (Figure 11-6).

The electron-deficient molecule, $BeCl_2$, is linear.

The electron-deficient molecule, BF_3, is trigonal planar.

11-4   The number of valence-shell electron pairs determines the shape of a molecule.

The arrangements of sets of electron pairs on the surface of spheres that minimize mutual repulsion between electron pairs are shown in Figure 11-6.

The five vertices of a trigonal bipyramid are not equivalent; the three lying on the equator are called equatorial vertices, and the two lying at the poles are called axial vertices (Figure 11-6d).

11-5 Molecules with six covalent bonds about a central atom are octahedral.

All six vertices of an octahedron are equivalent (Figure 11-8).

The bond angles for various molecular shapes are (Table 11-1):

linear	180°
trigonal planar	120°
tetrahedral	109.5°
trigonal bipyramidal	120° equatorial angles
	90°, 180° axial angles
octahedral	90°, 180°

11-6 Lone electron pairs in the valence shell affect the shapes of molecules.

Lone pairs are more spread out than bond pairs.

The repulsion between a lone pair and the electron pair in a covalent bond is greater than the repulsion between the electron pairs in two covalent bonds.

11-7 The values of m and n in the general formula AX_mE_n can be used to predict the shape of a molecule.

Many molecules can be classified using the formula AX_mE_n, where A represents the central atom, X represents an attached ligand, and E is a lone pair of electrons on the central atom.

The total number of electron pairs in the valence shell of the central atom determines the shape of a molecule.

Lone-pair–lone-pair   repulsion > lone-pair-bond-pair   repulsion > bond-pair–bond-pair repulsion (Equation 11-1).

The numbers of bonds and lone pairs of electrons around the central atom result in the molecular shapes (Figure 11-12).

AX_2	linear
AX_3	trigonal planar
AX_2E	bent
AX_4	tetrahedral
AX_3E	trigonal pyramidal
AX_2E_2	bent
AX_5	trigonal bipyramidal
AX_4E	seesaw
AX_3E_2	T-shaped
AX_2E_3	linear
AX_6	octahedral
AX_5E	square pyramidal
AX_4E_2	square planar

11-8 VSEPR theory is applicable to molecules that contain double or triple bonds.

A double or triple bond is counted simply as one bond connecting the ligand X to the central atom A.

Multiple bonds repel single bonds more strongly than single bonds repel other single bonds.

11-9 VSEPR theory can be applied to molecules that are described by resonance.

11-10 Lone-pair electrons occupy the equatorial vertices of a trigonal bipyramid.

An equatorial lone pair has only two neighbors at 90° (Figure 11-14).

AX_4E molecules are seesaw-shaped (Figure 11-15a).

AX_3E_2 molecules are T-shaped (Figure 11-15b).

AX_2E_3 molecules are linear (Figure 11-15c).

11-11 Two lone electron pairs occupy opposite vertices of an octahedron.

The-lone-pair–lone-pair repulsion is minimized when the two lone pairs occupy opposite vertices.

AX_5E molecules are square pyramidal (Figure 11-19b).

AX_4E_2 molecules are square planar (Figure 11-19c).

A summary of the results of VSEPR theory is given in Table 11-3.

B SELF-TEST

1 The four single bonds about a central carbon atom are directed toward _____.

2 All four vertices of a regular tetrahedron are equivalent. *True/False*

3 Dichloromethane has _____ geometrical isomers.

4 The shape of a molecule can be determined experimentally. *True/False*

5 The basis of the VSEPR theory is the postulate that the shape of a molecule is determined by _____
_____.

6 The shape of a molecule in which the central atom forms two bonds and has no lone electron pairs is _____.

7 The VSEPR theory predicts that two valence-shell electron pairs about a central atom lie _____.

8 The VSEPR theory predicts that three valence-shell electron pairs about a central atom lie _____.

9 The VSEPR theory predicts that four valence-shell electron pairs about a central atom lie _____.

10 The VSEPR theory predicts that five valence-shell electron pairs about a central atom lie _____.

11 The VSEPR theory predicts that six valence-shell electron pairs about a central atom lie _____.

12 The five vertices of a trigonal bipyramid are equivalent. *True/False*

13 The six vertices of an octahedron are equivalent. *True/False*

14 Axial vertices are the vertices of a _____ that lie _____.

15 Lone-electron pairs on the central atom in a molecule or ion do not affect the shape of the molecule or ion. *True/False*

16 The shape of ammonia, NH_3, is _____.

17 The H—N—H bond angle in ammonia is less than 109.5° because _____ _____.

18 The shape of the water molecule, H_2O, is _____.

19 The H—O—H bond angle in water is 109.5°. *True/False*

20 The symbol AX_3E indicates a molecule or ion that has _____ _____ around the central atom.

21 The shape of a molecule of class AX_3E is _____.

22 The symbol AX_4E indicates a molecule or ion that has _____ _____

around the central atom.

23 The lone electron pair in an AX_4E class of molecule is located at an (*axial/equatorial*) position on a trigonal bipyramid.

24 The shape of an AX_4E molecule is _____.

25 The shape of a molecule is described by the positions of the nuclei of the central atom and the ligands. *True/False*

26 The shape of an AX_3E_2 molecule is _____.

27 The shape of an AX_2E_3 molecule is _____.

28 In the molecule PCl_5, _____ is the central atom and _____ is a ligand.

29 The double bond in the formaldehyde molecule, H_2CO, is considered as two bonds in applying VSEPR theory. *True/False*

30 The formaldehyde molecule is an _____ class molecule.

31 The shape of the formaldehyde molecule is _____.

32 The F—Cl—F bond angle in the molecule ClF_3 is less than 90° because __

_____.

33 The symbol AX_5E indicates a molecule or ion that has _____

_____ around the central atom.

34 The shape of an AX_5E molecule is _____.

35 It makes no difference at which vertex the lone electron-pair in an AX_5E molecule is located. *True/False*

36 The shape of an AX_4E_2 molecule is _____.

37 The VSEPR theory cannot be applied to molecules that are described by resonance. *True/False*

38 The bond angles in a trigonal planar molecule are _____.

39 The bond angles in a trigonal bipyramidal molecule are _____,

_____, and _____.

40 The bond angles in a square pyramidal molecule are all exactly 90°. *True/False*

C CALCULATIONS YOU SHOULD KNOW HOW TO DO

There are no numerical calculations in this chapter. In Problems 11-1 through 11-42 you are asked to use VSEPR theory to predict molecular shapes.

D SOLUTIONS TO THE ODD-NUMBERED PROBLEMS

11-1 In this problem we first use VSEPR theory to predict the molecular shape and from the shape we determine if there are any 90° bond angles. (See Table 11-1.)

(a) TeF_6 is an AX_6 octahedral molecule and thus has 90° bond angles.
(b) $ZnCl_4^{2-}$ is an AX_4 tetrahedral molecule and thus has no 90° bond angles.
(c) $AsBr_5$ is an AX_5 trigonal bipyramidal molecule and thus has some 90° bond angles.
(d) $HgCl_2$ is an AX_2 linear molecule and thus has no 90° angles.
(e) GaI_3 is an AX_3 trigonal molecule and thus has no 90° angles.

11-3 (a) $HgCl_4^{2-}$ is an AX_4 tetrahedral molecule and thus has no 120° bond angles.
(b) $SbBr_6^-$ is an AX_6 octahedral molecule and thus has no 120° bond angles.
(c) $SbCl_5$ is an AX_5 trigonal bipyramidal molecule and thus has some 120° bond angles.

(d) $InCl_3$ is an AX_3 trigonal planar molecule and thus has 120° bond angles.

(e) $GeCl_4$ is an AX_4 tetrahedral molecule and thus has no 120° bond angles.

11-5 See Figure 11-12 or Table 11-3.

(a) :I—Cd—I: AX_2 linear

(b) :Br—Sn—Br: AX_2E bent

(c) :F—Kr—F: AX_2E_3 linear

(d) :F—O—F: AX_2E_2 bent

(e) :Cl—Te—Cl: AX_2E_2 bent

11-7 (a) 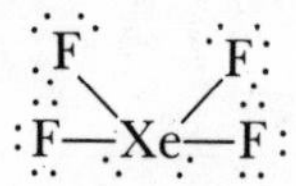 :F—Xe—F: AX_4E_2 square planar

(b) 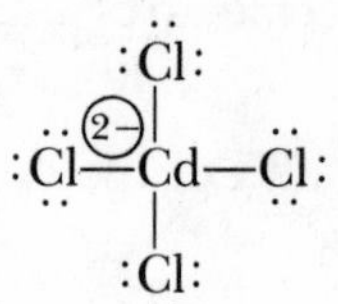 :Cl—Cd—Cl: AX_4 tetrahedral

(c) 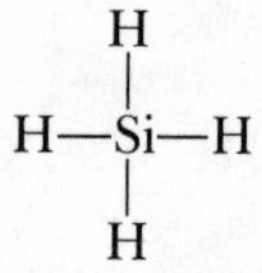 H—Si—H AX_4 tetrahedral

(d) 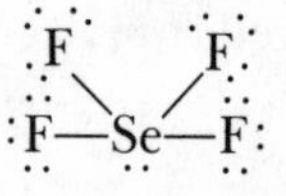 :F—Se—F: AX_4E seesaw

(e) 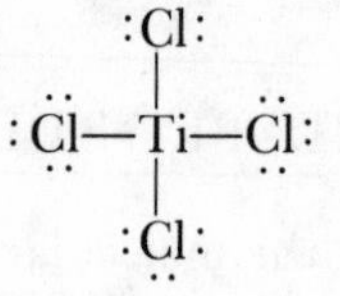 :Cl—Ti—Cl: AX_4 tetrahedral

11-9 (a) 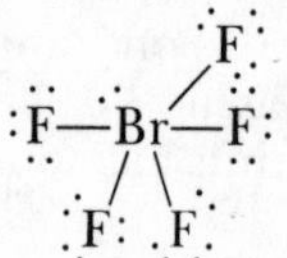 :F—Br—F: AX_5E square pyramidal

(b) 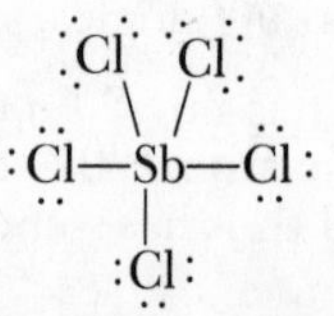 :Cl—Sb—Cl: AX_5 trigonal bipyramidal

(c) 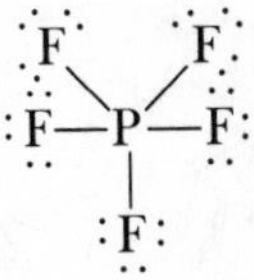 AX_5 trigonal bipyramidal

(d) 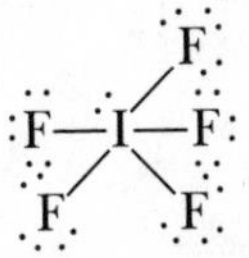 AX_5E square pyramidal

11-11 (a) 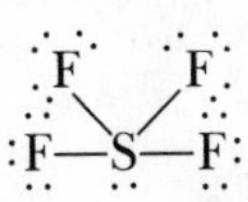 AX_4E seesaw

(b) 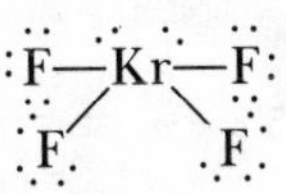 AX_4E_2 square planar

(c) 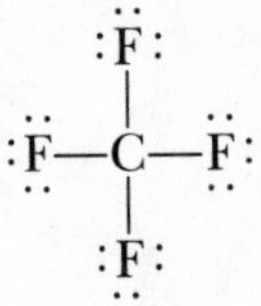 AX_4 tetrahedral

(d) 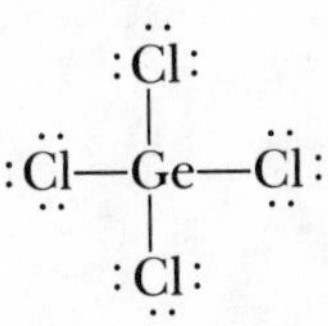 AX_4 tetrahedral

(e) 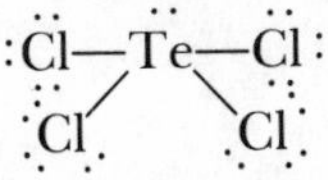 AX_4E seesaw

11-13 (a) 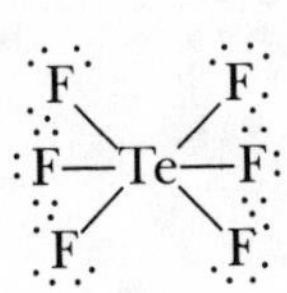 AX_6 octahedral   90° (1)

(b) 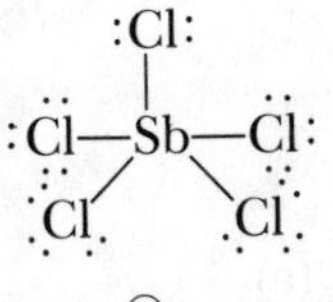 AX_5 trigonal bipyramidal   90°, 120° (1, 3)

(c) 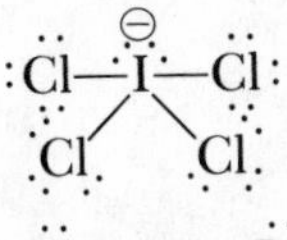 AX_4E_2 square planar   90° (1)

(d) 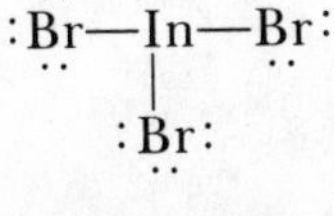 AX_3 trigonal planar   120° (3)

11-15 (a)

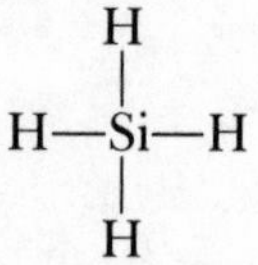

$$\begin{array}{c} H \\ | \\ H—Si—H \\ | \\ H \end{array}$$

AX_4 tetrahedral   109.5°
(2)

(b)

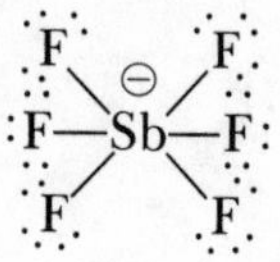

$$:\!F\!—\!Sb\!—\!F\!: \quad (\ominus)$$

AX_6 octahedral   90°
(1)

(c)

$$F\!—\!Br\!—\!F \quad (\ominus)$$

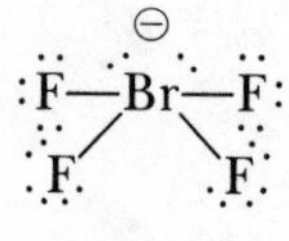

AX_4E_2 square planar   90°
(1)

(d)

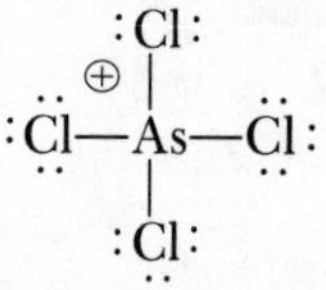

$$Cl\!—\!As\!—\!Cl \quad (\oplus)$$

AX_4 tetrahedral   109.5°
(2)

11-17 (a)

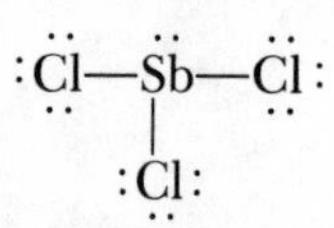

$$:\!Cl\!—\!Sb\!—\!Cl\!:$$

AX_3E trigonal pyramidal
(Figure 11-11)

(b)

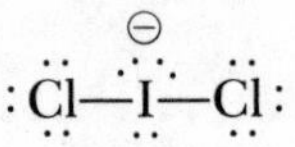

$$:\!Cl\!—\!I\!—\!Cl\!: \quad (\ominus)$$

AX_2E_3 linear
(Figure 11-18)

(c)

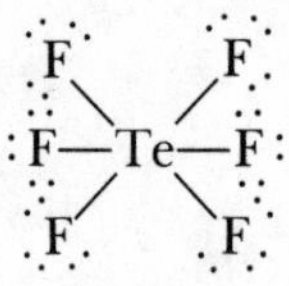

$$:\!F\!—\!Te\!—\!F\!:$$

AX_6 octahedral

(d)

$$:\!F\!—\!S\!—\!F\!:$$

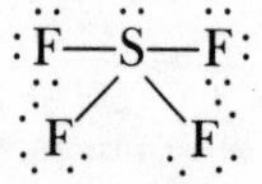

AX_4E seesaw
(Figure 11-16)

(e)

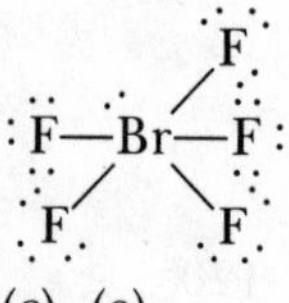

$$:\!F\!—\!Br\!—\!F\!:$$

AX_5E square pyramidal
(Figure 11-21)

(1) (c), (e)   (6) (d)
(2) (e), (d)   (7) none
(3) none   (8) (b), (c), (e)
(4) (a)   (9) (d), (e)
(5) none

11-19 AB compounds; for example

IF $:\!I\!—\!F\!:$ linear

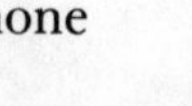

All AB compounds are linear.

AB_3 compounds; for example

IF$_3$:F̈—Ï—F̈: AX_3E_2 T-shaped
                |
              :F̈:

Thus BrF_3 and ClF_3 are T-shaped.

AB_5 compounds; for example

IF$_5$:F̈—Ï—F̈: AX_5E square pyramidal
         F̈. F

Thus BrF_5 and ClF_5 are square pyramidal.

11-21   Consult the text or the problems.

11-23   (a) :C̈l—Hg—C̈l: AX_2 linear (no dipole moment)

(b) :F̈—As—F̈: AX_5 trigonal bipyramidal (no dipole moment)
              |
            :F̈:

(c) :C̈l—S̈—C̈l: AX_2E_2 bent (has a dipole moment)

(d) :C̈l—Ö—C̈l: AX_2E_2 bent (has a dipole moment)

(e) :C̈l—Ga—C̈l: AX_3 trigonal planar (no dipole moment)
              |
            :C̈l:

11-25   (a) :B̈r—Te—B̈r: AX_4E seesaw
              | (has a dipole moment)
            :B̈r:

(b) :Ï—Cd—Ï: AX_2 linear
                                             (no dipole moment)

(c) :F̈—Se—F̈: AX_4E seesaw
              | (has a dipole moment)
            :F̈:

(d) :Cl—Sb—Cl: AX_5 trigonal bipyramidal
        (with Cl's above and below)   (no dipole moment)

(e) :F—I—F: AX_5E square pyramidal
        (with F's above and below)   (has a dipole moment)

11-27 (a) CF_4, AX_4, tetrahedral, nonpolar
       (b) PF_5, AX_5, trigonal bipyramidal, nonpolar
       (c) XeF_4, AX_4E_2, square planar, nonpolar
       (d) BF_3, AX_3, trigonal planar, nonpolar
       (e) SeF_4, AX_4E, seesaw, polar

11-29 We count the number of ligands and lone pairs on the central atom and treat the
       multiple bonds as single bonds

       (a) :O=S—Cl: AX_3E trigonal pyramidal
             |
            :Cl:

       (b) O=S—Cl: AX_4 tetrahedral
             ‖
            :Cl:

       (c) :O=Cl—F: AX_3E trigonal pyramidal
             ‖
            .O.

       (d) :O=Cl—F: AX_4 tetrahedral
             ‖
             O.

       (e) :Cl—P—Cl: AX_4 tetrahedral
             ‖
            :Cl:

11-31 (a) Cl   C=O: AX_3 trigonal planar
             Cl

(b)

$$\overset{\ominus}{:}\overset{..}{\underset{..}{S}}:$$
$$:\overset{..}{F}\overset{\oplus}{\underset{..}{-N}}\overset{..}{-F}:$$
$$:\overset{..}{F}:$$

AX$_4$ tetrahedral

(c)

$$\overset{\ominus}{:}\overset{..}{N}=\overset{\oplus}{N}=\overset{\ominus}{\underset{..}{N}}:$$

AX$_2$ linear

(d)

$$\overset{\ominus}{:}\overset{..}{O}-\overset{\oplus}{N}=\overset{..}{\underset{..}{O}}: \quad\longleftrightarrow\quad \overset{..}{O}=\overset{\oplus}{N}-\overset{..}{\underset{..}{O}}:\overset{\ominus}{}$$
$$:\overset{..}{\underset{..}{Cl}}: \qquad\qquad\qquad :\overset{..}{\underset{..}{Cl}}:$$

AX$_3$ trigonal planar

(e)

$$\overset{..}{\underset{..}{S}}$$
$$:\overset{..}{Cl}-P-\overset{..}{\underset{..}{Cl}}:$$
$$:\overset{..}{\underset{..}{Cl}}:$$

AX$_4$ tetrahedral

11-33 (a) $\overset{\ominus}{}\overset{..}{O}=\overset{..}{\underset{..}{Br}}=\overset{..}{\underset{..}{O}}$ AX$_2$E$_2$ bent

(b) $\overset{..}{O}=Si=\overset{..}{\underset{..}{O}}$ AX$_2$ linear

(c)

$$\overset{..}{\underset{..}{O}}$$
$$:\overset{..}{O}=\overset{||}{S}-\overset{..}{\underset{..}{Cl}}:\ +\ 2\ \text{resonance forms gives}$$
$$:\overset{..}{\underset{..}{O}}:\overset{\ominus}{}$$

$$\left[\ \overset{..}{\underset{..}{O}}\atop{:\overset{..}{O}=\!\!=\overset{||}{S}-\overset{..}{\underset{..}{Cl}}:}\atop{:\overset{..}{\underset{..}{O}}:}\ \right]^{-} \qquad \text{AX}_4 \qquad \text{tetrahedral}$$

(d) $\overset{\ominus}{}:\overset{..}{O}-\overset{\overset{O}{||}}{I}=\overset{..}{\underset{..}{O}}\ +\ 3\ \text{resonance forms gives}$

$$\left[\ :\overset{..}{O}=\!\!=\overset{\overset{..}{\underset{..}{O}}}{\underset{\overset{..}{\underset{..}{O}}}{I}}=\!\!=\overset{..}{\underset{..}{O}}:\ \right]^{-} \qquad \text{AX}_4 \qquad \text{tetrahedral}$$

(e) $^{\ominus}$:Ö—P—Ï: + 2 resonance forms gives

with O above and :Ö: $^{\ominus}$ below

$$\left[\begin{array}{c} \text{O} \\ \| \\ \text{O}{=}\text{P}{-}\text{Ï:} \\ \| \\ \text{O} \end{array} \right]^{2-} \qquad AX_4 \qquad \text{tetrahedral}$$

11-35 (a) :Ö=Xe=Ö: AX_3E trigonal pyramidal
             Ö

(b) :Ö=Xe=Ö: AX_4 tetrahedral
     (O above and O below)

(c) :F—Kr—F: AX_2E_3 linear

(d) $^{\ominus}$:Ö   Ö: $^{\ominus}$
     $^{\ominus}$:Ö—Xe—Ö: $^{\ominus}$ + other resonance forms gives
         Ö   Ö

$$\left[\begin{array}{ccc} :\text{Ö} & & \text{Ö:} \\ \text{O}{=}\!\!=\!\!\text{Xe}\!\!=\!\!\!=\text{O} \\ :\text{Ö} & & \text{Ö:} \end{array} \right]^{4-} \qquad AX_6 \qquad \text{octahedral}$$

(e) :F—Xe—F: AX_5E square pyramidal
     (⊕ charge, with F top, F F bottom)

11-37 (a) $^{\ominus}$:Ö—S—Ö: $^{\ominus}$ AX_2E_2 bent

(b) $^{\ominus}$:Ö—S—Ö: $^{\ominus}$ + 2 resonance forms gives
         Ö

$$\left[\text{O}{=}\!\!=\!\!\text{S}\!\!=\!\!\!=\text{O} \atop \text{O} \right]^{2-} \qquad AX_3E \qquad \text{trigonal pyramidal}$$

(c) $^{\ominus}\ddot{\text{O}}$—$\overset{\overset{\displaystyle \ddot{\text{O}}}{\|}}{\text{S}}$—$\ddot{\text{O}}\!:^{\ominus}$ + other resonance forms gives

$$\left[\begin{array}{c} \ddot{\text{O}} \\ \| \\ \ddot{\text{O}}\!=\!\!=\!\text{S}\!=\!\!=\!\ddot{\text{O}} \\ \| \\ \ddot{\text{O}} \end{array} \right]^{2-} \qquad AX_4 \qquad \text{tetrahedral}$$

11-39 (a) $\text{O}\!=\!\text{Xe}\!=\!\text{O}$ with F atoms AX_6 octahedral

(b) $\text{Xe}\!=\!\text{O}$ with F atoms AX_5E square pyramidal

(c) $\text{O}\!=\!\text{I}\!=\!\text{O}$ with F AX_3E trigonal pyramidal

(d) $\text{O}\!=\!\text{I}\!=\!\text{O}$ with F, O AX_4 tetrahedral

(e) $\text{O}\!=\!\text{I}\!=\!\text{O}$ with F, F AX_5 trigonal bipyramidal

11-41   The Lewis formula of the species NO_2^+ is

$$\ddot{\text{O}}\!=\!\overset{\oplus}{\text{N}}\!=\!\ddot{\text{O}}$$

Thus NO_2^+ is a linear molecule with a O—N—O bond angle of 180°. The Lewis formula of NO_2^- is

$$\left[\ddot{\text{O}}\!=\!\!=\!\dot{\text{N}}\!-\!\!-\!\ddot{\text{O}} \right]^{-}$$

Thus NO_2^- is a bent molecule with a predicted O—N—O bond angle of slightly less than 120°.

11-43 (a) All the vertices of a tetrahedron are equivalent, and thus it makes no difference where the ligand Y is placed. Therefore, there is only one possible arrangement of the ligands for tetrahedral AX_3Y molecules.

(b) There is only one possible arrangement of the ligands in tetrahedral AX_2YZ molecules.

(c) All the vertices of a square are equivalent, and thus it makes no difference where ligand Y is placed. Therefore, there is only one possible arrangement of the ligands in a square planar AX_3Y molecule.

(d) Two isomers with identical ligands either adjacent or opposite to one another:

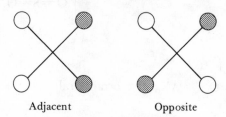

Adjacent   Opposite

11-45 (a) All octahedral vertices are equivalent. Thus there is only one possible arrangement for an octahedral AX_5Y molecule.

(b) Two isomers, one with the two Y's opposite and one with the two Y's adjacent:

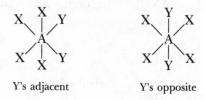

Y's adjacent   Y's opposite

(c) Two isomers, one with the three Y's on an octahedral face and one with the three Y's along three of the four vertices of a square:

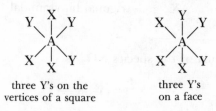

three Y's on the   three Y's
vertices of a square   on a face

11-47 (a) One isomer

(b) $Pt(NH_3)_5Cl^{3+}$ is an AX_5Y octahedral molecule; thus it has one isomer (Problem 11-45a).

(c) $Pt(NH_3)_4Cl_2^{2+}$ is an AX_4Y_2 octahedral molecule; thus it has two isomers. The two Cl atoms are adjacent in one isomer and the two Cl atoms are opposite one another in the other isomer (Problem 11-45b).

(d) $Pt(NH_3)_3Cl_3^+$ is an AX_3Y_3 octahedral molecule; thus it has two isomers. The three chlorine atoms lie on the vertices of a square in one isomer and the three chlorine atoms lie on a face in the other isomer (Problem 11-45c).

E   ANSWERS TO THE EVEN-NUMBERED PROBLEMS

11-2 AlF_6^{3-}, PCl_5

11-4 SeF_6, CdI_2, $AsCl_5$, ZnI_2

11-6 Br_3^- and ICl_2^- are linear; NH_2^-, PF_2^+, and IF_2^+ are bent

11-8 OH_3^+, PF_3, and NH_3

11-10 ICl_4^-

11-12 (a) square planar   (d) seesaw
           (b) tetrahedral   (e) tetrahedral
           (c) tetrahedral

11-14 (a) 109.5°; (b) 90°, 120°; (c) 120°; (d) 90°

11-16 (1) a; (2) c, d; (3) none; (4) b; (5) none; (6) none; (7) none; (8) a; (9) c, d

11-18 (1) d, e; (2) a; (3) b; (4) c; (5) none; (6) none; (7) none; (8) d, e; (9) a

11-20 (a) bent   (d) square planar
           (b) linear   (e) octahedral
           (c) seesaw

11-22 Consult the text or the problems.

11-24 (a) $\ddot{:}\overset{\displaystyle :\ddot{Cl}:}{\underset{\displaystyle :\ddot{Cl}:}{\overset{|}{\underset{|}{Cl—Ge—Cl}}}}\ddot{:}$ tetrahedral   no dipole moment

(b) $:\ddot{Cl}—Te—\ddot{Cl}:$ seesaw   dipole moment

(c) octahedral   no dipole moment

(d) $:\ddot{F}—Xe—\ddot{F}:$ linear   no dipole moment

(e) T-shaped   dipole moment

11-26 (a) octahedral, no dipole moment
           (b) square pyramidal, dipole moment
           (c) linear, no dipole moment
           (d) bent, dipole moment
           (e) T-shaped, dipole moment

11-28   TeCl$_4$ and PbCl$_2$ are polar.

11-30   (a) 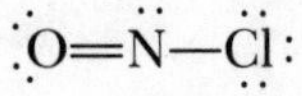 $\ddot{O}=N-\ddot{Cl}:$ bent

(b) 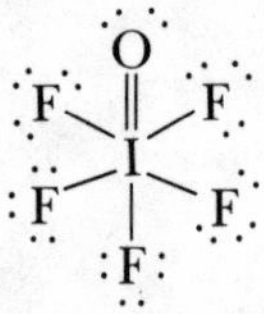   octahedral

(c) 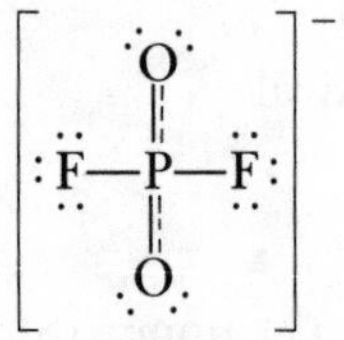   tetrahedral

(d) 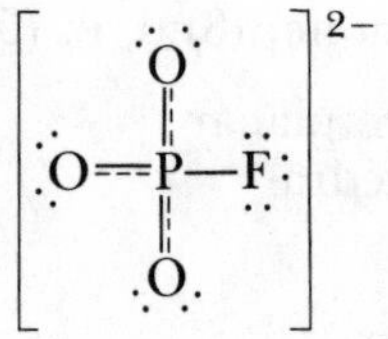   tetrahedral

(e) 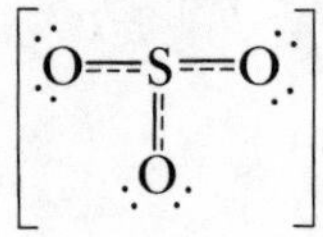   trigonal planar

11-32   (a) 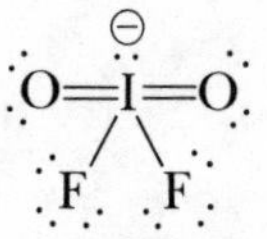   seesaw

(b) 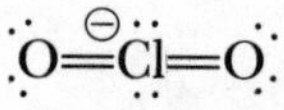 $\ddot{O}=\overset{\ominus}{\ddot{Cl}}=\ddot{O}:$ bent

(c) 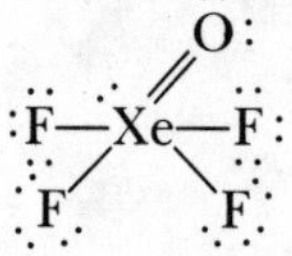   square pyramidal

(d) 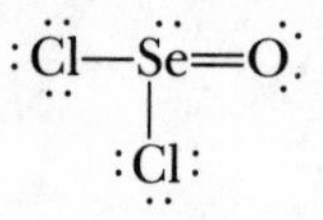   trigonal pyramidal

(e) 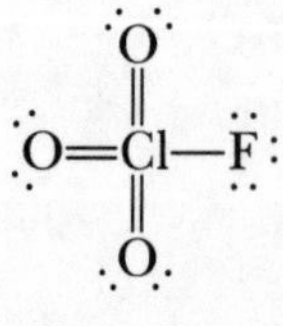   tetrahedral

11-34 (a) trigonal bipyramidal   (d) bent
        (b) tetrahedral   (e) tetrahedral
        (c) tetrahedral

11-36 (a) tetrahedral   (d) tetrahedral
        (b) octahedral   (e) tetrahedral
        (c) trigonal bipyramidal

11-38 (a) bent
        (b) trigonal pyramidal
        (c) tetrahedral

11-40 (a) 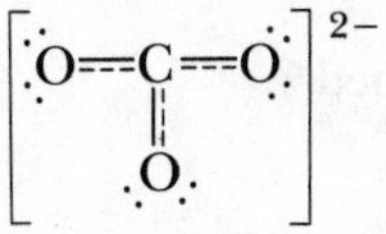 $\left[\ddot{O} = C = \ddot{O} \atop \ddot{O} \right]^{2-}$ trigonal planar

        (b) 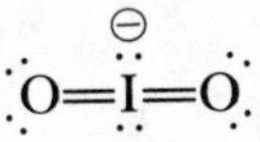 $\ddot{O} = \overset{\ominus}{\ddot{I}} = \ddot{O}$ bent

        (c) 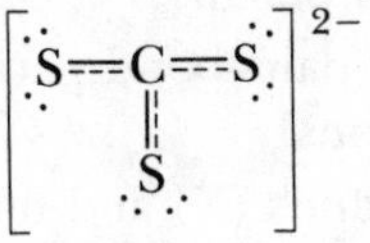 $\left[\ddot{S} = C = \ddot{S} \atop \ddot{S} \right]^{2-}$ trigonal planar

        (d) 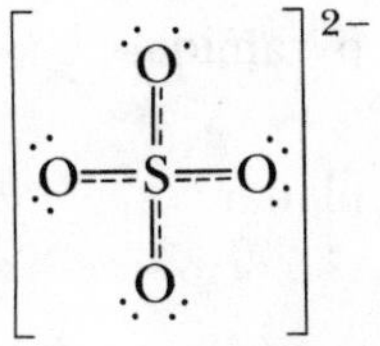 $\left[\ddot{O} = \overset{\ddot{O}}{\underset{\ddot{O}}{S}} = \ddot{O} \right]^{2-}$ tetrahedral

        (e) 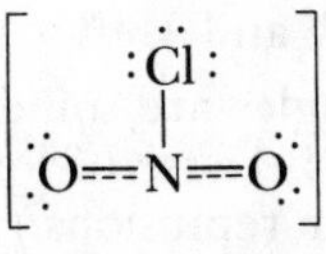 $\left[\ddot{O} = \overset{:\ddot{Cl}:}{N} = \ddot{O} \right]$ trigonal planar

11-42 (a) bent
        (b) trigonal planar
        (c) linear
        (d) tetrahedral

11-44 two

11-46 (a) two
        (b) two

11-48 (a) two isomers, Y axial and Y equatorial
        (b) three isomers; both Y's axial, both Y's equatorial, and one Y axial and one Y equatorial
        (c) three isomers; both X's axial, both X's equatorial, and one X axial and one X equatorial

F ANSWERS TO SELF-TEST

1 the vertices of a tetrahedron
2 true
3 no
4 true
5 mutual repulsion of bonding electron pairs and lone pairs in the valence shell of the central atom
6 linear
7 on a line containing the central atom, or at 180° from each other
8 at the vertices of an equilateral triangle
9 at the vertices of a tetrahedron
10 at the vertices of a trigonal bipyramid
11 at the vertices of an octahedron
12 false
13 true
14 trigonal bipyramid that lie at the poles (there are two axial vertices)
15 false
16 trigonal pyramidal (tripod)
17 lone-pair-bond-pair repulsions are greater than bond-pair-bond-pair repulsions
18 bent
19 false

20 three ligands (X) and a lone pair (E)
21 trigonal pyramidal
22 four ligands (X) and a lone pair (E)
23 equatorial
24 seesaw
25 true
26 T-shaped
27 linear
28 P; Cl
29 false
30 AX_3
31 trigonal planar
32 of lone-pair–bond-pair repulsions
33 five ligands (X) and one lone pair (E)
34 square pyramidal
35 true
36 square planar
37 false
38 120°
39 120°, 90°, and 180°
40 false (Angles are somewhat less than 90° because of lone-pair–bond-pair repulsions.)

12 / Bonding in Molecules

A   OUTLINE OF CHAPTER 12

12-1   The electrons in molecules are described by molecular orbitals.

The solution of the Schrödinger equation for H_2 gives the energies and wave functions that describe the two electrons.

A molecular orbital that encompasses both nuclei is shown in Figure 12-1.

The buildup of electron density between nuclei is responsible for attracting the nuclei together.

12-2   The bonding in polyatomic molecules can be described in terms of bond orbitals.

Localized bond orbitals describe the bonding electrons that are localized in covalent bonds.

12-3   A set of sp^3 orbitals point toward the vertices of a tetrahedron.

Hybrid atomic orbitals are formed by combining atomic orbitals on the same atom.

The sp^3 hybrid orbitals (Figure 12-4) are the four equivalent hybrid orbitals that result from combining the $2s$ orbital and the three $2p$ orbitals.

A σ orbital is circular in cross-section.

A σ bond occurs when two electrons of opposite spin occupy a σ orbital.

The bonding in CH_4 can be described by four localized bond orbitals, each of which is a combination of a sp^3 hybrid orbital on the central carbon atom and a $1s$ atomic orbital on the hydrogen atom (Figure 12-5).

The bonding in many molecules can be described in terms of sp^3 orbitals.

12-4   We use sp^3 orbitals to describe the bonding in molecules containing oxygen atoms.

The bonding in H_2O can be described in terms of sp^3 hybrid orbitals on the oxygen atom. Two of the sp^3 orbitals are used to form bonds with the hydrogen atoms, and the other two are occupied by the lone electron pairs on the oxygen atom (Figure 12-8).

The bonding in NH_3 can be described in terms of sp^3 orbitals on the nitrogen atom (Figure 12-9).

12-5 A double bond consists of a σ bond and a π bond.

The sp^2 hybrid orbitals are the three equivalent hybrid orbitals that are formed by combining a $2s$ orbital and two $2p$ orbitals.

The sp^2 hybrid orbitals (Figure 12-11) lie in a plane and are directed toward the vertices of an equilateral triangle.

The σ bonding in ethylene is described in terms of sp^2 orbitals on the carbon atoms.

The σ-bond framework (Figure 12-13) of a molecule indicates all the σ bonds in the molecule.

The combination of an sp^2 orbital on a carbon atom with a $1s$ orbital on a hydrogen atom or with an sp^2 or an sp^3 orbital on another carbon atom is a σ bond.

A π orbital is formed by the combination of two p orbitals.

A π orbital in cross section is similar to an atomic p orbital.

A π bond is formed when two electrons of opposite spins occupy a π orbital.

The double bond in ethylene consists of a σ bond (overlap of an sp^2 orbital from each carbon atom) and a π bond (overlap of a p orbital from each carbon atom) (Figure 12-14).

12-6 There is no rotation about carbon-carbon double bonds.

Cis and *trans* isomers are stereoisomers.

12-7 Physiological activity can be affected dramatically by molecular shape.

Vision involves a *cis-trans* isomerism.

12-8 A triple bond consists of one σ bond and two π bonds.

The sp hybrid orbitals (Figure 12-17) are the two equivalent hybrid orbitals that result from combining a $2s$ orbital and a $2p$ orbital.

The sp orbitals are directed 180° from each other.

There are three σ bonds in acetylene (Figure 12-18).

The carbon-carbon triple bond consists of one σ bond and two π bonds, and is cylindrically symmetric (Figure 12-20).

Table 12-1 summarizes the properties of the hybrid orbitals, sp^3, sp^2, and sp.

12-9 The π electrons in benzene are delocalized.

There are two principal resonance forms of benzene.

Benzene does not contain double bonds.

The six carbon-carbon bonds in benzene are equivalent.

Benzene is a planar, hexagonal molecule (Figure 12-23).

The π electrons in benzene are delocalized (Figure 12-22).

The three π orbitals in benzene are spread uniformly over the entire ring.

12-10   Molecular orbitals can be ordered according to their energies.

Molecular orbital theory is a theory of bonding.

Molecular orbitals are solutions to the Schrödinger equation for H_2^+.

The shapes of some of the molecular orbitals are shown in Figure 12-24.

12-11   Molecular orbitals are bonding or antibonding.

A molecular orbital that is concentrated in a region between two nuclei is a bonding orbital.

The molecular orbital of lowest energy is a bonding orbital and is designated 1σ.

A molecular orbital that is zero in a region between two nuclei is an antibonding orbital.

An antibonding orbital is designated by a superscript *.

Electrons are placed into molecular orbitals according to the Pauli exclusion principle.

The order of the molecular orbitals in terms of energy is given in Figure 12-27.

An antibonding electron annuls the effect of a bonding electron.

Bond order is given by Equation 12-1:

$$\text{bond order} = \frac{\left(\begin{array}{c}\text{number of electrons} \\ \text{in bonding orbitals}\end{array}\right) - \left(\begin{array}{c}\text{number of electrons} \\ \text{in antibonding orbitals}\end{array}\right)}{2}$$

12-12   Molecular orbital theory predicts that diatomic neon does not exist.

The ground-state electron configurations for the homonuclear diatomic molecules Li_2 through Ne_2 are given in Table 12-3.

12-13   A photoelectron spectrum demonstrates the existence of molecular orbitals.

12-14   Oxygen molecules are paramagnetic.

Electrons are placed in 1π and $1\pi^*$ orbitals according to Hund's rule.

O_2 contains two unpaired electrons, one in each of the $1\pi^*$ orbitals.

B   SELF-TEST

1   The covalent bond joining the two hydrogen atoms in H_2 is due to

_____ .

2   The localized bond orbitals that describe the electrons in a covalent bond are formed from _____ .

3   Hybrid atomic orbitals are obtained by _____

_____ .

4   The sp^3 orbitals are obtained by combining _____ .

5 The sp^3 orbitals are directed toward _____.

6 Each carbon-hydrogen bond orbital in methane, CH_4, is formed by _____

_____

_____.

7 A σ orbital is _____ in cross section when viewed along an internuclear axis.

8 A σ orbital may be occupied by _____ electrons.

9 The two electrons in a σ bond are of opposite spin. *True/False*

10 The carbon-carbon bond in ethane, C_2H_6, is a σ bond. *True/False*

11 The carbon-carbon bond in ethane is formed by _____

_____.

12 The bond orbital that describes the H—O bond in H_2O is a combination of

_____.

13 The sp^2 orbitals are obtained by combining _____

_____.

14 There are _____ sp^2 orbitals.

15 The sp^2 orbitals point to _____

_____.

16 A π orbital results when _____

_____.

17 A π orbital is circular in cross section when viewed along the internuclear axis. *True/False*

18 The double bond in ethylene, C_2H_4, consists of a _____ bond and a _____ bond.

19 How many valence electrons are there in ethylene? How many σ bonds and π bonds are there? _____

_____.

20 It is possible to have more than one double bond in a hydrocarbon, as in

How many valence electrons are there in this molecule? How many σ bonds and π bonds are there? _____

_____.

21 A double bond results from the formation of two σ bonds between two atoms. *True/False*

22 The carbon-oxygen double bond in formaldehyde, H_2CO, is formed by _____.

23 Rotation cannot occur about carbon-carbon double bonds. *True/False*

24 In *trans*-1,2-dichloroethene, $ClCH_2CH_2Cl$, the chlorine atoms lie _____ _____.

25 *Cis-trans* isomers are examples of _____ isomers.

26 The physical properties of *cis-trans* isomers are identical. *True/False*

27 The *sp* orbitals are obtained by combining _____ _____.

28 The *sp* orbitals are directed _____.

29 There are _____ *sp* orbitals.

30 The triple bond in acetylene, C_2H_2, is described by _____ bond and _____ bonds.

31 The number of valence electrons in $H—C\equiv C—CH_3$ is _____. There are _____ σ bonds and _____ π bonds.

32 All the carbon-carbon bond lengths in benzene are the same. *True/False*

33 The shape of the benzene molecule is _____ and _____.

34 The π electrons in benzene are said to be _____.

35 Each π orbital in benzene is located between two adjacent carbon atoms. *True/False*

36 Molecular orbitals are solutions of the Schrödinger equation for _____ _____.

37 All molecular orbitals have the same general shape. *True/False*

38 All molecular orbitals have the same energy. *True/False*

39 A bonding orbital is a molecular orbital that _____ _____.

40 An antibonding orbital is a molecular orbital that _____ _____.

41 The orbital designated by $1\sigma^*$ is the _____ _____.

42 The ground-state electron configuration of homonuclear diatomic molecules is constructed by placing all the electrons into the bonding orbital of lowest energy. *True/False*

43 A 2σ orbital may contain _____ electrons.

44 The set of 1π orbitals may contain a total of _____ electrons.

45 The bond order of a molecule is obtained from the Lewis formula of the molecule. *True/False*

46 A bond order of zero for a molecule indicates that the molecule does not exist. *True/False*

47 The bond order of B_2 is _____ where the ground state electron configuration of B_2 is $(1\sigma)^2(1\sigma*)^2(2\sigma)^2(2\sigma*)^2(1\pi)^2$.

48 The 1π electrons in B_2 occupy the same 1π orbital. *True/False*

49 The existence of molecular orbitals can be verified experimentally. *True/False*

50 The oxygen molecule is paramagnetic because _____

_____ .

C   CALCULATIONS YOU SHOULD KNOW HOW TO DO

The only numerical calculations in Chapter 12 involve the equation

$$\text{bond order} = \frac{\left(\begin{array}{c}\text{number of electrons}\\\text{in bonding orbitals}\end{array}\right) - \left(\begin{array}{c}\text{number of electrons}\\\text{in antibonding orbitals}\end{array}\right)}{2}$$

D   SOLUTIONS TO THE ODD-NUMBERED PROBLEMS

12-1 The interaction of two widely separated hydrogen atoms is zero because they are so far apart that they do not interact with each other. When the two hydrogen atoms are separated by 74 pm, they are joined by a covalent bond, and hence attract each other. Because they attract each other, their interaction energy is less than when they were widely separated; thus their interaction energy is negative.

12-3 (a) The Lewis formula for PCl_3 is

$$:\!\ddot{C}l\!-\!P\!-\!\ddot{C}l\!: \\ | \\ :\!\ddot{C}l\!:$$

There are 3 localized bonds and 10 lone pairs.

(b) The Lewis formula of SF_4 is

$$:\!\ddot{F}\!-\!S\!-\!\ddot{F}\!: \\ / \ \backslash \\ :\!\ddot{F} \quad \ddot{F}\!:$$

There are 4 localized bonds and 13 lone pairs.

(c) The Lewis formula for SiH_4 is

$$\begin{array}{c} H \\ | \\ H-Si-H \\ | \\ H \end{array}$$

There are 4 localized bonds and no lone pairs.

(d) The Lewis formula for OF_2 is

$$:\overset{..}{\underset{..}{F}}-\overset{..}{\underset{..}{O}}-\overset{..}{\underset{..}{F}}:$$

There are 2 localized bonds and 8 lone pairs.

(e) The Lewis formula for HOCl is

$$:\overset{..}{\underset{..}{Cl}}-\overset{..}{\underset{..}{O}}-H$$

There are 2 localized bonds and 5 lone pairs.

12-5 The Lewis formula for propane is

$$\begin{array}{c} H \quad H \quad H \\ | \quad\; | \quad\; | \\ H-C-C-C-H \\ | \quad\; | \quad\; | \\ H \quad H \quad H \end{array}$$

There are 10 localized bonds in propane. There are $3 \times 4 = 12$ valence electrons from the three carbon atoms and $8 \times 1 = 8$ valence electrons from the eight hydrogen atoms, giving a total of 20 valence electrons. The 20 valence electrons occupy the 10 localized bond orbitals.

12-7 The Lewis formula for carbon tetrafluoride is

$$\begin{array}{c} :\overset{..}{F}: \\ | \\ :\overset{..}{\underset{..}{F}}-C-\overset{..}{\underset{..}{F}}: \\ | \\ :\overset{..}{\underset{..}{F}}: \end{array}$$

We learned in Chapter 11 that VSEPR theory predicts that CF_4 is tetrahedral, and so we shall use sp^3 hybrid orbitals on the carbon atom. A fluorine atom has a $(1s)^2(2s)^2(2p_x)^2(2p_y)^2(2p_z)^1$ electron configuration, indicating that one of its $2p$ orbitals is occupied by only one electron. We form four equivalent localized bond orbitals by combining each sp^3 orbital on the carbon atom with a $2p$ orbital on each fluorine atom. There are $4 + (4 \times 7) = 32$ valence electrons in CF_4. Two valence electrons of opposite spin occupy each of the four localized bond orbitals. The remaining 24 valence electrons are lone electron pairs on the fluorine atoms. Each fluorine atom has three lone electron pairs.

12-9   The Lewis formula for carbon tetrachloride is

$$
\begin{array}{c}
:\ddot{Cl}: \\
| \\
:\ddot{Cl}\!-\!C\!-\!\ddot{Cl}: \\
| \\
:\ddot{Cl}:
\end{array}
$$

We shall use sp^3 hybrid orbitals on the carbon atom. A chlorine atom has a $[Ne]3s^2(3p_x)^2(3p_y)^2(3p_z)^1$ electron configuration, indicating that one of its $3p$ orbitals is occupied by only one electron. We form four equivalent localized bond orbitals by combining each sp^3 orbital on the carbon atom with a $3p$ orbital on each chlorine atom. Two valence electrons of opposite spin occupy each of the four localized bond orbitals. The remaining 24 valence electrons are lone electron pairs on the chlorine atom.

12-11   The structure of H_3O^+ can be represented by

$$
\begin{array}{c}
\ddot{O}^{\oplus} \\
H \quad\quad H \\
| \\
H \quad 110°
\end{array}
$$

Each of the three σ bonds is formed by combining an sp^3 orbital on the oxygen atom with a $1s$ hydrogen orbital. The lone electron pair occupies the remaining sp^3 orbital.

12-13   The Lewis formula for hydrazine is

$$
\begin{array}{c}
H\!-\!\ddot{N}\!-\!\ddot{N}\!-\!H \\
| \quad\quad | \\
H \quad\quad H
\end{array}
$$

We shall use sp^3 orbitals on each nitrogen atom. The three σ bonds on each nitrogen atom are formed by combining two of the sp^3 orbitals on the nitrogen atom with two $1s$ hydrogen orbitals and one of the sp^3 nitrogen orbitals with an sp^3 orbital on the other nitrogen atom. A lone electron pair occupies the remaining sp^3 orbital on each nitrogen atom.

12-15   The Lewis formula for methylamine is

$$
\begin{array}{c}
\ddot{} \\
H\!-\!N\!-\!H \\
| \\
H\!-\!C\!-\!H \\
| \\
H
\end{array}
$$

There are three covalent bonds and one lone pair on the nitrogen atom. Two bonds are formed by combining an sp^3 on the nitrogen atom with a $1s$ orbital on a hydrogen atom. The remaining bond is formed by combining an sp^3 orbital on the nitrogen atom with an sp^3 orbital on the carbon atom. The lone electron pair occupies the remaining sp^3 orbital. There are four covalent bonds on the carbon atom. Three bonds are formed by combining an sp^3 orbital on the carbon atom and a $1s$ orbital on a hydrogen atom. The shape around the carbon atom is tetrahedral; the shape around the nitrogen atom is trigonal pyramidal.

12-17 There are two covalent bonds and two lone electron pairs on the oxygen atom. One bond is formed by combining an sp^3 orbital on the oxygen atom with a $1s$ orbital on a hydrogen atom. The other bond is formed by combining an sp^3 orbital on the oxygen atom with an sp^3 orbital on the carbon atom. Each lone electron pair occupies an sp^3 orbital on the oxygen atom. There are four covalent bonds on the carbon atom. Three bonds are formed by combining an sp^3 orbital on the carbon atom with a $1s$ orbital on a hydrogen atom. The shape around the carbon atom is tetrahedral; the shape around the oxygen atom is bent.

12-19 There are two covalent bonds and two lone electron pairs on the oxygen atom. Each bond is formed by combining an sp^3 orbital on the oxygen atom with an sp^3 orbital on a carbon atom. Each lone electron pair occupies an sp^3 orbital on the oxygen atom. There are four covalent bonds on each carbon atom. Three bonds are formed by combining an sp^3 orbital on a carbon atom and a $1s$ orbital on a hydrogen atom.

12-21 The electron configuration of an arsenic atom is $[Ar](4s)^2(3d)^{10}(4p_x)^1(4p_y)^1(4p_z)^1$. Each $4p$ orbital is occupied by only one electron. To describe the bonding in AsH_3, use the $1s$ orbitals on the hydrogen atoms and the three $4p$ orbitals on the arsenic atom.

12-23 The three B—H bonds in BH_3 are σ bonds. Each σ bond is formed by combining an sp^2 hybrid orbital on the boron atom with a $1s$ hydrogen orbital. The remaining p orbital on the boron atom is empty.

12-25 There are eight σ bonds and one π bond in propene. There are $(6 \times 1) + (3 \times 4) = 18$ valence electrons, which occupy the nine bond orbitals.

12-27 (a) The Lewis formula for $Cl_2C{=}CH_2$ is

There are 5 σ bonds and 1 π bond.
(b) The Lewis formula for $H_2C{=}CHCH{=}CH_2$ is

There are 9 σ bonds and 2 π bonds.
(c) The Lewis formula for $H_2C{=}C{=}CH_2$ is

There are 6 σ bonds and 2 π bonds.

(d) The Lewis formula is

$$
\begin{array}{c}
\text{H} \qquad \text{H} \\
\diagdown\ \diagup \\
\text{C} \\
\diagup\ \diagdown \\
\text{H}-\text{C} \qquad \text{C}-\text{H} \\
\| \qquad \| \\
\text{H}-\text{C} \qquad \text{C}-\text{H} \\
\diagdown\ \diagup \\
\text{C} \\
\diagup\ \diagdown \\
\text{H} \qquad \text{H}
\end{array}
$$

There are 14 σ bonds and 2 π bonds.

12-29 The two C—H bonds on the first carbon atom are formed by combining an sp^2 orbital on the carbon atom with a $1s$ orbital on a hydrogen atom. The C—H bond on the middle carbon atom is formed by combining an sp^2 orbital on the carbon atom and a $1s$ orbital on the hydrogen atom. The C—C single bond is formed by combining an sp^2 orbital on the middle carbon atom and an sp^3 orbital on the last carbon atom. The C=C double bond is formed by combining sp^2 orbitals on each carbon atom and the remaining $2p$ orbitals on each carbon atom. The three C—H bonds on the last carbon atom are formed by combining an sp^3 orbital on the carbon atom and a $1s$ orbital on a hydrogen atom.

12-31 The Lewis formula of acetaldehyde is

$$
\begin{array}{c}
\text{H}_3\text{C} \\
\diagdown \\
\quad\ \text{C}=\ddot{\text{O}}: \\
\diagup \\
\text{H}
\end{array}
$$

The central carbon atom in acetaldehyde form a σ bonds to the other carbon atom, a σ bond to the hydrogen atom and a σ bond and π bond to the oxygen atom. The carbon-carbon σ bond is formed by combining an sp^2 orbital on the central carbon atom with an sp^3 orbital on the other carbon atom. The carbon-hydrogen σ bond is formed by combining an sp^2 orbital on the central carbon atom and a $1s$ orbital on the hydrogen atom. The carbon-oxygen σ bond is formed by combining the remaining sp^2 orbital of the central carbon atom with an sp^2 orbital on the oxygen atom. The π bond is formed by combining the remaining $2p$ orbital on the central carbon atom with the remaining $2p$ orbital on the oxygen atom. The two lone electron pairs on the oxygen atom occupy the other two sp^2 orbitals. The shape of acetaldehyde is trigonal planar around the central carbon atom.

12-33 The σ-bond framework of formamide is

$$
\begin{array}{c}
\qquad\qquad sp^3\text{-}sp^2 \\
\\
\text{H}-\text{N}-\text{C}-\text{H} \\
\\
1s\text{-}sp^3 \qquad \text{H} \quad \text{O} \qquad sp^2\text{-}1s \\
\\
\qquad\qquad\qquad sp^2\text{-}sp^2
\end{array}
$$

The remaining bond between the carbon atom and the oxygen atom is a π bond that is formed from the $2p$ orbitals on each atom.

12-35 The Lewis formula for ethylacetylene is

$$\underset{\underset{\displaystyle H}{|}}{\overset{\overset{\displaystyle H}{|}}{H-C}}-\underset{\underset{\displaystyle H}{|}}{\overset{\overset{\displaystyle H}{|}}{C}}-C\equiv C-H$$

There are nine σ bonds and two π bonds. There are $(6 \times 1) + (4 \times 4) = 22$ valence electrons, which occupy the 11 bond orbitals.

12-37 The Lewis formula of carbon monoxide is

$$:C \overset{\ominus}{\equiv} \overset{\oplus}{O}:$$

The σ bond between the carbon and oxygen atoms is formed by combining an sp orbital on the carbon atom and an sp orbital on the oxygen atom. Each of the two π bonds is formed by combining a $2p$ orbital on the carbon atom and a $2p$ orbital on the oxygen atom. One lone electron pair occupies an sp orbital on the carbon atom; the other pair occupies an sp orbital on the oxygen atom.

12-39 The σ-bond framework of methylacetylene is

The remaining bonds between the carbon atoms are two π bonds formed from the $2p$ orbitals on each atom. There are six σ bonds and two π bonds. There are $(4 \times 1) + (3 \times 4) = 16$ valence electrons which occupy the eight bond orbitals.

12-41 The Lewis formula for phenol is

The σ-bond framework is

The three π bonds are delocalized over the entire ring.

12-43   The Lewis formula for naphthalene is

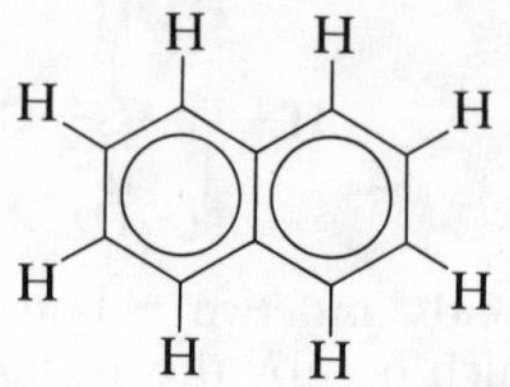

The σ-bond framework is

sp^2-1s

sp^2-sp^2

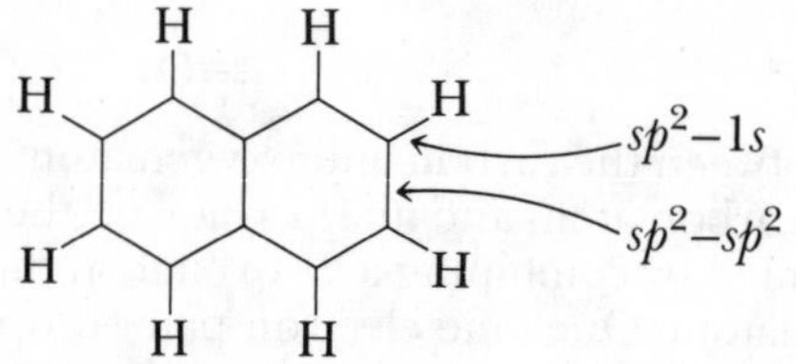

The five π bonds are delocalized over the entire two rings as indicated by the circles in the Lewis formula.

12-45   The Lewis formula for hexamethylbenzene is

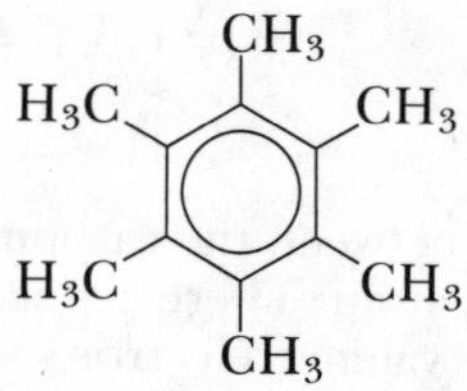

The σ-bond framework is

sp^3-1s

sp^2-sp^3

sp^2-sp^2

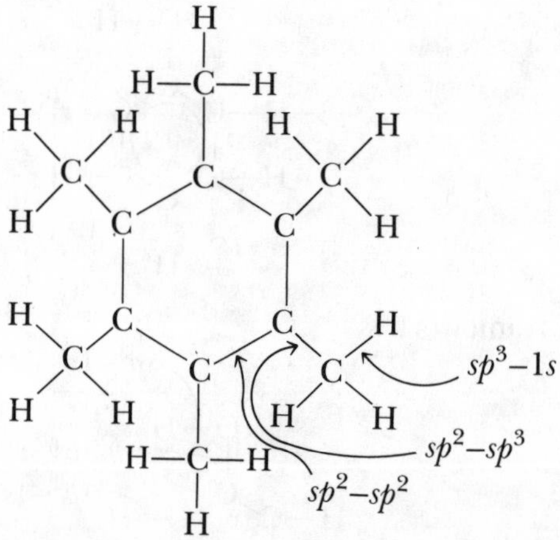

The three π bonds are spread uniformly over the entire ring. There are 30 σ bonds and 3 π bonds. There are $(18 \times 1) + (12 \times 4) = 66$ valence electrons which occupy the 33 bond orbitals.

12-47   There are eight electrons in diatomic beryllium. Using Figure 12-27, we see that the ground-state electron configuration of diatomic beryllium is $(1\sigma)^2(1\sigma*)^2(2\sigma)^2(2\sigma*)^2$. There are four electrons in bonding orbitals and four electrons in antibonding orbitals, and so Be_2 has no net bonding. We predict that Be_2 does not exist.

12-49 We find that the bond order of N_2 is 3 while the bond order of N_2^+ is $2\frac{1}{2}$ (Example 12-8). The bond energy increases as the bond order increases; therefore, the bond energy of N_2 is greater than that of N_2^+. However, we find that the bond order of O_2 is 2, while the bond order of O_2^+ is $2\frac{1}{2}$ (see page 456 in the text). Therefore, the bond energy of O_2 is less than that of O_2^+.

12-51 Using Figure 12-27 and Equation (12-1), we find that the ground-state electron configurations and bond orders of C_2 and C_2^{2-} are:

	Ground-state electron configuration	Bond order
C_2	$(1\sigma)^2(1\sigma*)^2(2\sigma)^2(2\sigma*)^2(1\pi)^4$	2
C_2^{2-}	$(1\sigma)^2(1\sigma*)^2(2\sigma)^2(2\sigma*)^2(1\pi)^4(3\sigma)^2$	3

Because the bond order of C_2^{2-} is greater than that of C_2, we predict that C_2^{2-} has a larger bond energy and a shorter bond length than C_2.

12-53 Carbon monoxide has $6 + 8 = 14$ electrons, and so the ground-state electron configuration of carbon monoxide is $(1\sigma)^2(1\sigma*)^2(2\sigma)^2(2\sigma*)^2(1\pi)^4(3\sigma)^2$. The bond order of CO is 3. The Lewis formula for CO is

$$^{\ominus}:C\equiv O:^{\oplus}$$

Both molecular orbital theory and the Lewis formula predict that there is a triple bond in CO.

E   ANSWERS TO THE EVEN-NUMBERED PROBLEMS

12-2 When the two hydrogen atoms are separated by less than the equilibrium distance (74 pm), they repel each other, which is reflected by positive values of the energy.

12-4 (a) 3 localized bonds, 1 lone pair
(b) 3 localized bonds, 4 lone pairs
(c) 3 localized bonds, 1 lone pair
(d) 2 localized bonds, 8 lone pairs
(e) 5 localized bonds, 2 lone pairs

12-6 13 bonds and 26 valence electrons

12-8 The Lewis formula for chloroform is

$$\ddot{:}\overset{\displaystyle ..}{\underset{..}{Cl}}\ddot{:}$$
$$|$$
$$:\ddot{Cl}-C-H$$
$$|$$
$$:\underset{..}{Cl}:$$

We learned that VSEPR theory predicts that $HCCl_3$ is tetrahedral, and we know that the sp^3 hybrid orbitals on a carbon atom will point to the vertices of a tetrahedron. A chlorine atom has a $[\text{Ne}](3s)^2(3p_x)^2(3p_y)^2(3p_z)^1$ electron configuration, indicating that one of its $3p$ orbitals is occupied by only one electron. We can form four equivalent localized bond orbitals by combining each sp^3 orbital on the carbon atom with a $1s$ orbital on the hydrogen atom and with a $3p$ orbital on each chlorine atom. There are $(4 \times 1) + (7 \times 3) + (1 \times 1) = 26$ valence electrons in HCCl_3. Two valence electrons of opposite spin occupy each of the four bond orbitals. The remaining 18 valence electrons are lone electron pairs on the three chlorine atoms. Each chlorine atom has three lone electron pairs.

12-10   The Lewis formula for OF_2 is

$$: \ddot{\text{F}} — \ddot{\text{O}} — \ddot{\text{F}} :$$

We shall use sp^3 hybrid orbitals on the oxygen atom. A fluorine atom has a $1s^2 2s^2 (2p_x)^2 (2p_y)^2 (2p_z)^1$ electron configuration, indicating that one of its $2p$ orbitals is occupied by only one electron. We form two equivalent localized bond orbitals by combining each sp^3 orbital on the oxygen atom with a $2p$ orbital on each fluorine atom. Two valence electrons of opposite spin occupy each of the two localized bond orbitals. The two lone electron pairs on the oxygen occupy the remaining two sp^3 orbitals on the oxygen atom. The remaining 12 valence electrons are lone electron pairs on the fluorine atoms.

12-12   The Lewis formula for NF_3 is

$$: \ddot{\text{F}} — \overset{..}{\text{N}} — \ddot{\text{F}} :$$
$$\mid$$
$$: \ddot{\text{F}} :$$

The three bonds are formed by combining an sp^3 orbital on the nitrogen atom with a $2p$ orbital on a fluorine atom. We use a $2p$ orbital on each fluorine atom because the electron configuration of a fluorine atom is $(1s)^2 (2s)^2 (2p_x)^2 (2p_y)^2 (2p_z)^1$, indicating that one of its $2p$ orbitals is occupied by only one electron. The lone electron pair on the nitrogen atom occupies the remaining sp^3 orbital. There are $(1 \times 5) + (3 \times 7) = 26$ valence electrons in NF_3.

12-14   The Lewis formula for hydrogen peroxide is

$$\text{H} — \ddot{\text{O}} — \ddot{\text{O}} — \text{H}$$

We shall use sp^3 orbitals on each oxygen atom. There are $(2 \times 1) + (2 \times 6) = 14$ valence electrons. There are three localized bonds. The H—O bond is formed by combining an sp^3 oxygen orbital with a $1s$ hydrogen orbital. The O—O bond is formed by combining an sp^3 orbital on one oxygen atom with an sp^3 orbital on the other oxygen atom. Six of the valence electrons occupy bond orbitals and eight valence electrons constitute the four lone pairs, two on each oxygen atom.

12-16   The Lewis formula for dimethylamine is

$$\begin{array}{ccccc} & \text{H} & & \text{H} & \\ & | & \overset{..}{} & | & \\ \text{H} — & \text{C} — & \text{N} — & \text{C} — & \text{H} \\ & | & | & | & \\ & \text{H} & \text{H} & \text{H} & \end{array}$$

There are nine σ bonds and one lone electron pair. There are $(7 \times 1) +$ $(2 \times 4) + (1 \times 5) = 20$ valence electrons. Two bonds on the nitrogen atom are formed by combining an sp^3 orbital on the nitrogen atom with an sp^3 orbital on a carbon atom. One bond on the nitrogen atom is formed by combining an sp^3 orbital on the nitrogen atom with a $1s$ orbital on a hydrogen atom. The lone electron pair occupies the remaining sp^3 orbital on the nitrogen atom. Each of the remaining six σ bonds is formed by combining an sp^3 orbital on a carbon atom and a $1s$ orbital on a hydrogen atom. The shape around the nitrogen atom is trigonal pyramidal. The shape around each carbon atom is tetrahedral.

12-18 The Lewis formula for ethyl alcohol is

$$
\begin{array}{ccccc}
& \text{H} & \text{H} & & \\
& | & | & \ddots & \\
\text{H}\!-\!\!& \text{C} & \!\!-\!\!\text{C}\!\!-\!\! & \ddot{\text{O}}\!\!-\!\!\text{H} & \\
& | & | & \ddots & \\
& \text{H} & \text{H} & &
\end{array}
$$

The two σ bonds on the oxygen atom are formed by combining an sp^3 oxygen orbital with a hydrogen $1s$ orbital and an sp^3 oxygen orbital with a carbon sp^3 orbital. The two lone electron pairs occupy the remaining two sp^3 orbitals on the oxygen atom. The σ bonds on the carbon atoms are formed by combining sp^3 carbon orbitals with $1s$ hydrogen orbitals, sp^3 carbon orbitals, or an sp^3 oxygen orbital. The shape of ethyl alcohol is tetrahedral around each carbon atom and bent around the oxygen atom. There are eight σ bonds, $(1 \times 6) + (2 \times 4) +$ $(6 \times 1) = 20$ valence electrons, and two lone electron pairs on the oxygen atom.

12-20 There are two covalent bonds and two lone electron pairs on the oxygen atom. Each C—O bond is formed by combining an sp^3 orbital on the oxygen atom with an sp^3 orbital on a carbon atom. Each lone electron pair occupies an sp^3 orbital on the oxygen atom. Each of the eight C—H bonds is formed by combining an sp^3 orbital on the carbon atom with a $1s$ orbital on a hydrogen atom. The C—C bond is formed by combining an sp^3 orbital on one carbon atom with an sp^3 orbital on the other carbon atom.

12-22 The electron configuration of a tellurium atom is

$$[\text{Kr}](5s)^2(4d)^{10}(5p_x)^2(5p_y)^1(5p_z)^1$$

indicating that two of the $5p$ orbitals are occupied by only one electron. To describe the bonding in H_2Te, use the $1s$ orbitals on the hydrogen atom and two of the $5p$ orbitals on the tellurium atom.

12-24 The three Al—Cl bonds in $AlCl_3$ are σ bonds. Each σ bond is formed by combining an sp^2 hybrid orbital on the aluminum atom with a $3p$ chlorine orbital.

12-26 There are eleven σ bonds and one π bond in 2-butene. There are $(8 \times 1) +$ $(4 \times 4) = 24$ valence electrons, which occupy the 12 bond orbitals.

12-28 (a) 5 σ bonds and 1 π bond
  (b) 8 σ bonds and 1 π bond
  (c) 6 σ bonds and 2 π bonds
  (d) 8 σ bonds and 2 π bonds

12-30   Each of the three C—H bonds is formed by combining an sp^2 orbital on a carbon atom and a $1s$ orbital on a hydrogen atom. The C—Cl bond is formed by combining an sp^2 orbital on the carbon atom and a $3p$ orbital on the chlorine atom. There are three lone electron pairs on the chlorine atom. The C=C double bond is formed by combining sp^2 orbitals on each carbon atom and by combining the remaining p orbitals on each carbon atom.

12-32   The central carbon atom in acetone forms two σ bonds to the two other carbon atoms and a σ bond and π bond to the oxygen atom. Each carbon-carbon σ bond is formed by combining an sp^2 orbital on the central carbon atom with an sp^3 orbital on the other carbon atom. The carbon-oxygen σ bond is formed by combining the remaining sp^2 orbital of the central carbon atom with an sp^2 orbital on the oxygen atom. The π bond is formed by combining the remaining $2p$ orbital on the central carbon atom with the remaining $2p$ orbital on the oxygen atom. The two lone electron pairs on the oxygen atom occupy the other two sp^2 orbitals. The shape of acetone is trigonal planar around the central carbon atom

$$ \overset{120°}{O=C} \begin{array}{c} CH_3 \\ \\ CH_3 \end{array} $$

12-34   The σ-bond framework of urea is

$$ \begin{array}{c} sp^3-sp^2 \qquad sp^2-sp^3 \\ 1s-sp^3 \\ H-N-C-N-H \qquad sp^3-1s \\ H \quad O \quad H \\ sp^2-sp^2 \end{array} $$

The remaining bond between the carbon atom and the oxygen atom is a π bond that is formed from the $2p$ orbitals on each atom.

12-36   There are five σ bonds and two π bonds. There are $(3 \times 1) + (2 \times 4) + (1 \times 5) = 16$ valence electrons, which occupy the seven bond orbitals, and one lone pair orbital on the nitrogen atom.

12-38   The Lewis formula for the acetylide ion is

$$:\overset{\ominus}{C}\equiv\overset{\ominus}{C}: $$

The σ bond between the carbon atoms is formed by combining an sp orbital on each of the carbon atoms. The two π bonds are formed by combining the $2p$ orbitals on each of the carbon atoms. Each lone electron pair occupies an sp orbital on a carbon atom.

12-40   The σ-bond framework of dimethylacetylene ($CH_3C\equiv CCH_3$) is

The remaining bonds between the middle two carbon atoms are two π bonds formed from the $2p$ orbitals on each carbon atom. The shape of the molecule is linear around the triple bond

$$C-C\equiv C-C$$

There are nine σ bonds and two π bonds. There are $(6 \times 1) + (4 \times 4) = 22$ valence electrons which occupy the 11 bond orbitals.

12-42   The Lewis formula for aniline is

The σ-bond framework is

The three π bonds are delocalized over the entire molecule.

12-44   The Lewis formula for anthracene is

which is a combination of several resonance forms. The σ-bond framework is

The seven π bonds are delocalized over the three rings.

12-46 The Lewis formula for pyridine is

The σ-bond framework of pyridine is

The three π bonds are delocalized over the entire ring. The lone electron pair on the nitrogen atom occupies the remaining sp^2 orbital.

12-48 We predict that B_2 is paramagnetic.

12-50 We predict that F_2^+ has a larger bond energy and a shorter bond length than F_2.

12-52 NF, NF^+ and NF^- are paramagnetic. Their bond orders are 2, $2\frac{1}{2}$, and $1\frac{1}{2}$, respectively.

12-54 The bond order is 3. The Lewis formula is

$$: C \equiv N :^{\ominus}$$

Both molecular orbital theory and the Lewis formula predict that there is a triple bond in CN^-.

F   ANSWERS TO THE SELF-TEST

1 the coalescing or overlapping of the two $1s$ atomic orbitals

2 combinations of atomic orbitals

3 combining atomic orbitals on the same atom

4 combining a $2s$ orbital and all three $2p$ orbitals

5 the vertices of a tetrahedron

6 combining a sp^3 orbital on the carbon atom with a hydrogen $1s$ atomic orbital

7 circular

8 two

9 true

10 true

11 combining an sp^3 orbital on one carbon atom with an sp^3 orbital on the other carbon atom

12 an sp^3 orbital on the oxygen atom with a hydrogen $1s$ atomic orbital

13 combining a $2s$ orbital with two of the $2p$ orbitals

14 three

15 the vertices of an equilateral triangle

16 p orbitals from different atoms are combined

17 false (It is similar to a p orbital in cross section.)

18 σ, π

19 $(2 \times 4) + (4 \times 1) = 12$ valence electrons; five σ bonds and one π bond

20 $(4 \times 4) + (6 \times 1) = 22$ valence electrons; nine σ bonds and two π bonds

21 false

22 combining a carbon sp^2 orbital and an oxygen sp^2 orbital to form a σ bond and combining a carbon p orbital and an oxygen p orbital to form a π bond

23 true

24 on opposite sides of the double bond

25 stereo

26 false

27 combining a $2s$ orbital with one of the $2p$ orbitals

28 $180°$ from each other

29 two

30 one σ bond and two π bonds

31 $(3 \times 4) + (4 \times 1) = 16$ valence electrons; six, two

32 true

33 planar, hexagonal

34 delocalized

35 false

36 H_2^+, the hydrogen molecular ion

37 false (See Figure 12-24.)

38 false (See Figure 12-27.)

39 is concentrated in the region between the two nuclei

40 is zero in the region between the two nuclei

41 antibonding orbital of lowest energy (See Figure 12-27.)

42 false (The electrons are placed into the molecular orbitals according to the Pauli exclusion principle and Hund's rule.)

43 two

44 four

45 false

46 true

47 one

48 false (Hund's rule)

49 true (photoelectron spectrum)

50 The two $1\pi^*$ electrons occupy separate $1\pi^*$ orbitals and are of the same spin (two electrons are unpaired).

13 / Liquids and Solids

A   OUTLINE OF CHAPTER 13

13-1   Interactions between molecules are much greater in the solid and liquid phases than in the gas phase.

Some of the properties of the gas, liquid, and solid phases are summarized on page 466.

Molecules translate, rotate, and vibrate freely in the gas phase, but not in the solid and liquid phases.

13-2   The processes of melting and boiling appear as horizontal lines on a heating curve.

Figure 13-4 shows a heating curve for one mole of water starting as ice at $-10°C$.

The molar enthalpy of fusion, $\Delta \bar{H}_{fus}$, is the heat required to melt one mole of a substance.

The molar enthalpy of vaporization, $\Delta \bar{H}_{vap}$, is the heat required to vaporize one mole of a substance.

The heat absorbed in raising the temperature of a substance from T_1 to T_2 without a change in phase is given by

$$q_P = n\bar{C}_P(T_2 - T_1) \tag{13-1}$$

where $\bar{C}_P$ is the molar heat capacity at constant pressure and n is the number of moles.

13-3   It requires energy to melt a solid or to vaporize a liquid.

The enthalpy of vaporization of a substance is greater than its enthalpy of fusion, or

$$\Delta \bar{H}_{vap} > \Delta \bar{H}_{fus}$$

The values of the melting point, boiling point, and molar enthalpies of vaporization and fusion of some substances are given in Table 13-1.

13-4   The van der Waals forces are attractive forces between molecules.

The value of $\Delta \bar{H}_{vap}$ is a measure of how strongly the molecules in a liquid attract each other.

Values of $\Delta \bar{H}_{vap}$ are relatively large for ionic compounds.

Polar molecules attract each other by a dipole-dipole force (Figure 13-7).

Water and some other compounds have relatively large values of $\Delta \bar{H}_{vap}$ because of hydrogen bonding (Figures 13-8, 13-9, 13-10, and 13-13).

All molecules attract each other by London forces (Figures 13-11 and 13-12).

The strengths of London forces depend upon the number of electrons in the two molecules.

13-5   The enthalpy of sublimation is a measure of the energy of interaction between the molecules in a solid.

Sublimation is the process whereby a solid is converted directly into a gas.

The molar enthalpy of sublimation, $\Delta \bar{H}_{sub}$, is the energy required to sublime one mole of a substance.

$$\Delta \bar{H}_{sub} = \Delta \bar{H}_{fus} + \Delta \bar{H}_{vap} \qquad (13\text{-}2)$$

13-6   The equilibrium between a liquid and its vapor is a dynamic equilibrium.

When the rate of evaporation of a liquid is equal to the rate of condensation of its vapor, a liquid-vapor equilibrium is established (Figures 13-15 and 13-16).

The equilibrium vapor pressure is the pressure of the vapor in equilibrium with the liquid.

13-7   A liquid has a unique equilibrium vapor pressure at each temperature.

The equilibrium vapor pressure of a liquid increases with temperature (Figure 13-18).

The normal boiling point of a liquid is the temperature at which its equilibrium vapor pressure is 1 atm.

The boiling point of a liquid decreases with increasing elevation (Figure 13-19).

13-8   Relative humidity is based upon the vapor pressure of water.

The relative humidity is a measure of the amount of water vapor in the atmosphere:

$$\text{relative humidity} = \frac{P_{H_2O}}{P^{\circ}_{H_2O}} \times 100 \qquad (13\text{-}3)$$

where P_{H_2O} is the partial pressure of the water vapor and $P^{\circ}_{H_2O}$ is the equilibrium vapor pressure at the same temperature (Table 13-2).

The dew point is the air temperature at which the relative humidity reaches 100 percent.

13-9   Surface tension minimizes the surface area of a liquid.

The surface tension is the net inward attraction of molecules on the surface of a liquid (Figure 13-20).

Surfactants lower surface tension.

Capillary action is the rise of a liquid in a thin tube (Figure 13-23).

13-10   X-ray diffraction patterns yield information about the structure of crystals.

The X-ray diffraction produced by a crystal is shown in Figure 13-24.

The unit cell is the smallest subunit of a crystal lattice that can be used to generate the entire lattice (Figures 13-27 and 13-28).

The three cubic unit cells are simple cubic, body-centered cubic, and face-centered cubic, as shown in Figures 13-29 and 13-30.

The unit cell of many metals is one of the three cubic unit cells.

The cubic closest-packed structure is the face-centered cubic arrangement (Figure 13-32).

The radii of atoms in a face-centered cubic structure can be calculated when the density is known.

The crystal structures of ionic solids often depend upon the differences in sizes of the cations and anions (Figure 13-33).

Molecular crystals come in a variety of structures (Figures 13-36 through 13-38).

13-11   A phase diagram displays the phase equilibrium lines simultaneously.

The phase diagrams of water and carbon dioxide are shown in Figures 13-39 and 13-40.

The critical point terminates the vapor pressure curve.

A gas with a temperature above its critical temperature cannot be liquified.

The sublimation pressure curve gives the temperature at which the solid and gas phases are in equilibrium at a particular pressure.

The melting point curve gives the temperature at which the solid and liquid phases are in equilibrium at a particular pressure.

The vapor pressure curve gives the temperature at which the liquid and gas phases are in equilibrium at a particular pressure.

The triple point is the temperature and pressure at which three phases coexist in equilibrium.

13-12   Diamond can be produced from graphite by applying very high pressure.

Diamond has a covalently bonded tetrahedral network (Figure 13-41).

Graphite has a layered structure (Figure 13-42).

The graphite-diamond phase equilibrium curve is shown in Figure 13-43.

B   SELF-TEST

1   The molecules in a solid move freely throughout the solid. *True/False*

2   The molecules in a liquid have no rotational motion. *True/False*

3   A liquid is easy to compress to smaller volumes. *True/False*

4 When heat is added to a liquid at a constant rate, the temperature will remain constant for a period of time at _____.

5 When heat is added to a solid at a constant rate, the temperature will remain constant for a period of time at _____.

6 The amount of energy as heat required to raise the temperature of a substance is determined by the _____ of the substance.

7 The energy as heat required to melt one mole of a solid is the _____ _____.

8 Energy as heat is required to melt a solid because _____ _____.

9 The energy as heat required to vaporize one mole of a liquid is the _____ _____.

10 Energy is required to vaporize a liquid because _____ _____.

11 For all substances, $\Delta \bar{H}_{vap}$ is (*greater/smaller*) than $\Delta \bar{H}_{fus}$.

12 The evaporation of water in perspiration (*adds/removes*) heat from the body.

13 There are attractive forces between all molecules or atoms. *True/False*

14 A large value of $\Delta \bar{H}_{vap}$ indicates a strong attraction between the particles in a liquid. *True/False*

15 The values of $\Delta \bar{H}_{vap}$ of ionic compounds are smaller than for other compounds. *True/False*

16 The attractive forces between polar molecules are due to _____ _____ attraction.

17 Ammonia, NH_3, has a lower value of $\Delta \bar{H}_{vap}$ than methane, CH_4. *True/False*

18 Hydrogen bonding is _____ _____.

19 The attractive forces between nonpolar molecules are called _____ _____.

20 No solid can be converted to a gas directly. *True/False*

21 The energy required to sublime one mole of a solid is the _____.

22 When a liquid is placed in a closed container, vapor from the liquid appears in the container. *True/False*

23 When the rate of condensation is equal to the rate of evaporation, the process of evaporation appears to cease. *True/False*

24 The system of a liquid in a closed container is at equilibrium when the rate _____.

25 A system is at equilibrium when no net observable change occurs. *True/False*

26 The equilibrium vapor pressure is the pressure _____

_____ .

27 The equilibrium vapor pressure of a substance is the same at all temperatures. *True/False*

28 The normal boiling point of a liquid is _____

_____ .

29 Water always boils at 100°C. *True/False*

30 Relative humidity is a measure of the amount _____

_____

_____ .

31 The dew point is _____

_____ .

32 The surface tension of a liquid is due to _____

_____ .

33 The surface tension tends to hold a drop of liquid in the form of a

_____ .

34 An X-ray diffraction pattern of a crystal can be used to determine the

_____ .

35 The unit cells of all ionic crystals are identical. *True/False*

36 The three types of cubic unit cells are _____

_____ .

37 Draw a simple cubic unit cell.

38 The cubic closest-packed structure represents _____

_____ .

39 Atomic or ionic radii can be calculated from crystal structures. *True/False*

40 Copper crystallizes as a face-centered cubic lattice. Copper atoms are located at the _____ and in the _____ .

41 The different crystal-packing arrangements for NaCl and CsCl are due to

_____ .

42 All molecular crystals have the same structure. *True/False*

43 A phase diagram can be used to determine the state of a substance at any pressure and temperature. *True/False*

44 The melting point curve separates the _____ phase and the _____ phase.

45 The melting point of water changes markedly with pressure. *True/False*

46 The critical temperature is _____

_____ .

47 A triple point is _____

_____ .

48 A gas can be liquified at all temperatures by applying sufficient pressure. *True/False*

49 Liquid carbon dioxide cannot exist at any temperature and pressure. *True/False*

50 The melting point of all substances decreases with pressure. *True/False*

51 A substance does not have a normal boiling point when its triple point

_____ .

52 Two crystalline structures of solid carbon are _____ and _____ .

C   CALCULATIONS YOU SHOULD KNOW HOW TO DO

1 Construct a heating curve for a substance that is heated at some given rate. You need the values of the heat capacities of the solid, liquid, and gas phases and the values of $\Delta \bar{H}_{fus}$ and $\Delta \bar{H}_{vap}$. See Example 13-1 and Problems 13-11 through 13-14.

2 Compute the quantity of heat that is absorbed or evolved in vaporization and fusion. See Example 13-2 and Problems 13-1 through 13-4, 13-9, and 13-10.

3 Compute the quantity of heat that is absorbed or evolved when a substance is heated or cooled through a phase change. See Example 13-3 and Problems 13-5 through 13-8.

4 Compute the quantity of heat that is absorbed or evolved in sublimation. See Problems 13-23 through 13-26.

5 Calculate the relative humidity and the dew point using the equation

$$\text{relative humidity} = \frac{P_{H_2O}}{P^{\circ}_{H_2O}} \times 100 \qquad (13\text{-}3)$$

and the data in Table 13-2. See Example 13-7 and Problems 13-35 through 13-38.

6 Calculate the length of an edge of a unit cell. See Example 13-9 and Problems 13-43, 13-44, 13-49, and 13-50.

7 Calculate the density of a substance, given the length of an edge of the unit cell. See Problems 13-45, 13-46, 13-53, and 13-54.

8 Calculate Avogadro's number, given the density and length of an edge of the unit cell. See Example 13-10 and Problems 13-47 and 13-48.

D   SOLUTIONS TO THE ODD-NUMBERED PROBLEMS

13-1   The amount of heat, q_P, evolved when 1.00 kg of rubidium condenses is

$$q_P = (1.00 \text{ kg})\left(\frac{1000 \text{ g}}{1 \text{ kg}}\right)\left(\frac{1 \text{ mol}}{85.47 \text{ g}}\right)(69 \text{ kJ} \cdot \text{mol}^{-1})$$

$$= 810 \text{ kJ}$$

13-3   The number of moles in 60.0 g of benzene is

$$n = (60.0 \text{ g})\left(\frac{1 \text{ mol}}{78.11 \text{ g}}\right) = 0.768 \text{ mol}$$

The molar heat of vaporization is the heat required to vaporize exactly 1 mole. If 26.2 kJ are required to vaporize 0.768 mol, then

$$\Delta \bar{H}_{vap} = \frac{26.2 \text{ kJ}}{0.768 \text{ mol}} = 34.1 \text{ kJ} \cdot \text{mol}^{-1}$$

13-5   The number of moles in 0.500 kg of ice is

$$n = (0.500 \text{ kg})\left(\frac{1000 \text{ g}}{1 \text{ kg}}\right)\left(\frac{1 \text{ mol}}{18.02 \text{ g}}\right) = 27.75 \text{ mol}$$

The heat absorbed when the ice melts is

$$q_P = n\Delta \bar{H}_{fus}; \quad \Delta \bar{H}_{fus} = 6.01 \text{ kJ} \cdot \text{mol}^{-1} \qquad \text{(from Table 13-1)}$$

$$q_P = (27.75 \text{ mol})(6.01 \text{ kJ} \cdot \text{mol}^{-1})$$

$$= 167 \text{ kJ}$$

The heat required to raise the temperature of water from 0° to 25°C is given by

$$q_P = n\bar{C}_P(T_2 - T_1) \tag{13-1}$$

The molar heat capacity of water is $75.3 \text{ J} \cdot \text{K}^{-1} \cdot \text{mol}^{-1}$ (Example 13-1):

$$q_P = (27.75 \text{ mol})(75.3 \text{ J} \cdot \text{K}^{-1} \cdot \text{mol}^{-1})(25 \text{ K})$$
$$= 52000 \text{ J} = 52 \text{ kJ}$$

The total heat required is

$$q_P = 167 \text{ kJ} + 52 \text{ kJ} = 219 \text{ kJ}$$

13-7 The number of moles in 20.1 g of mercury is

$$n = (20.1 \text{ g})\left(\frac{1 \text{ mol Hg}}{200.6 \text{ g}}\right) = 0.1002 \text{ mol}$$

The heat *released* when 0.1002 mol of mercury freezes at its melting point is (Table 13-1)

$$q_P = n(\Delta\bar{H}_{fus})$$
$$= (0.1002 \text{ mol})(2.30 \text{ kJ} \cdot \text{mol}^{-1}) = 0.230 \text{ kJ}$$

The heat *released* when 0.100 mol of mercury is cooled from 298 K to 234 K (the melting point of mercury) is given by

$$q_P = n\bar{C}_P(T_2 - T_1)$$
$$= (0.1002 \text{ mol})(28.0 \text{ J} \cdot \text{K}^{-1} \cdot \text{mol}^{-1})(64 \text{ K})$$
$$= 180 \text{ J} = 0.180 \text{ kJ}$$

The total heat released = 0.230 kJ + 0.180 kJ = 0.410 kJ.

13-9

$$q_P = n\Delta\bar{H}_{vap}$$
$$= (100 \text{ g})\left(\frac{1 \text{ mol}}{60.09 \text{ g}}\right)(42.1 \text{ kJ} \cdot \text{mol}^{-1})$$
$$= 70.1 \text{ kJ}$$

13-11 Mercury is a liquid at 300 K and boils at 630 K. It requires

$$q_P = n\bar{C}_P(T_2 - T_1) = (10.0 \text{ g})\left(\frac{1 \text{ mol}}{200.6 \text{ g}}\right)(28.0 \text{ J} \cdot \text{K}^{-1} \cdot \text{mol}^{-1})(330 \text{ K})$$
$$= 461 \text{ J}$$

to heat the liquid mercury from 300 K to its boiling point. If heat is supplied at $100 \text{ J} \cdot \text{min}^{-1}$, then the time required is

$$t = \frac{461 \text{ J}}{100 \text{ J} \cdot \text{min}^{-1}} = 4.61 \text{ min}$$

The heat required to vaporize the mercury is given by

$$q_P = n\Delta\bar{H}_{vap} = (10.0 \text{ g})\left(\frac{1 \text{ mol}}{200.6 \text{ g}}\right)(59.1 \text{ kJ} \cdot \text{mol}^{-1})$$

$$= 2.95 \text{ kJ} = 2950 \text{ J}$$

At a heating rate of $100 \text{ J} \cdot \text{min}^{-1}$, the time required is

$$t = \frac{2950 \text{ J}}{100 \text{ J} \cdot \text{min}^{-1}} = 29.5 \text{ min}$$

The heat required to heat the gaseous mercury from 630 K to 800 K is

$$q_P = n\bar{C}_P(T_2 - T_1) = (10.0 \text{ g})\left(\frac{1 \text{ mol}}{200.6 \text{ g}}\right)(20.8 \text{ J} \cdot \text{K}^{-1} \cdot \text{mol}^{-1})(170 \text{ K})$$

$$= 176 \text{ J}$$

and the time required is

$$t = \frac{176 \text{ J}}{100 \text{ J} \cdot \text{min}^{-1}} = 1.76 \text{ min}$$

The heating curve looks like that on the next page.

13-13 The melting point of lead is 327°C, and the temperature remains constant during the melting of the lead. The heat required to melt the lead is

$$q_P = (100 \text{ J} \cdot \text{min}^{-1})(2.30 \text{ min})$$

$$= 230 \text{ J}$$

The number of moles in 10.00 g of lead is

$$n = (10.00 \text{ g})\left(\frac{1 \text{ mol}}{207.2 \text{ g}}\right) = 0.04826 \text{ mol}$$

and so

$$\Delta\bar{H}_{fus} = \frac{230 \text{ J}}{0.04826 \text{ mol}} = 4770 \text{ J} \cdot \text{mol}^{-1} = 4.77 \text{ kJ} \cdot \text{mol}^{-1}$$

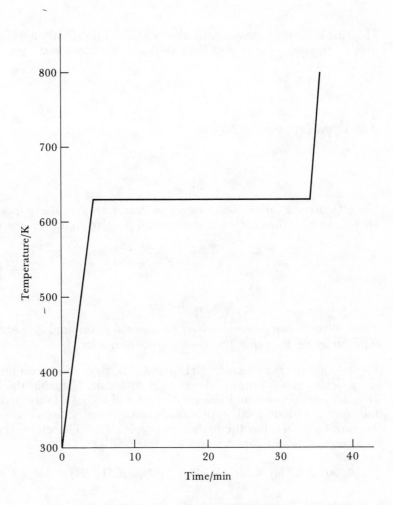

13-15   The only ionic compound is KBr. Thus we predict that KBr has the highest boiling point. The Lewis formulas of C_2H_5OH and C_2H_6 are

$$
\begin{array}{ccc}
\text{H} \quad \text{H} & & \text{H} \quad \text{H} \\
\mid \quad \mid & & \mid \quad \mid \\
\text{H}-\text{C}-\text{C}-\overset{\cdot\cdot}{\underset{\cdot\cdot}{\text{O}}}-\text{H} & \quad\text{and}\quad & \text{H}-\text{C}-\text{C}-\text{H} \\
\mid \quad \mid & & \mid \quad \mid \\
\text{H} \quad \text{H} & & \text{H} \quad \text{H}
\end{array}
$$

We see that liquid C_2H_5OH is hydrogen bonded and C_2H_6 is nonpolar. Helium is a smaller molecule than C_2H_6. Therefore, the predicted order is

$$T_b[\text{He}] < T_b[\text{C}_2\text{H}_6] < T_b[\text{C}_2\text{H}_5\text{OH}] < T_b[\text{KBr}]$$

13-17   NaF is an ionic compound, and so has ionic interactions.
The Lewis formula for ClF is

$$:\overset{\cdot\cdot}{\underset{\cdot\cdot}{\text{Cl}}}-\overset{\cdot\cdot}{\underset{\cdot\cdot}{\text{F}}}:$$

Fluorine is more electronegative than chlorine; therefore, the fluorine atom has a small negative charge and the chlorine atom has a small positive charge

$$\overset{\delta+}{:\!\ddot{Cl}}\!-\!\overset{\delta-}{\ddot{F}\!:}$$

The molecule is polar.
The Lewis formula for NF_3 is

$$:\!\ddot{F}\!-\!\ddot{N}\!-\!\ddot{F}\!:$$
$$|$$
$$:\!\ddot{F}\!:$$

Since fluorine is more electronegative than nitrogen, there is a small negative charge on each fluorine atom and a small positive charge on the nitrogen atom:

$$\overset{\delta-}{:\!\ddot{F}}\!-\!\overset{\delta+}{\ddot{N}}\!-\!\overset{\delta-}{\ddot{F}\!:}$$
$$|$$
$$:\!\ddot{F}\!:$$
$$\delta-$$

The molecule is polar because of its trigonal pyramidal shape.
The molecule F_2, being homonuclear, is nonpolar.

13-19 The two nonpolar molecules, CH_4 and C_2H_6, have the lowest molar enthalpies of vaporization. Of the two, the smaller molecule, CH_4, has the lower value of $\Delta\bar{H}_{vap}$. The two polar molecules, CH_3OH and C_2H_5OH, are hydrogen-bonded and have the highest values of molar enthalpies of vaporization. The larger of the two, C_2H_5OH, has the higher value of $\Delta\bar{H}_{vap}$. Therefore, the order of the molar enthalpies of vaporization is

$$\Delta\bar{H}_{vap}[CH_4] < \Delta\bar{H}_{vap}[C_2H_6] < \Delta\bar{H}_{vap}[CH_3OH] < \Delta\bar{H}_{vap}[C_2H_5OH]$$

13-21 The value of T_b for argon is 87 K; therefore,

$$\Delta\bar{H}_{vap} = (85 \text{ J} \cdot \text{K}^{-1} \cdot \text{mol}^{-1})T_b$$
$$= (85 \text{ J} \cdot \text{K}^{-1} \cdot \text{mol}^{-1})(87 \text{ K})$$
$$= 7400 \text{ J} \cdot \text{mol}^{-1} = 7.4 \text{ kJ} \cdot \text{mol}^{-1}$$

The experimental value is $\Delta\bar{H}_{vap} = 6.52 \text{ kJ} \cdot \text{mol}^{-1}$ (Table 13-1).

13-23 The heat absorbed by the sublimation of 100.0 g of $CO_2(s)$ is

$$q_P = (100.0 \text{ g})\left(\frac{1 \text{ mol}}{44.01 \text{ g}}\right)(25.2 \text{ kJ} \cdot \text{mol}^{-1})$$

$$= 57.3 \text{ kJ}$$

13-25 The enthalpy of sublimation can be calculated from the relation

$$\Delta\bar{H}_{sub} = \Delta\bar{H}_{fus} + \Delta\bar{H}_{vap}$$

(a) Using the data in Table 13-1, the enthalpy of sublimation of ammonia is

$$\Delta \bar{H}_{sub} = 5.65 \text{ kJ} \cdot \text{mol}^{-1} + 23.4 \text{ kJ} \cdot \text{mol}^{-1}$$
$$= 29.1 \text{ kJ} \cdot \text{mol}^{-1}$$

(b) Using the data in Table 13-1, the enthalpy of sublimation of methane is

$$\Delta \bar{H}_{sub} = 0.94 \text{ kJ} \cdot \text{mol}^{-1} + 8.17 \text{ kJ} \cdot \text{mol}^{-1}$$
$$= 9.11 \text{ kJ} \cdot \text{mol}^{-1}$$

13-27 Using Table 13-2 or Figure 13-18, the vapor pressure of water at 37°C is between 45 and 50 torr. The vapor pressure of water in exhaled air is between 45 and 50 torr.

13-29 Using Figure 13-18, the equilibrium vapor pressure of ethyl alcohol at 60°C is about 0.5 atm. If all the ethyl alcohol (CH_3CH_2OH) were to vaporize, then the pressure would be

$$P = \frac{nRT}{V} = \frac{\left[(0.50 \text{ g}) \left(\dfrac{1 \text{ mol}}{46.07 \text{ g}} \right) \right] (0.0821 \text{ L} \cdot \text{atm} \cdot \text{mol}^{-1} \cdot \text{K}^{-1})(333 \text{ K})}{0.250 \text{ L}}$$
$$= 1.2 \text{ atm}$$

This pressure is greater than the vapor pressure of ethyl alcohol at 60°C, and so vapor will condense until the vapor pressure is about 0.5 atm. Liquid will be present.

13-31 Using Table 13-2, the equilibrium vapor pressure of water is 0.50 atm at 82°C. Water will boil at 82°C at 18,000 feet.

13-33 The plot of atmospheric pressure versus altitude is

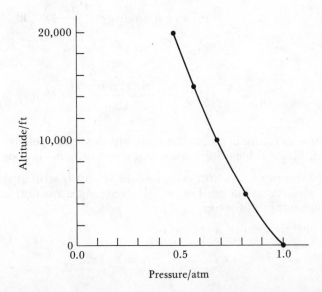

Use this plot to find the atmospheric pressure of each location. Use Table 13-2 to find the temperature at which this atmospheric pressure is the equilibrium vapor pressure of water.

Location	Atmospheric pressure/atm	Boiling point/°C
Denver	0.8	95
Mt. Kilimanjaro	0.5	80
Mt. Washington	0.8	95
The Matterhorn	0.6	85

13-35 From Table 13-2, the equilibrium vapor pressure of water at 40°C is 55.3 torr or 0.0728 atm. Relative humidity is given by the relation

$$\text{relative humidity} = \frac{P_{H_2O}}{P^\circ_{H_2O}} \times 100$$

Using this equation, we find P_{H_2O} according to

$$92 = \frac{P_{H_2O}}{55.3 \text{ torr}} \times 100$$

Solving for P_{H_2O},

$$P_{H_2O} = \frac{(92)(55.3 \text{ torr})}{100} = 51 \text{ torr}$$

13-37 The equilibrium vapor pressure of water at 30°C is 31.6 torr (Table 13-2). We can find the partial pressure of water from the definition of relative humidity

$$\text{relative humidity} = \frac{P_{H_2O}}{P^\circ_{H_2O}} \times 100$$

or

$$P_{H_2O} = \frac{(56)(31.6 \text{ torr})}{100} = 18 \text{ torr}$$

The temperature at which the equilibrium vapor pressure is 18 torr is the dew point. From Table 13-2 we see that the dew point is about 20°C.

13-39 The water molecules attract each other relatively strongly because of the hydrogen bonding in water. This relatively strong attraction accounts for the high surface tension of water.

13-41 The surface area of a sphere is

$$\text{Area} = 4\pi R^2$$

The area of a drop 2 mm in diameter is

$$\text{Area} = 4\pi(1 \text{ mm})^2 = 12.6 \text{ mm}^2$$

The energy of the surface is

$$\text{surface tension} = \frac{\text{energy}}{\text{area}}$$

or

$$\text{energy} = \text{surface tension} \times \text{area}$$

$$= (72 \text{ mJ} \cdot \text{m}^{-2})(12.6 \text{ mm}^2)\left(\frac{1 \text{ m}}{10^3 \text{ mm}}\right)^2$$

$$= 9.1 \times 10^{-4} \text{ mJ} = 0.91 \text{ } \mu\text{J}$$

When the drop is split into two drops, the total volume remains the same. We must find the volume of the drop

$$V = \tfrac{4}{3}\pi R^3$$

$$V = \tfrac{4}{3}\pi(1 \text{ mm})^3 = 4.2 \text{ mm}^3$$

The volume of each smaller drop is 2.1 mm^3. We now can find the radius of each of the small drops.

$$2.1 \text{ mm}^3 = \tfrac{4}{3}\pi R^3$$

$$R^3 = \frac{3}{4\pi}(2.1 \text{ mm}^3) = 0.50 \text{ mm}^3$$

$$R = 0.79 \text{ mm}$$

The surface area of each smaller drop is

$$\text{Area} = 4\pi(0.79 \text{ mm})^2 = 7.8 \text{ mm}^2$$

The total surface area of the smaller drops is

$$\text{Area} = (2)(7.8 \text{ mm}^2) = 15.6 \text{ mm}^2$$

The energy of the surface is

$$\text{energy} = \text{surface tension} \times \text{area}$$

$$= (72 \text{ mJ} \cdot \text{m}^{-2})(15.6 \text{ mm}^2)\left(\frac{1 \text{ m}}{10^3 \text{ mm}}\right)^2$$

$$= 1.1 \times 10^{-3} \text{ mJ} = 1.1 \text{ } \mu\text{J}$$

The energy required to change the drop to two drops is

$$\text{energy} = 1.1\ \mu\text{J} - 0.91\ \mu\text{J} = 0.2\ \mu\text{J}$$

13-43 The molar volume of platinum is given by

$$\bar{V} = \frac{\text{molar mass}}{\text{density}} = \frac{195.1\ \text{g} \cdot \text{mol}^{-1}}{21.45\ \text{g} \cdot \text{cm}^{-3}} = 9.0956\ \text{cm}^3 \cdot \text{mol}^{-1}$$

There are four platinum atoms per unit cell (Example 13-8), and so the number of unit cells per mole of platinum is

$$\text{unit cells per mole} = \frac{6.022 \times 10^{23}\ \text{atom} \cdot \text{mol}^{-1}}{4\ \text{atom/unit cell}} = 1.5055 \times 10^{23}\frac{\text{unit cells}}{\text{mol}}$$

The volume of a unit cell is

$$v = \frac{9.0956\ \text{cm}^3 \cdot \text{mol}^{-1}}{(1.5055 \times 10^{23})(\text{unit cell/mol})} = 6.0416 \times 10^{-23}\frac{\text{cm}^3}{\text{unit cell}}$$

The length of an edge of a unit cell is

$$\begin{aligned}\text{length} = (6.0416 \times 10^{-23}\ \text{cm}^3)^{1/3} &= 3.924 \times 10^{-8}\ \text{cm} \\ &= 392.4\ \text{pm}\end{aligned}$$

13-45 The volume of a unit cell of aluminum is

$$v = (405\ \text{pm})^3 = (4.05 \times 10^{-8}\ \text{cm})^3 = 6.643 \times 10^{-23}\ \text{cm}^3$$

There are four aluminum atoms per unit cell (Example 13-8) and the mass of the unit cell is

$$m = \left(\frac{4\ \text{atom}}{\text{unit cell}}\right)\left(\frac{26.98\ \text{g} \cdot \text{mol}^{-1}}{6.022 \times 10^{23}\ \text{atom} \cdot \text{mol}^{-1}}\right) = 1.792 \times 10^{-22}\frac{\text{g}}{\text{unit cell}}$$

The density

$$d = \frac{m}{v} = \frac{1.792 \times 10^{-22}\ \text{g/unit cell}}{6.643 \times 10^{-23}\ \text{cm}^3/\text{unit cell}} = 2.70\ \text{g} \cdot \text{cm}^{-3}$$

13-47 The molar volume of copper is

$$\bar{V} = \frac{\text{molar mass}}{\text{density}} = \frac{63.55\ \text{g} \cdot \text{mol}^{-1}}{8.93\ \text{g} \cdot \text{cm}^{-3}} = 7.116\ \text{cm}^3 \cdot \text{mol}^{-1}$$

The volume of a unit cell is

$$v = (361.5\ \text{pm})^3 = (3.615 \times 10^{-8}\ \text{cm})^3 = 4.724 \times 10^{-23}\ \text{cm}^3$$

The number of unit cells in a molar volume of copper is

$$\text{unit cells per mole} = \frac{\bar{V}}{v}$$

$$= \frac{7.116 \text{ cm}^3 \cdot \text{mol}^{-1}}{4.724 \times 10^{-23} \text{ cm}^3/\text{unit cell}} = 1.506 \times 10^{23} \frac{\text{unit cells}}{\text{mol}}$$

There are four copper atoms per unit cell, and so

$$\text{Avogadro's number} = \left(\frac{4 \text{ atoms}}{\text{unit cell}}\right)\left(1.506 \times 10^{23} \frac{\text{unit cell}}{\text{mol}}\right)$$

$$= 6.02 \times 10^{23} \text{ atom} \cdot \text{mol}^{-1}$$

13-49   The molar volume of KF is

$$\bar{V} = \frac{\text{molar mass}}{\text{density}} = \frac{58.10 \text{ g} \cdot \text{mol}^{-1}}{2.481 \text{ g} \cdot \text{cm}^{-3}} = 23.42 \text{ cm}^3 \cdot \text{mol}^{-1}$$

There are four KF formula units per unit cell (Example 13-11), and so there are

$$\text{unit cells per mole} = \frac{6.022 \times 10^{23} \text{ formula units/mol}}{4 \text{ formula units/unit cell}}$$

$$= 1.5055 \times 10^{23} \frac{\text{unit cells}}{\text{mol}}$$

The volume of a unit cell is

$$v = \frac{23.42 \text{ cm}^3 \cdot \text{mol}^{-1}}{1.5055 \times 10^{23} \dfrac{\text{unit cells}}{\text{mol}}} = 1.556 \times 10^{-22} \frac{\text{cm}^3}{\text{unit cell}}$$

The length of an edge of a unit cell is

$$l = (1.556 \times 10^{-22} \text{ cm}^3)^{1/3} = 5.378 \times 10^{-8} \text{ cm}$$

From Figure 13-33a we see that the nearest-neighbor distance is $l/2$, or 2.689×10^{-8} cm, or 268.9 pm.

13-51   The molar volume of CaO is

$$\bar{V} = \frac{\text{molar mass}}{\text{density}} = \frac{56.08 \text{ g} \cdot \text{mol}^{-1}}{3.25 \text{ g} \cdot \text{cm}^{-3}} = 17.26 \text{ cm}^3 \cdot \text{mol}^{-1}$$

The volume of a unit cell is

$$v = (481 \text{ pm})^3 = (4.81 \times 10^{-8} \text{ cm})^3 = 1.113 \times 10^{-22} \text{ cm}^3$$

The number of unit cells per mole is

$$\frac{\bar{V}}{v} = \frac{17.26 \text{ cm}^3 \cdot \text{mol}^{-1}}{1.113 \times 10^{-22} \dfrac{\text{cm}^3}{\text{unit cell}}} = 1.551 \times 10^{23} \frac{\text{unit cell}}{\text{mol}}$$

The result says that there are four $(6.02 \times 10^{23}/1.55 \times 10^{23})$ formula units of CaO in a unit cell, and so the unit cell must be the NaCl type.

13-53   The unit cell of cesium chloride is body-centered cubic. The volume of the unit cell of CsCl is

$$v = (412.1 \text{ pm})^3 = (4.121 \times 10^{-8} \text{ cm})^3 = 6.999 \times 10^{-23} \text{ cm}^3$$

A unit cell consists of one chloride ion and one cesium ion (Figure 13-34). The mass of the unit cell is

$$m = \left(\frac{1 \text{ formula unit}}{\text{unit cell}} \right) \left(\frac{168.4 \text{ g} \cdot \text{mol}^{-1}}{6.022 \times 10^{23} \text{ formula units} \cdot \text{mol}^{-1}} \right)$$

$$= 2.796 \times 10^{-22} \text{ g/unit cell}$$

The density is

$$d = \frac{\text{mass}}{\text{volume}}$$

$$= \frac{2.796 \times 10^{-22} \text{ g/unit cell}}{6.999 \times 10^{-23} \text{ cm}^3/\text{unit cell}}$$

$$= 3.995 \text{ g} \cdot \text{cm}^{-3}$$

13-55   (a) gas   (c) liquid
        (b) gas   (d) liquid

13-57   There are three triple points in the phase diagram of sulfur. When sulfur is heated from 40°C to 200°C at 1 atm, it goes from the rhombic form to the monoclinic form at 96°C and then melts at 119°C (see Interchapter D). Sulfur sublimes at a pressure less than 10^{-5} atm.

13-59   The Clausius-Clapeyron equation is

$$\log \frac{P_2}{P_1} = \frac{\Delta \bar{H}_{vap}}{2.3R} \left(\frac{1}{T_1} - \frac{1}{T_2} \right)$$

We let $P_1 = 1.00$ atm, $T_1 = 373$ K, $T_2 = 383$ K, and use the fact that $\Delta \bar{H}_{vap} = 40.7$ kJ $\cdot$ mol^{-1} to write

$$\log \frac{P_2}{1.00 \text{ atm}} = \frac{(40.7 \text{ kJ} \cdot \text{mol}^{-1})}{(2.3)(8.314 \text{ J} \cdot \text{K}^{-1} \cdot \text{mol}^{-1})} \left(\frac{10^3 \text{ J}}{1 \text{ kJ}} \right) \left(\frac{1}{373 \text{ K}} - \frac{1}{383 \text{ K}} \right)$$

$$= 0.15$$

Therefore,

$$\frac{P_2}{1.00 \text{ atm}} = 10^{0.15} = 1.4$$

$$P_2 = 1.4 \text{ atm}$$

13-61 The vapor pressure of the solid is equal to the vapor pressure of the liquid at the triple point. Therefore, we write

$$10.646 - \frac{2559.1 \text{ K}}{T_t} = 7.538 - \frac{1511 \text{ K}}{T_t}$$

Collecting terms gives

$$3.108 = \frac{1048 \text{ K}}{T_t}$$

and

$$T_t = \frac{1048 \text{ K}}{3.108} = 337.2 \text{ K}$$

The logarithm of the pressure at the triple point is given by

$$\log P_t = 7.538 - \frac{1511 \text{ K}}{337.2 \text{ K}} = 7.538 - 4.481$$

$$= 3.057$$

or

$$\log P_t = 10.646 - \frac{2559.1 \text{ K}}{337.2 \text{ K}}$$

$$= 3.057$$

The pressure at the triple point is

$$P_t = 10^{3.057} = 1140 \text{ torr}$$

E   ANSWERS TO THE EVEN-NUMBERED PROBLEMS

13-2 $5.08 \times 10^{-2} \text{ J}$

13-4 $\Delta \bar{H}_{vap} = 40.5 \text{ kJ} \cdot \text{mol}^{-1}$

13-6   1180 g

13-8   4.0 kJ

13-10 Your body must supply the energy (about $0.33 \text{ kJ} \cdot \text{g}^{-1}$) to melt the snow.

13-12 It would take longer to vaporize the water.

13-14 $\Delta \bar{H}_{vap} = 31.9 \text{ kJ} \cdot \text{mol}^{-1}$

13-16 $T_b[\text{Ar}] < T_b[\text{Kr}] < T_b[\text{NH}_3] < T_b[\text{NaCl}]$

13-18 HF and CH_3OH

13-20 $\Delta \bar{H}_{vap}[\text{CH}_4] < \Delta \bar{H}_{vap}[\text{CCl}_4] < \Delta \bar{H}_{vap}[\text{SiCl}_4] < \Delta \bar{H}_{vap}[\text{SiBr}_4]$

13-22 Water is strongly hydrogen bonded.

13-24 4.19 mol

13-26 $3120 \text{ g} \cdot \text{m}^{-2}$, or a thickness of 0.34 cm per m^2 of surface.

13-28 Approximately 370 K

13-30 $0.00128 \text{ mol} \cdot \text{L}^{-1}$

13-32 560 torr or 0.74 atm

13-34 The boiling point of water was used to determine the normal atmospheric pressure of Lhasa. Plots of normal atmospheric pressure versus altitude were used to find the altitude corresponding to the atmospheric pressure of Lhasa.

13-36 19%

13-38 The air near the surface of the glass is colder than the air in the room, and so is able to sustain less water vapor.

13-40 The surfactant lowers the surface tension of water, allowing the water to spread out, or "sheet."

13-42 8.1 mJ

13-44 3.302×10^{-8} cm or 330.2 pm

13-46 $0.533 \text{ g} \cdot \text{cm}^{-3}$

13-48 $6.02 \times 10^{23} \text{ atom} \cdot \text{mol}^{-1}$

13-50 Unit cell length is 4.30×10^{-8} cm or 430 pm; nearest neighbor (Cs—Cl) distance is 3.72×10^{-8} cm, or 372 pm.

13-52 Four formula units in a unit cell; the unit cell is the NaCl type.

13-54 $6.02 \times 10^{23} \text{ formula unit} \cdot \text{mol}^{-1}$

13-56 (a) gas   (c) gas
        (b) liquid   (d) solid

13-58 Oxygen does not melt under applied pressure.

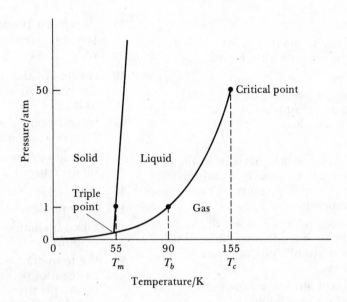

13-60 $\Delta \bar{H}_{vap} = 43.4 \text{ kJ} \cdot \text{mol}^{-1}$

13-62 $T_t = 172 \text{ K}$ and $P_t = 10.7$ torr

F ANSWERS TO THE SELF-TEST

1   false

2   false (They have hindered rotational motion.)

3   false

4   the boiling point of the liquid

5   the melting point of the solid

6   the heat capacity

7   molar enthalpy of fusion, $\Delta \bar{H}_{fus}$

8   the forces that hold the crystal into a lattice must be broken down

9   molar enthalpy of vaporization, $\Delta \bar{H}_{vap}$

10   attractive forces between the molecules must be overcome

11   greater

12   removes

13   true

14   true

15   false

16   dipole-dipole

17   false

18   an electrostatic intermolecular attraction between a hydrogen atom in one molecule and a highly electronegative atom (e.g., O or F) in another molecule.

19   London forces

20   false

21   molar enthalpy of sublimation, $\Delta \bar{H}_{sub}$

22   true

23   false (There is a dynamic equilibrium.)

24   of evaporation is equal to the rate of condensation

25 true

26 of the vapor that is in equilibrium with a liquid

27 false

28 the temperature at which the vapor pressure of the liquid is exactly 1 atm

29 false

30 of water vapor pressure in the air relative to the equilibrium water vapor pressure at that temperature

31 the temperature at which the relative humidity would be 100% for a given vapor pressure of water

32 inward attractive forces at the surface of a liquid

33 sphere

34 structure of the crystal

35 false

36 simple cubic, body-centered cubic, and face-centered cubic

37

38 the closest possible packing of layers of identical spheres

39 true

40 corners of the unit cell and in the center of each face of the unit cell

41 the different sizes of Cs^+ and Na^+ relative to Cl^-

42 false (They have a wide variety of structures.)

43 true

44 solid phase and the liquid phase

45 false (It changes by a small amount.)

46 the temperature above which a gas cannot be liquified regardless of the pressure applied

47 a temperature and pressure at which three phases coexist at equilibrium

48 false

49 false

50 false

51 lies at a pressure greater than 1 atm in the phase diagram

52 diamond and graphite

14 / Solutions

A   OUTLINE OF CHAPTER 14

14-1   A solution is a homogeneous mixture of two or more substances.

The solvent is the substance in which other substances are dissolved.

The solute is the dissolved substance.

The various types of solutions are given in Table 14-1.

14-2   Solubility involves a dynamic equilibrium.

Ions in aqueous solutions interact strongly with water molecules.

Dynamic equilibrium occurs when the number of ions being deposited onto the surface of the crystals is equal to the number of ions entering the solution at any instant (Figure 14-2).

A saturated solution contains the maximum quantity of solute that can be dissolved in the solvent.

An unsaturated solution is able to dissolve further quantities of solute.

The solubility of a solute is the maximum quantity of the solute that can be dissolved in a given quantity of solvent (Table 14-2).

The solubility of a solid in a liquid usually increases with increasing temperature (Figure 14-3).

14-3   The equilibrium vapor pressure of a pure liquid is always decreased when a substance is dissolved in the liquid.

Solution properties depend primarily on the ratio of the number of solute particles to the number of solvent particles.

A solute decreases the rate of evaporation of the solvent and thereby lowers the vapor pressure of the solvent (Figure 14-5).

14-4   The equilibrium vapor pressure of the solvent over a solution is proportional to the mole fraction of the solvent in the solution.

In an ideal solution the solvent and solute molecules are randomly distributed.

The mole fraction X_1 of the solvent in a solution is defined by the relation

$$X_1 = \frac{n_1}{n_1 + n_2} \qquad (14\text{-}1)$$

where n_1 is the number of moles of solvent and n_2 is the number of moles of solute in the solution.

In an ideal solution the vapor pressure of the solvent P_1 is directly proportional to the mole fraction of the solvent X_1 (Raoult's law).

Raoult's law states that $P_1 = X_1 P_1^\circ$, where P_1° is the vapor pressure of the pure solvent (Equation 14-3).

14-5 Colligative properties of solutions depend only on the solute particle concentration.

The major colligative properties are

(a) vapor pressure lowering
(b) boiling point elevation
(c) freezing point depression
(d) osmotic pressure

Molality, m, is the number of moles of solute per kilogram of solvent.

Molarity, M, is the number of moles of solute per liter of solution.

Colligative molality, m_c, is the molality times the number of solute particles per formula unit (Table 14-3).

14-6 Nonvolatile solutes increase the boiling point of a liquid.

The key to understanding colligative properties is the lowering of the solvent vapor pressure by the solute (Figure 14-7).

The boiling point elevation, $T_b - T_b^\circ$, is given by the equation

$$T_b - T_b^\circ = K_b m_c \qquad (14\text{-}4)$$

The boiling point elevation constant, K_b, depends on only the solvent properties (Table 14-4).

14-7 Solutes decrease the freezing point of a liquid.

The freezing point depression, $T_f^\circ - T_f$ is given by the equation

$$T_f^\circ - T_f = K_f m_c \qquad (14\text{-}5)$$

The freezing point depression constant K_f depends on only the solvent properties (Table 14-4).

14-8 The freezing point depression effect is the basis of the action of antifreeze.

Ethylene glycol is a commonly used antifreeze (Figure 14-8).

Antifreeze proteins in certain fishes have an enhanced capacity to lower the freezing point of water.

14-9   Only solvent molecules can pass through a semipermeable membrane.

The escaping tendency of water from pure water is greater than the escaping tendency of water from a solution.

The osmotic pressure is the pressure that must be applied to a solution to raise the escaping tendency of water in the solution to that of pure water (Figure 14-12).

The osmotic pressure π is computed from the expression

$$\pi = RTM_c \qquad\qquad (14\text{-}6)$$

where M_c is the colligative molarity.

Reverse osmosis is used to obtain pure water from seawater.

14-10   The molecular mass of proteins can be determined by osmotic pressure measurements.

Osmotic pressure is a large effect and is used to determine molecular masses of proteins.

14-11   Osmotic pressure plays a major role in living systems by keeping cells inflated.

Cell walls are permeable to water.

The net flow of water across cell walls is to the side with the larger colligative molarity (Figure 14-14).

14-12   The equilibrium concentration of a dissolved gas is proportional to the pressure of the gas over the solution.

Henry's law states that $P_{gas} = k_h M_{gas}$, where P_{gas} is the equilibrium gas pressure over a solution, M_{gas} is the molarity of the dissolved gas, and k_h is the Henry's law constant for the gas (Equation 14-7).

Henry's law constant, k_h, depends upon the gas and the solvent (Table 14-5).

The smaller the value of the Henry's law constant, k_h, for a gas, the greater is the solubility of the gas.

Gas solubility decreases with increasing temperature (Figure 14-17).

B   SELF-TEST

1   In a saturated solution the rate of crystallization is greater than the rate of dissolution. *True/False*

2   The vapor pressure of a liquid (*increases/decreases*) when a solute is dissolved in the liquid.

3   The rate of evaporation of the solvent from a solution is the same as the rate of evaporation from the pure solvent at the same temperature. *True/False*

4   A 1.0-m aqueous solution of sucrose has the same equilibrium vapor pressure as a 1.0-m aqueous solution of NaCl at the same temperature. *True/False*

5   Explain why the vapor pressure of a solution containing a nonvolatile solute is less than the vapor pressure of the pure solvent at the same temperature.

_____

6   The equilibrium vapor pressure of the solvent over a solution is proportional to _____ in the solution.

7   Raoult's law states that _____

_____ .

8   The colligative properties of a solution depend primarily upon _____

_____ .

9   The molality of a solution is defined as _____

_____ .

10 The molality of a solution is always the same as the molarity of the solution. *True/False*

11 A 1.0-m aqueous solution of glucose is prepared by dissolving 1.0 mol of glucose in _____ .

12 The colligative molality of a 1.0 m aqueous glucose solution is _____ m_c.

13 The colligative molality of a 1.0 m aqueous solution of KCl is _____ m_c.

14 The colligative molality of a 1.0 m aqueous solution of $Mg(NO_3)_2$ is _____ m_c.

15 Nonvolatile solutes (*increase/decrease*) the boiling point of the solvent.

16 Explain why a nonvolatile solute raises the boiling point of the solvent.

_____

_____

17 The boiling point elevation due to a dissolved solute is proportional to

_____ .

18 The boiling point elevation of a solution depends on the number of solute particles dissolved in the solvent. *True/False*

19 The boiling point elevation constant, K_b, depends upon the nature of the solute. *True/False*

20 Solutes (*increase/decrease*) the freezing point of the solvent.

21 Explain why a solute lowers the freezing point of the solvent.

_____

_____

22 The freezing point depression of a solution due to a solute is proportional to

_____ .

23 The freezing point depression of a solution depends primarily on the concentration of solute particles dissolved in the solvent. *True/False*

24 The freezing point depression constant, K_f, depends upon the nature of the solute. *True/False*

25 An antifreeze is added to water to _____ .

26 An antifreeze mixture cannot freeze regardless of the temperature. *True/False*

27 The freezing point of seawater is 0.0°C. *True/False*

28 If a beaker of water and a beaker of an aqueous solution of NaCl are placed under a Bell jar, then water transfers from the beaker of _____ to the beaker of

_____ .

29 If a 0.1-M aqueous solution of NaCl is separated from a 1.0-M aqueous solution of NaCl by a rigid semipermeable membrane, then water passes spontaneously from _____ to _____ .

30 The osmotic pressure of a solution is _____

_____

_____ .

31 The osmotic pressure is given by the equation $\pi =$ _____ .

32 The osmotic pressure of a solution is the equilibrium vapor pressure of the solution. *True/False*

33 The osmotic pressure of a solution depends primarily on the concentration of solute particles dissolved in the solvent. *True/False*

34 Pressure can be used to obtain pure water from seawater. *True/False*

35 Red blood cells will rupture when placed in pure water because

_____ .

36 The molecular masses of molecules can be determined from the colligative properties of a solution because colligative properties depend upon _____

_____ .

37 Explain why the osmotic pressure of a protein solution can be used to determine the molecular mass of a protein.

_____

_____

38 Boiling point elevation is useful for determining the formula mass of small compounds. *True/False*

39   The solubility of a gas (*increases/decreases*) if the equilibrium pressure of the gas over the solution is increased.

40   Henry's law states that _____

_____

41   The value of a Henry's law constant depends upon the gas. *True/False*

42   The solubility of a gas in water (*increases/decreases*) as the temperature increases.

C   CALCULATIONS YOU SHOULD KNOW HOW TO DO

1   Calculate mole fractions. See Example 14-1 and Problems 14-1 through 14-4

2   Calculate solvent vapor pressure and vapor pressure lowering using Raoult's law. See Example 14-2 and Problems 14-5 through 14-8.

3   Calculate molality and colligative molality of solutions. See Examples 14-3 and 14-4, and Problems 14-13 through 14-18.

4   Calculate the boiling-point elevation of solutions. See Problems 14-23 through 14-28.

5   Calculate the freezing point depression of solutions and molecular mass from the freezing point depression. See Examples 14-5 and 14-6 and Problems 14-29 through 14-40.

6   Calculate the osmotic pressure of solutions and molecular mass from the osmotic pressure. See Examples 14-7 through 14-9 and Problems 14-41 through 14-48.

7   Calculate the gas solubility in liquids using Henry's law. See Example 14-11 and Problems 14-49 through 14-54.

D   SOLUTIONS TO THE ODD-NUMBERED PROBLEMS

14-1   The mole fraction of water is given by

$$X_{H_2O} = \frac{n_{H_2O}}{n_{H_2O} + n_{C_2H_5OH}}$$

The mole fraction of water is

$$X_{H_2O} = \frac{(40.0 \text{ g})\left(\dfrac{1 \text{ mol } H_2O}{18.02 \text{ g } H_2O}\right)}{(40.0 \text{ g})\left(\dfrac{1 \text{ mol } H_2O}{18.02 \text{ g } H_2O}\right) + (25.0 \text{ g})\left(\dfrac{1 \text{ mol } C_2H_5OH}{46.07 \text{ g } C_2H_5OH}\right)}$$

$$= \frac{2.220 \text{ mol}}{2.220 \text{ mol} + 0.5427 \text{ mol}} = \frac{2.220 \text{ mol}}{2.763 \text{ mol}}$$

$$= 0.803$$

The mole fraction of ethyl alcohol is

$$X_{C_2H_5OH} = \frac{(25.0 \text{ g})\left(\dfrac{1 \text{ mol } C_2H_5OH}{46.07 \text{ g } C_2H_5OH}\right)}{2.220 \text{ mol} + 0.5427 \text{ mol}} = 0.196$$

14-3 The mole fraction is defined as

$$X_1 = \frac{n_1}{n_1 + n_2}$$

The mole fraction of acetone, A, is given as

$$X_A = \frac{n_A}{n_A + n_W} = 0.19$$

If we have a total of 100 moles of water and acetone, then 19 moles are acetone and 81 moles are water. The mass of acetone is

$$\text{mass} = (19 \text{ mol})\left(\frac{58.08 \text{ g acetone}}{1 \text{ mol acetone}}\right)$$
$$= 1100 \text{ g}$$

The mass of water is

$$\text{mass} = (81 \text{ mol})\left(\frac{18.02 \text{ g } H_2O}{1 \text{ mol } H_2O}\right)$$
$$= 1500 \text{ g}$$

Thus we dissolve 1100 g of acetone in 1500 g of water.

14-5 The mole fraction of water in the solution is

$$X_{H_2O} = \frac{n_{H_2O}}{n_{H_2O} + n_{glucose}}$$

$$= \frac{(100.0 \text{ g})\left(\dfrac{1 \text{ mol } H_2O}{18.02 \text{ g } H_2O}\right)}{(100.0 \text{ g})\left(\dfrac{1 \text{ mol } H_2O}{18.02 \text{ g } H_2O}\right) + (10.0 \text{ g})\left(\dfrac{1 \text{ mol glucose}}{180.16 \text{ g glucose}}\right)}$$

$$= 0.990$$

Raoult's law is

$$P_{H_2O} = X_{H_2O} P^{\circ}_{H_2O}$$

and thus

$$P_{H_2O} = (0.990)(47.1 \text{ torr}) = 46.6 \text{ torr}$$

The vapor pressure lowering is

$$P^\circ - P = 47.1 \text{ torr} - 46.6 \text{ torr} = 0.5 \text{ torr}$$

14-7 The mole fraction of water in the solution is

$$X_{H_2O} = \frac{n_{H_2O}}{n_{H_2O} + n_{sucrose}}$$

$$= \frac{(195 \text{ g})\left(\dfrac{1 \text{ mol } H_2O}{18.02 \text{ g } H_2O}\right)}{(195 \text{ g})\left(\dfrac{1 \text{ mol } H_2O}{18.02 \text{ g } H_2O}\right) + (30.0 \text{ g})\left(\dfrac{1 \text{ mol sucrose}}{342.30 \text{ g sucrose}}\right)}$$

$$= 0.992$$

From Raoult's law we compute

$$P_{H_2O} = X_{H_2O}P^\circ_{H_2O} = (0.992)(23.76 \text{ torr}) = 23.57 \text{ torr}$$

The vapor pressure lowering is

$$P^\circ_{H_2O} - P_{H_2O} = 23.76 \text{ torr} - 23.57 \text{ torr} = 0.19 \text{ torr}$$

14-9 If both the solvent and the solute are volatile, then we can apply Raoult's law to both substances. Thus we have

$$P_1 = P^\circ_1 X_1 \qquad P_2 = P^\circ_2 X_2$$

where the solvent is denoted by the subscript 1 and the solute is denoted by the subscript 2. The total pressure over the solution is given by Dalton's law of partial pressures

$$P_{total} = P_1 + P_2 = X_1 P^\circ_1 + X_2 P^\circ_2$$

14-11 Recall from Chapter 5 that the total pressure is the sum of the partial pressures:

$$P_{total} = P_1 + P_2$$

From Raoult's law, we have

$$P_{total} = X_1 P^\circ_1 + X_2 P^\circ_2$$

In a two component system

$$X_1 + X_2 = 1$$

Solving for X_2, we have

$$X_2 = 1 - X_1$$

Substituting $X_2 = 1 - X_1$ into the expression for P_{total}, we obtain

$$
\begin{aligned}
P_{total} &= X_1 P_1^\circ + (1 - X_1) P_2^\circ \\
&= X_1 P_1^\circ + P_2^\circ - X_1 P_2^\circ \\
&= P_2^\circ + X_1 (P_1^\circ - P_2^\circ)
\end{aligned}
$$

When $P_1^\circ = 348$ torr and $P_2^\circ = 270$ torr, we have

$$
\begin{aligned}
P_{total} &= 270 \text{ torr} + X_1 (348 \text{ torr} - 270 \text{ torr}) \\
&= 270 \text{ torr} + (78 \text{ torr}) X_1
\end{aligned}
$$

Notice that the expression for P_{total} has the same form as the equation for a straight line, $y = mx + b$. The slope of the line, m, is 78 torr and the y intercept b at $X_1 = 0$ is 270 torr.

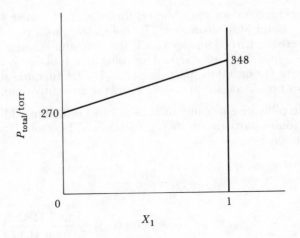

14-13   The number of moles of I_2 in 2.603 g of iodine is

$$n = (2.603 \text{ g}) \left(\frac{1 \text{ mol } I_2}{253.8 \text{ g } I_2} \right) = 0.01026 \text{ mol}$$

$$
\begin{aligned}
\text{molality} &= \frac{\text{moles of solute}}{\text{kilogram of solvent}} \\
&= \frac{0.01026 \text{ mol}}{0.1000 \text{ kg}} = 0.1026 \text{ m}
\end{aligned}
$$

14-15   The number of moles of sucrose in two teaspoons is

$$n = (2 \text{ teaspoons})\left(\frac{14 \text{ g}}{3 \text{ teaspoons}}\right)\left(\frac{1 \text{ mol}}{342.3 \text{ g sucrose}}\right)$$

$$= 0.0273 \text{ mol}$$

The mass of water in one cup is

$$\text{mass} = dV = (1.00 \text{ g} \cdot \text{mL}^{-1})(1 \text{ cup})\left(\frac{0.946 \text{ L}}{4 \text{ cups}}\right)\left(\frac{1000 \text{ mL}}{1 \text{ L}}\right)$$

$$= 240 \text{ g} = 0.240 \text{ kg}$$

The molality is

$$\text{molality} = \frac{\text{moles of solute}}{\text{kilogram of solvent}}$$

$$= \frac{0.0273 \text{ mol}}{0.240 \text{ kg}} = 0.11 \text{ m}$$

14-17   (a) There are two ions per $MgSO_4$ formula unit because $MgSO_4$ dissociates into Mg^{2+} and SO_4^{2-} in water. The colligative molality is thus 2.0 m_c.
   (b) There are three ions per $CuCl_2$ formula unit because $CuCl_2$ dissociates into Cu^{2+} and 2 Cl^- in water. The colligative molality is thus 3.0 m_c.
   (c) There is one solute particle per C_2H_5OH formula unit because C_2H_5OH does not dissociate in water. Thus the colligative molality is 1.0 m_c.

14-19   (a) The colligative molality of 0.25 m NaCl is 0.50 m_c. Thus there are 0.50 mol of solute particles in 1000 g of water. The mole fraction of water in the solution is

$$X_{H_2O} = \frac{n_{H_2O}}{n_{H_2O} + n_{solute}}$$

$$= \frac{(1000 \text{ g})\left(\frac{1 \text{ mol } H_2O}{18.02 \text{ g } H_2O}\right)}{(1000 \text{ g})\left(\frac{1 \text{ mol } H_2O}{18.02 \text{ g } H_2O}\right) + 0.50 \text{ mol}}$$

$$= 0.9911$$

The partial pressure of water is computed using Raoult's law:

$$P_{H_2O} = X_{H_2O}P^\circ_{H_2O} = (0.9911)(17.54 \text{ torr}) = 17.38 \text{ torr}$$

The vapor pressure lowering is

$$P^\circ_{H_2O} - P_{H_2O} = 17.54 \text{ torr} - 17.38 \text{ torr} = 0.16 \text{ torr}$$

(b) The colligative molality of 0.25 m $CaCl_2$ is 0.75 m_c. Thus there are 0.75 mol of solute particles in 1000 g of water. The mole fraction of water in the solution is

$$X_{H_2O} = \frac{(1000 \text{ g})\left(\dfrac{1 \text{ mol } H_2O}{18.02 \text{ g } H_2O}\right)}{(1000 \text{ g})\left(\dfrac{1 \text{ mol } H_2O}{18.02 \text{ g } H_2O}\right) + 0.75 \text{ mol}}$$

$$= 0.9867$$

The vapor pressure of water is

$$P_{H_2O} = X_{H_2O}P^{\circ}_{H_2O} = (0.9867)(17.54 \text{ torr}) = 17.31 \text{ torr}$$

The vapor pressure lowering is

$$P^{\circ}_{H_2O} - P_{H_2O} = 17.54 \text{ torr} - 17.31 \text{ torr} = 0.23 \text{ torr}$$

(c) The colligative molality of 0.25 m sucrose is 0.25 m_c. Thus there are 0.25 mol of solute particles in 1000 g of water. The mole fraction of water in the solution is

$$X_{H_2O} = \frac{(1000 \text{ g})\left(\dfrac{1 \text{ mol } H_2O}{18.02 \text{ g } H_2O}\right)}{(1000 \text{ g})\left(\dfrac{1 \text{ mol } H_2O}{18.02 \text{ g } H_2O}\right) + 0.25 \text{ mol}}$$

$$= 0.9955$$

The vapor pressure of water is

$$P_{H_2O} = X_{H_2O}P^{\circ}_{H_2O} = (0.9955)(17.54 \text{ torr}) = 17.46 \text{ torr}$$

The vapor pressure lowering is

$$P^{\circ}_{H_2O} - P_{H_2O} = 17.54 \text{ torr} - 17.46 \text{ torr} = 0.08 \text{ torr}$$

14-21 The mass of the solution prepared by dissolving 2.00 mol of NaOH in 1000 g of H_2O is

$$\text{mass} = \text{mass}_{NaOH} + \text{mass}_{H_2O}$$

Thus

$$\text{mass} = (2.00 \text{ mol})\left(\frac{40.00 \text{ g NaOH}}{1 \text{ mol NaOH}}\right) + 1000 \text{ g} = 1080 \text{ g}$$

The volume of the solution can be found from the density

$$d = \frac{\text{mass}}{V} \quad \text{or} \quad V = \frac{\text{mass}}{d}$$

$$V = \frac{1080 \text{ g}}{1.22 \text{ g} \cdot \text{mL}^{-1}} = 885 \text{ mL} = 0.885 \text{ L}$$

The molarity is

$$\text{molarity} = \frac{\text{moles of solute}}{\text{volume of solution}}$$

$$= \frac{2.00 \text{ mol}}{0.885 \text{ L}} = 2.26 \text{ M}$$

14-23   The colligative molality of the $Ca(NO_3)_2(aq)$ solution is

$$m_c = (3)(0.75 \text{ m}) = 2.25 \text{ m}_c$$

The boiling point elevation is

$$T_b - T_b^{\circ} = K_b m_c$$
$$= (0.52 \text{ K} \cdot \text{m}_c^{-1})(2.25 \text{ m}_c)$$
$$= 1.2 \text{ K} = 1.2°C$$

The boiling point of the solution is

$$T_b = 100.00°C + 1.2°C = 101.2°C$$

14-25   The molality of the solution is

$$m = \frac{(5.0 \text{ g})\left(\dfrac{1 \text{ mol picric acid}}{229.11 \text{ g picric acid}}\right)}{0.100 \text{ kg cyclohexane}} = 0.218 \text{ m}$$

$$m_c = m = 0.218 \text{ m}_c$$

The boiling point elevation is (Table 14-4)

$$T_b - T_b^{\circ} = K_b m_c = (2.79 \text{ K} \cdot \text{m}_c^{-1})(0.218 \text{ m}_c)$$
$$= 0.61 \text{ K} = 0.61°C$$

The boiling point is (Table 14-4)

$$T_b = 80.7°C + 0.61°C = 81.3°C$$

14-27   Ethyl alcohol is a temporary antifreeze because its equilibrium vapor pressure is much greater than one atmosphere at 100°C. Thus ethyl alcohol is much more readily lost by evaporation from the coolant system than a relatively high boiling liquid like ethylene glycol.

14-29   The molality of the solution is

$$m = \frac{(30.0 \text{ g})\left(\dfrac{1 \text{ mol glucose}}{180.16 \text{ g glucose}}\right)}{0.500 \text{ kg water}} = 0.333 \text{ m} = 0.333 \text{ m}_c$$

The freezing point depression is

$$T_f^\circ - T_f = K_f m_c = (1.86 \text{ K} \cdot \text{m}_c^{-1})(0.333 \text{ m}_c)$$
$$= 0.619 \text{ K} = 0.619°C$$

The freezing point is

$$T_f = 0.00°C - 0.62°C = -0.62°C$$

14-31   The molality of the solution is

$$m = \frac{(12.0 \text{ g})\left(\dfrac{1 \text{ mol CCl}_4}{153.81 \text{ g CCl}_4}\right)}{0.750 \text{ kg benzene}} = 0.104 \text{ m} = 0.104 \text{ m}_c$$

The freezing point depression is

$$T_f^\circ - T_f = K_f m_c = (5.10 \text{ K} \cdot \text{m}_c^{-1})(0.104 \text{ m}_c)$$
$$= 0.530 \text{ K} = 0.530°C$$

The freezing point is

$$T_f = 5.50°C - 0.530°C = 4.97°C$$

14-33   We can find the molality of the solution from the freezing point depression

$$T_f^\circ - T_f = K_f m_c$$
$$4.43 \text{ K} = (40.0 \text{ K} \cdot \text{m}_c^{-1}) \, m_c$$
$$m_c = \frac{4.43 \text{ K}}{40.0 \text{ K} \cdot \text{m}_c^{-1}} = 0.111 \text{ m}_c$$

Because the mass is given, we have the correspondence

$$0.111 \text{ mol} \cdot \text{kg}^{-1} \eqsim \frac{0.500 \text{ g}}{0.0100 \text{ kg}} = 50.0 \text{ g} \cdot \text{kg}^{-1}$$

and therefore

$$0.111 \text{ mol} \eqsim 50.0 \text{ g}$$

Dividing both sides by 0.111, we have

$$1.00 \text{ mol} \approx 450 \text{ g}$$

The molecular mass of vitamin K is 450.
     An alternative solution is to use the definition of molality

$$m_c = \frac{\text{moles of vitamin K}}{\text{kilogram of camphor}}$$

$$0.111 \text{ m} = \frac{(0.500 \text{ g})/(\text{molar mass})}{(0.0100 \text{ kg})}$$

Solving for the molar mass, we have

$$\text{molar mass} = \frac{0.500 \text{ g}}{(0.111 \text{ mol} \cdot \text{kg}^{-1})(0.0100 \text{ kg})} = 450 \text{ g} \cdot \text{mol}^{-1}$$

The molecular mass of vitamin K is 450.

14-35   We can find the colligative molality of the solution from the freezing point depression

$$T_f^\circ - T_f = K_f m_c$$
$$0.00°C - (-57°C) = (1.86 \text{ K} \cdot \text{m}_c^{-1})m_c$$
$$m_c = \frac{57 \text{ K}}{1.86 \text{ K} \cdot \text{m}_c^{-1}} = 30.6 \text{ m}_c$$

The concentration of $CaCl_2$ in the pond is

$$\text{molality} = \frac{m_c}{3} = \frac{30.6 \text{ m}_c}{3} = 10 \text{ m}$$

14-37   From Figure 14-8, the antifreeze mixture should be 52% ethylene glycol by volume. We can find the molality of the solution from the freezing point depression

$$T_f^\circ - T_f = K_f m_c$$
$$40 \text{ K} = (1.86 \text{ K} \cdot \text{m}_c^{-1})m_c$$
$$m_c = \frac{40 \text{ K}}{1.86 \text{ K} \cdot \text{m}_c^{-1}} = 21.5 \text{ m}_c$$

We know that there are 21.5 moles of ethylene glycol in 1000 g of water. The volume of 21.5 mol of ethylene glycol is found from the density.

$$\text{volume} = (21.5 \text{ mol})(\frac{62.07 \text{ g}}{1 \text{ mol}})(\frac{1 \text{ mL}}{1.116 \text{ g}})$$

$$= 1200 \text{ mL}$$

There are 1200 mL of ethylene glycol to 1000 mL of water. (The density of water is $1.00 \ g \cdot mL^{-1}$). The percent ethylene glycol by volume is

$$\frac{1200 \ mL}{1200 \ mL + 1000 \ mL} \times 100 = 55\%$$

14-39   The molality of the solution is

$$m = \frac{(40.7 \ g)\left(\dfrac{1 \ mol \ HgCl_2}{271.5 \ g \ HgCl_2}\right)}{0.100 \ kg}$$

$$= 1.50 \ m$$

If $HgCl_2$ were completely dissociated, then the colligative molality would be $4.50 \ m_c$. We can find the colligative molality from the freezing point depression

$$T_f^\circ - T_f = K_f m_c$$
$$2.83 \ K = (1.86 \ K \cdot m_c^{-1}) m_c$$
$$m_c = \frac{2.83 \ K}{1.86 \ K \cdot m_c^{-1}} = 1.52 \ m_c$$

This shows that the compound $HgCl_2$ is essentially undissociated.

14-41   The osmotic pressure is given by

$$\pi = RTM_c$$

Thus

$$\pi = (0.0821 \ L \cdot atm \cdot K^{-1} \cdot mol^{-1})(323 \ K)(0.50 \ mol \cdot L^{-1})$$
$$= 13 \ atm$$

14-43   The concentration of insulin in the aqueous solution is

$$M_c = \frac{\pi}{RT} = \frac{(0.853 \ atm)}{(0.0821 \ L \cdot atm \cdot K^{-1} \cdot mol^{-1})(298 \ K)}$$
$$= 3.49 \times 10^{-2} \ mol \cdot L^{-1}$$

The molecular mass can be calculated from the concentration. We have the correspondence

$$3.49 \times 10^{-2} \ mol \cdot L^{-1} \simeq \frac{2.00 \ g}{0.0100 \ L} = 200 \ g \cdot L^{-1}$$

and, therefore,

$$3.49 \times 10^{-2} \ mol \simeq 2.00 \times 10^2 \ g$$

Dividing both sides by 3.49×10^{-2}, we have

$$1.00 \text{ mol} \approx 5.73 \times 10^3 \text{ g}$$

The molecular mass of insulin is about 5730.

14-45 The concentration of immunoglobulin G in the aqueous solution is

$$M_c = \frac{\pi}{RT} = \frac{(6.19 \text{ torr})\left(\dfrac{1 \text{ atm}}{760 \text{ torr}}\right)}{(0.0821 \text{ L} \cdot \text{atm} \cdot \text{K}^{-1} \cdot \text{mol}^{-1})(298 \text{ K})}$$

$$= 3.33 \times 10^{-4} \text{ mol} \cdot \text{L}^{-1}$$

Thus we have the correspondence

$$3.33 \times 10^{-4} \text{ mol} \cdot \text{L}^{-1} \approx \frac{5.00 \text{ g}}{0.100 \text{ L}} = 50.0 \text{ g} \cdot \text{L}^{-1}$$

or

$$3.33 \times 10^{-4} \text{ mol} \approx 50.0 \text{ g}$$

Dividing both sides by 3.33×10^{-4}, we have

$$1.00 \text{ mol} \approx 1.50 \times 10^5 \text{ g}$$

The molecular mass of immunoglobulin G is about 150,000.

14-47 The concentration of a solution for which an applied pressure of 100 atm is just sufficient to cause reverse osmosis is

$$M_c = \frac{\pi}{RT} = \frac{100 \text{ atm}}{(0.0821 \text{ L} \cdot \text{atm} \cdot \text{K}^{-1} \cdot \text{mol}^{-1})(293 \text{ K})}$$

$$= 4.16 \text{ mol} \cdot \text{L}^{-1} = 4.16 \text{ M}_c$$

The concentration of sea water is 1.1 M_c. The number moles of ions in the sea water will remain the same after reverse osmosis:

moles ions before reverse osmosis = moles ions after reverse osmosis

$$M_B V_B = M_A V_A$$
$$(1.1 \text{ M}_c)V_B = (4.16 \text{ M}_c)V_A$$

We want 10 L of fresh water, that is $\Delta V = 10$ L:

$$V_B = 10 \text{ L} + V_A \qquad \text{or} \qquad V_A = V_B - 10 \text{ L}$$

$$(1.1 \text{ M}_c)V_B = (4.16 \text{ M}_c)(V_B - 10 \text{ L})$$

Solving for V_B, we have

$$41.6 \text{ L} = 3.06 V_B$$

$$V_B = \frac{41.6 \text{ L}}{3.06} = 13.6 \text{ L}$$

14-49 From Henry's law we have

$$P_{gas} = k_h M_{gas}$$

Thus

$$M_{gas} = \frac{P_{gas}}{k_h}$$

The Henry's law constant for N_2 is $1.6 \times 10^3 \text{ atm} \cdot \text{M}^{-1}$ (see Table 14-5):

$$M_{N_2} = \frac{1.0 \text{ atm}}{1.6 \times 10^3 \text{ atm} \cdot \text{M}^{-1}} = 6.3 \times 10^{-4} \text{ M}$$

14-51 The concentration of CO_2 is given by

$$M_{CO_2} = \frac{P_{CO_2}}{k_h}$$

Using the value of k_h for CO_2 given in Table 14-5, we have

$$M_{CO_2} = \frac{2.0 \text{ atm}}{29 \text{ atm} \cdot \text{M}^{-1}} = 6.9 \times 10^{-2} \text{ M} = 0.069 \text{ M}$$

14-53 The partial pressure of O_2 is (Table 14-5)

$$P_{O_2} = k_h M_{O_2} = (7.8 \times 10^2 \text{ atm} \cdot \text{M}^{-1})(1.28 \times 10^{-3} \text{ M})$$

$$= 1.0 \text{ atm}$$

Air is 20 percent O_2; the air pressure when the partial pressure of O_2 is 1.0 atm is

$$(0.20)P_{air} = P_{O_2}$$

$$P_{air} = \frac{1.0 \text{ atm}}{0.20} = 5.0 \text{ atm}$$

The increase in pressure is 4.0 atm. The depth of the dive is

$$\left(\frac{33 \text{ ft}}{1 \text{ atm}}\right)(4.0 \text{ atm}) = 130 \text{ ft}$$

E   ANSWERS TO THE EVEN-NUMBERED PROBLEMS

14-2 $X_{H_2CO} = 0.30$, $X_{CH_3OH} = 0.071$, $X_{H_2O} = 0.63$

14-4   0.814

14-6 $P_{H_2O} = 42.9$ torr, $P^{\circ}_{H_2O} - P_{H_2O} = 4.2$ torr

14-8 $P_{H_2O} = 0.873$ atm, $P^{\circ}_{H_2O} - P_{H_2O} = 0.13$ atm

14-10 $c = P^{\circ}_1$

14-12 $P_{C_6H_6} = 206$ torr, $P_{C_6H_5CH_3} = 64.2$ torr, $P_{total} = 270$ torr

14-14 Dissolve 457 g of $Ba(NO_3)_2$ in 100 g of water.

14-16 4.0 kg

14-18 (a) 1.0 m_c, (b) 4.0 m_c, (c) 3.0 m_c

14-20 46.8 torr

14-22 1.63 atm, 1.50 M

14-24 56 g NaCl

14-26 100.57°C, 12.5 torr

14-28 108.4°C

14-30 −0.56°C

14-32 325

14-34 328

14-36 −4.4°C (wine), −21°C (vodka)

14-38 155

14-40 $K_2HgI_4(aq) \longrightarrow 2K^+(aq) + HgI_4^{2-}(aq)$; $m_c = 3m$

14-42 28.0 atm

14-44 34,400

14-46 241,000, 4300 units

14-48 8.1 atm

14-50 CO_2

14-52 $[O_2] = 2.6 \times 10^{-4}$ M, $[N_2] = 4.9 \times 10^{-4}$ M

14-54 5.4% by volume

F   ANSWERS TO THE SELF-TEST

1	false (The rates are equal.)	3	false
2	decreases	4	false

5   The solute molecules decrease the rate of evaporation of the solvent relative to that of the pure solvent.

6   mole fraction of the solvent

7   the vapor pressure of the solvent P_1 is equal to $X_1 P_1^{\circ}$

8   the ratio of the number of solute particles to the number of solvent molecules, or to the colligative molality of the solution

9   moles of solute per kilogram of solvent

10 false

11 1000 grams (1 kg) of water

12 $1.0\ m_c$

13 $2.0\ m_c$

14 $3.0\ m_c$

15 increase

16 The solute lowers the vapor pressure of the solvent, and thus the temperature must be raised to increase the vapor pressure back to 1.0 atm, where the solution boils.

17 the colligative molality of the solution

18 true

19 false

20 decrease

21 The solute decreases the rate of crystallization of the solvent (the solute lowers the escaping tendency of the solvent).

22 the colligative molality of the solution

23 true

24 false

25 decrease the freezing point

26 false

27 false

28 pure water; NaCl in solution

29 the 0.1 M solution to the 1.0 M solution

30 the pressure required to increase the escaping tendency of the solvent in a solution to a value equal to that of the pure solvent

31 RTM_c

32 false

33 true

34 true

35 of the osmotic pressure that develops in the cells (Water enters the cells, thereby expanding the cell.)

36 the molar concentration of solute particles

37 Osmotic pressure is a large effect, and only a relatively small protein concentration is necessary for a molecular mass determination.

38 false (Boiling point elevation is a relatively small effect except for high solute concentrations and is not used for molecular mass determinations.)

39 increases

40 the solubility of a gas is proportional to the partial pressure of that gas over the solution $P_{gas} = k_h M_{gas}$

41 true

42 decreases

15 / Chemical Equilibrium

A   OUTLINE OF CHAPTER 15

15-1   A chemical equilibrium is a dynamic equilibrium.

An equilibrium state is attained when the rates of the forward and reverse processes are equal.

Double arrows ⇌ denote a reaction equilibrium.

A state of equilibrium can be attained from either direction.

Chemical equilibrium is attained when the forward reaction rate equals the reverse reaction rate.

15-2   A chemical equilibrium is approachable from either side.

Initial concentrations are denoted by the subscript zero, as in $[N_2O_4]_0$.

At equilibrium the reactant and the product concentrations remain constant (Figure 15-1).

The same equilibrium is attained starting from either the reactant side (left) or the product side (right) of the reaction (Table 15-1).

15-3   The equilibrium-constant expression for a chemical equation is equal to the ratio of product concentration terms to reactant concentration terms.

The equilibrium constant expression for the general equation

$$aA(g) + bB(soln) + cC(s) \rightleftharpoons xX(g) + yY(soln) + zZ(l)$$

is given by the law of concentration action (Guldberg and Waage) as

$$K_c = \frac{[X]^x[Y]^y}{[A]^a[B]^b} \tag{15-3}$$

The law of concentration action states that the equilibrium constant expression for a chemical reaction is formulated as the ratio of product concentrations to reactant concentrations, with each concentration factor raised to a power equal to the stoichiometric coefficient of that species in the balanced equation for the reaction. Pure liquids and solids, whose concentrations cannot be varied, do not appear in the equilibrium constant expression.

The subscript c in K_c denotes that the equilibrium constant is expressed in terms of concentrations.

The law of concentration action tells us how to write the equilibrium constant expression for any balanced chemical equation.

The key point is that at equilibrium the particular algebraic combination of concentration terms given by the law of concentration action for a reaction is equal to a constant called the equilibrium constant.

15-4 Equilibrium constants can be expressed in terms of pressures for gas phase reactions.

The pressure of a gas is equal to the concentration of the gas times RT,

$$P = [gas]RT \qquad (15\text{-}8)$$

The relation between K_c and K_p for a gas reaction is obtained using the K_c expression and the relation $P = [gas]RT$.

15-5 Equilibrium constants are used in a variety of calculations.

The reaction stoichiometry is used to find the relationship between the equilibrium concentration and the initial concentration of a reactant or a product.

The solutions to the quadratic equation $ax^2 + bx + c = 0$ are

$$x = \frac{-b \pm \sqrt{b^2 - 4ac}}{2a} \qquad (15\text{-}14)$$

15-6 A chemical reaction displaced from equilibrium proceeds toward a new equilibrium state in the direction that at least partially offsets the change in conditions.

Le Châtelier's principle (stated above) is used to predict the direction (left to right or right to left) in which an equilibrium shifts in response to a change in conditions that displaces the system from equilibrium.

The conditions whose change can affect a reaction equilibrium are

(a) the concentration of a reactant or product
(b) the reaction volume or applied pressure
(c) the temperature

15-7 A decrease in volume or increase in applied pressure shifts a reaction equilibrium toward the side with fewer moles of gas.

To predict the effect of a volume change on an equilibrium, it is important to focus on only the gaseous species in the reaction (Figure 15-3).

15-8 An increase in temperature shifts a reaction equilibrium in the direction in which heat is absorbed.

Endothermic reactions ($\Delta H^\circ_{rxn} > 0$) shift to the right with increasing temperature.

Exothermic reactions ($\Delta H^\circ_{rxn} < 0$) shift to the left with increasing temperature.

Table 15-2 gives a summary of possible shifts in reaction equilibria resulting from changes in reaction conditions.

15-9 Chemical reactions always proceed toward equilibrium.

The reaction quotient Q_c has the same algebraic form as the equilibrium constant expression K_c, but the concentration values inserted in Q_c need not be equilibrium values.

The value of Q_c depends on how the system is prepared.

The value of the ratio Q_c/K_c is used to determine the direction in which a reaction system proceeds toward equilibrium.

If $Q_c/K_c < 1$ then the reaction proceeds left to right to equilibrium. If $Q_c/K_c > 1$, then the reaction proceeds right to left to equilibrium.

A reaction that is not at equilibrium proceeds to equilibrium in the direction such that Q_c approaches K_c in magnitude.

At equilibrium, $Q_c = K_c$.

15-10 Equilibrium constants for chemical reactions can be combined to obtain equilibrium constants for other reactions.

The equilibrium constant for the reverse reaction is equal to the reciprocal of the equilibrium constant for the forward reaction, $K_r = 1/K_f$ (Equation 15-17).

If we add two equations, then the equilibrium constant for the resulting equation is equal to the product of the equilibrium constants for the two equations that are added together, $K_3 = K_1 K_2$ (Equation 15-18).

15-11 Le Châtelier's principle can be used to select the conditions that maximize the equilibrium yield of a reaction product.

B   SELF-TEST

1   Chemical equilibrium is attained when the rates of the forward reaction and the reverse reaction are zero. *True/False*

2   At equilibrium, the concentrations of reactants increase and the concentrations of the products decrease. *True/False*

3   A chemical equilibrium is a dynamic equilibrium. *True/False*

4   A chemical equilibrium can be approached from the reactant side of a reaction or from the product side. *True/False*

5   At equilibrium the rate of the forward reaction equals _____
_____ .

6   If we start a reaction with only reactants, then in time the concentrations of the reactants will (*decrease/increase/stay the same*).

7 If we start a reaction with only reactants, then in time the concentrations of products will (*decrease/increase/stay the same*).

8 At equilibrium the concentrations of the reactants and products are _____.

9 The value of the equilibrium constant of a reaction depends upon the initial values of the concentrations of the reactants. *True/False*

10 The value of the equilibrium constant of a reaction depends upon the direction in which the equilibrium is approached. *True/False*

11 The law of concentration action states that _____

_____

_____ .

12 For the balanced chemical equation

$$aA(g) + bB(soln) + cC(s) \rightleftharpoons xX(g) + yY(soln) + zZ(l)$$

the equilibrium constant expression is given by

$$K_c = \underline{\hspace{4cm}}$$

13 The equilibrium constant of a gas phase reaction can be expressed in terms of _____ or _____ .

14 For reactions involving gases, the equilibrium constant cannot be expressed in terms of pressure. *True/False*

15 Pure solid reactants and products do not appear in the K_p expression. *True/False*

16 An equilibrium constant cannot have a negative value. *True/False*

17 Given that the equilibrium value for the vapor pressure of water at 25°C is 0.031 atm, the value of K_p for the process $H_2O(l) \rightleftharpoons H_2O(g)$ is

_____ .

18 Given that $K_p = 1.00$ atm at 1200 K for the reaction

$$CaCO_3(s) \rightleftharpoons CaO(s) + CO_2(g)$$

the equilibrium partial pressure of $CO_2(g)$ over $CaCO_3(s)$ plus $CaO(s)$ mixture at 1200 K is _____ .

19 The K_c expression for the reaction

$$C(s) + CO_2(g) \rightleftharpoons 2CO(g)$$

is _____ .

20 The K_p expression for the reaction

$$C(s) + H_2O(g) \rightleftharpoons CO(g) + H_2(g)$$

is _____ .

21 Given that $K_c = 2.0$ at 25°C for the reaction

$$A(s) + B(g) \rightleftharpoons D(g)$$

when [D] = 2.0×10^{-4} M at equilibrium, the value of [B] is _____
_____ .

22 A change in the conditions of a reaction at equilibrium can cause the chemical system to shift to a new equilibrium state. *True/False*

23 Le Châtelier's principle states that _____
_____
_____ .

24 The conditions that can affect a reaction equilibrium are _____ ,
_____ , and _____ .

25 A decrease in the volume of a reaction at equilibrium shifts the equilibrium toward the side of the reaction with _____ .

26 An increase in temperature always shifts the reaction equilibrium toward the product side of a reaction. *True/False*

27 The reaction equilibrium

$$H_2(g) + I_2(g) \rightleftharpoons 2HI(g)$$

is unaffected by a change in the volume in which the reaction takes place. *True/False*

28 If the value of ΔH°_{rxn} is zero, then a chemical equilibrium is unaffected by a change in temperature. *True/False*

29 The equilibrium for an exothermic reaction shifts to the left with increasing temperature. *True/False*

30 Chemical reactions always proceed toward _____ .

31 The reaction quotient has the same algebraic form as the equilibrium constant expression for the reaction. *True/False*

32 For the balanced chemical equation

$$aA(g) + bB(soln) + cC(s) \rightleftharpoons xX(g) + yY(soln) + zZ(l)$$

the value of the reaction quotient is given by

$$Q_c = \underline{\hspace{5cm}}$$

where the subscript zeros denote _____.

33 The value of the ratio (Q_c/K_c) can be used to predict the direction in which a system will proceed spontaneously toward equilibrium. *True/False*

34 When the value of Q/K is less than 1, the reaction proceeds from _____ to _____ toward equilibrium.

35 Suppose that for the reaction

$$H_2(g) + I_2(g) \rightleftharpoons 2HI(g)$$

we take $[H_2]_0 = [I_2]_0 = 0.010 \text{ M}$ and $[HI]_0 = 0$. The value of Q_c is _____.

36 For the reaction system described in Question 35, which of the following relations is valid at equilibrium?
(a) $[H_2] = [I_2] = 0.010 - [HI]$
(b) $[H_2] = [I_2] = 0.010 - 2[HI]$
(c) $[H_2] = [I_2] = 0.010 - [HI]/2$
(d) $[HI] = 2[H_2]$

37 For the reaction system described in Question 35, which of the following relations is *not* valid at equilibrium?
(a) $[HI]^2 = K_c[I_2]^2$
(b) $[HI] = \sqrt{K_c}[H_2]$
(c) $\dfrac{(2x)^2}{(0.010 \text{ M} - x)^2} = K_c$, where $2x = [HI]$
(d) $2[HI]^2 = K_c[H_2]^2$

38 If the equilibrium constant for a forward reaction is K_f, then the equilibrium constant for the reverse reaction is given by $K_r = $ _____.

39 If an equation can be written as the sum of two equations whose equilibrium constants are K_1 and K_2, then the equilibrium constant of the new equation is given by $K_3 = $ _____.

C   CALCULATIONS YOU SHOULD KNOW HOW TO DO

1 Calculate the values of equilibrium constants from initial or equilibrium concentrations. See Examples 15-1 and 15-2 and Problems 15-11 through 15-20.

2 Use the law of concentration action to write expressions for K_c and K_p. See Examples 15-3 and 15-4 and Problems 15-1 through 15-10.

3 Compute equilibrium concentrations (or pressures) using K_c (or K_p) expressions together with initial concentrations. See Examples 15-6 through 15-8 and Problems 15-21 through 15-38.

4 Use Le Châtelier's principle. See Examples 15-9 through 15-12 and Problems 15-39 through 15-50.

5 Use Q_c/K_c to determine the direction in which a reaction proceeds toward equilibrium. See Examples 15-13 and 15-14 and Problems 15-51 through 15-56.

6 Calculate an equilibrium constant for a reaction from other equilibrium constants. See Examples 15-15 and 15-16 and Problems 15-57 through 15-60.

7 Use the van't Hoff equation to calculate equilibrium constants at different temperatures. See Problems 15-61 through 15-66.

The Quadratic Formula

The standard form for a quadratic equation in x is

$$ax^2 + bx + c = 0 \tag{1}$$

where a, b, and c are constants.

The two solutions to the quadratic equation are

$$x = \frac{-b \pm \sqrt{b^2 - 4ac}}{2a} \tag{15-14}$$

Equation (15-14) is called the quadratic formula. The quadratic formula is used to obtain the solutions to a quadratic equation in the standard form, that is, $ax^2 + bx + c = 0$.

For example, let's find the solutions to the quadratic equation

$$2x^2 - 2x - 3 = 0$$

In this case $a = 2$, $b = -2$, and $c = -3$, and Equation (15-14) gives

$$x = \frac{-(-2) \pm \sqrt{(-2)^2 - 4(2)(-3)}}{2(2)}$$

$$= \frac{2 \pm \sqrt{4 + 24}}{4}$$

$$= \frac{2 \pm 5.292}{4}$$

$$= 1.823 \text{ and } -0.823$$

To use the quadratic formula to solve a quadratic equation, it is first necessary to put the quadratic equation in the standard form so that we know the values of the constants a, b, and c to use in Equation (15-14). For example, consider the problem of solving for x in the quadratic equation

$$\frac{x^2}{0.35 - x} = 0.100$$

To identify the constants a, b, and c, we must write this equation in the standard form of the quadratic equation. Multiplying both sides by $0.35 - x$ yields

$$x^2 = (0.35 - x)(0.100)$$

or

$$x^2 = 0.035 - 0.100x$$

Rearrangement to the standard quadratic form yields

$$x^2 + 0.100x - 0.035 = 0$$

Thus $a = 1$, $b = 0.100$, and $c = -0.035$. Using Equation (15-14) we have

$$x = \frac{-0.100 \pm \sqrt{(0.10)^2 - 4(1)(-0.035)}}{2(1)}$$

from which we compute

$$x = \frac{-0.100 \pm \sqrt{0.15}}{2}$$

$$x = \frac{-0.100 \pm 0.387}{2}$$

Thus the solutions for x are

$$x = \frac{-0.100 + 0.387}{2} = 0.144$$

and

$$x = \frac{-0.100 - 0.387}{2} = -0.244$$

If x represents a concentration or gas pressure, then the only physically possible value of x is $+0.144$ because concentrations and pressures cannot have negative values.

Exercises

Solve the following equations for x.

1 $x^2 - 2x - 1 = 0$

2 $0.600x^2 - x - 0.450 = 0$

3 $x^2 + 2x - 0.285 = 0$

4 $\dfrac{x^2}{0.020 - x} = 0.0100$

5 $\dfrac{x^2}{0.150 - x} = 0.0250$

Answers

1 $1 \pm \sqrt{2}$ or 2.414; -0.414

2 2.04; -0.369

3 0.134; -2.13

4 0.010; -0.020

5 0.0500; -0.0750

D   SOLUTIONS TO THE ODD-NUMBERED PROBLEMS

For Problems 15-1 through 15-5, recall that each product concentration factor, raised to a power equal to its balancing coefficient, appears in the numerator of the K_c expression, and each reactant concentration factor, raised to a power equal to its balancing coefficient, appears in the denominator of the K_c expression. Pure solids and liquids do not appear in the K_c expression.

15-1 (a) $K_c = \dfrac{[H_2O]^2}{[H_2]^2}$

(b) $K_c = [POCl_3][HCl]^2$

15-3 (a) $K_c = \dfrac{[H_2]^2[S_2]}{[H_2S]^2}$

(b) $K_c = \dfrac{[C_2H_6]}{[C_2H_4][H_2]}$

15-5 (a) $K_c = \dfrac{[H_2O]^2}{[H_2]^2[O_2]}$

(b) $K_c = \dfrac{[O_2][NO_2]^4}{[N_2O_5]^2}$

(c) $K_c = [H_2O]^2$

15-7 (a) $K_p = \dfrac{P_{H_2O}^2}{P_{H_2}^2 P_{O_2}}$

(b) $K_p = \dfrac{P_{NO_2}^4 P_{O_2}}{P_{N_2O_5}^2}$

(c) $K_p = P_{H_2O}^2$

15-9 An equilibrium constant expression involves equilibrium concentration terms of reactants and products. The concentration of a substance cannot be negative; thus K_c cannot be negative.

15-11 We can write the equilibrium constant expression by applying the law of concentration action to the reaction

$$K_c = \frac{[CO][Cl_2]}{[COCl_2]}$$

Substituting the values of the equilibrium concentrations into the K_c expression, we have

$$K_c = \frac{(0.0456\ M)(0.0456\ M)}{(0.449\ M)}$$

$$K_c = 4.63 \times 10^{-3}\ M \text{ at } 527°C$$

15-13 The equilibrium constant expression for the reaction is

$$K_p = P_{NH_3}^2$$

The equilibrium pressure of $NH_3(g)$ in atmospheres is

$$P_{NH_3} = (62\ \text{torr})\left(\frac{1\ \text{atm}}{760\ \text{torr}}\right) = 8.2 \times 10^{-2}\ \text{atm}$$

Substituting this value of P_{NH_3} into K_p yields

$$K_p = (8.2 \times 10^{-2}\ \text{atm})^2 = 6.7 \times 10^{-3}\ \text{atm}^2)$$

15-15 The equilibrium constant expression for the reaction is

$$K_c = \frac{[HI]^2}{[H_2][I_2]}$$

We now set up a table of the initial concentrations and the equilibrium concentrations. For every H_2 (or I_2) molecule that reacts, two molecules of HI are produced. The decrease in the concentration of H_2 (or I_2) is therefore one half the increase in the concentration of HI.

	$H_2(g)$	$+$	$I_2(g)$	$\rightleftharpoons$	$2HI(g)$
Initial concentration	$\dfrac{1.00 \text{ mol}}{1.00 \text{ L}} = 1.00 \text{ M}$		1.00 M		0
Equilibrium concentration	$1.00 \text{ M} - (1.56/2) \text{ M}$ $= 0.22 \text{ M}$		$1.00 \text{ M} - (1.56/2) \text{ M}$ $= 0.22 \text{ M}$		$\dfrac{1.56 \text{ mol}}{1.00 \text{ L}} = 1.56 \text{ M}$

Substituting the values of the equilibrium concentrations into the K_c expression, we find that

$$K_c = \frac{[\text{HI}]^2}{[\text{H}_2][\text{I}_2]} = \frac{(1.56 \text{ M})^2}{(0.22 \text{ M})^2} = 50$$

15-17 The K_c expression for the reaction is

$$K_c = \frac{[\text{NH}_3]^2}{[\text{N}_2][\text{H}_2]^3}$$

The relation between K_c and K_p is obtained using the relation

$$P = [gas]RT \quad \text{or} \quad [gas] = P/RT \quad \text{for each gas}$$

$$K_c = \frac{\left(\dfrac{P_{\text{NH}_3}}{RT}\right)^2}{\left(\dfrac{P_{\text{N}_2}}{RT}\right)\left(\dfrac{P_{\text{H}_2}}{RT}\right)^3} = (RT)^2 \frac{P_{\text{NH}_3}^2}{P_{\text{N}_2}P_{\text{H}_2}^3} = (RT)^2 K_p$$

Substituting the values of R, T, and K_p, we have

$$K_c = [(0.0821 \text{ L} \cdot \text{atm} \cdot \text{K}^{-1} \cdot \text{mol}^{-1})(500 \text{ K})]^2(0.10 \text{ atm}^{-2})$$
$$= 170 \text{ M}^{-2} \text{ at } 227°\text{C}$$

15-19 We can write the equilibrium constant expression for the reaction by applying the law of concentration action:

$$K_c = \frac{[\text{CO}][\text{H}_2]}{[\text{H}_2\text{O}]}$$

Substituting in the values of the equilibrium concentrations, we find that

$$K_c = \frac{(6.75 \times 10^{-2} \text{ M})(6.75 \times 10^{-2} \text{ M})}{(5.70 \times 10^{-2} \text{ M})}$$
$$= 7.99 \times 10^{-2} \text{ M at } 800°\text{C}$$

The relation between K_c and K_p is

$$K_c = \frac{\left(\dfrac{P_{CO}}{RT}\right)\left(\dfrac{P_{H_2}}{RT}\right)}{\left(\dfrac{P_{H_2O}}{RT}\right)} = \frac{1}{RT}\left(\frac{P_{CO}P_{H_2}}{P_{H_2O}}\right) = \frac{1}{RT}K_p$$

Thus
$$K_p = RTK_c$$

and therefore

$$K_p = (0.0821 \text{ L} \cdot \text{atm} \cdot \text{K}^{-1} \cdot \text{mol}^{-1})(1073 \text{ K})(7.99 \times 10^{-2} \text{ mol} \cdot \text{L}^{-1})$$
$$= 7.04 \text{ atm at } 800°C$$

15-21 From the law of concentration action we have

$$K_c = \frac{[NO_2]^2}{[N_2O_4]}$$

Substituting in the values of the equilibrium concentration of N_2O_4 and of K_c, we have

$$0.20 \text{ M} = \frac{[NO_2]^2}{0.730 \text{ M}}$$

Thus
$$[NO_2]^2 = (0.20 \text{ M})(0.730 \text{ M}) = 0.146 \text{ M}^2$$

Taking the square root of both sides yields

$$[NO_2] = 0.38 \text{ M at equilibrium}$$

15-23 From the law of concentration action we have

$$K_c = \frac{[PCl_3][Cl_2]}{[PCl_5]}$$

We set up a table of initial concentrations and equilibrium concentrations. Let x be the number of moles per liter of PCl_3 that is produced by the decomposition of PCl_5. From the reaction stoichiometry $[PCl_3] = [Cl_2] = x$ and $[PCl_5] = 3.0 \text{ M} - x$ at equilibrium.

	$PCl_5(g)$	$\rightleftharpoons$ $PCl_3(g)$	$+$ $Cl_2(g)$
Initial concentrations	$\dfrac{1.50 \text{ mol}}{0.50 \text{ L}} = 3.0 \text{ M}$	0	0
Equilibrium concentrations	$3.0 \text{ M} - x$	x	x

Substituting the equilibrium concentration expressions into the K_c expression, we have

$$K_c = \frac{(x)(x)}{3.0 \text{ M} - x} = \frac{x^2}{3.0 \text{ M} - x} = 1.8 \text{ M}$$

or

$$x^2 = (1.8 \text{ M})(3.0 \text{ M} - x) = 5.4 \text{ M}^2 - (1.8 \text{ M})x$$

We rearrange this equation to the standard quadratic form

$$x^2 + (1.8 \text{ M})x - 5.4 \text{ M}^2 = 0$$

Using the quadratic formula, we have

$$x = \frac{-1.8 \text{ M} \pm \sqrt{(1.8 \text{ M})^2 - (4)(1)(-5.4 \text{ M}^2)}}{(2)(1)}$$

Taking the positive root, we obtain

$$x = 1.6 \text{ M}$$

We reject the negative value of x. Therefore, at equilibrium $[PCl_3] = 1.6$ M, $[Cl_2] = 1.6$ M, and $[PCl_5] = 3.0$ M $- 1.6$ M $= 1.4$ M.

15-25   From the law of concentration action we have

$$K_c = 2.51 \times 10^4 = \frac{[HCl]^2}{[H_2][Cl_2]}$$

Let x be the number of moles of H_2 or of Cl_2 that react. From the reaction stoichiometry, the number of moles of HCl produced is $2x$. Let V be the reaction volume. Thus the initial and equilibrium concentrations are:

	$H_2(g)$	$+$	$Cl_2(g)$	$\rightleftharpoons$ 2HCl(g)
Initial concentration	$\dfrac{0.250 \text{ mol}}{V}$		$\dfrac{0.250 \text{ mol}}{V}$	0
Equilibrium concentration	$\dfrac{0.250 \text{ mol} - x}{V}$		$\dfrac{0.250 \text{ mol} - x}{V}$	$\dfrac{2x}{V}$

Substituting the equilibrium concentrations into the K_c expression yields

$$\frac{\left(\dfrac{2x}{V}\right)^2}{\left(\dfrac{0.250 \text{ mol} - x}{V}\right)^2} = 2.51 \times 10^4$$

Taking the square root of both sides yields

$$\frac{\left(\dfrac{2x}{V}\right)}{\left(\dfrac{0.250 \text{ mol} - x}{V}\right)} = 1.58 \times 10^2$$

or after canceling V, the volume, in the denominator and the numerator, we have

$$2x = 158(0.250 \text{ mol} - x)$$

Collecting like terms

$$160x = 39.5 \text{ mol}$$

and solving for x gives

$$x = 0.247 \text{ mol}$$

The number of moles of HCl at equilibrium is $2x$ or 0.494 mol.

15-27   From the law of concentration action, we have

$$K_c = [NH_3][H_2S] = 1.81 \times 10^{-4} \text{ M}^2$$

We need K_p in order to calculate equilibrium pressures. The relation between K_c and K_p is

$$K_c = \left(\frac{P_{NH_3}}{RT}\right)\left(\frac{P_{H_2S}}{RT}\right) = \left(\frac{1}{RT}\right)^2 K_p$$

or

$$K_p = (RT)^2 K_c$$

Thus

$$K_p = [(0.0821 \text{ L} \cdot \text{atm} \cdot \text{K}^{-1} \cdot \text{mol}^{-1})(298 \text{ K})]^2 (1.81 \times 10^{-4} \text{ mol}^2 \cdot \text{L}^{-2})$$
$$= 0.108 \text{ atm}^2$$

From the reaction stoichiometry we have $P_{NH_3} = P_{H_2S}$ at equilibrium. Let x be the equilibrium pressure of NH_3. Thus

$$K_p = (x)(x) = x^2 = 0.108 \text{ atm}^2$$

Taking the square root yields

$$x = 0.329 \text{ atm}$$

At equilibrium $P_{H_2S} = P_{NH_3} = 0.329$ atm. The total pressure is the sum of the partial pressures of H_2S and NH_3

$$P_{tot} = P_{H_2S} + P_{NH_3} = 0.329 \text{ atm} + 0.329 \text{ atm}$$

$$= 0.658 \text{ atm}$$

15-29 From the law of concentration action we have

$$K_c = \frac{[Cl_2][I_2]}{[ICl]^2} = 0.11$$

We set up a table of initial concentrations and equilibrium concentrations. Let x be the number of moles per liter of I_2 or of Cl_2 that react. From the reaction stoichiometry the number of moles per liter of ICl produced is $2x$. Each mole of I_2 or Cl_2 that reacts produces two moles of ICl.

	$2ICl(g) \rightleftharpoons$	$I_2(g)$	+	$Cl_2(g)$
Initial concentration	0	$\frac{0.33 \text{ mol}}{1.5 \text{ L}} = 0.22 \text{ M}$		$\frac{0.33 \text{ mol}}{1.5 \text{ L}} = 0.22 \text{ M}$
Equilibrium concentration	$2x$	$0.22 \text{ M} - x$		$0.22 \text{ M} - x$

Substituting the equilibrium concentration expressions in the K_c expression yields

$$\frac{(0.22 \text{ M} - x)^2}{(2x)^2} = 0.11$$

Taking the square root of both sides, we obtain

$$\frac{0.22 \text{ M} - x}{2x} = 0.33$$

or

$$0.22 \text{ M} - x = (0.33)(2x) = 0.66x$$

Thus

$$x = \frac{0.22 \text{ M}}{1.66} = 0.13 \text{ M}$$

At equilibrium $[Cl_2] = [I_2] = 0.22 \text{ M} - 0.13 \text{ M} = 0.09 \text{ M}$ and $[ICl] = 0.26 \text{ M}$.

15-31 From the law of concentration action we have

$$K_c = \frac{[I_2][H_2]}{[HI]^2}$$

Let x be the number of moles per liter of H_2 that are produced from the decomposition of HI. Each mole of H_2 produced requires that two moles of HI decompose. We will set up a table of initial concentrations and equilibrium concentrations as before:

	$2HI(g)$	$\rightleftharpoons$	$H_2(g)$	$+$	$I_2(g)$
Initial concentrations	3.52 M + 1.00 M = 4.52 M		0.42 M		0.42 M
Equilibrium concentrations	4.52 M − 2x		0.42 M + x		0.42 M + x

Notice that the initial concentration of HI is the equilibrium concentration plus the concentration of the added HI. Substituting the equilibrium concentration expressions in the K_c expression, we have

$$K_c = \frac{(0.42 \text{ M} + x)(0.42 \text{ M} + x)}{(4.52 \text{ M} - 2x)^2}$$

We can calculate the value of K_c from the initial equilibrium concentrations

$$K_c = \frac{(0.42 \text{ M})(0.42 \text{ M})}{(3.52 \text{ M})^2} = 0.014$$

We now have

$$\frac{(0.42 \text{ M} + x)^2}{(4.52 \text{ M} - 2x)^2} = 0.014$$

Taking the square root of both sides, we obtain

$$\frac{0.42 \text{ M} + x}{4.52 \text{ M} - 2x} = 0.12$$

or

$$0.42 \text{ M} + x = (0.12)(4.52 \text{ M} - 2x) = 0.54 \text{ M} - 0.24x$$

$$1.24x = 0.12 \text{ M}$$

$$x = \frac{0.12 \text{ M}}{1.24} = 0.097 \text{ M}$$

Thus in the new equilibrium state we have

$$[HI] = 4.52 \text{ M} - 2x = 4.33 \text{ M}$$

$$[H_2] = 0.42 \text{ M} + x = 0.52 \text{ M}$$

$$[I_2] = 0.42 \text{ M} + x = 0.52 \text{ M}$$

15-33 From the law of concentration action we have

$$K_p = \frac{P_{NO_2}^2}{P_{N_2O_4}} = 4.90 \text{ atm}$$

We know from Dalton's law of partial pressures that

$$P_{tot} = P_{NO_2} + P_{N_2O_4} = 2.40 \text{ atm}$$

Solving for P_{NO_2}, we have

$$P_{NO_2} = 2.40 \text{ atm} - P_{N_2O_4}$$

Substituting this expression for P_{NO_2} into the K_p expression, we have

$$\frac{(2.40 \text{ atm} - P_{N_2O_4})^2}{P_{N_2O_4}} = \frac{5.76 \text{ atm}^2 - (4.80 \text{ atm})\, P_{N_2O_4} + P_{N_2O_4}^2}{P_{N_2O_4}} = 4.90 \text{ atm}$$

or

$$5.76 \text{ atm}^2 - (4.80 \text{ atm})\, P_{N_2O_4} + P_{N_2O_4}^2 = (4.90 \text{ atm})\, P_{N_2O_4}$$

Rearranging to the standard form of a quadratic equation, we have

$$P_{N_2O_4}^2 - (9.70 \text{ atm})\, P_{N_2O_4} + 5.76 \text{ atm}^2 = 0$$

The solution to the above equation from the quadratic formula is

$$P_{N_2O_4} = \frac{9.70 \text{ atm} \pm \sqrt{94.09 \text{ atm}^2 - (4)(1)(5.76 \text{ atm}^2)}}{2}$$

$$P_{N_2O_4} = \frac{9.70 \text{ atm} \pm 8.43 \text{ atm}}{2} = 9.065 \text{ atm and } 0.635 \text{ atm}$$

We can rule out the value 9.065 atm because it is larger than the total pressure. At equilibrium $P_{N_2O_4} = 0.635 \text{ atm}$ and $P_{NO_2} = 2.40 \text{ atm} - 0.635 \text{ atm} = 1.77$ atm.

15-35 From the law of concentration action we have

$$K_p = \frac{P_{CO_2}}{P_{CO}} = 600$$

The total pressure is equal to the sum of the partial pressures of $CO(g)$ and $CO_2(g)$:

$$P_{tot} = P_{CO} + P_{CO_2} = 11.8 \text{ atm}$$

Solving for P_{CO_2}, we have

$$P_{CO_2} = 11.8 \text{ atm} - P_{CO}$$

Substituting the expression for P_{CO_2} into the K_p expression we have that

$$\frac{11.8 \text{ atm} - P_{CO}}{P_{CO}} = 600$$

Thus

$$P_{CO} = \frac{11.8 \text{ atm}}{601} = 0.0196 \text{ atm}$$

The partial pressure of CO_2 is

$$P_{CO_2} = 11.8 \text{ atm} - P_{CO} = 11.8 \text{ atm} - 0.0196 \text{ atm} = 11.8 \text{ atm}$$

15-37 From the law of concentration action we have

$$K_p = \frac{P_{CH_3OH}}{P_{H_2}^2 P_{CO}} = 2.25 \times 10^4 \text{ atm}^{-2}$$

(a) Substituting the values of P_{H_2} and P_{CO} in the K_p expression, we have

$$\frac{P_{CH_3OH}}{(0.020 \text{ atm})^2(0.010 \text{ atm})} = 2.25 \times 10^4 \text{ atm}^{-2}$$

$$P_{CH_3OH} = (2.25 \times 10^4 \text{ atm}^{-2})(4.0 \times 10^{-6} \text{ atm}^3)$$

$$= 0.090 \text{ atm}$$

(b) The total pressure is equal to the sum of the partial pressures:

$$P_{tot} = P_{H_2} + P_{CO} + P_{CH_3OH} = 10.00 \text{ atm}$$

We have $P_{H_2} = 0.020$ atm; thus

$$0.020 \text{ atm} + P_{CO} + P_{CH_3OH} = 10.00 \text{ atm}$$

If we solve for P_{CO}, we have that

$$P_{CO} = 10.00 \text{ atm} - 0.020 \text{ atm} - P_{CH_3OH}$$

$$= 9.98 \text{ atm} - P_{CH_3OH}$$

Substituting the expression for P_{CO} and the value of P_{H_2} in the K_p expression, we have

$$\frac{P_{CH_3OH}}{(0.020 \text{ atm})^2 (9.98 \text{ atm} - P_{CH_3OH})} = 2.25 \times 10^4 \text{ atm}^{-2}$$

$$\frac{P_{CH_3OH}}{3.99 \times 10^{-3} \text{ atm}^3 - 4.00 \times 10^{-4} \text{ atm}^2 \, P_{CH_3OH}} = 2.25 \times 10^4 \text{ atm}^{-2}$$

or

$$P_{CH_3OH} = (2.25 \times 10^4 \text{ atm}^{-2})(3.99 \times 10^{-3} \text{ atm}^3 - 4.00 \times 10^{-4} \text{ atm}^2 \, P_{CH_3OH})$$
$$= 89.8 \text{ atm} - 9.00 \, P_{CH_3OH}$$

Collect like terms

$$10.00 \, P_{CH_3OH} = 89.8 \text{ atm}$$

and solve for P_{CH_3OH} to get

$$P_{CH_3OH} = \frac{89.8 \text{ atm}}{10.00} = 8.98 \text{ atm}$$

and

$$P_{CO} = 9.98 \text{ atm} - 8.98 \text{ atm} = 1.00 \text{ atm}$$

15-39 An increase in P_{H_2O} will cause a shift in the reaction equilibrium from right to left, because this is the direction in which P_{H_2O} will decrease. Thus P_{CO} will decrease and P_{CO_2} will increase.

15-41 An increase in the concentration of $Br_2(g)$ will cause the reaction equilibrium to shift to the right, thereby increasing the equilibrium concentration of NOBr and decreasing the equilibrium concentration of NO. An increase in the concentration of Br_2, which is a reactant, shifts the equilibrium from left to right.

15-43 (a) ⟵   The reaction is exothermic. An increase in temperature shifts the equilibrium to the left.

(b) ⟵   An increase in total volume leads to a decrease in the total number of moles per unit volume in the reaction mixture. A shift to the left causes an increase in the number of moles per unit volume.

(c) ⟶   A shift in equilibrium to the right will decrease the pressure of H_2.

(d) ⟶   A shift in equilibrium to the right will increase the pressure of CH_4.

(e) no change   The concentration of C(s) is independent of the amount of C(s), and thus the equilibrium concentrations are independent of the amount of C(s).

15-45 (a) $\longrightarrow$ The reaction is exothermic, and thus a decrease in temperature favors the evolution of heat.

(b) $\longleftarrow$ There are more moles of gas on the left than on the right, and thus a shift to the left will partially offset the decrease in the number of moles per unit volume.

(c) $\longrightarrow$ The addition of O_2 increases the concentration of O_2, which will be offset partially by a shift to the right.

(d) $\longleftarrow$ The removal of SO_2 decreases the concentration of SO_2, which then will be increased by a shift to the left.

15-47 (a) no change   There are the same number of moles of gaseous species on each side of the reaction.

(b) $\longleftarrow$ The reaction is exothermic.

(c) $\longrightarrow$ A shift to the right will decrease P_{NO_2}.

(d) $\longrightarrow$ A shift to the right will increase P_{SO_3} and P_{NO}.

15-49 (1)

$$K_c = \frac{[CO][H_2]}{[H_2O]}$$

An increase in temperature shifts the reaction equilibrium to the right (endothermic reaction). A decrease in reaction volume shifts the reaction equilibrium to the left ($\Delta n_{gas} = +1$).

(2)

$$K_c = \frac{[CO_2][H_2]}{[CO][H_2O]}$$

An increase in temperature shifts the reaction equilibrium to the left (exothermic reaction). A decrease in reaction volume has no effect ($\Delta n_{gas} = 0$).

(3)

$$K_c = \frac{[H_2O][CH_4]}{[CO][H_2]^3}$$

An increase in temperature shifts the equilibrium to the left (exothermic reaction). A decrease in the reaction volume shifts the equilibrium to the right ($\Delta n_{gas} = -2$).

15-51 The equilibrium constant expression is

$$K_c = \frac{[SO_3]^2}{[SO_2]^2[O_2]} = 13 \text{ M}^{-1} \text{ at equilibrium}$$

The Q_c expression is

$$Q_c = \frac{[SO_3]_0^2}{[SO_2]_0^2[O_2]_0}$$

The value of Q_c is calculated from the given initial concentrations:

	Q_c	Q_c/K_c	Direction that the reaction proceeds toward equilibrium
(a)	$\dfrac{(0.20\ M)^2}{(0.20\ M)^2(0.20\ M)} = 5.0\ M^{-1}$	$\dfrac{5\ M^{-1}}{13\ M^{-1}} = 0.38$	$\longrightarrow$
(b)	$\dfrac{(0.20\ M)^2}{(0.10\ M)^2(0.20\ M)} = 20\ M^{-1}$	$\dfrac{20\ M^{-1}}{13\ M^{-1}} = 1.5$	$\longleftarrow$

15-53   The Q_p expression is

$$Q_p = \frac{(P_{CO})_0(P_{H_2O})_0}{(P_{H_2})_0(P_{CO_2})_0}$$

Thus

$$Q_p = \frac{(1.25\ \text{atm})(0.50\ \text{atm})}{(0.50\ \text{atm})(0.25\ \text{atm})} = 5.0$$

Because Q_p does not equal K_p, the reaction is not at equilibrium

$$\frac{Q_p}{K_p} = \frac{5.0}{1.59} = 3.1$$

Because the value of Q/K is greater than 1, the reaction proceeds from right to left toward equilibrium.

15-55   The Q_p expression for the reaction is

$$Q_p = \frac{(P_{SO_3})_0^2}{(P_{SO_2})_0^2(P_{O_2})_0}$$

Thus

$$Q_p = \frac{(0.20\ \text{atm})^2}{(0.10\ \text{atm})^2(0.20\ \text{atm})} = 20\ \text{atm}^{-1}$$

$$\frac{Q_p}{K_p} = \frac{20\ \text{atm}^{-1}}{0.14\ \text{atm}^{-1}} = 140$$

Because $Q_p/K_p > 1$, the reaction proceeds right to left toward equilibrium.

15-57   The equation

$$CH_4(g) + 2H_2O(g) \rightleftharpoons CO_2(g) + 4H_2(g)$$

is the sum of the two given equations. Thus the equilibrium constant is given by

$$K = K_1K_2 = (1.44)(25.6\ \text{atm}^2) = 36.9\ \text{atm}^2$$

15-59 For the reverse of Equation (1),

(3) $\qquad$ $Cl_2(g) + MgO(s) \rightleftharpoons MgCl_2(s) + \frac{1}{2}O_2(g)$

we have

$$K_3 = \frac{1}{K_1} = \frac{1}{2.95 \text{ atm}^{1/2}}$$

Adding Equation (3) to Equation (2),

(2) $\qquad$ $MgCl_2(s) + H_2O(g) \rightleftharpoons MgO(s) + 2HCl(g)$

yields

(4) $\qquad$ $Cl_2(g) + H_2O(g) \rightleftharpoons 2HCl(g) + \frac{1}{2}O_2(g)$

Thus

$$K_4 = K_3K_2 = \left(\frac{1}{K_1}\right)(K_2) = \frac{8.40 \text{ atm}}{2.95 \text{ atm}^{1/2}} = 2.85 \text{ atm}^{1/2}$$

15-61 The van't Hoff equation is

$$\log \frac{K_2}{K_1} = \frac{\Delta H^\circ_{rxn}}{2.30R}\left(\frac{T_2 - T_1}{T_1T_2}\right)$$

Substituting the values of K_1, T_1, T_2, and ΔH°_{rxn} into the van't Hoff equation, we obtain

$$\log\left(\frac{K_2}{1.78 \text{ atm}}\right) = \frac{(92.9 \text{ kJ} \cdot \text{mol}^{-1})(1000 \text{ J} \cdot \text{kJ}^{-1})(673 \text{ K} - 523 \text{ K})}{(2.30)(8.31 \text{ J} \cdot \text{mol}^{-1} \cdot \text{K}^{-1})(523 \text{ K})(673 \text{ K})}$$

$$= 2.071$$

Taking the antilogarithm of both sides yields

$$\frac{K_2}{1.78 \text{ atm}} = 117.8$$

Thus

$$K_2 = (117.8)(1.78 \text{ atm}) = 210 \text{ atm}$$

15-63 Substituting in the values of K_1, T_1, T_2 and ΔH°_{rxn} into the van't Hoff equation (Problem 15-61), we have

$$\log \frac{K_2}{0.14 \text{ atm}^{-1}} = \frac{(-198 \text{ kJ} \cdot \text{mol}^{-1})(1000 \text{ J} \cdot \text{kJ}^{-1})(1273 \text{ K} - 900 \text{ K})}{(2.30)(8.31 \text{ J} \cdot \text{mol}^{-1} \cdot \text{K}^{-1})(1273 \text{ K})(900 \text{ K})}$$

$$= -3.373$$

Taking the antilogarithm of both sides, we have

$$\frac{K_2}{0.14 \text{ atm}^{-1}} = 4.24 \times 10^{-4}$$

$$K_2 = (4.24 \times 10^{-4})(0.14 \text{ atm}^{-1})$$

$$= 5.9 \times 10^{-5} \text{ atm}^{-1}$$

15-65   Using the property $\log a/b = \log a - \log b$, the van't Hoff equation can be written

$$\log \frac{K_2}{K_1} = \frac{\Delta H^\circ_{rxn}}{2.30R}\left(\frac{T_2 - T_1}{T_1 T_2}\right) = \log K_2 - \log K_1$$

Substituting the values of K_1, T_1, K_2, and T_2 into the van't Hoff equation yields

$$\frac{\Delta H^\circ_{rxn}(873 \text{ K} - 723 \text{ K})}{(2.30)(8.31 \text{ J} \cdot \text{mol}^{-1} \cdot \text{K}^{-1})(723 \text{ K})(873 \text{ K})} = -0.002 - (-0.706)$$

Thus

$$(1.24 \times 10^{-5} \text{ J}^{-1} \cdot \text{mol}) \, \Delta H^\circ_{rxn} = 0.704$$

Solving for ΔH°_{rxn}, we have

$$\Delta H^\circ_{rxn} = \frac{0.704}{1.24 \times 10^{-5} \text{ J}^{-1} \cdot \text{mol}}$$

$$= 5.66 \times 10^4 \text{ J} \cdot \text{mol}^{-1}$$

$$= 56.6 \text{ kJ} \cdot \text{mol}^{-1}$$

E   ANSWERS TO THE EVEN-NUMBERED PROBLEMS

15-2   (a) $K_c = \dfrac{[CH_3OH]}{[CO][H_2]^2}$

(b) $K_c = [CO_2][H_2O]$

15-4   (a) $K_c = \dfrac{[NO]^2}{[N_2][O_2]}$

(b) $K_c = [O_2]$

15-6   (a) $K_c = [CO_2][NH_3]^2$

(b) $K_c = \dfrac{[CO]^2}{[CO_2]}$

(c) $K_c = \dfrac{[N_2O_4]}{[N_2][O_2]^2}$

15-8 (a) $K_p = P_{NH_3}^2 P_{CO_2}$

(b) $K_p = \dfrac{P_{CO}^2}{P_{CO_2}}$

(c) $K_p = \dfrac{P_{N_2O_4}}{P_{N_2} P_{O_2}^2}$

15-10 $H_2SO_4(l) + 2NaCl(s) \longrightarrow 2HCl(g) + Na_2SO_4(s)$

$K_c = [HCl]^2 \qquad K_p = P_{HCl}^2$

15-12 $K_c = 1.8$ M

15-14 $K_p = 26$ atm^2

15-16 $K_p = 39$ atm

15-18 $K_p = 6.1$ atm

15-20 $K_c = 4.2 \times 10^{-4}$ M, $K_p = 5.1 \times 10^{-2}$ atm

15-22 $P_{CO_2} = 1.18$ atm

15-24 9.04 mol (688 g)

15-26 4.47 atm

15-28 $P_{CO_2} = P_{H_2O} = 0.50$ atm

15-30 $[COCl_2] = 0.15$ M, $[Cl_2] = 0.10$ M, $[CO] = 0.35$ M

15-32 $[H_2O] = [H_2] = 0.38$ M

15-34 $P_{H_2} = 1.3$ atm, $P_{HI} = 3.2$ atm

15-36 $P_{H_2} = 1.51$ atm, $P_{CH_4} = 0.60$ atm

15-38 (a) $P_{NH_3} = 1.6$ atm; (b) $X_{NH_3} = 0.0489$

15-40 No effect

15-42 Decreased

15-44 (a) $\longleftarrow$; (b) $\longleftarrow$; (c) $\longrightarrow$; (d) no change

15-46 (a) Right; (b) right; (c) left; (d) left

15-48 (a) Increased; (b) decreased

15-50 Low temperature and high pressure (small reaction volume)

15-52 $Q_p/K_p = 0.028$, not at equilibrium, proceeds left to right

15-54 $Q_p/K_p = 0.0475$, not at equilibrium, proceeds left to right

15-56 Right to left

15-58 $K_c = 2.2\ \text{M}^{-1/2}$; $K_p = 0.40\ \text{atm}^{-1/2}$

15-60 $K = 0.074\ \text{atm}^2$

15-62 $K = 269$

15-64 $K_P = 1 \times 10^{-31}$

15-66 $K = 3.69 \times 10^{-7}\ \text{atm}^{-2}$

F ANSWERS TO THE SELF-TEST

1 false (Forward and reverse rates are equal at equilibrium.)

2 false

3 true

4 true

5 the rate of the reverse reaction

6 decrease

7 increase

8 constant

9 false

10 false

11 The equilibrium constant expression for a reaction is given by the ratio of product equilibrium concentrations to reactant equilibrium concentrations, with each concentration factor raised to a power equal to the stoichiometric coefficient of that species in the balanced equation for the reaction.

12 $K_c = \dfrac{[X]^x[Y]^y}{[A]^a[B]^b}$

13 concentrations (K_c) or pressures (K_p)

14 false

15 true

16 true

17 0.031 atm

18 1.00 atm

19 $K_c = \dfrac{[CO]^2}{[CO_2]}$

20 $K_p = \dfrac{P_{CO}P_{H_2}}{P_{H_2O}}$

21 1.0×10^{-4} M

22 true

23 If a change in conditions displaces a reaction equilibrium, then the reaction proceeds toward equilibrium in the direction that at least partially offsets the change in conditions.

24 temperature, reaction volume, and concentrations of reactants and products

25 the smaller number of moles of gaseous species

26 false (only true for endothermic reactions)

27 true

28 true

29 true

30 equilibrium

31 true

32 $Q_c = \dfrac{[X]_0^x[Y]_0^y}{[A]_0^a[B]_0^b}$

where the subscript zeros denote initial values of the concentrations

33 true

34 left to right

35 zero

36 (c)

37 (d)

38 $1/K_f$

39 K_1K_2

16 / Rates and Mechanisms of Chemical Reactions

A   OUTLINE OF CHAPTER 16

16-1   A rate tells us how fast a quantity is changing with time.

For the reaction A → P, the rate of formation of product P is defined as

$$\text{rate} = \frac{\Delta[P]}{\Delta t} = \frac{[P]_2 - [P]_1}{t_2 - t_1} \tag{16-1}$$

The rate of consumption of reactant A is defined as

$$\text{rate} = -\frac{\Delta[A]}{\Delta t} = -\left(\frac{[A]_2 - [A]_1}{t_2 - t_1}\right) \tag{16-2}$$

The units of rate are $\text{mol} \cdot L^{-1} \cdot s^{-1}$ or $M \cdot s^{-1}$.

16-2   The rate law expresses the rate of a reaction in terms of the concentrations of the reactants.

The reaction rate constant is the proportionality constant between the reaction rate and the concentration terms on which the rate depends.

A reaction rate is said to be first order in the concentration of a species when the rate is proportional to the first power of the concentration of that species.

A first-order rate law is of the form rate = $k[A]$.

A second-order rate law is of the form rate = $k[A]^2$ or rate = $k[A][B]$.

If a reaction rate law is of the form rate = $k[A]^x[B]^y[C]^z$, then the rate law is x order in [A], y order in [B], and z order in [C]. The overall order is $x + y + z$.

Rate laws must be determined experimentally. There is no necessary relationship between the balancing coefficients in a chemical equation and the order of the various species concentrations in the reaction rate law.

The units of the rate constant depend on the order of the reaction (Example 16-5).

16-3 The method of initial rates is used to determine reaction rate laws.

The initial reaction rate is the reaction rate measured over a time interval that is short enough that the reactant concentrations do not change appreciably.

If the initial concentration of a reactant is doubled and the initial rate doubles, then the rate law is first order in the concentration of that reactant.

If the initial concentration of a reactant is doubled and the initial rate increases by a factor of 4, then the rate law is second order in the concentration of that reactant.

16-4 The half-life for a first-order rate law is given by $t_{1/2} = 0.693/k$.

If the rate law is rate $= k[A]$, then the dependence of $[A]$ on time is given by

$$\log[A] = \log [A]_0 - \frac{kt}{2.30} \qquad (16\text{-}7)$$

where $[A]_0$ is the concentration of A at time $t = 0$.

For a first-order reaction a plot of $\log [A]$ versus t is linear (Figure 16-3).

The half-life $t_{1/2}$ is the time required for the concentration of a reactant to decrease by a factor of 2 (Table 16-4 and Figure 16-4).

The half-life for a first-order reaction rate law is independent of the initial concentration of the reactant.

16-5 The half-life of a second-order rate law depends upon the initial concentration.

If a reaction rate is of the form rate $= k[A]^2$, then the dependence of $[A]$ on time is given by

$$\frac{1}{[A]} = \frac{1}{[A]_0} + kt \qquad (16\text{-}11)$$

For a second-order reaction a plot of $1/[A]$ versus t is a straight line (Figure 16-6).

The half-life for a second-order reaction is given by $t_{1/2} = 1/k[A]_0$ where k is the rate constant and $[A]_0$ is the initial concentration (Equation 16-12).

The properties of first-order and second-order reactions are summarized in Table 16-6.

16-6 A rate law cannot be deduced from the reaction stoichiometry.

An elementary process is a chemical reaction that occurs in a single step.

The rate law for an elementary process can be deduced from the stoichiometry of the reaction.

Most chemical reactions are not elementary processes.

A series of elementary processes that add up to give the overall reaction is called a reaction mechanism.

A slow step that controls the overall rate of a reaction is called the rate-determining step.

An intermediate is a species that appears in the reaction mechanism, but does not appear as a reactant or a product in the overall reaction.

16-7 Molecules must collide before they can react.

The collision theory of reaction rates postulates that only the more energetic collisions that occur with the correct relative orientations of the molecules lead to a reaction.

The reaction rate constant is given by

$$k = \begin{pmatrix} \text{fraction of collisions} \\ \text{with the required} \\ \text{relative orientations} \end{pmatrix} \times \begin{pmatrix} \text{collision} \\ \text{frequency} \end{pmatrix} \times \begin{pmatrix} \text{fraction of collisions} \\ \text{with the required} \\ \text{energy} \end{pmatrix}$$

The activation energy, E_a, is the minimum energy necessary to achieve a reaction between the colliding molecules (Figure 16-9).

16-8 The activation energy is an energy barrier that the reactants must surmount in order to react.

The Arrhenius equation

$$\log \left(\frac{k_2}{k_1} \right) = \frac{E_a}{2.30R} \left(\frac{T_2 - T_1}{T_1 T_2} \right) \tag{16-13}$$

describes the dependence of the reaction rate constant on temperature.

Reaction rate constants increase with increasing temperature because the activation energy is positive.

16-9 A catalyst is a substance that increases the reaction rate but is not consumed as a reactant.

A catalyst is a reaction rate facilitator that acts by providing a different and faster mechanism to the products (Figure 16-11).

A catalyst increases the rates of both the forward and reverse reactions.

A catalyst does not affect the equilibrium concentrations of reactants and products.

16-10 Many metal surfaces act as heterogeneous catalysts.

In heterogeneous catalysis the reactants bind to a solid surface and react more rapidly (Figure 16-12).

16-11 At equilibrium the forward reaction rate equals the reverse reaction rate.

The net reaction rate is the difference between the forward and the reverse reaction rates.

The equilibrium constant is equal to the ratio of the forward reaction rate constant to the reverse reaction rate constant, $K = k_f/k_r$ (Equation 16-16).

An equilibrium state is a dynamic state in which the forward and the reverse reactions continue to occur but at equal rates.

B   SELF-TEST

Questions 1 through 6 refer to the reaction

$$2H_2O_2(aq) \rightleftharpoons 2H_2O(l) + O_2(g)$$

1   (a) The rate at which oxygen is produced is defined as
_____.

     (b) The rate at which hydrogen peroxide, H_2O_2, is consumed is defined as
_____.

2   The reaction rate for the decomposition of hydrogen peroxide is always positive. *True/False*

3   The rate of the decomposition of hydrogen peroxide can be determined by measuring the increase in pressure due to oxygen. *True/False*

4   The rate of the decomposition of hydrogen peroxide can be determined by measuring the concentration of H_2O_2 at various times during the reaction. *True/False*

5   The rate for the decomposition of hydrogen peroxide can be expressed by
_____
_____.

6   From the stoichiometry of the decomposition of hydrogen peroxide, the reaction rate law must be rate = $k[H_2O_2]^2$. *True/False*

7   Reaction rates can be expressed in the units $M \cdot min^{-1}$. *True/False*

8   The rate law of a first-order reaction is rate = _____.

9   The units of the rate constant for a first-order reaction are _____.

10   Given that the decomposition of hydrogen peroxide is a first-order reaction in H_2O_2, the rate law is rate = _____.

11   The rate law of a second-order reaction is rate = _____.

12   The units of the rate constant for a second-order reaction are
_____.

13   The reaction $H^+(aq) + OH^-(aq) \longrightarrow H_2O(l)$ is an elementary process. The rate law is rate = _____.

14   The method of initial rates is used to determine _____.

15   If a reaction rate law is first-order in reactant A, then the initial reaction rate _____ when the concentration of A is doubled and the concentrations of all other reactants remain the same.

16　If a reaction rate law is second order in reactant B, then the initial reaction rate _____ when the concentration of B is doubled and the concentrations of all other reactants remain the same.

17　If a reaction rate law is zero-order in reactant C, then the initial reaction rate _____ when the concentration of C is doubled and the concentrations of all other reactants remain the same.

18　If a reaction is first-order, then the dependence of the concentration of A on time is given by $\log[A] =$ _____.

19　The decomposition of H_2O_2 is a first-order reaction in H_2O_2. A plot of _____ versus time is a straight line.

20　If a plot of the concentration of reactant A versus time is a straight line, then the reaction is first-order. *True/False*

21　The half-life of a reactant is defined as _____ _____ _____.

22　The half-life for a first-order reaction is (*independent of/dependent on*) the initial concentration of the reactant.

23　If the rate law is rate $= k[H_2O_2]$, then the time it takes for hydrogen peroxide to decrease from 0.50 M to 0.25 M is the same as to decrease from 0.25 M to 0.125 M. *True/False*

24　If a reaction is second-order, then the dependence of the concentration of A on time is given by $1/[A] =$ _____.

25　If a reaction rate law is second-order in [A], then a plot of _____ versus time will be a straight line.

26　If a plot of the concentration of reactant A versus time is a straight line, then the reaction is second-order. *True/False*

27　The half-life for a second-order reaction is (*independent of/dependent on*) the initial concentration of the reactant.

28　The reaction

$$NO_2(g) + CO(g) \longrightarrow NO(g) + CO_2(g)$$

is second-order. The rate law is rate $= k[NO_2]^2$. The time it takes for $[NO_2]$ to decrease from 0.50 M to 0.25 M is the same as to decrease from 0.25 M to 0.125 M. *True/False*

29　Most reactions are elementary processes. *True/False*

30 A series of elementary processes that add up to give an overall reaction is called the reaction _____.

31 The overall reaction rate may be controlled by a rate-determining step, which is the fastest step in the reaction mechanism. *True/False*

32 The reaction mechanism often involves intermediate species that do not appear in the overall reaction. *True/False*

33 The sum of the elementary processes for a reaction need not add up to the overall chemical equation. *True/False*

34 All collisions between reactant molecules lead to reaction. *True/False*

35 The activation energy is the minimum amount of kinetic energy that reactant molecules must have in order to react. *True/False*

36 Rate constants increase as the temperature increases. *True/False*

37 The temperature dependence of a rate constant is given by the Arrhenius equation, _____ = _____.

38 A catalyst acts by providing a new reaction pathway with a (*lower/higher*) activation energy.

39 A catalyst increases the rate of production of products without affecting the reverse reaction. *True/False*

40 Platinum metal is used as a catalyst for the reaction

$$C_2H_4(g) + H_2(g) \longrightarrow C_2H_6(g)$$

In this reaction, platinum is a heterogeneous catalyst. *True/False*

41 At equilibrium the net reaction rate is zero. *True/False*

42 The rate constants of the forward and reverse reactions, k_f and k_r, are related to the equilibrium constant, K. *True/False*

C   CALCULATIONS YOU SHOULD KNOW HOW TO DO

1 Express the reaction rate in terms of the reactant or product concentrations and calculate the reaction rate from the concentrations of reactants or products. See Examples 16-1 and 16-2 and Problems 16-5 through 16-14.

2 Determine the reaction rate law using the method of initial rates. See Examples 16-6 and 16-7 and Problems 16-15 through 16-26.

3 Determine the rate law and calculate the reaction rate constant and half-life for first-order reactions. See Example 16-3 and Problems 16-27 through 16-40.

4 Determine the rate law and calculate the reaction rate constant or half-life for second-order reactions. See Example 16-4 and Problems 16-41 through 16-46.

5 Determine the rate law from the reaction mechanism. See Examples 16-10 and 16-11 and Problems 16-47 through 16-58.

6 Use the Arrhenius equation to find the rate constant at some other temperature or to find the activation energy given the rate constants at two different temperatures. See Examples 16-12 and 16-13 and Problems 16-61 through 16-68.

7 Calculate the rate constant of the reverse reaction given the rate constant of the forward reaction and the equilibrium constant. See Problems 16-77 through 16-82.

A Review of Logarithms

Recall from Appendix A1 of the text that $100 = 10^2$, $1000 = 10^3$ and so on. Also recall that

$$\sqrt{10} = 10^{1/2} = 10^{0.50} = 3.16$$

By taking the square root of both sides of

$$10^{0.50} = 3.16$$

we find that

$$\sqrt{10^{0.50}} = 10^{(1/2)(0.50)} = 10^{0.25} = \sqrt{3.16} = 1.78$$

Furthermore, because

$$(10^x)(10^y) = 10^{x+y}$$

we can write

$$10^{0.25} \times 10^{0.50} = 10^{0.75} = (3.16)(1.78) = 5.62$$

By continuing this process, we would be able to express any number y as

$$y = 10^x \tag{1}$$

The number x to which 10 must be raised to get y is called the *logarithm* of y and is written as

$$x = \log y \tag{2}$$

Equations (1) and (2) are equivalent.

For example, we have shown above that

$$\log 1.78 = 0.25$$
$$\log 3.16 = 0.50$$
$$\log 5.62 = 0.75$$
$$\log 10.00 = 1.00$$

Logarithms of other numbers may be obtained from tables (Appendix C of the text) or more conveniently with a hand calculator. If you use tables, you must always write the number y in standard scientific notation. Thus, for example, you must write 42500 as 4.25×10^4, or 0.000465 as 4.65×10^{-4}. To take the logarithm of such numbers, we use the fact that

$$\log (ab) = \log a + \log b \tag{3}$$

Thus we write

$$\log 42500 = \log (4.25 \times 10^4) = \log 4.25 + \log 10^4$$
$$= \log 4.25 + 4.000$$

Log tables are set up so that the number a in $\log a$ is between 1 and 10 and the numbers within the tables are between 0 and 1. Thus, for example, from Appendix C we find that

$$\log 5.08 = 0.7059$$
$$\log 8.16 = 0.9117$$

and so on. If we look up $\log 4.25$ in Appendix C, then we find that $\log 4.25 = 0.6284$. Therefore,

$$\log 42500 = 0.6284 + 4.000$$
$$= 4.6284$$

If you use your calculator, you simply enter 42500 and push a LOG key to get 4.6284 directly. To find $\log 0.000465$, we write

$$\log 0.000465 = \log (4.65 \times 10^{-4}) = \log 4.65 + \log 10^{-4}$$
$$= \log 4.65 - 4.000$$

We find $\log 4.65 = 0.6675$ from Appendix C, and so

$$\log 0.000465 = 0.6675 - 4.000$$
$$= -3.3325$$

If you use your calculator, simply enter 0.000465 and push the LOG key to get -3.3325 directly. Although the use of a hand calculator is so much more convenient than a table of logarithms, you should be able to handle logarithms by either method.

Example 1 Evaluate
(a) $\log (6.64 \times 10^{-8})$
(b) $\log 0.00476$

Solution

(a) $\log (6.64 \times 10^{-8}) = \log 6.64 + \log 10^{-8}$
$$= 0.8222 - 8$$
$$= -7.1778$$

(b) $\log 0.00476 = \log (4.76 \times 10^{-3})$
$$= \log 4.76 + \log 10^{-3}$$
$$= 0.6776 - 3$$
$$= -2.3224$$

Both of these results can be obtained directly from your hand calculator by entering the number and pushing the LOG key.

Because logarithms are exponents ($y = 10^x$), logarithms have certain special properties such as

$$\log ab = \log a + \log b \tag{3}$$

$$\log \frac{a}{b} = \log a - \log b \tag{4}$$

$$\log a^n = n \log a \tag{5}$$

$$\log \sqrt[n]{a} = \log a^{1/n} = \frac{1}{n} \log a \tag{6}$$

If we let $a = 1$ in Equation 4, then we have

$$\log \frac{1}{b} = \log 1 - \log b$$

or, because $\log 1 = 0$,

$$\log \frac{1}{b} = -\log b \tag{7}$$

Thus we change the sign of a logarithm by taking the reciprocal of its argument.

Up to this point we have found the value of x in

$$y = 10^x$$

when y is given. It is often necessary to find the value of y when x is given. Because x is called the logarithm of y, y is called the antilogarithm of x. For example, suppose that $x = 6.1303$ and we wish to find y. We write

$$y = 10^{6.1303} = 10^{0.1303} \times 10^6$$

From the log table, we see that the number whose logarithm is 0.1303 is 1.35. Thus we find that

$$10^{6.1303} = 1.35 \times 10^6$$

You can obtain this result directly from your calculator. On a TI calculator, for example, enter 6.1303 and press the INV key (for inverse) and then the LOG key.

To obtain the antilogarithm of y using log tables, you must express y as

$$y = 10^a \times 10^n \tag{8}$$

where n is a positive or negative integer and a is between 0 and 1. The quantity a is found within the log table and the antilog of a is read from the table. As another example, let's find the antilog of 1.9509. We write

$$y = 10^{1.9509} = 10^{0.9509} \times 10^1$$

Find the value of 0.9509 within the log table and see that its antilog is 8.93. Thus we have

$$y = 10^{1.9509} = 8.93 \times 10^1 = 89.3$$

You should be able to obtain this result directly from your calculator. If your calculator has a 10^x key, then you can obtain the antilog of 1.9509 by entering 1.9509 and pressing the 10^x key. This operation is equivalent to using the INV key followed by the LOG key.

Exercises

1 Find the logarithms of the following numbers, using both the table of logarithms and your calculator:

(a) 3.12×10^{-10}
(b) 8.06×10^5
(c) 12.3
(d) 6.63×10^{-12}

(e) 4.23
(f) 0.0000291
(g) 556,000
(h) 1.02×10^{-3}

2 Find the antilogarithms of the following numbers, using both the table of logarithms and your calculator.

(a) 4.316
(b) 0.711

(c) 8.200
(d) 11.580

Answers

1 (a) −9.5058
   (b) 5.9063
   (c) 1.0899
   (d) −11.1785

   (e) 0.6263
   (f) −4.5361
   (g) 5.7451
   (h) −2.9914

2 (a) 2.07×10^4 (c) 1.58×10^8
    (b) 5.14 (d) 3.80×10^{11}

D   SOLUTIONS TO THE ODD-NUMBERED PROBLEMS

16-1   (a) The rate law for a second-order reaction is

$$\text{rate} = k[\text{A}]^2$$

Thus

$$k = \frac{\text{rate}}{[\text{A}]^2}$$

The units of k are

$$\frac{\text{M} \cdot \text{s}^{-1}}{\text{M}^2} = \text{M}^{-1} \cdot \text{s}^{-1}$$

(b) The rate law for a 3/2 order reaction is

$$\text{rate} = k[\text{A}]^{3/2}$$

Thus

$$k = \frac{\text{rate}}{[\text{A}]^{3/2}}$$

The units of k are

$$\frac{\text{M} \cdot \text{s}^{-1}}{\text{M}^{3/2}} = \text{M}^{-1/2} \cdot \text{s}^{-1}$$

16-3   (a) The ion $I_3^-(aq)$ forms a blue starch complex in solution. You could measure the concentration of I_3^- by the intensity of the color of the solution.
      (b) As the reaction proceeds, $H_2O(g)$ is consumed, thus decreasing the pressure of $H_2O(g)$. You could measure the rate of the reaction by measuring the rate of the decrease in the pressure of $H_2O(g)$.

16-5   We have

$$\text{rate} = (3.0 \times 10^6 \, \text{M}^{-1} \cdot \text{s}^{-1}) \, [\text{O}_3][\text{NO}]$$

Thus the initial rate is

$$\text{rate} = (3.0 \times 10^6 \, \text{M}^{-1} \cdot \text{s}^{-1})(2.0 \times 10^{-6} \, \text{M})(2.0 \times 10^{-6} \, \text{M})$$
$$= 1.2 \times 10^{-5} \, \text{M} \cdot \text{s}^{-1}$$

16-7 The rate of production of O_2 is 3/2 as great as the rate of loss of O_3 because three O_2 molecules are produced by the consumption of two O_3 molecules. Thus

$$\frac{\Delta[O_2]}{\Delta t} = -\tfrac{3}{2}\frac{\Delta[O_3]}{\Delta t} = \tfrac{3}{2}(6.3 \times 10^{-3} \text{ atm} \cdot \text{s}^{-1)}$$

$$= 9.5 \times 10^{-3} \text{ atm} \cdot \text{s}^{-1}$$

where we have expressed the concentration of O_2 as pressure.

16-9 The rate of decomposition of N_2O_5 is

$$\text{rate} = -\frac{\Delta[N_2O_5]}{\Delta t} = \frac{-([N_2O_5]_2 - [N_2O_5]_1)}{t_2 - t_1} = \frac{-[N_2O_5]_2 + [N_2O_5]_1}{t_2 - t_1}$$

The rate over the first 175 s is

$$\text{rate} = \frac{-1.32 \text{ M} + 1.48 \text{ M}}{175 \text{ s} - 0 \text{ s}} = 9.1 \times 10^{-4} \text{ M} \cdot \text{s}^{-1}$$

The rate from 845 s to 1202 s is

$$\text{rate} = \frac{-0.69 \text{ M} + 0.87 \text{ M}}{1202 \text{ s} - 845 \text{ s}} = 5.0 \times 10^{-4} \text{ M} \cdot \text{s}^{-1}$$

16-11 The total pressure P_{tot} in the reaction vessel is

$$P_{tot} = P_{CO} + P_{CO_2}$$

The increase in P_{CO_2} is one half of the decrease in P_{CO} because two molecules of CO react to form one molecule of CO_2. We start with only CO so that the pressure of CO_2 is due to the reaction of CO or

$$P_{CO_2} = \tfrac{1}{2}\Delta P_{CO}$$

Thus

$$P_{tot} = P_{CO} + \tfrac{1}{2}\Delta P_{CO}$$

Initially $P_{CO} = 250$ torr; therefore at any time t

$$P_{tot} = P_{CO} + \tfrac{1}{2}(250 \text{ torr} - P_{CO})$$

or

$$P_{tot} = \tfrac{1}{2}P_{CO} + 125 \text{ torr}$$

Thus

$$P_{CO} = 2(P_{tot} - 125 \text{ torr})$$

From the data given and the above equation for P_{CO} we compute

P_{CO}/torr	250	226	198	170
t/s	0	398	1002	1801

The rate of disappearance of CO is

$$\text{rate} = -\frac{\Delta P_{CO}}{\Delta t} = \frac{-P_{CO,2} + P_{CO,1}}{t_2 - t_1}$$

Thus for the three time intervals we have, respectively,

$$\text{rate} = \frac{-226 \text{ torr} + 250 \text{ torr}}{398 \text{ s} - 0 \text{ s}} = 6.0 \times 10^{-2} \text{ torr} \cdot \text{s}^{-1}$$

$$\text{rate} = \frac{-198 \text{ torr} + 226 \text{ torr}}{1002 \text{ s} - 398 \text{ s}} = 4.6 \times 10^{-2} \text{ torr} \cdot \text{s}^{-1}$$

$$\text{rate} = \frac{-170 \text{ torr} + 198 \text{ torr}}{1801 \text{ s} - 1002 \text{ s}} = 3.5 \times 10^{-2} \text{ torr} \cdot \text{s}^{-1}$$

The rate of appearance of CO_2 is

$$\text{rate} = \frac{\Delta P_{CO_2}}{\Delta t} = -\frac{1}{2} \frac{\Delta P_{CO}}{\Delta t}$$

We can use the results calculated above; thus for the three time intervals we have, respectively

$$\frac{\Delta P_{CO_2}}{\Delta t} = 3.0 \times 10^{-2} \text{ torr} \cdot \text{s}^{-1}$$

$$\frac{\Delta P_{CO_2}}{\Delta t} = 2.3 \times 10^{-2} \text{ torr} \cdot \text{s}^{-1}$$

$$\frac{\Delta P_{CO_2}}{\Delta t} = 1.8 \times 10^{-2} \text{ torr} \cdot \text{s}^{-1}$$

16-13 The data indicate that the rate is directly proportional to $[SO_2Cl_2]$. The rate doubles as $[SO_2Cl_2]$ is doubled. The order of the reaction is first-order. The first-order reaction rate law is

$$\text{rate} = k[SO_2Cl_2]$$

or

$$k = \frac{\text{rate}}{[SO_2Cl_2]}$$

To verify the prediction that the rate is first-order, let us show that the ratio of the rate to $[SO_2Cl_2]$ has a constant value.

$$\frac{\text{rate}}{[SO_2Cl_2]} = \frac{2.2 \times 10^{-6} \text{ M} \cdot \text{s}^{-1}}{0.10 \text{ M}} = 2.2 \times 10^{-5} \text{ s}^{-1}$$

$$= \frac{4.4 \times 10^{-6} \text{ M} \cdot \text{s}^{-1}}{0.20 \text{ M}} = 2.2 \times 10^{-5} \text{ s}^{-1}$$

$$= \frac{6.6 \times 10^{-6} \text{ M} \cdot \text{s}^{-1}}{0.30 \text{ M}} = 2.2 \times 10^{-5} \text{ s}^{-1}$$

$$= \frac{8.8 \times 10^{-6} \text{ M} \cdot \text{s}^{-1}}{0.40 \text{ M}} = 2.2 \times 10^{-5} \text{ s}^{-1}$$

16-15 The rate law is

$$\text{rate} = k[C_2H_5Cl]^x$$

When $[C_2H_5Cl]_0$ is doubled, the initial rate doubles. Thus the rate is first-order in $[C_2H_5Cl]$. The rate law is

$$\text{rate} = k[C_2H_5Cl]$$

The value of the rate constant is given by

$$k = \frac{\text{rate}}{[C_2H_5Cl]}$$

We can calculate k using the data from any of the runs

$$k = \frac{2.40 \times 10^{-30} \text{ M} \cdot \text{s}^{-1}}{0.33 \text{ M}} = 7.3 \times 10^{-30} \text{ s}^{-1}$$

$$k = \frac{4.80 \times 10^{-30} \text{ M} \cdot \text{s}^{-1}}{0.66 \text{ M}} = 7.3 \times 10^{-30} \text{ s}^{-1}$$

$$k = \frac{9.60 \times 10^{-30} \text{ M} \cdot \text{s}^{-1}}{1.32 \text{ M}} = 7.3 \times 10^{-30} \text{ s}^{-1}$$

16-17 The rate law is

$$\text{rate} = k[NOCl]^x$$

When $[NOCl]_0$ is doubled, the initial rate quadruples, and when $[NOCl]_0$ is tripled, the initial rate increases by a factor of 9. Thus the rate law is second-order in $[NOCl]$:

$$\text{rate} = k[NOCl]^2$$

The value of the rate constant is given by

$$k = \frac{\text{rate}}{[\text{NOCl}]^2}$$

We can calculate k using the data for any one of the three runs

$$k = \frac{1.75 \times 10^{-6}\ \text{M} \cdot \text{s}^{-1}}{(0.25\ \text{M})^2} = 2.8 \times 10^{-5}\ \text{M}^{-1} \cdot \text{s}^{-1}$$

$$k = \frac{7.00 \times 10^{-6}\ \text{M} \cdot \text{s}^{-1}}{(0.50\ \text{M})^2} = 2.8 \times 10^{-5}\ \text{M}^{-1} \cdot \text{s}^{-1}$$

$$k = \frac{1.57 \times 10^{-5}\ \text{M} \cdot \text{s}^{-1}}{(0.75\ \text{M})^2} = 2.8 \times 10^{-5}\ \text{M}^{-1} \cdot \text{s}^{-1}$$

16-19 When $[\text{Cr}(\text{H}_2\text{O})_6^{3+}]_0$ is increased by a factor of 10 and $[\text{SCN}^-]_0$ remains constant, the initial rate increases by a factor of 10. Thus the rate is first-order in $[\text{Cr}(\text{H}_2\text{O})_6^{3+}]$. When $[\text{SCN}^-]$ is increased by a factor of $0.5/0.2 = 2.5$ and $[\text{Cr}(\text{H}_2\text{O})_6^{3+}]_0$ remains the same, the initial rate increases by a factor of 2.5 $(1.5 \times 10^{-9}/6.0 \times 10^{-10})$. Thus the rate is first-order in $[\text{SCN}^-]$. The rate law is

$$\text{rate} = k[\text{Cr}(\text{H}_2\text{O})_6^{3+}][\text{SCN}^-]$$

We can calculate the rate constant using the data from any of the runs. The value of the rate constant is given by

$$k = \frac{\text{rate}}{[\text{Cr}(\text{H}_2\text{O})_6^{3+}][\text{SCN}^-]}$$

$$k = \frac{2.0 \times 10^{-11}\ \text{M} \cdot \text{s}^{-1}}{(1.0 \times 10^{-4}\ \text{M})(0.10\ \text{M})} = 2.0 \times 10^{-6}\ \text{M}^{-1} \cdot \text{s}^{-1}$$

$$k = \frac{2.0 \times 10^{-10}\ \text{M} \cdot \text{s}^{-1}}{(1.0 \times 10^{-3}\ \text{M})(0.10\ \text{M})} = 2.0 \times 10^{-6}\ \text{M}^{-1} \cdot \text{s}^{-1}$$

$$k = \frac{6.0 \times 10^{-10}\ \text{M} \cdot \text{s}^{-1}}{(1.5 \times 10^{-3}\ \text{M})(0.20\ \text{M})} = 2.0 \times 10^{-6}\ \text{M}^{-1} \cdot \text{s}^{-1}$$

$$k = \frac{1.5 \times 10^{-9}\ \text{M} \cdot \text{s}^{-1}}{(1.5 \times 10^{-3}\ \text{M})(0.50\ \text{M})} = 2.0 \times 10^{-6}\ \text{M}^{-1} \cdot \text{s}^{-1}$$

16-21 When $[\text{ClO}_3^-]_0$ is doubled and $[\text{I}^-]_0$ and $[\text{H}^+]_0$ remain the same, the initial rate doubles. Thus the rate is first-order in $[\text{ClO}_3^-]$ or

$$\text{rate} = k[\text{ClO}_3^-][\text{I}^-]^x[\text{H}^+]^y$$

When $[\text{I}^-]_0$ is doubled and $[\text{ClO}_3^-]_0$ and $[\text{H}^+]_0$ remain the same, the initial rate doubles. Thus the rate is first-order in $[\text{I}^-]$ or

$$\text{rate} = k[\text{ClO}_3^-][\text{I}^-][\text{H}^+]^y$$

When $[H^+]_0$ is doubled and $[ClO_3^-]_0$ and $[I^-]$ remain the same, the initial rate quadruples. Thus the rate is second-order in $[H^+]$ or

$$\text{rate} = k[ClO_3^-][I^-][H^+]^2$$

16-23 (a) The initial rate is

$$\text{rate} = (2.99 \times 10^6 \ M^{-1} \cdot s^{-1})(2.0 \times 10^{-6} \ M)(6.0 \times 10^{-5} \ M)$$
$$= 3.6 \times 10^{-4} \ M \cdot s^{-1}$$

(b) The rate of production of NO_2 is

$$\text{rate} = \frac{\Delta[NO_2]}{\Delta t} = 3.6 \times 10^{-4} \ M \cdot s^{-1}$$

The amount of NO_2 produced in one hour is

$$[NO_2] = \text{rate} \times \text{time}$$
$$= (3.6 \times 10^{-4} \ M \cdot s^{-1})\left(\frac{60 \ \text{min}}{1 \ \text{h}}\right)\left(\frac{60 \ \text{s}}{1 \ \text{min}}\right)$$
$$= 1.3 \text{ moles per liter per hour}$$

16-25 When $[NO_2]_0$ is doubled and $[O_3]_0$ remains the same, the initial rate doubles. Thus the rate law is first-order in $[NO_2]$. When $[O_3]_0$ is doubled and $[NO_2]_0$ remains the same, the initial rate doubles. Thus the rate law is first-order in $[O_3]$. The complete rate law is

$$\text{rate} = k[NO_2][O_3]$$

The value of the rate constant is given by

$$k = \frac{\text{rate}}{[NO_2][O_3]}$$
$$= \frac{5.0 \times 10^4 \ M \cdot s^{-1}}{(1.00 \ M)(1.00 \ M)} = 5.0 \times 10^4 \ M^{-1} \cdot s^{-1}$$
$$= \frac{1.0 \times 10^5 \ M \cdot s^{-1}}{(2.00 \ M)(1.00 \ M)} = 5.0 \times 10^4 \ M^{-1} \cdot s^{-1}$$
$$= \frac{2.0 \times 10^5 \ M \cdot s^{-1}}{(2.00 \ M)(2.00 \ M)} = 5.0 \times 10^4 \ M^{-1} \cdot s^{-1}$$

16-27 For a first-order reaction

$$\log \frac{[A]}{[A]_0} = -\frac{kt}{2.30}$$

The value of $[A]/[A]_0$ is $\frac{1}{10}$ and $k = 10 \text{ s}^{-1}$; thus we have

$$\log 0.10 = -\frac{(10 \text{ s}^{-1})t}{2.30}$$

$$-1.00 = -4.35 \text{ s}^{-1}t$$

Solving for t, we have

$$t = \frac{1.00}{4.35 \text{ s}^{-1}} = 0.23 \text{ s}$$

16-29   The half-life of the reaction is

$$t_{1/2} = \frac{0.693}{k}$$

$$= \frac{0.693}{2.2 \times 10^{-5} \text{ s}^{-1}} = 3.15 \times 10^4 \text{ s}$$

The number of half-lives in 5.0 hours is

$$\frac{(5.0 \text{ h})\left(\dfrac{60 \text{ min}}{1 \text{ h}}\right)\left(\dfrac{60 \text{ s}}{1 \text{ min}}\right)}{3.15 \times 10^4 \text{ s/half-life}} = 0.571 \text{ half-lives}$$

The fraction of SO_2Cl_2 remaining after 0.571 half-lives is given by

$$\frac{[A]}{[A]_0} = \left(\frac{1}{2}\right)^n$$

Thus

$$\text{fraction remaining} = \frac{[SO_2Cl_2]}{[SO_2Cl_2]_0} = \left(\frac{1}{2}\right)^{0.571}$$

$$= 0.67$$

An alternative solution is to use the equation

$$\log \frac{[A]}{[A]_0} = -\frac{kt}{2.30}$$

where $[A]/[A]_0$ is the fraction of SO_2Cl_2 remaining. Thus

$$\log \frac{[A]}{[A]_0} = -\frac{(2.2 \times 10^{-5} \text{ s}^{-1})\left(\dfrac{60 \text{ s}}{1 \text{ min}}\right)\left(\dfrac{60 \text{ min}}{1 \text{ h}}\right)(5.0 \text{ h})}{2.30}$$

$$= -0.1722$$

Taking antilogarithms, we have

$$\text{fraction remaining} = \frac{[A]}{[A]_0} = 0.67$$

16-31 We see from the data that the number of bacteria doubles every 15 min. The doubling time is independent of the number of bacteria; thus the rate law is first order (see also the plot of log (number of bacteria) versus t)

$$\text{rate of production} = k(\text{number of bacteria})$$

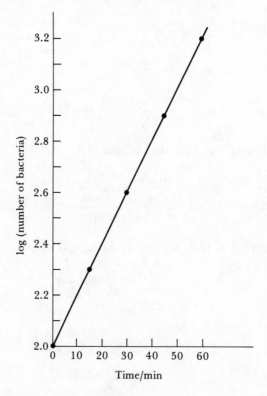

The half-life is equal to 15 min. There are

$$\frac{120 \text{ min}}{15 \text{ min/half-life}} = 8.0 \text{ half-lives}$$

in 2 hours. The number of bacteria after n half-lives is given by

$$\text{number of bacteria} = (\text{initial number of bacteria})(2)^n$$

or after 8 half-lives

$$\text{number of bacteria} = (100)(2)^8 = 2.56 \times 10^4 \text{ bacteria}$$

The rate constant is

$$k = \frac{0.693}{t_{1/2}} = \frac{0.693}{15 \text{ min}} = 4.6 \times 10^{-2} \text{ min}^{-1}$$

16-33   The fraction of a reactant remaining after time, t, is given by

$$\log \frac{[A]}{[A]_0} = -\frac{kt}{2.30}$$

Substituting the values of k and t, we have

$$\log \frac{[A]}{[A]_0} = -\frac{(4.0 \times 10^{-4} \text{ s}^{-1})(1 \text{ ms})\left(\dfrac{1 \text{ s}}{10^3 \text{ ms}}\right)}{2.30}$$

$$= -1.74 \times 10^{-7}$$

Taking antilogarithms, we have

$$\text{fraction remaining} = \frac{[A]}{[A]_0} = 1.00$$

16-35   The time for 99.9% of the reaction to take place is given by

$$\log \frac{[A]}{[A]_0} = -\frac{kt_1}{2.30}$$

where

$$\frac{[A]}{[A]_0} = 1 - 0.999 = 0.001$$

Thus we have

$$\log 0.001 = -\frac{kt_1}{2.30}$$

or

$$\frac{kt_1}{2.30} = 3.00$$

The time for 50% of the reaction to take place is given by

$$\log \frac{[A]}{[A]_0} = -\frac{kt_2}{2.30}$$

where

$$\frac{[A]}{[A]_0} = 1 - 0.50 = 0.50$$

Thus we have

$$\log 0.50 = -\frac{kt_2}{2.30}$$

or

$$\frac{kt_2}{2.30} = 0.301$$

Thus the ratio of t_1 to t_2 is given by

$$\frac{kt_1/2.30}{kt_2/2.30} = \frac{t_1}{t_2} = \frac{3.00}{0.301} = 10$$

16-37 If the reaction rate is first-order, then a plot of $\log [S_2O_8^{2-}]$ versus time is a straight line.

t/min	$\log [S_2O_8^{2-}]$
0	-1.00
17	-1.30
34	-1.60
51	-1.92

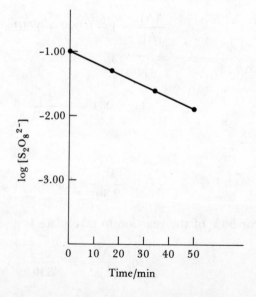

The reaction is first-order:

$$\text{rate} = k[S_2O_8^{2-}]$$

The equation for the straight line is

$$\log [A] = \log [A]_0 - \frac{kt}{2.30}$$

We can use the data at any of the time points to calculate k. At time $t = 17$ min, we have

$$-1.30 = -1.00 - \frac{k(17 \text{ min})}{2.30}$$

$$k = \frac{(0.30)(2.30)}{17 \text{ min}} = 0.041 \text{ min}^{-1}$$

Another approach is to realize that if the reaction is first-order, then the half-life, $t_{1/2}$, is independent of the initial concentration of the reactant.

$[S_2O_8^{2-}]$/M	t/min	$t_{1/2}$/min
0.100	0	
		17
0.050	17	
		17
0.025	34	
		17
0.012	51	

The $[S_2O_8^{2-}]$ is reduced by a factor of 2 every 17 minutes, so the half-life is 17 minutes. Thus the rate law is

$$\text{rate} = k[S_2O_8^{2-}]$$

We also can calculate k from the expression

$$t_{1/2} = \frac{0.693}{k}$$

$$k = \frac{0.693}{t_{1/2}} = \frac{0.693}{17 \text{ min}} = 0.041 \text{ min}^{-1}$$

16-39   The fraction of a reactant remaining after time t is given by

$$\log \frac{[A]}{[A]_0} = -\frac{kt}{2.30}$$

The fraction of material retained is $0.10 = 1 - 0.90$. The value of the rate constant is given by

$$k = \frac{0.693}{t_{1/2}} = \frac{0.693}{70d} = 0.0099d^{-1}$$

Thus

$$\log(0.10) = -\frac{(0.0099 d^{-1})t}{2.30}$$

$$t = \frac{(-1.00)(2.30)}{-0.0099 d^{-1}} = 230 d$$

16-41 The concentration of a reactant in a second-order reaction at a time t is given by

$$\frac{1}{[A]} = \frac{1}{[A]_0} + kt$$

Thus

$$\frac{1}{[NOBr]} = \frac{1}{0.052 \text{ M}} + (0.80 \text{ M}^{-1} \cdot \text{s}^{-1})(1 \text{ min})\left(\frac{60 \text{ s}}{1 \text{ min}}\right)$$

$$= 19 \text{ M}^{-1} + 48 \text{ M}^{-1} = 67 \text{ M}^{-1}$$

$$[NOBr] = \frac{1}{67 \text{ M}^{-1}} = 0.015 \text{ M}$$

16-43 The value of the half-life of a second-order reaction is given by

$$t_{1/2} = \frac{1}{k[A]_0}$$

Thus the rate constant is equal to

$$k = \frac{1}{t^{1/2}[N_2O]_0}$$

The half-life of the reaction is 4500 s when $[N_2O]_0$ is 2.0×10^{-2} M; therefore

$$k = \frac{1}{(4500 \text{ s})(2.0 \times 10^{-2} \text{ M})}$$

$$= 1.1 \times 10^{-2} \text{ M}^{-1} \cdot \text{s}^{-1}$$

16-45 (a) The rate law is first-order.
     (b) The rate law is zero-order.

(c) $$\frac{\text{rate 2}}{\text{rate 1}} = \frac{k[A]_2^x}{k[A]_1^x} = \left(\frac{[A]_2}{[A]_1}\right)^x = 1.41$$

Because $[A]_2 = 2[A]_1$, we have

$$1.41 = \left(\frac{2[A]_1}{[A]_1}\right)^x = 2^x$$

We solve for x by taking logarithms of both sides

$$\log 1.41 = \log 2^x = x \log 2$$

or

$$0.15 = 0.30x$$

Thus

$$x = 0.50$$

The order of the reaction rate law is $\frac{1}{2}$ order in [A].

16-47 (a) rate $= k[N_2O][O]$
       (b) rate $= k[O][O_3]$
       (c) rate $= k[ClCO][Cl_2]$

16-49 The overall reaction is given by the sum of the two equations, or

$$O_3(g) + O_3(g) + O(g) \longrightarrow O_2(g) + O(g) + 2O_2(g)$$

After combining and canceling like terms, we have

$$2O_3(g) \rightleftharpoons 3O_2(g)$$

16-51 The rate law is determined by the slow elementary step. The rate law for the slow step is

$$\text{rate} = k[CO_2][OH^-]$$

The experimental rate law is

$$\text{rate} = k[CO_2][OH^-]$$

Thus the mechanism is consistent with the rate equation, because the mechanism leads to the same rate law as is found experimentally.

16-53 To obtain the overall reaction, we add the three equations to obtain

$$2N_2O_5(g) + NO_2(g) + NO_3(g) + NO(g) + NO_3(g) \rightleftharpoons$$
$$2NO_2(g) + 2NO_3(g) + NO(g) + O_2(g) + NO_2(g) + 2NO_2(g)$$

or, after combining and canceling like terms,

$$2N_2O_5(g) \rightleftharpoons 4NO_2(g) + O_2(g)$$

The rate law is given by the slow elementary step

$$\text{rate} = k[NO_2][NO_3]$$

Both species, NO and NO_3, are intermediate species. The first reaction is fast and equilibrium is attained essentially instantaneously; thus we have

$$K = \frac{[NO_2]^2[NO_3]^2}{[N_2O_5]^2}$$

or

$$[NO_2][NO_3] = K^{1/2}[N_2O_5]$$

Thus the rate law is

$$\text{rate} = kK^{1/2}[N_2O_5]$$

If we let $k_1 = kK^{1/2}$, then we have

$$\text{rate} = k_1[N_2O_5]$$

16-55 The rate law for the elementary slow step is

$$\text{rate} = k[ClCO][Cl_2]$$

The species $ClCO(g)$ is an intermediate and its concentration is not easily measured. Because the reaction in step 2 is fast, the equilibrium adjusts instantaneously:

$$K_2 = \frac{[ClO]}{[Cl][CO]}$$

The species Cl is also an intermediate. We can eliminate [Cl] using the fast equilibrium in step 1:

$$K_1 = \frac{[Cl]^2}{[Cl_2]}$$

$$[Cl] = K_1^{1/2}[Cl_2]^{1/2}$$

Substituting the expression for [Cl] into the K_2 expression, we have

$$K_2 = \frac{[ClO]}{K_1^{1/2}[Cl_2]^{1/2}[CO]}$$

Thus

$$[ClO] = K_2K_1^{1/2}[Cl_2]^{1/2}[CO]$$

Substituting the expression for [ClO] into the rate law, we have

$$\text{rate} = kK_2K_1^{1/2}[Cl_2]^{1/2}[CO][Cl_2]$$

If we let $k_3 = kK_2K_1^{1/2}$, then we have

$$\text{rate} = k_3[Cl_2]^{3/2}[CO]$$

16-57 The rate law of the slow elementary step is

$$\text{rate} = k[NO_3][NO]$$

The species NO_3 is an intermediate. We can eliminate $[NO_3]$ from the rate law using the equilibrium expression in step 1. Because the equilibrium reaction is fast, we have

$$K = \frac{[NO_3]}{[NO][O_2]}$$

or

$$[NO_3] = K[NO][O_2]$$

Substituting the expression for $[NO_3]$ into the rate law, we have

$$\text{rate} = kK[NO][O_2][NO]$$

If we let $k' = kK$, then we have

$$\text{rate} = k'[NO]^2[O_2]$$

16-59 The formation of a covalent bond from two radicals does not involve any bond breaking process. For example, for two $CH_3 \cdot$ radicals,

$$2H_3C \cdot \longrightarrow H_3C\text{---}CH_3$$

Thus $E_a \simeq 0$. The only limitation to a reaction would be the orientations of the two radicals as they collide.

16-61 The Arrhenius equation is

$$\log\left(\frac{k_2}{k_1}\right) = \frac{E_a}{2.30R}\left(\frac{T_2 - T_1}{T_1 T_2}\right)$$

Thus

$$\log\left(\frac{9.15 \times 10^{-4}\,s^{-1}}{2.35 \times 10^{-4}\,s^{-1}}\right) = \frac{E_a}{(2.30)(8.31\,J \cdot K^{-1} \cdot mol^{-1})}\frac{(303\,K - 293\,K)}{(303\,K)(293\,K)}$$

$$0.590 = E_a(5.89 \times 10^{-6}\,J^{-1} \cdot mol)$$

$$E_a = \frac{0.590}{5.89 \times 10^{-6}\,J^{-1} \cdot mol} = 1.00 \times 10^5\,J \cdot mol^{-1}$$

$$= 100\,kJ \cdot mol^{-1}$$

16-63 The Arrhenius equation is

$$\log\left(\frac{k_2}{k_1}\right) = \frac{E_a}{2.30R}\left(\frac{T_2 - T_1}{T_1 T_2}\right)$$

Thus

$$\log\left(\frac{k_2}{6.07 \times 10^{-8}\ \text{s}^{-1}}\right) = \frac{(262 \times 10^3\ \text{J}\cdot\text{mol}^{-1})}{(2.30)(8.31\ \text{J}\cdot\text{K}^{-1}\cdot\text{mol}^{-1})}\frac{(800\ \text{K} - 600\ \text{K})}{(600\ \text{K})(800\ \text{K})}$$
$$= 5.712$$

Taking the antilogarithm of both sides, we have

$$\frac{k_2}{6.07 \times 10^{-8}\ \text{s}^{-1}} = 5.15 \times 10^5$$
$$k_2 = (5.15 \times 10^5)(6.07 \times 10^{-8}\ \text{s}^{-1})$$
$$= 3.13 \times 10^{-2}\ \text{s}^{-1}$$

16-65 The Arrhenius equation is

$$\log\left(\frac{k_2}{k_1}\right) = \frac{E_a}{2.30R}\left(\frac{T_2 - T_1}{T_1 T_2}\right)$$

The half-life, $t_{1/2}$, is related to the rate constant of a first-order process by

$$t_{1/2} = \frac{0.693}{k}$$

Thus the Arrhenius equation in terms of $t_{1/2}$ is

$$\log\left(\frac{t_{1/2,1}}{t_{1/2,2}}\right) = \frac{E_a}{2.30R}\left(\frac{T_2 - T_1}{T_1 T_2}\right)$$

Thus

$$\log\left(\frac{4.5\ \text{h}}{t_{1/2,2}}\right) = \frac{(586 \times 10^3\ \text{J}\cdot\text{mol}^{-1})(310.2\ \text{K} - 302.8\ \text{K})}{(2.30)(8.31\ \text{J}\cdot\text{K}^{-1}\cdot\text{mol}^{-1})(310.2\ \text{K})(302.8\ \text{K})}$$
$$= 2.416$$

Taking the antilogarithm of both sides, we have

$$\frac{4.5\ \text{h}}{t_{1/2,2}} = 260$$

$$t_{1/2} = \frac{4.5\ \text{h}}{260} = 0.017\ \text{h at 37°C}$$

16-67   We first must calculate $\log k$ and $1/T$.

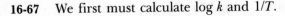

$\dfrac{1}{T}/10^{-3}$ K^{-1}	$\log k$
1.67	-0.155
1.60	0.262
1.54	0.649
1.43	1.34

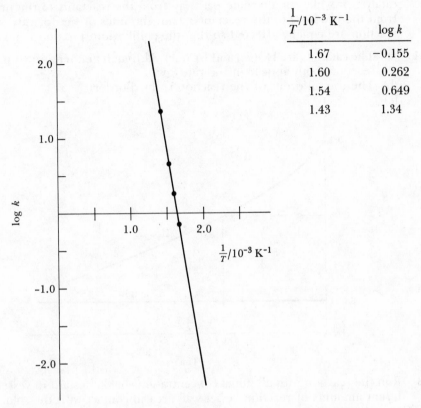

The plot of $\log k$ versus $1/T$ is a straight line. To estimate k at 500 K, we read the value of $\log k$ at $1/500$ K $= 2.0 \times 10^{-3}$ K^{-1} from the plot. We see that

$$\log k = -2.3$$
$$k = 10^{-2.3} = 5 \times 10^{-3} \text{ M}^{-1} \cdot \text{s}^{-1}$$

We can calculate E_a using the Arrhenius equation and any pair of data.

$$\log\left(\frac{k_2}{k_1}\right) = \frac{E_a}{2.30R}\left(\frac{T_2 - T_1}{T_1 T_2}\right)$$

$$\log\left(\frac{4.46 \text{ M}^{-1}\cdot\text{s}^{-1}}{1.83 \text{ M}^{-1}\cdot\text{s}^{-1}}\right) = \frac{E_a(650 \text{ K} - 625 \text{ K})}{(2.30)(8.31 \text{ J}\cdot\text{K}^{-1}\cdot\text{mol}^{-1})(650 \text{ K})(625 \text{ K})}$$

$$0.387 = (3.22 \times 10^{-6} \text{ J}^{-1}\cdot\text{mol})E_a$$

$$E_a = \frac{0.387}{3.22 \times 10^{-6} \text{ J}^{-1}\cdot\text{mol}} = 1.20 \times 10^{5} \text{ J}\cdot\text{mol}^{-1}$$

$$= 120 \text{ kJ}\cdot\text{mol}^{-1}$$

16-69 A catalyst cannot affect the position of equilibrium in a chemical reaction. A catalyst provides an alternate pathway from the reactants to the products and from the products to the reactants. Thus the rates of the forward and reverse reaction are equally affected so that the equilibrium position is unaffected.

16-71 (a) The catalysts are $H^+(aq)$ and $Br^-(aq)$. Although neither appear in the overall reaction, both appear in the rate law.
   (b) The overall order of the reaction is third-order.
   (c)

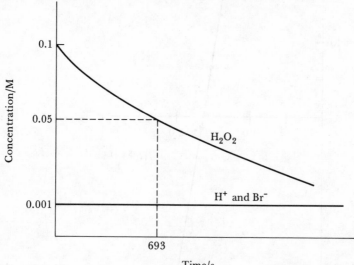

16-73 Run the reaction with all initial concentrations held constant in vessels with different amounts of reaction vessel wall area in contact with the solution. If the reaction rate increases as the wall surface in contact with the reaction mixture increases, then the reaction is catalyzed by the wall.

16-75 The mechanism outlined in Figure 16-12 can be written as

$$O_2(g) \longrightarrow O_2(surface) \qquad \text{fast}$$
$$O_2(surface) \longrightarrow 2O(surface) \qquad \text{slow}$$
$$SO_2(g) + O(surface) \longrightarrow SO_3(g) \qquad \text{fast}$$

Except at very low pressure, the platinum surface will be completely covered with oxygen molecules. Thus, the value of $[O_2(surface)]$ will be essentially constant and the rate-determining step will be independent on the pressure of $O_2(g)$. Furthermore, the oxygen atoms react rapidly with SO_2 molecules except when the number of SO_2 molecules present is very small (when the pressure of SO_2 is very low).

16-77 The equilibrium constant is related to the rate constants by

$$K = \frac{k_f}{k_r}$$

Thus

$$k_r = \frac{k_f}{K}$$

$$= \frac{6.7 \times 10^{-7} \text{ s}^{-1}}{0.14 \text{ M}} = 4.8 \times 10^{-6} \text{ M}^{-1} \cdot \text{s}^{-1}$$

16-79 At equilibrium, the rate of the reaction in the forward direction is equal to the rate in the reverse direction:

$$\text{rate}_f = \text{rate}_r$$

Thus

$$\text{rate}_f = k_f[\text{HI}]^2$$

The rate constant of the forward reaction is related to the rate constant of the reverse reaction through the equilibrium constant:

$$K = \frac{k_f}{k_r}$$

or

$$k_f = Kk_r$$

The equilibrium constant expression for the reaction is

$$K = \frac{[\text{H}_2][\text{I}_2]}{[\text{HI}]^2}$$

Thus

$$k_f = k_r \frac{[\text{H}_2][\text{I}_2]}{[\text{HI}]^2}$$

and

$$\text{rate}_r = \frac{k_r[\text{H}_2][\text{I}_2]}{[\text{HI}]^2}[\text{HI}]^2$$

$$= k_r[\text{H}_2][\text{I}_2]$$

16-81 At equilibrium

$$\text{rate}_f = \text{rate}_r$$

Thus

$$\text{rate}_r = k_f[\text{HCrO}_4^-][\text{HSO}_3^-]^2[\text{H}^+]$$

We also have

$$K = \frac{k_f}{k_r}$$

or

$$k_f = k_r K$$

The equilibrium constant expression for the reaction is

$$K = \frac{[\text{Cr}^{3+}]^2[\text{SO}_4^{2-}]^3}{[\text{HCrO}_4^-]^2[\text{HSO}_3^-]^3[\text{H}^+]^5}$$

Thus

$$\text{rate}_r = \frac{k_r[\text{Cr}^{3+}]^2[\text{SO}_4^{2-}]^3}{[\text{HCrO}_4^-]^2[\text{HSO}_3^-]^3[\text{H}^+]^5}[\text{HCrO}_4^-][\text{HSO}_3^-]^2[\text{H}^+]$$

$$= \frac{k_r[\text{Cr}^{3+}]^2[\text{SO}_4^{2-}]^3}{[\text{HCrO}_4^-][\text{HSO}_3^-][\text{H}^+]^4}$$

E   ANSWERS TO THE EVEN-NUMBERED PROBLEMS

16-2 (a) $\text{M} \cdot \text{s}^{-1}$ (b) $\text{M}^{-2} \cdot \text{s}^{-1}$

16-4 (a) pressure increase (b) color intensity due to Br_2

16-6 $5 \cdot 7 \, \text{M} \cdot \text{s}^{-1}$

16-8 $1.2 \, \text{torr} \cdot \text{s}^{-1}$

16-10 $7.1 \times 10^{-3} \, \text{M} \cdot \text{min}^{-1}$; $4.0 \times 10^{-3} \, \text{M} \cdot \text{min}^{-1}$; $2.8 \times 10^{-3} \, \text{M} \cdot \text{min}^{-1}$

$$-\frac{\Delta[\text{CH}_3\text{OH}]}{\Delta t} = -\frac{\Delta[\text{H}^+]}{\Delta t} = +\frac{\Delta[\text{CH}_3\text{Cl}]}{\Delta t}$$

16-12 $1.6 \times 10^{-2} \, \text{torr} \cdot \text{s}^{-1}$ and $1.4 \times 10^{-2} \, \text{torr} \cdot \text{s}^{-1}$, respectively

16-14 second-order in [NOBr]

16-16 rate $= (1.44 \times 10^{-4} \, \text{torr}^{-1} \cdot \text{s}^{-1})P_{\text{C}_5\text{H}_6}^2$

16-18 rate $= (6.0 \, \text{s}^{-1})P_{\text{N}_2\text{O}_3}$

16-20   rate = $(1.5 \ \text{M}^{-1} \cdot \text{s}^{-1})[\text{CoBr(NH}_3)_5^{2+}][\text{OH}^-]$, second-order overall

16-22   rate = $k[\text{BrO}_3^-][\text{I}^-]$

16-24   (1) $2.0 \times 10^{-4} \ \text{M} \cdot \text{s}^{-1}$ (2) $[\text{I}^-]_0 = 0.40 \ \text{M}$ (3) $[\text{C}_2\text{H}_4\text{Br}_2]_0 = 0.80 \ \text{M}$

16-26   rate = $(4.0 \times 10^{-3} \ \text{M}^{-1} \cdot \text{s}^{-1})[\text{CH}_3\text{COCH}_3][\text{H}^+]$

16-28   0.011 s

16-30 $t_{1/2} = 1.3 \times 10^3$ s; [cyclopropane] = 1.9×10^{-5} M at $t = 2.0$ h

16-32 1.4×10^6 bacteria/mL

16-34   1.00

16-36   Use the equation $\log \dfrac{[\text{A}]}{[\text{A}]_0} = -\dfrac{kt}{2.30}$.

16-38   rate = $kP_{\text{H}_2\text{C}_2\text{O}_4}$; $k = 2.8 \times 10^{-5} \ \text{s}^{-1}$

16-40   rate = 2×10^5 neurons $\cdot$ day^{-1}; 170 years

16-42 $[\text{NO}_2] = 0.015$ M

16-44 $t_{1/2} = 7.7 \times 10^{-9}$ s

16-46   (a) second-order   (b) second-order   (c) first-order

16-48   (a) rate = $k[\text{K}][\text{HCl}]$ (b) rate = $k[\text{Cl}][\text{ICl}]$ (c) rate = $k[\text{NO}_3][\text{CO}]$

16-50 $2\text{NO}_2(g) \longrightarrow 2\text{NO}(g) + \text{O}_2(g)$

16-52   mechanism (1)

16-54 $\text{H}_2\text{O}_2(aq) + 2\text{H}^+(aq) + 2\text{I}^-(aq) \longrightarrow \text{I}_2(aq) + 2\text{H}_2\text{O}(l)$; rate = $k[\text{H}_2\text{O}_2][\text{I}^-]$

16-62   149 kJ $\cdot$ mol^{-1}

16-64 $4.9 \times 10^{-3} \ \text{s}^{-1}$

16-66   41 beats $\cdot$ min^{-1}

16-68   The plot is a straight line; $E_a = 105$ kJ $\cdot$ mol^{-1}; $k = 6 \times 10^4 \ \text{s}^{-1}$ at 50°C.

16-70   A catalyst lowers the activation energy, thereby speeding up the reaction rates in both directions.

16-72   rate = $k[\text{H}_2\text{O}_2][\text{I}^-][\text{H}^+]^2$; the catalysts are $\text{H}^+(aq)$ and $\text{I}^-(aq)$.

16-74   Run the reaction under the same conditions except in the light and in the dark.

16-76   If the number of surface sites for adsorption of NH_3 is small compared to the number of $\text{NH}_3(g)$ molecules, then all surface sites will be occupied for a wide range of P_{NH_3} or $[\text{NH}_3]$ values. Thus the reaction rate will be independent of P_{NH_3} or $[\text{NH}_3]$.

16-78 $k_r = 1.0 \times 10^{-4} \ \text{s}^{-1}$

16-80 $k_r[\text{NO}_2^-]$

16-82   rate$_r = k_r[\text{NO}_3^-][\text{HNO}_2][\text{H}^+]$

F   ANSWERS TO THE SELF-TEST

1 (a) $\dfrac{\Delta[O_2]}{\Delta t}$ (b) $-\dfrac{\Delta[H_2O_2]}{\Delta t}$

2 true

3 true

4 true

5 the number of moles per liter of H_2O_2 consumed or of O_2 produced per second

6 false

7 true

8 $k[A]$

9 s^{-1}(more generally, reciprocal time)

10 $k[H_2O_2]$

11 $k[A]^2$ or $k[A][B]$

12 $M^{-1} \cdot s^{-1}$

13 $k[H^+][OH^-]$

14 the reaction rate law

15 doubles

16 quadruples

17 does not change

18 $\log [A]_0 - \dfrac{kt}{2.30}$

19 $\log [H_2O_2]$

20 false (In such a case the rate law is zero-order in [A].)

21 the time it takes for the concentration of the reactant to decrease by a factor of 2

22 independent of

23 true

24 $\dfrac{1}{[A]_0} + kt$

25 $\dfrac{1}{[A]}$

26 false

27 dependent on

28 false (It takes twice as long to decrease from 0.25 M to 0.125 M as to decrease from 0.50 M to 0.25 M.)

29 false

30 mechanism

31 false (The rate-determining step is the slowest step.)

32 true

33 false

34 false (Colliding molecules must have the proper orientations and sufficient energy to react.)

35 true

36 true

37 $\log \left(\dfrac{k_2}{k_1} \right) = \dfrac{E_a}{2.30R} \left(\dfrac{T_2 - T_1}{T_1 T_2} \right)$

38 lower

39 false (The catalyst also increases the reverse reaction rate.)

40 true

41 true

42 true

17 / Acids and Bases

A OUTLINE OF CHAPTER 17

17-1 An acid is a proton donor and a base is a proton acceptor.

In the Arrhenius acid-base classification, an acid produces $H^+(aq)$ and a base produces $OH^-(aq)$ in aqueous solution.

In the Brönsted-Lowry acid-base classification, an acid is a proton donor and a base is a proton acceptor.

In aqueous solution an acid donates a proton to the base water to produce the hydronium ion $H_3O^+(aq)$.

The hydronium ion is a hydrated proton (Figure 17-1).

$$HCl(aq) \longrightarrow H^+(aq) + Cl^-(aq) \qquad \text{(Arrhenius)}$$

$$HCl(aq) + H_2O(l) \longrightarrow H_3O^+(aq) + Cl^-(aq) \qquad \text{(Brönsted-Lowry)}$$

17-2 In any aqueous solution the ion concentration product $[H_3O^+][OH^-]$ is a constant.

The equilibrium constant expression for the reaction

$$H_2O(l) + H_2O(l) \rightleftharpoons H_3O^+(aq) + OH^-(aq)$$

is given by

$$K_w = [H_3O^+][OH^-] = 1.00 \times 10^{-14} M^2 \text{ at } 25°C \qquad (17\text{-}3)$$

K_w is called the ion product constant of water:

In a neutral solution, $\quad [H_3O^+] = [OH^-]$

In an acidic solution, $\quad [H_3O^+] > [OH^-]$

In a basic solution, $\quad [OH^-] > [H_3O^+]$

17-3 Strong acids and bases are completely dissociated in aqueous solutions.

Some strong acids and bases are given in Table 17-1.

Acids and bases that are incompletely dissociated in water are called weak acids and weak bases.

Most acids and bases are weak.

17-4 pH is a measure of the acidity of an aqueous solution.

$$pH \equiv -\log [H_3O^+] \qquad (17\text{-}4)$$

The pH of most aqueous solutions lies in the range 0 to 14, although pH values outside this range are occasionally encountered (Figure 17-2).

In a neutral aqueous solution at 25°C, pH = 7.0.

In an acidic aqueous solution at 25°C, pH < 7.0.

In a basic aqueous solution at 25°C, pH > 7.0.

17-5 Weak acids and weak bases react only partially with water.

The concentrations of $H_3O^+(aq)$ and $OH^-(aq)$ can be found from the pH of the solution and K_w.

$$[H_3O^+] = 10^{-pH} \qquad (17\text{-}5)$$

$$[OH^-] = \frac{K_w}{[H_3O^+]}$$

The percent dissociation of an acid is given by

$$\frac{[H_3O^+]}{[\text{acid}]} \times 100$$

17-6 The equilibrium constant for an acid dissociation reaction is denoted by K_a. For the reaction

$$HB(aq) + H_2O(l) \rightleftharpoons H_3O^+(aq) + B^-(aq)$$

$$K_a = \frac{[H_3O^+][B^-]}{[HB]} \qquad (17\text{-}12)$$

The larger the value of K_a, the stronger is the acid.

Table 17-2 gives some K_a values.

The pH of an aqueous solution of a weak acid can be found from the value of K_a and the K_a expression.

17-7 The larger the value of K_a, the stronger the acid.

17-8 The smaller the pK_a value for an acid, the stronger the acid

$$pK_a \equiv -\log K_a \qquad (17\text{-}9)$$

17-9   Bases react with water to produce hydroxide ions.

For the reaction

$$NH_3(aq) + H_2O(l) \rightleftharpoons NH_4^+(aq) + OH^-(aq)$$

$$K_b = \frac{[NH_4^+][OH^-]}{[NH_3]}$$

K_b is called the base protonation constant of ammonia.

The larger the value of K_b, the stronger is the base.

Table 17-3 gives some K_b values.

The pH of an aqueous solution of a weak base can be found from the value of K_b and the K_b expression.

$$pK_b \equiv -\log K_b \tag{17-10}$$

17-10   The acid-base pair HB, B$^-$ is called a conjugate acid-base pair.

For the dissociation of an acid in water

$$HB(aq) + H_2O(l) \rightleftharpoons H_3O^+(aq) + B^-(aq)$$

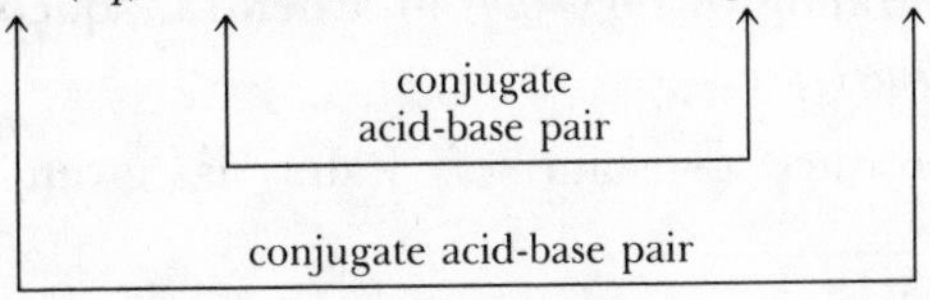

conjugate
acid-base pair

conjugate acid-base pair

For $HB(aq) + H_2O(l) \rightleftharpoons H_3O^+(aq) + B^-(aq)$

$$K_a = \frac{[H_3O)^+][B^-]}{[HB]} \tag{17-12}$$

For $B^-(aq) + H_2O(l) \rightleftharpoons HB(aq) + OH^-(aq)$

$$K_b = \frac{[HB][OH^-]}{[B^-]} \tag{17-13}$$

Therefore,

$$K_a K_b = K_w \tag{17-14}$$

The anion of a weak acid is itself a weak base.

Table 17-4 lists values of K_a and K_b for a number of conjugate acid-base pairs.

17-11   Aqueous solutions of many salts are either acidic or basic.

Various ions react with water to produce hydronium ions or hydroxide ions.

The acidic, neutral, or basic properties of a number of ions are given in Table 17-5.

The pH of aqueous salt solutions can be found from K_a or K_b expressions.

17-12   A Lewis acid is an electron-pair acceptor.

In the Lewis acid-base classification, an acid is an electron-pair acceptor and a base is an electron-pair donor.

In general, an electron-deficient species can act as a Lewis acid and a species with a lone pair of electrons can act as a Lewis base.

B   SELF-TEST

1   In the Brönsted-Lowry acid-base classification, an acid is _____.

2   In the Brönsted-Lowry acid-base classification, a base is _____.

3   Ammonia, NH_3, is an example of an acid. *True/False*

4   The hydronium ion is _____.

5   In aqueous solution the proton exists as a base proton. *True/False*

6   In aqueous solution the concentration of $OH^-(aq)$ does not depend upon the concentration of $H_3O^+(aq)$. *True/False*

7   The concentration of $OH^-(aq)$ in a neutral aqueous solution at 25°C is 1.0×10^{-14} M. *True/False*

8   The ion-product constant of water is given by the expression $K_w =$ _____.

9   The value of K_w at 25°C is _____.

10 The concentration of OH^- in an aqueous solution is 2.5×10^{-3} M; the solution is (*acidic/basic/neutral*).

11 The concentration of $H_3O^+(aq)$ in an aqueous solution is 2.5×10^{-11} M; the solution is (*acidic/basic/neutral*).

12 An aqueous solution of HBr contains the species HBr, Br^-, and $H_3O^+(aq)$. *True/False*

13 An aqueous solution of KOH contains the ionic species _____.

14 The concentration of $H_3O^+(aq)$ in an aqueous solution that is 0.032 M in HCl is _____.

15 The pH of a solution is defined as _____.

16 The pH scale compresses the wide range of the _____ scale.

17 The pH of a 0.010 M aqueous solution of HCl is _____.

18 Measurement of the pH of a solution can be used to find the concentration of $H_3O^+(aq)$ in the solution. *True/False*

19 The concentration of OH^- in an aqueous solution cannot be determined from pH measurements. *True/False*

20 The pH of pure water or of a neutral aqueous solution at 25°C is _____ .

21 Acidic solutions have pH values _____ .

22 Basic solutions have pH values _____ .

23 A weak acid is (*completely/partially*) dissociated in water.

24 A 0.10 M aqueous solution of the weak acid HF has the same pH as a 0.10 M aqueous solution of HCl. *True/False*

25 An aqueous solution of acetic acid, $HC_2H_3O_2$, contains no undissociated acid. *True/False*

26 An acid dissociation reaction is an example of a _____ reaction.

27 The equation for the acid dissociation reaction of hydrofluoric acid, HF, is
_____ .

28 The acid dissociation constant expression for hydrofluoric acid, HF, is $K_a =$
_____ .

29 The value of K_a indicates the extent of an acid's dissociation in water. *True/False*

30 An aqueous solution of nitrous acid, HNO_2, contains the species _____
_____ .

31 A weak base is a base that does not react completely with water. *True/False*

32 A 0.10 M aqueous solution of ammonia, NH_3, has the same pH as a 0.10 M aqueous solution of sodium hydroxide, NaOH. *True/False*

33 The protonation reaction of ammonia, NH_3, in water is _____
_____ .

34 The base-protonation equilibrium constant expression for ammonia, NH_3, is given by $K_b =$ _____ .

35 The value of the pK_a of an acid is given by $pK_a =$ _____ .

36 The stronger the acid, the (*smaller/larger*) is the pK_a value of the acid.

37 The value of the pK_b of a base is given by $pK_b =$ _____ .

38 Label the conjugate acid-base pairs in the proton transfer reaction

$$HNO_2(aq) + H_2O(l) \rightleftharpoons H_3O^+(aq) + NO_2^-(aq)$$

39 The conjugate _____ of $NH_3(aq)$ is $NH_4^+(aq)$.

40 The conjugate _____ of $HF(aq)$ is $F^-(aq)$.

41 The conjugate base of acetic acid, $HC_2H_3O_2$, reacts with water according to the equation _____.

42 The conjugate acid of NH_3 reacts with water according to the equation

_____.

43 The base protonation constant K_b for the conjugate base of an acid is related to the acid dissociation constant K_a of the acid by the relation $K_b =$ _____.

44 The aqueous solution of a salt is always neutral. *True/False*

45 The conjugate anionic base of a weak acid is a (*neutral/acidic/basic*) anion.

46 The conjugate cationic acid of a weak base is a (*neutral/acidic/basic*) cation.

47 An aqueous solution of NH_4Cl is (*neutral/acidic/basic*).

48 An aqueous solution of $NaNO_2$ is (*neutral/acidic/basic*).

49 An aqueous solution of $FeCl_3$ is (*neutral/acidic/basic*).

50 In the Lewis acid-base classification an acid is _____.

51 In the Lewis acid-base classification a base is _____.

52 An electron-deficient species can act as a Lewis _____.

53 A species with a lone pair of electrons can act as a Lewis _____.

C   CALCULATIONS YOU SHOULD KNOW HOW TO DO

1 Calculate the concentrations of various ionic species in solutions of strong acids or strong bases. See Examples 17-1 and 17-2 and Problems 17-1 through 17-6.

2 Calculate the pH given $[H_3O^+]$. See Example 17-3. (The use of logarithms is explained in Chapter 16 of this Study Guide.)

3 Calculate the pH of a solution of a strong base or a strong acid. See Example 17-5 and Problems 17-7 through 17-12.

4 Calculate $[H_3O^+]$ or $[OH^-]$ from the pH. See Example 17-4 and Problems 17-15 through 17-22. (The use of antilogarithms is explained following this section.)

5 Given the pH, calculate the percentage of weak-acid molecules that are dissociated or the percentage of weak-base molecules that are protonated. See Example 17-6 and Problems 17-29 through 17-32.

6 Calculate the value of K_a or K_b from the pH. See Problems 17-23 through 17-26, 17-41 and 17-42.

7 Calculate the pH of an acidic solution given the value of K_a. See Example 17-7 and Problems 17-33 through 17-40.

8 Calculate the pH of a basic solution given the value of K_b. See Example 17-9 and Problems 17-43 through 17-46.

9 Use Le Châtelier's principle to predict the effect of various changes in conditions on acid and base equilibria. See Problems 17-47 through 17-52.

10 Calculate K_a given K_b or calculate K_b given K_a for conjugate acid-base pairs. See Example 17-10 and Problems 17-59 and 17-60.

11 Calculate pK_a and pK_b values. See Example 17-8 and Problems 17-63 through 17-66.

12 Calculate the pH of aqueous salt solutions. See Example 17-11 and Problems 17-73 through 17-82.

Further Review of Logarithms

In Chapter 16 we reviewed the procedure for finding the value of the logarithm of a number. In this chapter we need to find the number when the logarithm is given, such as finding the concentration of $[H_3O^+]$ from the pH of the solution. We shall review finding the antilogarithm again.

Recall that we can write any number y as $y = 10^x$. Because x is called the logarithm of y, y is called the antilogarithm of x. For example, suppose that the logarithm of y is $x = 6.1303$ and we wish to find y. We write

$$y = 10^x = 10^{6.1303} = 10^{0.1303} \times 10^6$$

From the table of logarithms (Appendix C of the text) we see that the number whose logarithm is 0.1303 is 1.35. Thus we find that

$$10^{6.1303} = 1.35 \times 10^6$$

You can obtain this result directly on your hand calculator. On a TI calculator, for example, enter 6.1303, press the INV key (for inverse) and then the LOG key.

To obtain the antilogarithm of y using tables, you must express y as

$$y = 10^a \times 10^n \tag{1}$$

where n is a positive or negative integer and a is between 0 and 1. The quantity a is found within the logarithm table and the antilogarithm of a is read from the table. As another example, let's find the antilogarithm of 1.9509. We write

$$y = 10^{1.9509} = 10^{0.9509} \times 10^1$$

Find the value 0.9509 within the logarithm table, and you see that its antilogarithm is 8.93. Thus we have

$$y = 10^{1.9509} = 8.93 \times 10^1 = 89.3$$

You should be able to obtain this result directly on your hand calculator. If your calculator has a 10^x key, then you can obtain the antilogarithm of 1.9509 by entering 1.9509 and pressing the 10^x key. This operation is equivalent to using the INV key followed by the LOG key.

Example 1   Find the antilogarithms of the following numbers:
(a) 3.8401   (b) 6.7284

Solution

(a) $y = 10^{3.8401} = 10^{0.8401} \times 10^3$

From Appendix C, $10^{0.8401} = 6.92$, and so

$$y = 6.92 \times 10^3$$

(b) $y = 10^{6.7284} = 10^{0.7284} \times 10^6 = 5.35 \times 10^6$

You should learn how to evaluate antilogarithms using your hand calculator.

In many problems it is necessary to find the antilogarithm of negative numbers. For example, let's find the antilogarithm of -4.167, or the value of y, in

$$y = 10^{-4.167}$$

Even though the exponent is negative, we still must express y in the form of Equation (1). To do this, we write $-4.167 = 0.833 - 5.000$, so that

$$y = 10^{0.833} \times 10^{-5}$$

Now find 0.833 in a logarithm table, and see that its antilogarithm is 6.81. Thus

$$y = 6.81 \times 10^{-5}$$

You should be able to obtain this same result from your calculator by entering -4.167 and finding the inverse logarithm directly.

Example 2   Find the antilogarithm of
(a) -11.0899 (b) -2.3019

Solution

(a) $y = 10^{-11.0899} = 10^{0.9101} \times 10^{-12} = 8.13 \times 10^{-12}$
(b) $y = 10^{-2.3019} = 10^{0.6981} \times 10^{-3} = 4.99 \times 10^{-3}$

Exercises

Find the antilogarithms of the following numbers.

1	6.7324	**5**	-0.9788
2	21.0891	**6**	-6.7324
3	0.4152	**7**	-21.0891
4	-7.1586	**8**	-0.4152

Answers

1	5.400×10^6	**5**	1.050×10^{-1}
2	1.228×10^{21}	**6**	1.852×10^{-7}
3	2.601	**7**	8.145×10^{-22}
4	6.941×10^{-8}	**8**	3.844×10^{-1}

D   SOLUTIONS TO THE ODD-NUMBERED PROBLEMS

17-1   We can calculate the value of $[H_3O^+]$ from the K_w expression

$$K_w = [H_3O^+][OH^-] = 1.00 \times 10^{-14} \ M^2$$

If we solve for $[H_3O^+]$, then we get

$$[H_3O^+] = \frac{1.00 \times 10^{-14} \ M^2}{3.0 \times 10^{-3} \ M} = 3.3 \times 10^{-12} \ M$$

Because $[OH^-] > [H_3O^+]$, the solution is basic.

17-3   Because $HClO_4$ is a strong acid in water (see Table 17-1), it is completely dissociated and thus

$$[H_3O^+] = 0.050 \ M \quad \text{and} \quad [ClO_4^-] = 0.050 \ M$$

We can calculate $[OH^-]$ from the K_w expression

$$K_w = [H_3O^+][OH^-] = 1.00 \times 10^{-14} \ M^2$$

Solving for $[OH^-]$, we get

$$[OH^-] = \frac{1.00 \times 10^{-14} \ M^2}{[H_3O^+]} = \frac{1.00 \times 10^{-14} \ M^2}{0.050 \ M} = 2.0 \times 10^{-13} \ M$$

Because $[H_3O^+] > [OH^-]$, the solution is acidic.

17-5   We first must find the number of moles in 1.00 g of TlOH

$$n = (1.00 \ g)(\frac{1 \ mol}{221.4 \ g}) = 0.004517 \ mol$$

The molarity of the solution is

$$\text{molarity} = \frac{\text{moles of solute}}{\text{volume of solution}} = \frac{0.004517 \ mol}{0.500 \ L} = 0.00903 \ M$$

Because TlOH is a strong base, it is completely dissociated in aqueous solution and thus

$$[OH^-] = 9.03 \times 10^{-3} \text{ M} \quad \text{and} \quad [Tl^+] = 9.03 \times 10^{-3} \text{ M}$$

We can calculate $[H_3O^+]$ from the K_w expression

$$K_w = [H_3O^+][OH^-] = 1.00 \times 10^{-14} \text{ M}^2$$

to get

$$[H_3O^+] = \frac{1.00 \times 10^{-14} \text{ M}^2}{[OH^-]} = \frac{1.00 \times 10^{-14} \text{ M}^2}{9.03 \times 10^{-3} \text{ M}} = 1.11 \times 10^{-12} \text{ M}$$

17-7 Because HNO_3 is a strong acid in solution, it is completely dissociated and thus

$$[H_3O^+] = 0.050 \text{ M}$$

The pH is defined as

$$\text{pH} \equiv -\log [H_3O^+] = -\log (0.050) = 1.30$$

Because pH < 7, the solution is acidic.

17-9 Because both HCl and HBr are strong acids, they are completely dissociated in water. Thus from HCl

$$[H_3O^+] = 0.025 \text{ M}$$

and from HBr

$$[H_3O^+] = 0.025 \text{ M}$$

The total concentration of $H_3O^+(aq)$ is

$$[H_3O^+] = 0.025 \text{ M} + 0.025 \text{ M} = 0.050 \text{ M}$$

The pH of the solution is

$$\text{pH} = -\log [H_3O^+] = -\log (0.050) = 1.30$$

The solution is acidic because the pH < 7.

17-11 We first calculate the number of moles of KOH in 1.00 g:

$$n = (1.00 \text{ g}) \left(\frac{1 \text{ mol}}{56.11 \text{ g}} \right) = 1.78 \times 10^{-2} \text{ mol}$$

The molarity of the solution is

$$\text{molarity} = \frac{\text{moles of solute}}{\text{volume of solution}} = \frac{1.78 \times 10^{-2} \text{ mol}}{0.500 \text{ L}} = 3.56 \times 10^{-2} \text{ M}$$

Because KOH is a strong base, it is completely dissociated and thus

$$[OH^-] = 3.56 \times 10^{-2} \text{ M}$$

We can calculate $[H_3O^+]$ from the K_w expression

$$[H_3O^+] = \frac{1.00 \times 10^{-14} \text{ M}^2}{[OH^-]} = \frac{1.00 \times 10^{-14} \text{ M}^2}{3.56 \times 10^{-2} \text{ M}} = 2.81 \times 10^{-13} \text{ M}$$

The pH of the solution is

$$\text{pH} = -\log [H_3O^+] = -\log (2.81 \times 10^{-13}) = 12.55$$

17-13   The ion product constant for water at 0°C is

$$K_w = [H_3O^+][OH^-] = 0.12 \times 10^{-14} \text{ M}^2$$

In a neutral aqueous solution

$$[H_3O^+] = [OH^-]$$

Therefore, $$K_w = [H_3O^+]^2 = 0.12 \times 10^{-14} \text{ M}^2$$

Taking the square root of both sides, we get

$$[H_3O^+] = 3.5 \times 10^{-8} \text{ M}$$

The pH of a neutral aqueous solution at 0°C is

$$\text{pH} = -\log [H_3O^+] = -\log (3.5 \times 10^{-8}) = 7.46$$

At 0°C, an aqueous solution with a pH = 7.25 is acidic. The pH of the solution is less than 7.46, the pH of a neutral solution.

17-15   From the definition of pH

$$\text{pH} = -\log [H_3O^+]$$

We obtain, by taking the antilogarithm (antilogarithms are discussed on pages 333–334)

$$[H_3O^+] = 10^{-\text{pH}}$$

The pH of the muscle fluids is given as 6.8, and so

$$[H_3O^+] = 10^{-6.8} = 1.6 \times 10^{-7} \text{ M}$$

If you do not use a calculator to find $10^{-6.8}$, then write

$$[H_3O^+] = 10^{-6.8} = 10^{0.20} \times 10^{-7} = 1.6 \times 10^{-7} \text{ M}$$

17-17 From the definition of pH

$$pH = -\log [H_3O^+]$$

we write

$$[H_3O^+] = 10^{-pH}$$

The pH is 1.0 and so

$$[H_3O^+] = 10^{-1.0} = 0.10 \text{ M}$$

Because HCl is a strong acid, the concentration of HCl in the stomach is

$$[HCl] = [H_3O^+] = 0.10 \text{ M}$$

17-19 From the definition of pH

$$pH = -\log [H_3O^+]$$

we write

$$[H_3O^+] = 10^{-pH}$$

The pH of human blood is 7.4 and so

$$[H_3O^+] = 10^{-7.4} = 4.0 \times 10^{-8} \text{ M}$$

We can calculate $[OH^-]$ from the K_w expression

$$[OH^-] = \frac{1.00 \times 10^{-14} \text{ M}^2}{[H_3O^+]} = \frac{1.00 \times 10^{-14} \text{ M}^2}{4.0 \times 10^{-8} \text{ M}} = 2.5 \times 10^{-7} \text{ M}$$

17-21 From the definition of pH

$$pH = -\log [H_3O^+]$$

we write

$$[H_3O^+] = 10^{-pH}$$

The measured pH is 13.5 and so

$$[H_3O^+] = 10^{-13.5} = 3.16 \times 10^{-14} \text{ M}$$

We can calculate $[OH^-]$ from the K_w expression

$$[OH^-] = \frac{1.00 \times 10^{-14} \text{ M}^2}{[H_3O^+]} = \frac{1.00 \times 10^{-14} \text{ M}^2}{3.16 \times 10^{-14} \text{ M}} = 0.316 \text{ M}$$

Because one mole of $Sr(OH)_2$ dissociates and yields two moles of OH^-, the concentration of $Sr(OH)_2$ is

$$[Sr(OH)_2] = \tfrac{1}{2}[OH^-] = 0.16 \text{ M}$$

That is, 0.16 moles of $Sr(OH)_2$ dissolve per 1.00 L of solution. Solubility is often expressed as the number of grams per 100 mL of solution. The number of moles in 100 mL is

$$n = \text{molarity} \times \text{volume} = (0.16 \text{ mol} \cdot \text{L}^{-1})(0.100 \text{ L})$$
$$= 1.6 \times 10^{-2} \text{ mol}$$

The mass corresponding to 1.6×10^{-2} mol of $Sr(OH)_2$ is

$$\text{mass} = (1.6 \times 10^{-2} \text{ mol})\left(\frac{121.64 \text{ g}}{1 \text{ mol}}\right) = 1.9 \text{ g}$$

The solubility of $Sr(OH)_2$ is 1.9 g per 100 mL of solution.

17-23 The reaction is

$$HC_3H_5O_2(aq) + H_2O(l) \rightleftharpoons H_3O^+(aq) + C_3H_5O_2^-(aq)$$

The acid-dissociation constant expression is

$$K_a = \frac{[H_3O^+][C_3H_5O_2^-]}{[HC_3H_5O_2]}$$

We can find the value of $[H_3O^+]$ from the pH of the solution. We have

$$[H_3O^+] = 10^{-pH} = 10^{-3.09} = 8.13 \times 10^{-4} \text{ M}$$

From the reaction stoichiometry at equilibrium, $[H_3O^+] = [C_3H_5O_2^-]$, because we started with only $HC_3H_5O_2$. At equilibrium

$$[HC_3H_5O_2] = 0.050 \text{ M} - [H_3O^+] = 0.050 \text{ M} - 0.000813 \text{ M} = 0.050 \text{ M}$$

Substituting the values of the concentrations of H_3O^+, $C_3H_5O_2^-$, and $HC_3H_5O_2$ into the K_a expression, we have

$$K_a = \frac{(8.13 \times 10^{-4} \text{ M})(8.13 \times 10^{-4} \text{ M})}{(0.050 \text{ M})}$$
$$= 1.3 \times 10^{-5} \text{ M}$$

17-25 The reaction is

$$HC_2H_3O_2(aq) + H_2O(l) \rightleftharpoons H_3O^+(aq) + C_2H_3O_2^-(aq)$$

The acid-dissociation constant expression is

$$K_a = \frac{[H_3O^+][C_2H_3O_2^-]}{[HC_2H_3O_2]}$$

We can find the value of $[H_3O^+]$ from the pH:

$$[H_3O^+] = 10^{-pH} = 10^{-3.39} = 4.07 \times 10^{-4} \text{ M}$$

We can set up a table of initial concentrations and equilibrium concentrations.

	$HC_2H_3O_2(aq)$	+ $H_2O(l)$ $\rightleftharpoons$	$H_3O^+(aq)$	+	$C_2H_3O_2^-(aq)$
initial concentration	1.00×10^{-2} M	—	0		0
equilibrium concentration	1.00×10^{-2} M $-[H_3O^+]$ $= 0.96 \times 10^{-2}$ M	—	$[H_3O^+]$ $= 4.07 \times 10^{-4}$ M		$[C_2H_3O_2^-] = [H_3O^+]$ $= 4.07 \times 10^{-4}$ M

Substituting in the values of the equilibrium concentrations in the K_a expression, we have

$$K_a = \frac{(4.07 \times 10^{-4} \text{ M})(4.07 \times 10^{-4} \text{ M})}{0.96 \times 10^{-2} \text{ M}}$$

$$= 1.7 \times 10^{-5} \text{ M}$$

17-27 The acid-dissociation constant expression is

The ratio of the concentrations of the dissociated ion to the undissociated acid is

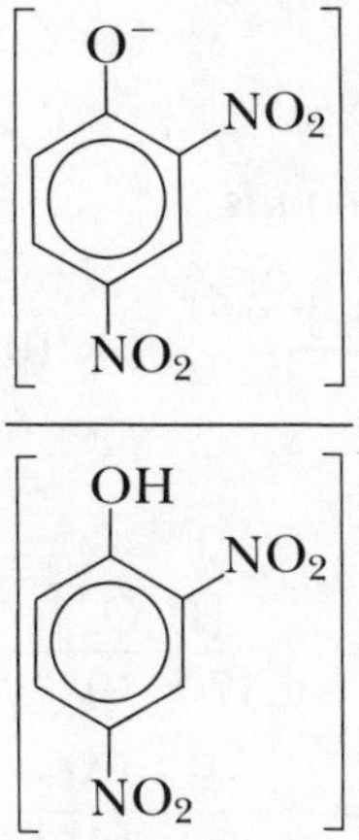

$$\frac{\left[\text{(2,4-dinitrophenolate ion)}\right]}{\left[\text{(2,4-dinitrophenol)}\right]} = \frac{K_a}{[\text{H}_3\text{O}^+]} = \frac{1.1 \times 10^{-4}\text{ M}}{[\text{H}_3\text{O}^+]}$$

We can find the value of $[\text{H}_3\text{O}^+]$ from the pH of the solution

$$[\text{H}_3\text{O}^+] = 10^{-\text{pH}} = 10^{-7.4} = 4.0 \times 10^{-8}\text{ M}$$

The value of the ratio is

$$\text{ratio} = \frac{1.1 \times 10^{-4}\text{ M}}{4.0 \times 10^{-8}\text{ M}} = 2.8 \times 10^3$$

17-29 The reaction is

$$\text{acetylsalicylic acid}(aq) + \text{H}_2\text{O}(l) \rightleftharpoons \text{H}_3\text{O}^+(aq) + \text{acetylsalicylate}(aq)$$

or

$$\text{acid}(aq) + \text{H}_2\text{O}(l) \rightleftharpoons \text{H}_3\text{O}^+(aq) + \text{anion}(aq)$$

The acid-dissociation constant expression is

$$K_a = \frac{[\text{anion}][\text{H}_3\text{O}^+]}{[\text{acid}]} = 2.75 \times 10^{-5}\text{ M}$$

The ratio of the dissociated acid to the undissociated acid is given by

$$\frac{[\text{anion}]}{[\text{acid}]} = \frac{K_a}{[\text{H}_3\text{O}^+]} = \frac{2.75 \times 10^{-5}\text{ M}}{[\text{H}_3\text{O}^+]}$$

The concentration of H_3O^+ is

$$[\text{H}_3\text{O}^+] = 10^{-\text{pH}} = 10^{-2.0} = 1.0 \times 10^{-2}\text{ M}$$

and so

$$\frac{[\text{anion}]}{[\text{acid}]} = \frac{2.75 \times 10^{-5} \text{ M}}{1.0 \times 10^{-2} \text{ M}} = 2.8 \times 10^{-3}$$

The percent of acid dissociated is 0.28%.

17-31 The acid-dissociation constant expression is

$$K_a = \frac{[\text{H}_3\text{O}^+][\text{NO}_2^-]}{[\text{HNO}_2]} = 4.47 \times 10^{-4} \text{ M}$$

from which we obtain

$$\frac{[\text{HNO}_2]}{[\text{NO}_2^-]} = \frac{[\text{H}_3\text{O}^+]}{K_a} = \frac{[\text{H}_3\text{O}^+]}{4.47 \times 10^{-4} \text{ M}}$$

$$= \frac{0.10 \text{ M}}{4.47 \times 10^{-4} \text{ M}} = 220$$

17-33 The reaction is

$$\text{HC}_7\text{H}_5\text{O}_2(aq) + \text{H}_2\text{O}(l) \rightleftharpoons \text{H}_3\text{O}^+(aq) + \text{C}_7\text{H}_5\text{O}_2^-(aq)$$

We can set up a table of initial and equilibrium concentrations.

	$\text{HC}_7\text{H}_5\text{O}_2(aq)$	$+ \text{H}_2\text{O}(l) \rightleftharpoons$	$\text{H}_3\text{O}^+(aq) +$	$\text{C}_7\text{H}_5\text{O}_2^-(aq)$
initial concentration	0.025 M	—	0	0
equilibrium concentration	0.025 M $-$ [H$_3$O$^+$]	—	[H$_3$O$^+$]	[C$_7$H$_5$O$_2^-$] = [H$_3$O$^+$]

Substituting the equilibrium concentration expressions in the K_a expression, we have

$$K_a = \frac{[\text{H}_3\text{O}^+][\text{C}_7\text{H}_5\text{O}_2^-]}{[\text{HC}_7\text{H}_5\text{O}_2]} = \frac{[\text{H}_3\text{O}^+]^2}{0.025 \text{ M} - [\text{H}_3\text{O}^+]} = 6.46 \times 10^{-5} \text{ M}$$

or

$$[\text{H}_3\text{O}^+]^2 + 6.46 \times 10^{-5} \text{ M} [\text{H}_3\text{O}^+] - 1.62 \times 10^{-6} \text{ M}^2 = 0$$

The quadratic formula (reviewed in Section C of Chapter 15 in this Study Guide) gives

$$[\text{H}_3\text{O}^+] = \frac{-6.46 \times 10^{-5} \text{ M} \pm \sqrt{4.17 \times 10^{-9} \text{ M}^2 - (4)(1)(-1.62 \times 10^{-6} \text{ M}^2)}}{(2)(1)}$$

$$= \frac{-6.46 \times 10^{-5} \text{ M} \pm 2.55 \times 10^{-3} \text{ M}}{2}$$

$$= 1.24 \times 10^{-3} \text{ M} \quad \text{and} \quad -1.36 \times 10^{-3} \text{ M}$$

We reject the negative root because concentrations are positive quantities. The pH of the solution is

$$pH = -\log [H_3O^+] = -\log (1.24 \times 10^{-3}) = 2.91$$

17-35 The reaction is

$$HC_2Cl_3O_2(aq) + H_2O(l) \rightleftharpoons H_3O^+(aq) + C_2Cl_3O_2^-(aq)$$

We can set up a table of initial and equilibrium concentrations.

	$HC_2Cl_3O_2(aq)$	$+ \quad H_2O(l) \rightleftharpoons$	$H_3O^+(aq) \ +$	$C_2Cl_3O_2^-(aq)$
initial concentration	0.010 M	—	0	0
equilibrium concentration	0.010 M − $[H_3O^+]$	—	$[H_3O^+]$	$[C_2Cl_3O_2^-] = [H_3O^+]$

Substituting the equilibrium concentration expressions in the K_a expression, we have

$$K_a = \frac{[H_3O^+][C_2Cl_3O_2^-]}{[HC_2Cl_3O_2]} = \frac{[H_3O^+]^2}{0.010 \text{ M} - [H_3O^+]} = 2.3 \times 10^{-1} \text{ M}$$

or

$$[H_3O^+]^2 + 2.3 \times 10^{-1} \text{ M } [H_3O^+] - 2.3 \times 10^{-3} \text{ M}^2 = 0$$

The quadratic formula gives

$$[H_3O^+] = \frac{-2.3 \times 10^{-1} \text{ M} \pm \sqrt{5.29 \times 10^{-2} \text{ M}^2 - (4)(1)(-2.3 \times 10^{-3} \text{ M}^2)}}{(2)(1)}$$

$$= \frac{-2.3 \times 10^{-1} \text{ M} \pm 2.5 \times 10^{-1} \text{ M}}{2}$$

$$= 1 \times 10^{-2} \text{ M}$$

The pH of the solution is

$$pH = -\log [H_3O^+] = -\log(1 \times 10^{-2}) = 2.0$$

17-37 The number of moles of benzoic acid in 6.15 g is

$$n = (6.15 \text{ g})\left(\frac{1 \text{ mol}}{122.12 \text{ g}}\right) = 0.05036 \text{ mol}$$

The molarity of the solution is

$$\text{molarity} = \frac{\text{moles of solute}}{\text{volume of solution}} = \frac{0.05036 \text{ mol}}{0.600 \text{ L}} = 0.0839 \text{ M}$$

We can set up a table of initial and equilibrium concentrations.

	$HC_7H_5O_2(aq)$	$+ \quad H_2O(l) \rightleftharpoons$	$H_3O^+(aq) \; +$	$C_7H_5O_2^-(aq)$
initial concentration	0.0839 M	—	0	0
equilibrium concentration	$0.0839 \text{ M} - [H_3O^+]$	—	$[H_3O^+]$	$[C_7H_5O_2^-] = [H_3O^+]$

Substituting the equilibrium concentration expressions in the K_a expression, we have

$$K_a = \frac{[H_3O^+][C_7H_5O_2^-]}{[HC_7H_5O_2]} = \frac{[H_3O^+]^2}{0.0839 \text{ M} - [H_3O^+]} = 6.46 \times 10^{-5} \text{ M}$$

or

$$[H_3O^+]^2 + 6.46 \times 10^{-5} \text{ M } [H_3O^+] - 5.42 \times 10^{-6} \text{ M}^2 = 0$$

The quadratic formula gives

$$[H_3O^+] = \frac{-6.46 \times 10^{-5} \text{ M} \pm \sqrt{4.17 \times 10^{-9} \text{ M}^2 - (4)(1)(-5.42 \times 10^{-6} \text{ M}^2)}}{(2)(1)}$$

$$= \frac{-6.46 \times 10^{-5} \text{ M} \pm 4.66 \times 10^{-3} \text{ M}}{2}$$

$$= 2.30 \times 10^{-3} \text{ M}$$

and the pH of the solution is

$$\text{pH} = -\log [H_3O^+] = -\log (2.30 \times 10^{-3}) = 2.64$$

17-39 We can set up a table of initial and equilibrium concentrations.

	$HO_3SNH_2(aq)$	$+ \quad H_2O(l) \rightleftharpoons$	$H_3O^+(aq) \; +$	$O_3SNH_2^-(aq)$
initial concentration	0.050 M	—	0	0
equilibrium concentration	$0.050 \text{ M} - [H_3O^+]$	—	$[H_3O^+]$	$[O_3SNH_2^-] = [H_3O^+]$

Substituting the equilibrium concentration expressions in the K_a expression, we have

$$K_a = \frac{[H_3O^+][O_3SNH_2^-]}{[HO_3SNH_2]} = \frac{[H_3O^+]^2}{0.050 \text{ M} - [H_3O^+]} = 0.10 \text{ M}$$

or

$$[H_3O^+]^2 + 0.10 \text{ M } [H_3O^+] - 0.0050 \text{ M}^2 = 0$$

The quadratic formula gives

$$[H_3O^+] = \frac{-0.10 \text{ M} \pm \sqrt{0.010 \text{ M}^2 - (4)(1)(-0.0050 \text{ M}^2)}}{(2)(1)}$$

$$= \frac{-0.10 \text{ M} \pm 0.17 \text{ M}}{2}$$

$$= 0.04 \text{ M}$$

The pH of the solution is

$$pH = -\log [H_3O^+] = -\log (0.04) = 1.4$$

17-41   The reaction is

$$NH_3(aq) + H_2O(l) \rightleftharpoons NH_4^+(aq) + OH^-(aq)$$

We can find the concentration of OH^- from the pH and the ion product constant of water

$$[H_3O^+] = 10^{-pH} = 10^{-11.12} = 7.59 \times 10^{-12} \text{ M}$$

$$[OH^-] = \frac{1.00 \times 10^{-14} \text{ M}^2}{[H_3O^+]} = \frac{1.00 \times 10^{-14} \text{ M}^2}{7.59 \times 10^{-12} \text{ M}} = 1.32 \times 10^{-3} \text{ M}$$

We can set up a table of initial and equilibrium concentrations.

	$NH_3(aq)$	$+ \; H_2O(l) \rightleftharpoons$	$NH_4^+(aq)$	$+ \quad OH^-(aq)$
initial concentration	0.100 M	—	0	0
equilibrium concentration	0.100 M − [OH⁻] = 9.9×10^{-2} M	—	$[NH_4^+] = [OH^-] =$ 1.32×10^{-3} M	$[OH^-] =$ 1.32×10^{-3} M

The base-protonation constant expression is

$$K_b = \frac{[NH_4^+][OH^-]}{[NH_3]} = \frac{(1.32 \times 10^{-3} \text{ M})(1.32 \times 10^{-3} \text{ M})}{9.9 \times 10^{-2} \text{ M}}$$

$$= 1.8 \times 10^{-5} \text{ M}$$

17-43   The reaction is

$$C_5H_5N(aq) + H_2O(l) \rightleftharpoons C_5H_5NH^+(aq) + OH^-(aq)$$

We can set up a table of initial and equilibrium concentrations.

	$C_5H_5N(aq)$	$+ \; H_2O(l) \rightleftharpoons$	$C_5H_5NH^+(aq)$	$+ \; OH^-(aq)$
initial concentration	0.600 M	—	0	0
equilibrium concentration	0.600 M − [OH⁻]	—	$[C_5H_5NH^+] = [OH^-]$	$[OH^-]$

The expression for K_b is

$$K_b = \frac{[C_5H_5NH^+][OH^-]}{[C_5H_5N]} = \frac{[OH^-]^2}{0.600\ M - [OH^-]} = 1.48 \times 10^{-9}\ M$$

Because K_b is so small, we expect that $[OH^-]$ will be small and thus negligible compared with 0.600 M. The expression for K_b becomes

$$\frac{[OH^-]^2}{0.600\ M} = 1.48 \times 10^{-9}\ M$$

$$[OH^-]^2 = 8.88 \times 10^{-10}\ M^2$$

$$[OH^-] = 2.98 \times 10^{-5}\ M$$

We can see that $[OH^-]$ is much smaller than 0.600 M. We can find $[H_3O^+]$ from the ion product constant of water

$$[H_3O^+] = \frac{1.00 \times 10^{-14}\ M^2}{[OH^-]} = \frac{1.00 \times 10^{-14}\ M^2}{2.98 \times 10^{-5}\ M} = 3.36 \times 10^{-10}\ M$$

The pH of the solution is

$$pH = -\log[H_3O^+] = -\log(3.36 \times 10^{-10}) = 9.47$$

17-45   We can set up a table of initial and equilibrium concentrations.

	$(CH_3)_2NH(aq)$	$+\ H_2O(l) \rightleftharpoons$	$(CH_3)_2NH_2^+(aq)$	$+\ OH^-(aq)$
initial concentration	0.050 M	—	0	0
equilibrium concentration	0.050 M $-$ [OH$^-$]	—	$[(CH_3)_2NH_2^+] = [OH^-]$	[OH$^-$]

The expression for K_b is

$$K_b = \frac{[(CH_3)_2NH_2^+][OH^-]}{[(CH_3)_2NH]} = \frac{[OH^-]^2}{0.050\ M - [OH^-]} = 5.81 \times 10^{-4}\ M$$

The value of K_b may not be small enough to ignore $[OH^-]$ in the denominator, and so we should use the quadratic formula

$$[OH^-]^2 + 5.81 \times 10^{-4}\ M\,[OH^-] - 2.91 \times 10^{-5}\ M^2 = 0$$

The quadratic formula gives

$$[OH^-] = \frac{-5.81 \times 10^{-4}\ M \pm \sqrt{3.38 \times 10^{-7}\ M^2 - (4)(1)(-2.91 \times 10^{-5}\ M^2)}}{(2)(1)}$$

$$= \frac{-5.81 \times 10^{-4}\ M \pm 1.08 \times 10^{-2}\ M}{2}$$

$$= 5.11 \times 10^{-3}\ M$$

$$[\text{H}_3\text{O}^+] = \frac{1.00 \times 10^{-14}\ \text{M}^2}{[\text{OH}^-]} = \frac{1.00 \times 10^{-14}\ \text{M}^2}{5.11 \times 10^{-3}\ \text{M}} = 1.96 \times 10^{-12}\ \text{M}$$

The pH of the solution is

$$\text{pH} = -\log\,[\text{H}_3\text{O}^+] = -\log\,(1.96 \times 10^{-12}) = 11.71$$

17-47 (a) The equilibrium is shifted from left to right.
(b) The equilibrium is shifted from right to left.
(c) The equilibrium is shifted from right to left.
(d) The equilibrium is shifted from right to left.

17-49 (a) The equilibrium shifts from left to right. The addition of OH^- to the solution removes $\text{H}_3\text{O}^+(aq)$ by the reaction between $\text{H}_3\text{O}^+(aq)$ and $\text{OH}^-(aq)$ to produce $\text{H}_2\text{O}(l)$.
(b) The equilibrium shifts from right to left because $\text{CHO}_2^-(aq)$ has been added.

17-51 (a) The equilibrium shifts from right to left.
(b) The equilibrium is not affected. Because $\Delta H^\circ_{rxn} \simeq 0$, the equilibrium constant does not change with temperature.
(c) The equilibrium shifts from right to left.
(d) The equilibrium shifts from left to right because the added $\text{NH}_3(aq)$ reacts with $\text{H}_3\text{O}^+(aq)$ according to

$$\text{NH}_3(aq) + \text{H}_3\text{O}^+(aq) \rightleftharpoons \text{NH}_4^+(aq) + \text{H}_2\text{O}(l)$$

(e) The equilibrium is shifted from right to left because $[\text{H}_3\text{O}^+]$ has increased.

17-53 (a) $\text{HC}_7\text{H}_5\text{O}_2(aq) + \text{H}_2\text{O}(l) \rightleftharpoons \text{H}_3\text{O}^+(aq) + \text{C}_7\text{H}_5\text{O}_2^-(aq)$

conjugate
acid-base pair

conjugate acid-base pair

(b) $\text{CH}_3\text{NH}_2(aq) + \text{H}_2\text{O}(l) \rightleftharpoons \text{CH}_3\text{NH}_3^+(aq) + \text{OH}^-(aq)$

conjugate acid-base pair

conjugate acid-base pair

(c) $\text{HCHO}_2(aq) + \text{H}_2\text{O}(l) \rightleftharpoons \text{H}_3\text{O}^+(aq) + \text{CHO}_2^-(aq)$

conjugate acid-base pair

conjugate acid-base pair

17-55 (a) $\text{NO}_2^-(aq)$ (c) $\text{H}_2\text{PO}_4^-(aq)$
(b) $\text{C}_2\text{H}_2\text{ClO}_2^-(aq)$ (d) $\text{HPO}_4^{2-}(aq)$

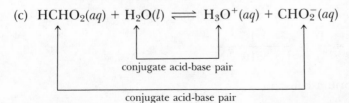

17-57 (a) $HCHO_2$ is an acid; CHO_2^- is its conjugate base.
(b) IO^- is a base; HIO is its conjugate acid.
(c) F^- is a base; HF is its conjugate acid.
(d) $CH_3NH_3^+$ is an acid; CH_3NH_2 is its conjugate base.
(e) $ClNH_2$ is a base; $ClNH_3^+$ is its conjugate acid.
(f) CN^- is a base; HCN is it conjugate acid.

17-59 We have that $K_b = \dfrac{K_w}{K_a}$

(a) $K_b = \dfrac{1.00 \times 10^{-14}\,M^2}{1.34 \times 10^{-5}\,M} = 7.46 \times 10^{-10}\,M$ for $C_3H_5O_2^-$

(b) $K_b = \dfrac{1.00 \times 10^{-14}\,M^2}{6.76 \times 10^{-4}\,M} = 1.48 \times 10^{-11}\,M$ for F^-

(c) $K_b = \dfrac{1.00 \times 10^{-14}\,M^2}{5.6 \times 10^{-10}\,M} = 1.8 \times 10^{-5}\,M$ for NH_3

(d) $K_b = \dfrac{1.00 \times 10^{-14}\,M^2}{5.9 \times 10^{-10}\,M} = 1.7 \times 10^{-5}\,M$ for $H_2BO_3^-$

17-61 (a) The equation is the sum of the two equations

(1) $HCHO_2(aq) + H_2O(l) \rightleftharpoons CHO_2^-(aq) + H_3O^+(aq)$

$\qquad K_1 = K_a = 1.8 \times 10^{-4}\,M$

(2) $NO_2^-(aq) + H_3O^+(aq) \rightleftharpoons HNO_2(aq) + H_2O(l)$

$\qquad K_2 = \dfrac{1}{K_a} = \dfrac{1}{4.5 \times 10^{-4}\,M}$

The equilibrium constant for a reaction whose equation is the sum of two equations is equal to the product of two equilibrium constants. Thus

$$K = K_1K_2 = \dfrac{1.8 \times 10^{-4}\,M}{4.5 \times 10^{-4}\,M} = 4.0 \times 10^{-1} = 0.40$$

(b) The equation is the sum of the two equations

(1) $CN^-(aq) + H_2O(l) \rightleftharpoons HCN(aq) + OH^-(aq)$

$\qquad K_1 = K_b = 2.1 \times 10^{-5}\,M$

(2) $NH_4^+(aq) + OH^-(aq) \rightleftharpoons NH_3(aq) + H_2O(l)$

$\qquad K_2 = \dfrac{1}{K_b} = \dfrac{1}{1.8 \times 10^{-5}\,M}$

The equilibrium constant is

$$K = K_1K_2 = \dfrac{2.1 \times 10^{-5}\,M}{1.8 \times 10^{-5}\,M} = 1.2$$

17-63 The value of pK_b is given by

$$pK_b = -\log K_b$$

(a) The value of K_b for $SO_3^{2-}(aq)$ is 1.6×10^{-7} M. Thus

$$pK_b = -\log(1.6 \times 10^{-7}) = 6.80$$

(b) The value of K_b for $HSO_3^-(aq)$ is 6.7×10^{-13} M. Thus

$$pK_b = -\log(6.7 \times 10^{-13}) = 12.17$$

17-65 From the definition of pK_a

$$pK_a = -\log K_a$$

we write

$$K_a = 10^{-pK_a}$$

Thus

$$K_a = 10^{-5.00} = 1.00 \times 10^{-5} \text{ M}$$

We have

$$K_b = \frac{K_w}{K_a}$$

Thus

$$K_b = \frac{1.00 \times 10^{-14} \text{ M}^2}{1.00 \times 10^{-5} \text{ M}} = 1.00 \times 10^{-9} \text{ M}$$

17-67 (a) acidic cation, neutral anion; acidic solution
(b) acidic cation, basic anion; cannot predict without calculations
(c) neutral cation, basic anion; basic solution
(d) neutral cation, neutral anion; neutral solution
(e) neutral cation, basic anion; basic solution

17-69 (a) neutral cation, basic anion; basic solution
(b) neutral cation, basic anion; basic solution
(c) acidic cation, neutral anion; acidic solution
(d) neutral cation, neutral anion; neutral solution
(e) acidic cation, neutral anion; acidic solution

17-71 The reaction that takes place in producing soap is

$$NaOH(aq) + HC_{18}H_{35}O_2(s) \rightleftharpoons \underset{\text{soap}}{NaC_{18}H_{35}O_2(s)} + H_2O(l)$$

Soap is made up of a neutral cation and a basic anion. The anion is the conjugate base of a weak acid and is a weak base. The soap solution is basic.

17-73 The salt NaClO dissociates completely in water to yield Na(*aq*) and ClO$^-$(*aq*). The reaction of the anion with water is

$$ClO^-(aq) + H_2O(l) \rightleftharpoons HClO(aq) + OH^-(aq)$$

The value of the equilibrium constant is (Table 17-4)

$$K_b = \frac{K_w}{K_a} = \frac{1.00 \times 10^{-14} \text{ M}}{3.0 \times 10^{-8} \text{ M}} = 3.3 \times 10^{-7} \text{ M}$$

We can set up a table of initial and equilibrium concentrations.

	ClO$^-$(*aq*)	+ H$_2$O(*l*) $\rightleftharpoons$	HClO(*aq*)	+ OH$^-$(*aq*)
initial concentration	0.050 M	—	0	0
equilibrium concentration	0.050 M − [OH$^-$]	—	[HClO] = [OH$^-$]	[OH$^-$]

The expression for K_b is

$$K_b = \frac{[HClO][OH^-]}{[ClO^-]} = \frac{[OH^-]^2}{0.050 \text{ M} - [OH^-]} = 3.3 \times 10^{-7} \text{ M}$$

We can neglect [OH$^-$] relative to 0.050 M because K_b is very small. We have

$$\frac{[OH^-]^2}{0.050 \text{ M}} = 3.3 \times 10^{-7} \text{ M}$$

Solving for [OH$^-$], we have

$$[OH^-] = 1.3 \times 10^{-4} \text{ M}$$

and so

$$[HClO] = 1.3 \times 10^{-4} \text{ M}$$

Using the ion product constant of water, we obtain

$$[H_3O^+] = \frac{1.00 \times 10^{-14} \text{ M}^2}{[OH^-]} = \frac{1.00 \times 10^{-14} \text{ M}^2}{1.3 \times 10^{-4} \text{ M}} = 7.7 \times 10^{-11} \text{ M}$$

The pH of the solution is

$$pH = -\log [H_3O^+] = -\log (7.7 \times 10^{-11}) = 10.11$$

17-75 The reaction is

$$CNO^-(aq) + H_2O(l) \rightleftharpoons HCNO(aq) + OH^-(aq)$$

The value of the equilibrium constant is (Table 17-2)

$$K_b = \frac{K_w}{K_a} = \frac{1.00 \times 10^{-14} \text{ M}}{2.19 \times 10^{-4} \text{ M}} = 4.57 \times 10^{-11} \text{ M}$$

We can set up a table of the initial and equilibrium concentrations.

	$CNO^-(aq)$	$+$	$H_2O(l)$	$\rightleftharpoons$	$HCNO(aq)$	$+$	$OH^-(aq)$
initial concentration	0.10 M		—		0		0
equilibrium concentration	$0.10 \text{ M} - [OH^-]$		—		$[HCNO] = [OH^-]$		$[OH^-]$

The K_b expression is

$$K_b = \frac{[HCNO][OH^-]}{[CNO^-]} = \frac{[OH^-]^2}{0.10 \text{ M} - [OH^-]} = 4.57 \times 10^{-11} \text{ M}$$

Neglecting $[OH^-]$ with respect to 0.10 M, we have

$$\frac{[OH^-]^2}{0.10 \text{ M}} = 4.57 \times 10^{-11} \text{ M}$$

$$[OH^-] = 2.14 \times 10^{-6} \text{ M}$$

and

$$[HCNO] = 2.14 \times 10^{-6} \text{ M}$$

and

$$[CNO^-] = 0.10 \text{ M} - [OH^-] = 0.10 \text{ M} - 2.14 \times 10^{-6} \text{ M} = 0.10 \text{ M}$$

Using the ion product constant of water, we obtain

$$[H_3O^+] = \frac{1.00 \times 10^{-14} \text{ M}^2}{[OH^-]} = \frac{1.00 \times 10^{-14} \text{ M}^2}{2.14 \times 10^{-6} \text{ M}} = 4.67 \times 10^{-9} \text{ M}$$

$$pH = -\log [H_3O^+] = -\log (4.67 \times 10^{-9}) = 8.33$$

17-77 The reaction is

$$C_5H_5NH^+(aq) + H_2O(l) \rightleftharpoons H_3O^+(aq) + C_5H_5N(aq)$$

We can set up a table of initial and equilibrium concentrations.

	$C_5H_5NH^+(aq)$	$+$	$H_2O(l)$	$\rightleftharpoons$	$H_3O^+(aq)$	$+$	$C_5H_5N(aq)$
initial concentration	0.30 M		—		0		0
equilibrium concentration	$0.30 \text{ M} - [H_3O^+]$		—		$[H_3O^+]$		$[C_5H_5N] = [H_3O^+]$

The K_a expression is (Table 17-4)

$$K_a = \frac{[H_3O^+][C_5H_5N]}{[C_5H_5NH^+]} = \frac{[H_3O^+]^2}{0.30\ M - [H_3O^+]} = 6.8 \times 10^{-6}\ M$$

Neglecting $[H_3O^+]$ with respect to 0.30 M, we have

$$\frac{[H_3O^+]^2}{0.30\ M} = 6.8 \times 10^{-6}\ M$$

$$[H_3O^+] = 1.4 \times 10^{-3}\ M$$

The pH of the solution is

$$pH = -\log[H_3O^+] = -\log(1.4 \times 10^{-3}) = 2.85$$

17-79 The number of moles in 23.7 g of NH_4ClO_4 is

$$n = (23.7\ g)\left(\frac{1\ mol}{117.49\ g}\right) = 0.202\ mol$$

The molarity of a saturated $NH_4ClO_4(aq)$ solution is

$$molarity = \frac{0.202\ mol}{0.100\ L} = 2.02\ M$$

The reaction is

$$NH_4^+(aq) + H_2O(l) \rightleftharpoons H_3O^+(aq) + NH_3(aq)$$

We have the following:

	$NH_4^+(aq)$	+	$H_2O(l)$	$\rightleftharpoons$	$H_3O^+(aq)$	+	$NH_3(aq)$
initial concentration	2.02 M		—		0		0
equilibrium concentration	2.02 M − $[H_3O^+]$		—		$[H_3O^+]$		$[NH_3] = [H_3O^+]$

The K_a expression is (Table 17-4)

$$K_a = \frac{[H_3O^+][NH_3]}{[NH_4^+]} = \frac{[H_3O^+]^2}{2.02\ M - [H_3O^+]} = 5.6 \times 10^{-10}\ M$$

Neglecting $[H_3O^+]$ relative to 2.02 M, we have

$$\frac{[H_3O^+]^2}{2.02\ M} = 5.6 \times 10^{-10}\ M$$

$$[H_3O^+] = 3.4 \times 10^{-5}\ M$$

The pH of the solution is

$$pH = -\log[H_3O^+] = -\log(3.4 \times 10^{-5}) = 4.47$$

17-81 In aqueous solution Fe^{3+} exists as $Fe(H_2O)_6^{3+}(aq)$.

$Fe(H_2O)_6^{3+}(aq)$	+	$H_2O(l)$	$\rightleftharpoons$	$H_3O^+(aq)$	+	$Fe(OH)(H_2O)_5^{2+}(aq)$
initial concentration	0.10 M		—	0		0
equilibrium concentration	0.10 M $- [H_3O^+]$		—	$[H_3O^+]$		$[Fe(OH)(H_2O)_5^{2+}]$ $= [H_3O^+]$

The K_a expression is

$$K_a = \frac{[H_3O^+][Fe(OH)(H_2O)_5^{2+}]}{[Fe(H_2O)_6^{3+}]} = \frac{[H_3O^+]^2}{0.10\ M - [H_3O^+]} = 1.0 \times 10^{-3}\ M$$

The value of K_a is not small enough to neglect $[H_3O^+]$ in the denominator, and so we must use the quadratic equation

$$[H_3O^+]^2 + 1.0 \times 10^{-3}\ M\ [H_3O^+] - 1.0 \times 10^{-4}\ M^2 = 0$$

The quadratic formula gives

$$[H_3O^+] = \frac{-1.0 \times 10^{-3}\ M \pm \sqrt{1.0 \times 10^{-6}\ M^2 - (4)(1)(-1.0 \times 10^{-4}\ M^2)}}{(2)(1)}$$

$$= \frac{-1.0 \times 10^{-3}\ M \pm 2.0 \times 10^{-2}\ M}{2}$$

$$= 9.5 \times 10^{-3}\ M$$

The pH of the solution is

$$pH = -\log[H_3O^+] = -\log(9.5 \times 10^{-3}) = 2.02$$

17-83 (a) HCl yields $H^+(aq)$ in aqueous solution and thus is an Arrhenius acid. HCl is a proton donor and thus is a Brönsted-Lowry acid. HCl is not electron deficient and thus is not a Lewis acid.

(b) $AlCl_3$ yields $H^+(aq)$ in aqueous solution and thus is an Arrhenius acid. $Al(H_2O)_6^{3+}(aq)$ is a proton donor and thus is a Brönsted-Lowry acid. $AlCl_3$ is an electron-deficient species and is a Lewis acid.

(c) BF_3 is neither an Arrhenius acid nor a Brönsted-Lowry acid. BF_3 can act as an electron-pair acceptor and hence is a Lewis acid.

17-85 (a) CH_3OCH_3 has two lone pairs of electrons and so can act as an electron-pair donor.

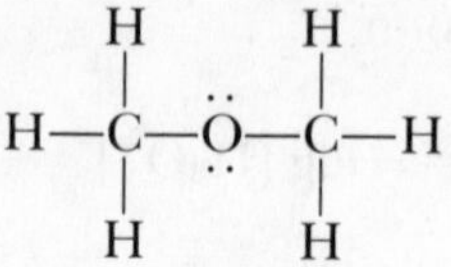

$$H-\underset{\underset{H}{|}}{\overset{\overset{H}{|}}{C}}-\overset{\cdot\cdot}{\underset{\cdot\cdot}{O}}-\underset{\underset{H}{|}}{\overset{\overset{H}{|}}{C}}-H$$

CH_3OCH_3 is a Lewis base.
(b) $GaCl_3$ is an electron-deficient species and thus is a Lewis acid.
(c) H_2O has two lone pairs of electrons and so can act as an electron-pair donor. H_2O is a Lewis base.

E   ANSWERS TO THE EVEN-NUMBERED PROBLEMS

17-2 4.0×10^{-11} M. The solution is acidic.

17-4 $[K^+] = [OH^-] = 0.25$ M; $[H_3O^+] = 4.0 \times 10^{-14}$ M. The solution is basic.

17-6 $[Ca^{2+}] = 5.4 \times 10^{-3}$ M; $[OH^-] = 1.1 \times 10^{-2}$ M; $[H_3O^+] = 9.3 \times 10^{-13}$ M

17-8 pH = 13.00. The solution is basic.

17-10 pH = 11.30. The solution is basic.

17-12 pH = 14.19

17-14 pH = 6.81. A solution of pH = 7.0 is basic at 37°C.

17-16 $[OH^-] = 1 \times 10^{-2}$ M; $NH_3(aq) + H_2O(l) \rightleftharpoons NH_4^+(aq) + OH^-(aq)$

17-18 Ratio = 400. The acidity of normal rain is due to dissolved CO_2.

17-20 $[H_3O^+] - 7.08 \times 10^{-9}$ M; $[OH^-] = 1.41 \times 10^{-6}$ M

17-22 1.66×10^{-4} M or 9.68×10^{-4} g per 100 mL of solution.

17-24 2.2×10^{-4} M

17-26 1.8×10^{-4} M

17-28 55.1

17-30 4.0

17-32 15

17-34 4.18

17-36 1.96

17-38 3.37

17-40 1.03

17-42 5.2×10^{-4} M

17-44 9.56

17-46 11.28

17-48 (a) The equilibrium is shifted toward $NH_4^+(aq)$. The added HCl decreases the concentration of $OH^-(aq)$.
(b) The equilibrium is shifted toward $NH_3(aq)$. The concentration of OH^- has been increased.
(c) The equilibrium is shifted toward $HCHO_2(aq)$. The concentration of $H_3O^+(aq)$ has been increased.
(d) The equilibrium is shifted away from $HCHO_2(aq)$. The added OH^- reacts with the $H_3O^+(aq)$ to produce $H_2O(l)$, thereby decreasing the concentration of $H_3O^+(aq)$.

17-50 (a) The equilibrium is shifted from left to right.
(b) The equilibrium is shifted from right to left.

17-52 (a) The equilibrium is shifted from right to left.
(b) The equilibrium is shifted from right to left.
(c) The equilibrium is shifted from left to right.
(d) The equilibrium is shifted from left to right.

17-54 (a) $NH_3(l) + NH_3(l) \rightleftharpoons NH_4^+(am) + NH_2^-(am)$

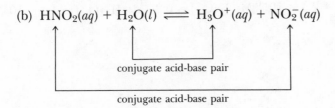

(b) $HNO_2(aq) + H_2O(l) \rightleftharpoons H_3O^+(aq) + NO_2^-(aq)$

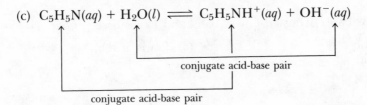

(c) $C_5H_5N(aq) + H_2O(l) \rightleftharpoons C_5H_5NH^+(aq) + OH^-(aq)$

conjugate acid-base pair

conjugate acid-base pair

17-56 (a) $NO_3^-(aq)$ (c) $C_6H_5O^-(aq)$
(b) $CHO_2^-(aq)$ (d) $CH_3NH_2(aq)$

17-58 (a) $HC_2H_2ClO_2$ is an acid; $C_2H_2ClO_2^-$ is its conjugate base.
(b) NH_3 is a base; NH_4^+ is its conjugate acid.
(c) ClO^- is a base; $HClO$ is its conjugate acid.
(d) CHO_2^- is a base; $HCHO_2$ is its conjugate acid.
(e) HN_3 is an acid; N_3^- is its conjugate base.
(f) NO_2^- is a base; HNO_2 is its conjugate acid.

17-60   (a) 6.7×10^{-6} M   (c) 2.2×10^{-4} M
       (b) 4.8×10^{-10} M   (d) 9.1×10^{-8} M

17-62   (a) 3.5×10^{-5} M   (b) 6.7×10^{4} M

17-64   (a) 9.25   (b) 1.92

17-66 $\log (K_a K_b) = \log K_w = \log (1.00 \times 10^{-14}) = -14.00$
      $\log (K_a K_b) = \log K_a + \log K_b = -14.00$
      $-\log K_a - \log K_b = 14.00$
      $\mathrm{p}K_a + \mathrm{p}K_b = 14.00$

17-68   (a) acidic cation, neutral anion; acidic solution
       (b) neutral cation, neutral anion; neutral solution
       (c) neutral cation, acidic anion; acidic solution
       (d) neutral cation, basic anion; basic solution
       (e) acidic cation, basic anion; cannot predict without calculations

17-70   (a) acidic cation, basic anion; cannot predict without calculations
       (b) neutral cation, basic anion; basic solution
       (c) acidic cation, neutral anion; acidic solution
       (d) neutral cation, acidic anion; acidic solution
       (e) neutral cation, neutral anion; neutral solution

17-72   The salts produce acid solutions because $Al^{3+}(aq)$ is an acidic cation.

17-74   9.09

17-76 $[OH^-] = [HNO_2] = 2.4 \times 10^{-6}$ M; $[NO_2^-] = 0.25$ M; $[H_3O^+] = 4.2 \times 10^{-9}$ M;
      pH = 8.38

17-78   11.25

17-80   9.03

17-82   1.3

17-84   (a) Arrhenius base, Brönsted-Lowry base, and Lewis base
       (b) Lewis base
       (c) Arrhenius base, Brönsted-Lowry base, and Lewis base

17-86   (a) Lewis base   (c) Lewis acid
       (b) Lewis acid

F   ANSWERS TO THE SELF-TEST

1 a proton donor

2 a proton acceptor

3 false

4 a hydrated proton and is designated by $H_3O^+(aq)$

5 false (Protons are hydrated in aqueous solution.)

6 false ($[H_3O^+][OH^-] = 1.0 \times 10^{-14}$ M^2 at 25°C.)

7 false ($[OH^-] = 1.0 \times 10^{-7}$ M in a neutral aqueous solution at 25°C.)

8 $[H_3O^+][OH^-]$

9 1.00×10^{-14} M^2

10 basic

11 basic

12 false (HBr is completely dissociated.)

13 $K^+(aq)$, $OH^-(aq)$, and $H_3O^+(aq)$

14 0.032 M

15 $pH \equiv -\log [H_3O^+]$

16 $[H_3O^+]$ or hydronium ion concentration

17 2.0

18 true

19 false

20 7.0

21 less than 7.0 (at 25°C)

22 greater than 7.0 (at 25°C)

23 partially

24 false

25 false

26 proton-transfer

27 $HF(aq) + H_2O(l) \rightleftharpoons$ $H_3O^+(aq) + F^-(aq)$

28 $\dfrac{[H_3O^+][F^-]}{[HF]}$

29 true

30 $HNO_2(aq)$, $H_3O^+(aq)$, $NO_2^-(aq)$, and $OH^-(aq)$

31 true

32 false

33 $NH_3(aq) + H_2O(l) \rightleftharpoons$ $NH_4^+(aq) + OH^-(aq)$

34 $\dfrac{[NH_4^+][OH^-]}{[NH_3]}$

35 $-\log K_a$

36 smaller

37 $-\log K_b$

38 $HNO_2(aq) + H_2O(l) \rightleftharpoons H_3O^+(aq) + NO_2^-(aq)$

conjugate acid-base pair

conjugate acid-base pair

39 acid

40 base

41 $C_2H_3O_2^-(aq) + H_2O(l) \rightleftharpoons$ $HC_2H_3O_2(aq) + OH^-(aq)$

42 $NH_4^+(aq) + H_2O(l) \rightleftharpoons$ $H_3O^+(aq) + NH_3(aq)$

43 $\dfrac{K_w}{K_a}$

44 false

45 basic

46 acidic

47 acidic

48 basic

49 acidic

50 an electron-pair acceptor

51 an electron-pair donor

52 acid

53 base

18 / Titrations, Buffers, and Polyprotic Acids

A weak base can be titrated with a strong acid.

A titration curve of a weak base with a strong acid is shown in Figure 18-7.

The equivalence point does not occur at pH = 7.0 in the titrations of weak acids or weak bases.

18-4 The pH of a buffer solution can be computed using the Henderson-Hasselbalch equation.

A solution that is resistant to changes in pH upon the addition of an acid or a base is called a buffer.

A solution of a conjugate acid and its conjugate base is a buffer.

The pH of a buffer is estimated by the Henderson-Hasselbalch equation:

$$pH \approx pK_a + \log \frac{[\text{base}]_0}{[\text{acid}]_0} \qquad (18\text{-}14)$$

18-5 A buffer solution suppresses pH changes when acid or base is added.

The capacity of a buffer to resist changes in pH is not unlimited.

Buffers resist changes in pH upon dilution with solvent.

The resistance of a buffer to change in pH is shown in Table 18-3.

18-6 Buffers control the pH of blood.

18-7 Polyprotic acids can donate more than one proton.

Phosphoric acid has three distinct acid dissociation constants.

Step 1: $H_3PO_4(aq) + H_2O(l) \rightleftharpoons H_3O^+(aq) + H_2PO_4^-(aq)$

$$K_{a1} = \frac{[H_3O^+][H_2PO_4^-]}{[H_3PO_4]}$$

Step 2: $H_2PO_4^-(aq) + H_2O(l) \rightleftharpoons H_3O^+(aq) + HPO_4^{2-}(aq)$

$$K_{a2} = \frac{[H_3O^+][HPO_4^{2-}]}{[H_2PO_4^-]}$$

Step 3: $HPO_4^{2-}(aq) + H_2O(l) \rightleftharpoons H_3O^+(aq) + PO_4^{3-}(aq)$

$$K_{a3} = \frac{[H_3O^+][PO_4^{3-}]}{[HPO_4^{2-}]}$$

The pK_a values for some polyprotic acids are given in Table 18-4.

Because K_{a1} is much greater than K_{a2}, the second and third dissociations of H_3PO_4 can be neglected in calculations of the pH of a $H_3PO_4(aq)$ solution.

Distribution diagrams give the various species that result from the dissociation of a polyprotic acid as a function of pH.

The distribution diagrams for H_3PO_4, H_2CO_3, and $HC_2H_3O_2$ are given in Figure 18-8.

A titration curve of $H_3PO_4(aq)$ with $KOH(aq)$ is shown in Figure 18-9.

B   SELF-TEST

1   An indicator is a weak organic _____ that changes color with pH.

2   Indicators come in a variety of colors. *True/False*

3   Indicators can be used to estimate the _____ of a solution from the colors of the indicators.

4   The pH at which an indicator changes color is approximately equal to _____ of the indicator.

5   Methyl orange is red in the acid form and yellow in the base form. Methyl orange is _____ in the pH transition region.

6   The color of litmus paper is _____ in basic solution.

7   Explain how you would use litmus paper to test whether a solution is acidic or basic. _____
    _____
    _____ .

8   By referring to Figure 18-2, estimate the pH of a colorless aqueous solution that turns red when o-cresol red is added and yellow when thymol blue is added.
    _____

9   In a titration of a solution of HCl(*aq*) with a solution of NaOH(*aq*), the solution of _____ is added slowly to the solution of _____ .

10 In a titration of a solution of HCl(*aq*) with a solution of KOH(*aq*), the titrant is _____ .

11 The titration curve of a titration of a solution of HCl(*aq*) with a solution of NaOH(*aq*) is a plot of _____ versus _____ .

12 The equivalence point of a titration of a solution of HCl(*aq*) with a solution of NaOH(*aq*) is the point _____
    _____ .

13 The equivalence point of a titration always occurs at pH = 7.0. *True/False*

14 In the titration of a solution of HCl(*aq*) with a solution of NaOH(*aq*), phenol-phthalein is added to the solution of HCl(*aq*) to signal _____ .

15 The end point of a titration is indicated by _____
    _____ .

16 In the titration of a solution of HCl(*aq*) with a solution of NaOH(*aq*), the pH changes very little around the equivalence point. *True/False*

17 In the titration of a solution of acetic acid, $HC_2H_3O_2(aq)$, with a solution of $NaOH(aq)$, the equivalence point occurs at a pH greater than 7.0. *True/False*

18 Explain why the equivalence point of a titration of a solution of $HC_2H_3O_2(aq)$ with a solution of $NaOH(aq)$ does not occur at pH = 7.0. _____

_____

19 Referring to Figure 18-2, determine which indicator(s) you would use in a titration in which the equivalence point occurs at a pH of 10. _____

_____

20 If bromthymol blue were used as an indicator in a titration, then the end point occurs at a pH of _____.

21 The equilibrium constant for the reaction of a weak acid such as acetic acid with a strong base is very large. *True/False*

22 A solution that contains a mixture of a weak acid and its conjugate base can be used as a buffer. *True/False*

23 A buffer is resistant to changes in pH upon the addition of an acid but not upon the addition of a base. *True/False*

24 The pH of a buffer can be estimated using the _____ _____ equation.

25 The Henderson-Hasselbalch equation cannot be used to calculate the pH of a buffer when _____

_____.

26 The pH of a buffer is resistant to change upon addition of solvent. *True/False*

27 A buffer can resist changes in pH regardless of the amount of acid or base added. *True/False*

28 The pH of a buffer solution (*decreases/increases/remains the same*) when the solution is diluted.

29 A polyprotic acid has more than one acid dissociation constant. *True/False*

30 One mole of phosphoric acid, H_3PO_4, requires _____ moles of sodium hydroxide, NaOH, for complete neutralization.

31 Explain why the value of the second acid dissociation constant is less than the value of the first acid dissociation constant.

32 A distribution diagram can be used to find the relative amounts of the species of a polyprotic acid present at a given pH. *True/False*

33 The species arising from the dissociation of the polyprotic acid $H_3PO_4(aq)$ are _____, _____, _____, and _____.

34 A solution of $H_3PO_4(aq)$ contains appreciable amounts of $H_3PO_4(aq)$, $H_2PO_4^-(aq)$, and $HPO_4^{2-}(aq)$ at all values of pH. *True/False*

35 The titration curve of a solution of the diprotic acid, oxalic acid, with a solution of $NaOH(aq)$ has (*one/two/three*) equivalence points.

36 A solution containing $H_2PO_4^-(aq)$ and $HPO_4^-(aq)$ can be used as a buffer. *True/False*

37 The ratio of successive acid dissociation constants of polyprotic acids is often about _____.

38 Upon addition of NaOH to an aqueous solution of NaH_2PO_4, the pH will (*increase/decrease*).

39 A buffer is formed by mixing equal volumes of 1.0 M solutions of $HC_2H_3O_2$ and $NaC_2H_3O_2$. The reaction that occurs when $HCl(aq)$ is added to this mixture is _____.

40 In a buffer formed by mixing $K_3PO_4(aq)$ and $K_2HPO_4(aq)$, the conjugate base is _____.

C CALCULATIONS YOU SHOULD KNOW HOW TO DO

1 Calculate the points on a titration curve of a strong acid with a strong base. See text pages 702 through 705, Table 18-1, and Problems 18-9 through 18-12, 18-17, 18-18, 18-63, and 18-64.

2 Calculate the quantity of strong acid or base that is required to neutralize a given amount of strong base or acid. See Problems 18-13 through 18-16.

3 Calculate a few special points on a titration curve of a weak acid with a strong base. You should be able to calculate the initial pH and the pH at the equivalence point. See Section 18-3 and Problems 18-19 through 18-20.

4 Determine the molecular mass of an unknown acid or base by titrating to the equivalence point. See Problems 18-21 through 18-26.

5 Estimate the pH of a buffer using the Henderson-Hasselbalch equation. See Examples 18-7 and 18-8 and Problems 18-27 through 18-38.

6 Use the Henderson-Hasselbalch equation to calculate the pH of a buffer before and after the addition of small amounts of strong acid or base. See Example 18-9 and Problems 18-39 through 18-46.

7   Use a distribution diagram to determine which species are present in a solution of a polyprotic acid at a given pH. See Problems 18-49 through 18-52.

8   Calculate the quantity of strong base required to neutralize a given quantity of a weak polyprotic acid. See Problems 18-53 and 18-54.

9   Determine the molecular mass of a weak polyprotic acid by titrating to the equivalence point. See Problems 18-55 and 18-56.

10 Calculate the pH of a solution of a weak polyprotic acid. See Problems 18-57 and 18-58.

D   SOLUTIONS TO THE ODD-NUMBERED PROBLEMS

18-1   Using Figure 18-2 we see that phenolphthalein is red when the pH is greater than 10 and that Poirrier's blue is blue-violet when the pH is less than 11. Combining these two facts, we conclude that the pH of solution is between 10 and 11.

18-3   Using Figure 18-2 we see that the pH at which Nile blue is blue is less than 10, the pH at which neutral red is yellow is greater than 8 and the pH at which thymol blue is green is between 8 and 9.5. Therefore, the pH of the solution is between 8 and 9.5. To obtain a better estimate of the pH, we should use an indicator that changes color at a pH around 9 such as tropeolin OOO.

18-5   We see from Figure 18-2 that the middle of the transition color range of bromcresol green is pH = 5. When bromcresol green is added to the medium, a green color indicates that the pH is around 5. When the color changes, the pH is either too high or too low. Methyl red would also be suitable.

18-7   At the middle of the color change the two forms HIn(aq) and In$^-$(aq) are present in equal amounts. At this pH

$$K_{ai} \approx [H_3O^+]$$

In the case of Congo red, the middle of the color change occurs at pH = 4. The concentration of H$_3$O$^+$(aq) is

$$[H_3O^+] = 10^{-pH} = 10^{-4} = 1 \times 10^{-4} \text{ M}$$

$$K_{ai} \approx 1 \times 10^{-4} \text{ M}$$

18-9   The number of moles of H$_3$O$^+$(aq) in 50.0 mL of 0.100 M HCl(aq) is

$$\text{moles of H}_3\text{O}^+(aq) = MV = (0.100 \text{ mol} \cdot \text{L}^{-1})(0.0500 \text{ L})$$
$$= 5.00 \times 10^{-3} \text{ mol}$$

The number of moles of OH$^-$(aq) in 51.0 mL of 0.100 M NaOH(aq) is

$$\text{moles of OH}^-(aq) = MV = (0.100 \text{ mol} \cdot \text{L}^{-1})(0.0510 \text{ L})$$
$$= 5.10 \times 10^{-3} \text{ mol}$$

We see that we have added an excess of $OH^-(aq)$. All the $H_3O^+(aq)$ is consumed in the reaction

$$H_3O^+(aq) + OH^-(aq) \rightleftharpoons 2H_2O(l)$$

The number of moles of $OH^-(aq)$ that remain unreacted after adding the NaOH solution is

$$\text{moles of unreacted } OH^-(aq) = 5.10 \times 10^{-3} \text{ mol} - 5.00 \times 10^{-3} \text{ mol}$$
$$= 0.10 \times 10^{-3} \text{ mol} = 1.0 \times 10^{-4} \text{ mol}$$

The volume of the solution after the addition of NaOH solution is 50.0 mL + 51.0 mL = 101.0 mL. The concentration of $OH^-(aq)$ is

$$[OH^-] = \frac{1.0 \times 10^{-4} \text{ mol}}{0.1010 \text{ L}} = 9.9 \times 10^{-4} \text{ M}$$

The concentration of $[H_3O^+]$ is

$$[H_3O^+] = \frac{K_w}{[OH^-]} = \frac{1.00 \times 10^{-14} \text{ M}}{9.9 \times 10^{-4} \text{ M}} = 1.0 \times 10^{-11} \text{ M}$$

The pH of the solution is

$$pH = -\log [H_3O^+] = -\log (1.0 \times 10^{-11}) = 11.00$$

18-11 The $OH^-(aq)$ concentration in a 0.100 M NaOH(aq) solution is

$$[OH^-] = 0.100 \text{ M}$$

The $H_3O^+(aq)$ concentration in this solution is

$$[H_3O^+] = \frac{K_w}{[OH^-]} = \frac{1.00 \times 10^{-14} \text{ M}^2}{0.100 \text{ M}} = 1.00 \times 10^{-13} \text{ M}$$

and the pH is

$$pH = -\log [H_3O^+] = -\log (1.00 \times 10^{-13}) = 13.00$$

Because NaOH is a strong base and HCl is a strong acid, the pH at the equivalence point (50.0 mL of HCl(aq) added) is 7.0. The pH when 100.0 mL of HCl(aq) is added can be obtained by realizing that once the equivalence point is reached, any additional HCl(aq) remains as $H_3O^+(aq)$. Thus when 100.0 mL of HCl(aq) is added there are

$$\text{mol } H_3O^+(aq) = MV_{\text{excess}}$$
$$= (0.10 \text{ mol} \cdot L^{-1})(0.050 \text{ L})$$
$$= 5.0 \times 10^{-3} \text{ mol}$$

The total volume of the solution is 50.0 mL $+ 100.0$ mL $= 150.0$ mL, and so $[H_3O^+]$ is given by

$$[H_3O^+] = \frac{5.0 \times 10^{-3} \text{ mol}}{0.1500 \text{ L}} = 0.033 \text{ M}$$

The pH is

$$pH = -\log (0.033) = 1.48$$

The titration curve looks like

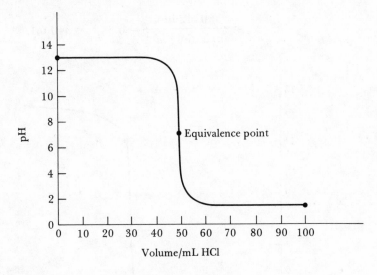

18-13   At the equivalence point we have the condition

$$\text{moles of acid} = \text{moles of base}$$

or

$$M_a V_a = M_b V_b$$

Therefore

$$M_a = \frac{M_b V_b}{V_a} = \frac{(0.150 \text{ M})(32.1 \text{ mL})}{(25.0 \text{ mL})} = 0.193 \text{ M}$$

Note that we can use the units mL because the volume units cancel.

18-15   The number of moles in 1.00 g of $Mg(OH)_2$ is

$$n = (1.00 \text{ g})\left(\frac{1 \text{ mol}}{58.33 \text{ g}}\right) = 0.0171 \text{ mol}$$

At neutralization (the equivalence point)

$$\text{moles of OH}^-(aq) = \text{moles of H}_3\text{O}^+(aq)$$

There are two moles of OH$^-$(aq) per mole of Mg(OH)$_2$(aq), and so we have

$$\text{moles of OH}^-(aq) = \left(\frac{2 \text{ mol OH}^-}{1 \text{ mol Mg(OH)}_2} \right)(0.0171 \text{ mol Mg(OH)}_2)$$

$$= M_a V_a = (0.10 \text{ mol} \cdot \text{L}^{-1})(V_a)$$

Solving for V_a, we get

$$V_a = \frac{0.0342 \text{ mol}}{0.10 \text{ mol} \cdot \text{L}^{-1}} = 0.34 \text{ L} = 340 \text{ mL}$$

18-17

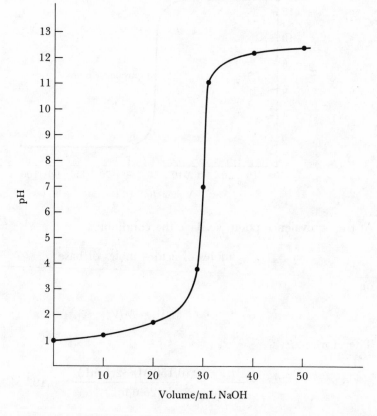

18-19   The volume of NaOH(aq) added to reach the equivalence point is given by

$$V_b = \frac{M_a V_a}{M_b} = \frac{(0.100 \text{ M})(50.0 \text{ mL})}{(0.100 \text{ M})} = 50.0 \text{ mL}$$

The reaction is

$$HC_2H_6AsO_2(aq) + OH^-(aq) \rightleftharpoons C_2H_6AsO_2^-(aq) + H_2O(l)$$

$\qquad$ cacodylic acid $\qquad\qquad\qquad\qquad\qquad$ cacodylate

At the equivalence point

$$\text{moles of } C_2H_6AsO_2^- = \text{initial moles of } HC_2H_6AsO_2$$

$$= MV = (0.100 \text{ M})(0.0500 \text{ L}) = 5.00 \times 10^{-3} \text{ mol}$$

The volume of the solution at the equivalence point is 50.0 mL + 50.0 mL = 100.0 mL. The concentration of cacodylate is

$$[C_2H_6AsO_2^-] = \frac{5.00 \times 10^{-3} \text{ mol}}{0.1000 \text{ L}} = 5.00 \times 10^{-2} \text{ M}$$

The cacodylate ion is a weak base because it is the conjugate base of a weak acid. The reaction of the cacodylate ion with water is

$$C_2H_6AsO_2^-(aq) + H_2O(l) \rightleftharpoons HC_2H_6AsO_2(aq) + OH^-(aq)$$

The value of K_b is

$$K_b = \frac{K_w}{K_a} = \frac{1.00 \times 10^{-14} \text{ M}^2}{5.4 \times 10^{-7} \text{ M}} = 1.85 \times 10^{-8} \text{ M}$$

At equilibrium we have

$$[HC_2H_6AsO_2] = [OH^-]$$

$$[C_2H_6AsO_2^-] = 5.00 \times 10^{-2} \text{ M} - [OH^-]$$

We shall calculate the value of $[OH^-]$ using the expression for K_b. The expression for K_b is

$$K_b = \frac{[HC_2H_6AsO_2][OH^-]}{[C_2H_6AsO_2^-]} = \frac{[OH^-]^2}{5.00 \times 10^{-2} \text{ M} - [OH^-]} = 1.85 \times 10^{-8} \text{ M}$$

Neglecting $[OH^-]$ compared to 5.00×10^{-2} M, we have

$$\frac{[OH^-]^2}{5.00 \times 10^{-2} \text{ M}} = 1.85 \times 10^{-8} \text{ M}$$

$$[OH^-]^2 = 9.25 \times 10^{-10} \text{ M}^2$$

$$[OH^-] = 3.04 \times 10^{-5} \text{ M}$$

The $H_3O^+(aq)$ concentration is

$$[H_3O^+] = \frac{K_w}{[OH^-]} = \frac{1.00 \times 10^{-14} \text{ M}^2}{3.04 \times 10^{-5} \text{ M}} = 3.29 \times 10^{-10} \text{ M}$$

The pH of the solution at the equivalence point is

$$\text{pH} = -\log [H_3O^+] = -\log (3.29 \times 10^{-10}) = 9.48$$

Referring to Figure 18-2, we see that thymolphthalein or phenolphthalein is a suitable indicator.

18-21 At the equivalence point

$$\text{moles of acid} = \text{moles of base added}$$

The number of moles of acid is given by

$$\text{moles of acid} = M_b V_b = (0.250 \text{ mol} \cdot \text{L}^{-1})(0.0341 \text{ L})$$
$$= 0.00853 \text{ mol}$$

We have the correspondence

$$1.50 \text{ g of ascorbic acid} \backsim 0.00853 \text{ mol of ascorbic acid}$$

Dividing by 0.00853, we have

$$176 \text{ g} \backsim \text{one mole}$$

Thus the molecular mass of ascorbic acid, Vitamin C, is 176.

18-23 Both acids have only one dissociable proton per molecule. Thus, at the equivalence point

$$\text{moles of acid} = \text{moles of base} = M_b V_b$$
$$= (1.00 \text{ mol} \cdot \text{L}^{-1})(0.01549 \text{ L}) = 0.01549 \text{ mol}$$

We have the correspondence

$$1.89 \text{ g acid} \backsim 0.01549 \text{ mol acid}$$

Dividing both sides by 0.01549, we have

$$122 \text{ g} \backsim \text{one mole}$$

Thus the molecular mass of the acid is 122. The molecular mass of benzoic acid, $HC_7H_5O_2$, is 122.12; the molecular mass of chlorobenzoic acid, $HC_7H_4ClO_2$, is 156.56. The acid must be benzoic acid.

18-25   At the equivalence point

$$\text{moles of acid} = \text{moles of base}$$

The concentration of acetic acid in the vinegar solution is given by

$$M_a = \frac{M_b V_b}{V_a} = \frac{(0.400 \text{ M})(38.5 \text{ mL})}{(21.0 \text{ mL})} = 0.733 \text{ M}$$

We now calculate the mass percentage of the acetic acid. For convenience, consider a 100-mL sample of vinegar. The number of moles of acetic acid in 100 mL of vinegar is

$$n = MV = (0.733 \text{ mol} \cdot \text{L}^{-1})(0.100 \text{ L}) = 0.0733 \text{ mol}$$

The mass of acetic acid in 100 mL of vinegar is

$$\text{mass} = (0.0733 \text{ mol})\left(\frac{60.05 \text{ g}}{1 \text{ mol}}\right) = 4.40 \text{ g}$$

The mass of 100 mL of vinegar solution is

$$\text{mass} = dV = (1.060 \text{ g} \cdot \text{mL}^{-1})(100 \text{ mL}) = 106.0 \text{ g}$$

The mass percentage of acetic acid is

$$\text{mass \%} = \frac{\text{mass of acetic acid}}{\text{mass of vinegar solution}} \times 100$$

$$= \frac{4.40 \text{ g}}{106.0 \text{ g}} \times 100 = 4.15\%$$

18-27   We first identify the acid and the base:

$$\text{acid:} \quad HC_2H_3O_2 \quad \text{base:} \quad C_2H_3O_2^- \quad \text{(from } NaC_2H_3O_2\text{)}$$

The stoichiometric concentrations of the acid and base forms are

$$[\text{acid}]_0 = 0.050 \text{ M} \qquad [\text{base}]_0 = 0.050 \text{ M}$$

The pK_a of acetic acid is

$$pK_a = -\log K_a = -\log (1.74 \times 10^{-5}) = 4.76$$

From the Henderson-Hasselbalch equation we have

$$pH = pK_a + \log \frac{[\text{base}]_0}{[\text{acid}]_0} = 4.76 + \log \frac{0.050 \text{ M}}{0.050 \text{ M}}$$

$$= 4.76 + 0.00 = 4.76$$

18-29 The stoichiometric concentrations of the acid and base forms are

$$[\text{acid}]_0 = [\text{HCHO}_2]_0 = 0.25 \text{ M}$$

$$[\text{base}]_0 = [\text{CHO}_2^-]_0 = 0.20 \text{ M}$$

The pK_a of formic acid is

$$pK_a = -\log K_a = -\log (1.8 \times 10^{-4}) = 3.74$$

From the Henderson-Hasselbalch equation we have

$$pH = pK_a + \log \frac{[\text{base}]_0}{[\text{acid}]_0} = 3.74 + \log \left(\frac{0.20 \text{ M}}{0.25 \text{ M}} \right)$$

$$= 3.74 - 0.097 = 3.64$$

18-31 The stoichiometric concentrations of conjugate acid and base are

$$[\text{acid}]_0 = [\text{NH}_4^+] = 0.10 \text{ M}$$

$$[\text{base}]_0 = [\text{NH}_3] = 0.20 \text{ M}$$

From the Henderson-Hasselbalch equation we have

$$pH = pK_a + \log \frac{[\text{base}]_0}{[\text{acid}]_0} = 9.24 + \log \left(\frac{0.20 \text{ M}}{0.10 \text{ M}} \right)$$

$$= 9.24 + 0.30 = 9.54$$

18-33 We shall estimate the pH of the solution using the Henderson-Hasselbalch equation

$$pH = pK_a + \log \frac{[\text{base}]_0}{[\text{acid}]_0}$$

The reaction in each case is

$$\text{H}_2\text{PO}_4^-(aq) + \text{H}_2\text{O}(l) \rightleftharpoons \text{H}_3\text{O}^+(aq) + \text{HPO}_4^{2-}(aq)$$

Thus we see that $\text{H}_2\text{PO}_4^-(aq)$ is the conjugate acid and $\text{HPO}_4^{2-}(aq)$ is the conjugate base. The value of pK_a for H_2PO_4^- is

$$pK_a = -\log K_a = -\log (6.2 \times 10^{-8} \text{ M}) = 7.21$$

We can now do each part in turn:

(a) $[\text{acid}]_0 = 0.050 \text{ M}$ $[\text{base}]_0 = 0.050 \text{ M}$

$$pH = 7.21 + \log \left(\frac{0.050 \text{ M}}{0.050 \text{ M}} \right) = 7.21 + 0.00 = 7.21$$

(b) $[acid]_0 = 0.050$ M $[base]_0 = 0.10$ M

$$pH = 7.21 + \log\left(\frac{0.10 \text{ M}}{0.050 \text{ M}}\right) = 7.21 + 0.30 = 7.51$$

(c) $[acid]_0 = 0.10$ M $[base]_0 = 0.050$ M

$$pH = 7.21 + \log\left(\frac{0.050 \text{ M}}{0.10 \text{ M}}\right) = 7.21 - 0.30 = 6.91$$

18-35 We must first calculate the concentrations of KH_2PO_4 and Na_2HPO_4 in the buffer solution:

$$[KH_2PO_4] = \frac{(3.40 \text{ g})\left(\dfrac{1 \text{ mol}}{136.09 \text{ g}}\right)}{1.00 \text{ L}} = 0.0250 \text{ M}$$

$$[Na_2HPO_4] = \frac{(3.55 \text{ g})\left(\dfrac{1 \text{ mol}}{141.96 \text{ g}}\right)}{1.00 \text{ L}} = 0.0250 \text{ M}$$

The stoichiometric concentrations of the acid and base forms are

$$[acid]_0 = [H_2PO_4^-]_0 = 0.0250 \text{ M}$$
$$[base]_0 = [HPO_4^{2-}]_0 = 0.0250 \text{ M}$$

From the Henderson-Hasselbalch equation we have

$$pH = pK_a + \log\frac{[base]_0}{[acid]_0} = 7.21 + \log\left(\frac{0.0250 \text{ M}}{0.0250 \text{ M}}\right)$$

$$= 7.21 + 0.00 = 7.21$$

18-37 One equilibrium that is established in the solution is

$$HC_2H_3O_2(aq) + H_2O(l) \rightleftharpoons H_3O^+(aq) + C_2H_3O_2^-(aq)$$

$$K_a = \frac{[C_2H_3O_2^-][H_3O^+]}{[HC_2H_3O_2]} = 1.74 \times 10^{-5} \text{ M}$$

We can set up a table of initial and equilibrium concentrations.

	$HC_2H_3O_2(aq)$	$+$ $H_2O(l)$ $\rightleftharpoons$	$C_2H_3O_2^-(aq)$	$+$ $H_3O^+(aq)$
initial concentration	0.100 M	—	0.100 M	0
equilibrium concentration	0.100 M $-$ $[H_3O^+]$	—	0.100 M $+$ $[H_3O^+]$	$[H_3O^+]$

Note that $[C_2H_3O_2^-]$ is not equal to $[H_3O^+]$ in this case. The K_a expression is

$$K_a = \frac{(0.100 \text{ M} + [H_3O^+]) [H_3O^+]}{0.100 \text{ M} - [H_3O^+]} = 1.74 \times 10^{-5} \text{ M}$$

If we neglect $[H_3O^+]$ with respect to 0.100 M, then we find that

$$[H_3O^+] = 1.74 \times 10^{-5} \text{ M}$$

The equilibrium concentrations are

$$[HC_2H_3O_2] = 0.100 \text{ M} - 1.74 \times 10^{-5} \text{ M} = 0.100 \text{ M}$$
$$[C_2H_3O_2^-] = 0.100 \text{ M} + 1.74 \times 10^{-5} \text{ M} = 0.100 \text{ M}$$

and so we see that

$$[HC_2H_3O_2] \approx [HC_2H_3O_2]_0$$
$$[C_2H_3O_2^-] \approx [C_2H_3O_2^-]_0$$

These relations arise because $[H_3O^+]$ is negligible compared to either $[HC_2H_3O_2]$ or $[C_2H_3O_2^-]$.

18-39 The number of moles of $H_3O^+(aq)$ in 10.0 mL of 0.10 M HCl(aq) is

$$\text{moles of } H_3O^+ = MV = (0.10 \text{ mol} \cdot \text{L}^{-1})(0.0100 \text{ L}) = 0.0010 \text{ mol}$$

The concentration of $H_3O^+(aq)$ before the addition of the 10.0 mL of HCl(aq) is

$$[H_3O^+] = 10^{-\text{pH}} = 10^{-4.76} = 1.74 \times 10^{-5} \text{ M}$$

The number of moles of $H_3O^+(aq)$ before the addition of HCl(aq) is

$$\text{moles of } H_3O^+ = MV = (1.74 \times 10^{-5} \text{ mol} \cdot \text{L}^{-1})(0.100 \text{ L}) = 1.74 \times 10^{-6} \text{ mol}$$

The final number of moles of $H_3O^+(aq)$ in the solution is

$$1.0 \times 10^{-3} \text{ mol} + 1.74 \times 10^{-6} \text{ mol} = 1.0 \times 10^{-3} \text{ mol}$$

The concentration of $H_3O^+(aq)$ is

$$[H_3O^+] = \frac{1.0 \times 10^{-3} \text{ mol}}{0.110 \text{ L}} = 9.1 \times 10^{-3} \text{ M}$$

The pH of the solution is

$$\text{pH} = -\log [H_3O^+] = -\log (9.1 \times 10^{-3}) = 2.04$$

The change in pH is $4.76 - 2.04 = 2.72$ pH units.

18-41$\quad$If we use equal concentrations of conjugate acid and base, then

$$pH = pK_a + \log \frac{[base]_0}{[acid]_0}$$

$$= pK_a$$

To obtain a pH buffered at 3.29, we want $pK_a = 3.29$, or

$$K_a = 10^{-3.29} = 5.1 \times 10^{-4} \text{ M}$$

From Table 17-4 we find that $K_a = 5.1 \times 10^{-4}$ M for nitrous acid, and so a solution of equal concentrations of $HNO_2(aq)$ and $NaNO_2(aq)$ would act as a buffer at pH = 3.29.

18-43$\quad$The number of moles in 1.00 g of KOH is

$$n = (1.00 \text{ g}) \left(\frac{1 \text{ mol}}{56.11 \text{ g}} \right) = 0.0178 \text{ mol}$$

The $OH^-(aq)$ reacts with $NH_4^+(aq)$ in the buffer via the reaction

$$NH_4^+(aq) + OH^-(aq) \longrightarrow NH_3(aq) + H_2O(l)$$

(a)$\quad$The number of moles of ammonium ion in the buffer solution before adding KOH is

$$\text{moles of } NH_4^+ = MV = (0.10 \text{ mol} \cdot L^{-1})(0.500 \text{ L}) = 0.050 \text{ mol}$$

The number of moles of NH_4^+ after the addition of 0.0178 mol of KOH is

$$\text{moles of } NH_4^+ = \text{moles of } NH_4^+ \text{ before} - \text{moles of } OH^- \text{ added}$$

$$= 0.050 \text{ mol} - 0.0178 \text{ mol} = 0.032 \text{ mol}$$

The number of moles of ammonia in the buffer solution before adding KOH is

$$\text{moles of } NH_3 = MV = (0.10 \text{ M})(0.500 \text{ L}) = 0.050 \text{ mol}$$

The number of moles of NH_3 after the addition of 0.0178 mol of KOH is

$$\text{moles of } NH_3 = \text{moles of } NH_3 \text{ before} + \text{moles of } OH^- \text{ added}$$

$$= 0.050 \text{ mol} + 0.0178 \text{ mol} = 0.068 \text{ mol}$$

The pH of the original buffer is

$$pH = pK_a + \log \frac{[base]_0}{[acid]_0} = 9.24 + \log \left(\frac{0.10 \text{ M}}{0.10 \text{ M}} \right) = 9.24$$

The pH of the final buffer is

$$\text{pH} = \text{p}K_a + \log \frac{[\text{base}]_0}{[\text{acid}]_0} = 9.24 + \log \left(\frac{0.068 \text{ mol}}{0.032 \text{ mol}} \right) = 9.57$$

The change in pH is $9.57 - 9.24 = 0.33$.

(b) The number of moles of ammonium ion in the buffer solution before adding KOH is

$$\text{moles of NH}_4^+ = MV = (1.00 \text{ mol} \cdot \text{L}^{-1})(0.500 \text{ L}) = 0.500 \text{ mol}$$

The number of moles of $\text{NH}_4^+(aq)$ after the addition of 0.0178 mol of KOH is

$$\text{moles of NH}_4^+ = \text{moles of NH}_4^+ \text{ before} - \text{moles of OH}^- \text{ added}$$
$$= 0.500 \text{ mol} - 0.0178 \text{ mol} = 0.482 \text{ mol}$$

The number of moles of ammonia in the buffer solution before adding KOH is

$$\text{moles of NH}_3 = MV = (1.00 \text{ mol} \cdot \text{L}^{-1})(0.500 \text{ L}) = 0.500 \text{ mol}$$

The number of moles of $\text{NH}_3(aq)$ after the addition of 0.0178 mol of KOH is

$$\text{moles of NH}_3 = \text{moles of NH}_3 \text{ before} + \text{moles of KOH added}$$
$$= 0.500 \text{ mol} + 0.0178 \text{ mol} = 0.518 \text{ mol}$$

The pH of the final solution is

$$\text{pH} = \text{p}K_a + \log \frac{[\text{base}]_0}{[\text{acid}]_0} = 9.24 + \log \frac{0.518 \text{ mol}}{0.482 \text{ mol}} = 9.27$$

The change in pH is $9.27 - 9.24 = 0.03$. The pH change in the more concentrated buffer solution is much less than the pH change in the more dilute buffer solution.

18-45 The number of moles of $\text{OH}^-(aq)$ added is

$$\text{moles of OH}^- = MV = (0.200 \text{ mol} \cdot \text{L}^{-1})(0.0200 \text{ L}) = 4.00 \times 10^{-3} \text{ mol}$$

The $\text{OH}^-(aq)$ reacts with $\text{HC}_2\text{H}_3\text{O}_2(aq)$ in the buffer solution according to

$$\text{HC}_2\text{H}_3\text{O}_2(aq) + \text{OH}^-(aq) \rightleftharpoons \text{C}_2\text{H}_3\text{O}_2^-(aq) + \text{H}_2\text{O}(l)$$

The number of moles of $\text{HC}_2\text{H}_3\text{O}_2(aq)$ in the buffer solution before the addition of $\text{NaOH}(aq)$ is

$$\text{moles of HC}_2\text{H}_3\text{O}_2 = MV = (0.150 \text{ mol} \cdot \text{L}^{-1})(0.0500 \text{ L})$$
$$= 7.50 \times 10^{-3} \text{ mol}$$

The number of moles of $HC_2H_3O_2(aq)$ in the buffer solution after the addition of $NaOH(aq)$ is

$$\text{moles of } HC_2H_3O_2 = \text{moles of } HC_2H_3O_2 \text{ before } - \text{ moles of } OH^- \text{ added}$$
$$= 7.50 \times 10^{-3} \text{ mol} - 4.00 \times 10^{-3} \text{ mol}$$
$$= 3.50 \times 10^{-3} \text{ mol}$$

The concentration of $HC_2H_3O_2(aq)$ after the addition of $NaOH(aq)$ is

$$[HC_2H_3O_2] = \frac{3.50 \times 10^{-3} \text{ mol}}{0.0700 \text{ L}} = 5.0 \times 10^{-2} \text{ M}$$

The number of moles of $C_2H_3O_2^-(aq)$ in the buffer solution before the addition of $NaOH(aq)$ is

$$\text{moles of } C_2H_3O_2^- = MV = (0.150 \text{ mol} \cdot L^{-1})(0.0500 \text{ L})$$
$$= 7.50 \times 10^{-3} \text{ mol}$$

The number of moles of $C_2H_3O_2^-(aq)$ in the buffer solution after the addition of $NaOH(aq)$ is

$$\text{moles of } C_2H_3O_2^- = \text{moles of } C_2H_3O_2^- \text{ before } + \text{ moles of } OH^- \text{ added}$$
$$= 7.50 \times 10^{-3} \text{ mol} + 4.00 \times 10^{-3} \text{ mol}$$
$$= 11.50 \times 10^{-3} \text{ mol}$$

The concentration of $C_2H_3O_2^-(aq)$ after the addition of $NaOH(aq)$ is

$$[C_2H_3O_2^-] = \frac{11.50 \times 10^{-3} \text{ mol}}{0.0700 \text{ L}} = 1.64 \times 10^{-1} \text{ M}$$

Calculating the new pH using the Henderson-Hasselbalch equation, we have

$$pH = pK_a + \log \frac{[\text{base}]_0}{[\text{acid}]_0} = 4.76 + \log \left(\frac{0.164 \text{ M}}{0.050 \text{ M}} \right) = 5.28$$

In order to justify the use of the Henderson-Hasselbalch equation, we shall now calculate the pH of the solution using the K_a expression. Set up a table of initial and equilibrium concentrations.

	$HC_2H_3O_2(aq)$	$+ H_2O(l) \rightleftharpoons$	$C_2H_3O_2^-(aq)$	$+ H_3O^+(aq)$
initial concentration	$\dfrac{0.00350 \text{ mol}}{0.0700 \text{ L}} =$	—	$\dfrac{0.0115 \text{ mol}}{0.0700 \text{ L}} =$	≈ 0
	0.0500 M		0.164 M	
equilibrium concentration	$0.0500 \text{ M} - [H_3O^+]$	—	$0.164 \text{ M} + [H_3O^+]$	$[H_3O^+]$

$$K_a = \frac{[C_2H_3O_2^-][H_3O^+]}{[HC_2H_3O_2]} = \frac{(0.164 \text{ M} + [H_3O^+])[H_3O^+]}{0.0500 \text{ M} - [H_3O^+]}$$

$$= 10^{-4.76} = 1.74 \times 10^{-5} \text{ M}$$

Neglecting $[H_3O^+]$ compared to 0.0500 M and 0.164 M, we have

$$\frac{(0.164 \text{ M})[H_3O^+]}{0.0500 \text{ M}} = 1.74 \times 10^{-5} \text{ M}$$

$$[H_3O^+] = 5.30 \times 10^{-6} \text{ M}$$

$$\text{pH} = -\log [H_3O^+] = -\log (5.30 \times 10^{-6}) = 5.28$$

The pH calculated using the Henderson-Hasselbalch equation agrees with the pH calculated using the K_a expression.

18-47 (a) The two reactions corresponding to K_{a1} and K_{a2} are

$$H_2CO_3(aq) + H_2O(l) \rightleftharpoons H_3O^+(aq) + HCO_3^-(aq) \qquad K_{a1}$$

$$HCO_3^-(aq) + H_2O(l) \rightleftharpoons H_3O^+(aq) + CO_3^{2-}(aq) \qquad K_{a2}$$

Add these two equations to get

$$H_2CO_3(aq) + 2H_2O(l) \rightleftharpoons 2H_3O^+(aq) + CO_3^{2-}(aq) \qquad K = K_{a1}K_{a2}$$

and

$$K = \frac{[H_3O^+]^2[CO_3^{2-}]}{[H_2CO_3]} = K_{a1}K_{a2}$$

But according to the stoichiometry of the reaction

$$2HCO_3^-(aq) \rightleftharpoons CO_3^{2-}(aq) + H_2CO_3(aq)$$

We have $[CO_3^{2-}] = [H_2CO_3]$, and so

$$\frac{[H_3O^+]^2[\cancel{CO_3^{2-}}]}{[\cancel{H_2CO_3}]} = K_{a1}K_{a2}$$

$$[H_3O^+]^2 = K_{a1}K_{a2}$$

$$[H_3O^+] = (K_{a1}K_{a2})^{1/2}$$

(b) A $NaHCO_3(aq)$ solution acts as a buffer through the reactions

$NaHCO_3$ acting as a base:

$$HCO_3^-(aq) + H_3O^+(aq) \rightleftharpoons H_2CO_3(aq) + H_2O(l)$$

$NaHCO_3$ acting as an acid:

$$HCO_3^-(aq) + OH^-(aq) \rightleftharpoons CO_3^{2-}(aq) + H_2O(l)$$

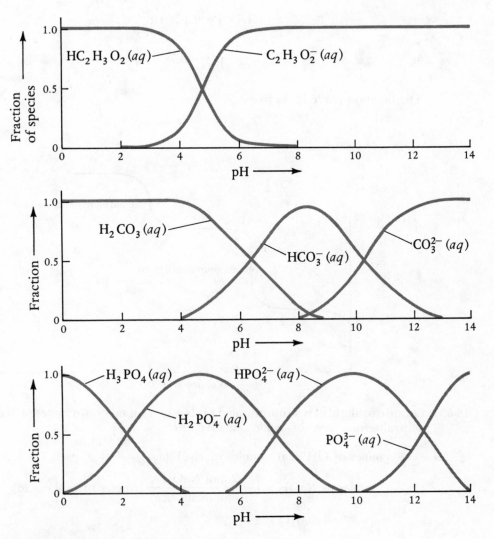

18-49 Referring to Figure 18-8 (above), we see that
(a) $H_3PO_4(aq)$ and $H_2PO_4^-(aq)$
(b) $H_2PO_4^-(aq)$
(c) $H_2PO_4^-(aq)$ and $HPO_4^{2-}(aq)$
(d) $HPO_4^{2-}(aq)$

18-51 We see from Figure 18-8 (above) that the pH at which H_2CO_3 is completely reacted to HCO_3^- is slightly greater than 8. The first equivalence point is at a pH that is slightly greater than 8. We see from Figure 18-8 that the pH at which HCO_3^- is completely reacted to CO_3^{2-} is 13. Thus, the second equivalence point is at a pH of 13. The pH of a 0.10 M $H_2CO_3(aq)$ solution is given by

$$K_{a1} = \frac{[HCO_3^-][H_3O^+]}{[H_2CO_3]} = \frac{[H_3O^+]^2}{0.10 \text{ M}} = 4.5 \times 10^{-7} \text{ M}$$

or $[H_3O^+] = 2.1 \times 10^{-4}$ M

or   pH = 3.7

The titration curve looks like

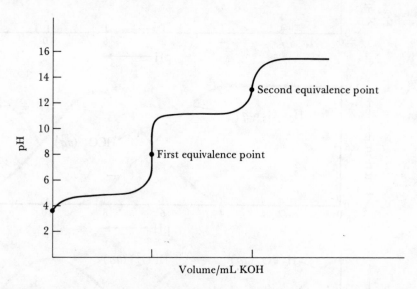

Volume/mL KOH

18-53 Because oxalic acid is a diprotic acid (Table 18-4), it takes two moles of NaOH to neutralize one mole of oxalic acid. We have

$$\text{moles of OH}^-(aq) = \text{moles of H}_3O^+(aq)$$

$$\text{moles of NaOH} = \left(\frac{2 \text{ mol NaOH}}{1 \text{ mol oxalic acid}}\right)(\text{moles of oxalic acid})$$

$$M_b V_b = 2 M_a V_a$$

$$V_b = \frac{2 M_a V_a}{M_b} = \frac{(2)(0.10 \text{ M})(25.0 \text{ mL})}{(0.10 \text{ M})} = 50.0 \text{ mL}$$

18-55 The number of moles of NaOH(aq) used to neutralize the oxalic acid is

$$\text{moles of NaOH} = MV = (0.250 \text{ mol} \cdot \text{L}^{-1})(0.0444 \text{ L}) = 0.0111 \text{ mol}$$

Because oxalic is a diprotic acid, it takes two moles of NaOH to neutralize one mole of oxalic acid. Thus the number of moles of oxalic acid is

moles of oxalic acid

$$= \left(\frac{1 \text{ mol oxalic acid}}{2 \text{ mol NaOH}}\right)(\text{moles of NaOH}) = 5.55 \times 10^{-3} \text{ mol}$$

Thus we have the correspondence

$$0.500 \text{ g oxalic acid} \backsimeq 0.00555 \text{ mol oxalic acid}$$

Dividing both sides by 0.00555, we have

$$90.1 \text{ g oxalic acid} \backsimeq \text{one mole oxalic acid}$$

The molecular mass of oxalic acid is 90.1.

18-57 The reaction is

$$H_3AsO_4(aq) + H_2O(l) \rightleftharpoons H_3O^+(aq) + H_2AsO_4^-(aq)$$

The value of K_{a1} is

$$K_{a1} = 10^{-pK_{a1}} = 10^{-2.22} = 6.03 \times 10^{-3} \text{ M}$$

The K_{a1} expression is

$$K_{a1} = \frac{[H_3O^+][H_2AsO_4^-]}{[H_3AsO_4]} = \frac{[H_3O^+]^2}{0.100 \text{ M} - [H_3O^+]} = 6.03 \times 10^{-3} \text{ M}$$

or

$$[H_3O^+]^2 + 6.03 \times 10^{-3} \text{ M}[H_3O^+] - 6.03 \times 10^{-4} \text{ M}^2 = 0$$

The quadratic formula gives

$$[H_3O^+] = \frac{-6.03 \times 10^{-3} \text{ M} \pm \sqrt{3.64 \times 10^{-5} \text{ M}^2 - (4)(1)(-6.03 \times 10^{-4} \text{ M}^2)}}{(2)(1)}$$

$$= \frac{-6.03 \times 10^{-3} \text{ M} \pm 4.95 \times 10^{-2} \text{ M}}{2}$$

$$= 2.17 \times 10^{-2} \text{ M}$$

The pH of the solution is

$$pH = -\log[H_3O^+] = -\log(2.17 \times 10^{-2}) = 1.66$$

18-59 For the reaction

$$NH_4^+(aq) + H_2O(l) \rightleftharpoons H_3O^+(aq) + NH_3(aq)$$

$$K_a = \frac{[H_3O^+][NH_3]}{[NH_4^+]} = 10^{-9.24} = 5.75 \times 10^{-10} \text{ M}$$

The pH at which the fraction of NH_4^+ is 0.50 or

$$[NH_3] = [NH_4^+]$$

is given by

$$K_a = \frac{[H_3O^+][NH_3]}{[NH_4^+]} = [H_3O^+] = 5.75 \times 10^{-10} \text{ M}$$

$$\text{pH} = -\log [H_3O^+] = -\log (5.75 \times 10^{-10}) = 9.24$$

The pH at which the fraction of NH_4^+ is 0.90 is obtained from

$$\frac{[NH_4^+]}{[NH_4^+] + [NH_3]} = 0.90$$

or

$$[NH_3] = \tfrac{1}{9}[NH_4^+]$$

Thus we write

$$K_a = \frac{[H_3O^+][NH_3]}{[NH_4^+]} = \frac{\tfrac{1}{9}[H_3O^+][NH_4^+]}{[NH_4^+]} = \tfrac{1}{9}[H_3O^+] = 5.75 \times 10^{-10} \text{ M}$$

or

$$[H_3O^+] = 5.18 \times 10^{-9} \text{ M}$$

from which

$$\text{pH} = 8.29$$

The pH at which the fraction of NH_4^+ is 0.10 is obtained using

$$\frac{[NH_4^+]}{[NH_4^+] + [NH_3]} = 0.10$$

or

$$[NH_3] = 9[NH_4^+]$$

Thus we have

$$K_a = \frac{[H_3O^+][NH_3]}{[NH_4^+]} = \frac{9[H_3O^+][NH_4^+]}{[NH_4^+]} = 9[H_3O^+] = 5.75 \times 10^{-10} \text{ M}$$

or

$$[H_3O^+] = 6.39 \times 10^{-11} \text{ M}$$

from which

$$pH = 10.20$$

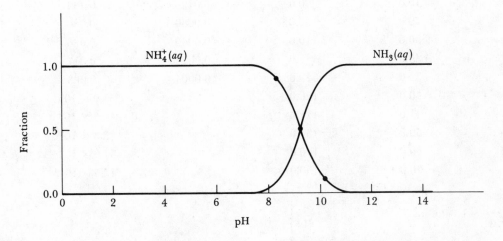

18-61 $3HCO_3^-(aq) + H_3C_6H_5O_7(aq) \rightleftharpoons 3H_2CO_3(aq) + C_6H_5O_7^{3-}(aq)$
$$\downharpoonleft\upharpoonright$$
$$CO_2(aq) + H_2O(l)$$
$$\downharpoonleft\upharpoonright$$
$$CO_2(g)$$

or

$$3HCO_3^-(aq) + H_3C_6H_5O_7(aq) \rightleftharpoons 3CO_2(g) + C_6H_5O_7^{3-}(aq) + 3H_2O(l)$$

18-63   The number of moles of $OH^-(aq)$ at the start of the titration is

moles of $OH^- = MV = (0.200 \; mol \cdot L^{-1})(0.0800 \; L) = 0.0160 \; mol$

Until the KOH is neutralized, the number of moles of $OH^-(aq)$ is given by

moles of OH^- = moles of OH^- at start $-$ moles of HCl added

After neutralization of KOH, the number of moles of $H_3O^+(aq)$ is given by

moles of H_3O^+ = moles of HCl added $-$ moles of OH^- at start

The concentration of OH^- is

$$[OH^-] = \frac{K_w}{[H_3O^+]} = \frac{1.00 \times 10^{-14} \; M^2}{[H_3O^+]}$$

Volume of HCl solution added/mL	Total volume of resulting solution/mL	Moles of $OH^-(aq)$ in solution/mol	$[OH^-]/M$	pH
10.0	90.0	0.0120	0.133	13.12
20.0	100.0	0.0080	0.080	12.90
30.0	110.0	0.0040	0.036	12.56
35.0	115.0	0.0020	0.017	12.23
39.0	119.0	0.0004	0.003	11.48
40.0	120.0		1.0×10^{-7}	7.00
41.0	121.0		3×10^{-12}	2.48
50.0	130.0		3.3×10^{-13}	1.52
60.0	140.0		1.8×10^{-13}	1.26
70.0	150.0		1.25×10^{-13}	1.10

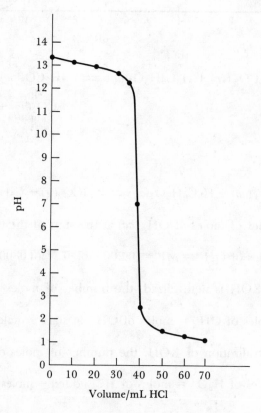

E   ANSWERS TO THE EVEN-NUMBERED PROBLEMS

18-2   4.5 to 5

18-4   3 to 4.5; bromcresol green

18-6   neutral red

18-8 3.2×10^{-11} M

18-10   12.63

18-12

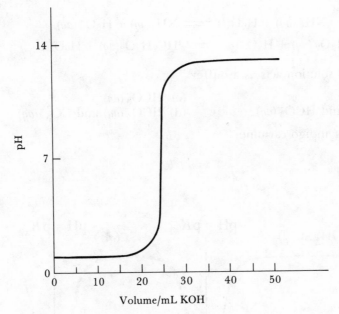

18-14   0.289 M

18-16   190 mL

18-18   10.40

18-20   8.02; thymol blue or phenolphthalein

18-22   122

18-24   88.1

18-26   180

18-28   5.06

18-30   3.57

18-32   8.94

18-34   5.07

18-36   7.49

18-38   (a) yes   (b) no   (c) no   (d) yes

18-40   7.20 pH units

18-42   equal concentrations of pyridinium ion and pyridine

18-44   0.04 pH units in both cases

18-46   Measure the pH of the original solution. Dilute the solution and measure the pH of the diluted solution. The pH of a buffer would not be affected by dilution.

18-48   The two reactions are

$$NH_4^+(aq) + H_2O(l) \rightleftharpoons NH_3(aq) + H_3O^+(aq)$$
$$C_2H_3O_2^-(aq) + H_3O^+(aq) \rightleftharpoons HC_2H_3O_2(aq) + H_2O(l)$$

$NH_4C_2H_3O_2(aq)$ solution acts as a buffer.

18-50   (a) $H_2CO_3(aq)$ (c) $HCO_3^-(aq)$
             (b) $H_2CO_3(aq)$ and $HCO_3^-(aq)$ (d) $HCO_3^-(aq)$ and $CO_3^{2-}(aq)$

18-52   Poirrier's blue or indigo carmine

18-54   200 mL

18-56   116

18-58   3.39

18-60

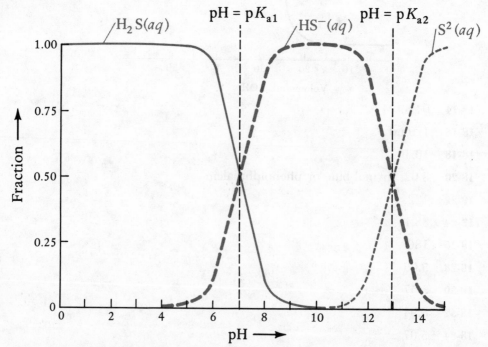

18-62   2.62 g

18-64

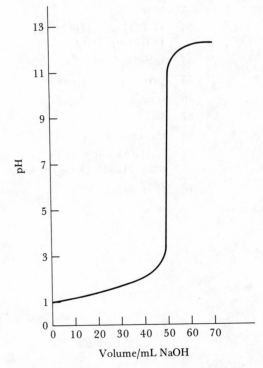

F   ANSWERS TO THE SELF-TEST
───

1   acid

2   true

3   pH

4   pK_a

5   orange

6   blue

7   Litmus is red in acidic solutions and blue in basic solutions.

8   between 7 and 8

9   NaOH(aq); HCl(aq)

10 KOH(aq)

11 pH versus the volume of NaOH(aq) added

12 at which the number of moles of NaOH(aq) that has been added is exactly equal to the number of moles of HCl(aq) initially present

13 false

14 the end-point of the titration

15 a change in color of the indicator

16 false

17 true

18 The salt present at the equivalence point, sodium acetate ($NaC_2H_3O_2$), is a basic salt.

19 Nile blue, alizarin yellow, or thymolphthalein

20 6 to 7

21 true

22 true

23 false

24 Henderson-Hasselbalch

25 when the stoichiometric concentrations of buffer components are not equal to their actual concentrations, as when a large quantity of acid or base is added

26 true

27 false (See Question 25.)

28 remains the same

29 true

30 three

31 It requires more energy to remove a proton from an anion because of the electrical attraction between the two.

32 true

33 $H_2PO_4^-(aq)$, $HPO_4^{2-}(aq)$, $PO_4^{3-}(aq)$, $H_3O^+(aq)$

34 false

35 two

36 true

37 10^{-5}

38 increase

39 $C_2H_3O_2^-(aq) + H_3O^+(aq) \rightleftharpoons HC_2H_3O_2(aq) + H_2O(l)$

40 $PO_4^{3-}(aq)$

19 / Solubility and Precipitation Reactions

19-3   The solubility of an ionic solid is decreased when a common ion is present in the solution.

The solubility of an ionic solid is decreased when a common ion is present in the solution.

At equilibrium the K_{sp} expression for an ionic solid must always hold if the solid phase is in contact with the solution.

The decrease in salt solubility arising from the presence of a common ion in the solution is understood readily in terms of Le Châtelier's principle.

The solubility of an ionic solid is increased by a chemical species that acts to decrease the concentration of a constituent ion of the salt, for example, through the formation of a complex ion.

19-4   The magnitude of the ratio Q_{sp}/K_{sp} is used to predict whether an ionic solid will precipitate.

The Q_{sp} expression has the same algebraic form as the K_{sp} expression, but the concentration values used in the Q_{sp} expression need not be equilibrium values.

If $Q_{sp}/K_{sp} > 1$, then precipitation will occur.

If $Q_{sp}/K_{sp} < 1$, then precipitation cannot occur.

If $Q_{sp} = K_{sp}$, then the ionic solid is in equilibrium with the solution.

19-5   Salts of weak acids are more soluble in acidic solutions than in neutral or basic solutions.

The increase in solubility of a salt of a weak acid with increased $[H_3O^+]$ is a consequence of the formation of the conjugate acid of the anion of the salt (Figure 19-3).

19-6   Some metal cations can be separated from a mixture by the formation of an insoluble hydroxide of one of them.

The solubility of a metal hydroxide depends on both the K_{sp} value and on the pH of the solution (Figure 19-4).

19-7   Insoluble sulfides are separated by adjustment of solution pH.

Because $S^{2-}(aq)$ is a conjugate base of a weak acid, HS^-, the solubility of a metal sulfide is greater the greater the value of $[H_3O^+]$.

The solubility of a saturated solution of $H_2S(aq)$ is 0.10 M at 25°C.

The value of $[S^{2-}]$ in a solution is controlled by controlling the pH of the solution with suitable buffers (Figure 19-5).

The value of $[S^{2-}]$ when $[H_2S] = 0.10$ M is given by

$$[S^{2-}] = \frac{1.1 \times 10^{-21} \text{ M}^3}{[H_3O^+]^2} \tag{19-18}$$

19-8   Amphoteric hydroxides dissolve in both highly acidic and highly basic solutions.

Amphoteric hydroxides dissolve in highly basic solutions by the formation of soluble hydroxy complexes; for example,

$$Al(OH)_3(s) + OH^-(aq) \rightleftharpoons Al(OH)_4^-(aq)$$

The values of the equilibrium constants for some amphoteric hydroxides are given in Table 19-4.

19-9 Qualitative analysis is the determination of the species present in a sample.

The sample to be analyzed is called the unknown.

19-10 Precipitation reactions are used to separate mixtures of ions.

A reagent is added that precipitates certain cations but not others.

A mixture of KNO_3 and $AgNO_3$ is analyzed by adding

(a) $HCl(aq)$ to precipitate $Ag^+(aq)$ as $AgCl(s)$
(b) $Na_3Co(NO_2)_6(aq)$ to precipitate $K^+(aq)$ as $K_3Co(NO_2)_6(s)$ after the removal of $Ag^+(aq)$

19-11 Many qualitative analysis schemes involve the separation of cations as insoluble sulfides.

Many cations are precipitated as insoluble sulfides by adding H_2S to the solution (Table 19-5).

Selective precipitation of the metal sulfides is achieved by adjusting the pH of the solution.

The different colors of the metal sulfides can be used to identify the cations. (Figure 19-13)

19-12 Amphoteric metal hydroxides are separated by dissolution in strong base.

Separations of certain cations are achieved by the formation of insoluble hydroxides at controlled pH values (Table 19-5).

19-13 Qualitative analysis schemes involve sequential separation of small groups of cations.

An essential feature of a qualitative analysis scheme is the successive removal of subgroups of ions by precipitation reactions.

An outline of a simplified qualitative analysis scheme is given in Figure 19-15.

B   SELF-TEST

1   All Na^+, K^+, and NH_4^+ salts are (*soluble/insoluble*) in water.

2   The salt $AgClO_4(s)$ is (*soluble/insoluble*) in water.

3   The salt $Hg_2(NO_3)_2(s)$ is (*soluble/insoluble*) in water.

4   The salt $Pb(NO_3)_2(s)$ is (*soluble/insoluble*) in water.

5   The salt $CaSO_4(s)$ is (*soluble/insoluble*) in water.

6   The salt $PbF_2(s)$ is (*soluble/insoluble*) in water.

7   The salt $FeSO_4$ is (*soluble/insoluble*) in water.

8   Complete and balance

$$(NH_4)_2CO_3(aq) + CaCl_2(aq) \longrightarrow$$

9 Complete and balance

$$Na_2S(aq) + Zn(NO_3)_2(aq) \longrightarrow$$

10 The solubility product constant expression for calcium carbonate, $CaCO_3$, is $K_{sp} =$ _____.

11 The solubility product constant expression for magnesium hydroxide, $Mg(OH)_2$, is $K_{sp} =$ _____.

12 The value of K_{sp} determines the solubility of an ionic solid in pure water. *True/False*

13 The solubility of $PbCl_2(s)$ in water is equal to the concentration of $Pb^{2+}(aq)$. *True/False*

14 The solubility of $Fe(OH)_2(s)$ in water is equal to the concentration of $OH^-(aq)$. *True/False*

15 The solubility of $CaSO_4(s)$ is greater in a 0.10 M $Na_2SO_4(aq)$ solution than in water. *True/False*

16 The solubility product constant for $AgCl(s)$ is not $K_{sp} = [Ag^+][Cl^-]$ when $AgCl(s)$ is in equilibrium with a 0.25 M $NaCl(aq)$ solution. *True/False*

17 The common-ion effect is _____
_____.

18 The solubility of $AgCl(s)$ is (*increased/decreased*) by the addition of NaCl to the solution.

19 The solubility of $AgCl(s)$ is (*increased/decreased*) by the addition of $NH_3(aq)$ to the solution.

20 If the value of the ratio Q_{sp}/K_{sp} for $Cu(OH)_2(s)$ is 10 when a solution of $NaOH(aq)$ is mixed with a solution of $Cu(NO_3)_2(aq)$, then a precipitate of _____ (*will/will not*) form.

21 The value of the ratio Q_{sp}/K_{sp} for $Ag_2SO_4(s)$ is 0.032 when a solution of $AgNO_3(aq)$ is added to a solution of $K_2SO_4(aq)$. A precipitate of _____ (*will/will not*) form.

22 The increased solubility of $AgCl(s)$ in $NH_3(aq)$ relative to the solubility of $AgCl(s)$ in water is a result of the reaction _____
_____.

23 Addition of $HNO_3(aq)$ to an aqueous solution of $Ag(NH_3)_2Cl(aq)$ results in the formation of a precipitate of _____.

24 Salts of weak acids are more soluble the higher the pH of the solution. *True/False*

25 The salt $BaCO_3(s)$ is (*more/less*) soluble when the pH of the solution is 2.0 than when the pH of the solution is 7.0.

26 Using a chemical equation, explain why the solubility of silver benzoate, $AgC_7H_5O_2$, increases as the pH of the solution decreases. _____

_____ .

27 Water-insoluble metal carbonates, such as $CaCO_3(s)$, dissolve in $HCl(aq)$ with evolution of the gas _____ .

28 The solubility of a metal sulfide depends on the pH of the solution. *True/False*

29 The net reaction for $FeS(s)$ dissolving in a buffered solution with pH = 2 is

_____ .

30 For the reaction

$$2H_2O(l) + H_2S(aq) \rightleftharpoons 2H_3O^+(aq) + S^{2-}(aq)$$

$K = 1.1 \times 10^{-20}$ M^2 at 25°C. The value of $[S^{2-}]$ in a buffered solution with $[H_3O^+] = 0.010$ M and $[H_2S] = 0.10$ M is 1.1×10^{-17} M. *True/False*

31 For $ZnS(s)$, $K_{sp} = 1.6 \times 10^{-24}$ M^2. If a solution with $[Zn^{2+}] = 0.01$ M is buffered and treated with H_2S such that $[S^{2-}] = 1.1 \times 10^{-17}$ M, then $ZnS(s)$ will precipitate. *True/False*

32 For $PbS(s)$, $K_{sp} = 8.0 \times 10^{-28}$ M^2 and for $ZnS(s)$, $K_{sp} = 1.6 \times 10^{-24}$ M^2; $ZnS(s)$ is more soluble than $PbS(s)$ in an acidic solution. *True/False*

33 The solubility of a metal hydroxide depends on the pH of the solution. *True/False*

34 Amphoteric hydroxides are more soluble in both acidic and basic solutions than in water. *True/False*

35 Aluminum hydroxide, $Al(OH)_3$, is insoluble at any pH. *True/False*

36 The equation for the solubility reaction for $Al(OH)_3(s)$ in water is _____

_____ .

37 The equation for the reaction for $Al(OH)_3(s)$ dissolving in a highly acidic aqueous solution is_____ .

38 The equation for the reaction for $Al(OH)_3(s)$ dissolving in a highly basic solution is _____ .

39 Zinc hydroxide, $Zn(OH)_2$, is soluble when the pH of the solution is 14.0 because of the reaction

_____ .

40 For the reactions

$$AgCl(s) \rightleftharpoons Ag^+(aq) + Cl^-(aq) \qquad K = K_{sp,AgCl}$$
$$AgBr(s) \rightleftharpoons Ag^+(aq) + Br^-(aq) \qquad K = K_{sp,AgBr}$$

The equilibrium constant for the reaction

$$AgCl(s) + Br^-(aq) \rightleftharpoons AgBr(s) + Cl^-(aq)$$

is

$$K = \frac{K_{sp,AgCl}}{K_{sp,AgBr}}$$

True/False

41 Qualitative analysis is the determination of the _____ _____ in a sample.

42 In a solution of $AgNO_3(aq)$ and $KNO_3(aq)$, $Ag^+(aq)$ can be separated from $K^+(aq)$ by adding $HCl(aq)$ to precipitate _____ as _____.

43 In a solution containing both $Ag^+(aq)$ and $K^+(aq)$, $Ag^+(aq)$ must be removed before testing for the presence of $K^+(aq)$ with $Na_3Co(NO_2)_6(aq)$. *True/False*

44 Many metal cations form insoluble metal sulfides. *True/False*

45 All metal sulfides are black. *True/False*

46 The metal sulfides, FeS and SnS, may be separated by adjusting the _____ of the solution.

47 All metal sulfides are insoluble when $[H_3O^+] = 0.3$ M. *True/False*

48 The insoluble hydroxide, $Al(OH)_3$, can be made soluble by adjusting the _____ of the solution.

49 The steps in a qualitative analysis scheme may be carried out in any order. *True/False*

50 A qualitative analysis scheme often utilizes the differences in solubilities at various pH values. *True/False*

51 Mercury(II) can be separated from copper(II) by adding $HCl(aq)$ to a solution containing both cations. *True/False*

52 Zinc(II) can be separated from iron(II) in a solution containing both cations by adding excess $NaOH(aq)$. The precipitate will be _____ and the solution will contain _____.

C   CALCULATIONS YOU SHOULD KNOW HOW TO DO

1 Calculate the value of K_{sp} for a salt given the solubility of the salt. See Problems 19-13, 19-14, 19-17, and 19-18.

2 Calculate the solubility of a salt given the value of K_{sp} of the salt. See Examples

19-3, 19-4, and 19-5 and Problems 19-11, 19-12, 19-15, 19-16, and 19-19 through 19-28.

3 Use Q_{sp}/K_{sp} to determine whether precipitation of an ionic solid will occur. See Example 19-6 and Problems 19-31 through 19-36.

4 Calculate the solubility of certain salts at a given pH of the solution. See Example 19-7 and Problems 19-41 through 19-44 and 19-47 through 19-50.

5 Calculate the solubilities of metal sulfides at a given pH of the solution. See Problems 19-51 through 19-56.

6 Calculate the solubility of amphoteric hydroxides at a given pH of the solution. See Example 19-8 and Problems 19-57 through 19-64.

D SOLUTIONS TO THE ODD-NUMBERED PROBLEMS

19-1 $AgBr$ Insoluble—rule 3: All Ag^+ salts are insoluble.
$PbSO_4$ Insoluble—rule 3: All Pb^{2+} salts are insoluble.
NH_4Cl Soluble—rule 1: All NH_4^+ salts are soluble.
KNO_3 Soluble—rule 1: All K^+ salts are soluble.
$BaSO_4$ Insoluble—rule 6: $BaSO_4$ is insoluble.

19-3 $CaCO_3$ Insoluble—rule 5: All carbonates are insoluble.
$Ca(NO_3)_2$ Soluble—rule 2: All nitrates are soluble.
$CaCl_2$ Soluble—rule 4: All chlorides are soluble.
CaS Insoluble—rule 5: All sulfides are insoluble.
$CaSO_4$ Insoluble—rule 6: $CaSO_4$ is insoluble.

19-5 (a) The possible double-replacement products are AgI and $NaClO_4$. Although $NaClO_4$ is soluble, AgI is insoluble (rule 3):

$$AgClO_4(aq) + NaI(aq) \longrightarrow NaClO_4(aq) + AgI(s)$$

The corresponding net ionic equation is

$$Ag^+(aq) + I^-(aq) \longrightarrow AgI(s)$$

(b) The possible double-replacement products are Hg_2SO_4 and KNO_3. Although KNO_3 is soluble (rule 1), Hg_2SO_4 is insoluble (rule 3):

$$Hg_2(NO_3)_2(aq) + K_2SO_4(aq) \longrightarrow 2KNO_3(aq) + Hg_2SO_4(s)$$

$$Hg_2^{2+}(aq) + SO_4^{2-}(aq) \longrightarrow Hg_2SO_4(s)$$

(c) The possible double-replacement products are $PbCrO_4$ and $LiNO_3$. Although $LiNO_3$ is soluble (rule 2), $PbCrO_4$ is insoluble (rule 3):

$$Pb(NO_3)_2(aq) + Li_2CrO_4(aq) \longrightarrow 2LiNO_3(aq) + PbCrO_4(s)$$

$$Pb^{2+}(aq) + CrO_4^{2-}(aq) \longrightarrow PbCrO_4(s)$$

(d) The possible double-replacement products are $ZnCO_3$ and NaCl. Although NaCl is soluble (rule 1), $ZnCO_3$ is insoluble (rule 5):

$$ZnCl_2(aq) + Na_2CO_3(aq) \longrightarrow 2NaCl(aq) + ZnCO_3(s)$$
$$Zn^{2+}(aq) + CO_3^{2-}(aq) \longrightarrow ZnCO_3(s)$$

(e) The possible double-replacement products are $BaSO_4$ and $ZnCl_2$. Although $ZnCl_2$ is soluble (rule 4), $BaSO_4$ is insoluble (rule 6):

$$BaCl_2(aq) + ZnSO_4(aq) \longrightarrow ZnCl_2(aq) + BaSO_4(s)$$
$$Ba^{2+}(aq) + SO_4^{2-}(aq) \longrightarrow BaSO_4(s)$$

19-7 (a) $Hg_2(ClO_4)_2(aq) + 2NaBr(aq) \longrightarrow 2NaClO_4(aq) + Hg_2Br_2(s)$ (rule 3)
(b) $Fe(ClO_4)_3(aq) + 3NaOH(aq) \longrightarrow 3NaClO_4(aq) + Fe(OH)_3(s)$ (rule 5)
(c) $CaCl_2(aq) + H_2SO_4(aq) \longrightarrow 2HCl(aq) + CaSO_4(s)$ (rule 6)
(d) $Pb(NO_3)_2(aq) + 2LiIO_3(aq) \longrightarrow 2LiNO_3(aq) + Pb(IO_3)_2(s)$ (rule 3)
(e) $H_2SO_4(aq) + Pb(NO_3)_2(aq) \longrightarrow 2HNO_3(aq) + PbSO_4(s)$ (rule 3)

19-9 The $Pb^{2+}(aq)$ is removed from solution by the formation of insoluble $PbSO_4(s)$, which passes out of the body through the large intestine.

19-11 The solubility equilibrium is

$$PbCrO_4(s) \rightleftharpoons Pb^{2+}(aq) + CrO_4^{2-}(aq)$$

The K_{sp} expression is

$$K_{sp} = [Pb^{2+}][CrO_4^{2-}] = 2.8 \times 10^{-13} \text{ M}^2$$

If $PbCrO_4$ is equilibrated with pure water, then at equilibrium we have

$$[Pb^{2+}] = [CrO_4^{2-}] = s$$

where s is the solubility of $PbCrO_4$ in pure water. Thus

$$K_{sp} = (s)(s) = s^2 = 2.8 \times 10^{-13} \text{ M}^2$$
$$s = 5.3 \times 10^{-7} \text{ M}$$

The solubility in grams per liter is

$$s = (5.3 \times 10^{-7} \text{ mol} \cdot \text{L}^{-1}) \left(\frac{323.2 \text{ g}}{1 \text{ mol}} \right) = 1.7 \times 10^{-4} \text{ g} \cdot \text{L}^{-1}$$

19-13 The solubility equilibrium is

$$AgBr(s) \rightleftharpoons Ag^+(aq) + Br^-(aq)$$

The solubility of AgBr is

$$(1.33 \times 10^{-4} \text{ g} \cdot \text{L}^{-1})\left(\frac{1 \text{ mol}}{187.8 \text{ g}}\right) = 7.082 \times 10^{-7} \text{ M}$$

From the reaction stoichiometry, we have

$$\text{solubility of AgBr} = [\text{Ag}^+] = [\text{Br}^-] = 7.082 \times 10^{-7} \text{ M}$$

Using the K_{sp} expression, we compute

$$K_{sp} = [\text{Ag}^+][\text{Br}^-] = (7.082 \times 10^{-7} \text{ M})^2$$
$$= 5.02 \times 10^{-13} \text{ M}^2$$

19-15 The solubility equilibrium is

$$\text{Mg(OH)}_2(s) \rightleftharpoons \text{Mg}^{2+}(aq) + 2\text{OH}^-(aq)$$

The solubility product constant expression is

$$K_{sp} = [\text{Mg}^{2+}][\text{OH}^-]^2 = 1.8 \times 10^{-11} \text{ M}^3$$

When $\text{Mg(OH)}_2(s)$ is in equilibrium with pure water, we have

$$[\text{OH}^-] = 2\,[\text{Mg}^{2+}]$$

The solubility of $\text{Mg(OH)}_2(s)$ in pure water is equal to $[\text{Mg}^{2+}]$ because each mole of Mg(OH)_2 that dissolves yields one mole of $\text{Mg}^{2+}(aq)$. The solubility of $\text{Mg(OH)}_2(s)$ is

$$s = [\text{Mg}^{2+}] = \frac{[\text{OH}^-]}{2}$$

or $[\text{OH}^-] = 2s$ where we have neglected the $[\text{OH}^-]$ arising from the dissociation of $\text{H}_2\text{O}(l)$.

Combining these results with the K_{sp} expression, we have

$$K_{sp} = (s)(2s)^2 = 4s^3 = 1.8 \times 10^{-11} \text{ M}^3$$
$$s = \left(\frac{1.8 \times 10^{-11} \text{ M}^3}{4}\right)^{1/3} = 1.7 \times 10^{-4} \text{ M}$$

The solubility in grams per liter is

$$s = (1.7 \times 10^{-4} \text{ mol} \cdot \text{L}^{-1})\left(\frac{58.33 \text{ g}}{1 \text{ mol}}\right) = 9.9 \times 10^{-3} \text{g} \cdot \text{L}^{-1}$$

19-17   The solubility equilibrium is

$$KClO_4(s) \rightleftharpoons K^+(aq) + ClO_4^-(aq)$$

The K_{sp} expression is

$$K_{sp} = [K^+][ClO_4^-]$$

From the reaction stoichiometry, at equilibrium $[K^+] = [ClO_4^-] =$ solubility of $KClO_4$. The solubility of $KClO_4$ is

$$s = \frac{0.75 \text{ g}}{0.100 \text{ L}} = (7.5 \text{ g} \cdot \text{L}^{-1})\left(\frac{1 \text{ mol}}{138.55 \text{ g}}\right) = 0.054 \text{ M}$$

Substituting the values of $[K^+]$ and $[ClO_4^-]$ into the K_{sp} expression, we have

$$K_{sp} = (0.054 \text{ M})(0.054 \text{ M}) = 2.9 \times 10^{-3} \text{ M}^2$$

19-19   The solubility equilibrium is

$$Zn(OH)_2(s) \rightleftharpoons Zn^{2+}(aq) + 2OH^-(aq)$$

The K_{sp} expression is

$$K_{sp} = [Zn^{2+}][OH^-]^2 = 1.0 \times 10^{-15} \text{ M}^3 \qquad \text{(Table 19-1)}$$

From the reaction stoichiometry, at equilibrium we have

$$[OH^-] = 2[Zn^{2+}] \quad \text{or} \quad [Zn^{2+}] = \tfrac{1}{2}[OH^-]$$

Substituting $[Zn^{2+}] = \tfrac{1}{2}[OH^-]$ in the K_{sp} expression, we have

$$K_{sp} = \tfrac{1}{2}[OH^-][OH^-]^2 = \tfrac{1}{2}[OH^-]^3 = 1.0 \times 10^{-15} \text{ M}^3$$
$$[OH^-] = (2.0 \times 10^{-15} \text{ M}^3)^{1/3} = 1.3 \times 10^{-5} \text{ M}$$

From the K_w expression for water we have

$$[H_3O^+] = \frac{K_w}{[OH^-]} = \frac{1.00 \times 10^{-14} \text{ M}^2}{1.3 \times 10^{-5} \text{ M}} = 7.7 \times 10^{-10} \text{ M}$$

The pH of the solution is

$$\text{pH} = -\log[H_3O^+] = -\log(7.7 \times 10^{-10}) = 9.11$$

19-21   The equilibrium expression that describes the solubility of silver sulfate is

$$Ag_2SO_4(s) \rightleftharpoons 2Ag^+(aq) + SO_4^{2-}(aq)$$

and the solubility product expression is

$$K_{sp} = [Ag^+]^2[SO_4^{2-}] = 1.4 \times 10^{-5} \ M^3 \qquad \text{(Table 19-1)}$$

The only source of $SO_4^{2-}(aq)$ is from the $Ag_2SO_4(s)$ that dissolves. If we let s be the solubility of $Ag_2SO_4(s)$ in 1.00 M $AgNO_3(aq)$, then

$$[SO_4^{2-}] = s$$

The $Ag^+(aq)$ is due to the 1.00 M $AgNO_3(aq)$ and the $Ag_2SO_4(s)$ that dissolves. Because each $Ag_2SO_4(s)$ that dissolves yields two $Ag^+(aq)$, we have at equilibrium

$$[Ag^+] = \underset{\substack{\text{from} \\ AgNO_3}}{1.00 \ M} + \underset{\substack{\text{from} \\ Ag_2SO_4}}{2s}$$

If we substitute the expressions for $[Ag^+]$ and $[SO_4^{2-}]$ into the K_{sp} expression, then we obtain

$$K_{sp} = (1.00 \ M + 2s)^2(s) = 1.4 \times 10^{-5} \ M^3$$

Because Ag_2SO_4 is a slightly soluble salt, we expect the value of s to be small. Therefore, we neglect $2s$ compared to 1.00 M, and we write

$$(1.00 \ M)^2(s) \approx 1.4 \times 10^{-5} \ M^3$$

$$s \approx \frac{1.4 \times 10^{-5} \ M^3}{1.00 \ M^2} = 1.4 \times 10^{-5} \ M$$

Note that s is small relative to 1.00 M, and so our approximation 1.00 M + $2s \approx$ 1.00 M is acceptable. The solubility of $Ag_2SO_4(s)$ in $g \cdot L^{-1}$ is

$$s = (1.4 \times 10^{-5} \ mol \cdot L^{-1})\left(\frac{311.9 \ g}{1 \ mol}\right) = 4.4 \times 10^{-3} \ g \cdot L^{-1}$$

19-23 The equilibrium expression that describes the solubility of barium fluoride is

$$BaF_2(s) \rightleftharpoons Ba^{2+}(aq) + 2F^-(aq)$$

The solubility product expression is

$$K_{sp} = [Ba^{2+}][F^-]^2 = 1.0 \times 10^{-6} \ M^3$$

The only source of $Ba^{2+}(aq)$ is from the $BaF_2(s)$ that dissolves. If we let s be the solubility of $BaF_2(s)$ in 0.25 M $NaF(aq)$, then

$$[Ba^{2+}] = s$$

The $F^-(aq)$ is due to the 0.25 M $NaF(aq)$ and the $BaF_2(s)$ that dissolves. Because each mole of $BaF_2(s)$ that dissolves yields two moles of $F^-(aq)$, we have

$$[F^-] = 0.25 \text{ M} + 2s$$

If we substitute the expressions for $[Ba^{2+}]$ and $[F^-]$ into the K_{sp} expression, we have

$$K_{sp} = (s)(0.25 \text{ M} + 2s)^2 = 1.0 \times 10^{-6} \text{ M}^3$$

Because BaF_2 is only slightly soluble, we expect the value of s to be small. Therefore, we neglect $2s$ compared to 0.25 M and write

$$(s)(0.25 \text{ M})^2 = 1.0 \times 10^{-6} \text{ M}^3$$

$$s = \frac{1.0 \times 10^{-6} \text{ M}^3}{0.0625 \text{ M}^2} = 1.6 \times 10^{-5} \text{ M}$$

The solubility in grams per liter is

$$s = (1.6 \times 10^{-5} \text{ mol} \cdot \text{L}^{-1})\left(\frac{175.3 \text{ g}}{1 \text{ mol}}\right) = 2.8 \times 10^{-3} \text{ g} \cdot \text{L}^{-1}$$

19-25   The equilibrium expression that describes the solubility of $AgCl(s)$ is

$$AgCl(s) \rightleftharpoons Ag^+(aq) + Cl^-(aq)$$

The solubility product expression is

$$K_{sp} = [Ag^+][Cl^-] = 1.8 \times 10^{-10} \text{ M}^2 \qquad \text{(Table 19-1)}$$

The only source of $Ag^+(aq)$ is $AgCl(s)$; thus the solubility s is equal to

$$s = [Ag^+]$$

The $Cl^-(aq)$ in solution is due to 0.50 M $CaCl_2(aq)$ plus the dissolved AgCl. Because $CaCl_2$ dissociates completely, we have

$$[Cl^-] = (2 \times 0.50 \text{ M}) + s$$

Substitution of the above expressions for $[Ag^+]$ and $[Cl^-]$ into the K_{sp} expression yields

$$s(1.00 \text{ M} + s) = 1.8 \times 10^{-10} \text{ M}^2$$

Assuming that s is small compared to 1.00 M yields

$$s = \frac{1.8 \times 10^{-10} \text{ M}^2}{1.00 \text{ M}} = 1.8 \times 10^{-10} \text{ M}$$

The solubility in grams per liter is

$$s = (1.8 \times 10^{-10} \text{ mol} \cdot \text{L}^{-1}) \left(\frac{143.4 \text{ g}}{1 \text{ mol}} \right) = 2.6 \times 10^{-8} \text{ g} \cdot \text{L}^{-1}$$

19-27 The equilibrium expression that describes the solubility of CuBr(s) in water is

(1) $\text{CuBr}(s) \rightleftharpoons \text{Cu}^+(aq) + \text{Br}^-(aq)$ $K_{sp} = 5.3 \times 10^{-9} \text{ M}^2$ (Table 19-1)

Furthermore, $\text{Cu}^+(aq)$ reacts with $\text{NH}_3(aq)$ according to

(2) $\text{Cu}^+(aq) + 2\text{NH}_3(aq) \rightleftharpoons \text{Cu(NH}_3)_2^+(aq)$ $K_2 = 6.3 \times 10^{10} \text{ M}^{-2}$

The sum of these two equations is

(3) $\text{CuBr}(s) + 2\text{NH}_3(aq) \rightleftharpoons \text{Cu(NH}_3)_2^+(aq) + \text{Br}^-(aq)$

This reaction represents the dissolution of CuBr(s) in an ammonia solution. The equilibrium constant for reaction (3) is equal to the product of the equilibrium constants for reactions (1) and (2):

$$K_3 = K_{sp}K_2 = (5.3 \times 10^{-9} \text{ M}^2)(6.3 \times 10^{10} \text{ M}^{-2}) = 334$$

Thus

$$K_3 = \frac{[\text{Cu(NH}_3)_2^+][\text{Br}^-]}{[\text{NH}_3]^2} = 334$$

From the reaction (3) stoichiometry we have

$$[\text{Cu(NH}_3)_2^+] = [\text{Br}^-]$$

Also we have assumed that $[\text{Cu}^+] \ll [\text{Cu(NH}_3)_2^+]$ because $K_{sp} \ll K_3$, and thus essentially all of the Cu^+ in solution is in the form $\text{Cu(NH}_3)_2^+$. If we let s be the solubility of CuBr(s) in $\text{NH}_3(aq)$, then

$$s = [\text{Br}^-]$$

and we have

$$K_3 = \frac{(s)(s)}{[\text{NH}_3]^2}$$

The equilibrium value of $[\text{NH}_3]$ is given as 0.185 M. Therefore,

$$\frac{s^2}{(0.185 \text{ M})^2} = 334$$

Thus

$$s^2 = 11.4 \text{ M}^2$$

and

$$s = 3.4 \text{ M}$$

We see that CuBr(s) is quite soluble in an ammonia solution.

19-29 (a) Solubility is increased; an increase in the concentration of $S_2O_3^{2-}$ shifts the equilibrium from left to right.

(b) Solubility remains unchanged; the amount of a solid reactant has no effect on the equilibrium concentrations.

(c) Solubility is decreased; an increase in the concentration of $Br^-(aq)$ shifts the equilibrium from right to left.

(d) Solubility remains unchanged; neither $Na^+(aq)$ nor $NO_3^-(aq)$ reacts with the species involved.

19-31 The concentration of $Cl^-(aq)$ after mixing is found from

$$M_b V_b = M_a V_a$$

where b stands for before and a stands for after. Thus

$$[Cl^-]_0 = \frac{(0.25 \text{ M})(0.100 \text{ L})}{(0.100 \text{ L} + 0.0050 \text{ L})} = 0.24 \text{ M}$$

The concentration of $Ag^+(aq)$ after mixing is

$$[Ag^+]_0 = \frac{(0.10 \text{ M})(0.0050 \text{ L})}{0.105 \text{ L}} = 4.8 \times 10^{-3} \text{ M}$$

and NO_3^- is a spectator ion. The value of Q_{sp} is

$$Q_{sp} = [Ag^+]_0[Cl^-]_0 = (4.8 \times 10^{-3} \text{ M})(0.24 \text{ M}) = 1.2 \times 10^{-3} \text{ M}^2$$

The value of K_{sp} for AgCl(s) is $1.8 \times 10^{-10} \text{ M}^2$ (Table 19-1); thus,

$$\frac{Q_{sp}}{K_{sp}} = \frac{1.2 \times 10^{-3} \text{ M}^2}{1.8 \times 10^{-10} \text{ M}^2} = 6.7 \times 10^6 > 1$$

Thus AgCl(s) will precipitate from the solution.

19-33 The concentration of $Pb^{2+}(aq)$ after mixing is

$$[Pb^{2+}]_0 = \frac{(3.00 \text{ M})(0.0500 \text{ L})}{0.0750 \text{ L}} = 2.00 \text{ M}$$

The concentration of $I^-(aq)$ after mixing is

$$[I^-]_0 = \frac{(2.00 \times 10^{-3} \text{ M})(0.0250 \text{ L})}{0.0750 \text{ L}} = 6.67 \times 10^{-4} \text{ M}$$

The value of Q_{sp} is

$$Q_{sp} = [Pb^{2+}]_0[I^-]_0^2 = (2.00 \text{ M})(6.67 \times 10^{-4} \text{ M})^2 = 8.90 \times 10^{-7} \text{ M}^3$$

The value of K_{sp} is $7.1 \times 10^{-9} \text{ M}^3$ (Table 19-1); thus

$$\frac{Q_{sp}}{K_{sp}} = \frac{8.90 \times 10^{-7} \text{ M}^3}{7.1 \times 10^{-9} \text{ M}^3} = 130 > 1$$

Because $Q_{sp}/K_{sp} > 1$, $PbI_2(s)$ will precipitate from the solution. Because $[Pb^{2+}]_0 \gg [I^-]_0$, essentially all of the $I^-(aq)$ is precipitated as $PbI_2(s)$, and the final equilibrium value of $[Pb^{2+}]$ will still be 2.00 M. Thus we have at equilibrium following the precipitation of $PbI_2(s)$

$$[Pb^{2+}]_0[I^-]^2 \simeq K_{sp} = 7.1 \times 10^{-9} \text{ M}^3$$

Therefore,

$$[I^-] = \left(\frac{7.1 \times 10^{-9} \text{ M}^3}{2.00 \text{ M}}\right)^{1/2} = 6.0 \times 10^{-5} \text{ M}$$

The moles of I^- that precipitates is given by

$$\begin{pmatrix} \text{moles of } I^- \\ \text{precipitated} \end{pmatrix} = \begin{pmatrix} \text{initial} \\ \text{moles of } I^- \end{pmatrix} - \begin{pmatrix} \text{final moles} \\ \text{of } I^- \end{pmatrix}$$

$$= (6.67 \times 10^{-4} \text{ M} - 6.0 \times 10^{-5} \text{ M})(0.0750 \text{ L})$$

$$= 4.55 \times 10^{-5} \text{ mol } I^-$$

The moles of $PbI_2(s)$ that precipitates is equal to one-half the moles of I^- that precipitates because each mole of $PbI_2(s)$ contains 2 moles of I^-. Thus

$$\text{moles of } PbI_2(s) = \tfrac{1}{2}(4.55 \times 10^{-5} \text{ mol}) = 2.28 \times 10^{-5} \text{ mol}$$

The equilibrium concentrations following the precipitation of $PbI_2(s)$ are

$$[Pb^{2+}] = 2.00 \text{ M} \qquad\qquad [NO_3^-] = 2[Pb^{2+}]_0 = 4.00 \text{ M}$$

$$[Na^+] = [I^-]_0 = 6.67 \times 10^{-4} \text{ M} \qquad [I^-] = 6.0 \times 10^{-5} \text{ M}$$

19-35 The concentration of $Cl^-(aq)$ after mixing is

$$[Cl^-]_0 = \frac{(2.00 \text{ M})(0.100 \text{ L})}{0.200 \text{ L}} = 1.00 \text{ M}$$

The concentration of $Ag^+(aq)$ after mixing is

$$[Ag^+]_0 = \frac{(0.020 \text{ M})(0.100 \text{ L})}{0.200 \text{ L}} = 0.010 \text{ M}$$

The value of K_{sp} for AgCl(s) is 1.8×10^{-10} M^2. Because AgCl(s) is only very slightly soluble, essentially all of the Ag$^+$(aq) will precipitate from the solution as AgCl(s). The number of moles of AgCl(s) that precipitates is equal to the number of moles of Ag$^+$(aq) initially present.

(a) moles of AgCl(s) = moles of Ag$^+$(aq) = (0.010 M)(0.200 L)

$$= 2.0 \times 10^{-3} \text{ mol}$$

The number of grams of AgCl in 2.0×10^{-3} mol is

$$\text{mass} = (2.0 \times 10^{-3} \text{ mol})\left(\frac{143.4 \text{ g}}{1 \text{ mol}}\right) = 0.29 \text{ g}$$

(b) The concentration of Cl$^-$(aq) at equilibrium is

$$[\text{Cl}^-] = 1.00 \text{ M} - 0.010 \text{ M} = 0.99 \text{ M}$$

The concentration of Ag$^+$ at equilibrium can be found from the K_{sp} expression

$$K_{sp} = [\text{Ag}^+][\text{Cl}^-] = [\text{Ag}^+][0.99 \text{ M}] = 1.8 \times 10^{-10} \text{ M}^2$$

$$[\text{Ag}^+] = \frac{1.8 \times 10^{-10} \text{ M}^2}{0.99 \text{ M}} = 1.8 \times 10^{-10} \text{ M}$$

This confirms the statement that essentially all of the Ag$^+$(aq) is precipitated as AgCl(s).

19-37   The equilibrium expression is

$$\text{CaF}_2(s) \rightleftharpoons \text{Ca}^{2+}(aq) + 2\text{F}^-(aq)$$

Recall that HF is a weak acid, and a saturated CaF$_2$ solution would contain some HF(aq).

(a) The solubility is increased; a decrease in pH is an increase in [H$_3$O$^+$]. The added H$_3$O$^+$(aq) reacts with F$^-$(aq) to form HF, thereby reducing the concentration of F$^-$(aq) and causing a shift in the equilibrium from left to right.

(b) A slight decrease in solubility owing to the shift to the left in the equilibrium

$$\text{F}^-(aq) + \text{H}_2\text{O}(l) \rightleftharpoons \text{HF}(aq) + \text{OH}^-(aq)$$

which leads to an increase in [F$^-$].

(c) The solubility is decreased, an increase in [Ca^{2+}] shifts the equilibrium from right to left (common ion effect).

19-39   CaCO$_3$; CO$_3^{2-}$(aq) is the conjugate base of the weak acid HCO$_3^-$(aq).

PbSO$_3$; SO$_3^{2-}$(aq) is the conjugate base of the weak acid HSO$_3^-$(aq).

Fe(OH)$_3$; OH$^-$(aq) reacts with H$_3$O$^+$(aq) so that [OH$^-$] is decreased.

ZnS; S^{2-}(aq) is the conjugate base of the weak acid HS$^-$(aq).

19-41 The equilibrium expression is

$$Mg(OH)_2(s) \rightleftharpoons Mg^{2+}(aq) + 2OH^-(aq)$$

The K_{sp} expression is

$$K_{sp} = [Mg^{2+}][OH^-]^2 = 1.8 \times 10^{-11} \; M^3 \qquad \text{(Table 19-1)}$$

At pH = 9.0

$$[H_3O^+] = 10^{-9.0} = 1.0 \times 10^{-9} \; M$$

Thus

$$[OH^-] = \frac{K_w}{[H_3O^+]} = \frac{1.00 \times 10^{-14} \; M^2}{1.0 \times 10^{-9} \; M} = 1.0 \times 10^{-5} \; M$$

Let s be the solubility of $Mg(OH)_2$. Then

$$[Mg^{2+}] = s$$
$$K_{sp} = (s)(1.0 \times 10^{-5} \; M)^2 = 1.8 \times 10^{-11} \; M^3$$
$$s = \frac{1.8 \times 10^{-11} \; M^3}{1.0 \times 10^{-10} \; M^2} = 0.18 \; M$$

19-43 The equilibrium expression is

$$Cu(OH)_2(s) \rightleftharpoons Cu^{2+}(aq) + 2OH^-(aq)$$

The K_{sp} expression is

$$K_{sp} = [Cu^{2+}][OH^-]^2 = 2.2 \times 10^{-20} \; M^3 \qquad \text{(Table 19-1)}$$

At pH = 8.0

$$[H_3O^+] = 10^{-pH} = 10^{-8.0} = 1.0 \times 10^{-8} \; M$$

and thus

$$[OH^-] = \frac{K_w}{[H_3O^+]} = \frac{1.00 \times 10^{-14} \; M^2}{1.0 \times 10^{-8} \; M} = 1.0 \times 10^{-6} \; M$$

Let s be the solubility of $Cu(OH)_2$. We have

$$[Cu^{2+}] = s$$

Therefore,

$$K_{sp} = (s)(1.0 \times 10^{-6} \; M)^2 = 2.2 \times 10^{-20} \; M^3$$

and $\qquad\qquad\qquad\qquad\qquad\qquad s = 2.2 \times 10^{-8}$ M

19-45 (a) $\qquad\qquad\qquad\qquad$ $ZnS(s) \rightleftharpoons Zn^{2+}(aq) + S^{2-}(aq)$

The solubility increases. The $H_3O^+(aq)$ from the added HNO_3 reacts with S^{2-} to form HS^-, thereby decreasing the concentration of $S^{2-}(aq)$. A decrease in $[S^{2-}]$ shifts the equilibrium from left to right.

(b) $\qquad\qquad\qquad\qquad$ $MgCO_3(s) \rightleftharpoons Mg^{2+}(aq) + CO_3^{2-}(aq)$

The solubility decreases. The CO_2 forms a small amount of $CO_3^{2-}(aq)$ in water. An increase in $[CO_3^{2-}]$ shifts the equilibrium from right to left.

(c) $\qquad\qquad\qquad\qquad$ $AgI(s) \rightleftharpoons Ag^+(aq) + I^-(aq)$

The solubility increases. Ammonia, NH_3, reacts with Ag^+ to form the soluble ion $Ag(NH_3)_2^+$, thereby reducing the amount of $Ag^+(aq)$. A decrease in $[Ag^+]$ shifts the equilibrium from left to right.

(d) $\qquad\qquad\qquad\qquad$ $CdS(s) \rightleftharpoons Cd^{2+}(aq) + S^{2-}(aq)$

The $S^{2-}(aq)$ ion reacts with water to form $HS^-(aq)$:

$$S^{2-}(aq) + H_2O(l) \rightleftharpoons HS^-(aq) + OH^-(aq)$$

Addition of $OH^-(aq)$ shifts this equilibrium to the left and thus increases $[S^{2-}]$. The increase in $[S^{2-}]$ leads to a shift in the solubility equilibrium to the left, thereby decreasing the solubility of $CdS(s)$.

19-47 The solubility product expression of $Cr(OH)_3(s)$ is

$$K_{sp} = [Cr^{3+}][OH^-]^3 = 6.3 \times 10^{-31} \text{ M}^4 \qquad \text{(Table 19-1)}$$

$$\text{solubility of } Cr(OH)_3 = s = [Cr^{3+}] = \frac{6.3 \times 10^{-31} \text{ M}^4}{[OH^-]^3}$$

$$= \frac{6.3 \times 10^{-31} \text{ M}^4[H_3O^+]^3}{K_w^3}$$

At pH = 5.0

$$[H_3O^+] = 10^{-pH} = 10^{-5.0} = 1.0 \times 10^{-5} \text{ M}$$

Thus the solubility of $Cr(OH)_3$ is

$$s = \frac{(6.3 \times 10^{-31} \text{ M}^4)(1.0 \times 10^{-5} \text{ M})^3}{(1.00 \times 10^{-14} \text{ M}^2)^3} = 6.3 \times 10^{-4} \text{ M}$$

The solubility product expression of $Ni(OH)_2$ is

$$K_{sp} = [Ni^{2+}][OH^-]^2 = 2.0 \times 10^{-15} \text{ M}^3$$

$$\text{solubility of Ni(OH)}_2 = s = [\text{Ni}^{2+}] = \frac{2.0 \times 10^{-15} \text{ M}^3}{[\text{OH}^-]^2}$$

$$= \frac{2.0 \times 10^{-15} \text{ M}^3[\text{H}_3\text{O}^+]^2}{K_w^2}$$

Thus at pH = 5.0

$$s = \frac{(2.0 \times 10^{-15} \text{ M}^3)(1.0 \times 10^{-5} \text{ M})^2}{(1.00 \times 10^{-14} \text{ M}^2)^2} = 2.0 \times 10^3 \text{ M}$$

At pH = 5.0, $\text{Ni(OH)}_2(s)$ is very soluble, while $\text{Cr(OH)}_3(s)$ is only slightly soluble; thus a separation of $\text{Ni}^{2+}(aq)$ and $\text{Cr}^{3+}(aq)$ can be achieved by buffering the solution at pH = 5, where the $\text{Cr(OH)}_3(s)$ will precipitate and the $\text{Ni}^{2+}(aq)$ will remain in solution.

19-49 The solubility product expression for $\text{Pb(OH)}_2(s)$ is

$$K_{sp} = [\text{Pb}^{2+}][\text{OH}^-]^2 = 1.2 \times 10^{-15} \text{ M}^3 \qquad \text{(Table 19-1)}$$

Thus we have for the solubility as a function of $[\text{H}_3\text{O}^+]$

$$s = [\text{Pb}^{2+}] = \frac{1.2 \times 10^{-15} \text{ M}^3}{[\text{OH}^-]^2} = \frac{1.2 \times 10^{-15} \text{ M}^3[\text{H}_3\text{O}^+]^2}{K_w^2}$$

$$= \frac{1.2 \times 10^{-15} \text{ M}^3[\text{H}_3\text{O}^+]^2}{(1.00 \times 10^{-14} \text{ M}^2)^2} = 1.2 \times 10^{13} \text{ M}^{-1}[\text{H}_3\text{O}^+]^2$$

The solubility product expression for $\text{Sn(OH)}_2(s)$ is

$$K_{sp} = [\text{Sn}^{2+}][\text{OH}^-]^2 = 1.4 \times 10^{-28} \text{ M}^3 \qquad \text{(Table 19-1)}$$

Thus we have for the solubility as a function of $[\text{H}_3\text{O}^+]$

$$s = [\text{Sn}^{2+}] = \frac{1.4 \times 10^{-28} \text{ M}^3}{[\text{OH}^-]^2} = \frac{1.4 \times 10^{-28} \text{ M}^3[\text{H}_3\text{O}^+]^2}{K_w^2}$$

$$= \frac{1.4 \times 10^{-28} \text{ M}^3[\text{H}_3\text{O}^+]^2}{(1.00 \times 10^{-14} \text{ M}^2)^2} = 1.4 \text{ M}^{-1}[\text{H}_3\text{O}^+]^2$$

From the above expressions for s we see that $\text{Pb(OH)}_2(s)$ is much more soluble at a given pH than is $\text{Sn(OH)}_2(s)$. Let's find the pH at which s for $\text{Sn(OH)}_2(s)$ (the less-soluble hydroxide) is 1×10^{-6} M.

$$s = 1 \times 10^{-6} \text{ M} = 1.4 \text{ M}^{-1}[\text{H}_3\text{O}^+]^2$$

$$[\text{H}_3\text{O}^+]^2 = \frac{1 \times 10^{-6} \text{ M}}{1.4 \text{ M}^{-1}}$$

Thus $$[\text{H}_3\text{O}^+] = 8.5 \times 10^{-4} \text{ M}$$

and

$$pH = 3.1$$

When the pH is greater than 3.1, the solubility of $Sn(OH)_2(s)$ is less than 10^{-6} M. The solubility of $Pb(OH)_2$ at pH = 3.1 is

$$s = 1.2 \times 10^{13}\ M^{-1}[H_3O^+]^2$$
$$= (1.2 \times 10^{13}\ M^{-1})(8.5 \times 10^{-4}\ M)^2 = 7.6 \times 10^6\ M$$

Thus at pH = 3.1 an effective separation can be achieved. If the pH is too high, then we would have to consider the formation of hydroxyl complexes.

19-51 The K_{sp} expression for CuS(s) is

$$K_{sp} = [Cu^{2+}][S^{2-}] = 6.3 \times 10^{-36}\ M^2 \qquad \text{(Table 19-1)}$$

The solubility of CuS is

$$s = [Cu^{2+}] = \frac{6.3 \times 10^{-36}\ M^2}{[S^{2-}]}$$

From Equation (19-18)

$$[S^{2-}] = \frac{1.1 \times 10^{-21}\ M^3}{[H_3O^+]^2} \qquad (19\text{-}18)$$

At pH = 2.0

$$[H_3O^+] = 10^{-2.0} = 1.0 \times 10^{-2}\ M$$

and thus

$$[S^{2-}] = \frac{1.1 \times 10^{-21}\ M^3}{(1.0 \times 10^{-2}\ M)^2} = 1.1 \times 10^{-17}\ M$$

Therefore, the solubility of CuS is

$$s = \frac{6.3 \times 10^{-36}\ M^2}{1.1 \times 10^{-17}\ M} = 5.7 \times 10^{-19}\ M$$

19-53 The solubility product expression for PbS is

$$K_{sp} = [Pb^{2+}][S^{2-}] = 8.0 \times 10^{-28}\ M^2 \qquad \text{(Table 19-1)}$$

Thus the solubility of PbS is

$$s = [Pb^{2+}] = \frac{8.0 \times 10^{-28}\ M^2}{[S^{2-}]}$$

Substituting Equation (19-18) into the above equation for s, we obtain

$$s = \frac{8.0 \times 10^{-28} \text{ M}^2[\text{H}_3\text{O}^+]^2}{1.1 \times 10^{-21} \text{ M}^3} = 7.3 \times 10^{-7} \text{ M}^{-1}[\text{H}_3\text{O}^+]^2$$

Proceeding in an analogous manner, we find for the solubility of MnS as a function of $[\text{H}_3\text{O}^+]$

$$K_{sp} = [\text{Mn}^{2+}][\text{S}^{2-}] = 2.5 \times 10^{-13} \text{ M}^2 \qquad \text{(Table 19-1)}$$

$$s = [\text{Mn}^{2+}] = \frac{2.5 \times 10^{-13} \text{ M}^2}{[\text{S}^{2-}]} = \frac{2 \ 5 \times 10^{-13} \text{ M}^2[\text{H}_3\text{O}^+]^2}{1.1 \times 10^{-21} \text{ M}^3}$$

$$= 2.3 \times 10^8 \text{ M}^{-1}[\text{H}_3\text{O}^+]^2$$

The $[\text{H}_3\text{O}^+]$ at which the solubility of PbS is 1×10^{-6} M is given by

$$1 \times 10^{-6} \text{ M} = 7.3 \times 10^{-7} \text{ M}^{-1}[\text{H}_3\text{O}^+]^2$$

Thus

$$[\text{H}_3\text{O}^+]^2 = \frac{1 \times 10^{-6} \text{ M}}{7.3 \times 10^{-7} \text{ M}^{-1}} = 1.37 \text{ M}^2$$

$$[\text{H}_3\text{O}^+] = 1.2 \text{ M}$$

or

$$\text{pH} = -0.08$$

The solubility of MnS at $[\text{H}_3\text{O}^+] = 1.2$ M is

$$s = (2.3 \times 10^8 \text{ M}^{-1})(1.2 \text{ M})^2 = 3.3 \times 10^8 \text{ M}$$

which is much greater than 0.025 M

At a pH of -0.08, essentially all of the $\text{Pb}^{2+}(aq)$ precipitates as PbS(s), and all the $\text{Mn}^{2+}(aq)$ remains in solution.

19-55 The concentration of $[\text{S}^{2-}]$ is given by Equation (19-18):

$$[\text{S}^{2-}] = \frac{1.1 \times 10^{-21} \text{ M}^3}{[\text{H}_3\text{O}^+]^2}$$

At pH = 3.0, $[\text{H}_3\text{O}^+] = 1.0 \times 10^{-3}$ M and

$$[\text{S}^{2-}] = \frac{1.1 \times 10^{-21} \text{ M}^3}{(1.0 \times 10^{-3} \text{ M})^2} = 1.1 \times 10^{-15} \text{ M}$$

At pH = 6.0, $[H_3O^+] = 1.0 \times 10^{-6}$ M and

$$[S^{2-}] = \frac{1.1 \times 10^{-21} \text{ M}^3}{(1.0 \times 10^{-6} \text{ M})^2} = 1.1 \times 10^{-9} \text{ M}$$

The solubility product expression of HgS(s) is

$$K_{sp} = [Hg^{2+}][S^{2-}] = 4 \times 10^{-53} \text{ M}^2 \qquad \text{(Table 19-1)}$$

Thus the solubility of HgS is

$$s = [Hg^{2+}] = \frac{4 \times 10^{-53} \text{ M}^2}{[S^{2-}]}$$

At pH = 3.0, the solubility of HgS is

$$s = \frac{4 \times 10^{-53} \text{ M}^2}{1.1 \times 10^{-15} \text{ M}} = 4 \times 10^{-38} \text{ M}$$

and at pH = 6.0

$$s = \frac{4 \times 10^{-53} \text{ M}^2}{1.1 \times 10^{-9} \text{ M}} = 4 \times 10^{-44} \text{ M}$$

The solubility product expression for CdS(s) is

$$K_{sp} = [Cd^{2+}][S^{2-}] = 8.0 \times 10^{-27} \text{ M}^2 \qquad \text{(Table 19-1)}$$

Thus the solubility of CdS is

$$s = [Cd^{2+}] = \frac{8.0 \times 10^{-27} \text{ M}^2}{[S^{2-}]}$$

At pH = 3.0, the solubility of CdS(s) is

$$s = \frac{8.0 \times 10^{-27} \text{ M}^2}{1.1 \times 10^{-15} \text{ M}} = 7.3 \times 10^{-12} \text{ M}$$

and at pH = 6.0

$$s = \frac{8.0 \times 10^{-27} \text{ M}^2}{1.1 \times 10^{-9} \text{ M}} = 7.3 \times 10^{-18} \text{ M}$$

19-57   The precipitation reaction is

$$Pb(NO_3)_2(aq) + 2NaOH(aq) \rightleftharpoons Pb(OH)_2(s) + 2NaNO_3(aq)$$

The precipitate dissolves via the reaction

$$Pb(OH)_2(s) + OH^-(aq) \rightleftharpoons Pb(OH)_3^-(aq)$$

19-59 The solution is basic and thus the reaction is

$$Sn(OH)_2(s) + OH^-(aq) \rightleftharpoons Sn(OH)_3^-(aq)$$

From Table 19-4, the equilibrium constant expression for the reaction is

$$K = \frac{[Sn(OH)_3^-]}{[OH^-]} = 0.01 = \frac{s}{[OH^-]}$$

Note that the solubility of $Sn(OH)_2$ is equal to $[Sn(OH)_3^-]$. At pH = 13.0, $[H_3O^+] = 1.0 \times 10^{-13}$ M, and

$$[OH^-] = \frac{K_w}{[H_3O^+]} = \frac{1.00 \times 10^{-14} \text{ M}^2}{1.0 \times 10^{-13} \text{ M}} = 1.0 \times 10^{-1} \text{ M}$$

Thus $s = (0.01)[OH^-] = (0.01)(0.10 \text{ M}) = 1 \times 10^{-3}$ M

19-61 The solubility of $Al(OH)_3(s)$ in basic solution is

$$s = [Al(OH)_4^-] = 40[OH^-]$$

which is derived from the equilibrium expression. At pH = 12.0, $[H_3O^+] = 1.0 \times 10^{-12}$ M and

$$[OH^-] = \frac{K_w}{[H_3O^+]} = \frac{1.00 \times 10^{-14} \text{ M}^2}{1.0 \times 10^{-12} \text{ M}} = 1.0 \times 10^{-2} \text{ M}$$

Thus $s = (40)(1.0 \times 10^{-2} \text{ M}) = 0.40$ M

19-63 The solubility of $Cr(OH)_3(s)$ in acidic solution is determined primarily by the reaction

$$Cr(OH)_3(s) \rightleftharpoons Cr^{3+}(aq) + 3OH^-(aq)$$

The solubility of $Cr(OH)_3(s)$ due to this reaction is

$$s = [Cr^{3+}] = \frac{K_{sp}}{[OH^-]^3} = \frac{6.3 \times 10^{-31} \text{ M}^4}{[OH^-]^3}$$

At pH = 3.0, $[H_3O^+] = 1.0 \times 10^{-3}$ M and

$$[OH^-] = \frac{K_w}{[H_3O^+]} = \frac{1.00 \times 10^{-14} \text{ M}^2}{1.0 \times 10^{-3} \text{ M}} = 1.0 \times 10^{-11} \text{ M}$$

Thus $$s = \frac{6.3 \times 10^{-31} \text{ M}^4}{(1.0 \times 10^{-11} \text{ M})^3} = 6.3 \times 10^2 \text{ M}$$

At pH = 6.0, $[H_3O^+] = 1.0 \times 10^{-6}$ M and

$$[OH^-] = \frac{K_w}{[H_3O^+]} = \frac{1.00 \times 10^{-14} \text{ M}^2}{1.0 \times 10^{-6} \text{ M}} = 1.0 \times 10^{-8} \text{ M}$$

$$s = \frac{6.3 \times 10^{-31} \text{ M}^4}{(1.0 \times 10^{-8} \text{ M})^3} = 6.3 \times 10^{-7} \text{ M}$$

The solubility of $Cr(OH)_3(s)$ in basic solution is determined primarily by the reaction

$$Cr(OH)_3(s) + OH^-(aq) \rightleftharpoons Cr(OH)_4^-(aq)$$

The solubility of $Cr(OH)_3(s)$ due to this reaction is

$$s = [Cr(OH)_4^-] = 0.04[OH^-]$$

At pH = 9.0, $[H_3O^+] = 1.0 \times 10^{-9}$ M and

$$[OH^-] = \frac{K_w}{[H_3O^+]} = \frac{1.0 \times 10^{-14} \text{ M}^2}{1.0 \times 10^{-9} \text{ M}} = 1.0 \times 10^{-5} \text{ M}$$

$$s = (0.04)(1.0 \times 10^{-5} \text{ M}) = 4 \times 10^{-7} \text{ M}$$

At pH = 12.0, $[H_3O^+] = 1.0 \times 10^{-12}$ M and

$$[OH^-] = \frac{K_w}{[H_3O^+]} = \frac{1.00 \times 10^{-14} \text{ M}^2}{1.0 \times 10^{-12} \text{ M}} = 1.0 \times 10^{-2} \text{ M}$$

and $$s = (0.04)(1.0 \times 10^{-2} \text{ M}) = 4 \times 10^{-4} \text{ M}$$

E   ANSWERS TO THE EVEN-NUMBERED PROBLEMS

19-2   Insoluble, soluble, soluble, soluble, insoluble

19-4 $AgCl$, Ag_2S, and Ag_2CO_3 are insoluble.

19-6   (a) $Pb(NO_2)_2(s)$ (d) $Hg_2(C_7H_5O_2)_2(s)$
           (b) $CaSO_4(s)$ (e) $Ag_2SO_4(s)$
           (c) No reaction

19-8   (a) No reaction   (d) $CaCO_3(s) + 2NaCl(aq)$
           (b) $Hg_2Cl_2(s) + 2KNO_3(aq)$ (e) $Cu(OH)_2(s) + 2LiClO_4(aq)$
           (c) $ZnS(s) + 2NaClO_4(aq)$

19-10 The $CaC_2O_4(s)$ that is formed is insoluble and is removed by vomiting. The excess $Ca^{2+}(aq)$ is removed by excretion as $CaSO_4$ formed by the addition of $MgSO_4$.

19-12 $TlCl(s) \rightleftharpoons Tl^+(aq) + Cl^-(aq)$, 1.3×10^{-2} M; $3.1 \text{ g} \cdot \text{L}^{-1}$

19-14 $K_{sp} = 2.60 \times 10^{-13} \text{ M}^3$

19-16 2.2×10^{-2} M; $7.9 \text{ g} \cdot \text{L}^{-1}$

19-18 $K_{sp} = 1.1 \times 10^{-2} \text{ M}^2$

19-20 1.41×10^{-2} M; $1.04 \text{ g} \cdot \text{L}^{-1}$

19-22 $5.5 \times 10^{-7} \text{ g} \cdot \text{L}^{-1}$

19-24 4.2×10^{-4} M; $0.19 \text{ g} \cdot \text{L}^{-1}$

19-26 3.6×10^{-5} M; $5.0 \times 10^{-3} \text{ g} \cdot \text{L}^{-1}$

19-28 1.1 M

19-30 (a) Increased   (b) no effect   (c) increased

19-32 $Q_{sp}/K_{sp} = 14$ and $Ag_2SO_4(s)$ will precipitate.

19-34 5.00×10^{-6} mol of $AgBr(s)$ precipitate. $[Ag^+] = 0.25$ M $= [NO_3^-]$; $[Na^+] = 5.00 \times 10^{-5}$ M; $[Br^-] = 2.0 \times 10^{-12}$ M

19-36 (a) 0.19 mg   (b) $[Zn^{2+}] = 0.15$ M, $[S^{2-}] = 1.1 \times 10^{-23}$ M

19-38 Increased; slightly decreased; decreased

19-40 All but $Hg_2I_2(s)$ are more soluble at lower pH.

19-42 8.0×10^{-3} M

19-44 2.5×10^{-4} M

19-46 (a) $\longrightarrow$ (b) $\longleftarrow$ (c) no change   (d) $\longleftarrow$

19-48 The solubilities at pH = 4.0 are 2.2 M for $Cu(OH)_2(s)$ and "1.0×10^5 M" (that is, very large) for $Zn(OH)_2(s)$, and thus a separation cannot be achieved using $M(OH)_2(s)$ solubility differences at pH = 4.0. The solubilities are both large.

19-50 pH = 11.6 gives a good separation.

19-52 $s = 9.1 \times 10^{-9}$ M (Use Equation (19-18) for $[S^{2-}]$ as a function of $[H_3O^+]$.)

19-54 Adjust pH to -0.07, where the solubility of $PbS(s)$ is 1×10^{-6} M and the solubility of $FeS(s)$ is 8×10^3 M.

19-56 $[Mn^{2+}] = [Fe^{2+}] = 0.01$ M; $[Cd^{2+}] = 7 \times 10^{-7}$ M

19-58 $Zn^{2+}(aq) + 2OH^-(aq) \longrightarrow Zn(OH)_2(s)$
$Zn(OH)_2(s) + 2OH^-(aq) \longrightarrow Zn(OH)_4^{2-}(aq)$

19-60 8×10^{-3} M

19-62 5.0×10^{-4} M

19-64 1.2×10^7 M (pH = 3.0); 12 M (pH = 6.0); 8×10^{-4} M (pH = 12.0)
At higher pH, the solubility of $Pb(OH)_2$ would be greater.

F   ANSWERS TO THE SELF-TEST

1 soluble

2 soluble

3 soluble

4 soluble

5 insoluble

6 insoluble

7 soluble

8 $(NH_4)_2CO_3(aq) + CaCl_2(aq) \longrightarrow$ $CaCO_3(s) + 2NH_4Cl(aq)$

9 $Na_2S(aq) + Zn(NO_3)_2(aq) \longrightarrow$ $ZnS(s) + 2NaNO_3(aq)$

10 $K_{sp} = [Ca^{2+}][CO_3^{2-}]$

11 $K_{sp} = [Mg^{2+}][OH^-]^2$

12 true

13 true

14 false $(s = [OH^-]/2)$

15 false (common-ion effect)

16 false $([Ag^+][Cl^-] = K_{sp}$ in any aqueous solution in contact with solid AgCl.)

17 the decrease in the solubility of an ionic solid that results when one of the constituent ions of the salt is added to the solution

18 decreased

19 increased, due to $Ag(NH_3)_2^+(aq)$ formation

20 $Cu(OH)_2(s)$ will form.

21 $Ag_2SO_4(s)$ will not form.

22 $AgCl(s) + 2NH_3(aq) \rightleftharpoons$ $Ag(NH_3)_2^+(aq) + Cl^-(aq)$

23 $AgCl(s)$ (The reaction is $Ag(NH_3)_2^+(aq) + 2H_3O^+(aq) +$ $Cl^-(aq) \rightleftharpoons AgCl(s) +$ $2NH_4^+(aq) + 2H_2O(l).)$

24 false

25 more (because CO_3^{2-} is the conjugate base of a weak acid)

26 because of the reaction

$AgC_7H_5O_2(s) + H_3O^+(aq) \rightleftharpoons$ $Ag^+(aq) + HC_7H_5O_2(aq) + H_2O(l)$

27 CO_2

28 true

29 $FeS(s) + 2H_3O^+(aq) \rightleftharpoons$ $Fe^{2+}(aq) + H_2S(aq) + 2H_2O(l)$

30 true

31 true

32 true

33 true

34 true

35 false $(Al(OH)_3$ is soluble in strong acids and strong bases.)

36 $Al(OH)_3(s) \rightleftharpoons$ $Al^{3+}(aq) + 3OH^-(aq)$

37 $Al(OH)_3(s) + 3H_3O^+(aq) \rightleftharpoons$ $Al^{3+}(aq) + 6H_2O(l)$

38 $Al(OH)_3(s) + OH^-(aq) \rightleftharpoons$ $Al(OH)_4^-(aq)$

39 $Zn(OH)_2(s) + 2OH^-(aq) \rightleftharpoons$ $Zn(OH)_4^{2-}(aq)$

40 true

41 the species present; that is, the anions and cations

42 $Ag^+(aq)$, as $AgCl(s)$

43 true

44 true

45 false (Metal sulfides have a variety of colors.)

46 pH

47 false (e.g., HgS is insoluble)

48 pH

49 false

50 true

51 false (Both cations are soluble in $HCl(aq)$.)

52 $Fe(OH)_2(s)$; $Zn(OH)_4^{2-}(aq)$ (Iron(II) does not form a hydroxyl ion.)

20 / Oxidation–Reduction Reactions

A   OUTLINE OF CHAPTER 20

20-1   An oxidation state can be assigned to each atom in a chemical species.

The rules for the assignment of oxidation states to the elements in a chemical species are given on page 782.

20-2   Oxidation states can be assigned using Lewis formulas.

A general method for assigning oxidation states from Lewis formulas is given.

Fluorine, the most electronegative element, is assigned an oxidation state of -1 in compounds..

20-3   Oxidation-reduction reactions involve the transfer of electrons from one reactant to another.

A decrease in oxidation state is called reduction.

An increase in oxidation state is called oxidation.

The reactant that contains the element that is reduced is called the oxidizing agent.

The reactant that contains the element that is oxidized is called the reducing agent.

An oxidizing agent acts as an electron acceptor.

A reducing agent acts as an electron donor.

20-4   Electron-transfer reactions can be separated into two half-reactions.

Oxidation-reduction reactions can be written as the sum of two half-reactions.

The half-reaction in which electrons appear on the right-hand side is the oxidation half-reaction.

The half-reaction in which electrons appear on the left-hand side is the reduction half-reaction. For example,

$$Zn(s) \longrightarrow Zn^{2+}(aq) + 2e^- \qquad \text{(oxidation half-reaction)}$$
$$Cu^{2+}(aq) + 2e^- \longrightarrow Cu(s) \qquad \text{(reduction half-reaction)}$$

20-5 Equations for oxidation-reduction reactions can be balanced by balancing each half-reaction separately.

The procedure for balancing equations by the method of half-reactions is discussed in detail (pages 790 through 792).

The procedure also applies to balancing half-reactions (Example 20-8).

20-6 Chemical equations for reactions occurring in basic solution should not contain $H^+(aq)$.

The procedure for balancing equations that occur in basic solution requires one more step than for reactions that occur in acidic solution.

If any $H^+(aq)$ appears in the balanced equation for a reaction in basic solution, then enough $OH^-(aq)$ is added to both sides to neutralize all the $H^+(aq)$.

20-7 Bleaches and disinfectants are strong oxidizing agents.

B SELF-TEST

1 The oxidation state of a free element is _____.

2 The alkali metals in compounds are always assigned an oxidation state of _____.

3 The alkaline earth metals in compounds are assigned an oxidation state of _____.

4 Oxygen in compounds usually is assigned an oxidation state of _____.

5 Hydrogen in compounds usually is assigned an oxidation state of _____.

6 The sum of the oxidation states of each atom in a chemical species is equal to the charge on the species. *True/False*

7 The name of NaH is _____.

8 The oxidation state of hydrogen in NaH is _____.

9 The oxidation state of chlorine in NaCl is _____.

10 The oxidation state of sulfur in K_2S is _____.

11 The name of Na_2O_2 is _____.

12 The oxidation state of oxygen in Na_2O_2 is _____.

13 The oxidation state of sulfur in SO_4^{2-} is _____.

14 The oxidation state of an element in a compound is always equal to the actual charge on the atom. *True/False*

15 Oxidation states can be assigned using the Lewis formula of a chemical species and the _____ of the atoms.

16 The most electronegative element is _____.

17 Fluorine in compounds is always assigned an oxidation state of _____.

18 The oxidation state of chlorine in ClF_3 is _____.

19 Oxidation-reduction reactions involve the transfer of _____ between reactants.

20 Oxidation is an (*increase/decrease*) in oxidation state.

21 An oxidizing agent is the reactant that contains _____
_____.

22 An oxidizing agent acts as an electron (*donor/acceptor*).
Consider the following reaction for questions 23 through 28.

$$2AgNO_3(aq) + Ni(s) \longrightarrow Ni(NO_3)_2(aq) + 2Ag(s)$$

23 The element oxidized is _____.

24 The element reduced is _____.

25 The oxidizing agent is _____.

26 The reducing agent is _____.

27 The electron donor is _____.

28 The electron acceptor is _____.
Consider the following reaction for questions 29 through 34.

$$FeCl_2(aq) + CeCl_4(aq) \longrightarrow FeCl_3(aq) + CeCl_3(aq)$$

29 The element oxidized is _____.

30 The element reduced is _____.

31 The oxidizing agent is _____.

32 The reducing agent is _____.

33 The oxidation half-reaction is _____.

34 The reduction half-reaction is _____.
Consider the following half-reaction for questions 35 through 38.

$$NO_3^-(aq) \longrightarrow N_2(g)$$

35 The equation when balanced with respect to nitrogen is _____
_____.

36 Now balance the equation with respect to oxygen.
_____.

37 Now balance the equation with respect to hydrogen in an acidic solution.
_____.

38 The equation balanced with respect to charge is _____
_____.

39 In a balanced oxidation-reduction equation, the number of electrons donated by the oxidation half-reaction must equal _____
_____.

40 Reactions occurring in basic solutions may contain $H^+(aq)$ in the balanced equation. *True/False*

41 In reactions occurring in basic solution, the $H^+(aq)$ in the solution reacts with $OH^-(aq)$ to produce $H_2O(l)$. *True/False*

42 Bleaches are reducing agents. *True/False*

C   CALCULATIONS YOU SHOULD KNOW HOW TO DO

1 Assign oxidation states to each atom in a molecule or an ion. This is done either by
(a) applying the rules given in Section 20-1. See Examples 20-1 and 20-2 and Problems 20-1 through 20-8.
(b) writing out the Lewis formula. See Examples 20-3 and Problems 20-9 and 20-10.
(c) analogy within the periodic table. See Example 20-4.

2 Use the method of half-reactions to balance oxidation-reduction equations. See Example 20-7 and Problems 20-19 through 20-32 and 20-39 through 20-46.

3 Balance half-reactions. See Examples 20-8 through 20-10 and Problems 20-33 through 20-38.

4 Carry out stoichiometric calculations involving oxidation-reduction reactions. See Problems 20-47 through 20-52.

D   SOLUTIONS TO THE ODD-NUMBERED PROBLEMS

20-1 (a) $Cr_2O_7^{2-}$ We assign oxygen an oxidation state of -2 (rule 6). The oxidation state, x, of chromium is thus given by (rule 2)

$$2x + 7(-2) = -2$$

or $x = +6$. The oxidation state of chromium in $Cr_2O_7^{2-}$ is $+6$.

(b) MoO_4^{2-} We assign oxygen an oxidation state of -2 (rule 6). The oxidation state, x, of molybdenum is thus given by (rule 2)

$$x + 4(-2) = -2$$

or $x = +6$. The oxidation state of molybdenum in MoO_4^{2-} is $+6$.

(c) $Cr(OH)_4^-$ We assign oxygen a state of -2 (rule 6) and hydrogen a state of $+1$ (rule 5). The oxidation state, x, of chromium is given by (rule 2)

$$x + 4(-2) + 4(+1) = -1$$

or $x = +3$. The oxidation state of chromium in $Cr(OH)_4^-$ is $+3$.

(d) VO_2^+ We assign oxygen an oxidation state of -2 (rule 6). The oxidation state, x, of vanadium is given by (rule 2)

$$x + 2(-2) = +1$$

or $x = +5$. The oxidation state of vanadium in VO_2^+ is $+5$.

(e) MnO_4^- We assign oxygen an oxidation state of -2 (rule 6). The oxidation state, x, of manganese is given by (rule 2)

$$x + 4(-2) = -1$$

or $x = +7$. The oxidation state of manganese in MnO_4^- is $+7$.

20-3 (a) Na_2SeO_3 We assign sodium an oxidation state of $+1$ (rule 3) and oxygen an oxidation state of -2 (rule 6). The oxidation state, x, of selenium is given by (rule 2) $2(+1) + x + 3(-2) = 0$ or $x = +4$. The oxidation state of selenium in Na_2SeO_3 is $+4$.

(b) H_3PO_4 We assign hydrogen an oxidation state of $+1$ (rule 5) and oxygen an oxidation state of -2 (rule 6). The oxidation state, x, of phosphorus is given by (rule 2) $3(+1) + x + 4(-2) = 0$ or $x = +5$. The oxidation state of phosphorus in H_3PO_4 is $+5$.

(c) Na_2SiF_6 We assign sodium an oxidation state of $+1$ (rule 3) and fluorine an oxidation state of -1. The oxidation state, x, of silicon is given by (rule 2) $2(+1) + x + 6(-1) = 0$ or $x = +4$. The oxidation state of silicon in Na_2SiF_6 is $+4$.

(d) $NaBrO_3$ We assign sodium an oxidation state of $+1$ (rule 3) and oxygen an oxidation state of -2 (rule 6). The oxidation state, x, of bromine is given by (rule 2) $+1 + x + 3(-2) = 0$ or $x = +5$. The oxidation state of bromine in $NaBrO_3$ is $+5$.

(e) $HAsO_2$ We assign hydrogen an oxidation state of $+1$ (rule 5) and oxygen an oxidation state of -2 (rule 6). The oxidation state, x, of arsenic is given by (rule 2) $+1 + x + 2(-2) = 0$ or $x = +3$. The oxidation state of arsenic in $HAsO_2$ is $+3$.

20-5 (a) NO_2 We assign oxygen an oxidation state of -2 (rule 6). The oxidation state, x, of nitrogen is (rule 2) $x + 2(-2) = 0$ or $x = +4$.

(b) N_2 We assign nitrogen an oxidation state of 0 (rule 1).

(c) N_2O We assign oxygen an oxidation state of -2 (rule 6). The oxidation state, x, of nitrogen is (rule 2) $2x + 1(-2) = 0$ or $x = +1$.

(d) NO_3^- We assign oxygen an oxidation state of -2 (rule 6). The oxidation state, x, of nitrogen is (rule 2) $x + 3(-2) = -1$ or $x = +5$.

(e) NO_2^- We assign oxygen an oxidation state of -2 (rule 6). The oxidation state, x, of nitrogen is (rule 2) $x + 2(-2) = -1$ or $x = +3$.

20-7   (a) H_2CO We assign oxygen an oxidation state of -2 (rule 6) and hydrogen an oxidation state of $+1$ (rule 5). The oxidation state, x, of carbon is given by (rule 2) $2(+1) + x + 1(-2) = 0$ or $x = 0$.

(b) CH_4 We assign hydrogen an oxidation state of $+1$ (rule 5). The oxidation state, x, of carbon is given by (rule 2) $x + 4(+1) = 0$ or $x = -4$.

(c) CH_3OH We assign oxygen an oxidation state of -2 (rule 6) and hydrogen an oxidation state of $+1$ (rule 5). The oxidation state, x, of carbon is given by (rule 2) $x + 3(+1) + 1(-2) + 1(+1) = 0$ or $x = -2$.

(d) $HCHO_2$ We assign oxygen an oxidation state of -2 (rule 6) and hydrogen an oxidation state of $+1$ (rule 5). The oxidation state, x, of carbon is given by (rule 2) $+1 + x + 1 + 2(-2) = 0$ or $x = +2$.

(e) CO_2 We assign oxygen an oxidation state of -2 (rule 6). The oxidation state, x, of carbon is given by (rule 2) $x + 2(-2) = 0$ or $x = +4$.

20-9   (a) $SbCl_3$ The Lewis formula for $SbCl_3$ is

$$:\overset{..}{\underset{..}{Cl}}—\overset{..}{Sb}—\overset{..}{\underset{..}{Cl}}:$$
$$|$$
$$:\overset{..}{\underset{..}{Cl}}:$$

Because chlorine is more electronegative than antimony, we assign the electrons in each of the three covalent bonds to the chlorine atoms. Therefore, the oxidation state of antimony is $5 - 2 = +3$.

(b) Sb_4O_6 We assign oxygen an oxidation state of -2 (rule 6). The oxidation state, x, of antimony is given by (rule 2) $4x + 6(-2) = 0$ or $x = +3$.

(c) SbF_5^{2-} The Lewis formula of SbF_5^{2-} is

$$\left[\begin{array}{c} :\overset{..}{F}: \\ :F—Sb—F: \\ :\overset{..}{F}: \quad \overset{..}{F}: \end{array} \right]^{2-}$$

Because fluorine is more electronegative than antimony, we assign the electrons in each of the five covalent bonds to fluorine. Therefore, the oxidation state of antimony is $5 - 2 = +3$.

(d) $SbCl_6^{3-}$ The Lewis formula of $SbCl_6^{3-}$ is

$$\left[\begin{array}{c} \overset{..}{Cl} \quad :\overset{..}{Cl}: \\ :Cl—Sb—Cl: \\ :\overset{..}{Cl}: \quad :\overset{..}{Cl}: \end{array} \right]^{3-}$$

Because chlorine is more electronegative than antimony, we assign the electrons in each of the six covalent bonds to the chlorine atom. Therefore, the oxidation state of antimony is $5 - 2 = +3$.

(e) Sb_2O_4 We assign oxygen an oxidation state of -2 (rule 6). The oxidation state, x, of antimony is given by $2x + 4(-2) = 0$ or $x = +4$.

20-11 The oxidation state of iodine decreases from $+5$ in I_2O_5 to 0 in I_2. Thus iodine is reduced and I_2O_5 acts as the oxidizing agent. The oxidation state of carbon increases from $+2$ in CO to $+4$ in CO_2. Thus carbon is oxidized and CO acts as the reducing agent.

20-13 The oxidation state of nitrogen decreases from $+5$ in $NaNO_3$ to $+3$ in $NaNO_2$. Thus nitrogen is reduced; $NaNO_3$ is the oxidizing agent. The oxidation state of lead increases from 0 in Pb to $+2$ in PbO. Thus lead is oxidized; Pb is the reducing agent.

20-15 (a) The oxidation state of vanadium increases from 0 in V to $+2$ in V^{2+}. Thus vanadium is oxidized and acts as the reducing agent. The oxidation state of nickel decreases from $+2$ in Ni^{2+} to 0 in Ni. Thus $Ni^{2+}(aq)$ is reduced and acts as the oxidizing agent. The half-reactions are

$$V(s) \longrightarrow V^{2+}(aq) + 2e^- \qquad \text{(oxidation half-reaction)}$$
$$Ni^{2+}(aq) + 2e^- \longrightarrow Ni(s) \qquad \text{(reduction half-reaction)}$$

(b) The oxidation state of titanium increases from $+2$ in Ti^{2+} to $+3$ in Ti^{3+}. Thus Ti^{2+} is oxidized and acts as the reducing agent. The oxidation state of cobalt decreases from $+2$ in Co^{2+} in 0 in Co. Thus $Co^{2+}(aq)$ is reduced and acts as the oxidizing agent. The half-reactions are

$$Ti^{2+}(aq) \longrightarrow Ti^{3+}(aq) + e^- \qquad \text{(oxidation half-reaction)}$$
$$Co^{2+}(aq) + 2e^- \longrightarrow Co(s) \qquad \text{(reduction half-reaction)}$$

20-17 The oxygen in KO_2 is in an unusual oxidation state $(-\frac{1}{2})$. The common oxidation state of oxygen is -2, and so the oxygen in KO_2 is easily reduced from $-\frac{1}{2}$ to -2, thus making KO_2 a strong oxidizing agent.

20-19 (a) The oxidation state of chromium decreases from $+6$ to $+3$ and the oxidation state of chlorine increases from -1 to $+3$. The oxidation half-reaction and the reduction half-reaction are

$$Cl^- \longrightarrow ClO_2^- \qquad \text{(oxidation)}$$
$$CrO_4^{2-} \longrightarrow Cr^{3+} \qquad \text{(reduction)}$$

Each half-reaction is balanced with respect to Cl and Cr. We add $2H_2O$ to the left side of the oxidation half-reaction and $4H_2O$ to the right side of the reduction half-reaction in order to balance the oxygen atoms:

$$2H_2O + Cl^- \longrightarrow ClO_2^- \qquad \text{(oxidation)}$$
$$CrO_4^{2-} \longrightarrow Cr^{3+} + 4H_2O \qquad \text{(reduction)}$$

To balance the hydrogen atoms, we now add $4H^+$ to the right side of the oxidation half-reaction and $8H^+$ to the left side of the reduction half-reaction:

$$Cl^- + 2H_2O \longrightarrow ClO_2^- + 4H^+ \qquad \text{(oxidation)}$$

$$CrO_4^{2-} + 8H^+ \longrightarrow Cr^{3+} + 4H_2O \qquad \text{(reduction)}$$

We add 4 electrons to the right-hand side of the oxidation half-reaction to balance the charge; we add 3 electrons to the left-hand side of the reduction half-reaction to balance the charge:

$$Cl^- + 2H_2O \longrightarrow ClO_2^- + 4H^+ + 4e^- \qquad \text{(oxidation)}$$

$$CrO_4^{2-} + 8H^+ + 3e^- \longrightarrow Cr^{3+} + 4H_2O \qquad \text{(reduction)}$$

If we multiply the oxidation half-reaction by 3 and the reduction half-reaction by 4, each reaction will involve 12 electrons:

$$3Cl^- + 6H_2O \longrightarrow 3ClO_2^- + 12H^+ + 12e^- \qquad \text{(oxidation)}$$

$$4CrO_4^{2-} + 32H^+ + 12e^- \longrightarrow 4Cr^{3+} + 16H_2O \qquad \text{(reduction)}$$

If we add the half-reactions and indicate the various phases, then we have the balanced equation

$$4CrO_4^{2-}(aq) + 3Cl^-(aq) + 20H^+(aq) \longrightarrow$$

$$3ClO_2^-(aq) + 4Cr^{3+}(aq) + 10H_2O(l)$$

(b) The oxidation state of iodine decreases from $+5$ to -1 and the oxidation state of chromium increases from $+3$ to $+6$. The oxidation half-reaction and the reduction half-reaction are

$$Cr(OH)_4^- \longrightarrow CrO_4^{2-} \qquad \text{(oxidation)}$$

$$IO_3^- \longrightarrow I^- \qquad \text{(reduction)}$$

Both half-reactions are balanced with respect to Cr and I. To balance the oxygen atoms, we add $3H_2O$ to the right side of the reduction half-reaction. Notice that the oxidation half-reaction is already balanced with respect to oxygen.

$$Cr(OH)_4^- \longrightarrow CrO_4^{2-} \qquad \text{(oxidation)}$$

$$IO_3^- \longrightarrow I^- + 3H_2O \qquad \text{(reduction)}$$

To balance the hydrogen atoms, we add $4H^+$ to the right side of the oxidation half-reaction and $6H^+$ to the left side of the reduction half-reaction:

$$Cr(OH)_4^- \longrightarrow CrO_4^{2-} + 4H^+ \qquad \text{(oxidation)}$$

$$IO_3^- + 6H^+ \longrightarrow I^- + 3H_2O \qquad \text{(reduction)}$$

To balance the charges, we add 3 electrons to the right side of the oxidation half-reaction and 6 electrons to the left side of the reduction half-reaction

$$Cr(OH)_4^- \longrightarrow CrO_4^{2-} + 4H^+ + 3e^- \qquad \text{(oxidation)}$$

$$IO_3^- + 6H^+ + 6e^- \longrightarrow I^- + 3H_2O \qquad \text{(reduction)}$$

If we multiply the oxidation half-reaction by 2, then both half-reactions involve 6 electrons.

$$2Cr(OH)_4^- \longrightarrow 2CrO_4^{2-} + 8H^+ + 6e^- \qquad \text{(oxidation)}$$

$$IO_3^- + 6H^+ + 6e^- \longrightarrow I^- + 3H_2O \qquad \text{(reduction)}$$

If we add the two reactions and indicate the various phases, then we have

$$IO_3^-(aq) + 2Cr(OH)_4^-(aq) \longrightarrow I^-(aq) + 2CrO_4^{2-}(aq) + 2H^+(aq) + 3H_2O(l)$$

We cannot have H^+ in basic solution. If we add $2OH^-$ to both sides of the reaction, we have the balanced equation in basic solution

$$IO_3^-(aq) + 2Cr(OH)_4^-(aq) + 2OH^-(aq) \longrightarrow$$
$$I^-(aq) + 2CrO_4^{2-}(aq) + \underbrace{2H^+(aq) + 2OH^-(aq)}_{2H_2O} + 3H_2O(l)$$

or

$$IO_3^-(aq) + 2Cr(OH)_4^-(aq) + 2OH^-(aq) \longrightarrow I^-(aq) + 2CrO_4^{2-}(aq) + 5H_2O(l)$$

(c) The oxidation state of arsenic increases from $+3$ to $+5$. The oxidation state of iodine increases from $-\frac{1}{3}$ to -1. The oxidation half-reaction and reduction half-reaction are

$$HAsO_2 \longrightarrow H_3AsO_4 \qquad \text{(oxidation)}$$

$$I_3^- \longrightarrow I^- \qquad \text{(reduction)}$$

We must balance the iodine in the reduction half-reaction:

$$HAsO_2 \longrightarrow H_3AsO_4 \qquad \text{(oxidation)}$$

$$I_3^- \longrightarrow 3I^- \qquad \text{(reduction)}$$

We add $2H_2O$ to the left side of the oxidation half-reaction to balance the oxygen atoms:

$$HAsO_2 + 2H_2O \longrightarrow H_3AsO_4 \qquad \text{(oxidation)}$$

$$I_3^- \longrightarrow 3I^- \qquad \text{(reduction)}$$

To balance the hydrogen atoms, we add $2H^+$ to the right side of the oxidation half-reaction:

$$HAsO_2 + 2H_2O \longrightarrow H_3AsO_4 + 2H^+ \qquad \text{(oxidation)}$$
$$I_3^- \longrightarrow 3I^- \qquad \text{(reduction)}$$

To balance charges, we add 2 electrons to the right side of the oxidation half-reaction and 2 electrons to the left side of the reduction half-reaction:

$$HAsO_2 + 2H_2O \longrightarrow H_3AsO_4 + 2H^+ + 2e^- \qquad \text{(oxidation)}$$
$$I_3^- + 2e^- \longrightarrow 3I^- \qquad \text{(reduction)}$$

Each reaction involves two electrons. If we add the two half-reactions and indicate phases, then we have the balanced equation

$$HAsO_2(aq) + I_3^-(aq) + 2H_2O(l) \longrightarrow H_3AsO_4(aq) + 3I^-(aq) + 2H^+(aq)$$

20-21   (a) The two half-reactions are

$$NO_2^- \longrightarrow NO_3^- \qquad \text{(oxidation)}$$
$$BrO_3^- \longrightarrow Br^- \qquad \text{(reduction)}$$

We add H_2O to the left side of the oxidation half-reaction and $3H_2O$ to the right side of the reduction half-reaction:

$$NO_2^- + H_2O \longrightarrow NO_3^- \qquad \text{(oxidation)}$$
$$BrO_3^- \longrightarrow Br^- + 3H_2O \qquad \text{(reduction)}$$

Now we add $2H^+$ to the right side of the first half-reaction and $6H^+$ to the left side of the second:

$$NO_2^- + H_2O \longrightarrow NO_3^- + 2H^+ \qquad \text{(oxidation)}$$
$$BrO_3^- + 6H^+ \longrightarrow Br^- + 3H_2O \qquad \text{(reduction)}$$

We add 2 electrons to the right side of the oxidation half-reaction and 6 electrons to the left side of the reduction half-reaction:

$$NO_2^- + H_2O \longrightarrow NO_3^- + 2H^+ + 2e^- \qquad \text{(oxidation)}$$
$$BrO_3^- + 6H^+ + 6e^- \longrightarrow Br^- + 3H_2O \qquad \text{(reduction)}$$

If we multiply the oxidation half-reaction by 3, then both reactions involve 6 electrons:

$$3NO_2^- + 3H_2O \longrightarrow 3NO_3^- + 6H^+ + 6e^- \qquad \text{(oxidation)}$$
$$BrO_3^- + 6H^+ + 6e^- \longrightarrow Br^- + 3H_2O \qquad \text{(reduction)}$$

If we add the two half-reactions and indicate the various phases, then we have the balanced equation

$$BrO_3^-(aq) + 3NO_2^-(aq) \longrightarrow 3NO_3^-(aq) + Br^-(aq)$$

(b) The two half-reactions are

$$Sb \longrightarrow Sb_2O_3 \qquad \text{(oxidation)}$$
$$MnO_4^- \longrightarrow MnO_2 \qquad \text{(reduction)}$$

We first balance with respect to Sb:

$$2Sb \longrightarrow Sb_2O_3 \qquad \text{(oxidation)}$$
$$MnO_4^- \longrightarrow MnO_2 \qquad \text{(reduction)}$$

Now balance with respect to oxygen atoms:

$$2Sb + 3H_2O \longrightarrow Sb_2O_3 \qquad \text{(oxidation)}$$
$$MnO_4^- \longrightarrow MnO_2 + 2H_2O \qquad \text{(reduction)}$$

Now balance the hydrogen atoms:

$$2Sb + 3H_2O \longrightarrow Sb_2O_3 + 6H^+ \qquad \text{(oxidation)}$$
$$MnO_4^- + 4H^+ \longrightarrow MnO_2 + 2H_2O \qquad \text{(reduction)}$$

Add electrons to balance the charges:

$$2Sb + 3H_2O \longrightarrow Sb_2O_3 + 6H^+ + 6e^- \qquad \text{(oxidation)}$$
$$MnO_4^- + 4H^+ + 3e^- \longrightarrow MnO_2 + 2H_2O \qquad \text{(reduction)}$$

Multiply the reduction half-reaction by 2:

$$2Sb + 3H_2O \longrightarrow Sb_2O_3 + 6H^+ + 6e^- \qquad \text{(oxidation)}$$
$$2MnO_4^- + 8H^+ + 6e^- \longrightarrow 2MnO_2 + 4H_2O \qquad \text{(reduction)}$$

Add these two half-reactions to obtain the balanced equation:

$$2MnO_4^-(aq) + 2Sb(s) + 2H^+(aq) \longrightarrow Sb_2O_3(s) + 2MnO_2(s) + H_2O(l)$$

(c) The two half-reactions are

$$Cr^{2+} \longrightarrow Cr^{3+} \qquad \text{(oxidation)}$$
$$H_2MoO_4 \longrightarrow Mo \qquad \text{(reduction)}$$

Balance the oxygen atoms by adding H_2O:

$$Cr^{2+} \longrightarrow Cr^{3+} \qquad \text{(oxidation)}$$
$$H_2MoO_4 \longrightarrow Mo + 4H_2O \qquad \text{(reduction)}$$

Balance the hydrogen atoms by adding H^+:

$$Cr^{2+} \longrightarrow Cr^{3+} \qquad \text{(oxidation)}$$
$$H_2MoO_4 + 6H^+ \longrightarrow Mo + 4H_2O \qquad \text{(reduction)}$$

Now balance the charges by adding electrons:

$$Cr^{2+} \longrightarrow Cr^{3+} + e^- \qquad \text{(oxidation)}$$
$$H_2MoO_4 + 6H^+ + 6e^- \longrightarrow Mo + 4H_2O \qquad \text{(reduction)}$$

Multiply the oxidation half-reaction by 6:

$$6Cr^{2+} \longrightarrow 6Cr^{3+} + 6e^- \qquad \text{(oxidation)}$$
$$H_2MoO_4 + 6H^+ + 6e^- \longrightarrow Mo + 4H_2O \qquad \text{(reduction)}$$

and add to obtain the balanced equation

$$H_2MoO_4(aq) + 6Cr^{2+}(aq) + 6H^+(aq) \longrightarrow Mo(s) + 6Cr^{3+}(aq) + 4H_2O(l)$$

20-23 (a) The two half-reactions are

$$Fe(OH)_2 \longrightarrow Fe(OH)_3 \qquad \text{(oxidation)}$$
$$O_2 \longrightarrow OH^- \qquad \text{(reduction)}$$

We are able to include the OH^- on the right side of the reduction half-reaction because the reaction takes place in basic solution. Oxygen is reduced in the reduction half-reaction and so must be treated specially. We balance the oxygen atoms in the reduction half-reaction first to obtain

$$Fe(OH)_2 \longrightarrow Fe(OH)_3 \qquad \text{(oxidation)}$$
$$O_2 \longrightarrow 2OH^- \qquad \text{(reduction)}$$

We now add H_2O to the left side of the oxidation half-reaction to balance the oxygen atoms:

$$Fe(OH)_2 + H_2O \longrightarrow Fe(OH)_3 \qquad \text{(oxidation)}$$
$$O_2 \longrightarrow 2OH^- \qquad \text{(reduction)}$$

Add H^+ to balance hydrogen atoms:

$$Fe(OH)_2 + H_2O \longrightarrow Fe(OH)_3 + H^+ \qquad \text{(oxidation)}$$
$$O_2 + 2H^+ \longrightarrow 2OH^- \qquad \text{(reduction)}$$

We add electrons to balance charges:

$$Fe(OH)_2 + H_2O \longrightarrow Fe(OH)_3 + H^+ + e^- \quad \text{(oxidation)}$$
$$O_2 + 2H^+ + 4e^- \longrightarrow 2OH^- \quad \text{(reduction)}$$

If we multiply the oxidation half-reaction by 4, then both half-reactions involve 4 electrons:

$$4Fe(OH)_2 + 4H_2O \longrightarrow 4Fe(OH)_3 + 4H^+ + 4e^- \quad \text{(oxidation)}$$
$$O_2 + 2H^+ + 4e^- \longrightarrow 2OH^- \quad \text{(reduction)}$$

If we add the two half-reactions, then we have the balanced equation

$$4Fe(OH)_2 + O_2 + 4H_2O \longrightarrow 4Fe(OH)_3 + \underbrace{2H^+ + 2OH^-}_{2H_2O}$$

Indicating various phases, we have

$$4Fe(OH)_2(s) + O_2(g) + 2H_2O(l) \longrightarrow 4Fe(OH)_3(s)$$

(b) The two half-reactions are

$$Cu \longrightarrow Cu^{2+} \quad \text{(oxidation)}$$
$$NO_3^- \longrightarrow NO \quad \text{(reduction)}$$

Adding H_2O and H^+ to balance the oxygen atoms and hydrogen atoms gives

$$Cu \longrightarrow Cu^{2+} \quad \text{(oxidation)}$$
$$NO_3^- + 4H^+ \longrightarrow NO + 2H_2O \quad \text{(reduction)}$$

Adding electrons to balance charges gives

$$Cu \longrightarrow Cu^{2+} + 2e^- \quad \text{(oxidation)}$$
$$NO_3^- + 4H^+ + 3e^- \longrightarrow NO + 2H_2O \quad \text{(reduction)}$$

Multiply the first half-reaction by 3 and the second by 2 to get

$$3Cu \longrightarrow 3Cu^{2+} + 6e^- \quad \text{(oxidation)}$$
$$2NO_3^- + 8H^+ + 6e^- \longrightarrow 2NO + 4H_2O \quad \text{(reduction)}$$

Add these two half-reactions to obtain the balanced equation

$$3Cu(s) + 2NO_3^-(aq) + 8H^+(aq) \longrightarrow 2NO(g) + 3Cu^{2+}(aq) + 4H_2O(l)$$

(c) The two half-reactions are

$$Bi_2O_3 \longrightarrow 2BiO_3^- \quad \text{(oxidation)}$$
$$ClO^- \longrightarrow Cl^- \quad \text{(reduction)}$$

Addition of H_2O and H^+ gives

$$Bi_2O_3 + 3H_2O \longrightarrow 2BiO_3^- + 6H^+ \quad \text{(oxidation)}$$
$$ClO^- + 2H^+ \longrightarrow Cl^- + H_2O \quad \text{(reduction)}$$

Addition of electrons gives

$$Bi_2O_3 + 3H_2O \longrightarrow 2BiO_3^- + 6H^+ + 4e^- \quad \text{(oxidation)}$$
$$ClO^- + 2H^+ + 2e^- \longrightarrow Cl^- + H_2O \quad \text{(reduction)}$$

Multiplication of the reduction half-reaction by 2 gives

$$Bi_2O_3 + 3H_2O \longrightarrow 2BiO_3^- + 6H^+ + 4e^- \quad \text{(oxidation)}$$
$$2ClO^- + 4H^+ + 4e^- \longrightarrow 2Cl^- + 2H_2O \quad \text{(reduction)}$$

Addition of these two half-reactions gives the balanced equation (in acid solution)

$$Bi_2O_3 + 2ClO^- + H_2O \longrightarrow 2BiO_3^- + 2Cl^- + 2H^+$$

Addition of OH^- to eliminate H^+ gives

$$Bi_2O_3 + 2ClO^- + H_2O + 2OH^- \longrightarrow 2BiO_3^- + 2Cl^- + \underbrace{2H^+ + 2OH^-}_{2H_2O}$$

or finally

$$Bi_2O_3(s) + 2ClO^-(aq) + 2OH^-(aq) \longrightarrow 2BiO_3^-(aq) + 2Cl^-(aq) + H_2O(l)$$

20-25 (a) The various steps are

$$NH_4^+ \longrightarrow N_2O \quad \text{(oxidation)}$$
$$NO_3^- \longrightarrow N_2O \quad \text{(reduction)}$$

$$2NH_4^+ \longrightarrow N_2O \quad \text{(oxidation)}$$
$$2NO_3^- \longrightarrow N_2O \quad \text{(reduction)}$$

$$2NH_4^+ + H_2O \longrightarrow N_2O + 10H^+ \quad \text{(oxidation)}$$
$$2NO_3^- + 10H^+ \longrightarrow N_2O + 5H_2O \quad \text{(reduction)}$$

$$2NH_4^+ + H_2O \longrightarrow N_2O + 10H^+ + 8e^- \quad \text{(oxidation)}$$
$$2NO_3^- + 10H^+ + 8e^- \longrightarrow N_2O + 5H_2O \quad \text{(reduction)}$$

$$2NH_4^+(aq) + 2NO_3^-(aq) \longrightarrow 2N_2O(g) + 4H_2O(l)$$

or
$$NH_4^+(aq) + NO_3^-(aq) \longrightarrow N_2O(g) + 2H_2O(l)$$

(b) The oxidation state of sulfur does not change in the reaction.

$$Hg \longrightarrow Hg_2SO_4 \qquad \text{(oxidation)}$$
$$Cr_2O_7^{2-} \longrightarrow Cr^{3+} \qquad \text{(reduction)}$$

$$2Hg \longrightarrow Hg_2SO_4 \qquad \text{(oxidation)}$$
$$Cr_2O_7^{2-} \longrightarrow 2Cr^{3+} \qquad \text{(reduction)}$$

Sulfur is balanced by using H_2SO_4:

$$2Hg + H_2SO_4 \longrightarrow Hg_2SO_4 + 2H^+ \qquad \text{(oxidation)}$$
$$Cr_2O_7^{2-} + 14H^+ \longrightarrow 2Cr^{3+} + 7H_2O \qquad \text{(reduction)}$$

$$2Hg + H_2SO_4 \longrightarrow Hg_2SO_4 + 2H^+ + 2e^- \qquad \text{(oxidation)}$$
$$Cr_2O_7^{2-} + 14H^+ + 6e^- \longrightarrow 2Cr^{3+} + 7H_2O \qquad \text{(reduction)}$$

$$6Hg + 3H_2SO_4 \longrightarrow 3Hg_2SO_4 + 6H^+ + 6e^- \qquad \text{(oxidation)}$$
$$Cr_2O_7^{2-} + 14H^+ + 6e^- \longrightarrow 2Cr^{3+} + 7H_2O \qquad \text{(reduction)}$$

$$6Hg(l) + 3H_2SO_4(aq) + Cr_2O_7^{2-}(aq) + 8H^+(aq) \longrightarrow$$
$$3Hg_2SO_4(s) + 2Cr^{3+}(aq) + 7H_2O(l)$$

(c) The notation $\cdot 3H_3O$ signifies three waters of hydration:

$$Fe \longrightarrow Fe_2O_3 \cdot 3H_2O \qquad \text{(oxidation)}$$
$$O_2 \longrightarrow OH^- \qquad \text{(reduction)}$$

$$2Fe \longrightarrow Fe_2O_3 \cdot 3H_2O \qquad \text{(oxidation)}$$
$$O_2 \longrightarrow 2OH^- \qquad \text{(reduction)}$$

$$2Fe + 6H_2O \longrightarrow Fe_2O_3 \cdot 3H_2O + 6H^+ \qquad \text{(oxidation)}$$
$$O_2 + 2H^+ \longrightarrow 2OH^- \qquad \text{(reduction)}$$

$$2Fe + 6H_2O \longrightarrow Fe_2O_3 \cdot 3H_2O + 6H^+ + 6e^- \qquad \text{(oxidation)}$$
$$O_2 + 2H^+ + 4e^- \longrightarrow 2OH^- \qquad \text{(reduction)}$$

$$4Fe + 12H_2O \longrightarrow 2Fe_2O_3 \cdot 3H_2O + 12H^+ + 12e^- \qquad \text{(oxidation)}$$
$$3O_2 + 6H^+ + 12e^- \longrightarrow 6OH^- \qquad \text{(reduction)}$$

$$4Fe + 3O_2 + 12H_2O \longrightarrow 2Fe_2O_3 \cdot 3H_2O + \underbrace{6H^+ + 6OH^-}_{6H_2O}$$

or

$$4Fe(s) + 3O_2(g) + 6H_2O(l) \longrightarrow 2Fe_2O_3 \cdot 3H_2O(s)$$

20-27 (a) The various steps are

$$MnO \longrightarrow MnO_4^- \qquad \text{(oxidation)}$$
$$PbO_2 \longrightarrow Pb^{2+} \qquad \text{(reduction)}$$

$$MnO + 3H_2O \longrightarrow MnO_4^- + 6H^+ \qquad \text{(oxidation)}$$
$$PbO_2 + 4H^+ \longrightarrow Pb^{2+} + 2H_2O \qquad \text{(reduction)}$$

$$MnO + 3H_2O \longrightarrow MnO_4^- + 6H^+ + 5e^- \qquad \text{(oxidation)}$$
$$PbO_2 + 4H^+ + 2e^- \longrightarrow Pb^{2+} + 2H_2O \qquad \text{(reduction)}$$

$$2MnO + 6H_2O \longrightarrow 2MnO_4^- + 12H^+ + 10e^- \qquad \text{(oxidation)}$$
$$5PbO_2 + 20H^+ + 10e^- \longrightarrow 5Pb^{2+} + 10H_2O \qquad \text{(reduction)}$$

$$2MnO(s) + 5PbO_2(s) + 8H^+(aq) \longrightarrow 2MnO_4^-(aq) + 5Pb^{2+}(aq) + 4H_2O(l)$$

electron donor	MnO
electron acceptor	PbO$_2$
oxidizing agent	PbO$_2$
reducing agent	MnO
species oxidized	Mn
species reduced	Pb

(b) The oxidation state of arsenic does not change in this reaction. The various steps are

$$As_2S_5 \longrightarrow HSO_4^- \qquad \text{(oxidation)}$$
$$NO_3^- \longrightarrow NO_2 \qquad \text{(reduction)}$$

We balance arsenic by adding H_3AsO_4.

$$As_2S_5 \longrightarrow 5HSO_4^- + 2H_3AsO_4 \qquad \text{(oxidation)}$$
$$NO_3^- \longrightarrow NO_2 \qquad \text{(reduction)}$$

$$As_2S_5 + 28H_2O \longrightarrow 5HSO_4^- + 2H_3AsO_4 + 45H^+ \qquad \text{(oxidation)}$$
$$NO_3^- + 2H^+ \longrightarrow NO_2 + H_2O \qquad \text{(reduction)}$$

$$As_2S_5 + 28H_2O \longrightarrow 5HSO_4^- + 2H_3AsO_4 + 45H^+ + 40e^- \qquad \text{(oxidation)}$$
$$NO_3^- + 2H^+ + e^- \longrightarrow NO_2 + H_2O \qquad \text{(reduction)}$$

$$As_2S_5 + 28H_2O \longrightarrow 5HSO_4^- + 2H_3AsO_4 + 45H^+ + 40e^- \qquad \text{(oxidation)}$$
$$40NO_3^- + 80H^+ + 40e^- \longrightarrow 40NO_2 + 40H_2O \qquad \text{(reduction)}$$

$$As_2S_5(s) + 40NO_3^-(aq) + 35H^+(aq) \longrightarrow$$
$$5HSO_4^-(aq) + 2H_3AsO_4(aq) + 40NO_2(g) + 12H_2O(l)$$

electron donor	As_2S_5
electron acceptor	NO_3^-
oxidizing agent	NO_3^-
reducing agent	As_2S_5
species oxidized	S
species reduced	N

20-29

$$Zn \longrightarrow ZnO_2^{2-} \qquad \text{(oxidation)}$$
$$2MnO_2 \longrightarrow Mn_2O_3 \cdot H_2O \qquad \text{(reduction)}$$

$$Zn + 2H_2O \longrightarrow ZnO_2^{2-} + 4H^+ \qquad \text{(oxidation)}$$
$$2MnO_2 + 2H^+ \longrightarrow Mn_2O_3 \cdot H_2O \qquad \text{(reduction)}$$

$$Zn + 2H_2O \longrightarrow ZnO_2^{2-} + 4H^+ + 2e^- \qquad \text{(oxidation)}$$
$$2MnO_2 + 2H^+ + 2e^- \longrightarrow Mn_2O_3 \cdot H_2O \qquad \text{(reduction)}$$

$$Zn + 2MnO_2 + 2H_2O \longrightarrow ZnO_2^{2-} + Mn_2O_3 \cdot H_2O + 2H^+$$

or, adding OH^-,

$$Zn + 2MnO_2 + 2H_2O + 2OH^- \longrightarrow ZnO_2^{2-} + Mn_2O_3 \cdot H_2O + \underbrace{2H^+ + 2OH^-}_{2H_2O}$$

or finally

$$Zn(s) + 2MnO_2(s) + 2OH^-(aq) \longrightarrow ZnO_2^{2-}(aq) + Mn_2O_3 \cdot H_2O(s)$$

20-31 The two half-reactions are

$$CrI_3 \longrightarrow CrO_4^{2-} + IO_4^- \qquad \text{(oxidation)}$$
$$Cl_2 \longrightarrow Cl^- \qquad \text{(reduction)}$$

First balance the iodine atoms and the chlorine atoms:

$$CrI_3 \longrightarrow CrO_4^{2-} + 3IO_4^- \qquad \text{(oxidation)}$$
$$Cl_2 \longrightarrow 2Cl^- \qquad \text{(reduction)}$$

Now add H_2O and H^+ to balance the oxygen atoms and hydrogen atoms:

$$CrI_3 + 16H_2O \longrightarrow CrO_4^{2-} + 3IO_4^- + 32H^+ \qquad \text{(oxidation)}$$
$$Cl_2 \longrightarrow 2Cl^- \qquad \text{(reduction)}$$

Add electrons to balance charges

$$CrI_3 + 16H_2O \longrightarrow CrO_4^{2-} + 3IO_4^- + 32H^+ + 27e^- \quad \text{(oxidation)}$$
$$Cl_2 + 2e^- \longrightarrow 2Cl^- \quad \text{(reduction)}$$

Multiply the reduction half-reaction by 27 and the oxidation half-reaction by 2:

$$2CrI_3 + 32H_2O \longrightarrow 2CrO_4^{2-} + 6IO_4^- + 64H^+ + 54e^- \quad \text{(oxidation)}$$
$$27Cl_2 + 54e^- \longrightarrow 54Cl^- \quad \text{(reduction)}$$

Add to obtain the balanced equation

$$2CrI_3(s) + 27Cl_2(g) + 32H_2O(l) \longrightarrow$$
$$2CrO_4^{2-}(aq) + 6IO_4^-(aq) + 54Cl^-(aq) + 64H^+(aq)$$

Add OH^- to obtain

$$2CrI_3(s) + 27Cl_2(g) + 64OH^-(aq) \longrightarrow$$
$$2CrO_4^{2-}(aq) + 6IO_4^-(aq) + 54Cl^-(aq) + 32H_2O(l)$$

20-33 (a) We add $2H_2O$ to the right side of the reaction to balance the oxygen atoms and $4H^+$ to the left side to balance the hydrogen atoms:

$$PbO_2 + 4H^+ \longrightarrow Pb^{2+} + 2H_2O$$

We now add 2 electrons to the left side to balance the charge:

$$PbO_2(s) + 4H^+(aq) + 2e^- \longrightarrow Pb^{2+}(aq) + 2H_2O(l)$$

Note that the charge on each side of the equation is +2.

(b) We add $2H_2O$ to the right side of the reaction to balance the oxygen atoms and $4H^+$ to the left side to balance the hydrogen atoms:

$$MnO_2 + 4H^+ \longrightarrow Mn^{2+} + 2H_2O$$

We now add 2 electrons to the left side to balance the charge:

$$MnO_2(s) + 4H^+(aq) + 2e^- \longrightarrow Mn^{2+}(aq) + 2H_2O(l)$$

(c) We add $2H_2O$ to the left side of the reaction to balance the oxygen atoms and $4H^+$ to the right side to balance the hydrogen atoms:

$$NO + 2H_2O \longrightarrow NO_3^- + 4H^+$$

We now add 3 electrons to the right side to balance the charge:

$$NO(g) + 2H_2O(l) \longrightarrow NO_3^-(aq) + 4H^+(aq) + 3e^-$$

20-35 These half-reactions are balanced in a manner similar to those in Problem 20-33. The steps are

(a) $2WO_3 \longrightarrow W_2O_5$

$2WO_3 + 2H^+ \longrightarrow W_2O_5 + H_2O$

$2WO_3(s) + 2H^+(aq) + 2e^- \longrightarrow W_2O_5(s) + H_2O(l)$

(b) $U^{4+} + 2H_2O \longrightarrow UO_2^+ + 4H^+$

$U^{4+}(aq) + 2H_2O(l) \longrightarrow UO_2^+(aq) + 4H^+(aq) + e^-$

(c) $Zn + 4H_2O \longrightarrow Zn(OH)_4^{2-} + 4H^+$

$Zn + 4H_2O \longrightarrow Zn(OH)_4^{2-} + 4H^+ + 2e^-$

$Zn + 4H_2O + 4OH^- \longrightarrow Zn(OH)_4^{2-} + \underbrace{4H^+ + 4OH^-}_{4H_2O} + 2e^-$

$Zn(s) + 4OH^-(aq) \longrightarrow Zn(OH)_4^{2-}(aq) + 2e^-$

20-37 These half-reactions are balanced in a manner similar to those in Problem 20-33. The steps are

(a) $2SO_3^{2-} \longrightarrow S_2O_4^{2-}$

$2SO_3^{2-} + 4H^+ \longrightarrow S_2O_4^{2-} + 2H_2O$

$2SO_3^{2-} + 4H^+ + 2e^- \longrightarrow S_2O_4^{2-} + 2H_2O$

$2SO_3^{2-} + \underbrace{4H^+ + 4OH^-}_{4H_2O} + 2e^- \longrightarrow S_2O_4^{2-} + 2H_2O + 4OH^-$

$2SO_3^{2-}(aq) + 2H_2O(l) + 2e^- \longrightarrow S_2O_4^{2-}(aq) + 4OH^-(aq)$

(b) $2Cu(OH)_2 \longrightarrow Cu_2O$

$2Cu(OH)_2 + 2H^+ \longrightarrow Cu_2O + 3H_2O$

$2Cu(OH)_2 + 2H^+ + 2e^- \longrightarrow Cu_2O + 3H_2O$

$2Cu(OH)_2 + \underbrace{2H^+ + 2OH^-}_{2H_2O} + 2e^- \longrightarrow Cu_2O + 3H_2O + 2OH^-$

$2Cu(OH)_2(s) + 2e^- \longrightarrow Cu_2O(s) + H_2O(l) + 2OH^-(aq)$

(c) $2AgO \longrightarrow Ag_2O$

$2AgO + 2H^+ \longrightarrow Ag_2O + H_2O$

$2AgO + 2H^+ + 2e^- \longrightarrow Ag_2O + H_2O$

$2AgO + \underbrace{2H^+ + 2OH^-}_{2H_2O} + 2e^- \longrightarrow Ag_2O + H_2O + 2OH^-$

$2AgO(s) + H_2O(l) + 2e^- \longrightarrow Ag_2O(s) + 2OH^-(aq)$

(d) $HgO + 2H^+ \longrightarrow Hg + H_2O$

$HgO + 2H^+ + 2e^- \longrightarrow Hg + H_2O$

$HgO + \underbrace{2H^+ + 2OH^-}_{2H_2O} + 2e^- \longrightarrow Hg + H_2O + 2OH^-$

$HgO(s) + H_2O(l) + 2e^- \longrightarrow Hg(l) + 2OH^-(aq)$

20-39 The steps are

$$Au + Cl^- \longrightarrow AuCl_4^- \qquad \text{(oxidation)}$$

$$NO_3^- \longrightarrow NO_2 \qquad \text{(reduction)}$$

$$Au + 4Cl^- \longrightarrow AuCl_4^- \qquad \text{(oxidation)}$$

$$NO_3^- + 2H^+ \longrightarrow NO_2 + H_2O \qquad \text{(reduction)}$$

$$Au + 4Cl^- \longrightarrow AuCl_4^- + 3e^- \qquad \text{(oxidation)}$$
$$NO_3^- + 2H^+ + e^- \longrightarrow NO_2 + H_2O \qquad \text{(reduction)}$$

$$Au + 4Cl^- \longrightarrow AuCl_4^- + 3e^- \qquad \text{(oxidation)}$$
$$3NO_3^- + 6H^+ + 3e^- \longrightarrow 3NO_2 + 3H_2O \qquad \text{(reduction)}$$

$$Au(s) + 3NO_3^-(aq) + 4Cl^-(aq) + 6H^+(aq) \longrightarrow$$
$$AuCl_4^-(aq) + 3NO_2(g) + 3H_2O(l)$$

20-41   The steps are

$$P \longrightarrow P_4O_{10} \qquad \text{(oxidation)}$$
$$BaSO_4 \longrightarrow BaS \qquad \text{(reduction)}$$

$$4P + 10H_2O \longrightarrow P_4O_{10} + 20H^+ \qquad \text{(oxidation)}$$
$$BaSO_4 + 8H^+ \longrightarrow BaS + 4H_2O \qquad \text{(reduction)}$$

$$4P + 10H_2O \longrightarrow P_4O_{10} + 20H^+ + 20e^- \qquad \text{(oxidation)}$$
$$BaSO_4 + 8H^+ + 8e^- \longrightarrow BaS + 4H_2O \qquad \text{(reduction)}$$

$$8P + 20H_2O \longrightarrow 2P_4O_{10} + 40H^+ + 40e^- \qquad \text{(oxidation)}$$
$$5BaSO_4 + 40H^+ + 40e^- \longrightarrow 5BaS + 20H_2O \qquad \text{(reduction)}$$

$$8P(s) + 5BaSO_4(s) \longrightarrow 2P_4O_{10}(s) + 5BaS(s)$$

The $8P(s)$ can be written as $2P_4(s)$.

20-43
$$SO_2 \longrightarrow H_2SO_4 \qquad \text{(oxidation)}$$
$$O_2 \longrightarrow H_2O \qquad \text{(reduction)}$$

$$SO_2 + 2H_2O \longrightarrow H_2SO_4 + 2H^+ \qquad \text{(oxidation)}$$
$$O_2 + 4H^+ \longrightarrow 2H_2O \qquad \text{(reduction)}$$

$$SO_2 + 2H_2O \longrightarrow H_2SO_4 + 2H^+ + 2e^- \qquad \text{(oxidation)}$$
$$O_2 + 4H^+ + 4e^- \longrightarrow 2H_2O \qquad \text{(reduction)}$$

$$2SO_2 + 4H_2O \longrightarrow 2H_2SO_4 + 4H^+ + 4e^- \qquad \text{(oxidation)}$$
$$O_2 + 4H^+ + 4e^- \longrightarrow 2H_2O \qquad \text{(reduction)}$$

$$2SO_2(g) + O_2(g) + 2H_2O(l) \longrightarrow 2H_2SO_4(aq)$$

and the reaction for the corrosion of iron by H_2SO_4 is

$$H_2SO_4(aq) + Fe(s) \longrightarrow FeSO_4(s) + H_2(g)$$

20-45

$$Na_2B_4O_7 \longrightarrow 4NaBO_3 \qquad \text{(oxidation)}$$

$$Na_2O_2 \longrightarrow 2H_2O \qquad \text{(reduction)}$$

$$H_2O_2 \longrightarrow 2H_2O \qquad \text{(reduction)}$$

Notice that there are two reduction half-reactions. We use Na^+ to balance sodium.

$$Na_2B_4O_7 + 5H_2O + 2Na^+ \longrightarrow 4NaBO_3 + 10H^+ \qquad \text{(oxidation)}$$

$$Na_2O_2 + 4H^+ \longrightarrow 2H_2O + 2Na^+ \qquad \text{(reduction)}$$

$$H_2O_2 + 2H^+ \longrightarrow 2H_2O \qquad \text{(reduction)}$$

$$Na_2B_4O_7 + 5H_2O + 2Na^+ \longrightarrow 4NaBO_3 + 10H^+ + 8e^- \text{(oxidation)}$$

$$Na_2O_2 + 4H^+ + 2e^- \longrightarrow 2H_2O + 2Na^+ \qquad \text{(reduction)}$$

$$H_2O_2 + 2H^+ + 2e^- \longrightarrow 2H_2O \qquad \text{(reduction)}$$

We want the Na^+ to cancel and so we write

$$Na_2B_4O_7 + 5H_2O + 2Na^+ \longrightarrow 4NaBO_3 + 10H^+ + 8e^- \text{(oxidation)}$$

$$Na_2O_2 + 4H^+ + 2e^- \longrightarrow 2H_2O + 2Na^+ \qquad \text{(reduction)}$$

$$3H_2O_2 + 6H^+ + 6e^- \longrightarrow 6H_2O \qquad \text{(reduction)}$$

$$Na_2B_4O_7(aq) + Na_2O_2(aq) + 3H_2O_2(aq) \longrightarrow 4NaBO_3(aq) + 3H_2O(l)$$

20-47 The number of moles of BrO_3^- is

$$n = MV = (0.125 \text{ mol} \cdot L^{-1})(0.0437 \text{ L}) = 5.46 \times 10^{-3} \text{ mol}$$

The number of moles of antimony that reacts with 5.46×10^{-3} mol of BrO_3^- is

$$\text{mol of } Sb^{3+} = (5.46 \times 10^{-3} \text{ mol } BrO_3^-)\left(\frac{3 \text{ mol } Sb^{3+}}{1 \text{ mol } BrO_3^-}\right)$$

$$= 1.64 \times 10^{-2} \text{ mol}$$

The number of grams of antimony that reacts is

$$\text{mass} = (1.64 \times 10^{-2} \text{ mol})\left(\frac{121.8 \text{ g}}{1 \text{ mol}}\right) = 2.00 \text{ g}$$

$$\% \text{ antimony} = \frac{2.00 \text{ g Sb}}{7.70 \text{ g ore}} \times 100 = 25.9\%$$

20-49

$$\text{moles of } I_3^- = MV = (0.400 \text{ mol} \cdot L^{-1})(0.0495 \text{ L}) = 1.98 \times 10^{-2} \text{ mol}$$

$$\text{moles of } Sn^{2+} = (1.98 \times 10^{-2} \text{ mol } I_3^-)\left(\frac{1 \text{ mol } Sn^{2+}}{1 \text{ mol } I_3^-}\right) = 1.98 \times 10^{-2} \text{ mol}$$

$$\text{mass of tin} = (1.98 \times 10^{-2} \text{ mol Sn})\left(\frac{118.7 \text{ g}}{1 \text{ mol}}\right) = 2.35 \text{ g}$$

$$\% \text{ tin} = \frac{2.35 \text{ g Sn}}{10.0 \text{ g ore}} \times 100 = 23.5\%$$

20-51 $\text{moles of Na}_2\text{S}_2\text{O}_3 = MV = (0.250 \text{ mol} \cdot \text{L}^{-1})(0.0487 \text{ L}) = 0.01218 \text{ mol}$

$$\text{moles of I}_3^- = (0.01218 \text{ mol Na}_2\text{S}_2\text{O}_3)\left(\frac{1 \text{ mol I}_3^-}{2 \text{ mol Na}_2\text{S}_2\text{O}_3}\right)$$

$$= 6.09 \times 10^{-3} \text{ mol}$$

The concentration of $\text{I}_3^-(aq)$ is

$$M = \frac{\text{moles of I}_3^-}{\text{volume}} = \frac{6.09 \times 10^{-3} \text{ mol}}{0.0150 \text{ L}} = 0.406 \text{ M}$$

E   ANSWERS TO THE EVEN-NUMBERED PROBLEMS

20-2   (a) -2 (b) $+6$ (c) 0 (d) $+4$ (e) $+6$

20-4   (a) $+1$ (b) $+7$ (c) -1 (d) $-\frac{1}{2}$ (e) $+3$

20-6   (a) $+1$ (b) $+3$ (c) $+4$ (d) $+4$ (e) $+6$

20-8   (a) $+3$ (b) $+\frac{7}{2}$ (c) $+4$ (d) $+\frac{9}{2}$ (e) $+5$

20-10 (a) $+2$ (b) $+6$ (c) 0 (d) $+6$ (e) $+6$

20-12 The oxidizing agent is $\text{Na}_2\text{SO}_4(s)$; the reducing agent is $\text{C}(s)$.

20-14 The oxidizing agent is $\text{ClO}_2(g)$; the reducing agent is $\text{C}(s)$.

20-16 (a) The oxidizing agent is $\text{Cu}^{2+}(aq)$; the reducing agent is $\text{Cr}^{2+}(aq)$.

$$\text{Cr}^{2+}(aq) \longrightarrow \text{Cr}^{3+}(aq) + \text{e}^- \qquad \text{(oxidation)}$$
$$\text{Cu}^{2+}(aq) + 2\text{e}^- \longrightarrow \text{Cu}(s) \qquad \text{(reduction)}$$

(b) The oxidizing agent is $\text{Fe}^{3+}(aq)$; the reducing agent is $\text{In}^+(aq)$.

$$\text{In}^+(aq) \longrightarrow \text{In}^{3+}(aq) + 2\text{e}^- \qquad \text{(oxidation)}$$
$$\text{Fe}^{3+}(aq) + \text{e}^- \longrightarrow \text{Fe}^{2+}(aq) \qquad \text{(reduction)}$$

20-18 The hydrogen in LiAlH_4 is in an unusual oxidation state (-1). The common oxidation state of hydrogen is $+1$, and so the hydrogen in LiAlH_4 is easily oxidized from -1 to $+1$, thus making LiAlH_4 a strong reducing agent.

20-20 (a) $\text{Co(OH)}_2(s) + \text{SO}_3^{2-}(aq) \longrightarrow \text{SO}_4^{2-}(aq) + \text{Co}(s) + \text{H}_2\text{O}(l)$
(b) $3\text{GeO}(s) + \text{IO}_3^-(aq) \longrightarrow 3\text{GeO}_2(s) + \text{I}^-(aq)$
(c) $\text{NO}_3^-(aq) + \text{PbO}(s) \longrightarrow \text{NO}_2^-(aq) + \text{PbO}_2(s)$

20-22 (a) $\text{BrO}_3^-(aq) + \text{F}_2(g) + 2\text{OH}^-(aq) \longrightarrow \text{BrO}_4^-(aq) + 2\text{F}^-(aq) + \text{H}_2\text{O}(l)$
(b) $\text{H}_3\text{AsO}_3(aq) + \text{I}_2(aq) + \text{H}_2\text{O}(l) \longrightarrow \text{H}_3\text{AsO}_4(aq) + 2\text{I}^-(aq) + 2\text{H}^+(aq)$
(c) $2\text{MnO}_4^-(aq) + 5\text{C}_2\text{O}_4^{2-}(aq) + 16\text{H}^+(aq) \longrightarrow$
$$2\text{Mn}^{2+}(aq) + 10\text{CO}_2(aq) + 8\text{H}_2\text{O}(l)$$

20-24 (a) $MnO_2(s) + 2Cl^-(aq) + 4H^+(aq) \longrightarrow Mn^{2+}(aq) + Cl_2(g) + 2H_2O(l)$
(b) $Cr_2O_7^{2-}(aq) + 6I^-(aq) + 14H^+(aq) \longrightarrow 2Cr^{3+}(aq) + 3I_2(s) + 7H_2O(l)$
(c) $3CuS(s) + 2NO_3^-(aq) + 8H^+(aq) \longrightarrow$
$$3Cu^{2+}(aq) + 3S(s) + 2NO(g) + 4H_2O(l)$$

20-26 (a) $2CoCl_2(s) + Na_2O_2(aq) + 2H_2O(l) + 2OH^-(aq) \longrightarrow$
$$2Co(OH)_3(s) + 4Cl^-(aq) + 2Na^+(aq)$$
(b) $N_2H_4(aq) + 2Cu(OH)_2(s) \longrightarrow N_2(g) + 2Cu(s) + 4H_2O(l)$
(c) $C_2O_4^{2-}(aq) + MnO_2(s) + 4H^+(aq) \longrightarrow Mn^{2+}(aq) + 2CO_2(g) + 2H_2O(l)$

20-28 (a) $3ZnS(s) + 2NO_3^-(aq) + 8H^+(aq) \longrightarrow$
$$3Zn^{2+}(aq) + 3S(s) + 2NO(g) + 4H_2O(l)$$

electron donor	ZnS
electron acceptor	NO_3^-
oxidizing agent	NO_3^-
reducing agent	ZnS
species oxidized	sulfur
species reduced	nitrogen

(b) $2MnO_4^-(aq) + 5HNO_2(aq) + H^+(aq) \longrightarrow 5NO_3^-(aq) + 2Mn^{2+}(aq) + 3H_2O(l)$

electron donor	HNO_2
electron acceptor	MnO_4^-
oxidizing agent	MnO_4^-
reducing agent	HNO_2
species oxidized	nitrogen
species reduced	manganese

20-30 $2NiO_2H(s) + Cd(s) + 2H_2O(l) \longrightarrow Cd(OH)_2(s) + 2Ni(OH)_2(s)$

20-32 $3C_2H_5OH(aq) + 5H_2O(l) + 14I_3^-(aq) \longrightarrow$
$$2CO_2(g) + 2CHO_2^-(aq) + 2HCI_3(aq) + 36I^-(aq) + 24H^+(aq)$$

Answer is not unique because of the involvement of three different half-reactions.

20-34 (a) $H_2BO_3^-(aq) + 8H^+(aq) + 8e^- \longrightarrow BH_4^-(aq) + 3H_2O(l)$
(b) $2ClO_3^-(aq) + 12H^+(aq) + 10e^- \longrightarrow Cl_2(g) + 6H_2O(l)$
(c) $Cl_2(g) + 2H_2O(l) \longrightarrow 2HClO(aq) + 2H^+(aq) + 2e^-$

20-36 (a) $OsO_4(s) + 8H^+(aq) + 8e^- \longrightarrow Os(s) + 4H_2O(l)$
(b) $S(s) + 6OH^-(aq) \longrightarrow SO_3^{2-}(aq) + 3H_2O(l) + 4e^-$
(c) $Sn(s) + 3OH^-(aq) \longrightarrow HSnO_2^-(aq) + H_2O(l) + 2e^-$

20-38 (a) $Au(CN)_2^-(aq) + e^- \longrightarrow Au(s) + 2CN^-(aq)$
(b) $PbO_2(s) + SO_4^{2-}(aq) + 4H^+(aq) + 2e^- \longrightarrow PbSO_4(s) + 2H_2O(l)$
(c) $MnO_4^-(aq) + 4H^+(aq) + 3e^- \longrightarrow MnO_2(s) + 2H_2O(l)$
(d) $Cr(OH)_3(s) + 5OH^-(aq) \longrightarrow CrO_4^{2-}(aq) + 4H_2O(l) + 3e^-$

20-40 $3C(s) + 2KNO_3(s) + S(s) \longrightarrow 3CO_2(g) + N_2(g) + K_2S(s)$

The reducing agent is C; the oxidizing agents are KNO_3 and S.

20-42 $4KO_2(s) + 2H_2O(l) \longrightarrow 4KOH(s) + 3O_2(g)$
$KOH(s) + CO_2(g) \longrightarrow KHCO_3(s)$

20-44 $2Fe(s) + 2CrO_4^{2-}(aq) + 2H_2O(l) \longrightarrow Fe_2O_3(s) + Cr_2O_3(s) + 4OH^-(aq)$

20-46 $2Al(s) + 6H_2O(l) + 2OH^-(aq) \longrightarrow 2Al(OH)_4^-(aq) + 3H_2(g)$

20-48   0.565 g; 11.3%

20-50 $4NaOH(aq) + Ca(OH)_2(aq) + C(s) + 4ClO_2(g) \longrightarrow$
$$4NaClO_2(aq) + CaCO_3(s) + 3H_2O(l)$$

746 kg

20-52   0.124 M; 173 mg

F   ANSWERS TO THE SELF-TEST

1	0	**24**	silver
2	+1	**25**	$AgNO_3(aq)$
3	+2	**26**	$Ni(s)$
4	−2	**27**	$Ni(s)$
5	+1	**28**	$AgNO_3(aq)$
6	true	**29**	iron
7	sodium hydride	**30**	cerium
8	−1	**31**	$CeCl_4(aq)$
9	−1	**32**	$FeCl_2(aq)$
10	−2	**33**	$Fe^{2+}(aq) \longrightarrow Fe^{3+}(aq) + e^-$
11	sodium peroxide	**34**	$Ce^{4+}(aq) + e^- \longrightarrow Ce^{3+}(aq)$
12	−1	**35**	$2NO_3^-(aq) \longrightarrow N_2(g)$
13	+6	**36**	$2NO_3^-(aq) \longrightarrow N_2(g) + 6H_2O(l)$
14	false	**37**	$2NO_3^-(aq) + 12H^+(aq) \longrightarrow$ $N_2(g) + 6H_2O(l)$
15	electronegativities		
16	fluorine	**38**	$2NO_3^-(aq) + 12H^+(aq) + 10e^- \longrightarrow$ $N_2(g) + 6H_2O(l)$
17	−1		
18	+3	**39**	the number of electrons that are accepted in the reduction half-reaction
19	electrons		
20	increase		
21	the element that is reduced	**40**	false
22	acceptor	**41**	true
23	nickel	**42**	false

21 / Electrochemical Cells

21-1   An electrochemical cell produces electricity directly from a chemical reaction.

An electrochemical cell enables us to obtain an electric current from an oxidation-reduction reaction (Figure 21-2).

An electrochemical cell involves an oxidation half-reaction and a reduction half-reaction.

Electrodes are used to enable electrons to enter or leave an electrochemical cell. The electron transfer processes occur at the electrodes.

Salt bridges are used to separate two different electrolyte solutions in a cell. Current in the form of moving ions can pass through the salt bridge from one electrolyte solution to the other.

Current within the cell electrolyte(s) is carried by ions.

A cell must be designed so that the reducing agent and the oxidizing agent are physically separated.

Discharge denotes that current is drawn from the cell.

Electric current flows spontaneously through metallic conductors from a region of negative electric potential to a region of positive electric potential.

21-2   A cell diagram represents an electrochemical cell.

By convention, the half-reaction of the left electrode of a cell is written as an oxidation half-reaction, and the half-reaction for the right electrode of a cell is written as a reduction half-reaction (oxidation at the left electrode, reduction at the right electrode).

The net cell reaction is given by the sum of the two electrode half-reactions adjusted so that the number of electrons is the same in both half-reactions.

21-3   The cell voltage depends on the concentrations of reactants and products of the cell reaction.

The cell voltage is a quantitative measure of the driving force of the cell reaction.

The effect of a change in the concentration of a reactant or product on the cell voltage can be predicted by applying Le Châtelier's principle.

The Nernst equation is

$$E = -\frac{2.303RT}{nF}\log\left(\frac{Q}{K}\right) \qquad (21\text{-}2)$$

Faraday's constant, F, is the charge of one mole of electrons and is equal to 96,500 coulombs per mole.

At 25°C, the Nernst equation is

$$E = -\left(\frac{0.0592 \text{ V}}{n}\right)\log\left(\frac{Q}{K}\right) \qquad (21\text{-}5)$$

If $E_{\text{cell}} > 0$, then the cell reaction is spontaneous from left to right as written.

If $E_{\text{cell}} < 0$, then the cell reaction is spontaneous from right to left as written.

If $E_{\text{cell}} = 0$, then the cell reaction is at equilibrium.

21-4 The Nernst equation can be written in terms of a standard cell voltage.

The standard cell voltage E^0 is the voltage of the cell when $Q = 1$.

The relation between the standard cell voltage and the equilibrium constant for the cell reaction at 25°C is given by

$$E^0 = \left(\frac{0.0592 \text{ V}}{n}\right)\log K \qquad (21\text{-}8)$$

Another form of the Nernst equation is

$$E = E^0 - \left(\frac{0.0592 \text{ V}}{n}\right)\log Q \qquad (21\text{-}9)$$

A plot of E versus $\log Q$ is shown in Figure 21-4.

21-5 E^0 values can be assigned to half-reactions.

A standard cell voltage is the difference in standard voltages between the two cell electrodes:

$$E^0_{\text{cell}} = E^0_{\text{right}} - E^0_{\text{left}}$$

By convention for the half-reaction

$$2H^+(aq, 1 \text{ M}) + 2e^- \longrightarrow H_2(g, 1 \text{ atm}) \qquad E^0 \equiv 0 \text{ V}$$

Some standard electrode reduction voltages are given in Table 21-1.

The more positive the E^0 value for a half-reaction, the stronger is the oxidizing agent in the half-reaction.

The more negative the E^0 value for a half-reaction, the stronger is the reducing agent in the half-reaction.

21-6　Electrochemical cells are used to determine concentrations of ions.

If E^0 is known and if E is measured and if all the concentration terms in Q but one are known, then the unknown concentration can be calculated.

21-7　The pH of a solution can be determined by electrochemical cell measurements.

The voltage of a cell involving a hydrogen gas electrode or a hydrogen glass electrode (Figure 21-5) depends on the pH.

$$E = (59.2 \text{ mV}) \text{pH} \quad \text{at} \quad 25°C$$

Potentiometric titrations of acids and bases can be carried out with a hydrogen glass electrode (Figure 21-6).

21-8　A battery is an electrochemical cell or group of cells designed for use as a power source.

Primary batteries such as the dry cell are not rechargeable.

Secondary batteries such as the lead storage battery are rechargeable.

The dry cell, the lead storage battery, the nickel-cadmium battery, and the mercury battery are described.

21-9　An electrolysis is a chemical reaction that occurs as a result of the passage of an electric current.

Reduction occurs at the cathode.

Oxidation occurs at the anode.

Cations move toward the cathode.

Anions move toward the anode.

The decomposition voltage is the minimum voltage necessary to cause an electrolysis reaction to occur.

21-10　Metals are obtained from salts by electrochemical processes.

The unit of electric current is ampere.

One ampere is the flow of one coulomb of charge per second.

$$\text{coulombs} = \text{amperes} \times \text{seconds} \tag{21-16}$$

Electrons combine with metal ions to form the metal during the passage of the electric current.

Faraday's laws are summarized as

$$\text{mass deposited} = \frac{\text{current} \times \text{time} \times \text{atomic mass}}{\text{Faraday's constant} \times \text{ionic charge}} \tag{21-18}$$

21-11　Many chemicals are produced on an industrial scale by electrolysis.

The chlor-alkali process involves the electrolysis of $NaCl(aq)$ to produce $Cl_2(g)$ and $NaOH(aq)$ (Figure 21-9).

The Hall process involves the electrolysis of $Al_2O_3(s)$ dissolved in cryolite, Na_3AlF_6, to produce aluminum metal (Figure 21-10).

B   SELF-TEST

1   An electric current can be obtained from an oxidation-reduction reaction.
    True/False

2   In an electrochemical cell, the _____ reaction is
    separated from the _____ reaction.

3   In an electrochemical cell, electrons flow spontaneously in the external circuit
    from the (*positive/negative*) electrode to the (*positive/negative*) electrode.

4   The function of a salt bridge in an electrochemical cell is _____
    _____
    _____.

5   Consider the electrochemical cell whose cell diagram is

$$Cd(s)\,|\,Cd(NO_3)_2(aq)\,\|\,Pb(NO_3)_2(aq)\,|\,Pb(s)$$

    (a) Oxidation occurs at the _____ electrode.
    (b) The oxidation half-reaction is _____.
    (c) The reduction half-reaction is _____.

6   The voltage of a cell prepared by placing a cadmium rod and a lead rod in an
    aqueous solution containing $Cd(NO_3)_2(aq)$ and $Pb(NO_3)_2(aq)$ is _____.

7   Consider the cell diagram

$$Zn(s)\,|\,ZnSO_4(aq)\,|\,Hg_2SO_4(s)\,|\,Hg(l)$$

    (a) The electrolyte solution is _____.
    (b) The substances in contact with $ZnSO_4(aq)$ are _____,
    _____, and _____.
    (c) The salt bridge is _____.

8   The function of platinum in a hydrogen gas electrode is _____
    _____.

9   The measured voltage of an electrochemical cell depends on the size of the
    electrodes. *True/False*

10 Consider the cell whose cell diagram is

$$Zn(s)\,|\,ZnSO_4(aq)\,\|\,CuSO_4(aq)\,|\,Cu(s)$$

    (a) The measured voltage _____ when the concentration of
    $ZnSO_4(aq)$ is increased.
    (b) The measured voltage _____ when the concentration of
    $CuSO_4(aq)$ is increased.

(c) The measured voltage _____ when the amount of Zn(s) is increased.

(d) The measured voltage _____ when the salt bridge is removed.

11 The sign of the cell voltage is _____ when the cell reaction is spontaneous, left to right.

12 The equation for the relationship between the standard cell voltage, E^0, and the equilibrium constant of a reaction at 25°C is given by $E^0 =$ _____.

13 The standard cell voltage is the measured cell voltage when _____ _____.

14 If $E^0_{cell} = 0$, then $K =$ _____.

15 If $K < 1$, then E^0 is (*less than/greater than*) zero.

16 The Nernst equation, which relates the cell voltage, E, and the reaction concentration quotient, Q, at 25°C, is given by $E =$ _____.

17 The measured cell voltage is always equal to E^0. *True/False*

18 The measured cell voltage when the cell reaction is at equilibrium is _____.

19 The standard voltage of a half-reaction is a directly measured quantity. *True/False*

20 The standard cell voltage is always a positive quantity. *True/False*

21 The standard reduction voltage of the hydrogen electrode is set equal to _____.

22 Standard electrode voltages are tabulated for the (*oxidation/reduction*) half-reactions.

23 A large, positive standard electrode voltage indicates a strong oxidizing agent in the half-reaction. *True/False*

24 The stronger the reducing agent the more (*negative/positive*) is the half-reaction E^0 value.

25 The standard cell voltage, E^0_{cell}, for a reaction can be calculated from the standard electrode voltages of the half-reactions of the reaction. *True/False*

26 The value of E^0_{cell} is unchanged when the cell reaction is multiplied by a factor of two. *True/False*

27 Measurement of the cell voltage can be used to calculate the concentration of a species in solution by using _____ equation.

28 The pH of a solution can be measured using a _____ or a _____ electrode.

29   The pH of a solution is related to the _____ of the hydrogen electrode.

30   The dry cell is a primary battery. *True/False*

31   The nickel-cadmium battery is a secondary battery. *True/False*

32   Water can be decomposed by passing a current through a dilute aqueous solution of Na_2SO_4. *True/False*

33   In the electrolysis of water, electrons pass through the solution from the cathode to the anode. *True/False*

34   During electrolysis of a solution of $AgNO_3(aq)$, silver metal is deposited from solution at the (*anode/cathode*).

35   The amount of silver deposited by the electrolysis of a $AgNO_3(aq)$ solution depends upon the amount of charge that flows through the solution. *True/False*

36   The amount of charge that flows is related to the current by the relationship: charge = _____.

37   The amount of charge contained in one mole of electrons is _____.

38   Faraday's constant is _____.

39   The chlor-alkali process is used industrially to prepare _____ and _____ by the electrolysis of _____.

40   The Hall process is used industrially to prepare _____ by the electrolysis of _____.

C   CALCULATIONS YOU SHOULD KNOW HOW TO DO

1   Write cell reactions and cell diagrams. See Examples 21-1 through 21-3, and Problems 21-1 through 21-12 and 21-41 through 21-46.

2   Use Le Châtelier's principle to predict effects on the cell voltage. See Example 21-4 and Problems 21-13 through 21-18.

3   Use the Nernst equation to calculate the value of E^0 or the value of K, the equilibrium constant. See Examples 21-5 and 21-6 and Problems 21-21 through 21-30.

4   Use the E^0 values for half-reactions given in Table 21-1 to calculate E^0 values for cell reactions. See Examples 21-7 and 21-8 and Problems 21-31 through 21-40.

5   Use the Nernst equation to determine the concentration of an ion in solution. See Example 21-9 and Problems 21-57 through 21-60.

6   Calculate the current required to deposit a given amount of a metal or the amount of metal deposited during the passage of a given amount of current. See Examples 21-13 and 21-14 and Problems 21-47 through 21-56.

D   SOLUTIONS TO THE ODD-NUMBERED PROBLEMS

21-1

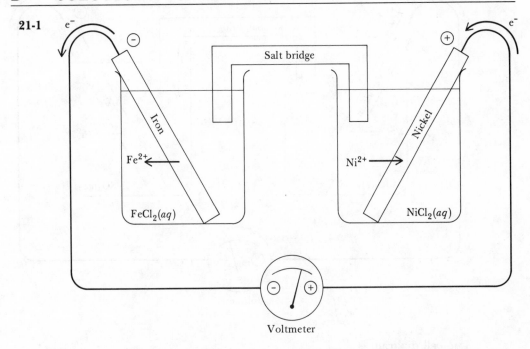

Voltmeter

Electrons flow from the negative electrode to the positive electrode in the external circuit. The reaction at the negative electrode is

$$Fe(s) \longrightarrow Fe^{2+}(aq) + 2e^-$$

Positive ions, $Fe^{2+}(aq)$ are produced at the negative electrode. The reaction at the positive electrode is

$$Ni^{2+}(aq) + 2e^- \longrightarrow Ni(s)$$

Positive ions, $Ni^{2+}(aq)$, are consumed at the positive electrode. We write the cell diagram with the oxidation half-reaction occurring at the left electrode and the reduction half-reaction occurring at the right electrode. Thus the cell diagram is

$$Fe(s) \,|\, FeCl_2(aq) \,\|\, NiCl_2(aq) \,|\, Ni(s)$$

21-3   The reaction at the negative electrode is

$$V(s) \longrightarrow V^{2+}(aq) + 2e^-$$

The reaction at the positive electrode is

$$Zn^{2+}(aq) + 2e^- \longrightarrow Zn(s)$$

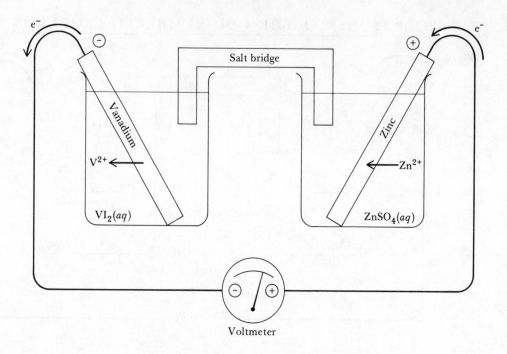

The cell diagram is

$$V(s) \mid VI_2(aq) \parallel ZnSO_4(aq) \mid Zn(s)$$

21-5 Oxidation takes place at the left electrode. Thus the half-reaction at the left electrode is

$$Ag(s) + I^-(aq) \longrightarrow AgI(s) + e^-$$

The reaction is not $Ag(s) \rightarrow Ag^+(aq) + e^-$ because the oxidized silver is in the form of $AgI(s)$. The half-reaction at the right electrode is

$$2H^+(aq) + 2e^- \longrightarrow H_2(g)$$

The net cell reaction is

$$2Ag(s) + 2HI(aq) \longrightarrow 2AgI(s) + H_2(g)$$

21-7 Oxidation takes place at the left electrode; thus

$$Cd(s) \longrightarrow Cd^{2+}(aq) + 2e^-$$

The reaction that occurs at the right electrode is

$$Re^{3+}(aq) + 3e^- \longrightarrow Re(s)$$

The number of electrons that are lost in the oxidation half-reaction must equal the number of electrons that are gained in the reduction half-reaction; therefore

$$3Cd(s) \longrightarrow 3Cd^{2+}(aq) + 6e^-$$
$$2Re^{3+}(aq) + 6e^- \longrightarrow 2Re(s)$$

The net cell reaction is the sum of the two electrode reactions:

$$3Cd(s) + 2Re^{3+}(aq) \longrightarrow 3Cd^{2+}(aq) + 2Re(s)$$

A sketch of the cell is as follows

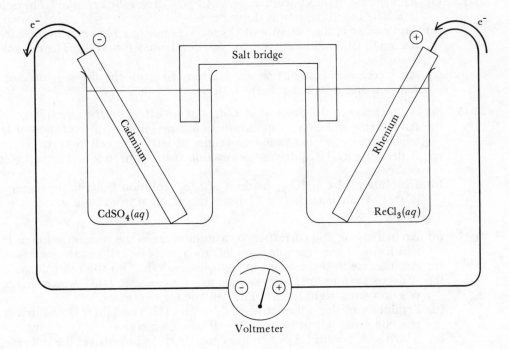

Voltmeter

21-9 The half-reaction that occurs at the left electrode is

$$H_2(g) \longrightarrow 2H^+(aq) + 2e^- \qquad \text{(oxidation)}$$

Platinum is an inert electrode. The half-reaction that occurs at the right electrode is

$$PbSO_4(s) + 2e^- \longrightarrow Pb(s) + SO_4^{2-}(aq) \qquad \text{(reduction)}$$

The net cell reaction is

$$H_2(g) + PbSO_4(s) \longrightarrow Pb(s) + 2H^+(aq) + SO_4^{2-}(aq)$$

21-11   The oxidation half-reaction (left electrode) is

$$La(s) \longrightarrow La^{3+}(aq) + 3e^-$$

The reduction half-reaction (right electrode) is

$$Cu^{2+}(aq) + 2e^- \longrightarrow Cu(s)$$

Oxidation takes place at the left electrode and reduction at the right electrode. We shall connect the cell compartments in which the half-reactions occur by a salt bridge. The cell diagram is

$$La(s)\,|\,LaCl_3(aq)\,\|\,CuCl_2(aq)\,|\,Cu(s)$$

21-13   (a) An increase in the concentration of $Cl^-(aq)$ drives the reaction from right to left. The cell voltage thus decreases.

(b) An increase in the pressure of Cl_2 corresponds to an increase in the concentration of Cl_2 and thus drives the reaction from left to right. The cell voltage increases.

(c) An increase in a solid reactant has no effect on the driving force of the reaction and thus has no effect on the cell voltage.

21-15   (a) An increase in the amount of $Ca(s)$ has no effect on the cell voltage.

(b) An increase in P_{H_2} corresponds to an increase in the concentration of $H_2(g)$ which drives the reaction from right to left. The cell voltage decreases.

(c) A decrease in [HCl] drives the reaction from right to left. The cell voltage decreases.

(d) Dissolution of $Ca(NO_3)_2$ in the $CaCl_2(aq)$ solution leads to an increase in $[Ca^{2+}]$. An increase in $[Ca^{2+}]$ drives the reaction from right to left. The cell voltage decreases.

21-17   (a) An increase in P_{H_2} corresponds to an increase in the concentration of $H_2(g)$ which drives the reaction from left to right. The cell voltage increases.

(b) An increase in the amount of $Pb(s)$ has no effect on the cell voltage.

(c) A decrease in the pH corresponds to an increase in $[H^+]$, which drives the reaction from right to left. The cell voltage decreases.

(d) A dilution of the cell electrolyte decreases $[H^+]$ and $[SO_4^{2-}]$ and drives the reaction from left to right. The cell voltage increases.

(e) The dissolution of $Na_2SO_4(s)$ increases $[SO_4^{2-}]$ which drives the cell reaction from right to left. The cell voltage decreases.

(f) A decrease in the amount of $PbSO_4(s)$ has no effect on the cell voltage as long as at least some $PbSO_4(s)$ remains.

(g) Added NaOH reacts with $H^+(aq)$, thereby causing a decrease in $[H^+]$. A decrease in $[H^+]$ drives the reaction from left to right. The cell voltage increases.

21-19   (a) To obtain the balanced chemical equation, we write the oxidation half-reaction and the reduction half-reaction with the same number of electrons in each.

$$3Cu(s) \longrightarrow 3Cu^{2+}(aq) + 6e^-$$
$$2Fe^{3+}(aq) + 6e^- \longrightarrow 2Fe(s)$$

Thus the number of electrons transferred is 6 or $n = 6$.

(b) The oxidation half-reaction is

$$Cr^{2+}(aq) \longrightarrow Cr^{3+}(aq) + e^-$$

The reduction half-reaction is

$$Cu^{2+}(aq) + e^- \longrightarrow Cu^+(aq)$$

The number of electrons in the two half-reactions is the same, and thus the number of electrons transferred is one, or $n = 1$.

21-21 The relation between E^0 and K is

$$E^0 = \left(\frac{0.0592 \text{ V}}{n}\right) \log K$$

Solving for $\log K$, we have

$$\log K = \frac{nE^0}{0.0592 \text{ V}}$$

The value of n for the reaction is 2 and thus

$$\log K = \frac{(2)(0.463 \text{ V})}{(0.0592 \text{ V})} = 15.64$$

or

$$K = 10^{15.64} = 4.38 \times 10^{15}$$

21-23 We first calculate E^0 using the Nernst equation:

$$E = E^0 - \left(\frac{0.0592 \text{ V}}{n}\right) \log Q$$

Thus, using the given reaction,

$$E = E^0 - \left(\frac{0.0592 \text{ V}}{n}\right) \log \left(\frac{[Cd^{2+}]}{[Pb^{2+}]}\right)$$

For this reaction $n = 2$. Thus using the given concentrations, we have

$$0.293 \text{ V} = E^0 - \left(\frac{0.0592 \text{ V}}{2}\right) \log \left(\frac{0.0250 \text{ M}}{0.150 \text{ M}}\right)$$

$$0.293 \text{ V} = E^0 + 0.023 \text{ V}$$

$$E^0 = 0.293 \text{ V} - 0.023 \text{ V} = 0.270 \text{ V}$$

The relationship between E^0 and K is

$$E^0 = \left(\frac{0.0592 \text{ V}}{n}\right) \log K$$

Thus

$$\log K = \frac{nE^0}{0.0592 \text{ V}}$$

and using the above value of E^0, we compute

$$\log K = \frac{(2)(0.270 \text{ V})}{0.0592 \text{ V}} = 9.12$$

Thus

$$K = 10^{9.12} = 1.32 \times 10^9$$

21-25 Application of the Nernst equation to the cell reaction yields ($n = 3$)

$$E = E^0 - \left(\frac{0.0592 \text{ V}}{3}\right) \log \left(\frac{[Al^{3+}]}{[Fe^{3+}]}\right)$$

Thus

$$1.59 \text{ V} = E^0 - \left(\frac{0.0592 \text{ V}}{3}\right) \log \left(\frac{0.250 \text{ M}}{0.0050 \text{ M}}\right)$$

$$1.59 \text{ V} = E^0 - 0.0335 \text{ V}$$

and

$$E^0 = 1.59 \text{ V} + 0.034 \text{ V} = 1.62 \text{ V}$$

The relationship between E^0 and K is

$$\log K = \frac{nE^0}{0.0592 \text{ V}}$$

Thus

$$\log K = \frac{(3)(1.62 \text{ V})}{0.0592 \text{ V}} = 82.09$$

$$K = 10^{82.09} = 1.2 \times 10^{82}$$

21-27 The oxidation half-reaction is

$$Zn(s) \longrightarrow Zn^{2+}(aq) + 2e^-$$

The reduction half-reaction is

$$Hg_2Cl_2(s) + 2e^- \longrightarrow 2Hg(l) + 2Cl^-(aq)$$

The cell reaction is

$$Zn(s) + Hg_2Cl_2(s) \longrightarrow 2Hg(l) + Zn^{2+}(aq) + 2Cl^-(aq)$$

Application of the Nernst equation to the cell reaction ($n = 2$) yields

$$E = E^0 - \left(\frac{0.0592 \text{ V}}{2}\right) \log \left([Zn^{2+}][Cl^-]^2\right)$$

Thus

$$E = 1.03 \text{ V} - \left(\frac{0.0592 \text{ V}}{2}\right) \log (0.010)(0.020)^2$$

$$= 1.03 \text{ V} + 0.16 \text{ V} = 1.19 \text{ V}$$

21-29 We shall use the Nernst equation in the form

$$E = -\frac{2.30RT}{nF} \log \left(\frac{Q}{K}\right)$$

The cell reaction will take place until $Q = K$ when equilibrium has been reached:

$$E = -\frac{2.30 \, RT}{nF} \log (1) = 0$$

21-31 We see that Cr^{2+} is oxidized to Cr^{3+}:

$$Cr^{2+}(aq) \longrightarrow Cr^{3+}(aq) + e^-$$

and that chlorine in hypochlorous acid is reduced

$$HClO(aq) + H^+(aq) + 2e^- \longrightarrow Cl^-(aq) + H_2O(l)$$

The E_{cell}^0 value for the complete cell is given by

$$E_{cell}^0 = E_{right}^0(\text{reduction}) - E_{left}^0(\text{oxidation})$$

or

$$E_{cell}^0 = E_{HClO/Cl^-}^0 - E_{Cr^{3+}/Cr^{2+}}^0$$

From Table 21-1 we obtain

$$E_{Cr^{3+}/Cr^{2+}}^0 = -0.41 \text{ V}$$

Thus
$$1.80 \text{ V} = E^0_{\text{HClO/Cl}^-} - (-0.41 \text{ V})$$
$$E^0_{\text{HClO/Cl}^-} = 1.80 \text{ V} - 0.41 \text{ V} = 1.39 \text{ V}$$

21-33 The oxidation half-reaction is

$$\text{Pb}(s) \longrightarrow \text{Pb}^{2+}(aq) + 2e^- \qquad \text{(left electrode)}$$

The reduction half-reaction is

$$\text{Cd}^{2+}(aq) + 2e^- \longrightarrow \text{Cd}(s) \qquad \text{(right electrode)}$$

The E^0_{cell} value for the complete cell reaction is given by

$$E^0_{\text{cell}} = E^0_{\text{right}} - E^0_{\text{left}}$$

or
$$E^0_{\text{cell}} = E^0_{\text{Cd}^{2+}/\text{Cd}} - E^0_{\text{Pb}^{2+}/\text{Pb}}$$

From Table 21-1 we obtain

$$E^0_{\text{cell}} = -0.40 \text{ V} - (-0.13 \text{ V}) = -0.27 \text{ V}$$

The net reaction

$$\text{Cd}^{2+}(aq) + \text{Pb}(s) \longrightarrow \text{Pb}^{2+}(aq) + \text{Cd}(s)$$

does not occur spontaneously. Lead will not displace cadmium from $\text{Cd}(\text{C}_2\text{H}_3\text{O}_2)_2(aq)$ under standard conditions.

21-35 The value of E^0_{cell} is given by

$$E^0_{\text{cell}} = E^0_{\text{right}}(\text{reduction}) - E^0_{\text{left}}(\text{oxidation})$$

Thus
$$E^0_{\text{cell}} = E^0_{\text{H}^+/\text{H}_2} - E^0_{\text{V}^{3+}/\text{V}^{2+}}$$

From Table 21-1 we obtain

$$E^0_{\text{H}^+/\text{H}_2} = 0 \qquad \text{and} \qquad E^0_{\text{V}^{3+}/\text{V}^{2+}} = -0.24 \text{ V}$$

Thus
$$E^0_{\text{cell}} = 0 - (-0.24 \text{ V}) = 0.24 \text{ V}$$

From the relation between E^0 and K, we have

$$\log K = \frac{nE^0_{\text{cell}}}{0.0592 \text{ V}}$$

$$= \frac{(1)(0.24 \text{ V})}{0.0592 \text{ V}} = 4.05$$

$$K = 10^{4.05} = 1.12 \times 10^4$$

21-37 The value of E^0_{cell} is given by

$$E^0_{cell} = E^0_{right}(\text{reduction}) - E^0_{left}(\text{oxidation})$$
$$= E^0_{O_2/H_2O} - E^0_{Zn^{2+}/Zn}$$

From Table 21-1 we obtain

$$E^0_{cell} = 1.23 \text{ V} - (-0.76 \text{ V}) = 1.99 \text{ V}$$

Application of the Nernst equation

$$E = E^0 - \left(\frac{0.0592 \text{ V}}{n}\right) \log Q$$

to the cell reaction yields ($n = 4$)

$$E = E^0 - \left(\frac{0.0592 \text{ V}}{4}\right) \log \left(\frac{[Zn^{2+}]^2}{P_{O_2}[H^+]^4}\right)$$

Thus
$$E = 1.99 \text{ V} - \left(\frac{0.0592 \text{ V}}{4}\right) \log \left(\frac{(0.0010)^2}{(0.20)(0.20)^4}\right)$$
$$= 1.99 \text{ V} + 0.037 \text{ V} = 2.03 \text{ V}$$

21-39 The oxidation half-reaction is

$$S_2O_3^{2-}(aq) + 3H_2O(l) \longrightarrow 2SO_3^{2-}(aq) + 6H^+(aq) + 4e^-$$

However, the reaction occurs in basic solution, so we convert the half-reaction to basic solution:

$$S_2O_3^{2-}(aq) + 6OH^-(aq) \longrightarrow 2SO_3^{2-}(aq) + 3H_2O(l) + 4e^-$$

The reduction half-reaction in basic solution is

$$O_2(g) + 2H_2O(l) + 4e^- \longrightarrow 4OH^-(aq)$$

From Table 21-1 we obtain

$$E^0_{O_2/OH^-} = 0.40 \text{ V}$$

We can obtain the value of $E^0_{SO_3^{2-}/S_2O_3^{2-}}$ from the E^0_{cell} value:

$$E^0_{cell} = E^0_{right} - E^0_{left}$$
$$= E^0_{O_2/OH^-} - E^0_{SO_3^{2-}/S_2O_3^{2-}}$$

Thus
$$0.98 \text{ V} = 0.40 \text{ V} - E^0_{SO_3^{2-}/S_2O_3^{2-}}$$
$$E^0_{SO_3^{2-}/S_2O_3^{2-}} = -0.98 \text{ V} + 0.40 \text{ V} = -0.58 \text{ V}$$

21-41 Replacing cadmium with iron in the nickel-cadmiun battery, we have

$$\ominus \text{steel} \,|\, \text{Fe}(s) \,|\, \text{Fe(OH)}_2(s) \,|\, \text{LiOH}(aq) \,|\, \text{NiOOH}(s), \, \text{Ni(OH)}_2(s) \,|\, \text{steel} \oplus$$

21-43 The oxidation reaction is

$$\text{Zn}(s) \longrightarrow \text{Zn}^{2+}(aq) + 2e^-$$

The reduction reaction is

$$\text{Hg}_2\text{SO}_4(s) + 2e^- \longrightarrow 2\text{Hg}(l) + \text{SO}_4^-(aq)$$

The cell diagram is

$$\ominus \text{Zn}(s) \,|\, \text{ZnSO}_4(aq) \,|\, \text{Hg}_2\text{SO}_4(s) \,|\, \text{Hg}(l) \oplus$$

21-45 The oxidation half-reaction is

$$\text{Mg}(s) + \text{O}^{2-}(soln) \longrightarrow \text{MgO}(s) + 2e^-$$

The reduction half-reaction is

$$2\text{CuO}(s) + 2e^- \longrightarrow \text{Cu}_2\text{O}(s) + \text{O}^{2-}(soln)$$

The cell reaction is the sum of the two half-reactions

$$\text{Mg}(s) + 2\text{CuO}(s) \longrightarrow \text{MgO}(s) + \text{Cu}_2\text{O}(s)$$

The cell diagram

$$\ominus \text{Mg}(s) \,|\, \text{MgO}(s) \,|\, \text{LiCl} + \text{KCl}(soln) \,|\, \text{CuO}(s), \, \text{Cu}_2\text{O}(s) \,|\, \text{steel} \oplus$$

21-47 The number of moles of copper that are deposited is

$$\text{moles of Cu} = MV = (0.250 \text{ mol} \cdot \text{L}^{-1})(0.740 \text{ L}) = 0.185 \text{ mol}$$

Copper is reduced according to

$$\text{Cu}^{2+}(aq) + 2e^- \longrightarrow \text{Cu}(s)$$

The number of moles of electrons required to deposit 0.185 mol of Cu is

$$\text{moles of electrons} = (0.185 \text{ mol Cu})\left(\frac{2 \text{ mol of electrons}}{1 \text{ mol of Cu}}\right)$$

$$= 0.370 \text{ mol}$$

The charge on 0.370 mol of electrons is

$$\text{charge} = (0.370 \text{ mol})(96,500 \text{ C} \cdot \text{mol}^{-1})$$

$$= 3.57 \times 10^4 \text{ C}$$

We also have that

$$\underset{\text{(coulombs)}}{\text{charge}} = \underset{\text{(amperes)}}{\text{current}} \times \underset{\text{(seconds)}}{\text{time}}$$

Thus

$$3.57 \times 10^4 \text{ C} = (3.64 \text{ A})(\text{time})$$

Using the fact that $1 \text{ A} = 1 \text{ C} \cdot \text{s}^{-1}$, we have

$$\text{time} = \frac{3.57 \times 10^4 \text{ C}}{3.64 \text{ C} \cdot \text{s}^{-1}} = 9.81 \times 10^3 \text{ s}$$

$$= (9.81 \times 10^3 \text{ s})\left(\frac{1 \text{ h}}{3600 \text{ s}}\right) = 2.73 \text{ h}$$

21-49   The total charge is given by

$$\text{charge} = \text{current} \times \text{time}$$

$$= (1.0 \text{ C} \cdot \text{s}^{-1})(1.0 \text{ h})\left(\frac{60 \text{ min}}{1 \text{ h}}\right)\left(\frac{60 \text{ s}}{1 \text{ min}}\right)$$

$$= 3.6 \times 10^3 \text{ C}$$

The number of moles of electrons that correspond to 3.6×10^3 C is

$$\text{moles of electrons} = (3.6 \times 10^3 \text{ C})\left(\frac{1}{96,500 \text{ C} \cdot \text{mol}^{-1}}\right)$$

$$= 0.0373 \text{ mol}$$

The reaction is

$$Cs^+(l) + e^- \longrightarrow Cs(s)$$

The number of moles of cesium that are deposited is

$$\text{moles of Cs} = (0.0373 \text{ mol electrons})\left(\frac{1 \text{ mol Cs}}{1 \text{ mol e}^-}\right)$$

$$= 0.0373 \text{ mol}$$

The mass of cesium deposited is

$$\text{mass of Cs} = (0.0373 \text{ mol})\left(\frac{132.9 \text{ g}}{1 \text{ mol}}\right)$$

$$= 4.96 \text{ g}$$

21-51 The total charge is

$$\text{charge} = \text{current} \times \text{time}$$

$$= (1500\ \text{C} \cdot \text{s}^{-1})(24\ \text{h})\left(\frac{60\ \text{min}}{1\ \text{h}}\right)\left(\frac{60\ \text{s}}{1\ \text{min}}\right)$$

$$= 1.296 \times 10^8\ \text{C}$$

The number of moles of electrons that correspond to 1.296×10^8 C is

$$\text{moles of electrons} = \frac{1.296 \times 10^8\ \text{C}}{9.65 \times 10^4\ \text{C} \cdot \text{mol}^{-1}}$$

$$= 1.343 \times 10^3\ \text{mol}$$

The reaction is

$$2\text{F}^-(KF) \longrightarrow \text{F}_2(g) + 2e^-$$

The number of moles of fluorine produced is

$$\text{moles of F}_2 = (1.343 \times 10^3\ \text{mol electrons})\left(\frac{1\ \text{mol F}_2}{2\ \text{mol e}^-}\right)$$

$$= 6.715 \times 10^2\ \text{mol}$$

The mass of fluorine produced is

$$\text{mass of F}_2 = (6.715 \times 10^2\ \text{mol})\left(\frac{38.00\ \text{g}}{1\ \text{mol}}\right)$$

$$= 2.552 \times 10^4\ \text{g}$$

$$= 25.52\ \text{kg}$$

Hydrogen fluoride, HF, is a covalent compound and is a poor conductor of electricity. Liquid HF is also volatile and very toxic.

21-53 The number of moles of gold deposited is

$$\text{moles of Au} = (0.200\ \text{g})\left(\frac{1\ \text{mol}}{197.0\ \text{g}}\right) = 0.001015\ \text{mol}$$

The number of moles of electrons required to deposit 0.001015 mol of gold is

$$\text{moles of electrons} = (0.001015\ \text{mol Au})\left(\frac{1\ \text{mol e}^-}{1\ \text{mol Au}}\right)$$

$$= 0.001015\ \text{mol}$$

The charge that corresponds to 0.001015 mol of electrons is

$$\text{charge} = (0.001015 \text{ mol})(96{,}500 \text{ C} \cdot \text{mol}^{-1})$$
$$= 97.97 \text{ C}$$

We also have that

$$\text{charge} = \text{current} \times \text{time}$$
$$97.97 \text{ C} = (30 \text{ mC} \cdot \text{s}^{-1})\left(\frac{1 \text{ C}}{1000 \text{ mC}}\right)(\text{time})$$

Thus
$$\text{time} = \frac{97.97 \text{ C}}{0.030 \text{ C} \cdot \text{s}^{-1}} = 3266 \text{ s} = 54 \text{ min}$$

21-55 The number of moles in one metric ton of copper is

$$\text{moles of Cu} = (1 \text{ metric ton})\left(\frac{1000 \text{ kg}}{1 \text{ metric ton}}\right)\left(\frac{1000 \text{ g}}{1 \text{ kg}}\right)\left(\frac{1 \text{ mol}}{63.55 \text{ g}}\right)$$
$$= 1.574 \times 10^4 \text{ mol}$$

The number of electrons required to deposit 1.574×10^4 mol of copper is

$$\text{moles of electrons} = (1.574 \times 10^4 \text{ mol Cu})\left(\frac{2 \text{ mol e}^-}{1 \text{ mol Cu}}\right)$$
$$= 3.148 \times 10^4 \text{ mol}$$

The charge that corresponds to 3.148×10^4 moles of electrons is

$$\text{charge} = (3.148 \times 10^4 \text{ mol})(96{,}500 \text{ C} \cdot \text{mol}^{-1})$$
$$= 3.038 \times 10^9 \text{ C}$$

One ampere-hour is a current of one ampere that flows for one hour. Thus the number of coulombs in 1A·h is

$$1\text{A}\cdot\text{h} = (1 \text{ C} \cdot \text{s}^{-1})(1 \text{ h})\left(\frac{3600 \text{ s}}{1 \text{ h}}\right) = 3.600 \times 10^3 \text{ C}$$

The number of A·h in 3.038×10^9 C is

$$\frac{3.038 \times 10^9 \text{ C}}{3.600 \times 10^3 \text{ C/A}\cdot\text{h}} = 8.44 \times 10^5 \text{ A}\cdot\text{h}$$

21-57 Because the cell voltage is negative, the oxidation reaction is

$$\text{Ag}(s) \longrightarrow \text{Ag}^+(aq) + \text{e}^-$$

and the reduction reaction is

$$AgBr(s) + e^- \longrightarrow Ag(s) + Br^-(aq)$$

The net reaction is

$$AgBr(s) \longrightarrow Ag^+(aq) + Br^-(aq)$$

The equilibrium constant for this cell is K_{sp} for $AgBr(s)$

$$K = [Ag^+][Br^-] = K_{sp}$$

We can find the value of K_{sp} from the Nernst equation

$$\log K = \frac{nE^0}{0.0592 \text{ V}}$$

We see that $n = 1$ for this reaction; thus

$$\log K_{sp} = \frac{(1)(-0.728 \text{ V})}{0.0592 \text{ V}} = -12.30$$

$$K_{sp} = 10^{-12.30} = 5.0 \times 10^{-13} \text{ M}^2$$

21-59   The oxidation half-reaction is

$$H_2(g) \longrightarrow 2H^+(aq) + 2e^-$$

By definition, $E^0 = 0$ for this half-reaction. The reduction half-reaction is

$$Hg_2Cl_2(s) + 2e^- \longrightarrow 2Hg(l) + 2Cl^-(aq)$$

$$E^0 = 0.2415 \text{ V}$$

The cell reaction is

$$H_2(g) + Hg_2Cl_2(s) \longrightarrow 2Hg(l) + 2H^+(aq) + 2Cl^-(aq)$$

The value of E^0_{cell} is

$$E^0_{cell} = E^0_{right} - E^0_{left} = E^0_{Hg_2Cl_2/Hg} - E^0_{H^+/H_2}$$
$$= 0.2415 \text{ V} - 0 = +0.2415 \text{ V}$$

Application of the Nernst equation to the cell reaction yields

$$E = E^0 - \left(\frac{0.0592 \text{ V}}{2}\right) \log \left(\frac{[H^+]^2}{P_{H_2}}\right)$$

Because the solution of $KCl(aq)$ is saturated, the concentration of $Cl^-(aq)$ remains constant and so does not appear in the above expression. If the pressure of H_2 gas is held constant at 1.00 atm, then

$$E = E^0 - \left(\frac{0.0592 \text{ V}}{2}\right) \log [H^+]^2$$

Using the property of logarithms that $\log y^a = a \log y$, we have

$$E = E^0 - (0.0592 \text{ V}) \log [H^+]$$
$$= +0.2415 \text{ V} - (0.0592 \text{ V}) \log [H^+]$$

The voltage of the cell depends only upon the concentration of $H^+(aq)$. In terms of pH,

$$pH = -\log [H^+]$$

we have

$$E = +0.2415 \text{ V} + (0.0592 \text{ V}) \text{ pH}$$

or

$$pH = \frac{E - 0.2415 \text{ V}}{0.0592 \text{ V}}$$

Thus the pH can be computed from a measured value of E.

E   ANSWERS TO THE EVEN-NUMBERED PROBLEMS

21-2 $Mn(s) \longrightarrow Mn^{2+}(aq) + 2e^-$ (negative electrode)
            $Cr^{2+}(aq) + 2e^- \longrightarrow Cr(s)$ (positive electrode)

$Mn(s) \,|\, MnSO_4(aq) \,\|\, CrSO(aq) \,|\, Cr(s)$

21-4 $Co(s) \longrightarrow Co^{2+}(aq) + 2e^-$ (negative electrode)
            $Pb^{2+}(aq) + 2e^- \longrightarrow Pb(s)$ (positive electrode)

$Co(s) \,|\, Co(NO_3)_2(aq) \,\|\, Pb(NO_3)_2(aq) \,|\, Pb(s)$

21-6 $Cu(s) + 2AgClO_4(aq) \longrightarrow Cu(ClO_4)_2(aq) + 2Ag(s)$

21-8 $Sn(s) \longrightarrow Sn^{2+}(aq) + 2e^-$ (left electrode)
            $Ag^+(aq) + e^- \longrightarrow Ag(s)$ (right electrode)

21-10 $Pb(s) + Hg_2SO_4(s) \longrightarrow 2Hg(l) + PbSO_4(s)$

21-12 $Pt(s) \,|\, H_2(g) \,|\, HCl(aq) \,|\, AgCl(s) \,|\, Ag(s)$

21-14 (a) increase   (b) no change   (c) increase

21-16 (a) increase   (b) no change   (c) decrease   (d) decrease

21-18 (a) increase   (b) decrease   (c) no change   (d) no change
            (e) decrease   (f) decrease

CHAPTER 21

21-20 (a) $n = 2$ (b) $n = 2$

21-22 $K = 2.7 \times 10^7$

21-24 $E^0 = 0.140$ V; $K = 5.4 \times 10^4$

21-26 $E^0 = 1.55$ V; $K = 2.3 \times 10^{52}$

21-28 $Cd(s) + 2H^+(aq) \longrightarrow Cd^{2+}(aq) + H_2(g)$

21-30 $E = 0$ V; the cell is short-circuited.

21-32 $E^0_{NO_3^-/NO_2} = +0.80$ V

21-34 $E^0_{cell} = +0.23$ V; $S_2O_8^{2-}(aq)$ is unstable.

21-36 $E^0_{cell} = 0.46$ V; $K = 3.5 \times 10^{15}$ M^{-1}

21-38 $E = 0.30$ V

21-40 $BH_4^-(aq) + 8OH^-(aq) \longrightarrow H_2BO_3^-(aq) + 5H_2O(l) + 8e^-$
$O_2(g) + e^- \longrightarrow O_2^-(aq)$

$E^0_{H_2BO_3^-/BH_4^-} = -1.24$ V

21-42 $Cd(Hg) + Hg_2SO_4(s) \rightleftharpoons 2Hg(l) + CdSO_4(aq)$

The value of $[Cd^{2+}][SO_4^{2-}]$ is fixed because the solution is saturated; thus E is fixed.

21-44 (a) $Zn(s) + 4KOH(aq) \longrightarrow K_2ZnO_2(s) + 2H_2O(l) + 2K^+(aq) + 2e^-$
(b) $Ag_2O_2(s) + 4K^+(aq) + 2H_2O(l) + 4e^- \longrightarrow 2Ag(s) + 4KOH(aq)$
(c) $2Zn(s) + Ag_2O_2(s) + 4KOH(aq) \longrightarrow 2Ag(s) + 2K_2ZnO_2(s) + 2H_2O(l)$

21-46 $^\ominus Mg(s) | MgCl_2(s) | KSCN(NH_3) | AgCl(s) | Ag(s)^\oplus$
$Mg(s) + 2AgCl(s) \rightleftharpoons MgCl_2(s) + 2Ag(s)$

21-48 0.201 g

21-50 0.84 g

21-52 1.74×10^6 C; 483 A · h

21-54 106, palladium

21-56 17 million tons

21-58 $Ag(s) | AgNO_3(aq) \| NaCl(aq) | AgCl(s) | Ag(s)$

21-60 See solution to Problem 21-59. A measurement of the cell voltage gives $[H^+]$ in the $HC_2H_3O_2(aq) + NaC_2H_3O_2(aq)$ solution from which K_a can be calculated.

F   ANSWERS TO THE SELF-TEST

1 true

2 oxidation half-reaction, reduction half-reaction

3 negative, positive

4 to provide an ionic current path between the separated solutions

5 (a) left (negative)
   (b) $Cd(s) \longrightarrow Cd^{2+}(aq) + 2e^-$
   (c) $Pb^{2+}(aq) + 2e^- \longrightarrow Pb(s)$

6 0 V (The cell is short-circuited.)

7 (a) $ZnSO_4(aq)$
   (b) $Zn(s)$, $Hg_2SO_4(s)$, $Hg(l)$
   (c) There is no salt bridge in this cell.

8 To act as a metallic surface on which the electron transfer half-reaction $2H^+(aq) + 2e^- \rightleftharpoons H_2(g)$ can occur.

9 false

10 (a) decreases   (b) increases
   (c) remains unchanged
   (d) eventually becomes zero

11 positive

12 $E^0 = \left(\dfrac{0.0592 \text{ V}}{n} \right) \log K$

13 $Q = 1$ or when all species are in their standard states

14 1

15 less than

16 $E = E^0 - \left(\dfrac{0.0592 \text{ V}}{n} \right) \log Q$

17 false

18 0

19 false (A reference half-reaction must be defined.)

20 false

21 zero

22 reduction

23 true

24 negative

25 true

26 true

27 the Nernst

28 hydrogen gas or a hydrogen glass

29 voltage

30 true

31 true

32 true

33 false (The current in solution is carried by ions.)

34 cathode

35 true

36 charge = current × time

37 96,500 coulombs or one Faraday

38 $96,500 \text{ C} \cdot \text{mol}^{-1}$ (the charge on one mole of electrons)

39 chlorine, $Cl_2(g)$, and sodium hydroxide and hydrogen, $H_2(g)$; $NaCl(aq)$

40 aluminum metal; $Al_2O_3(s)$ dissolved in $Na_3AlF_6(l)$

22 / Entropy and Gibbs Energy

A   OUTLINE OF CHAPTER 22

22-1   An evolution of energy does not guarantee reaction spontaneity.

Exothermic reactions are energetically downhill (Figures 22-1 and 22-2).

Highly exothermic reactions are spontaneous.

$\Delta H°_{rxn} < 0$ is not sufficient to guarantee reaction spontaneity.

22-2   Entropy is a measure of the amount of disorder or randomness in a system.

Entropy arises from positional disorder and thermal disorder.

The entropy of a perfect crystal is zero at absolute zero.

The entropy of a substance at fixed pressure increases as the temperature increases (Figure 22-4).

The greater the number of ways that the energy can be distributed among the energy levels of a substance, the greater is the entropy of the substance.

22-3   There is a jump in entropy at a phase transition.

The entropy of the liquid phase of a substance at a given temperature and pressure is greater than the entropy of the solid phase.

The molar entropy change upon fusion is given by

$$\Delta \bar{S}_{fus} = \Delta \bar{H}_{fus}/T_m \tag{22-1}$$

The entropy of the gaseous phase of a substance at a given temperature and pressure is greater than the entropy of the liquid phase.

The molar entropy change upon vaporization is given by

$$\Delta \bar{S}_{vap} = \Delta \bar{H}_{vap}/T_b \tag{22-2}$$

Gases are more disordered than liquids and liquids are more disordered than solids.

The units of entropy are $J \cdot K^{-1}$ or $J \cdot K^{-1} \cdot mol^{-1}$.

$$\Delta \overline{S}_{vap} > \Delta \overline{S}_{fus}$$

22-4   The molar entropy of a substance depends on the number, masses, and arrangement of the atoms in the molecule.

$\overline{S}°$ denotes a standard (1 atm) molar entropy.

Greater mass leads to a greater capacity to take up energy and thus to a higher entropy.

The more atoms of a given mass in a molecule, the higher the entropy.

The more complex a molecule is, the higher the molar entropy.

22-5 $\Delta S°_{rxn}$ equals the entropy of the products minus the entropy of the reactants.

For the reaction $a\text{A} + b\text{B} \longrightarrow y\text{Y} + z\text{Z}$

$$\Delta \overline{S}°_{rxn} = (y\overline{S}°_Y + z\overline{S}°_Z) - (a\overline{S}°_A + b\overline{S}°_B) \qquad (22\text{-}3)$$

Values of $\overline{S}°$ for some compounds are given in Table 22-1.

If there are more moles of gaseous products than reactants, then $\Delta S°_{rxn} > 0$.

22-6   Nature acts to minimize the energy and to maximize the entropy of all processes.

Reactions with $\Delta S_{rxn} > 0$ are entropy driven and are said to be entropy favored.

Reactions with $\Delta H_{rxn} < 0$ are energy (enthalpy) favored.

If $\Delta H_{rxn} < 0$ and $\Delta S_{rxn} > 0$, then the reaction is spontaneous.

If $\Delta H_{rxn} > 0$ and $\Delta S_{rxn} < 0$, then the reaction is not spontaneous.

22-7   The sign of the Gibbs free energy change determines whether or not a reaction is spontaneous.

The Gibbs free energy change for a reaction that occurs at constant temperature is given by

$$\Delta G_{rxn} = \Delta H_{rxn} - T\Delta S_{rxn} \qquad (22\text{-}4)$$

Chemical reactions seek a compromise between energy minimization and entropy maximization (Table 22-2).

The Gibbs criteria for spontaneity are:

if $\Delta G_{rxn} < 0$, then the reaction is spontaneous

if $\Delta G_{rxn} > 0$, then the reaction is not spontaneous

if $\Delta G_{rxn} = 0$, then the reaction is at equilibrium

The standard Gibbs free energy change, denoted by $\Delta G°_{rxn}$, is equal to ΔG_{rxn} when the reactants and products are at standard conditions.

The value of $\Delta G°_{rxn}$ is given by

$$\Delta G°_{rxn} = \Delta H°_{rxn} - T\Delta S°_{rxn}$$

22-8   The value of ΔG_{rxn} is equal to the maximum amount of work that can be obtained from the reaction.

The Gibbs free energy change for an oxidation-reduction reaction is related to the cell voltage by

$$\Delta G_{rxn} = -nFE \qquad (22\text{-}5)$$

If ΔG_{rxn} is negative, then the magnitude of ΔG_{rxn} is equal to the maximum amount of work that can be obtained from the reaction.

If ΔG_{rxn} is positive, then ΔG_{rxn} is equal to the minimum amount of work that must be done to make the reaction occur.

22-9   The value of ΔG_{rxn} depends upon the ratio Q/K.

$$\Delta G_{rxn} = 2.30\,RT\log(Q/K) \qquad (22\text{-}6)$$

If $Q/K < 1$, then $\Delta G_{rxn} < 0$.
If $Q/K > 1$, then $\Delta G_{rxn} > 0$.
If $Q/K = 1$, then $\Delta G_{rxn} = 0$.

The standard Gibbs free energy change for a reaction is related to the equilibrium constant by

$$\Delta G^\circ_{rxn} = -2.30RT\log K \qquad (22\text{-}8)$$

Spontaneous is not synonymous with immediate.

For a reaction to occur, ΔG_{rxn} must be less than zero, but $\Delta G_{rxn} < 0$ does not guarantee that the reaction will occur at an appreciable rate.

22-10 ΔG°_{rxn} can be calculated from tabulated $\Delta \bar{G}^\circ_f$ values.

The standard Gibbs free energy of formation of a compound, denoted by $\Delta \bar{G}^\circ_f$, is equal to the value of ΔG°_{rxn} for the reaction in which the compound is formed from its constituent elements at standard conditions.

For the reaction $a\text{A} + b\text{B} \longrightarrow y\text{Y} + z\text{Z}$.

$$\Delta G^\circ_{rxn} = (y\Delta\bar{G}^\circ_f[\text{Y}] + z\Delta\bar{G}^\circ_f[\text{Z}]) - (a\Delta\bar{G}^\circ_f[\text{A}] + b\Delta\bar{G}^\circ_f[\text{B}]) \qquad (22\text{-}9)$$

Values of $\Delta\bar{G}^\circ_f$ for some compounds are given in Table 22-1.

22-11   It is the sign of ΔG_{rxn} and not ΔG°_{rxn} that determines reaction spontaneity.

ΔG_{rxn} and ΔG°_{rxn} are related by

$$\Delta G_{rxn} = \Delta G^\circ_{rxn} + 2.30RT\log Q \qquad (22\text{-}10)$$

If $Q = 1$, then $\Delta G_{rxn} = \Delta G^\circ_{rxn}$.

B   SELF-TEST

1   All exothermic processes are spontaneous processes. *True/False*

2   All processes that lead to an increase in entropy are spontaneous. *True/False*

3   Entropy arises from _____ disorder and _____ disorder.

4 The entropy of liquid water increases when the temperature is raised from 25°C to 50°C at constant pressure because _____
_____.

5 The entropy of water vapor (*increases/decreases*) when the volume of the gas is increased from 0.50 L to 1.0 L at 200°C.

6 The entropy of a substance increases upon melting because _____
_____.

7 The entropy of a substance increases upon vaporization because _____
_____.

8 The value of the molar entropy change of fusion is given by $\Delta \bar{S}_{fus} =$
_____.

9 The value of the molar entropy change of vaporization is given by $\Delta \bar{S}_{vap} =$
_____.

10 The molar entropy of $H_2O(l)$ is (*greater than/less than/the same as*) the molar entropy of $H_2O(g)$ at the same temperature and pressure.

11 The entropy of gaseous molecules at 25°C and 1 atm is greater the greater the _____ of the molecule and the larger the number of _____ in the molecule.

12 The molar entropy of $C_2H_2(g)$ is less than the molar entropy of $C_2H_6(g)$ at the same temperature and pressure because _____
_____.

13 The standard entropy change of the reaction

$$2H_2O(l) \longrightarrow 2H_2(g) + O_2(g)$$

is (*positive/negative*).

14 The standard molar entropy change of the reaction

$$2H_2O(l) \longrightarrow 2H_2(g) + O_2(g)$$

in terms of the standard molar entropies of products and reactants is given by $\Delta S_{rxn}^\circ =$ _____.

15 Isothermal processes that lead to a decrease in the Gibbs free energy are spontaneous processes. *True/False*

16 If $\Delta G_{rxn} < 0$, then the reaction is _____.

17 If $\Delta G_{rxn} > 0$, then the reaction is _____.

18 If $\Delta G_{rxn} = 0$, then the reaction is _____.

19   If a spontaneous reaction is endothermic, then the change in entropy for the reaction must be (*positive/negative*).

20   The value of the Gibbs free energy change of a reaction run at constant temperature is related to the changes in enthalpy and entropy of the reaction by the equation $\Delta G_{rxn} =$ _____.

21   A spontaneous endothermic reaction is _____ driven.

22   A spontaneous reaction for which the entropy change is negative is _____ driven.

23   If the value of ΔG_{rxn} is 123 kJ, then the reaction (*is/is not*) spontaneous.

24   All reactions with $\Delta H_{rxn} < 0$ and $\Delta S_{rxn} > 0$ are _____.

25   All reactions with $\Delta H_{rxn} > 0$ and $\Delta S_{rxn} < 0$ are _____.

26   The value of ΔG_{rxn} is independent of temperature. *True/False*

27   The maximum amount of work that can be obtained from a reaction is equal to

_____.

28   The value of ΔG_{rxn} for the combustion of a certain fuel is -2030 kJ. The maximum amount of work that can be obtained from the utilization of the fuel is

_____.

29   The Gibbs free energy change for an oxidation-reduction reaction is related to the corresponding cell voltage by the equation $\Delta G_{rxn} =$

_____.

30   The cell voltage for an oxidation-reduction reaction is 1.21 V. The reaction (*is/is not*) spontaneous.

31   Electric energy can be used to drive a reaction for which ΔG_{rxn} is positive. *True/False*

32   The relation between ΔG_{rxn} and Q/K is $\Delta G_{rxn} =$ _____.

33   A reaction for which $Q/K < 1$ (*is/is not*) spontaneous.

34   The standard Gibbs free energy change of a reaction is the Gibbs free energy change of the reaction when _____.

35   The standard Gibbs free energy change of a reaction is related to the equilibrium constant of the reaction by the equation $\Delta G_{rxn}^{\circ} =$

_____.

36   The equilibrium constant at 25°C for the dissociation of acetic acid is 1.7×10^{-5} M. The dissociation reaction (*is/is not*) spontaneous when run under standard conditions.

37   Tables of standard molar Gibbs free energies of formation of compounds can be set up. *True/False*

38 The standard Gibbs energy change of the reaction

$$2H_2O(l) \longrightarrow 2H_2(g) + O_2(g)$$

can be calculated using tables of standard molar Gibbs free energies of formation and the relationship ΔG_{rxn}° = _____.

39 The value of ΔG_{rxn}° for the dissociation of acetic acid is 27.1 kJ. The reaction is not spontaneous under any conditions. *True/False*

40 The value of ΔG_{rxn} for a reaction is -342 kJ. The reaction must proceed rapidly toward equilibrium. *True/False*

41 The value of $\Delta \bar{G}_f^{\circ}$ for $O_2(g)$ at 25°C is 0 kJ $\cdot$ mol^{-1}. *True/False*

42 The value of $\Delta \bar{H}_f^{\circ}$ for $O_2(g)$ at 25°C is 0 kJ $\cdot$ mol^{-1}. *True/False*

43 The value of $\bar{S}^{\circ}$ for $O_2(g)$ at 25°C is 0 J $\cdot$ K^{-1} $\cdot$ mol^{-1}. *True/False*

C   CALCULATIONS YOU SHOULD KNOW HOW TO DO

1 Calculate the values of $\Delta \bar{S}_{fus}$ and $\Delta \bar{S}_{vap}$ using Equations (22-1) and (22-2). See Example 22-1 and Problems 22-1 through 22-8.

2 Predict relative entropies. See Example 22-2 and Problems 22-9 through 22-14.

3 Calculate ΔS_{rxn}° from $\bar{S}^{\circ}$ values of the reactants and products. See Example 22-3 and Problems 22-21 through 22-24.

4 Predict the sign of ΔS_{rxn}°. See Example 22-4 and Problems 22-15 through 22-18.

5 Calculate ΔG_{rxn} using the equation $\Delta G_{rxn} = \Delta H_{rxn} - T\Delta S_{rxn}$. See Example 22-5 and Problems 22-25 through 22-32.

6 Calculate ΔG_{rxn} or the cell voltage, using the relation $\Delta G_{rxn} = -nFE$. See Example 22-6 and Problems 22-33 through 22-40.

7 Calculate ΔG_{rxn}° and ΔG_{rxn} given the equilibrium constant using the equations $\Delta G_{rxn}^{\circ} = -2.30RT \log K$ and $\Delta G_{rxn} = 2.30RT \log (Q/K)$. See Examples 22-7 and 22-8 and Problems 22-41 through 22-54.

8 Calculate ΔG_{rxn}° using tabulated $\Delta \bar{G}_f^{\circ}$ values of the reactants and products. See Example 22-9 and Problems 22-55 through 22-72.

D   SOLUTIONS TO THE ODD-NUMBERED PROBLEMS

22-1 We calculate $\Delta \bar{S}_{fus}$ from the relationship

$$\Delta \bar{S}_{fus} = \frac{\Delta \bar{H}_{fus}}{T_m}$$

Using the values of T_m and $\Delta\bar{H}_{fus}$ given, we have

LiCl $\Delta\bar{S}_{fus} = \dfrac{19.8 \times 10^3 \text{ J} \cdot \text{mol}^{-1}}{887 \text{ K}} = 22.3 \text{ J} \cdot \text{K}^{-1} \cdot \text{mol}^{-1}$

NaCl $\Delta\bar{S}_{fus} = \dfrac{28.2 \times 10^3 \text{ J} \cdot \text{mol}^{-1}}{1073 \text{ K}} = 26.3 \text{ J} \cdot \text{K}^{-1} \cdot \text{mol}^{-1}$

KCl $\Delta\bar{S}_{fus} = \dfrac{26.8 \times 10^3 \text{ J} \cdot \text{mol}^{-1}}{1043 \text{ K}} = 25.7 \text{ J} \cdot \text{K}^{-1} \cdot \text{mol}^{-1}$

We calculate $\Delta\bar{S}_{vap}$ from the relationship

$$\Delta\bar{S}_{vap} = \frac{\Delta\bar{H}_{vap}}{T_b}$$

Using the values of T_b and $\Delta\bar{H}_{vap}$ given, we have

LiCl $\Delta\bar{S}_{vap} = \dfrac{161.4 \times 10^3 \text{ J} \cdot \text{mol}^{-1}}{1598 \text{ K}} = 101.0 \text{ J} \cdot \text{K}^{-1} \cdot \text{mol}^{-1}$

NaCl $\Delta\bar{S}_{vap} = \dfrac{181.7 \times 10^3 \text{ J} \cdot \text{mol}^{-1}}{1686 \text{ K}} = 107.8 \text{ J} \cdot \text{K}^{-1} \cdot \text{mol}^{-1}$

KCl $\Delta\bar{S}_{vap} = \dfrac{172.8 \times 10^3 \text{ J} \cdot \text{mol}^{-1}}{1773 \text{ K}} = 97.46 \text{ J} \cdot \text{K}^{-1} \cdot \text{mol}^{-1}$

22-3   We calculate $\Delta\bar{S}_{fus}$ using the relationship

$$\Delta\bar{S}_{fus} = \frac{\Delta\bar{H}_{fus}}{T_m}$$

Using the values of T_m and $\Delta\bar{H}_{fus}$ given, we have

CH_2Cl_2 $\Delta\bar{S}_{fus} = \dfrac{1.434 \times 10^3 \text{ J} \cdot \text{mol}^{-1}}{178.01 \text{ K}} = 8.056 \text{ J} \cdot \text{K}^{-1} \cdot \text{mol}^{-1}$

$CHCl_3$ $\Delta\bar{S}_{fus} = \dfrac{8.800 \times 10^3 \text{ J} \cdot \text{mol}^{-1}}{209.6 \text{ K}} = 41.99 \text{ J} \cdot \text{K}^{-1} \cdot \text{mol}^{-1}$

CCl_4 $\Delta\bar{S}_{fus} = \dfrac{3.275 \times 10^3 \text{ J} \cdot \text{mol}^{-1}}{250.2 \text{ K}} = 13.09 \text{ J} \cdot \text{K}^{-1} \cdot \text{mol}^{-1}$

We calculate $\Delta\bar{S}_{vap}$ using the relationship

$$\Delta\bar{S}_{vap} = \frac{\Delta\bar{H}_{vap}}{T_b}$$

Using the values of T_b and $\Delta\bar{H}_{vap}$ given, we have

$$\text{CH}_2\text{Cl}_2 \qquad \Delta\bar{S}_{vap} = \frac{31.68 \times 10^3 \text{ J} \cdot \text{mol}^{-1}}{313.2 \text{ K}} = 101.2 \text{ J} \cdot \text{K}^{-1} \cdot \text{mol}^{-1}$$

$$\text{CHCl}_3 \qquad \Delta\bar{S}_{vap} = \frac{31.38 \times 10^3 \text{ J} \cdot \text{mol}^{-1}}{334.9 \text{ K}} = 93.70 \text{ J} \cdot \text{K}^{-1} \cdot \text{mol}^{-1}$$

$$\text{CCl}_4 \qquad \Delta\bar{S}_{vap} = \frac{31.92 \times 10^3 \text{ J} \cdot \text{mol}^{-1}}{349.69 \text{ K}} = 91.28 \text{ J} \cdot \text{K}^{-1} \cdot \text{mol}^{-1}$$

22-5 We calculate $\Delta\bar{S}_{fus}$ using the relationship

$$\Delta\bar{S}_{fus} = \frac{\Delta\bar{H}_{fus}}{T_m}$$

Using the value of T_m and $\Delta\bar{H}_{fus}$ given, we have

$$\text{Li} \qquad \Delta\bar{S}_{fus} = \frac{2.99 \times 10^3 \text{ J} \cdot \text{mol}^{-1}}{454 \text{ K}} = 6.59 \text{ J} \cdot \text{K}^{-1} \cdot \text{mol}^{-1}$$

$$\text{Na} \qquad \Delta\bar{S}_{fus} = \frac{2.60 \times 10^3 \text{ J} \cdot \text{mol}^{-1}}{371 \text{ K}} = 7.01 \text{ J} \cdot \text{K}^{-1} \cdot \text{mol}^{-1}$$

$$\text{K} \qquad \Delta\bar{S}_{fus} = \frac{2.33 \times 10^3 \text{ J} \cdot \text{mol}^{-1}}{336 \text{ K}} = 6.93 \text{ J} \cdot \text{K}^{-1} \cdot \text{mol}^{-1}$$

$$\text{Rb} \qquad \Delta\bar{S}_{fus} = \frac{2.34 \times 10^3 \text{ J} \cdot \text{mol}^{-1}}{312 \text{ K}} = 7.50 \text{ J} \cdot \dot{\text{K}}^{-1} \cdot \text{mol}^{-1}$$

$$\text{Cs} \qquad \Delta\bar{S}_{fus} = \frac{2.10 \times 10^3 \text{ J} \cdot \text{mol}^{-1}}{302 \text{ K}} = 6.95 \text{ J} \cdot \text{K}^{-1} \cdot \text{mol}^{-1}$$

22-7 $\text{H}_2\text{S} \qquad \Delta\bar{S}_{fus} = \dfrac{\Delta\bar{H}_{fus}}{T_m} = \dfrac{2.38 \times 10^3 \text{ J} \cdot \text{mol}^{-1}}{187.6 \text{ K}} = 12.7 \text{ J} \cdot \text{K}^{-1} \cdot \text{mol}^{-1}$

$$\Delta\bar{S}_{vap} = \frac{\Delta\bar{H}_{vap}}{T_b} = \frac{18.7 \times 10^3 \text{ J} \cdot \text{mol}^{-1}}{212.5 \text{ K}} = 88.0 \text{ J} \cdot \text{K}^{-1} \cdot \text{mol}^{-1}$$

From Example 22-1 we have

$$\text{H}_2\text{O} \qquad \Delta\bar{S}_{fus} = 22.1 \text{ J} \cdot \text{K}^{-1} \cdot \text{mol}^{-1}$$
$$\Delta\bar{S}_{vap} = 109 \text{ J} \cdot \text{K}^{-1} \cdot \text{mol}^{-1}$$

The larger values of $\Delta\bar{S}_{fus}$ and $\Delta\bar{S}_{vap}$ for H_2O are a result of the breaking of hydrogen bonds in the processes solid → liquid and liquid → gas. The hydrogen bonds make for a higher degree of order and thus their breaking produces a greater increase in disorder.

22-9 (a) The mass of PF_3 is less than the mass of PCl_3. Thus we predict that

$$\overline{S}°(PF_3) < \overline{S}°(PCl_3)$$

(b) Cyclopropane has almost the same mass, but has less freedom of movement than propane because of its ring structure. Thus we predict that

$$\overline{S}°(\text{cyclopropane}) < \overline{S}°(\text{propane})$$

(c) Dioxane has less freedom of movement than butyric acid because of its ring structure. We predict that

$$\overline{S}°(\text{dioxane}) < \overline{S}°(\text{butyric acid})$$

(d) n-Pentane is a more flexible molecule than neopentane and thus we predict that

$$\overline{S}°(\text{neopentane}) < \overline{S}°(n\text{-pentane})$$

22-11 The number of carbon atoms is the same in each compound but the number of chlorine atoms varies. We expect the total molar entropy to increase with increasing total mass and increasing number of atoms. Thus we predict that

$$\overline{S}°(C_2Cl_2) < \overline{S}°(C_2Cl_4) < \overline{S}°(C_2Cl_6)$$

22-13 The compound $SO_3(g)$ has more atoms and a greater mass than $SO_2(g)$ and so is able to take up energy more easily. Thus we would predict that

$$\overline{S}°(SO_2) < \overline{S}°(SO_3)$$

22-15 Iodine molecules in $I_2(s)$ are restricted to movements around their lattice sites, while iodine molecules in $I_2(g)$ are free to move through the gas. The positional disorder in the gaseous state is greater than in the solid state; thus the entropy of iodine is greater in the gaseous state than in the solid state.

22-17 (a) The argon atoms have a greater freedom of movement in the gaseous state. The entropy will increase.

(b) The oxygen atoms have a greater freedom of movement at lower pressure. The entropy will decrease.

(c) Copper atoms have a greater thermal disorder at a higher temperature. The entropy will increase.

(d) The water molecules have a greater freedom of movement in the gaseous state. The entropy will decrease.

22-19 (a) We have the same number of moles of gaseous reactant and gaseous product ($\Delta n = 0$).

(b) We have three moles of gaseous reactants and two moles of gaseous products ($\Delta n = -1$).

(c) We have four moles of gaseous reactants and two moles of gaseous products ($\Delta n = -2$).

(d) We have one mole of gaseous reactant and two moles of gaseous products ($\Delta n = +1$).

The value of ΔS°_{rxn} increases as the net change in the number of moles of gas increases, thus

$$\Delta S^{\circ}_{rxn}(c) < \Delta S^{\circ}_{rxn}(b) < \Delta S^{\circ}_{rxn}(a) < \Delta S^{\circ}_{rxn}(d)$$

22-21 The value of ΔS°_{rxn} is given by

$$\Delta S^{\circ}_{rxn} = \bar{S}^{\circ}(\text{products}) - \bar{S}^{\circ}(\text{reactants})$$

(a) $\Delta S^{\circ}_{rxn} = 2\bar{S}^{\circ}[NO_2(g)] + 3\bar{S}^{\circ}[H_2O(g)] - 2\bar{S}^{\circ}[NH_3(g)] - \frac{7}{2}\bar{S}^{\circ}[O_2(g)]$

$\Delta S^{\circ}_{rxn} = (2 \text{ mol})(240.4 \text{ J} \cdot \text{K}^{-1} \cdot \text{mol}^{-1}) + (3 \text{ mol})(188.7 \text{ J} \cdot \text{K}^{-1} \cdot \text{mol}^{-1})$
$- (2 \text{ mol})(192.5 \text{ J} \cdot \text{K}^{-1} \cdot \text{mol}^{-1}) - (\frac{7}{2} \text{ mol})(205.0 \text{ J} \cdot \text{K}^{-1} \cdot \text{mol}^{-1})$

$= -55.6 \text{ J} \cdot \text{K}^{-1}$

(b) $\Delta S^{\circ}_{rxn} = \bar{S}^{\circ}[CH_3OH(l)] - \bar{S}^{\circ}[CO(g)] - 2\bar{S}^{\circ}[H_2(g)]$

$= (1 \text{ mol})(126.9 \text{ J} \cdot \text{K}^{-1} \cdot \text{mol}^{-1}) - (1 \text{ mol})(197.8 \text{ J} \cdot \text{K}^{-1} \cdot \text{mol}^{-1})$
$- (2 \text{ mol})(130.6 \text{ J} \cdot \text{K}^{-1} \cdot \text{mol}^{-1})$

$= -332.1 \text{ J} \cdot \text{K}^{-1}$

(c) $\Delta S^{\circ}_{rxn} = \bar{S}^{\circ}[CO(g)] + \bar{S}^{\circ}[H_2(g)] - \bar{S}^{\circ}[C(s)] - \bar{S}^{\circ}[H_2O(g)]$

$= (1 \text{ mol})(197.8 \text{ J} \cdot \text{K}^{-1} \cdot \text{mol}^{-1}) + (1 \text{ mol})(130.6 \text{ J} \cdot \text{K}^{-1} \cdot \text{mol}^{-1})$
$- (1 \text{ mol})(5.74 \text{ J} \cdot \text{K}^{-1} \cdot \text{mol}^{-1}) - (1 \text{ mol})(188.7 \text{ J} \cdot \text{K}^{-1} \cdot \text{mol}^{-1})$

$= 134.0 \text{ J} \cdot \text{K}^{-1}$

The graphite form of $C(s)$ is used here.

(d) $\Delta S^{\circ}_{rxn} = \bar{S}^{\circ}[CH_4(g)] + \bar{S}^{\circ}[H_2O(g)] - \bar{S}^{\circ}[CO(g)] - 3\bar{S}^{\circ}[H_2(g)]$

$= (1 \text{ mol})(186.2 \text{ J} \cdot \text{K}^{-1} \cdot \text{mol}^{-1}) + (1 \text{ mol})(188.7 \text{ J} \cdot \text{K}^{-1} \cdot \text{mol}^{-1})$
$- (1 \text{ mol})(197.8 \text{ J} \cdot \text{K}^{-1} \cdot \text{mol}^{-1}) - (3 \text{ mol})(130.6 \text{ J} \cdot \text{K}^{-1} \cdot \text{mol}^{-1})$

$= -214.7 \text{ J} \cdot \text{K}^{-1}$

22-23 The value of ΔS°_{rxn} is given by

$$\Delta S^{\circ}_{rxn} = \bar{S}^{\circ}(\text{products}) - \bar{S}^{\circ}(\text{reactants})$$

(a) $\Delta S^{\circ}_{rxn} = \bar{S}^{\circ}[CO_2(g)] - \bar{S}^{\circ}[C(s)] - \bar{S}^{\circ}[O_2(g)]$

$= (1 \text{ mol})(213.6 \text{ J} \cdot \text{K}^{-1} \cdot \text{mol}^{-1}) - (1 \text{ mol})(5.74 \text{ J} \cdot \text{K}^{-1} \cdot \text{mol}^{-1})$
$- (1 \text{ mol})(205.0 \text{ J} \cdot \text{K}^{-1} \cdot \text{mol}^{-1})$

$= 2.9 \text{ J} \cdot \text{K}^{-1}$

(b) $\Delta S^{\circ}_{rxn} = 2\bar{S}^{\circ}[SO_3(g)] - 2\bar{S}^{\circ}[SO_2(g)] - \bar{S}^{\circ}[O_2(g)]$

$= (2 \text{ mol})(256.3 \text{ J} \cdot \text{K}^{-1} \cdot \text{mol}^{-1}) - (2 \text{ mol})(248.4 \text{ J} \cdot \text{K}^{-1} \cdot \text{mol}^{-1})$
$- (1 \text{ mol})(205.0 \text{ J} \cdot \text{K}^{-1} \cdot \text{mol}^{-1})$

$= -189.2 \text{ J} \cdot \text{K}^{-1}$

(c) $\Delta S^{\circ}_{rxn} = \bar{S}^{\circ}[CO_2(g)] + 2\bar{S}^{\circ}[H_2O(l)] - \bar{S}^{\circ}[CH_4(g)] - 2\bar{S}^{\circ}[O_2(g)]$

$= (1 \text{ mol})(213.6 \text{ J} \cdot \text{K}^{-1} \cdot \text{mol}^{-1}) + (2 \text{ mol})(69.9 \text{ J} \cdot \text{K}^{-1} \cdot \text{mol}^{-1})$
$- (1 \text{ mol})(186.2 \text{ J} \cdot \text{K}^{-1} \cdot \text{mol}^{-1}) - (2 \text{ mol})(205.0 \text{ J} \cdot \text{K}^{-1} \cdot \text{mol}^{-1})$

$= -242.8 \text{ J} \cdot \text{K}^{-1}$

(d) $\Delta S_{rxn}^{\circ} = \bar{S}^{\circ}[C_2H_4(g)] - \bar{S}^{\circ}[C_2H_2(g)] - \bar{S}^{\circ}[H_2(g)]$

$\quad = (1 \text{ mol})(219.6 \text{ J} \cdot \text{K}^{-1} \cdot \text{mol}^{-1}) - (1 \text{ mol})(200.8 \text{ J} \cdot \text{K}^{-1} \cdot \text{mol}^{-1})$

$\quad - (1 \text{ mol})(130.6 \text{ J} \cdot \text{K}^{-1} \cdot \text{mol}^{-1})$

$\quad = -111.8 \text{ J} \cdot \text{K}^{-1}$

22-25 The reaction is spontaneous. Because the reaction is spontaneous, the sign of ΔG_{rxn} is negative. We learned in Chapter 6 that it requires energy to vaporize a liquid. Thus the sign of ΔH_{rxn} is positive. $\Delta \bar{S}_{vap}$ is also positive (liquid → gas). Vaporization is entropy driven.

22-27 The value of ΔS_{rxn}° is given by

$$\Delta \bar{S}_{rxn}^{\circ} = \bar{S}^{\circ}(\text{products}) - \bar{S}^{\circ}(\text{reactants}) = \bar{S}^{\circ}[C_6H_6(l)] - 3\bar{S}^{\circ}[C_2H_2(g)]$$

$$= (1 \text{ mol})(172.8 \text{ J} \cdot \text{K}^{-1} \cdot \text{mol}^{-1}) - (3 \text{ mol})(200.8 \text{ J} \cdot \text{K}^{-1} \cdot \text{mol}^{-1})$$

$$= -429.6 \text{ J} \cdot \text{K}^{-1}$$

We can calculate ΔG_{rxn}° using the relationship

$$\Delta G_{rxn}^{\circ} = \Delta H_{rxn}^{\circ} - T\Delta S_{rxn}^{\circ}$$

$$= -631 \text{ kJ} - (298 \text{ K})(-429.6 \text{ J} \cdot \text{K}^{-1})\left(\frac{1 \text{ kJ}}{1000 \text{ J}}\right)$$

$$= -503 \text{ kJ}$$

The reaction is spontaneous at 1 atm and 25°C in the direction

$$3C_2H_2(g) \longrightarrow C_6H_6(l)$$

22-29 $\Delta S_{rxn}^{\circ} = 2\bar{S}^{\circ}[CO_2(g)] + 2\bar{S}^{\circ}[H_2O(g)] - \bar{S}^{\circ}[C_2H_4(g)] - 3\bar{S}^{\circ}[O_2(g)]$

$\quad = (2 \text{ mol})(213.6 \text{ J} \cdot \text{K}^{-1} \cdot \text{mol}^{-1}) + (2 \text{ mol})(188.7 \text{ J} \cdot \text{K}^{-1} \cdot \text{mol}^{-1})$

$\quad - (1 \text{ mol})(219.6 \text{ J} \cdot \text{K}^{-1} \cdot \text{mol}^{-1}) - (3 \text{ mol})(205.0 \text{ J} \cdot \text{K}^{-1} \cdot \text{mol}^{-1})$

$\quad = -30.0 \text{ J} \cdot \text{K}^{-1}$

We calculate ΔG_{rxn}° using

$$\Delta G_{rxn}^{\circ} = \Delta H_{rxn}^{\circ} - T\Delta S_{rxn}^{\circ}$$

$$= -1323 \text{ kJ} - (298 \text{ K})(-30.0 \text{ J} \cdot \text{K}^{-1})\left(\frac{1 \text{ kJ}}{1000 \text{ J}}\right)$$

$$= -1314 \text{ kJ}$$

The reaction is spontaneous in the direction

$$C_2H_4(g) + 3O_2(g) \longrightarrow 2CO_2(g) + 2H_2O(g)$$

22-31 The process cannot work without energy input because for the process

$$H_2O(l) \longrightarrow H_2(g) + \tfrac{1}{2}O_2(g)$$

ΔG_{rxn}° (= 237 kJ) is large and positive, and thus the reaction is not spontaneous at one atm. A catalyst does not affect ΔG_{rxn}; it increases only the reaction rate.

22-33   The value of ΔG_{rxn} is given by

$$\Delta G_{rxn} = -nFE$$

Two moles of electrons are transferred in this reaction; thus $n = 2$.

$$\Delta G_{rxn} = -(2 \text{ mol})(96{,}500 \text{ C} \cdot \text{mol}^{-1})(1.05 \text{ V})$$
$$= -203{,}000 \text{ J} = -203 \text{ kJ}$$

22-35   The value of ΔG_{rxn}° is given by

$$\Delta G_{rxn}^{\circ} = -nFE^{\circ}$$

In the reaction one mole of copper is oxidized from an oxidation state of zero to an oxidation state of $+2$. Thus the reaction requires two moles of electrons, and so $n = 2$.

$$\Delta G_{rxn}^{\circ} = -(2 \text{ mol})(96{,}500 \text{ C} \cdot \text{mol}^{-1})(0.65 \text{ V})$$
$$= -130{,}000 \text{ J} = -130 \text{ kJ}$$

22-37   (a) The oxidation half-reaction is

$$2\text{Ag}(s) \longrightarrow 2\text{Ag}^+(aq) + 2e^-$$

The reduction half-reaction is

$$\text{F}_2(g) + 2e^- \longrightarrow 2\text{F}^-(aq)$$

The standard cell voltage E° is given by

$$E^{\circ} = E^{\circ}_{\text{F}_2/\text{F}^-} - E^{\circ}_{\text{Ag}^+/\text{Ag}}$$
$$= 2.87 \text{ V} - 0.80 \text{ V} = 2.07 \text{ V}$$

The value of ΔG_{rxn}° is given by

$$\Delta G_{rxn}^{\circ} = -nFE^{\circ}$$

Two electrons are transferred in this reaction, thus

$$\Delta G_{rxn}^{\circ} = -(2 \text{ mol})(96{,}500 \text{ C} \cdot \text{mol}^{-1})(2.07 \text{ V})$$
$$= -400{,}000 \text{ J} = -400 \text{ kJ}$$

   (b) The oxidation half-reaction is

$$\tfrac{1}{2} \text{H}_2(g) \longrightarrow \text{H}^+(aq) + e^-$$

The reduction half-reaction is

$$Fe^{3+}(aq) + e^- \longrightarrow Fe^{2+}(aq)$$

The standard cell voltage, $E°$, is

$$E° = E°_{Fe^{3+}/Fe^{2+}} - E°_{H^+/H_2}$$
$$= 0.77 \text{ V} - 0 \text{ V} = 0.77 \text{ V}$$

The value of $\Delta G°_{rxn}$ is given by

$$\Delta G°_{rxn} = -nFE°$$

One electron is transferred in this reaction; thus $n = 1$.

$$\Delta G°_{rxn} = -(1 \text{ mol})(96,500 \text{ C} \cdot \text{mol}^{-1})(0.77 \text{ V})$$
$$= -74,000 \text{ J} = -74 \text{ kJ}$$

22-39 The value of the standard cell voltage is

$$E° = E°_{Cd^{2+}/Cd} - E°_{Zn^{2+}/Zn}$$
$$= -0.40 \text{ V} - (-0.76 \text{ V}) = 0.36 \text{ V}$$

The value of $\Delta G°_{rxn}$ is $\qquad \Delta G°_{rxn} = -nFE°$

In the reaction two moles of electrons are transferred from one mole of zinc to one mole of cadmium; thus $n = 2$.

$$\Delta G°_{rxn} = -(2 \text{ mol})(96,500 \text{ C} \cdot \text{mol}^{-1})(0.36 \text{ V})$$
$$= -69,000 \text{ J} = -69 \text{ kJ}$$

The value of ΔG_{rxn} is given by

$$\Delta G_{rxn} = \Delta G°_{rxn} + 2.30RT \log Q$$
$$= \Delta G°_{rxn} + 2.30RT \log \frac{[Zn^{2+}]}{[Cd^{2+}]}$$
$$= -69 \text{ kJ} + (2.30)(8.31 \text{ J} \cdot \text{K}^{-1})(298 \text{ K}) \log \left(\frac{0.01}{0.050} \right)$$
$$= -69 \text{ kJ} - 3.98 \text{ kJ} = -73 \text{kJ}$$

The value of E for the cell under the conditions given is

$$E = -\frac{\Delta G_{rxn}}{nF}$$
$$= -\frac{-73 \times 10^3 \text{ J}}{(2 \text{ mol})(96,500 \text{ C} \cdot \text{mol}^{-1})}$$
$$= 0.38 \text{ V}$$

The reaction is

$$Zn(s) + Cd^{2+}(aq) \longrightarrow Zn^{2+}(aq) + Cd(s)$$

22-41 The value of ΔG°_{rxn} and the equilibrium constant are related by

$$\Delta G^{\circ}_{rxn} = -2.30RT \log K$$

(a) The sign of the $\log K$ is negative; thus ΔG°_{rxn} is positive.
(b) The sign of the $\log K$ is positive; thus ΔG°_{rxn} is negative.

22-43 We have
$$\Delta G^{\circ}_{rxn} = -2.30RT \log K$$

At 250°C, we have

$$\Delta G^{\circ}_{rxn} = -(2.30)(8.31 \text{ J} \cdot \text{K}^{-1})(523 \text{ K}) \log (1.8)$$
$$= -2550 \text{ J} = -2.55 \text{ kJ}$$

The reaction is spontaneous in the direction

$$PCl_5(g) \longrightarrow PCl_3(g) + Cl_2(g)$$

when PCl_5, PCl_3, and Cl_2 are at standard conditions. The value of ΔG_{rxn} at other conditions is given by

$$\Delta G_{rxn} = 2.30RT \log Q - 2.30RT \log K$$
$$= 2.30RT \log Q + \Delta G^{\circ}_{rxn}$$
$$= \Delta G^{\circ}_{rxn} + 2.30RT \log \frac{[PCl_3]_0[Cl_2]_0}{[PCl_5]_0}$$
$$= -2.55 \text{ kJ} + (2.30)(8.31 \text{ J} \cdot \text{K}^{-1})(523 \text{ K}) \log \frac{(0.25)(0.25)}{(0.010)}$$
$$= 5.41 \text{ kJ}$$

The reaction to the right is not spontaneous under these conditions.

22-45 The value of ΔG°_{rxn} is given by

$$\Delta G^{\circ}_{rxn} = -2.30RT \log K$$
$$= -(2.30)(8.31 \text{ J} \cdot \text{K}^{-1})(298 \text{ K}) \log (4.5 \times 10^{-4})$$
$$= 1.91 \times 10^4 \text{ J} = 19.1 \text{ kJ}$$

Because $\Delta G^{\circ}_{rxn} > 0$, nitrous acid will not dissociate spontaneously when $[NO_3^-] = [H^+] = [HNO_2] = 1.00$ M (standard conditions). The value of ΔG_{rxn} at any other conditions is given by

$$\Delta G_{rxn} = 2.30RT \log \frac{Q}{K}$$

Thus

$$\Delta G_{rxn} = 2.30RT \log \left(\dfrac{\dfrac{[NO_2^-][H^+]}{[HNO_2]}}{K} \right)$$

$$= (2.30)(8.31 \text{ J} \cdot \text{K}^{-1})(298 \text{ K}) \log \left(\dfrac{\dfrac{(1.0 \times 10^{-5})(1.0 \times 10^{-5})}{(1.0)}}{4.5 \times 10^{-4}} \right)$$

$$= -3.79 \times 10^4 \text{ J}$$

Because $\Delta G_{rxn} < 0$, nitrous acid will dissociate spontaneously under these conditions.

22-47 The value of ΔG_{rxn}° is given by

$$\Delta G_{rxn}^\circ = -2.30RT \log K$$

$$= -(2.30)(8.31 \text{ J} \cdot \text{K}^{-1})(298 \text{ K}) \log (1.35 \times 10^{-3})$$

$$= 1.63 \times 10^4 \text{ J}$$

Chloroacetic acid will not dissociate spontaneously when $[C_2H_2ClO_2^-] = [H^+] = [HC_2H_2ClO_2] = 1.0 \text{ M}$. The value of ΔG_{rxn} at any other conditions is given by

$$\Delta G_{rxn} = 2.30RT \log \dfrac{Q}{K}$$

Thus

$$\Delta G_{rxn} = 2.30RT \log \left(\dfrac{\dfrac{[C_2H_2ClO_2^-][H^+]}{[HC_2H_2ClO_2]}}{K} \right)$$

$$= (2.30)(8.31 \text{ J} \cdot \text{K}^{-1})(298 \text{ K}) \log \left(\dfrac{\dfrac{(0.0010)(1.0 \times 10^{-5})}{0.10}}{1.35 \times 10^{-3}} \right)$$

$$= -2.35 \times 10^4 \text{ J}$$

Chloroacetic acid will dissociate spontaneously under these conditions.

22-49 The value of ΔG_{rxn}° is given by

$$\Delta G_{rxn}^\circ = -2.30RT \log K$$

Thus

$$\Delta G_{rxn}^\circ = -(2.30)(8.31 \text{ J} \cdot \text{K}^{-1})(298 \text{ K}) \log (1.78 \times 10^{-10})$$

$$= 5.55 \times 10^4 \text{ J} = 55.5 \text{ kJ}$$

The reaction is spontaneous right to left when $[Ag^+] = [Cl^-] = 1.0$ M (standard conditions). Therefore, it is not possible to prepare a solution that is 1.0 M in $Ag^+(aq)$ and $Cl^-(aq)$. Insoluble AgCl will precipitate out of the solution.

22-51 The value of ΔG°_{rxn} is given by

$$\Delta G^\circ_{rxn} = -2.30RT \log K$$

Thus

$$\Delta G^\circ_{rxn} = -(2.30)(8.31 \text{ J} \cdot \text{K}^{-1})(298 \text{ K}) \log (2.5 \times 10^3)$$
$$= -1.94 \times 10^4 \text{ J}$$

The reaction is spontaneous left to right when $Ag^+(aq)$, $NH_3(aq)$, and $Ag(NH_3)_2^+(aq)$ are at standard conditions. The value of ΔG_{rxn} at any other condition is given by

$$\Delta G_{rxn} = 2.30RT \log \frac{Q}{K}$$

Thus

$$\Delta G_{rxn} = 2.30RT \log \left(\frac{\dfrac{[Ag(NH_3)_2^+]}{[Ag^+][NH_3]^2}}{K} \right)$$

$$= (2.30)(8.31 \text{ J} \cdot \text{K}^{-1})(298 \text{ K}) \log \left(\frac{\dfrac{(1.0 \times 10^{-3})}{(1.0 \times 10^{-3})(0.10)^2}}{2.5 \times 10^{-3}} \right)$$

$$= -7.96 \times 10^3 \text{ J}$$

The reaction is spontaneous left to right.

22-53 No, because if K is infinite, then ΔG°_{rxn} is infinite, and thus an infinite amount of work could be obtained from the reaction, which is impossible.

22-55 The value of ΔG°_{rxn} is calculated using the data in Table 22-1 and the relationship

$$\Delta G^\circ_{rxn} = \Delta G^\circ_f(\text{products}) - \Delta G^\circ_f(\text{reactants})$$

(a) $\Delta G^\circ_{rxn} = \Delta \bar{G}^\circ_f[CH_3OH(l)] - \Delta \bar{G}^\circ_f[CO(g)] - 2\Delta \bar{G}^\circ_f[H_2(g)]$
$$= (1 \text{ mol})(-166.3 \text{ kJ} \cdot \text{mol}^{-1}) - (1 \text{ mol})(-137.2 \text{ kJ} \cdot \text{mol}^{-1})$$
$$- (2 \text{ mol})(0 \text{ kJ} \cdot \text{mol}^{-1})$$
$$= -29.1 \text{ kJ}$$

Using the relationship $\Delta G^\circ = -2.30RT \log K$, we have

$$\log K = -\frac{\Delta G^\circ_{rxn}}{2.30RT} = -\frac{(-29.1 \times 10^3 \text{ J})}{(2.30)(8.31 \text{ J} \cdot \text{K}^{-1})(298 \text{ K})} = 5.11$$

Thus
$$K = 1.29 \times 10^5$$

(b) $\Delta G^\circ_{rxn} = \Delta \bar{G}^\circ_f[CO(g)] + \Delta \bar{G}^\circ_f[H_2(g)] - \Delta \bar{G}^\circ_f[C(s)] - \Delta \bar{G}^\circ_f[H_2O(g)]$

$\qquad = (1 \text{ mol})(-137.2 \text{ kJ} \cdot \text{mol}^{-1}) + (1 \text{ mol})(0 \text{ kJ} \cdot \text{mol}^{-1})$

$\qquad \quad - (1 \text{ mol})(0 \text{ kJ} \cdot \text{mol}^{-1}) - (1 \text{ mol})(-228.6 \text{ kJ} \cdot \text{mol}^{-1})$

$\qquad = 91.4 \text{ kJ}$

From the relation $\Delta G^\circ_{rxn} = -2.30RT \log K$, we have

$$\log K = - \frac{\Delta G^\circ_{rxn}}{2.30RT} = - \frac{(91.4 \times 10^3 \text{ J})}{(2.30)(8.31 \text{ J} \cdot \text{K}^{-1})(298 \text{ K})} = -16.047$$

Thus
$$K = 8.97 \times 10^{-17}$$

(c) $\Delta G^\circ_{rxn} = \Delta \bar{G}^\circ_f[CH_4(g)] + \Delta \bar{G}^\circ_f[H_2O(g)] - \Delta \bar{G}^\circ_f[CO(g)] - 3\Delta \bar{G}^\circ_f[H_2(g)]$

$\qquad = (1 \text{ mol})(-50.75 \text{ kJ} \cdot \text{mol}^{-1}) + (1 \text{ mol})(-228.6 \text{ kJ} \cdot \text{mol}^{-1})$

$\qquad \quad - (1 \text{ mol})(-137.2 \text{ kJ} \cdot \text{mol}^{-1}) - (3 \text{ mol})(0 \text{ kJ} \cdot \text{mol}^{-1})$

$\qquad = -142.2 \text{ kJ}$

From the relation $\Delta G^\circ_{rxn} = -2.30RT \log K$, we compute

$$\log K = - \frac{\Delta G_{rxn}}{2.30RT} = - \frac{(-142.2 \times 10^3 \text{ J})}{(2.30)(8.31 \text{ J} \cdot \text{K}^{-1})(298 \text{ K})} = 24.966$$

$$K = 9.25 \times 10^{24}$$

22-57 The value of ΔG°_{rxn} is given by

$$\Delta G^\circ_{rxn} = \Delta G^\circ_f(\text{products}) - \Delta G^\circ_f(\text{reactants})$$

Thus

$\Delta G^\circ_{rxn} = 2\Delta \bar{G}^\circ_f[HF(g)] + \Delta \bar{G}^\circ_f[Cl_2(g)] - 2\Delta \bar{G}^\circ_f[HCl(g)] - \Delta \bar{G}^\circ_f[F_2(g)]$

$\qquad = (2 \text{ mol})(-273 \text{ kJ} \cdot \text{mol}^{-1}) + (1 \text{ mol})(0 \text{ kJ} \cdot \text{mol}^{-1})$

$\qquad \quad - (2 \text{ mol})(-95.30 \text{ kJ} \cdot \text{mol}^{-1}) - (1 \text{ mol})(0 \text{ kJ} \cdot \text{mol}^{-1}) = -355 \text{ kJ}$

The value of ΔH°_{rxn} is given by

$$\Delta H^\circ_{rxn} = \Delta H^\circ_f(\text{products}) - \Delta H^\circ_f(\text{reactants})$$

Thus

$\Delta H^\circ_{rxn} = 2\Delta \bar{H}^\circ_f[HF(g)] + \Delta \bar{H}^\circ_f[Cl_2(g)] - 2\Delta \bar{H}^\circ_f[HCl(g)] - \Delta \bar{H}^\circ_f[F_2(g)]$

$\qquad = (2 \text{ mol})(-271.1 \text{ kJ} \cdot \text{mol}^{-1}) + (1 \text{ mol})(0 \text{ kJ} \cdot \text{mol}^{-1})$

$\qquad \quad - (2 \text{ mol})(-92.31 \text{ kJ} \cdot \text{mol}^{-1}) - (1 \text{ mol})(0 \text{ kJ} \cdot \text{mol}^{-1}) = -357.6 \text{ kJ}$

From the relation $\Delta G_{rxn}^{\circ} = -2.30RT \log K$ we have

$$\log K = -\frac{\Delta G_{rxn}^{\circ}}{2.30RT} = -\frac{(-355 \times 10^3 \text{ J})}{(2.30)(8.31 \text{ J} \cdot \text{K}^{-1})(298 \text{ K})}$$

$$= 62.328$$

$$K = 2.1 \times 10^{62}$$

22-59 The value of ΔG_{rxn}° is given by

$$\begin{aligned}
\Delta G_{rxn}^{\circ} &= \Delta G_f^{\circ}(\text{products}) - \Delta G_f^{\circ}(\text{reactants}) \\
&= 2\Delta \bar{G}_f^{\circ}[SO_3(g)] - 2\Delta \bar{G}_f^{\circ}[SO_2(g)] - \Delta \bar{G}_f^{\circ}[O_2(g)] \\
&= (2 \text{ mol})(-371.1 \text{ kJ} \cdot \text{mol}^1) - (2 \text{ mol})(-300.2 \text{ kJ} \cdot \text{mol}^{-1}) \\
&\quad - (1 \text{ mol})(0 \text{ kJ} \cdot \text{mol}^{-1}) \\
&= -141.8 \text{ kJ}
\end{aligned}$$

The value of ΔH_{rxn}° is given by

$$\begin{aligned}
\Delta H_{rxn}^{\circ} &= \Delta H_f^{\circ}(\text{products}) - \Delta H_f^{\circ}(\text{reactants}) \\
&= 2\Delta \bar{H}_f^{\circ}[SO_3(g)] - 2\Delta \bar{H}_f^{\circ}[SO_2(g)] - \Delta \bar{H}_f^{\circ}[O_2(g)] \\
&= (2 \text{ mol})(-395.7 \text{ kJ} \cdot \text{mol}^{-1}) - (2 \text{ mol})(-296.8 \text{ kJ} \cdot \text{mol}^{-1}) \\
&\quad - (1 \text{ mol})(0 \text{ kJ} \cdot \text{mol}^{-1}) \\
&= -197.8 \text{ kJ}
\end{aligned}$$

The value of $\log K$ is given by

$$\log K = -\frac{\Delta G_{rxn}^{\circ}}{2.30RT} = -\frac{(-141.8 \times 10^3 \text{ J})}{(2.30)(8.31 \text{ J} \cdot \text{K}^{-1})(298 \text{ K})}$$

$$= 24.896$$

$$K = 7.87 \times 10^{24}$$

To estimate $K_{400°C}$, we first calculate $\Delta G_{rxn(400°C)}^{\circ}$. The value of ΔS_{rxn}° is given by

$$\begin{aligned}
\Delta S_{rxn}^{\circ} &= S^{\circ}(\text{products}) - S^{\circ}(\text{reactants}) \\
&= 2\bar{S}^{\circ}[SO_3(g)] - 2\bar{S}^{\circ}[SO_2(g)] - \bar{S}^{\circ}[O_2(g)] \\
&= (2 \text{ mol})(256.3 \text{ J} \cdot \text{K}^{-1} \cdot \text{mol}^{-1}) - (2 \text{ mol})(248.4 \text{ J} \cdot \text{K}^{-1} \cdot \text{mol}^{-1}) \\
&\quad - (1 \text{ mol})(205.0 \text{ J} \cdot \text{K}^{-1} \cdot \text{mol}^{-1}) \\
&= -189.2 \text{ J} \cdot \text{K}^{-1}
\end{aligned}$$

We can find the value of ΔG_{rxn}° at some other temperature from

$$\Delta G_{rxn}^{\circ} = \Delta H_{rxn}^{\circ} - T\Delta S_{rxn}^{\circ}$$

Thus at 400°C

$$\Delta G_{rxn}^\circ = (-197.8 \text{ kJ}) - (673 \text{ K})(-0.1892 \text{ kJ} \cdot \text{K}^{-1})$$
$$= -70.5 \text{ kJ}$$

The value of the equilibrium constant at 400°C is given by

$$\log K = -\frac{\Delta G_{rxn}^\circ}{2.30RT} = -\frac{(-70.5 \times 10^3 \text{ J})}{(2.30)(8.31 \text{ J} \cdot \text{K}^{-1} \cdot \text{mol}^{-1})(673 \text{ K})}$$
$$= 5.481$$

Therefore,

$$K = 3.03 \times 10^5$$

22-61 The value of ΔG_{rxn}° is given by

$$\Delta G_{rxn}^\circ = \Delta G_f^\circ(\text{products}) - \Delta G_f^\circ(\text{reactants})$$
$$= \Delta \bar{G}_f^\circ[\text{H}_2\text{O}(g)] + \Delta \bar{G}_f^\circ[\text{CO}(g)] - \Delta \bar{G}_f^\circ[\text{H}_2(g)] - \Delta \bar{G}_f^\circ[\text{CO}_2(g)]$$
$$= (1 \text{ mol})(-228.6 \text{ kJ} \cdot \text{mol}^{-1}) + (1 \text{ mol})(-137.2 \text{ kJ} \cdot \text{mol}^{-1})$$
$$- (1 \text{ mol})(0 \text{ kJ} \cdot \text{mol}^{-1}) - (1 \text{ mol})(-394.4 \text{ kJ} \cdot \text{mol}^{-1}) = 28.6 \text{ kJ}$$

The value of ΔH_{rxn}° is given by

$$\Delta H_{rxn}^\circ = \Delta H_f^\circ(\text{products}) - \Delta H_f^\circ(\text{reactants})$$

Thus

$$\Delta H_{rxn}^\circ = \Delta \bar{H}_f^\circ[\text{H}_2\text{O}(g)] + \Delta \bar{H}_f^\circ[\text{CO}(g)] - \Delta \bar{H}_f^\circ[\text{H}_2(g)] - \Delta \bar{H}_f^\circ[\text{CO}_2(g)]$$
$$= (1 \text{ mol})(-241.8 \text{ kJ} \cdot \text{mol}^{-1}) + (1 \text{ mol})(-110.5 \text{ kJ} \cdot \text{mol}^{-1})$$
$$- (1 \text{ mol})(0 \text{ kJ} \cdot \text{mol}^{-1}) - (1 \text{ mol})(-393.5 \text{ kJ} \cdot \text{mol}^{-1}) = 41.2 \text{ kJ}$$

The value of ΔS_{rxn}° is given by

$$\Delta S_{rxn}^\circ = S^\circ(\text{products}) - S^\circ(\text{reactants})$$

Thus

$$\Delta S_{rxn}^\circ = \bar{S}^\circ[\text{H}_2\text{O}(g)] + \bar{S}^\circ[\text{CO}(g)] - \bar{S}^\circ[\text{H}_2(g)] - \bar{S}^\circ[\text{CO}_2(g)]$$
$$= (1 \text{ mol})(188.7 \text{ J} \cdot \text{K}^{-1} \cdot \text{mol}^{-1}) + (1 \text{ mol})(197.8 \text{ J} \cdot \text{K}^{-1} \cdot \text{mol}^{-1})$$
$$- (1 \text{ mol})(130.6 \text{ J} \cdot \text{K}^{-1} \cdot \text{mol}^{-1}) - (1 \text{ mol})(213.6 \text{ J} \cdot \text{K}^{-1} \cdot \text{mol}^{-1})$$
$$= 42.3 \text{ J} \cdot \text{K}^{-1}$$

Because $\Delta G_{rxn}^\circ = +28.6 \text{ kJ}$ the reaction is spontaneous right to left. The reaction is enthalpy driven to the left.

22-63 $\Delta G_{rxn}^{\circ} = -2.30RT \log K$

Thus

(a) $\Delta G_{rxn}^{\circ} > 0$ requires $K < 1$

(b) $\Delta G_{rxn}^{\circ} = 0$ requires $K = 1$

(c) $\Delta G_{rxn}^{\circ} < 0$ requires $K > 1$

22-65 The value of ΔG_{rxn}° for the reaction

(1)
$$H_2(g) + O_2(g) \rightleftharpoons H_2O_2(l)$$

is given by

$$\begin{aligned}
\Delta G_{rxn}^{\circ} &= \Delta \bar{G}_f^{\circ}[H_2O_2(l)] - \Delta \bar{G}_f^{\circ}[H_2(g)] - \Delta \bar{G}_f^{\circ}[O_2(g)] \\
&= (1 \text{ mol})(120.4 \text{ kJ} \cdot \text{mol}^{-1}) - (1 \text{ mol})(0 \text{ kJ} \cdot \text{mol}^{-1}) \\
&\quad - (1 \text{ mol})(0 \text{ kJ} \cdot \text{mol}^{-1}) \\
&= -120.4 \text{ kJ}
\end{aligned}$$

The value of ΔG_{rxn}° for the reaction

(2)
$$2H_2O(l) + O_2(g) \rightleftharpoons 2H_2O_2(l)$$

is given by

$$\begin{aligned}
\Delta G_{rxn}^{\circ} &= 2\Delta \bar{G}_f^{\circ}[H_2O_2(l)] - 2\Delta \bar{G}_f^{\circ}[H_2O(l)] - \Delta \bar{G}_f^{\circ}[O_2(g)] \\
&= (2 \text{ mol})(-120.4 \text{ kJ} \cdot \text{mol}^{-1}) - (2 \text{ mol})(-237.2 \text{ kJ} \cdot \text{mol}^{-1}) \\
&\quad - (1 \text{ mol})(0 \text{ kJ} \cdot \text{mol}^{-1}) \\
&= 233.6 \text{ kJ}
\end{aligned}$$

The reaction between hydrogen and oxygen is the more energy efficient because $\Delta G_{rxn}^{\circ}(1) < \Delta G_{rxn}^{\circ}(2)$.

22-67 The equation for the combustion of ethane is

$$C_2H_6(g) + \tfrac{7}{2}O_2(g) \longrightarrow 2CO_2(g) + 3H_2O(l)$$

The value of ΔG_{rxn}° is given by

$$\Delta G_{rxn}^{\circ} = \Delta G_f^{\circ}(\text{products}) - \Delta G_f^{\circ}(\text{reactants})$$

Thus

$$\begin{aligned}
\Delta G_{rxn}^{\circ} &= 2\Delta \bar{G}_f^{\circ}[CO_2(g)] + 3\Delta \bar{G}_f^{\circ}[H_2O(l)] - \Delta \bar{G}_f^{\circ}[C_2H_6(g)] - \tfrac{7}{2}\Delta \bar{G}_f^{\circ}[O_2(g)] \\
&= (2 \text{ mol})(-394.4 \text{ kJ} \cdot \text{mol}^{-1}) + (3 \text{ mol})(-237.2 \text{ kJ} \cdot \text{mol}^{-1}) \\
&\quad - (1 \text{ mol})(-32.89 \text{ kJ} \cdot \text{mol}^{-1}) - (\tfrac{7}{2} \text{ mol})(0 \text{ kJ} \cdot \text{mol}^{-1}) = -1467.5 \text{ kJ}
\end{aligned}$$

The maximum amount of work that can be obtained when $CO_2(g)$, $H_2O(l)$, $C_2H_6(g)$, and $O_2(g)$ are at standard conditions is 1467.5 kJ.

22-69   The reaction that takes place in an ethane-oxygen cell is

$$C_2H_6(g) + \tfrac{7}{2}O_2(g) \rightleftharpoons 2CO_2(g) + 3H_2O(l)$$

The value of ΔG_{rxn}° is given by

$$\Delta G_{rxn}^{\circ} = 2\Delta \bar{G}_f^{\circ}[CO_2(g)] + 3\Delta \bar{G}_f^{\circ}[H_2O(l)] - \Delta \bar{G}_f^{\circ}[C_2H_6(g)] - \tfrac{7}{2}\Delta \bar{G}_f^{\circ}[O_2(g)]$$

Thus

$$\Delta G_{rxn}^{\circ} = (2 \text{ mol})(-394.4 \text{ kJ} \cdot \text{mol}^{-1}) + (3 \text{ mol})(-237.2 \text{ kJ} \cdot \text{mol}^{-1})$$
$$- (1 \text{ mol})(-32.89 \text{ kJ} \cdot \text{mol}^{-1}) - (\tfrac{7}{2} \text{ mol})(0 \text{ kJ} \cdot \text{mol}^{-1}) = -1467.5 \text{ kJ}$$

The value of the standard voltage of the cell is given by

$$E^{\circ} = -\frac{\Delta G_{rxn}^{\circ}}{nF}$$

The oxidation state of carbon is increased from -3 to $+4$, thus fourteen (2×7) moles of electrons are involved and

$$E^{\circ} = -\frac{(-1467.5 \times 10^3 \text{ J})}{(14 \text{ mol})(96,500 \text{ C} \cdot \text{mol}^{-1})}$$
$$= 1.086 \text{ V}$$

22-71   The reaction for which we wish to calculate an equilibrium constant is

$$AgCl(s) \rightleftharpoons Ag^+(aq) + Cl^-(aq) \qquad K = K_{sp}$$

The value of ΔG_{rxn}° is given by

$$\Delta G_{rxn}^{\circ} = \Delta \bar{G}_f^{\circ}[Ag^+(aq)] + \Delta \bar{G}_f^{\circ}[Cl^-(aq)] - \Delta \bar{G}_f^{\circ}[AgCl(s)]$$

Thus

$$\Delta G_{rxn}^{\circ} = (1 \text{ mol})(77.1 \text{ kJ} \cdot \text{mol}^{-1}) + (1 \text{ mol})(-131.2 \text{ kJ} \cdot \text{mol}^{-1})$$
$$- (1 \text{ mol})(-109.7 \text{ kJ} \cdot \text{mol}^{-1}) = 55.6 \text{ kJ}$$

The equilibrium constant, K_{sp}, can be calculated using the relation

$$\log K_{sp} = -\frac{\Delta G_{rxn}^{\circ}}{2.30RT} = -\frac{(55.6 \times 10^3 \text{ J})}{(2.30)(8.31 \text{ J} \cdot \text{K}^{-1})(298 \text{ K})}$$
$$= -9.762$$

Thus

$$K_{sp} = 1.73 \times 10^{-10} \text{ M}^2$$

22-73 Omitting the *rxn* subscript from ΔG°_{rxn}, ΔH°_{rxn}, and ΔS°_{rxn}, we write

$$\Delta G^\circ_2 = \Delta H^\circ - T_2 \Delta S^\circ$$
$$\Delta G^\circ_1 = \Delta H^\circ - T_1 \Delta S^\circ$$

We also have

$$\Delta G^\circ_2 = -2.30 R T_2 \log K_2$$
$$\Delta G^\circ_1 = -2.30 R T_1 \log K_1$$

We equate the two expressions for ΔG°_1 to obtain

$$-2.30 R T_2 \log K_2 = \Delta H^\circ - T_2 \Delta S^\circ$$
$$-2.30 R T_1 \log K_1 = \Delta H^\circ - T_1 \Delta S^\circ$$

Solving each equation for $\log K$, we have

$$\log K_2 = -\frac{\Delta H^\circ}{2.30 R T_2} + \frac{\Delta S^\circ}{2.30 R}$$

$$\log K_1 = -\frac{\Delta H^\circ}{2.30 R T_1} + \frac{\Delta S^\circ}{2.30 R}$$

If we subtract the expression for $\log K_1$ from the expression for $\log K_2$, then we have

$$\log K_2 - \log K_1 = -\frac{\Delta H^\circ}{2.30 R T_2} + \frac{\Delta S^\circ}{2.30 R} + \frac{\Delta H^\circ}{2.30 R T_1} - \frac{\Delta S^\circ}{2.30 R}$$

$$= -\frac{\Delta H^\circ}{2.30 R T_2} + \frac{\Delta H^\circ}{2.30 R T_1}$$

Thus

$$\log K_2 - \log K_1 = \log \frac{K_2}{K_1} = -\frac{\Delta H^\circ}{2.30 R T_2} + \frac{\Delta H^\circ}{2.30 R T_1}$$

We can factor out the term $\dfrac{\Delta H^\circ}{2.30 R}$ on the right side of this equation to obtain

$$\log \frac{K_2}{K_1} = \frac{\Delta H^\circ}{2.30 R} \left(-\frac{1}{T_2} + \frac{1}{T_1} \right)$$

$$= \frac{\Delta H^\circ}{2.30 R} \left(\frac{1}{T_1} - \frac{1}{T_2} \right)$$

Thus

$$\log \frac{K_2}{K_1} = \frac{\Delta H^\circ_{rxn}}{2.30 R} \left(\frac{T_2 - T_1}{T_1 T_2} \right)$$

22-75   A plot of the data in the form $1/T$ versus $\log K_p$ is a straight line.

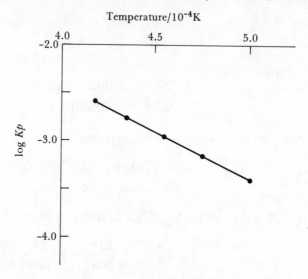

Thus we can use any set of data and the van't Hoff equation to calculate ΔH°_{rxn}.

$$\log\left(\frac{16.9 \times 10^{-4}}{6.86 \times 10^{-4}}\right) = \frac{\Delta H^{\circ}_{rxn}\,(2300\ \text{K} - 2100\ \text{K})}{(2.30)(8.31\ \text{J}\cdot\text{K}^{-1})(2300\ \text{K})(2100\ \text{K})}$$

$$0.3916 = (2.167 \times 10^{-6}\ \text{J}^{-1})\,\Delta H^{\circ}_{rxn}$$

$$\Delta H^{\circ}_{rxn} = 1.81 \times 10^{5}\ \text{J} = 181\ \text{kJ}$$

22-77   A plot of the data in form $1/T$ versus $\log K$ is a straight line. Thus we can use any set of data and the van't Hoff equation to calculate ΔH°_{rxn}.

$$\log\left(\frac{1.77}{1.34}\right) = \frac{\Delta H^{\circ}_{rxn}\,(1273\ \text{K} - 1173\ \text{K})}{(2.30)(8.31\ \text{J}\cdot\text{K}^{-1})(1273\ \text{K})(1173\ \text{K})}$$

$$0.1209 = (3.504 \times 10^{-6}\ \text{J}^{-1})\,\Delta H^{\circ}_{rxn}$$

$$\Delta H^{\circ}_{rxn} = 3.45 \times 10^{4}\ \text{J} = 34.5\ \text{kJ}$$

22-79   The value of ΔH°_{rxn} is given by

$$\Delta H^{\circ}_{rxn} = \Delta \bar{H}^{\circ}_{f}[\text{PCl}_5(g)] - \Delta \bar{H}^{\circ}_{f}[\text{PCl}_3(g)] - \Delta \bar{H}^{\circ}_{f}[\text{Cl}_2(g)]$$

$$= (1\ \text{mol})(-375.0\ \text{kJ}\cdot\text{mol}^{-1}) - (1\ \text{mol})(-306.4\ \text{kJ}\cdot\text{mol}^{-1})$$
$$\quad - (1\ \text{mol})(0\ \text{kJ}\cdot\text{mol}^{-1})$$

$$= -68.6\ \text{kJ}$$

Using the van't Hoff equation, we have

$$\log\left(\frac{K_p}{0.562\ \text{atm}^{-1}}\right) = \frac{(-68.6 \times 10^{3}\ \text{J})(673\ \text{K} - 523\ \text{K})}{(2.30)(8.31\ \text{J}\cdot\text{K}^{-1})(673\ \text{K})(523\ \text{K})}$$

$$= -1.5296$$

Thus

$$\frac{K_p}{0.562 \text{ atm}^{-1}} = 2.954 \times 10^{-2}$$

$$K_p = 0.0166 \text{ atm}^{-1} \quad \text{at} \quad 400°C$$

22-81 For an exothermic reaction, $\Delta H°_{rxn} < 0$. Thus $\log K_2/K_1 < 0$ when $T_2 > T_1$. Because $\log K_2/K_1$ is negative, $K_2/K_1 < 1$. In other words, $K_1 > K_2$, or the equilibrium constant at a higher temperature is less than that at a lower temperature.

22-83 We rewrite the van't Hoff equation in the form

$$\log \frac{K_2}{K_1} = \frac{\Delta H°_{rxn}}{2.30R} \left(\frac{1}{T_1} - \frac{1}{T_2} \right)$$

If we hold T_1 fixed; then we have

$$\log \frac{K}{K_1} = \frac{\Delta H°_{rxn}}{2.30R} \left(\frac{1}{T_1} - \frac{1}{T} \right)$$

or

$$\log K - \log K_1 = \frac{\Delta H°_{rxn}}{2.30RT_1} - \frac{\Delta H°_{rxn}}{2.30RT}$$

Since $\log K_1$ and $\dfrac{\Delta H°_{rxn}}{2.30RT_1}$ have a fixed value, we have

$$\log K = -\frac{\Delta H°_{rxn}}{2.30RT} + \text{constant}$$

If we let $y = \log K$ and $x = 1/T$, then we have the equation

$$y = \left(-\frac{\Delta H°_{rxn}}{2.30R} \right) x + \text{constant}$$

which is the equation of a straight line.

E ANSWERS TO THE EVEN-NUMBERED PROBLEMS

22-2

Compound	$\Delta \bar{S}_{fus}/ \text{ J} \cdot \text{K}^{-1} \cdot \text{mol}^{-1}$	$\Delta \bar{S}_{vap}/ \text{ J} \cdot \text{K}^{-1} \cdot \text{mol}^{-1}$
HF	24.08	86.03
HCl	12.53	93.10
HBr	12.92	93.45
HI	12.92	88.99

22-4

Compound	$\Delta\bar{S}_{fus}/$ J$\cdot$K$^{-1}\cdot$mol^{-1}	$\Delta\bar{S}_{vap}/$ J$\cdot$K$^{-1}\cdot$mol^{-1}
CH_3OH	18.11	111.1
C_2H_5OH	31.64	115.1
C_3H_7OH	35.32	117.7

22-6 Li (83.41 J$\cdot$K$^{-1}\cdot$mol^{-1}), Na (77.5 J$\cdot$K$^{-1}\cdot$mol^{-1}), K (74.6 J$\cdot$K$^{-1}\cdot$mol^{-1}), Rb (72 J$\cdot$K$^{-1}\cdot$mol^{-1}), Cs (70 J$\cdot$K$^{-1}\cdot$mol^{-1})

22-8 $CH_4 < NH_3 < H_2O$

22-10 (a) PCl_5 (b) CH_3CH_2OH (c) $CH_3CH_2CH_2CH_2NH_2$

22-12 $\bar{S}°(CH_4) < \bar{S}°(CH_3OH) < \bar{S}°(CH_3Cl)$

22-14 Fe_3O_4 has a greater mass than Fe_2O_3.

22-16 Gases are more disordered than liquids.

22-18 (a) decrease (b) increase (c) increase (d) decrease

22-20 (b) $\approx$ (d) < (c) < (a)

22-22 (a) 605 J$\cdot$K^{-1} (b) 24.7 J$\cdot$K^{-1} (c) -323.6 J$\cdot$K^{-1} (d) -120.7 J$\cdot$K^{-1}

22-24 (a) 144.1 J$\cdot$K^{-1} (b) 171.6 J$\cdot$K^{-1} (c) 12.5 J$\cdot$K^{-1} (d) -85.4 J$\cdot$K^{-1}

22-26 Reaction is spontaneous and entropy driven; ΔG_{rxn} is negative, ΔH_{rxn} is positive, and ΔS_{rxn} is positive.

22-28 $\Delta S°_{rxn} = -128.7$ J$\cdot$K^{-1}, $\Delta G°_{rxn} = 3.0$ kJ; reaction is spontaneous right to left.

22-30 $\Delta S°_{rxn} = 176.3$ J$\cdot$K^{-1}, $\Delta G°_{rxn} = 119$ kJ; reaction is spontaneous right to left.

22-32 no effect

22-34 -392 kJ

22-36 -320 kJ

22-38 (a) -212 kJ (b) 3 kJ

22-40 $Co(s) + 2Ag^+(aq) \longrightarrow Co^{2+}(aq) + 2Ag(s)$; $E = 1.14$ V; $\Delta G_{rxn} = -220$ kJ; and $\Delta G°_{rxn} = -208$ kJ

22-42 (a) negative (b) positive

22-44 $\Delta G°_{rxn} = +35.7$ kJ (spontaneous right to left); $\Delta G_{rxn} = +60.2$ kJ (spontaneous right to left)

22-46 $\Delta G°_{rxn} = +42.8$ kJ (not spontaneous); $\Delta G_{rxn} = -19.8$ kJ (spontaneous)

22-48 $\Delta G°_{rxn} = +27.1$ kJ (spontaneous right to left); yes, $\Delta G_{rxn} = -33.8$ kJ (spontaneous left to right)

22-50 $\Delta G°_{rxn} = +48.7$ kJ; $CaCO_3(s)$ will precipitate.

22-52 $\Delta G°_{rxn} = -41.6$ kJ (spontaneous left to right); $\Delta G_{rxn} = -39.3$ kJ (spontaneous left to right)

22-54 no

22-56 (a) $\Delta G^\circ_{rxn} = -822.6$ kJ, $K = 2.7 \times 10^{144}$

(b) $\Delta G^\circ_{rxn} = +173.38$ kJ, $K = 3.62 \times 10^{-31}$

(c) $\Delta G^\circ_{rxn} = -231.1$ kJ, $K = 3.76 \times 10^{40}$

22-58 $\Delta G^\circ_{rxn} = 226$ kJ; $\Delta H^\circ_{rxn} = +331$ kJ; $K = 2.09 \times 10^{-40}$

22-60 $\Delta G^\circ_{rxn} = -16.0$ kJ; $\Delta H^\circ_{rxn} = -10.2$ kJ, $K_{25°C} = 6.44 \times 10^2$; $K_{100°C} = 3.69 \times 10^2$

22-62 $\Delta \bar{G}^\circ_f = -65.3$ kJ $\cdot$ mol^{-1}; $\Delta \bar{H}^\circ_f = -135.4$ kJ $\cdot$ mol^{-1}

22-64 -5.70 kJ

22-66 -2874 kJ

22-68 818.1 kJ (Use $H_2O(l)$.)

22-70 $E° = 1.060$ V (Use $H_2O(l)$.)

22-72 $K_{sp} = 3.29 \times 10^{-13}$ M^2

22-74 ΔG°_{rxn} (at 25°C) $= 4.86$ kJ
$\Delta H^\circ_{rxn} = 11.8$ kJ
$\Delta S^\circ_{rxn} = 23.3$ J $\cdot$ K^{-1}

22-76 193 kJ

22-78 -188 kJ

22-80 45.8

22-82 $\log K_2/K_1 > 0$ when $T_2 > T_1$

22-84 181 kJ

F   ANSWERS TO THE SELF-TEST

1 false

2 false

3 positional, thermal

4 of the increased energy that is distributed among the molecules (increase in thermal disorder)

5 increases

6 of the increased positional disorder of the molecules

7 of the increased positional disorder of the molecules

8 $\Delta \bar{S}_{fus} = \Delta \bar{H}_{fus}/T_m$

9 $\Delta \bar{S}_{vap} = \Delta \bar{H}_{vap}/T_b$

10 less than

11 mass, atoms

12 of lower molecular mass and smaller number of atoms in C_2H_2

13 positive

14 $= 2\bar{S}°[H_2(g)] + \bar{S}°[O_2(g)] - 2\bar{S}°[H_2O(l)]$

15 true

16 spontaneous

17 not spontaneous

18 at equilibrium

19 positive

20 $\Delta H_{rxn} - T\Delta S_{rxn}$

21 entropy

22 energy (enthalpy)

23 is not

24 spontaneous

25 not spontaneous

26 false

27 the magnitude of ΔG_{rxn}

28 2030 kJ

29 $-nFE$

30 is

31 true

32 $2.30RT \log (Q/K)$

33 is

34 the reactants and products are at standard conditions

35 $-2.30RT \log K$

36 is not $(\Delta G_{rxn}^\circ = (2.30)(8.31 \text{ J} \cdot \text{K}^{-1})(298 \text{ K}) \log (1.7 \times 10^{-5})$ and $\Delta G_{rxn}^\circ > 0)$

37 true

38 $2\Delta \bar{G}_f^\circ[\text{H}_2(g)] + \Delta \bar{G}_f^\circ[\text{O}_2(g)] - 2\Delta \bar{G}_f^\circ[\text{H}_2\text{O}(l)]$

39 false

40 false

41 true

42 true

43 false

23 / Transition Metal Complexes

A   OUTLINE OF CHAPTER 23

23-1   There are 10 elements in each d transition metal series

There are five d orbitals for each value of the principal quantum number.

$l = 2$ and $m_l = 0$, ± 1, or ± 2 for d orbitals.

The shapes and relative orientations of the five d orbitals are shown in Figure 23-2.

Sc–Zn form the $3d$ transition metal series. ⎫
Y–Cd form the $4d$ transition metal series. ⎬   Figure 23-1
Lu–Hg form the $5d$ transition metal series. ⎭

The electron configurations of the M(II) transition metal ions are strictly regular in the sense that the $n = 1$ level is filled first, then the $n = 2$ level is filled, then the $n = 3$ level is completely filled, and so on.

23-2   Transition metal ions with x electrons in the outer d orbitals are called d^x ions.

Moving from left to right across a d transition metal series, d electrons are added one at a time for each successive element.

For the first d transition metal series

d^1	d^2	d^3	d^4	d^5
Sc(II)	Ti(II)	V(II)	Cr(II)	Mn(II)
21	22	23	24	25

d^6	d^7	d^8	d^9	d^{10}
Fe(II)	Co(II)	Ni(II)	Cu(II)	Zn(II)
26	27	28	29	30

The number of d electrons in the M(II) ion is the same as the position of the element within the d transition metal series.

23-3 Ligands are anions or neutral molecules that bind to metal ions to form complexes.

The complex ion $[Fe(CN)_6]^{4-}$ has an octahedral structure with six cyanide ions bonded to the central iron atom (Figure 23-3).

The complex ion $[Ni(CN)_4]^{2-}$ has a square-planar structure with four cyanide ions bonded to the central nickel atom (page 913 of the text).

The complex ion $[CoCl_4]^{2-}$ has a tetrahedral structure with four chloride ions bonded to the central cobalt atom (page 913 of the text).

The complex ion $[Ag(NH_3)_2]^+$ has a linear structure with two nitrogen atoms bonded to the central silver atom.

Some examples of complex ions are listed in Table 23-1.

Some common ligands are listed in Table 23-2.

23-4 Transition metal complexes have a systematic nomenclature.

The rules for naming transition metal complexes are given on pages 914 and 915 of the text.

The names of some common ligands are given in Table 23-2.

The chemical formula of a complex ion can be written when its name is given (Example 23-7).

23-5 Certain octahedral and square-planar transition metal complexes can exist in isomeric forms.

cis-trans isomers of square-planar and octahedral complexes exist. For example:

cis-diamminedichloroplatinum(II)   trans-diamminedichloroplatinum(II)

cis- designates the structure in which the identical ligands are adjacent to each other.

trans- designates the structure in which identical ligands are opposite to each other.

23-6 Some ligands bind to more than one coordination position around the metal ion.

Ligands that attach to a metal ion at more than one coordination position are called polydentate ligands or chelating agents.

The prefixes *bis-* and *tris-* are used in the nomenclature of complexes that contain chelating agents.

The oxalate ion (ox) and ethylenediamine (en) are examples of bidentate ligands.

23-7 The five d orbitals of a transition-metal ion in an octahedral complex are split into two groups by the ligands.

The five d orbitals are split into the two sets:

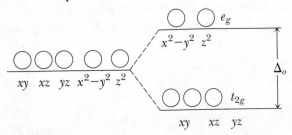

The magnitude of Δ_o depends upon the central metal ion, its charge, and the ligands.

This splitting pattern arises from the orientation of the d orbitals relative to the ligands as shown in Figure 23-5.

23-8 The colors of most transition metal complexes arise from transitions of electrons in the metal d orbitals.

The energy difference, Δ_o, corresponds to the visible region of the spectrum.

The visible absorption spectrum of a complex ion is shown in Figure 23-6.

23-9 The colors of many gemstones are due to transition metal ions.

23-10 d-Orbital electron configuration is the key to understanding the chemistry of the d transition metals.

Electrons are placed into the sets of d orbitals according to Hund's rule and the value of Δ_o.

Certain octahedral complexes can be either high-spin or low-spin.

The value of Δ_o determines whether a d-electron configuration will be low-spin or high-spin.

If Δ_o is small, then the d electrons will occupy the e_g orbitals before they pair up in the t_{2g} orbitals.

If Δ_o is large, then the d electrons will fill the t_{2g} orbitals completely before occupying the higher-energy e_g orbitals.

The various possible ground-state d-electron configurations for octahedral ions are given in Figure 23-7.

23-11 Ligands can be ordered according to their ability to split the transition metal d orbitals.

The spectrochemical series orders ligands according to the magnitude of the splitting of the d orbitals that they cause (Figure 23-9).

The spectrochemical series can be used to predict whether a given complex will be low-spin or high-spin.

23-12 Transition metal complexes are classified as either inert or labile.

Taube's rules say that t_{2g}^3, t_{2g}^4, t_{2g}^5, and t_{2g}^6 octahedral complexes are inert, whereas all other octahedral complexes are labile.

Taube's rules are used to predict whether a complex is inert or labile.

Some examples of inert and labile complexes are listed in Table 23-6.

CHAPTER 23

23-13 The *d*-orbital splitting patterns in square-planar and tetrahedral complexes are different from those in octahedral complexes.

The splitting patterns for the *d* orbitals are

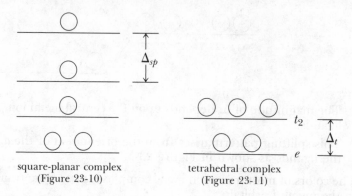

square-planar complex
(Figure 23-10)

tetrahedral complex
(Figure 23-11)

All d^8 square-planar complexes are low-spin because Δ_{sp} is relatively large.

There are no low-spin tetrahedral complexes because Δ_t is relatively small.

23-14 Transition metal complexes with unpaired *d* electrons are paramagnetic.

Molecules with no unpaired electrons cannot be magnetized by an external magnetic field and are called diamagnetic.

Molecules with unpaired electrons can be magnetized by an external magnetic field and are called paramagnetic.

Paramagnetic substances are drawn into a magnetic field (Figure 23-13).

Magnetic studies can determine whether a complex is square-planar or tetrahedral or whether an octahedral complex is low-spin or high-spin.

B SELF-TEST

1 There is a total of _____ metals in each *d* transition metal series.

2 Iron(II) is a d^6 ion; iron(II) has _____ *d* electrons.

3 Chromium(II) is a $d^{(\ \ )}$ ion.

4 Platinum(II) is a $d^{(\ \ )}$ ion.

5 Iron(III) is a $d^{(\ \ )}$ ion.

6 Transition metals often have more than one oxidation state. *True/False*

7 In the complex ion $[Fe(CN)_6]^{4-}$, the metal ion is _____ and the ligands are
_____.

8 When the compound $K_4[Fe(CN)_6]$ is dissolved in water, the compound produces K^+ ions, Fe^{2+} ions, and CN^- ions. *True/False*

9 Most transition metal complexes are colored due to the electronic transitions of

_____ .

10 All nickel(II) complexes are the same color. *True/False*

11 The ligands NH_3 in $[Ni(NH_3)_6]^{2+}$ are arranged around the nickel atom in an

_____ structure.

12 The ligands CN^- in $[Pt(CN)_4]^{2-}$ are arranged around the platinum atom in a

_____ structure.

13 In any complex ion or complex molecule, name the _____

first and then the _____ .

14 The name of the ligand NH_3 is _____ .

15 The name of the ligand CO is _____ .

16 The number of ligands of a particular type in a complex ion or complex molecule is denoted by _____ .

17 The name tetrachlorocobaltate(II) indicates that the complex is an anion. *True/False*

18 The oxidation state of the metal atom in a complex is denoted by

_____ .

19 *cis*-diamminedichloroplatinum(II) is identical in physical properties to *trans*-diamminedichloroplatinum(II). *True/False*

20 The two Cl^- ligands in $[Pt(NH_3)_2Cl_2]$ in the *cis*-isomer are located _____ in the square-planar structure.

21 Geometrical isomers in octahedral complexes may exist. *True/False*

22 A chelating ligand is a _____ .

23 Ethylenediamine is an example of a bidentate ligand. *True/False*

24 The number of chelating ligands in a complex is indicated by _____

_____ .

25 The five *d* orbitals in a metal ion without any attached ligands have the same energy. *True/False*

26 The five *d* orbitals in a metal ion with attached ligands have the same energy. *True/False*

27 The *d* orbitals of a transition metal ion in an octahedral complex are split into a lower set, called _____ , and an upper set, called _____ .

28 The t_{2g} set of orbitals can accommodate a maximum of _____ electrons.

29 The difference in energy between the t_{2g} and e_g orbitals is the same in all octahedral complexes. *True/False*

30 The difference in energy between the t_{2g} and e_g orbitals in an octahedral complex is denoted by _____.

31 If the value of Δ_o is small compared to the pairing energy, then the d electrons will pair up in the t_{2g} orbitals before occupying the e_g orbitals. *True/False*

32 The d-electron configuration of an octahedral complex is high-spin when

_____.

33 If the value of Δ_o is small compared to the pairing energy, then the d-electron configuration is (*low/high*)-spin.

34 The value of Δ_o depends upon the nature of the ligands in an octahedral complex. *True/False*

35 The value of Δ_o for the ligand Cl^- is (*greater than/less than*) for the ligand CN^-.

36 The rate at which an octahedral complex exchanges its ligands depends on the d-electron configuration of the transition metal ion. *True/False*

37 A t_{2g}^5 octahedral complex is (*inert/labile*).

38 The d-orbital splitting pattern for a square-planar transition metal complex is

39 The d-orbital splitting pattern for a tetrahedral transition metal complex is

40 A paramagnetic molecule behaves like a magnet in an externally applied magnetic field. *True/False*

41 A paramagnetic molecule contains (*paired/unpaired*) electrons.

42 A high-spin d^6 complex is (*paramagnetic/diamagnetic*).

C CALCULATIONS YOU SHOULD KNOW HOW TO DO

Although there are no numerical calculations in Chapter 23, here are some things that you should be able to do.

1 Determine electron configurations of transition-metal ions. See Examples 23-2 and 23-3 and Problems 23-1 through 23-6.

2 Determine the oxidation states of the metal atoms in complexes. See Example 23-5 and Problems 23-7 through 23-10.

3 Write the name of a complex from its chemical formula. See Example 23-6, Problems 23-17 through 23-22, and Problems 23-29 and 23-30.

4 Write the chemical formula of a complex from its name. See Examples 23-7 and 23-9, Problems 23-23 through 23-28, and Problems 23-31 and 23-32.

5 Draw structures of the geometrical isomers of complexes. See Example 23-8 and Problems 23-33 through 23-38.

6 Write d-orbital electron configurations of metals in octahedral ions. See Example 23-11 and Problems 23-39 and 23-40.

7 Using the spectrochemical series, predict whether a given complex is high-spin or low-spin. See Example 23-12 and Problems 23-41 through 23-44.

8 Using Taube's rules, predict whether a given complex is inert or labile. See Example 23-13 and Problems 23-45 through 23-48.

9 Predict whether or not a given complex is paramagnetic. See Examples 23-14, 23-15 and 23-16 and Problems 23-51 through 23-54.

D SOLUTIONS TO THE ODD-NUMBERED PROBLEMS

23-1 (a) There are $24 - 2 = 22$ electrons in Cr^{2+}. The electron configuration of $Cr^{2+}(g)$ is $1s^2 2s^2 2p^6 3s^2 3p^6 3d^4$.

(b) There are $29 - 1 = 28$ electrons in Cu^+. The electron configuration of $Cu^+(g)$ is $1s^2 2s^2 2p^6 3s^2 3p^6 3d^{10}$.

(c) There are $40 - 2 = 38$ electrons in Zr^{2+}. The electron configuration of $Zr^{2+}(g)$ is $1s^2 2s^2 2p^6 3s^2 3p^6 3d^{10} 4s^2 4p^6 4d^2$.

(d) There are $42 - 3 = 39$ electrons in Mo^{3+}. The electron configuration of $Mo^{3+}(g)$ is $1s^2 2s^2 2p^6 3s^2 3p^6 3d^{10} 4s^2 4p^6 4d^3$.

(e) There are $78 - 4 = 74$ electrons in Pt^{4+}. The electron configuration of $Pt^{4+}(g)$ is $1s^2 2s^2 2p^6 3s^2 3p^6 3d^{10} 4s^2 4p^6 4d^{10} 4f^{14} 5s^2 5p^6 5d^6$.

23-3 (a) Iron(III) has one less electron than iron(II) and thus has five d electrons.

(b) Palladium is below nickel in the periodic table and so Pd^{2+} has eight d electrons.

(c) Molybdenum is below chromium in the periodic table and Mo^{3+} has one less electron than Mo^{2+}; thus Mo^{3+} has three d electrons.

(d) Iridium is below cobalt in the periodic table and Ir^{3+} has one less electron than Ir^{2+}; thus Ir^{3+} has six d electrons.

(e) Copper(II) is the ninth transition metal in the $3d$ series, and so Cu(II) has nine d electrons.

23-5 (a) For an M(III) ion to be a d^7 ion, the corresponding M(II) ion must be a d^8 ion. The M(III) d^7 ions are Ni(III), Pd(III) and Pt(III).

(b) For an M(IV) ion to be a d^3 ion, the corresponding M(II) ion must be a d^5 ion. The M(IV) d^3 ions are Mn(IV), Tc(IV) and Re(IV).

(c) The M(II) d^{10} ions are Zn(II), Cd(II) and Hg(II).

23-7 (a) There are six H_2O ligands around the cobalt atom. The charge on the H_2O ligand is zero. Denoting the charge on Co as x, we have $x + 6(0) = +2$ or $x = +2$. The oxidation state of cobalt is $+2$.

(b) The charge on the NH_3 ligand is zero and the charge on the Cl^- ligand is -1. Denoting the charge of Cr as x, we have $x + 4(0) + 2(-1) = +1$ or $x = +3$. The oxidation state of chromium is $+3$.

(c) The charge on the CN^- ligand is -1. Denoting the charge on Cr as x, we have $x + 6(-1) = -3$ or $x = +3$. The oxidation state of chromium is $+3$.

(d) The charge on the F^- ligand is -1. Denoting the charge on Co as x, we have $x + 6(-1) = -3$ or $x = +3$. The oxidation state of cobalt is $+3$.

(e) The charge on the NH_3 ligand is zero. Denoting the charge on Ag as x, we have $x + 2(0) = +1$ or $x = +1$. The oxidation state of silver is $+1$.

23-9 (a) The charge on the CN^- ligand is -1. Denoting the charge on Zn as x, we have $x + 4(-1) = -2$ or $x = +2$. The oxidation state of zinc is $+2$.

(b) The charge on the NH_3 ligand is zero. Denoting the charge on Ni as x, we have $x + 6(0) = +2$ or $x = +2$. The oxidation state of nickel is $+2$.

(c) The charge on the I^- ligand is -1. Denoting the charge on Cd as x, we have $x + 4(-1) = -2$ or $x = +2$. The oxidation state of cadmium is $+2$.

(d) The charge on the CN^- ligand is -1. Denoting the charge on Fe as x, we have $x + 6(-1) = -3$ or $x = +3$. The oxidation state of iron is $+3$.

(e) The charge on the CN^- ligand is -1. Denoting the charge on Fe as x, we have $x + 6(-1) = -4$ or $x = +2$. The oxidation state of iron is $+2$.

23-11 The equation for dissolving the compound in water is

$$[Pt(NH_3)_5Cl]Cl_3(s) \xrightarrow{H_2O(l)} [Pt(NH_3)_5Cl]^{3+}(aq) + 3Cl^-(aq)$$

Thus there is a total of four moles of ions in solution when one mole of $[Pt(NH_3)_5Cl]Cl_3$ is dissolved in water.

23-13 (a) three moles of $K^+(aq)$ and one mole of $[Fe(CN)_6]^{3-}(aq)$
         (b) one mole of $[Ir(NH_3)_2Cl_2]^+(aq)$ and one mole of $NO_3^-(aq)$
         (c) one mole of $[Pt(NH_3)_4Cl_2]^{2+}(aq)$ and two moles of $Cl^-(aq)$
         (d) one mole of $[Ru(NH_3)_6]^{3+}(aq)$ and three moles of $Br^-(aq)$

23-15 The key point is that only the chloride ions that exist in solution as $Cl^-(aq)$, and
         not the chloride ions that are complexed with the platinum ions, are precipitated
         by $Ag^+(aq)$ as $AgCl(s)$. Let's look at each case in turn.

$PtCl_4 \cdot 6NH_3$ Because all four chloride ions per formula unit are precipitated by $Ag^+(aq)$, all four chloride ions must exist in solution as $Cl^-(aq)$. The chemical formula of the complex salt must be $[Pt(NH_3)_6]Cl_4$.

$PtCl_4 \cdot 5NH_3$ One of the four chloride ions must be complexed to the platinum ion because it is not precipitated by $Ag^+(aq)$. The chemical formula of the complex salt must be $[Pt(NH_3)_5Cl]Cl_3$.

$PtCl_4 \cdot 4NH_3$ Two of the four chloride ions must be complexed to the platinum ion because they are not precipitated by $Ag^+(aq)$. The chemical formula of the complex salt must be $[Pt(NH_3)_4Cl_2]Cl_2$.

$PtCl_4 \cdot 3NH_3$ Three of the four chloride ions must be complexed to the platinum ion because they are not precipitated by $Ag^+(aq)$. The chemical formula of the complex salt must be $[Pt(NH_3)_3Cl_3]Cl$.

$PtCl_4 \cdot 2NH_3$ All four of the chloride ions must be complexed to the platinum ion because none are precipitated by $Ag^+(aq)$. The chemical formula of the complex salt must be $[Pt(NH_3)_2Cl_4]$.

23-17 (a) Denoting the oxidation state of chromium as x, we have $x + 5(0) + 1(-1) = +2$ or $x = +3$. The complex ion is called pentaamminechlorochromium(III).
         (b) Denoting the oxidation state of tungsten as x, we have $x + 3(0) + 3(0) = +2$ or $x = +2$. The complex ion is called triamminetriaquatungsten(II).
         (c) Denoting the oxidation state of iron as x, we have $x + 6(0) = +3$ or $x = +3$. The complex ion is called hexaaquairon(III).
         (d) Denoting the oxidation state of iron as x, we have $x + 4(-1) = -1$ or $x = +3$. The complex ion is called tetrachloroferrate(III).

23-19 (a) Denoting the oxidation state of cobalt as x, we have $x + 6(-1) = -3$ or $x = +3$. The compound is called ammonium hexanitritocobaltate(III).
         (b) Denoting the oxidation state of iridium as x, we have $x + 4(0) + 2(-1) = +1$ or $x = +3$. The compound is called tetraamminedibromoiridium(III) bromide.
         (c) Denoting the oxidation state of copper as x, we have $x + 4(-1) = -2$ or $x = +2$. The compound is called potassium tetrachlorocuprate(II).
         (d) Denoting the oxidation state of ruthenium as x, we have $x + 5(0) = 0$ or $x = 0$. The molecule is called pentacarbonylruthenium(0).

23-21 (a) Denoting the oxidation state of iron as x, we have $x + 5(-1) + 0 = -3$ or $x = +2$. The compound is called sodium carbonylpentacyanoferrate(II).
         (b) Denoting the oxidation state of platinum as x, we have $x + 4(0) + 2(-1) = +2$ or $x = +4$. The compound is called *trans*-tetraamminedichloroplatinum(IV) iodide.

(c) Denoting the oxidation state of molybdenum as x, we have $x + 6(-1) = -2$ or $x = +4$. The compound is called potassium hexaisothiocyanatomolybdate(IV).

(d) Denoting the oxidation state of manganese as x, we have $x + 4(-1) = -2$ or $x = +2$. The compound is called ammonium tetrachloromanganate(II).

23-23 (a) The complex anion has five CN^- ligands with a total charge of $5(-1) = -5$, one CO ligand with zero charge, and one iron atom in an oxidation state $+2$. The net charge on the complex anion is $-5 + 0 + 2 = -3$. The formula of the complex anion is $[Fe(CN)_5(CO)]^{3-}$.

(b) The complex anion has two Cl^- ligands with a charge of $2(-1) = -2$, two I^- ligands with a charge of $2(-1) = -2$, and one gold atom in an oxidation state $+3$. The net charge on the complex anion is $-2 - 2 + 3 = -1$. The formula of the complex anion is $[AuCl_2I_2]^-$.

(c) The anion has six CN^- ligands with a charge of $6(-1) = -6$ and one cobalt atom in an oxidation state $+3$. The net charge on the complex anion is $-6 + 3 = -3$ and the formula of the complex anion is $[Co(CN)_6]^{3-}$.

(d) The anion has six NO_2^- ligands with a charge of $6(-1) = -6$ and a cobalt atom in an oxidation state $+3$. The net charge on the complex anion is $-6 + 3 = -3$. The formula of the complex ion is $[Co(NO_2)_6]^{3-}$.

23-25 (a) The complex cation has six NH_3 ligands with zero charge and one cobalt atom in an oxidation state $+3$. The net charge on the complex cation is $+3$. The formula for the complex cation is $[Co(NH_3)_6]^{3+}$.

(b) The complex has four CO ligands with zero charge and one nickel atom in an oxidation state 0. The net charge on the complex is 0. The formula for the complex is $[Ni(CO)_4]$.

(c) The complex anion has six SCN^- ligands with a charge of $6(-1) = -6$ and a manganese atom in an oxidation state $+2$. The net charge on the complex anion is -4. The formula for the complex anion is $[Mn(SCN)_6]^{4-}$.

(d) The complex cation has two NH_3 ligands with zero charge and one copper atom in an oxidation state $+1$. The net charge on the complex cation is $+1$. The formula for the complex cation is $[Cu(NH_3)_2]^+$.

23-27 (a) The charge on the anion is $4(-2) + 6+ = -2$. The formula for the compound is $K_2[CrO_4]$.

(b) The charge on the cation is $4(0) + 2 = +2$. The formula for the compound is $[Ni(NH_3)_4](NO_3)_2$.

(c) The charge on the cation is $2(0) + 1 = +1$. The formula for the compound is $[Ag(NH_3)_2]Cl$.

(d) The charge on the anion is $6(-1) + 3 = -3$. The formula for the compound is $Ca_3[Mn(CN)_6]_2$.

(e) The charge on the anion is $4(-1) + 2 = -2$. The formula for the compound is $Na_2[Cd(SCN)_4]$.

23-29 (a) The oxidation state x of ruthenium is given by $x + 3(0) = +3$ or $x = +3$. The name of the complex ion is tris(ethylenediamine)ruthenium(III).

(b) The oxidation state x of cobalt is given by $x + 2(0) = +2$ or $x = +2$. The name of the complex ion is bis(ethylenediamine)cobalt(II).

(c) The oxidation state x of molybdenum is given by $x + 2(-2) + 2(-1) = -3$ or $x = +3$. The name of the complex ion is diiodobis(oxalato)molybdate(III).

(d) The oxidation state x of cobalt is given by $x + 2(0) + 1(0) + 2(-1) = +1$ or $x = +3$. The name of the complex ion is diamminedichloroethylenediaminecobalt(III).

23-31 (a) The complex anion has three $C_2O_4^{2-}$ ligands and an iron atom in an oxidation state $+3$. The net charge on the complex anion is $3(-2) + 3 = -3$. The formula for the complex anion is $[Fe(C_2O_4)_3]^{3-}$ or $[Fe(ox)_3]^{3-}$.

(b) The complex cation has three $H_2NCH_2CH_2NH_2$ ligands and a chromium atom in an oxidation state $+3$. The net charge on the complex cation is $+3$. The formula for the complex cation is $[Cr(H_2NCH_2CH_2NH_2)_3]^{3+}$ or $[Cr(en)_3]^{3+}$.

(c) The complex cation has three $H_2NCH_2CH_2NH_2$ ligands and a ruthenium atom in an oxidation state $+2$. The net charge on the complex cation is $+2$. The formula for the complex cation is $[Ru(H_2NCH_2CH_2NH_2)_3]^{2+}$ or $[Ru(en)_3]^{2+}$.

(d) The complex cation has two Cl^- ligands, two $H_2NCH_2CH_2NH_2$ ligands, and one platinum atom in an oxidation state $+4$. The net charge on the complex cation is $2(-1) + (0) + 4 = +2$. The formula for the complex cation is $[Pt(H_2NCH_2CH_2NH_2)_2Cl_2]^{2+}$ or $[Pt(en)_2Cl_2]^{2+}$.

23-33 The structure of the complex ion is octahedral. The possible arrangements around the central platinum ion are

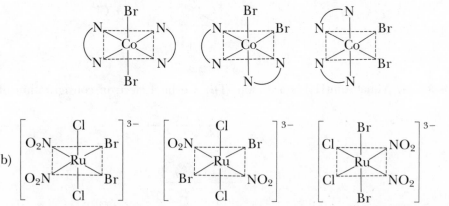

23-35 (a) The structure of the complex is octahedral. The possible arrangements of the ligands around the central cobalt ion are

(b)

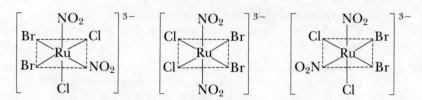

These structures are easier to visualize if you make a model of an octahedron as given in Appendix D of the text..

23-37 (a) The complex is square planar:

$$\left[\begin{array}{c} N \quad\quad Cl \\ Pt \\ Cl \quad\quad N \end{array}\right]^{2+} + 2Cl^-$$

trans

(b) The complex is square planar:

$$K^+ + \left[\begin{array}{c} I \quad\quad Cl \\ Au \\ Cl \quad\quad I \end{array}\right]^-$$

trans

(c) The complex is octahedral:

$$\begin{array}{c} Cl \\ H_3N \quad\quad Cl \\ Co \\ H_3N \quad\quad Cl \\ NH_3 \end{array}$$

cis,cis

(d) The complex is octahedral:

$$\left[\begin{array}{c} Cl \\ H_3N \quad\quad NH_3 \\ Pt \\ H_3N \quad\quad Cl \\ Cl \end{array}\right]^+ + Cl^-$$

cis,trans

23-39 (a) Vanadium(III) is a d^2 ion. The d-orbital electron configuration of V^{3+} is

$$\frac{\bigcirc \quad \bigcirc}{x^2-y^2 \quad z^2} \quad e_g^0$$

$$\frac{\uparrow \quad \uparrow \quad \bigcirc}{xy \quad xz \quad yz} \quad t_{2g}^2$$

or simply t_{2g}^2.

(b) Chromium(II) is a d^4 ion. If Δ_o is greater than the energy that is required to pair electrons, then the d-orbital electron configuration of Cr^{2+} is

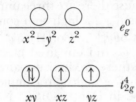

or t_{2g}^4.

(c) Manganese(II) is a d^5 ion. If Δ_o is less than the energy that is required to pair electrons, then the d-orbital electron configuration of Mn^{2+} is

$$\underline{\quad\uparrow\quad\uparrow\quad}_{\;x^2-y^2\;\;z^2}\quad e_g^2$$

$$\underline{\quad\uparrow\quad\uparrow\quad\uparrow\quad}_{\;xy\;\;xz\;\;yz}\quad t_{2g}^3$$

or $t_{2g}^3 e_g^2$.

(d) Copper(I) is a d^{10} ion. The d-orbital electron configuration of Cu^+ is

$$\underline{\quad\uparrow\downarrow\quad\uparrow\downarrow\quad}_{\;x^2-y^2\;\;z^2}\quad e_g^4$$

$$\underline{\quad\uparrow\downarrow\quad\uparrow\downarrow\quad\uparrow\downarrow\quad}_{\;xy\;\;xz\;\;yz}\quad t_{2g}^6$$

or $t_{2g}^6 e_g^4$.

(e) Cobalt(III) is a d^6 ion. The d-orbital electron configuration of a low-spin Co^{3+} complex is

$$\underline{\quad\bigcirc\quad\bigcirc\quad}_{\;x^2-y^2\;\;z^2}\quad e_g^0$$

$$\underline{\quad\uparrow\downarrow\quad\uparrow\downarrow\quad\uparrow\downarrow\quad}_{\;xy\;\;xz\;\;yz}\quad t_{2g}^6$$

or t_{2g}^6.

23-41 (a) The iron in $[\mathrm{Fe(CN)_6}]^{4-}$ is Fe(II), a d^6 ion. The two possible d-electron configurations are t_{2g}^6 (no unpaired electrons) and $t_{2g}^4 e_g^2$ (four unpaired electrons). Because there are no unpaired electrons the d-electron configuration must be t_{2g}^6, a low-spin complex.

(b) The iron in $[\mathrm{Fe(CN)_6}]^{3-}$ is Fe(III), a d^5 ion. The two possible d-electron configurations are $t_{2g}^5 e_g^0$ (one unpaired electron) or $t_{2g}^3 e_g^2$ (five unpaired electrons). Because there is one unpaired electron, the d-electron configuration must be $t_{2g}^5 e_g^0$, a low-spin complex.

(c) The cobalt in $[Co(NH_3)_6]^{2+}$ is Co(II), a d^7 ion. The two possible d-electron configurations are $t_{2g}^6 e_g^1$ (one unpaired electron) and $t_{2g}^5 e_g^2$ (three unpaired electrons). Because there are three unpaired electrons, the d-electron configuration must be $t_{2g}^5 e_g^2$, a high-spin complex.

(d) The cobalt in $[CoF_6]^{3-}$ is Co(III), a d^6 ion. The two possible d-electron configurations are t_{2g}^6 (no unpaired electrons) and $t_{2g}^4 e_g^2$ (four unpaired electrons). Because there are four unpaired electrons, the d-electron configuration must be $t_{2g}^4 e_g^2$, a high-spin complex.

(e) The manganese in $[Mn(H_2O)_6]^{2+}$ is Mn(II), a d^5 ion. The two possible d-electron configurations are t_{2g}^5 (one unpaired electron) and $t_{2g}^3 e_g^2$ (five unpaired electrons). Because there are five unpaired electrons, the d-electron configuration must be $t_{2g}^3 e_g^2$, a high-spin complex.

23-43 (a) The complex involves iron(II), which is a d^6 ion. Referring to the spectrochemical series, we see that CN^- produces a relatively large Δ_o value. We predict that the complex is low-spin with the d-electron configuration t_{2g}^6.

(b) The complex involves manganese(II), which is a d^5 ion. Because F^- produces a relatively small Δ_o value, we predict that the complex is high-spin with the d-electron configuration $t_{2g}^3 e_g^2$.

(c) The complex involves cobalt(III), which is a d^6 ion. Because NO_2^- produces a relatively large Δ_o value, we predict that the complex is low-spin with the d-electron configuration t_{2g}^6.

(d) The complex involves iron(III), which is a d^5 ion. Because there are no low-spin tetrahedral complexes, we predict that the complex is high-spin with the d-electron configuration $e^2 t_2^3$.

23-45 (a) The F^- ligand is a high-spin ligand. The d-electron configuration of high-spin iron(III), a d^5 ion, is $t_{2g}^3 e_g^2$. According to Taube's rules, we predict that $[FeF_6]^{3-}$ is a labile complex.

(b) The d-electron configuration of nickel(II), a d^8 ion, is $t_{2g}^6 e_g^2$. Therefore we predict that $[Ni(H_2O)_6]^{2+}$ is a labile complex.

(c) The d-electron configuration of chromium(III), a d^3 ion, is t_{2g}^3. Thus we predict that $[Cr(H_2O)_6]^{3+}$ is an inert complex.

(d) The d-electron configuration of vanadium(III), a d^2 ion, is t_{2g}^2. Therefore we predict that $[V(H_2O)_6]^{3+}$ is a labile complex.

23-47 (a) The d-electron configuration of chromium(III), a d^3 ion, is t_{2g}^3. Therefore we predict that $[Cr(NH_3)_6]^{3+}$ is an inert complex.

(b) The d-electron configuration of low-spin cobalt(III), a d^6 ion, is t_{2g}^6. Thus we predict that $[Co(en)_3]^{3+}$ is an inert complex.

(c) The d-electron configuration of molybdenum(IV), a d^2 ion, is t_{2g}^2. Thus we predict that $[Mo(NCS)_6]^{2-}$ is a labile complex.

(d) The d-electron configuration of scandium(III), a d^0 ion, is t_{2g}^0. Therefore we predict that $[Sc(H_2O)_6]^{3+}$ is a labile complex.

23-49 (a) Palladium(II) is a d^8 ion. The d-electron configuration is $e^4 t_2^4$. We predict that there are no unpaired electrons in $[Pd(CN)_4]^{2-}$.

(b) Ruthenium(III) is a d^5 ion. The low-spin d-electron configuration is

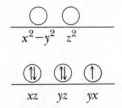

We predict that there is one unpaired electron in $[Ru(NH_3)_6]^{3+}$.

(c) Manganese(II) is a d^5 ion. The CN^- ligand is a low-spin ligand, and the low-spin d-electron configuration is

We predict that there is one unpaired electron in $[Mn(CN)_6]^{4-}$.

(d) Iron(III) is a d^5 ion. The F^- ligand is a high-spin ligand. The high-spin d-electron configuration is

We predict that there are five unpaired electrons in $[FeF_6]^{3-}$.

23-51 (a) Cobalt(III) is a d^6 ion. The d-electron configuration of low-spin Co(III) is t_{2g}^6. There are no unpaired electrons; thus $[Co(en)_3]^{3+}$ is diamagnetic.

(b) Iron(II) is a d^6 ion. The CN^- ligand is a low-spin ligand, and the d-electron configuration of low-spin Fe(II) is t_{2g}^6. There are no unpaired electrons; thus $[Fe(CN)_6]^{4-}$ is diamagnetic.

(c) Nickel(II) is a d^8 ion. The d-electron configuration is

There are two unpaired electrons; thus $[NiF_4]^{2-}$ is paramagnetic.

(d) Cobalt(II) is a d^7 ion. The d-electron configuration is

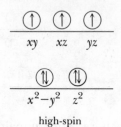

high-spin

and so $[CoBr_4]^{2-}$ is paramagnetic. Tetrahedral complexes are high-spin because Δ_t is less than the pairing energy.

23-53 Each complex ion could be either square-planar or tetrahedral. Nickel(II) is a d^8 ion, and the two possible d-electron configurations of $[NiF_4]^{2-}$ are

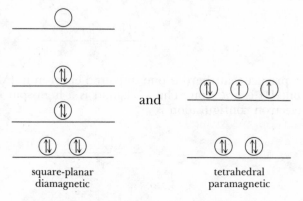

and

square-planar
diamagnetic

tetrahedral
paramagnetic

We conclude that $[NiF_4]^{2-}$ is tetrahedral. The two possibilities for $[Ni(CN)_4]^{2-}$ are the same as shown above. Because $[Ni(CN)_4]^{2-}$ is diamagnetic, we predict that it is square-planar.

E   ANSWERS TO THE EVEN-NUMBERED PROBLEMS

23-2 (a) $1s^22s^22p^63s^23p^63d^8$
(b) $1s^22s^22p^63s^23p^63d^{10}4s^24p^64d^5$
(c) $1s^22s^22p^63s^23p^63d^{10}4s^24p^64d^{10}4f^{14}5s^25p^65d^1$
(d) $1s^22s^22p^63s^23p^63d^{10}4s^24p^64d^{10}4f^{14}5s^25p^65d^{10}$
(e) $1s^22s^22p^63s^23p^63d^{10}4s^24p^64d^{10}$

23-4 (a) 10   (b) 2   (c) 1   (d) 4   (e) 10

23-6 (a) Cr(II), Mo(II), and W(II)
(b) Cu(III), Ag(III), and Au(III)
(c) Ti(IV), Zr(IV), and Hf(IV)

23-8 (a) +2   (b) +2   (c) +3   (d) +3   (e) +2

23-10   (a) +3   (b) +3   (c) +3   (d) +3   (e) +3

23-12   three

23-14   (a) one mole of $[Co(NH_3)_6]^{3+}(aq)$ and three moles of $Br^-(aq)$
(b) one mole of $[Pt(NH_3)_3Cl_3]^+(aq)$ and one mole of $Cl^-(aq)$
(c) one mole of $[Cr(H_2O)_6]^{3+}(aq)$ and three moles of $Br^-(aq)$
(d) four moles of $K^+(aq)$ and one mole of $[Cr(CN)_6]^{4-}(aq)$

23-16   The chloride ions that exist in solution as $Cl^-(aq)$ but not the chloride ions that are complexed with the platinum atoms are precipitated by $Ag^+(aq)$ as $AgCl(s)$.

$[Pt(NH_3)_4]Cl_2$; $[Pt(NH_3)_3Cl]Cl$; $[Pt(NH_3)_2Cl_2]$

23-18   (a) hexacyanoferrate(III)
(b) tetracarbonylnickel(0)
(c) pentaaquathiocyanatoiron(III)
(d) diamminetetraaquacobalt(II)

23-20   (a) sodium tetracyanoaurate(III)
(b) hexaaquachromium(III) chloride
(c) pentacarbonylmanganese(I) chloride
(d) hexaamminecopper(II) chloride

23-22   (a) pentaamminechlororuthenium(III) chloride
(b) sodium hexacyanocobaltate(III)
(c) sodium hexafluororhenate(IV)
(d) pentaaquathiocyanatoiron(III) nitrate

23-24   (a) $[NiBrCl(CN)_2]^{2-}$
(b) $[Co(SCN)_4]^{2-}$
(c) $[VCl_6]^{3-}$
(d) $[Cr(NH_3)_5Cl]^{2+}$

23-26   (a) $[Co(H_2O)_6]^{2+}$
(b) $[Cu(NH_3)_4]^{2+}$
(c) $[Cr(CO)_6]$
(d) $[WCl_2O_2]$

23-28   (a) $(NH_4)_2[CoCl_4]$
(b) $K_4[Fe(CN)_6]$
(c) $Na_2[Os(OH)_4O_2]$
(d) $[Fe(H_2O)_5SCN]Cl_2$
(e) $K_3[IrCl_6]$

23-30   (a) *trans*-dichlorobis(ethylenediamine)cobalt(III)
(b) tetraammineethylenediamineruthenium(III)
(c) tris(oxalato)molybdate(III)
(d) diaquabis(ethylenediamine)iron(III)

23-32   (a) $[CoCl(OH)(en)_2]^+$
(b) $[Cd(en)_2(ox)]$
(c) $[Pt(NO_2)_2(C_2O_4)_2]^{2-}$
(d) $[V(en)_2(C_2O_4)]^+$

23-34 The structure of the complex is square planar. The possible arrangements around the central platinum atom are

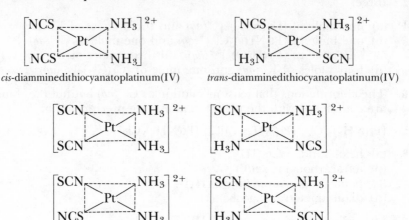

cis-diamminedithiocyanatoplatinum(IV)   trans-diamminedithiocyanatoplatinum(IV)

23-36 (a) The structure of the complex is octahedral. The possible arrangements around the central paladium atom are

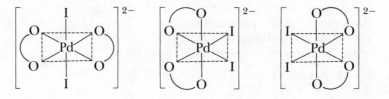

(b) The structure of the complex is octahedral. The possible arrangements around the central platinum are are

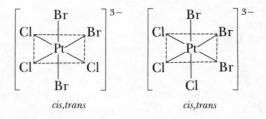

cis,trans   cis,trans

23-38 (a) *cis* and *trans*
(b) only one form
(c) only one form with bonding through the nitrogen atom of NCS⁻
(d) *cis* and *trans*

23-40 (a) $t_{2g}^5 e_g^2$ (b) $t_{2g}^3 e_g^2$ (c) t_{2g}^5 (d) t_{2g}^0 (e) $t_{2g}^6 e_g^2$

23-42 (a) low-spin   (b) low-spin   (c) high-spin   (d) high-spin   (e) low-spin

23-44 (a) low-spin   (b) high-spin   (c) low-spin   (d) high-spin
t_{2g}^4 $t_{2g}^4 e_g^2$ t_{2g}^6 $e_g^2 t_2^3$

23-46 a and b are inert; c and d are labile.

23-48 a is inert; b, c, and d are labile.

23-50 (a) 2   (b) 3   (c) 2   (d) 0

23-52 a, b, and c are paramagnetic.

23-54 $[Fe(H_2O)_6]^{2+}$ is a high-spin complex; $[Fe(CN)_6]^{4-}$ is a low-spin complex.

F   ANSWERS TO THE SELF-TEST

1	10	30	Δ_o
2	six	31	false
3	4	32	the value of Δ_o is less than the energy that is required to pair electrons
4	8		
5	5		
6	true	33	high
7	iron; the cyanide ions	34	true
8	false	35	less than
9	the d electrons	36	true
10	false	37	inert
11	octahedral	38	
12	square-planar		
13	ligands; metal atom		
14	ammine		
15	carbonyl		
16	a Greek prefix		
17	true		
18	a roman numeral in parentheses		
19	false		
20	on adjacent corners		
21	true		
22	polydentate ligand	39	
23	true		
24	a prefix such as *bis* or *tris*		
25	true		
26	false		
27	t_{2g}; e_g	40	true
28	6	41	unpaired
29	false	42	paramagnetic

For 38:

- x^2-y^2: ◯ (one electron)
- xy: ◯ (one electron)
- z^2: ◯ (one electron)
- xz ◯ xy ◯ (two electrons)

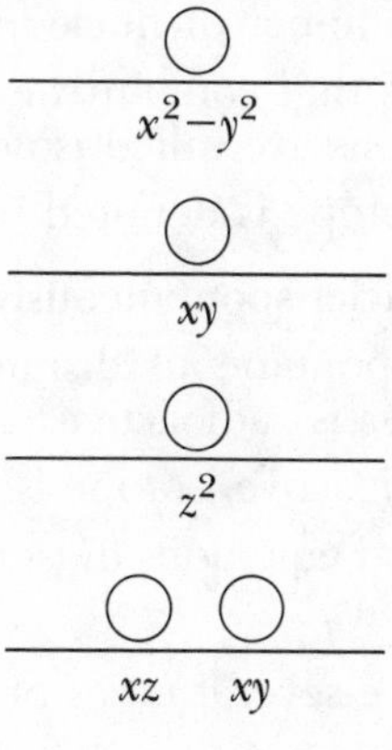

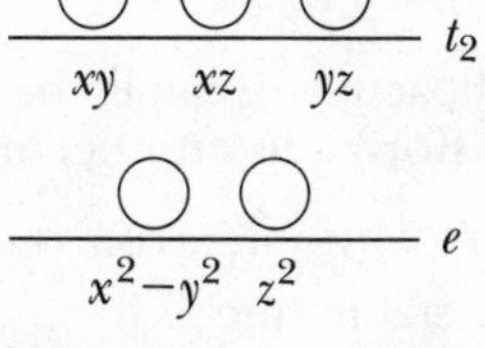

For 39:

- t_2: xy ◯ xz ◯ yz ◯
- e: x^2-y^2 ◯ z^2 ◯

24 / Nuclear and Radiochemistry

24-5   Only a few stable nuclei have odd numbers of protons and neutrons.

The number of stable nuclei with even and odd numbers of protons and neutrons are given in Table 24-3.

Predictions if certain nuclei are stable or radioactive can be made from the proton-neutron ratio and the number of protons and neutrons in the nuclei.

24-6   The rate of decay of a radioactive isotope is specified by its half-life.

Radioactive decay is a first-order rate process.

Different radioisotopes have different half-lives.

The half-lives of some radioisotopes are listed in Table 24-4.

The number of nuclei remaining, N, after a decay time, t, is given

$$\log \frac{N_0}{N} = \frac{0.301t}{t_{1/2}} \qquad (24\text{-}1)$$

where N_0 is the initial number of nuclei and $t_{1/2}$ is the half-life of the radioisotope.

24-7   Radioactivity can be used to determine the age of rocks.

The age of a rock can be determined by its uranium-238 and lead-206 content (Example 24-7).

The age of ores or rocks can also be determined by the rubidium-strontium method or the potassium-argon method.

24-8   Carbon-14 can be used to date certain archaeological objects.

Radiocarbon dating is useful for objects less than about 30,000 years old.

Living organisms contain a fixed percentage of carbon-14. The radiation due to carbon-14 in all living organisms is 15.3 disintegrations per minute per gram of total carbon.

The age of a carbon containing object is given by

$$t = (1.90 \times 10^4 \text{ years}) \log \left(\frac{15.3}{R} \right) \qquad (24\text{-}4)$$

where R is the number of disintegrations per minute per gram of carbon in the object.

24-9   Radioisotopes can be produced in the laboratory.

Radioisotopes that are not found in nature but are produced in the laboratory are called artificial radioisotopes.

Some of the many radioisotopes that are used in medicine are listed in Table 24-5.

24-10 Nuclear chemistry can be used to detect extremely small quantities of the elements.

In neutron-activation analysis the sample is irradiated by a beam of neutrons. The frequencies of the γ-rays emitted are characteristic of the isotopes present in the sample.

In a *PIXE* (*p*roton *i*nduced *X*-ray *e*mission) analysis the sample is irradiated by a beam of protons. The energies of the X-rays emitted are characteristic of the elements present in the sample (Figure 24-5).

24-11 Elements beyond uranium in the periodic table are produced artificially.

The elements beyond uranium in the periodic table are called the transuranium elements.

The transuranium elements and the reactions used to produce them are given in Table 24-6.

24-12 Enormous amounts of energy accompany nuclear reactions.

Nuclear reactions are about a million times more energetic than chemical reactions.

The mass lost in a nuclear reaction is converted into energy.

The relation between mass lost and energy produced is given by

$$\Delta E = c^2 \Delta m \tag{24-6}$$

where c is the speed of light, $3.00 \times 10^8 \ \mathrm{m \cdot s^{-1}}$.

24-13 Energy is required to break up a nucleus.

The energy required to break up a nucleus into its constituent protons and neutrons is called the binding energy.

The binding energy is calculated by calculating Δm for the reaction and then using the equation $\Delta E = c^2 \Delta m$.

The graph of the binding energy per nucleon versus the mass number, called a binding energy curve, is shown in Figure 24-7.

24-14 Some nuclei fragment in nuclear reactions.

A nuclear reaction in which a nucleus splits into two smaller fragments is called a fission reaction.

Energy is released in the $^{235}_{92}\mathrm{U}$ fission reaction.

24-15 The fission of uranium-235 can initiate a chain reaction.

A chain reaction occurs when uranium-235 undergoes a fission reaction after absorbing a neutron (Figure 24-9).

The smallest quantity of fissionable material that can support a chain reaction is called the critical mass.

24-16 A nuclear reactor utilizes a controlled chain reaction.

The chain reaction in a nuclear reactor is controlled by control rods, which are made out of substances that absorb neutrons readily (Figure 24-11).

The heat produced by a nuclear reaction in the core of the reactor is used to generate electricity (Figure 24-12).

24-17 A breeder reactor is designed to produce more fissionable material than it consumes.

Uranium-238 is converted to the fissionable material, plutonium-239, in a nuclear reactor.

24-18 Fusion reactions release more energy than fission reactions.

A nuclear reaction in which small nuclei join to form larger nuclei is called a fusion reaction.

The sun's energy is due to a nuclear reaction involving the fusion of four protons into a helium-4 nucleus and two positrons.

The hydrogen bomb utilizes a fusion reaction.

24-19 Exposure to radiation damages cells, tissues, and genes.

A measure of the activity of a radioactive substance is its specific activity.

The specific activity of a radioisotope is inversely proportional to its half-life, $t_{1/2}$.

The specific activity of a radioisotope is given by

$$\text{specific activity} = \frac{4.2 \times 10^{23} \text{ disintegrations} \cdot \text{g}^{-1}}{Mt_{1/2}} \tag{24-8}$$

where M is the atomic mass of the isotope and $t_{1/2}$ is the half-life in seconds.

The quantity 3.7×10^{10} disintegrations per second is called a curie and is designated by Ci.

The specific activities of some important radioisotopes are listed in Table 24-7.

The extent of the damage produced by radiation depends upon the energy and type of radiation.

B   SELF-TEST

1 A radioisotope is _____.

2 Alpha particles are _____.

3 Beta particles are _____.

4 Gamma rays are _____.

5 Uranium-238 is an α-emitter. The nuclear equation for the disintegration of uranium-238 is $^{238}_{92}\text{U} \rightarrow$ _____.

6 Indium-116 is a β-emitter. The nuclear equation for the disintegration of indium-116 is $^{116}_{49}\text{In} \rightarrow$ _____.

7 Nuclei contain electrons as well as protons and neutrons. *True/False*

8 Potassium-38 is a positron emitter. The nuclear equation for the disintegration of potassium-38 is $^{38}_{19}\text{K} \rightarrow$ _____.

9 Describe an electron-capture process. _____

_____.

10 Nuclei that lie above the band of stability emit _____.

11   Nuclei that lie below the band of stability emit _____.

12   Nuclei with $Z \geq 84$ emit _____.

13   Elements with an odd number of protons usually have only one or two stable isotopes. *True/False*

14   A nucleus containing an even number of both protons and neutrons is likely to be unstable. *True/False*

15   Nuclei that contain a magic number of protons or neutrons are usually stable. *True/False*

16   All nuclei with $Z \geq$ ____ are radioactive.

17   All radioactive nuclei decay at the same rate. *True/False*

18   The rate of radioactive decay varies with temperature. *True/False*

19   Radioactive decay is a _____-order rate process.

20   The half-life of a radioactive sample is the time _____ _____.

21   The age of a uranium-containing rock can be determined by measuring the masses of _____ and _____ in the rock sample.

22   Rocks containing potassium can be dated using the_____- _____ method.

23   Carbon-14 dating is used to determine the age of once-living material. *True/False*

24   All living organisms contain carbon-14. *True/False*

25   The rate of β-decay in living organisms is _____ disintegrations per minute per gram of carbon.

26   Objects of any age can be dated by the carbon-14 method. *True/False*

27   The source of carbon-14 in living organisms is _____.

28   Radioisotopes that are made in the laboratory are called _____.

29   Neutron activation analysis is used to measure trace quantities of elements. *True/False*

30   To carry out a neutron activation analysis, the sample is irradiated by a beam of _____.

31   In the PIXE analytical method, the sample is irradiated by a beam of _____.

32   The transuranium elements are laboratory-made. *True/False*

33   The mass lost in a nuclear reaction is converted into _____.

34 The relation between mass and energy is given by _____.

35 The value of ΔE for a typical nuclear reaction is similar to that for a typical chemical reaction. *True/False*

36 Energy is (*absorbed/evolved*) when a nucleus is broken up into its constituent protons and neutrons.

37 The binding energy per nucleon is the same for all nuclei. *True/False*

38 A binding energy curve is a plot of _____ versus _____.

39 In the uranium-235 fission reaction, when uranium-235 absorbs a neutron, the uranium-235 nucleus _____.

40 The uranium-235 fission reaction can support a chain reaction because _____.

41 A quantity of uranium-235 less than the critical mass will not support a chain reaction. *True/False*

42 In a reactor the rate of the uranium-235 fission reactions can be controlled by inserting material that absorbs neutrons. *True/False*

43 The uranium-235 fission reaction can be used in a nuclear reactor to produce energy. *True/False*

44 A breeder reactor is designed to produce more fissionable material than is consumed. *True/False*

45 The major source of the sun's energy is the fusion of _____ into _____.

46 The specific activity of a radioactive substance is _____.

47 The specific activity of a radioisotope is related to the half-life and the atomic mass of the isotope by the equation specific activity = _____.

48 One curie is equal to _____.

C   CALCULATIONS YOU SHOULD KNOW HOW TO DO

1 Complete and balance nuclear equations. See Examples 24-1 and 24-2 and Problems 24-3 through 24-10.

2 Calculate the quantity of a radioisotope that remains after a certain time. See Example 24-5, Problems 24-21 through 24-28, and Problems 24-31 and 24-32.

3 Calculate the half-life of a given radioisotope from its rate-of-decay data. See Example 24-6 and Problems 24-29 and 24-30.

4   Use Equation 24-4 to determine the ages of objects by radio-carbon dating. See Example 24-8 and Problems 24-33 through 24-38.

5   Determine the ages of rocks by uranium-lead dating, rubidium-strontium dating or potassium-argon dating. See Example 24-7 and Problems 24-39 through 24-44.

6   Calculate the binding energy and the binding energy per nucleon of a given nucleus. See Example 24-10 and Problems 24-45 through 24-48.

7   Calculate the energy released in nuclear reactions. See Problems 24-49 through 24-54 and 24-57 through 24-60.

8   Calculate the quantity of mass lost in exothermic chemical reactions. See Example 24-9 and Problems 24-55 and 24-56.

9   Calculate the specific activity of a radioisotope from its half-life. See Problems 24-61 through 24-64.

10 Use given decay rates to calculate solubility products and concentrations of radioisotopes. See Problems 24-65 through 24-72.

D   SOLUTIONS TO THE ODD-NUMBERED PROBLEMS

24-1 (a) 71 protons and $177 - 71 = 106$ neutrons
          (b) 90 protons and $233 - 90 = 143$ neutrons
          (c) 40 protons and $92 - 40 = 52$ neutrons
          (d) 32 protons and $68 - 32 = 36$ neutrons
          (e) 98 protons and $252 - 98 = 154$ neutrons

24-3 (a) $^{32}_{15}P \longrightarrow {}^{0}_{-1}e + {}^{32}_{16}S$
          (b) $^{210}_{84}Po \longrightarrow {}^{4}_{2}He + {}^{206}_{82}Pb$
          (c) $^{52}_{26}Fe \longrightarrow {}^{0}_{+1}e + {}^{52}_{25}Mn$
          (d) $^{67}_{31}Ga + {}^{0}_{-1}e \longrightarrow {}^{67}_{30}Zn$

24-5 (a) $^{12}_{6}C + {}^{12}_{6}C \longrightarrow {}^{23}_{11}Na + {}^{1}_{1}H$
          (b) $^{12}_{6}C + {}^{12}_{6}C \longrightarrow {}^{20}_{10}Ne + {}^{4}_{2}He$
          (c) $^{18}_{8}O + {}^{1}_{1}H \longrightarrow {}^{15}_{7}N + {}^{4}_{2}He$
          (d) $^{17}_{9}F \longrightarrow {}^{17}_{8}O + {}^{0}_{+1}e$
          (e) $^{249}_{98}Cf + {}^{18}_{8}O \longrightarrow {}^{263}_{106}Unh + 4{}^{1}_{0}n$
               (See Appendix E of the text.)

24-7 (a) $^{9}_{4}Be + {}^{4}_{2}He \longrightarrow {}^{12}_{6}C + {}^{1}_{0}n$
          (b) $^{7}_{3}Li + {}^{1}_{1}H \longrightarrow {}^{4}_{2}He + {}^{4}_{2}He$
          (c) $^{63}_{29}Cu + {}^{1}_{1}H \longrightarrow {}^{63}_{30}Zn + {}^{1}_{0}n$
          (d) $^{14}_{7}N + {}^{1}_{0}n \longrightarrow {}^{14}_{6}C + {}^{1}_{1}H$
          (e) $^{54}_{26}Fe + {}^{2}_{1}H \longrightarrow {}^{55}_{27}Co + {}^{1}_{0}n$

24-9 (a) $^{12}_{6}C + ^{1}_{1}H \longrightarrow ^{13}_{7}N + \gamma$

(b) $^{13}_{7}N \longrightarrow ^{13}_{6}C + ^{0}_{+1}e$

(c) $^{13}_{6}C + ^{1}_{1}H \longrightarrow ^{14}_{7}N + \gamma$

(d) $^{14}_{7}N + ^{1}_{1}H \longrightarrow ^{15}_{8}O + \gamma$

(e) $^{15}_{8}O \longrightarrow ^{15}_{7}N + ^{0}_{+1}e$

(f) $^{15}_{7}N + ^{1}_{1}H \longrightarrow ^{12}_{6}C + ^{4}_{2}He$

The net reaction is

$$4^{1}_{1}H \longrightarrow ^{4}_{2}He + 2^{0}_{+1}e + 3\gamma$$

24-11 The proton-neutron ratio in sodium-20 is $11/9 = 1.2$. The nucleus lies above the band of stability, and so we predict that sodium-20 decays by positron emission.

24-13 The proton-neutron ratio in technetium-93 is $43/50 = 0.86$. Referring to Figure 24-1, we see that the nucleus lies above the band of stability, and we predict that technetium-93 decays by positron emission.

24-15 (a) The proton-neutron ratio in tin-130 is $50/80 = 0.63$. The nucleus lies below the band of stability and so we predict that ^{130}Sn decays by β-emission.

(b) The proton-neutron ratio in iron-52 is $26/26 = 1.0$. The nucleus lies above the band of stability and so we predict that ^{52}Fe decays by positron emission.

(c) All nuclei with $Z \geq 84$ are radioactive. We predict that ^{239}Pu decays by α-emission.

(d) The proton-neutron ratio in argon-34 is $18/16 = 1.1$. The nucleus lies above the band of stability and so we predict that ^{34}Ar decays by positron emission.

(e) The proton-neutron ratio in calcium-50 is $20/30 = 0.68$. The nucleus lies below the band of stability, and so we predict that ^{50}Ca decays by β-emission.

24-17 (a) The atomic number of thorium is greater than 84; thus we predict that thorium-215 is radioactive.

(b) Magnesium-24 has an even number of protons and neutrons; thus we predict that magnesium-24 is a stable isotope.

(c) The proton-neutron ratio in nitrogen-12 is $7/5 = 1.4$, which is greater than 1; thus we predict that nitrogen-12 is radioactive.

(d) Sodium-22 has an odd number of both protons and neutrons; thus we predict that sodium-22 is radioactive.

(e) Germanium-72 has an even number of protons and neutrons and its proton-neutron ratio is 0.80; thus we predict that germanium-72 is a stable isotope.

24-19 (a) Sodium-24 has an odd number of both neutrons and protons. We predict that sodium-24 is radioactive.

(b) Antimony-118 has an odd number of both neutrons and protons. We predict that antimony-118 is radioactive.

(c) Tin-118 has an even number of both neutrons and protons and a magic number of protons. We predict that tin-118 is stable.

(d) Aluminum-26 has an odd number of both neutrons and protons. We predict that aluminum-26 is radioactive.

24-21   If we use Equation (24-1), then we have

$$\log \frac{N_0}{N} = \frac{0.301t}{t_{1/2}} = \frac{(0.301)(12.0 \text{ h})}{7.2 \text{ h}} = 0.5017$$

$$\frac{N_0}{N} = 3.17$$

The fraction remaining is

$$\frac{N}{N_0} = 0.315$$

From Example 24-6 we have

$$\frac{N}{N_0} = \frac{\text{present mass of At-211}}{\text{initial mass of At-211}}$$

Thus

$$\text{present mass of At-211} = (0.315)(0.10 \text{ mg})$$
$$= 0.032 \text{ mg}$$

24-23   If we use Equation (24-1), then we have

$$\log \frac{N_0}{N} = \frac{0.301t}{t_{1/2}} = \frac{(0.301)(1 \text{ day})\left(\dfrac{24 \text{ h}}{1 \text{ day}}\right)\left(\dfrac{60 \text{ min}}{1 \text{ h}}\right)}{110 \text{ min}}$$
$$= 3.94$$
$$\frac{N_0}{N} = 8720$$

Inverting both sides gives the fraction remaining

$$\frac{N}{N_0} = 0.000115 = 1.15 \times 10^{-4}$$

24-25   We have

$$\log \frac{N_0}{N} = \frac{0.301t}{t_{1/2}}$$

When an isotope decays to 10 percent of its original value, then $N/N_0 = 0.10$. If $N/N_0 = 0.10$, then

$$\frac{N_0}{N} = \frac{1}{0.10} = 10$$

and we have

$$\log 10 = \frac{0.301t}{36 \text{ h}}$$

Solving for t, we have

$$t = \frac{(\log 10)(36 \text{ h})}{0.301} = 120 \text{ h or } 5.0 \text{ days}$$

24-27   We have

$$\log \frac{N_0}{N} = \frac{0.301t}{t_{1/2}} = \frac{(0.301)(10 \text{ h})}{2.84 \text{ h}} = 1.06$$

$$\frac{N_0}{N} = 11.48$$

or

$$\frac{N}{N_0} = 0.0871$$

Recall that the rate of decay is proportional to the number of nuclei present:

$$\text{rate} \propto N$$

Thus

$$\frac{N}{N_0} = \frac{\text{rate}}{\text{rate}_0}$$

$$\text{rate after 10 h} = (0.0871)(10,000 \text{ disintegrations} \cdot \text{min}^{-1})$$
$$= 870 \text{ disintegrations} \cdot \text{min}^{-1}$$

24-29   Recall that the rate of radioactive decay is proportional to the number of nuclei present:

$$\text{rate} \propto N$$

The ratio of N_0/N is, therefore, equal to the ratio of the rates

$$\frac{N_0}{N} = \frac{\text{rate}_0}{\text{rate}}$$

Thus the equation

$$\log \frac{N_0}{N} = \frac{0.301t}{t_{1/2}}$$

becomes

$$\log\left(\frac{\text{rate}_0}{\text{rate}}\right) = \frac{0.301t}{t_{1/2}}$$

Substituting in the values of rate_0, rate, and t, we have

$$\log\left(\frac{8500 \text{ dpm}}{2780 \text{ dpm}}\right) = \frac{(0.301)(20.0 \text{ h})}{t_{1/2}}$$

Solving for $t_{1/2}$, we have

$$t_{1/2} = \frac{(0.301)(20.0 \text{ h})}{0.4854} = 12.4 \text{ h}$$

24-31   We have

$$\log\frac{N_0}{N} = \frac{0.301t}{t_{1/2}} = \frac{(0.301)(220 \text{ h})}{(14.28 \text{ days})\left(\dfrac{24 \text{ h}}{1 \text{ day}}\right)} = 0.1932$$

$$\frac{N_0}{N} = 1.560$$

or

$$\frac{N}{N_0} = 0.6409$$

Recall that the rate of decay is proportional to the number of nuclei present:

$$\text{rate} \propto N$$

Thus

$$\frac{N}{N_0} = \frac{\text{rate}}{\text{rate}_0}$$

$$\text{rate after } 220 \text{ h} = (0.6409)(40,000 \text{ disintegrations} \cdot \text{min}^{-1})$$
$$= 25,600 \text{ disintegrations} \cdot \text{min}^{-1}$$

24-33   Using Equation (24-4), we have

$$t = (1.90 \times 10^4 \text{ years}) \log\left(\frac{15.3}{R}\right)$$

$$= (1.90 \times 10^4 \text{ years}) \log\left(\frac{15.3}{12.8}\right)$$
$$= 1.47 \times 10^3 \text{ years}$$

The lintels are about 1500 years old ($\sim$500 AD).

24-35 Using Equation (24-4), we have

$$t = (1.90 \times 10^4 \text{ years}) \log \left(\frac{15.3}{13.19} \right)$$

$$= 1.22 \times 10^3 \text{ years}$$

The log is about 1220 years old (~760 AD).

24-37 The ratio of carbon-14 content is equal to the ratio of the rates of decay:

$$\frac{^{14}C_{\text{living}}}{^{14}C_{\text{bone}}} = \frac{(\text{rate of decay})_{\text{living}}}{(\text{rate of decay})_{\text{bone}}} = \frac{15.3 \text{ disintegrations per min per gram C}}{R}$$

We are given that

$$\frac{^{14}C_{\text{bone}}}{^{14}C_{\text{living}}} = 0.30$$

Using Equation (24-4), we have

$$t = (1.90 \times 10^4 \text{ years}) \log \left(\frac{15.3}{R} \right)$$

$$= (1.90 \times 10^4 \text{ years}) \log \left(\frac{1}{0.30} \right)$$

$$= 9.9 \times 10^3 \text{ years} = 9,900 \text{ years old (about 8000 BC)}$$

24-39 The age of the uranite is given by

$$t = \frac{t_{1/2}}{0.301} \log \frac{N_0}{N}$$

where

$$\frac{N_0}{N} = \frac{\text{initial mass of } ^{238}U}{\text{present mass of } ^{238}U}$$

The initial mass of ^{238}U is the sum of the present mass and the mass that has decayed:

$$\frac{N_0}{N} = \frac{\text{mass of } ^{238}U \text{ that has decayed} + \text{present mass of } ^{238}U}{\text{present mass of } ^{238}U}$$

$$= \frac{\text{mass of } ^{238}U \text{ that has decayed}}{\text{present mass of } ^{238}U} + 1$$

The mass of lead resulting from the decay of uranium is

$$\text{mass of } ^{206}\text{Pb} = \left(\frac{206}{238}\right)(\text{mass of } ^{238}\text{U that has decayed})$$

and the mass ratio $^{206}\text{Pb}/^{238}\text{U}$ is

$$\text{mass ratio} = \frac{\text{mass of } ^{206}\text{Pb}}{\text{present mass of } ^{238}\text{U}} = 0.420$$

or

$$\frac{\left(\dfrac{206}{238}\right)(\text{mass of } ^{238}\text{U that has decayed})}{\text{present mass of } ^{238}\text{U}} = 0.420$$

Therefore,

$$\frac{\text{mass of } ^{238}\text{U that has decayed}}{\text{present mass of } ^{238}\text{U}} = \left(\frac{238}{206}\right)(0.420)$$

and

$$\frac{N_0}{N} = \left(\frac{238}{206}\right)(0.420) + 1 = 1.485$$

and the age of the uranite is

$$t = \frac{4.51 \times 10^9 \text{ years}}{0.301} \log 1.485$$
$$= 2.57 \times 10^9 \text{ years}$$

24-41 The age of the meteorite is given by

$$t = \frac{t_{1/2}}{0.301} \log \frac{N_0}{N}$$

where

$$\frac{N_0}{N} = \frac{\text{initial mass of } ^{87}\text{Rb}}{\text{present mass of } ^{87}\text{Rb}}$$

The initial mass of ^{87}Rb is the sum of the present mass and the mass that has decayed:

$$\frac{N_0}{N} = \frac{\text{mass of } ^{87}\text{Rb that has decayed} + \text{present mass of } ^{87}\text{Rb}}{\text{present mass of } ^{87}\text{Rb}}$$

$$= \frac{\text{mass of } ^{87}\text{Rb that has decayed}}{\text{present mass of } ^{87}\text{Rb}} + 1$$

The mass ratio $^{87}Sr/^{87}Rb$ is given by

$$\text{mass ratio} = \frac{\text{mass of } ^{87}Sr}{\text{present mass of } ^{87}Rb}$$

The mass of ^{87}Sr is derived from the decay of ^{87}Rb. Thus

$$\text{mass of } ^{87}Sr = \text{mass of } ^{87}Rb \text{ that has decayed}$$

We have

$$\text{mass ratio} = \frac{\text{mass of } ^{87}Rb \text{ that has decayed}}{\text{present mass of } ^{87}Rb} = 0.0038$$

Therefore,

$$\frac{N_0}{N} = 0.0038 + 1 = 1.0038$$

and the age of the meteorite is

$$t = \frac{4.9 \times 10^{10} \text{ years}}{0.301} \log 1.0038$$

$$= 2.7 \times 10^8 \text{ years}$$

24-43   The age of the rock is given by

$$t = \frac{t_{1/2}}{0.301} \log \frac{N_0}{N}$$

$$\frac{N_0}{N} = \frac{\text{initial mass of } ^{40}K}{\text{present mass of } ^{40}K}$$

The initial mass of ^{40}K is the sum of the present mass and the mass that has decayed:

$$\frac{N_0}{N} = \frac{\text{mass of } ^{40}K \text{ that has decayed} + \text{present mass of } ^{40}K}{\text{present mass of } ^{40}K}$$

$$= \frac{\text{mass of } ^{40}K \text{ that has decayed}}{\text{present mass of } ^{40}K} + 1$$

We shall use the measured mass ratio, $^{40}Ar/^{40}K$, to determine the ratio of mass of ^{40}K that has decayed to the present mass. Only 0.107 (10.7%) of the ^{40}K decays to ^{40}Ar. The mass of argon produced from the decay of ^{40}K is

$$\text{mass of } ^{40}Ar = (0.107)\left(\frac{40}{40}\right)(\text{mass of } ^{40}K \text{ that has decayed})$$

The mass ratio, $^{40}Ar/^{40}K$, is given to be 1.05, and so

$$1.05 = \frac{(0.107)\left(\dfrac{40}{40}\right)(\text{mass of } ^{40}K \text{ that has decayed})}{\text{present mass of } ^{40}K}$$

Thus

$$\frac{\text{mass of } ^{40}K \text{ that has decayed}}{\text{present mass of } ^{40}K} = \frac{(1.05)}{(0.107)(1)} = 9.81$$

Therefore, we have

$$\frac{N_0}{N} = 9.81 + 1.00 = 10.81$$

and the age of the lunar rock is

$$t = \left(\frac{1.3 \times 10^9 \text{ years}}{0.301}\right) \log 10.81$$
$$= 4.5 \times 10^9 \text{ years}$$

24-45   Referring to Section 24-13, we find the following masses:

$$\begin{aligned} ^1_1H &\quad 1.0078 \text{ amu} \\ ^1_0n &\quad 1.0087 \text{ amu} \end{aligned}$$

The mass difference between $^{57}_{27}Co$ and its constituent particles is

$$\Delta m = (27 \times 1.0078 \text{ amu}) + (30 \times 1.0087 \text{ amu}) - 56.9363 \text{ amu}$$
$$= 0.5353 \text{ amu}$$

which corresponds to an energy of

$$\Delta E = c^2 \Delta m = (9.00 \times 10^{16} \text{ m}^2 \cdot \text{s}^{-2})(0.5353 \text{ amu})(1.66 \times 10^{-27} \text{ kg} \cdot \text{amu}^{-1})$$
$$= 8.00 \times 10^{-11} \text{ J}$$

The binding energy per nucleon is

$$\frac{8.00 \times 10^{-11} \text{ J}}{57 \text{ nucleons}} = 1.40 \times 10^{-12} \text{ J} \cdot \text{nucleon}^{-1}$$

24-47   We have the masses

$$\begin{aligned} ^1_1H &\quad 1.0078 \text{ amu} \\ ^1_0n &\quad 1.0087 \text{ amu} \end{aligned}$$

The mass difference between $^{35}_{17}Cl$ and its constituent particles is

$$\Delta m = (17 \times 1.0078 \text{ amu}) + (18 \times 1.0087 \text{ amu}) - 34.9689 \text{ amu}$$
$$= 0.3203 \text{ amu}$$

which corresponds to an energy

$$\Delta E = c^2 \Delta m = (9.00 \times 10^{16} \text{ m}^2 \cdot \text{s}^{-2})(0.3203 \text{ amu})(1.66 \times 10^{-27} \text{ kg} \cdot \text{amu}^{-1})$$
$$= 4.79 \times 10^{-11} \text{ J}$$

The binding energy per nucleon is

$$\frac{4.79 \times 10^{-11} \text{ J}}{35 \text{ nucleons}} = 1.37 \times 10^{-12} \text{ J} \cdot \text{nucleon}^{-1}$$

24-49 The difference in mass between products and reactants is

$$\Delta m = 4.0026 \text{ amu} - (2 \times 2.0141 \text{ amu})$$
$$= -0.0256 \text{ amu}$$

The loss of mass corresponds to an energy of

$$\Delta E = c^2 \Delta m = (9.00 \times 10^{16} \text{ m}^2 \cdot \text{s}^{-2})(0.0256 \text{ amu})(1.66 \times 10^{-27} \text{ kg} \cdot \text{amu}^{-1})$$
$$= 3.82 \times 10^{-12} \text{ J per atom of helium}$$

The energy released per mole of helium is

$$\Delta E = (3.82 \times 10^{-12} \text{ J} \cdot \text{atom}^{-1})(6.022 \times 10^{23} \text{ atom} \cdot \text{mol}^{-1})$$
$$= 2.30 \times 10^{12} \text{ J} \cdot \text{mol}^{-1}$$

The energy released per gram of helium is

$$\Delta E = (2.30 \times 10^{12} \text{ J} \cdot \text{mol}^{-1})\left(\frac{1 \text{ mol}}{4.0026 \text{ g}}\right) = 5.75 \times 10^{11} \text{ J} \cdot \text{g}^{-1}$$

The number of moles of octane that must be burned to produce this amount of energy is

$$\text{moles of octane} = \frac{5.75 \times 10^{11} \text{ J}}{5.45 \times 10^6 \text{ J} \cdot \text{mol}^{-1}} = 1.06 \times 10^5 \text{ mol}$$

The mass of octane is

$$\text{mass of octane} = (1.06 \times 10^5 \text{ mol})\left(\frac{114.22 \text{ g}}{1 \text{ mol}}\right)$$
$$= 1.21 \times 10^7 \text{ g} = 1.21 \times 10^4 \text{ kg} = 12.1 \text{ metric ton}$$

24-51   The *nuclear* masses are

$$^1_1\text{H} \qquad 1.0078 \text{ amu} - m_e = 1.0078 \text{ amu} - 0.00055 \text{ amu}$$
$$= 1.0073 \text{ amu}$$

$$^4_2\text{He} \qquad 4.0026 \text{ amu} - 2m_e = 4.0026 \text{ amu} - 0.0011 \text{ amu}$$
$$= 4.0015 \text{ amu}$$

The difference in mass between the products and reactants is

$$\Delta m = 4.0015 \text{ amu} + (2 \times 0.00055 \text{ amu}) - (4 \times 1.0073 \text{ amu})$$
$$= -0.0266 \text{ amu}$$

The loss in mass corresponds to an energy of

$$\Delta E = c^2 \Delta m = (9.00 \times 10^{16} \text{ m}^2 \cdot \text{s}^{-2})(0.0266 \text{ amu})(1.66 \times 10^{-27} \text{ kg} \cdot \text{amu}^{-1})$$
$$= 3.97 \times 10^{-12} \text{ J}$$

The energy released by the production of one helium nucleus is 3.97×10^{-12} J. The number of helium nuclei formed to produce 8.0×10^{22} kJ is

$$\text{number of } ^4_2\text{He} \atop \text{formed per second} = \frac{8.0 \times 10^{25} \text{ J} \cdot \text{s}^{-1}}{3.97 \times 10^{-12} \text{ J} \cdot \text{nuclei}^{-1}}$$
$$= 2.0 \times 10^{37} \text{ nuclei} \cdot \text{s}^{-1}$$

$$\text{moles of } ^4_2\text{He} \atop \text{formed per second} = \frac{2.0 \times 10^{37} \text{ nuclei} \cdot \text{s}^{-1}}{6.022 \times 10^{23} \text{ nuclei} \cdot \text{mol}^{-1}}$$
$$= 3.3 \times 10^{13} \text{ mol} \cdot \text{s}^{-1}$$

$$\text{mass of } ^4_2\text{He} \atop \text{formed per second} = (3.3 \times 10^{13} \text{ mol})\left(\frac{4.0026 \text{ g}}{1 \text{ mol}}\right) = 1.3 \times 10^{14} \text{ g} \cdot \text{s}^{-1}$$

$$= 1.3 \times 10^{11} \text{ kg} \cdot \text{s}^{-1} = 1.3 \times 10^8 \text{ metric tons per second}$$

24-53   The rate of energy release is

$$(148 \text{ J} \cdot \text{h}^{-1})\left(\frac{1 \text{ h}}{60 \text{ min}}\right)\left(\frac{1 \text{ min}}{60 \text{ s}}\right) = 4.11 \times 10^{-2} \text{ J} \cdot \text{s}^{-1}$$

The rate of decay is 3.7×10^{10} disintegrations $\cdot$ s^{-1}. Thus each disintegration must release energy of

$$E = \frac{4.11 \times 10^{-2} \text{ J} \cdot \text{s}^{-1}}{3.7 \times 10^{10} \text{ disintegrations} \cdot \text{s}^{-1}} = 1.1 \times 10^{-12} \text{ J} \cdot \text{disintegration}^{-1}$$

The mass difference between products and reactants is

$$\Delta m = 222.0154 \text{ amu} + 4.0026 \text{ amu} - 226.0254 \text{ amu}$$
$$= -0.0074 \text{ amu}$$

The energy released by the loss of this mass is

$$\Delta E = c^2 \Delta m = (9.00 \times 10^{16} \text{ m}^2 \cdot \text{s}^{-2})(0.0074 \text{ amu})(1.66 \times 10^{-27} \text{ kg} \cdot \text{amu}^{-1})$$
$$= 1.1 \times 10^{-12} \text{ J}$$

This energy is in excellent agreement with that calculated above.

24-55   The energy released per mole of carbon is

$$\Delta E = 3.96 \times 10^5 \text{ J} \cdot \text{mol}^{-1}$$

The mass loss that corresponds to this energy is

$$\Delta m = \frac{\Delta E}{c^2} = \frac{3.96 \times 10^5 \text{ J} \cdot \text{mol}^{-1}}{9.00 \times 10^{16} \text{ m}^2 \cdot \text{s}^{-2}}$$
$$= 4.40 \times 10^{-12} \text{ kg per mole of carbon that reacts}$$

24-57   The energy released by the fusion of hydrogen is

$$\Delta E = 6.4 \times 10^{11} \text{ J} \cdot \text{g}^{-1}$$

The number of grams of ^1H required to supply 85×10^{15} kJ is

$$\text{mass of } {}^1\text{H} = \frac{85 \times 10^{18} \text{ J}}{6.4 \times 10^{11} \text{ J} \cdot \text{g}^{-1}} = 1.33 \times 10^8 \text{ g}$$

The mass of water required is

mass of H_2O

$$= (1.33 \times 10^8 \text{ g } {}^1\text{H})\left(\frac{0.99985 \text{ mol } {}^1\text{H}}{1.0078 \text{ g } {}^1\text{H}}\right)\left(\frac{1 \text{ mol } H_2O}{2 \text{ mol } {}^1\text{H}}\right)\left(\frac{18.02 \text{ g } H_2O}{1 \text{ mol } H_2O}\right)$$
$$= 1.2 \times 10^9 \text{ g} = 1.2 \times 10^6 \text{ kg}$$
$$= 1.2 \times 10^3 \text{ metric tons}$$

We obtained the factor 0.99985 from Table 1-9.

24-59   The thermal energy produced by the plant in one month is

$$E_{thermal} = (3.00 \times 10^9 \text{ J} \cdot \text{s}^{-1})\left(\frac{60 \text{ s}}{1 \text{ min}}\right)\left(\frac{60 \text{ min}}{1 \text{ h}}\right)\left(\frac{24 \text{ h}}{1 \text{ day}}\right)\left(\frac{30 \text{ days}}{1 \text{ month}}\right)(1 \text{ month})$$
$$= 7.78 \times 10^{15} \text{ J}$$

The available thermal energy per mole of ^{235}U that disintegrates is

$$E_{thermal} = (2.9 \times 10^{-11} \text{ J} \cdot \text{atom}^{-1})(6.022 \times 10^{23} \text{ atom} \cdot \text{mol}^{-1})$$
$$= 1.75 \times 10^{13} \text{ J} \cdot \text{mol}^{-1}$$

The number of moles of ^{235}U that are required in one month to produce 7.8×10^{15} J is

$$\text{moles of } ^{235}\text{U} = \frac{7.78 \times 10^{15} \text{ J}}{1.75 \times 10^{13} \text{ J} \cdot \text{mol}^{-1}} = 4.4 \times 10^2 \text{ mol}$$

24-61 The specific activity is given by

$$\text{specific activity} = \left(\frac{4.2 \times 10^{23} \text{ disintegrations} \cdot \text{g}^{-1}}{M t_{1/2}} \right)$$

We first must convert the half-life to seconds:

$$t_{1/2} = (1.40 \times 10^{10} \text{ years}) \left(\frac{365 \text{ days}}{1 \text{ year}} \right) \left(\frac{24 \text{ h}}{1 \text{ day}} \right) \left(\frac{60 \text{ min}}{1 \text{ h}} \right) \left(\frac{60 \text{ s}}{1 \text{ min}} \right)$$
$$= 4.42 \times 10^{17} \text{ s}$$

The specific activity of thorium-232 is given by

$$\text{specific activity} = \frac{4.2 \times 10^{23} \text{ disintegrations} \cdot \text{g}^{-1}}{(232)(4.42 \times 10^{17} \text{ s})}$$
$$= 4.10 \times 10^3 \text{ disintegrations} \cdot \text{s}^{-1} \cdot \text{g}^{-1}$$

In terms of curies, we have

$$\text{specific activity} = \frac{4.10 \times 10^3 \text{ disintegrations} \cdot \text{s}^{-1} \cdot \text{g}^{-1}}{3.7 \times 10^{10} \text{ disintegrations} \cdot \text{s}^{-1} \cdot \text{Ci}^{-1}}$$
$$= 1.1 \times 10^{-7} \text{ Ci} \cdot \text{g}^{-1}$$

24-63 We first must convert the half-life to seconds:

$$t_{1/2} = (87 \text{ days}) \left(\frac{24 \text{ h}}{1 \text{ day}} \right) \left(\frac{60 \text{ min}}{1 \text{ h}} \right) \left(\frac{60 \text{ s}}{1 \text{ min}} \right) = 7.52 \times 10^6 \text{ s}$$

The specific activity of sulfur-35 is given by

$$\text{specific activity} = \frac{4.2 \times 10^{23} \text{ disintegrations} \cdot \text{g}^{-1}}{(35)(7.52 \times 10^6 \text{ s})}$$
$$= 1.6 \times 10^{15} \text{ disintegrations} \cdot \text{s}^{-1} \cdot \text{g}^{-1}$$
$$= \frac{1.6 \times 10^{15} \text{ disintegrations} \cdot \text{s}^{-1} \cdot \text{g}^{-1}}{3.7 \times 10^{10} \text{ disintegrations} \cdot \text{s}^{-1} \cdot \text{Ci}^{-1}}$$
$$= 4.3 \times 10^4 \text{ Ci} \cdot \text{g}^{-1}$$

24-65   We first must convert the half-life to seconds:

$$t_{1/2} = (78 \text{ h})\left(\frac{60 \text{ min}}{\text{h}}\right)\left(\frac{60 \text{ s}}{1 \text{ min}}\right) = 2.81 \times 10^5 \text{ s}$$

The specific activity of gallium-67 is

$$\text{specific activity} = \frac{4.2 \times 10^{23} \text{ disintegrations} \cdot \text{g}^{-1}}{(67)(2.81 \times 10^5 \text{ s})}$$

$$= 2.23 \times 10^{16} \text{ disintegrations} \cdot \text{s}^{-1} \cdot \text{g}^{-1}$$

The activity of the sample is

$$\text{activity} = (200 \text{ mCi})\left(\frac{1 \text{ Ci}}{1000 \text{ mCi}}\right)(3.7 \times 10^{10} \text{ disintegrations} \cdot \text{s}^{-1} \cdot \text{Ci}^{-1})$$

$$= 7.40 \times 10^9 \text{ disintegrations} \cdot \text{s}^{-1}$$

The number of grams of gallium-67 required to produce this activity is

$$\text{mass of } ^{67}\text{Ga} = \frac{7.40 \times 10^9 \text{ disintegrations} \cdot \text{s}^{-1}}{2.23 \times 10^{16} \text{ disintegrations} \cdot \text{s}^{-1} \cdot \text{g}^{-1}}$$

$$= 3.32 \times 10^{-7} \text{ g}$$

The mass of $^{67}\text{GaCl}_3$ is

$$\text{mass} = (3.32 \times 10^{-7} \text{g} \, ^{67}\text{Ga})\left(\frac{1 \text{ mol } ^{67}\text{Ga}}{67 \text{ g } ^{67}\text{Ga}}\right)\left(\frac{1 \text{ mol } ^{67}\text{GaCl}_3}{1 \text{ mol } ^{67}\text{Ga}}\right)\left(\frac{173 \text{ g } ^{67}\text{GaCl}_3}{1 \text{ mol } ^{67}\text{GaCl}_3}\right)$$

$$= 8.6 \times 10^{-7} \text{ g} = 8.6 \times 10^{-4} \text{ mg}$$

24-67   We first must convert the half-life to seconds:

$$t_{1/2} = (87.2 \text{ days})\left(\frac{24 \text{ h}}{1 \text{ day}}\right)\left(\frac{60 \text{ min}}{1 \text{ h}}\right)\left(\frac{60 \text{ s}}{1 \text{ min}}\right) = 7.53 \times 10^6 \text{ s}$$

The specific activity of sulfur-35 is

$$\text{specific activity} = \frac{4.2 \times 10^{23} \text{ disintegrations} \cdot \text{g}^{-1}}{(35)(7.53 \times 10^6 \text{ s})}$$

$$= 1.59 \times 10^{15} \text{ disintegrations} \cdot \text{s}^{-1} \cdot \text{g}^{-1}$$

The number of grams of sulfur-35 that has an activity of 3.23×10^{11} disintegrations $\cdot \text{s}^{-1}$ is

$$\text{mass of } ^{35}\text{S} = \frac{3.23 \times 10^{11} \text{ disintegrations} \cdot \text{s}^{-1}}{1.59 \times 10^{15} \text{ disintegrations} \cdot \text{s}^{-1} \cdot \text{g}^{-1}}$$

$$= 2.03 \times 10^{-4} \text{ g}$$

The number of grams of sulfur in 10.0 g of SO_2 is

$$\text{mass of S in } SO_2 = (10.0 \text{ g } SO_2)\left(\frac{1 \text{ mol } SO_2}{64.06 \text{ g } SO_2}\right)\left(\frac{1 \text{ mol S}}{1 \text{ mol } SO_2}\right)\left(\frac{32.06 \text{ g S}}{1 \text{ mol S}}\right)$$

$$= 5.00 \text{ g}$$

The fraction of ^{35}S in the SO_2 sample is

$$\text{fraction} = \frac{\text{mass of } ^{35}S}{\text{mass of S}} = \frac{2.03 \times 10^{-4} \text{ g}}{5.00 \text{ g}}$$

$$= 4.1 \times 10^{-5} \text{ or } 0.0041\%$$

24-69 The number of moles of thallium-204 in the water sample is

$$\text{moles of } ^{204}Tl = \frac{563 \text{ disintegrations} \cdot \text{min}^{-1}}{1.13 \times 10^8 \text{ disintegrations} \cdot \text{min}^{-1} \cdot \text{mol}^{-1}}$$

$$= 4.98 \times 10^{-6} \text{ mol}$$

The number of moles of oxygen in the water sample is

$$\text{moles of } O_2 = (4.98 \times 10^{-6} \text{ mol } ^{204}Tl)\left(\frac{1 \text{ mol } O_2}{4 \text{ mol } Tl^+}\right)$$

$$= 1.25 \times 10^{-6} \text{ mol}$$

The concentration of O_2 is

$$[O_2] = \frac{1.25 \times 10^{-6} \text{ mol}}{0.010 \text{ L}} = 1.25 \times 10^{-4} \text{ M}$$

24-71 The total activity of iodine-131 is

$$\text{activity} = (20,000 \text{ disintegrations} \cdot \text{min}^{-1} \cdot \text{mL}^{-1})(50.0 \text{ mL})$$

$$= 1.00 \times 10^6 \text{ disintegrations} \cdot \text{min}^{-1}$$

The total number of moles of iodine is

$$\text{moles of iodine} = (0.15 \text{ M})(0.0500 \text{ L}) = 7.50 \times 10^{-3} \text{ mol}$$

The molar activity of iodine-131 is

$$\text{molar activity} = \frac{1.00 \times 10^6 \text{ disintegrations} \cdot \text{min}^{-1}}{7.5 \times 10^{-3} \text{ mol}}$$

$$= 1.33 \times 10^8 \text{ disintegrations} \cdot \text{min}^{-1} \cdot \text{mol}^{-1}$$

The total activity of iodine-131 in solution after the two solutions are mixed is

$$\text{activity} = (320 \text{ disintegrations} \cdot \text{min}^{-1} \cdot \text{mL}^{-1})(100 \text{ mL})$$
$$= 3.20 \times 10^4 \text{ disintegrations} \cdot \text{min}^{-1}$$

The number of moles of iodide ion in solution is

$$\text{moles of iodide} = \frac{3.20 \times 10^4 \text{ disintegrations} \cdot \text{min}^{-1}}{1.33 \times 10^8 \text{ disintegrations} \cdot \text{min}^{-1} \cdot \text{mol}^{-1}}$$
$$= 2.41 \times 10^{-4} \text{ mol}$$

The concentration of iodide ion is

$$[\text{I}^-] = \frac{2.41 \times 10^{-4} \text{ mol}}{0.100 \text{ L}} = 2.41 \times 10^{-3} \text{ M}$$

and that of lead ion is

$$[\text{Pb}^{2+}] = \tfrac{1}{2} \times 2.41 \times 10^{-3} \text{ M} = 1.21 \times 10^{-3} \text{ M}$$

The solubility product of PbI_2 is given by

$$K_{sp} = [\text{Pb}^{2+}][\text{I}^-]^2$$
$$= (1.21 \times 10^{-3} \text{ M})(2.41 \times 10^{-3} \text{ M})^2$$
$$= 7.0 \times 10^{-9} \text{ M}^3$$

E   ANSWERS TO THE EVEN-NUMBERED PROBLEMS

24-2 (a) 34 protons and $82 - 34 = 48$ neutrons
(b) 30 protons and $70 - 30 = 40$ neutrons
(c) 74 protons and $180 - 74 = 106$ neutrons
(d) 88 protons and $223 - 88 = 135$ neutrons
(e) 97 protons and $245 - 97 = 148$ neutrons

24-4 (a) $_{-1}^{0}e$ (b) $_{17}^{37}\text{Cl}$ (c) $_{85}^{204}\text{At}$ (d) $_{37}^{83}\text{Rb}$

24-6 (a) $_{1}^{1}\text{H}$ (b) $_{2}^{3}\text{He}$ (c) $_{1}^{2}\text{H}$ (d) $_{36}^{81}\text{Kr}$ (e) $_{100}^{249}\text{Fm}$

24-8 (a) $_{8}^{16}\text{O} + _{1}^{1}\text{H} \longrightarrow _{9}^{17}\text{F} + \gamma$
(b) $_{10}^{20}\text{Ne} + _{1}^{1}\text{H} \longrightarrow _{11}^{21}\text{Na} + \gamma$
(c) $_{8}^{17}\text{O} + _{1}^{1}\text{H} \longrightarrow _{7}^{14}\text{N} + _{2}^{4}\text{He}$
(d) $_{11}^{22}\text{Na} + _{1}^{1}\text{H} \longrightarrow _{10}^{19}\text{Ne} + _{2}^{4}\text{He}$
(e) $_{8}^{18}\text{O} + _{2}^{4}\text{He} \longrightarrow _{10}^{21}\text{Ne} + _{0}^{1}\text{n}$

24-10 $^{27}_{13}\text{Al} + ^{4}_{2}\text{He} \longrightarrow ^{30}_{15}\text{P} + ^{1}_{0}\text{n}$

Phosphorus-30 decays by positron emission.

24-12   positron emission

24-14   positron emission

24-16   (a) α-emission   (b) positron emission   (c) β-emission
(d) positron emission   (e) β-emission

24-18   a, c, and e are stable.

24-20   a and d are radioactive; b and c are stable.

24-22   0.042 mg

24-24   0.63

24-26   201 years

24-28 3.57×10^{-3}

24-30   2.8 h

24-32   0.46 disintegration $\cdot$ min^{-1}

24-34   7400 years old

24-36   3800 disintegrations $\cdot$ s^{-1}

24-38   3550 years old

24-40 1.97×10^{9} years

24-42 3.9×10^{9} years

24-44 1.1×10^{6} years

24-46   binding energy = 7.91×10^{-11} J
binding energy per nucleon = 1.41×10^{-12} J $\cdot$ nucleon^{-1}

24-48   binding energy = 2.58×10^{-11} J
binding energy per nucleon = 1.29×10^{-12} J $\cdot$ nucleon^{-1}

24-50 $\Delta E = 1.67 \times 10^{12}$ J $\cdot$ mol^{-1} of lithium; 5.00×10^{3} kg octane

24-52 $\Delta E = 2.45 \times 10^{-11}$ J $\cdot$ atom^{-1} of uranium-235; 1.99 kg

24-54 1.64×10^{-13} J; 1.24×10^{20} s^{-1}

24-56 3.30×10^{-12} kg per mole of sulfur that reacts

24-58 5×10^{5} metric tons annually of naturally occurring uranium; 2 years

24-60 7.4×10^{11} J; 1.4×10^{5} kg

24-62 3.2×10^{3} Ci $\cdot$ g^{-1}

24-64   0.019 Ci $\cdot$ g^{-1}

24-66 2.0×10^{-9} mg

24-68   5.0 L

24-70 3.3×10^{-5} M

24-72 1.7×10^{-8} M^2

F   ANSWERS TO THE SELF-TEST

1   a radioactive isotope

2   helium-4 nuclei, that are emitted from radioactive nuclei

3   electrons that are emitted from radioactive nuclei

4   electromagnetic radiation of short wavelength or high frequency

5 $^{4}_{2}$He $+ \, ^{234}_{90}$Th

6 $^{116}_{50}$Sn $+ \, ^{0}_{-1}$e

7   false (There are no electrons in nuclei.)

8 $^{38}_{18}$Ar $+ \, ^{0}_{+1}$e

9   In an electron-capture process an orbital electron is captured by the nucleus and combines with a proton to produce a neutron.

10 positrons

11 β-particles

12 α-particles

13 true

14 false

15 true

16 84

17 false

18 false

19 first

20 that is required for one half of the nuclei to decay

21 uranium-238 and lead-206

22 potassium-argon

23 true

24 true

25 15.3

26 false

27 carbon dioxide, $^{14}CO_2$

28 artificial radioisotopes

29 true

30 neutrons

31 protons

32 true

33 energy

34 $\Delta E = c^2 \Delta m$ or $E = mc^2$

35 false (It is about 10^6 times larger.)

36 absorbed

37 false

38 binding energy per nucleon versus number of nucleons (mass number)

39 splits into two roughly equal fragments

40 neutrons are produced when a uranium-235 nucleus undergoes fission

41 true

42 true

43 true

44 true

45 protons into helium-4 nuclei

46 the number of disintegrations per second per gram of material

47 specific activity $=$
$$\frac{4.2 \times 10^{23} \text{ disintegrations} \cdot \text{g}^{-1}}{M t_{1/2}}$$

48 3.7×10^{10} disintegrations $\cdot$ s^{-1}

25 / Organic Chemistry

A OUTLINE OF CHAPTER 25

25-1 Alkanes are hydrocarbons that contain only single bonds.

Hydrocarbons consist of only hydrogen and carbon.

The bonding in alkanes is described in terms of sp^3 hybrid orbitals on the carbon atoms.

25-2 Molecules that have the same chemical formula but different structures are called structural isomers.

Condensed structural formulas are more compact than Lewis formulas.

Structural isomers have different chemical and physical properties.

Further hydrogen atoms cannot be bonded to carbon atoms in alkanes.

Alkanes are saturated hydrocarbons.

Rotation can occur about carbon-carbon single bonds.

25-3 The number of structural isomers increases with the number of carbon atoms in an alkane.

The names and physical properties of the first 10 straight-chain alkanes are given in Table 25-1.

The number of structural isomers versus the number of carbon atoms is given in Table 25-2.

25-4 The principal sources of saturated hydrocarbons are petroleum and natural gas deposits.

25-5 Alkanes are relatively unreactive.

Alkanes react with oxygen in combustion reactions.

Alkane combustion reactions are highly exothermic.

The substitution reaction between an alkane and a halogen in the presence of ultraviolet light yields an alkyl halide.

25-6   Alkanes and substituted alkanes can be named systematically according to IUPAC rules.

The IUPAC rules for naming alkanes and their derivatives are given on pages 990 and 991.

The names of some common groups are listed in Table 25-4.

The formula of a compound can be written from the IUPAC name of the compound (Example 25-5).

25-7   Hydrocarbons that contain double bonds are called alkenes.

In an unsaturated hydrocarbon not all the carbon atoms are bonded to four other atoms.

Alkenes are unsaturated hydrocarbons that contain one or more double bonds.

The double bond in an alkene forces the alkene to have a planar region.

cis-trans isomers of alkenes may exist.

The IUPAC nomenclature for alkenes and their derivatives is given on page 996.

25-8   Alkenes undergo addition reactions.

Alkenes undergo combustion and substitution reactions.

Alkenes undergo these addition reactions:

   (a) addition of hydrogen in the presence of a catalyst and high temperature and pressure
   (b) addition of chlorine or bromine
   (c) addition of hydrogen chloride
   (d) addition of water in the presence of acid

Markovnikov's rule states that when HX adds to an alkene, the hydrogen atom becomes bonded to the carbon atom in the double bond already bearing the larger number of hydrogen atoms.

Markovnikov's rule is used to predict the product in addition reactions.

25-9   Alcohols are organic compounds that contain an —OH group.

The IUPAC nomenclature for alcohols is given on page 999.

The bonding in an alcohol in terms of sp^3 hybrid orbitals is shown in Figure 25-8.

25-10   Hydrocarbons that contain a triple bond are called alkynes.

The IUPAC nomenclature for alkynes and their derivatives is given on page 1001.

Alkynes undergo combustion reactions and the addition reactions that alkenes undergo.

25-11   Benzene belongs to a class of hydrocarbons called aromatic hydrocarbons.

Aromatic hydrocarbons have rings that are stabilized by π-electron delocalization.

Benzene is represented by the structure

A common way of naming disubstituted benzene is the *ortho-*, *meta-*, and *para-* system.

The benzene ring is stable and undergoes few reactions.

Benzene undergoes the substitution reactions that alkanes do.

25-12 Aldehydes and ketones contain a carbon-oxygen double bond.

Aldehydes have the general formula RCHO.

The bonding in an aldehyde in terms of hybrid orbitals is described in Example 25-11.

The aldehyde group —CHO is planar.

A primary alcohol is an alcohol in which the —OH-bearing carbon atom is bonded to only one other carbon atom.

Aldehydes are obtained from the oxidation of primary alcohols.

A secondary alcohol is an alcohol in which the —OH-bearing carbon atom is bonded to two other carbon atoms.

Secondary alcohols are oxidized to ketones.

A ketone has the general formula

A tertiary alcohol is an alcohol in which the —OH-bearing carbon atom is bonded to three other carbon atoms.

Tertiary alcohols cannot be oxidized to a molecule containing a carbon-oxygen double bond.

25-13 Organic carboxylic acids contain a —COOH group.

An organic carboxylic acid can be obtained by the oxidation of an aldehyde or a primary alcohol.

Carboxylic acids produce $H_3O^+(aq)$ in water.

Carboxylic acids are neutralized by bases.

A carboxylate ion is the anion that results from the dissociation or neutralization of a carboxylic acid.

The carboxylate ion is stabilized by charge delocalization.

25-14 Esters are produced by the reaction of organic acids with alcohols.

The general formula of an ester is

$$R\diagdown C{=}O \diagup_{R'O}$$

where the R' group comes from the alcohol.
The IUPAC nomenclature for esters is given on page 1010.

B   SELF-TEST

1   Alkanes contain carbon-carbon _____ bonds.

2   The bonding in alkanes can be described in terms of _____ hybrid orbitals on the carbon atoms.

3   Structural isomers have the same physical properties. *True/False*

4   The molecules whose formulas are

$$CH_3CH_2CH_3 \quad \text{and} \quad CH_3CH_2 \atop \underset{CH_3}{|}$$

are structural isomers. *True/False*

5   Ethane, CH_3CH_3, is a planar molecule. *True/False*

6   The number of isomers of pentane is (*greater than/less than/the same as*) the number of isomers of heptane.

7   Alkanes undergo a great variety of reactions. *True/False*

8   Alkanes react with oxygen in a combustion reaction to form _____ and _____.

9   Hydrocarbons are used as fuels because _____ _____.

10   The reaction between chlorine and an alkane is an example of a _____ reaction.

11   The reaction between chlorine and an alkane requires _____ for the reaction to occur.

12   The reaction between chlorine and an alkane produces an _____

13 In the IUPAC system for naming saturated hydrocarbons, the carbons in the main chain are numbered starting at the end that _____ _____.

14 If two methyl groups are attached to the same carbon atom in an alkane, then only one number is necessary in the IUPAC name. *True/False*

15 Formulas can be drawn from IUPAC names. *True/False*

16 Alkenes are saturated hydrocarbons. *True/False*

17 Alkenes contain one or more carbon-carbon _____ bonds.

18 The double bond in an alkene consists of a _____ bond and a _____ bond.

19 The bonding in the double bond in an alkene can be described in terms of _____ and _____ orbitals.

20 The region around the double bond in an alkene has a _____ _____ shape.

21 In the *cis*-isomer of 1,2-dichloroethene the two chlorine atoms lie _____.

22 Alkenes are named by _____ and _____.

23 The position of the double bond in an alkene is designated by _____.

24 The reaction between hydrogen and an alkene is an example of an _____ reaction.

25 The reaction between hydrogen and ethene in the presence of a catalyst produces _____.

26 The reaction between chlorine and ethene produces _____.

27 The reaction between hydrogen chloride and ethene produces _____.

28 The reaction between water and ethene in the presence of acid produces _____.

29 Markovnikov's rule is used to predict the product of the addition of HCl(g) or H_2O(l) to the double bond of an alkene. *True/False*

30 Markovnikov's rule states that _____ _____ _____.

31 An alcohol contains the _____ group.

32 An alcohol is named by _____
and _____ .

33 The position of the —OH group must be designated by a number in the IUPAC name for an alcohol. *True/False*

34 The bonding in methanol can be described in terms of _____
_____ on the carbon and oxygen atoms.

35 Alkynes contain one or more carbon-carbon _____ bonds.

36 Alkynes undergo reactions similar to alkenes. *True/False*

37 Alkynes are named by _____
and _____ .

38 The position of the triple bond in an alkyne must be designated by a number. *True/False*

39 A compact way of writing the benzene structure is _____ .

40 Benzene contains three double bonds. *True/False*

41 Benzene undergoes the same reactions as an alkene. *True/False*

42 Derivatives of benzene are named by numbering the carbon atoms in benzene according to _____ .

43 The designation *ortho-* in *o*-dichlorobenzene indicates that the two chlorine atoms are in the _____ and _____ positions on the benzene ring.

44 The designation *para-* in *p*-dichlorobenzene indicates that the two chlorine atoms are in the _____ and _____ positions on the benzene ring.

45 Aromatic hydrocarbons are stabilized by _____
_____ .

46 Aldehydes have the general formula _____ .

47 Ketones have the general formula _____ .

48 Aldehydes and ketones contain a carbon-oxygen _____ bond.

49 The aldehyde group has a _____ shape.

50 Aldehydes are obtained from the oxidation of _____ .

51 Ketones are obtained from the oxidation of _____ .

52 Organic carboxylic acids have the general formula _____ .

53 Carboxylic acids contain the _____ group.

54 Carboxylic acids can be obtained from the oxidation of ＿＿＿＿＿＿ or ＿＿＿＿＿＿＿＿＿.

55 Carboxylic acids dissociate in water to produce ＿＿＿＿＿＿＿＿ and ＿＿＿＿＿＿＿＿＿＿＿.

56 The two carbon-oxygen bonds in a carboxylate ion are identical. *True/False*

57 The two carbon-oxygen bonds in the carboxyl group are identical. *True/False*

58 The reaction between a carboxylic acid and a base yields a ＿＿＿＿＿＿＿＿＿ and ＿＿＿＿＿＿＿＿＿.

59 The reaction between a carboxylic acid and an alcohol yields an ＿＿＿＿＿＿＿＿＿ and ＿＿＿＿＿＿＿＿＿＿.

60 An ester has the general formula ＿＿＿＿＿＿＿＿＿ where ＿＿＿＿＿＿＿＿＿＿＿.

C   CALCULATIONS YOU SHOULD KNOW HOW TO DO

There are no calculations in this chapter. You should know how to do the following:

1 Name according to IUPAC rules

(a) alkanes (See Examples 25-2 through 25-4 and Problems 25-7 through 25-11.)
(b) alkenes (See Problem 25-17.)
(c) alcohols (See Problem 25-31.)
(d) alkynes (See Problem 25-39.)
(e) benzene derivatives (See Problem 25-46.)
(f) aldehydes (See Problem 25-47.)
(g) carboxylic acids (See Problem 25-52.)

2 Write formulas from the IUPAC names of

(a) alkanes (See Example 25-5 and Problems 25-12 through 25-16.)
(b) alkenes (See Problem 25-18.)
(c) alcohols (See Problem 25-32.)
(d) alkynes (See Problem 25-40.)
(e) benzene derivatives (See Example 25-10 and Problem 25-45.)
(f) aldehydes (See Problem 25-48.)
(g) carboxylic acids (See Problem 25-51.)

3 Write chemical equations for the reaction involving

(a) alkanes (See Example 25-1 and Problems 25-1 and 25-2.)
(b) alkenes (See Examples 25-7 and 25-8 and Problems 25-19 through 25-28.)
(c) alkynes (See Example 25-9 and Problems 25-41 through 25-44.)
(d) aldehydes and ketones (See Example 25-12 and Problems 25-49 and 25-50.)
(e) carboxylic acids (See Examples 25-13 and 25-14 and Problems 25-53 through 25-58.)

D SOLUTIONS TO THE ODD-NUMBERED PROBLEMS

25-1 (a) The reaction for the combustion of C_4H_{10} is

$$2C_4H_{10}(g) + 13O_2(g) \longrightarrow 8CO_2(g) + 10H_2O(l)$$

(b) $C_6H_{14}(l) + NaOH(aq) \longrightarrow$ N.R.

(c) Chlorine and propane do not react under dark conditions:

$$C_3H_8(g) + Cl_2(g) \xrightarrow{\text{(dark)}} \text{N.R.}$$

(d) $C_2H_6(g) + Cl_2(g) \xrightarrow{\text{UV}} C_2H_5Cl(l) + HCl(g)$

Because this is a free-radical reaction, dichloroethanes are also formed.

25-3 (a) The molecules are identical: One can be rotated 180° to superimpose upon the other.

(b) The molecules are identical. The chlorine atom is attached to the second carbon atom in each molecule.

(c) The molecules are different. They represent structural isomers because the chlorine atom is attached to a different carbon atom in each molecule.

(d) The molecules are identical. The groups in one molecule may be rotated around a carbon-carbon bond so that it is identical to the other molecule.

25-5 The formula for *n*-pentane is

$$\overset{1}{C}H_3\overset{2}{C}H_2\overset{3}{C}H_2\overset{4}{C}H_2\overset{5}{C}H_3$$

We can substitute a chlorine atom for a hydrogen atom on carbon atoms 1, 2, or 3 to obtain three different isomers. The isomers are

$ClCH_2CH_2CH_2CH_2CH_3$ 1-chloropentane

$$CH_3\overset{\overset{\displaystyle Cl}{|}}{C}HCH_2CH_2CH_3 \qquad \text{2-chloropentane}$$

$$CH_3CH_2\overset{\overset{\displaystyle Cl}{|}}{C}HCH_2CH_3 \qquad \text{3-chloropentane}$$

Notice that 4-chloropentane is the same as 2-chloropentane and that 5-chloropentane is the same as 1-chloropentane.

25-7 (a) The longest consecutive chain of carbon atoms is four:

$$\overset{1}{C}H_3 - \overset{2}{C}\overset{|}{H} - \overset{3}{C}H_2 - \overset{4}{C}H_3$$

And so we shall name this molecule as a derivative of butane. The IUPAC name is 2-chlorobutane.

(b) The longest consecutive chain of carbon atoms is four:

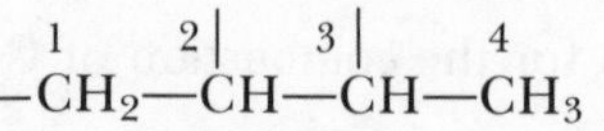

$$\overset{1}{—}CH_2\overset{2}{—}\overset{|}{C}H\overset{3}{—}\overset{|}{C}H\overset{4}{—}CH_3$$

The IUPAC name is 1,2,3-trichlorobutane.

(c) The longest consecutive chain of carbon atoms is six:

$$\overset{1}{C}H_3\overset{2}{—}CH_2\overset{3}{—}\overset{|}{C}\overset{4}{—}CH_2\overset{5}{—}CH_2\overset{6}{—}CH_3$$

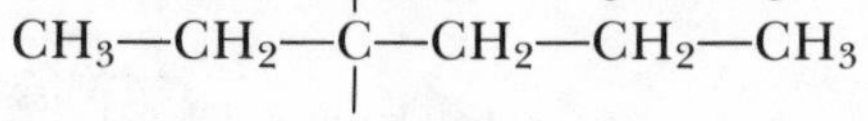

And so we shall name this molecule as a derivative of hexane. The IUPAC name is 3-iodo-3-methylhexane.

(d) The longest consecutive chain of carbon atoms is six (not four):

$$CH_3—CH_2—CH_2—CH_2—CH_2—CH_3$$

The IUPAC name is hexane.

25-9 (a) The name violates rule 3. The chain was not numbered to give the lowest number to the carbon atom that has an attached group. The correct IUPAC name is 2-methylpentane.

(b) The formula for 2-ethylbutane is

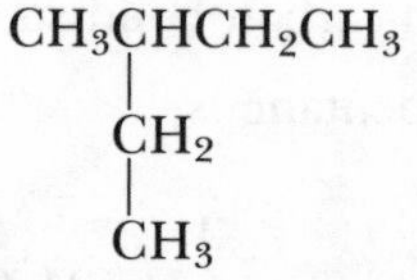

$$CH_3CHCH_2CH_3$$
$$|$$
$$CH_2$$
$$|$$
$$CH_3$$

This name violates rule 2. The correct IUPAC name is 3-methylpentane.

(c) The formula for 2-propylhexane is

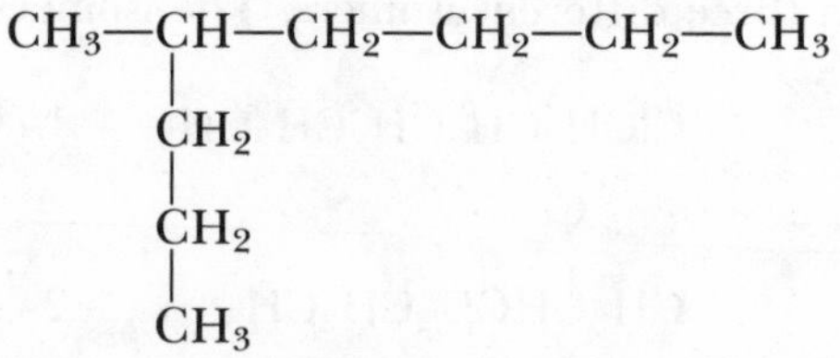

$$CH_3—CH—CH_2—CH_2—CH_2—CH_3$$
$$|$$
$$CH_2$$
$$|$$
$$CH_2$$
$$|$$
$$CH_3$$

This name violates rule 2. The correct IUPAC name is 4-methyloctane.

(d) One of the methyl groups has not been numbered (rule 6). The correct IUPAC name is 2,2-dimethylpropane.

25-11 According to Table 25-2, hexane has five isomers, which are

$$CH_3—CH_2—CH_2—CH_2—CH_2—CH_3 \qquad \text{hexane}$$

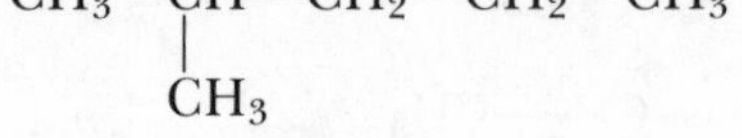

$$CH_3—CH—CH_2—CH_2—CH_3 \qquad \text{2-methylpentane}$$
$$\quad\;\;|$$
$$\quad\;CH_3$$

$$CH_3—CH_2—CH—CH_2—CH_3 \qquad \text{3-methylpentane}$$
$$\qquad\qquad\;\;|$$
$$\qquad\qquad CH_3$$

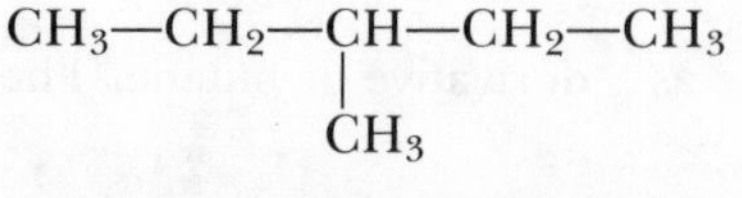

$$CH_3—CH_2—\underset{\underset{CH_3}{|}}{\overset{\overset{CH_3}{|}}{C}}—CH_3$$ 2,2-dimethylbutane

$$CH_3—\underset{\underset{CH_3}{|}}{CH}—\underset{\underset{CH_3}{|}}{CH}—CH_3$$ 2,3-dimethylbutane

25-13 (a) $CH_3—\underset{\underset{CH_3}{|}}{CH}—CH_2—CH_3$ 2-methylbutane

(b) $Cl—CH_2—CH_2—Br$ 1-bromo-2-chloroethane
2-bromo-1-chloroethane

(c) $CH_3—\underset{\underset{Cl}{|}}{\overset{\overset{Cl}{|}}{C}}—\underset{\underset{Cl}{|}}{\overset{\overset{Cl}{|}}{C}}—Cl$ 1,1,1,2,2-pentachloropropane

(d) $CH_3—\underset{\underset{CH_3}{|}}{\overset{\overset{CH_3}{|}}{C}}—CH_3$ 2,2-dimethylpropane

25-15 (a) The parent alkane is butane. The name indicates that a methyl group is bonded to the second and third carbon atoms. Thus the structural formula is

$$CH_3—\underset{\underset{CH_3}{|}}{CH}—\underset{\underset{CH_3}{|}}{CH}—CH_3$$

(b) The parent alkane is butane. The name indicates that two methyl groups are bonded to the second carbon atom and one methyl group is bonded to the third carbon atom. The structural formula is

$$CH_3—\underset{\underset{CH_3}{|}}{\overset{\overset{CH_3}{|}}{C}}—\underset{\underset{CH_3}{|}}{CH}—CH_3$$

(c) The parent alkane is hexane. The name indicates that two methyl groups are bonded to the third carbon atom and an ethyl group is bonded to the fourth carbon atom. The structural formula is

$$CH_3—CH_2—\underset{\underset{CH_3}{|}}{\overset{\overset{CH_3}{|}}{C}}—\underset{\underset{\underset{\underset{CH_3}{|}}{CH_2}}{|}}{CH}—CH_2—CH_3$$

(d) The parent alkane is octane. The name indicates that an isopropyl group is bonded to the fourth carbon atom. The structural formula is

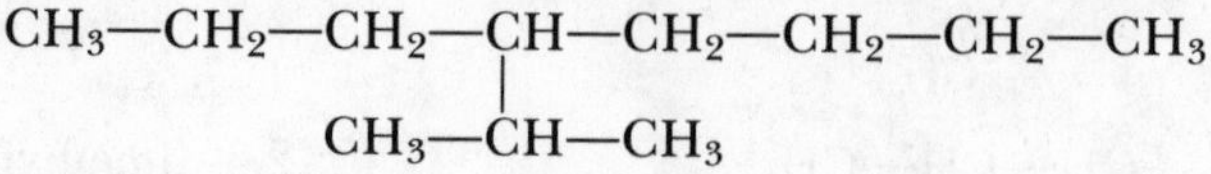

$$CH_3{-}CH_2{-}CH_2{-}CH{-}CH_2{-}CH_2{-}CH_2{-}CH_3$$
$$CH_3{-}CH{-}CH_3$$

25-17 (a) 3-methyl-1-butene
(b) 2-methyl-2-butene
(c) 2-methyl-1-butene
(d) 4-methyl-2-hexene

25-19 (a) The reaction is

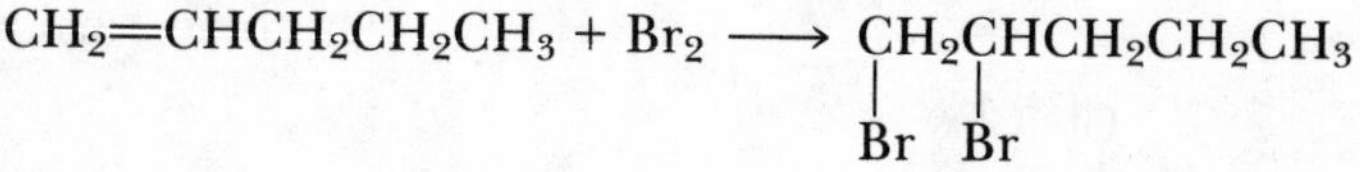

$$CH_2{=}CHCH_2CH_2CH_3 + Br_2 \longrightarrow CH_2CHCH_2CH_2CH_3$$
$$\quad\quad Br\ \ Br$$

1,2-dibromopentane

(b) The reaction is

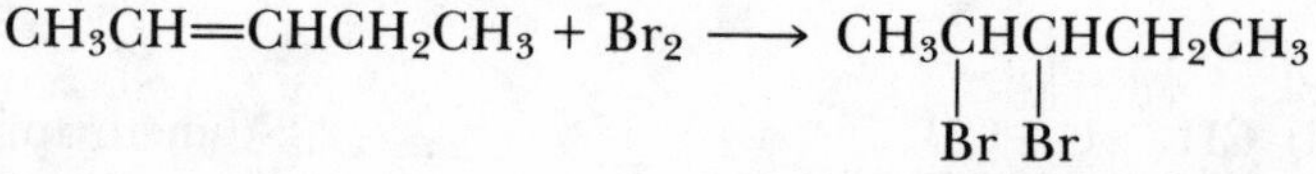

$$CH_3CH{=}CHCH_2CH_3 + Br_2 \longrightarrow CH_3CHCHCH_2CH_3$$
$$\quad\quad Br\ Br$$

2,3-dibromopentane

(c) The reaction is

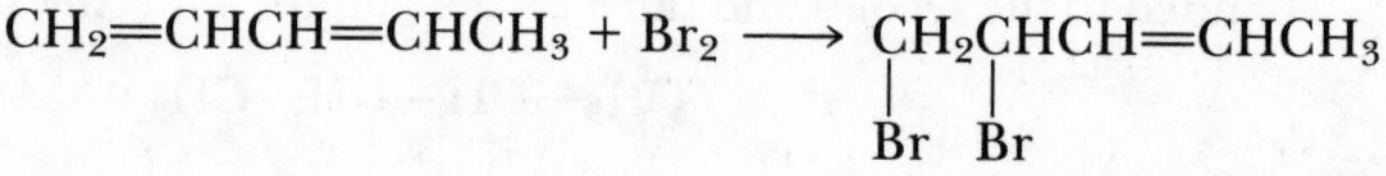

$$CH_2{=}CHCH{=}CHCH_3 + Br_2 \longrightarrow CH_2CHCH{=}CHCH_3$$
$$\quad\quad Br\ \ Br$$

1,2-dibromo-3-pentene
(4,5-dibromo-2-pentene)

and

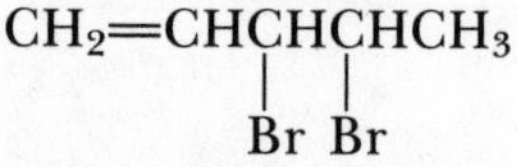

$$CH_2{=}CHCHCHCH_3$$
$$\quad\quad Br\ Br$$

3,4-dibromo-1-pentene
(2,3-dibromo-4-pentene)

25-21 The Lewis formula for 1-butene is

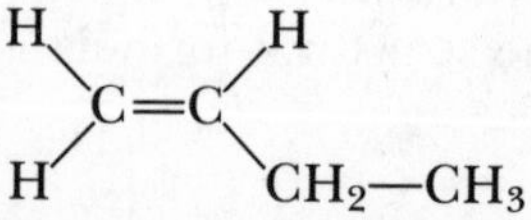

$$\begin{array}{ccc} H & & H \\ & C{=}C & \\ H & & CH_2{-}CH_3 \end{array}$$

(a) 1-butene + $Cl_2(g) \longrightarrow Cl{-}CH_2{-}CH{-}CH_2{-}CH_3$
$$\quad\quad\quad\quad\quad\quad\quad Cl$$

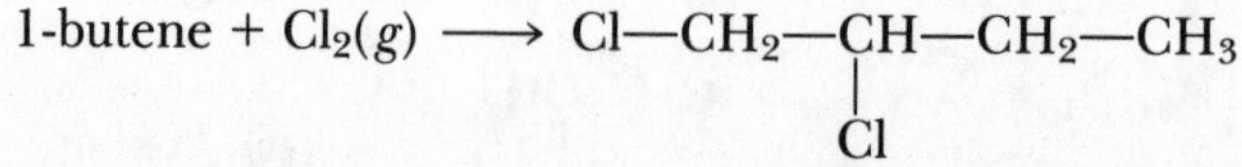

1,2-dichlorobutane

(b) We must use Markovnikov's rule in this case:

$$\text{1-butene} + \text{HCl}(g) \longrightarrow \text{CH}_3\!-\!\underset{\underset{\text{Cl}}{|}}{\text{CH}}\!-\!\text{CH}_2\!-\!\text{CH}_3$$

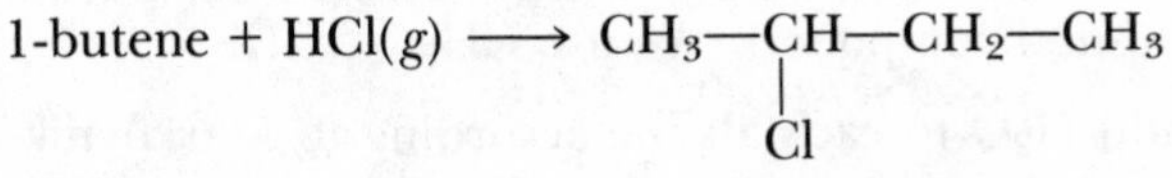

2-chlorobutane

(c) We must use Markovnikov's rule in this case:

$$\text{1-butene} + \text{H}_2\text{O}(l) \xrightarrow{\text{acid}} \text{CH}_3\!-\!\underset{\underset{\text{OH}}{|}}{\text{CH}}\!-\!\text{CH}_2\!-\!\text{CH}_3$$

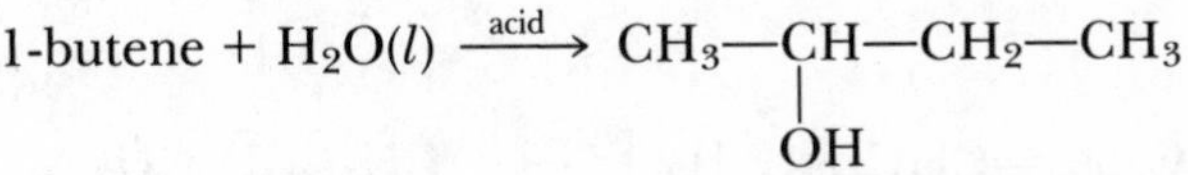

2-butanol

(d) $\text{1-butene} + \text{H}_2(g) \xrightarrow{\text{Pt}} \text{CH}_3\!-\!\text{CH}_2\!-\!\text{CH}_2\!-\!\text{CH}_3$

butane

25-23 (a)

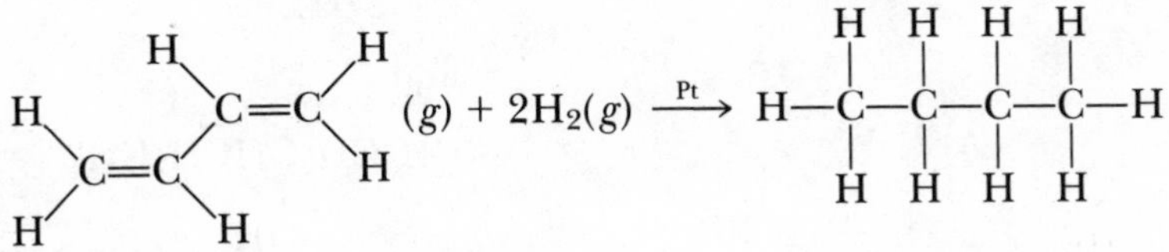

(b)

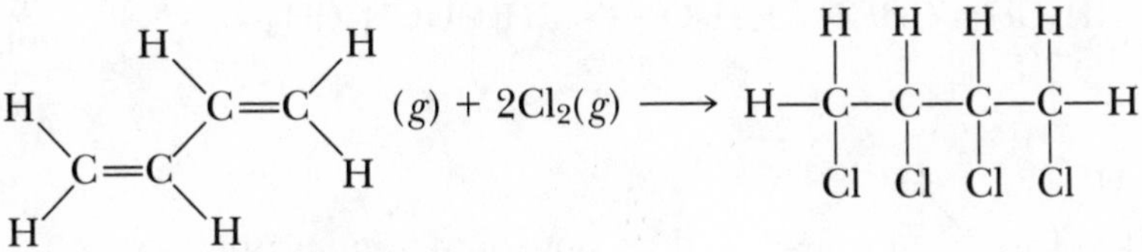

(c) We must use Markovnikov's rule.

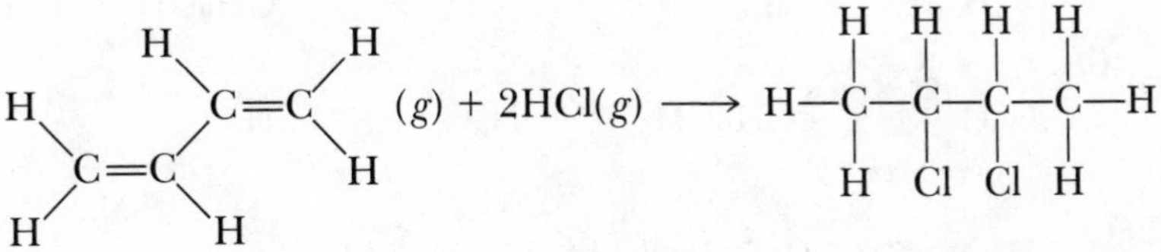

25-25 (a) We shall react H_2O in the presence of an acid with an alkene in accord with Markovnikov's rule to obtain the desired alcohol. We use the alkenes

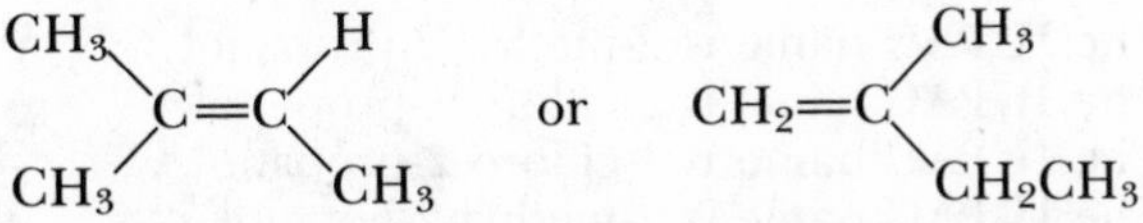

(b) We react H_2O in the presence of an acid with an alkene in accord with Markovnikov's rule to obtain the desired alcohol. We use the alkene $\text{CH}_2\!=\!\text{CHCH}_3$.

(c) We react one mole of H_2 with the corresponding alkyne $CH_3C{\equiv}CCH_3$.

(d) We react HBr with an alkyne in accord with Markovnikov's rule to obtain the desired compound. We use $CH_3C{\equiv}CH$.

25-27 We add H_2O to each alkene according to Markovnikov's rule

(a) $CH_2{=}CHCHCH_3 + H_2O \xrightarrow{\text{acid}} CH_3CHCHCH_3$
$\qquad\qquad |\qquad\qquad\qquad\qquad\quad\; |\;\; |$
$\qquad\qquad CH_3 \qquad\qquad\qquad\quad OHCH_3$

(b) $CH_3C{=}CHCH_3 + H_2O \xrightarrow{\text{acid}} CH_3\overset{\displaystyle OH}{\underset{\displaystyle CH_3}{C}}CH_2CH_3$
$\qquad\qquad |$
$\qquad\qquad CH_3$

(c) $CH_3CH{=}CHCH_2CH_3 + H_2O \xrightarrow{\text{acid}} CH_3CHCH_2CH_2CH_3$
$\qquad\qquad\qquad\qquad\qquad\qquad\qquad\qquad\qquad |$
$\qquad\qquad\qquad\qquad\qquad\qquad\qquad\qquad\;\; OH$

and

$\qquad\qquad CH_3CH_2CHCH_2CH_3$
$\qquad\qquad\qquad\qquad\qquad |$
$\qquad\qquad\qquad\qquad\;\; OH$

(d) $CH_3CH{=}CHCH_3 + H_2O \xrightarrow{\text{acid}} CH_3CHCH_2CH_3$
$\qquad\qquad\qquad\qquad\qquad\qquad\qquad\qquad |$
$\qquad\qquad\qquad\qquad\qquad\qquad\qquad OH$

25-29 (a)
$$\text{H}\diagdown\;\;\diagup\text{H}$$
$$\text{C=C}$$
$$\text{H}\diagup\;\;\diagdown\text{CH}_2\text{CH}_3$$
does not show *cis-trans* isomerism

(b)
$$\text{H}\diagdown\;\;\diagup\text{H}\qquad\qquad\text{H}\diagdown\;\;\diagup\text{CH}_2\text{CH}_3$$
$$\text{C=C}\qquad\qquad\qquad\text{C=C}$$
$$\text{H}_3\text{C}\diagup\;\;\diagdown\text{CH}_2\text{CH}_3\quad\text{H}_3\text{C}\diagup\;\;\diagdown\text{H}$$
$$\quad\quad cis\qquad\qquad\qquad\qquad trans$$

(c)
$$\text{H}\diagdown\;\;\diagup\text{CH}_2\text{CH}_3$$
$$\text{C=C}$$
$$\text{H}\diagup\;\;\diagdown\text{CH}_3$$
does not show *cis-trans* isomerism

25-31 (a) The IUPAC name is 2-methyl-2-propanol.
(b) The IUPAC name is 2-chloro-1-propanol.
(c) The IUPAC name is 1-chloro-2-propanol.
(d) The IUPAC name is 2-methyl-2-butanol.

25-33 (a) a primary alcohol
(b) a secondary alcohol
(c) a secondary alcohol
(d) a tertiary alcohol

25-35 The reaction between water and an alkali metal is

$$2H_2O(l) + 2M(s) \longrightarrow 2M^+OH^-(s) + H_2(g)$$

Notice the similarity to the following reactions:

$$2CH_3CH_2OH(l) + 2Na(s) \longrightarrow 2Na^+CH_3CH_2O^-(s) + H_2(g)$$

$$2CH_3CH_2CH_2OH(l) + 2Na(s) \longrightarrow 2Na^+CH_3CH_2CH_2O^-(s) + H_2(g)$$

25-37 (a) $C_2H_5NH_2(aq) + HBr(aq) \longrightarrow C_2H_5NH_3^+Br^-(aq)$
(b) $2(CH_3)_2NH(aq) + H_2SO_4(aq) \longrightarrow [(CH_3)_2NH_2^+]_2SO_4^{2-}(aq)$

(c)

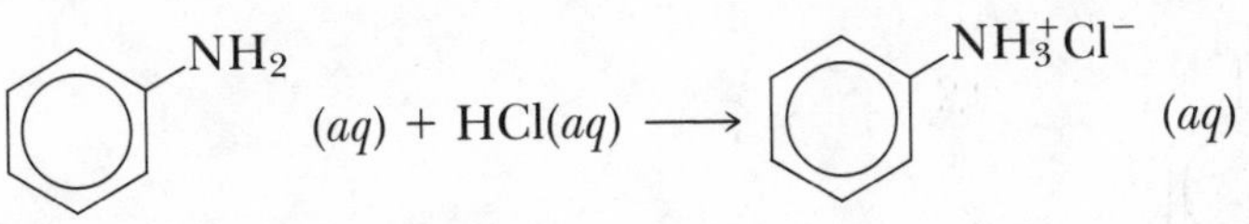

(d) $(C_2H_5)_3N(aq) + HCl(aq) \longrightarrow (C_2H_5)_3NH^+Cl^-(aq)$

25-39 (a) 1-butyne
(b) 2-butyne
(c) 4,4-dimethyl-2-heptyne
(d) 3,4-dimethyl-1-hexyne

25-41 We can break the reaction down into two steps. We shall use Markovnikov's rule to predict the product of each step. The first step is

$$CH_3C\!\equiv\!CH(g) + HBr(g) \longrightarrow CH_3\underset{\underset{Br}{|}}{C}\!=\!CH_2(g)$$

The second step is

$$CH_3\underset{\underset{Br}{|}}{C}\!=\!CH_2(g) + HBr(g) \longrightarrow CH_3\overset{\overset{Br}{|}}{\underset{\underset{Br}{|}}{C}}CH_3(l)$$

The product is 2,2-dibromopropane.

25-43 (a) $CH_3C\!\equiv\!CH(g) + 4O_2(g) \longrightarrow 3CO_2(g) + 2H_2O(l)$
(b) This reaction can be broken down into two steps. We shall use Markovnikov's rule to predict the product in each step. The first step is

$$CH_3C\!\equiv\!CH(g) + HCl(g) \longrightarrow CH_3\underset{\underset{Cl}{|}}{C}\!=\!CH_2(g)$$

The second step is

$$CH_3\underset{\underset{Cl}{|}}{C}\!=\!CH_2(g) + HCl(g) \longrightarrow CH_3\overset{\overset{Cl}{|}}{\underset{\underset{Cl}{|}}{C}}CH_3(l)$$

(c) $CH_3C\equiv CH(g) + 2Br_2(l) \longrightarrow CH_3\overset{\displaystyle Br}{\underset{\displaystyle Br}{\overset{\displaystyle |}{\underset{\displaystyle |}{C}}}}CHBr_2(l)$

25-45   (a)

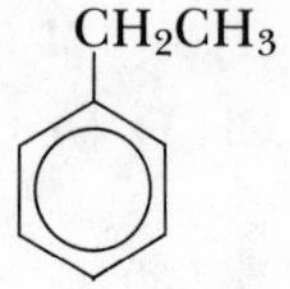

CH$_2$CH$_3$

(b)

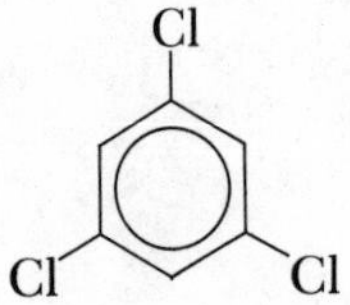

Cl

Cl   Cl

(c)

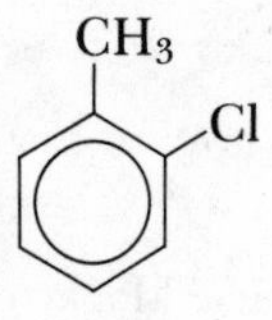

CH$_3$
        Cl

(d)

Cl

        Br

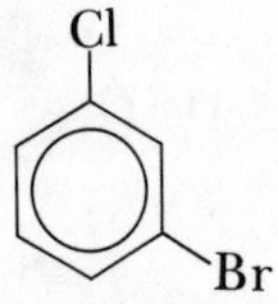

25-47   (a) butanal
       (b) 3-methylbutanal
       (c) methanal
       (d) 3,4-dimethylpentanal

25-49   (a) The aldehyde is

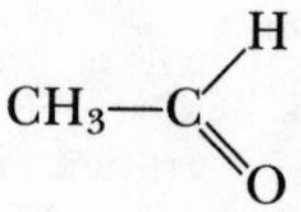

$$CH_3-\overset{\displaystyle H}{\underset{\displaystyle O}{C}} \qquad or \qquad CH_3CHO$$

We would use ethanol, CH_3CH_2OH.
       (b) The aldehyde is

$$CH_3CHCHO$$
$$|$$
$$CH_3$$

We would use 2-methylpropanol, CH_3CHCH_2OH.
$$|$$
$$CH_3$$

(c) The aldehyde is

$$\underset{\underset{CH_3}{|}}{\overset{\overset{CH_3}{|}}{CH_3CCHO}}$$

We would use 2,2-dimethylpropanol, $\underset{\underset{CH_3}{|}}{\overset{\overset{CH_3}{|}}{CH_3CCH_2OH}}$.

25-51 (a) CH_3CH_2COOH or $CH_3CH_2-\overset{\overset{O}{\|}}{C}-OH$

(b) $\underset{\underset{CH_3}{|}}{CH_3CHCOOH}$ or $\underset{\underset{CH_3}{|}}{CH_3CH}-\overset{\overset{O}{\|}}{C}-OH$

(c) $\underset{\underset{CH_3}{|}}{\overset{\overset{CH_3}{|}}{CH_3CCH_2COOH}}$ or $\underset{\underset{CH_3}{|}}{\overset{\overset{CH_3}{|}}{CH_3CCH_2}}-\overset{\overset{O}{\|}}{C}-OH$

(d) $\underset{\underset{CH_3}{|}}{CH_3CH_2CHCH_2COOH}$ or $\underset{\underset{CH_3}{|}}{CH_3CH_2CHCH_2}-\overset{\overset{O}{\|}}{C}-OH$

25-53 $\underset{\text{acetic acid}}{CH_3COOH(aq)} + \underset{\text{1-octanol}}{CH_3CH_2CH_2CH_2CH_2CH_2CH_2CH_2OH(aq)} \longrightarrow$

$$\underset{\text{octyl acetate}}{CH_3CH_2CH_2CH_2CH_2CH_2CH_2CH_2O}\overset{\overset{CH_3}{\diagdown}}{\diagup}C=O(aq) + H_2O(l)$$

25-55 (a) This is a neutralization reaction. The balanced equation is

$$HCOOH(aq) + NaOH(aq) \longrightarrow NaHCOO(aq) + H_2O(l)$$

(b) The reaction between an acid and an alcohol yields an ester. The balanced equation is

$$HCOOH(aq) + CH_3OH(aq) \longrightarrow \underset{CH_3O}{\overset{H}{\diagdown}}{\diagup}C=O(aq) + H_2O(l)$$

(c) This is a neutralization reaction. The balanced equation is

$$2HCOOH(aq) + Ca(OH)_2(aq) \longrightarrow Ca(HCOO)_2(aq) + 2H_2O(l)$$

25-57 (a) $CH_3CH_2COOH(aq) + KOH(aq) \longrightarrow KCH_3CH_2COO(aq) + H_2O(l)$
potassium propanoate

(b) $\underset{\underset{CH_3}{|}}{CH_3CHCOOH}(aq) + KOH(aq) \longrightarrow \underset{\underset{CH_3}{|}}{KCH_3CHCOO}(aq) + H_2O(l)$
potassium 2-methylpropanoate

(c) $2Cl_2CHCOOH(aq) + Ca(OH)_2(aq) \longrightarrow Ca(Cl_2CHCOO)_2(aq) + 2H_2O(l)$
calcium 2,2-dichloroethanoate

E   ANSWERS TO THE EVEN-NUMBERED PROBLEMS

25-2 (a) $C_3H_8(g) + H_2SO_4(aq) \longrightarrow$ N.R.
(b) $C_5H_{12}(g) + 8O_2(g) \longrightarrow 5CO_2(g) + 6H_2O(l)$
(c) $C_2H_6(g) + HCl(aq) \longrightarrow$ N.R.

(d) $C_5H_{12}(l) + Cl_2(g) \xrightarrow{UV} C_5H_{11}Cl(l) + HCl(g)$ and higher chloropentanes

25-4 (a) identical   (c) different
(b) identical   (d) identical

25-6

$\underset{\underset{Cl}{|}}{CH_3CH_2CHCl}$ 1,1-dichloropropane

$\underset{\underset{Cl}{|}}{\overset{\overset{Cl}{|}}{CH_3CCH_3}}$ 2,2-dichloropropane

$\underset{\underset{Cl}{|}}{CH_3CHCH_2Cl}$ 1,2-dichloropropane

$ClCH_2CH_2CH_2Cl$ 1,3-dichloropropane

25-8 (a) 3-chloropentane
(b) 2,2-dimethyl-3-nitrobutane
(c) 2-chlorobutane
(d) 2-methylbutane

25-10 (a) It violates rule 3; 1,2-dichloropropane.
(b) It violates rules 2 and 3; 1-bromo-2-methylbutane.
(c) It violates rule 2; 2-methylpentane.
(d) It violates rule 6; 2,2-dimethylbutane or 2,3-dimethylbutane.

25-12   do not differ; differ; are the same compound

25-14   (a) $CH_3CH_2CH_2CH_2CH_2CH_3$ hexane

(b) $CH_3\overset{|}{C}HCH_2CH_2\overset{|}{C}HCH_3$ 2,5-dimethylhexane
$\quad\quad\;\; CH_3\quad\quad\quad CH_3$

(c) $CH_3\overset{\overset{\textstyle CH_3}{|}}{\underset{\underset{\textstyle CH_3}{|}}{C}}CH_3$ 2,2-dimethylpropane

(d) $CH_3\overset{\overset{\textstyle Cl}{|}}{C}H\overset{\overset{\textstyle }{}}{\underset{\underset{\textstyle Cl\;\;Cl}{|\;\;|}}{C}}CCl_3$ 1,1,1,2,2,3-hexachlorobutane

25-16   (a) $Cl_2CH\underset{\underset{\textstyle Cl}{|}}{C}HCH_2CH_3$

(b) Cl_3CCH_3

(c) $ClCH_2\underset{\underset{\textstyle Cl\;\;Cl}{|\;\;|}}{CHCH}CH_2CH_3$

(d) $CH_3\overset{\overset{\textstyle Cl}{|}}{\underset{\underset{\textstyle Cl\quad Cl}{|\quad\;|}}{C}}CH_2CHCH_2CH_3$

25-18   (a) $CH_3\overset{\overset{\textstyle CH_3}{|}}{C}HCH{=}CHCH_2CH_3$

(b) $CH_2{=}\overset{\overset{\textstyle CH_3}{|}}{C}CH_2CH_2CH_3$

(c) $CH_3\overset{\overset{\textstyle H_3C}{|}}{C}{=}\overset{\overset{\textstyle CH_3}{|}}{C}CH_3$

(d) $CH_3CH{=}\overset{\overset{\textstyle CH_3}{|}}{C}CH_2CH_3$

25-20   (a) $BrCH_2\underset{\underset{\textstyle Br}{|}}{C}HCH_2CH_3$ 1,2-dibromobutane

(b) $CH_3\underset{\underset{\textstyle Br\;\;Br}{|\;\;|}}{CHCH}CH_3$ 2,3-dibromobutane

(c) $BrCH_2CHCH\!=\!CHCH_2CH_3$ 1,2-dibromo-3-hexene
$\overset{\displaystyle |}{Br}$

$CH_2\!=\!CHCHCHCH_2CH_3$ 3,4-dibromo-1-hexene
$\overset{\displaystyle |\ \ |}{Br\ Br}$

25-22 (a) $CH_3CHCHCH_2CH_3$ 2,3-dichloropentane
$\overset{\displaystyle |\ \ |}{Cl\ Cl}$

(b) $CH_3CH_2CHCH_2CH_3$ 3-chloropentane
$\overset{\displaystyle |}{Cl}$

$CH_3CHCH_2CH_2CH_3$ 2-chloropentane
$\overset{\displaystyle |}{Cl}$

(c) $CH_3CH_2CHCH_2CH_3$ 3-pentanol
$\overset{\displaystyle |}{OH}$

$CH_3CHCH_2CH_2CH_3$ 2-pentanol
$\overset{\displaystyle |}{OH}$

(d) $CH_3CH_2CH_2CH_2CH_3$ pentane

25-24 (a)

$$\begin{array}{c}CH_3 \\ \\ CH_3\end{array}\!\!\!\!C\!=\!C\!\!\!\!\begin{array}{c}H \\ \\ CH_3\end{array}(l) + Br_2(l) \longrightarrow CH_3\overset{\displaystyle \overset{CH_3}{|}}{C}\!-\!\underset{\displaystyle \underset{Br\ Br}{|\ \ |}}{CH}CH_3(l)$$

(b)

$$\begin{array}{c}CH_3 \\ \\ CH_3\end{array}\!\!\!\!C\!=\!C\!\!\!\!\begin{array}{c}H \\ \\ CH_3\end{array}(l) + HCl(g) \longrightarrow CH_3\overset{\displaystyle \overset{CH_3}{|}}{\underset{\displaystyle \underset{Cl}{|}}{C}}CH_2CH_3(l)$$

(c)

$$\begin{array}{c}CH_3 \\ \\ CH_3\end{array}\!\!\!\!C\!=\!C\!\!\!\!\begin{array}{c}H \\ \\ CH_3\end{array}(l) + H_2O(l) \xrightarrow{\ acid\ } CH_3\overset{\displaystyle \overset{CH_3}{|}}{\underset{\displaystyle \underset{OH}{|}}{C}}CH_2CH_3(l)$$

25-26 (a) $CH_3CH\!=\!CHCH_3 + Br_2$
(b) $CH_3C\!\equiv\!CCH_3 + 2Cl_2$
(c) $CH_3C\!=\!CH_2 + H_2O$
$\overset{\displaystyle |}{CH_3}$

(d) $CH_3CHCH\!=\!CH_2 + Br_2$
$\overset{\displaystyle |}{CH_3}$

25-28   (a) $CH_3CHCHCH_3$
                     | |
                    Cl Cl

      (b) $BrCH_2CHCH_2CH_3$ and $BrCH_2CH_2CHCH_3$
                         | |
                        Cl Cl

                        CH_3
                        |
      (c) CH_3CCH_3
                        |
                        Cl

      (d) $ClCH_2CHCH_3$ and $Cl_2CHCH_2CH_3$
                              |
                            Cl

25-30   (b)

                        CH_3
                        |
25-32   (a) $CH_3CH_2CCH_2OH$
                        |
                        CH_3

      (b) $CH_3CHCH_2CH_2CHCH_3$
                       | |
                    OH CH_3

      (c) $ClCH_2CHCH_2CH_2CH_2CH_3$
                       |
                    OH

      (d) $ClCH_2CHCHCH_2CH_3$
                       | |
                    Cl OH

25-34   (a) tertiary alcohol
      (b) secondary alcohol
      (c) primary alcohol
      (d) primary alcohol

25-36 $CH_3O^-(aq) + H_2O(l) \longrightarrow CH_3OH(aq) + OH^-(aq)$

25-38 $^-Br^+H_3NCH_2CH_2NH_3^+Br^-(aq)$

25-40   (a) $CH_3C{\equiv}CH$
      (b) $CH_3CH_2C{\equiv}CCH_2CH_3$
      (c) $CH_3CH_2C{\equiv}CCHCH_2CH_2CH_3$
                                    |
                                 CH_2CH_3

                        CH_3
                        |
      (d) $CH_3CC{\equiv}CCH_2CH_3$
                        |
                        CH_3

25-42   (a) $\underset{\underset{\text{Br}}{|}}{\overset{\overset{\text{Br}}{|}}{\text{CH}_3\text{CH}_2\text{CCH}_3}}$ 2,2-dibromobutane

25-44   (a) $\text{CH}_3\text{C}\equiv\text{CCH}_3(g) + 2\text{HCl}(g) \longrightarrow \underset{\underset{\text{Cl}}{|}}{\overset{\overset{\text{Cl}}{|}}{\text{CH}_3\text{CCH}_2\text{CH}_3}}(l)$

         (b) $\text{CH}_3\text{C}\equiv\text{CCH}_3(g) + 2\text{H}_2(g) \xrightarrow{\text{Ni}(s)} \text{CH}_3\text{CH}_2\text{CH}_2\text{CH}_3(g)$

         (c) $\text{CH}_3\text{C}\equiv\text{CCH}_3(g) + 2\text{Cl}_2(g) \longrightarrow \underset{\underset{\text{Cl}}{|}\ \underset{\text{Cl}}{|}}{\overset{\overset{\text{Cl}}{|}\ \overset{\text{Cl}}{|}}{\text{CH}_3\text{C}-\text{CCH}_3}}(l)$

25-46   (a)   1-nitro-3-chlorobenzene
         (b)   hexamethylbenzene
         (c)   1,4-dichlorobenzene or *p*-dichlorobenzene
         (d)   1,2-dichlorobenzene or *o*-dichlorobenzene

25-48   (a) $\text{CH}_3\text{CH}_2\text{CHO}$
         (b) $\underset{\underset{\text{CH}_3}{|}}{\text{CH}_3\text{CH}_2\text{CH}_2\text{CHCHO}}$

         (c) $\underset{\underset{\text{CH}_3}{|}}{\text{CH}_3\text{CHCH}_2\text{CH}_2\text{CHO}}$

         (d) $\underset{\underset{\text{CH}_3}{|}}{\overset{\overset{\text{CH}_3}{|}}{\text{CH}_3\text{CH}_2\text{CH}_2\text{CCH}_2\text{CHO}}}$

25-50   (a) $\text{CH}_3\text{CH}_2\text{CHO}$
         (b) $\underset{\underset{\text{CH}_3}{|}}{\text{CH}_3\text{CHCHO}}$

         (c) $\underset{\underset{\text{CH}_3}{|}}{\overset{\overset{\text{CH}_3}{|}}{\text{CH}_3\text{CH}_2\text{CCHO}}}$

25-52   (a)   3-chlorobutanoic acid
         (b)   2,2-dimethylpropanoic acid
         (c)   4-chloro-3-methylpentanoic acid
         (d)   2,2,3,3,3-pentachloropropanoic acid

25-54 $CH_3CH_2CH_2COOH(aq) + CH_3CH_2OH(aq) \longrightarrow$

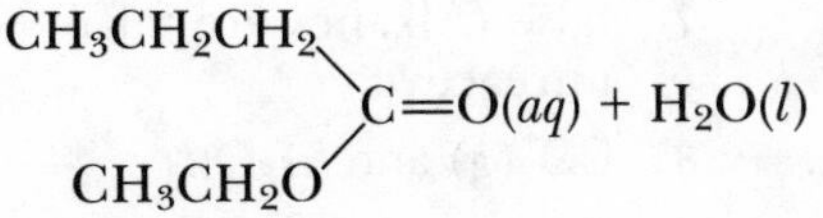

$$\begin{array}{c} CH_3CH_2CH_2 \\ \\ CH_3CH_2O \end{array}\!\!\!\!C\!=\!\!O(aq) + H_2O(l)$$

25-56   (a) $CH_3CH_2COOH(aq) + NH_3(aq) \longrightarrow NH_4CH_3CH_2COO(aq)$

   (b) $CH_3CH_2COOH(aq) + CH_3OH(aq) \longrightarrow$ $\begin{array}{c} CH_3CH_2 \\ \\ CH_3O \end{array}\!\!\!\!C\!=\!\!O(aq) + H_2O(l)$

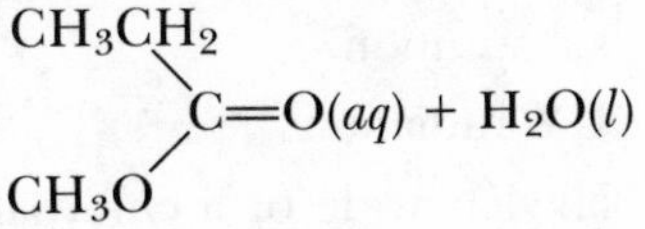

   (c) $CH_3CH_2COOH(aq) + CH_3CH_2OH(aq) \longrightarrow$

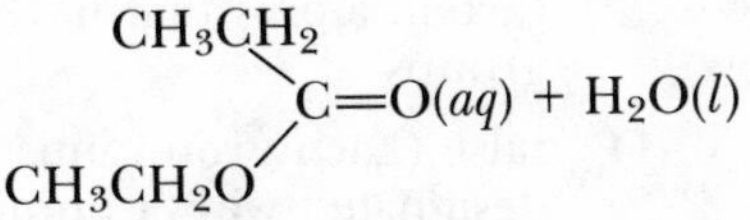

$$\begin{array}{c} CH_3CH_2 \\ \\ CH_3CH_2O \end{array}\!\!\!\!C\!=\!\!O(aq) + H_2O(l)$$

25-58   (a) $Na^+ \left[\begin{array}{c} \overset{\displaystyle\ddot{O}:}{\underset{\displaystyle\overset{|}{Cl}}{CH_3CH\!-\!C}} \\ \ddot{O}: \end{array} \right]^-$

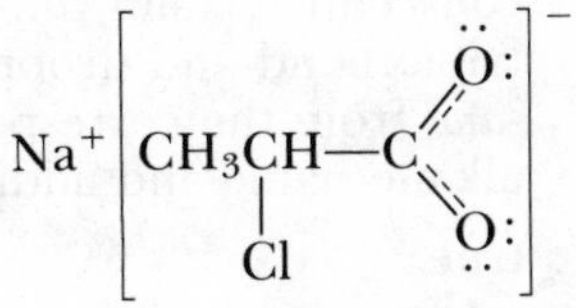

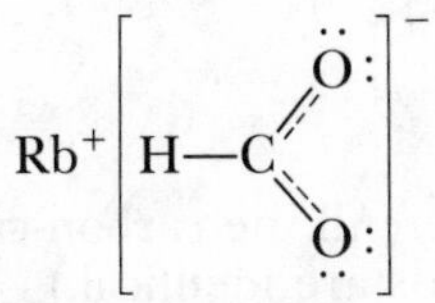

   (b) $Rb^+ \left[\begin{array}{c} \overset{\displaystyle\ddot{O}:}{H\!-\!C} \\ \ddot{O}: \end{array} \right]^-$

   (c) $Sr^{2+} \left[\begin{array}{c} CH_3 \\ \overset{\displaystyle|}{\underset{\displaystyle\overset{|}{CH_3}}{CH_3C\!-\!C}}\overset{\displaystyle\ddot{O}:}{} \\ \ddot{O}: \end{array} \right]^-_2$

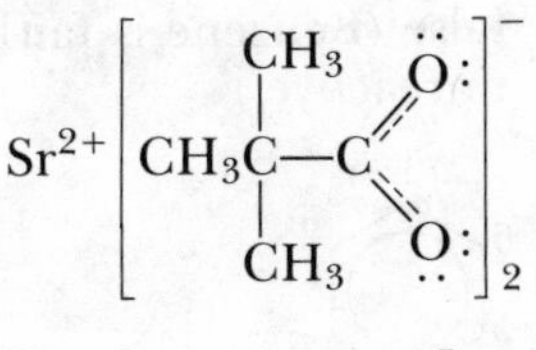

   (d) $La^{3+} \left[\begin{array}{c} \overset{\displaystyle\ddot{O}:}{CH_3\!-\!C} \\ \ddot{O}: \end{array} \right]^-_3$

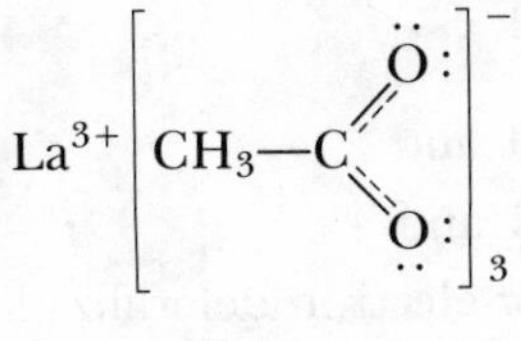

F   ANSWERS TO THE SELF-TEST

1   single

2   sp^3

3   false

4   false

5   false (The bonding around each carbon atom is tetrahedral.)

6   less than

7   false (Alkanes are fairly unreactive.)

8   $CO_2(g)$ and $H_2O(l)$

9   their combustion reactions are highly exothermic

10 substitution

11 UV radiation

12 alkylchloride or a chloroalkane

13 gives the lowest numbers to the carbon atoms that have attached groups

14 false (Each group must be designated with a number.)

15 true

16 false

17 double

18 σ; π

19 sp^2 hybrid orbitals and p orbitals on the carbon atoms in the double bonds

20 planar

21 on the same side of the double bond, or adjacent to one another

22 identifying the longest consecutive chain containing the double bond and dropping the -ane from the name of the main chain and adding -ene

23 the number of the first carbon atom in the double bond

24 addition

25 ethane

26 1,2-dichloroethane

27 chloroethane

28 ethanol (the alcohol CH_3CH_2OH)

29 true

30 when HX adds to an alkene, the hydrogen atom becomes bonded to the carbon atom in the double bond already bearing the larger number of hydrogen atoms

31 —OH

32 identifying the longest consecutive chain containing the carbon atom bearing the —OH group and dropping the -e from the corresponding alkane name and adding -ol

33 true

34 sp^3 hybrid orbitals

35 triple

36 true

37 identifying the longest consecutive chain containing the triple bond and dropping the -ane from the corresponding alkane name and adding -yne

38 true

39

40 false (All the carbon-carbon bonds are identical.)

41 false (Benzene is fairly unreactive.)

42

43 1 and 2

44 1 and 4

45 π-electron delocalization

46 RCHO

47

48 double

49 planar or trigonal planar

50 primary alcohols

51   secondary alcohols

52   RCOOH

53   —COOH

54   aldehydes or primary alcohols

55   carboxylate ions and hydronium
     ions

56   true

57   false

58   salt and water

59   ester and water

60
$$\begin{array}{c} R \\ \end{array} \!\!\! \diagdown \\ \qquad C{=}O \\ R'O \diagup$$

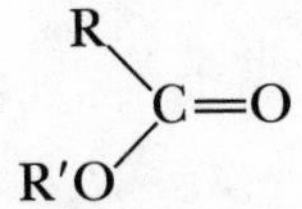

where R' is derived from the
alcohol

26 / Biochemistry

A   OUTLINE OF CHAPTER 26

26-1 Amino acids have an amino group and a carboxyl group attached to a central carbon atom.

Amino acids have the general formula

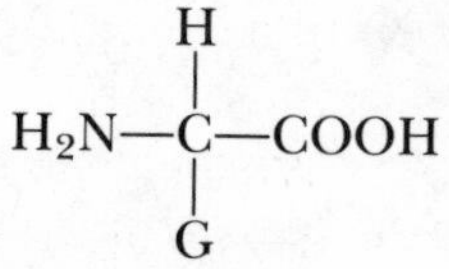

$$H_2N-\underset{\underset{G}{|}}{\overset{\overset{H}{|}}{C}}-COOH$$

where G is called the side group (Table 26-1).

Amino acids are the monomers from which proteins are built. Only 20 different amino acids are commonly found in proteins.

26-2 The amino acids have optical isomers.

Optical isomers are nonsuperimposable mirror-image molecules (Figure 26-1).

The two optical isomers are distinguished by the letters D and L.

The L-isomers of amino acids occur in proteins.

26-3 Amino acids are the monomers of proteins.

Proteins are formed by condensation reactions between the carboxyl group (—COOH) on one amino acid and the amino group (—NH$_2$) on another amino acid.

Two amino acids become linked through a peptide bond:

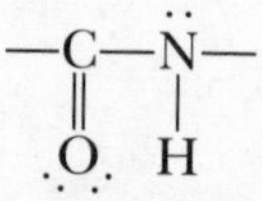

$$-\underset{\underset{\ddot{\cdot}\ddot{O}\cdot}{\|}}{C}-\underset{\underset{H}{|}}{\ddot{N}}-$$

It is necessary to specify the order of the amino acids in a peptide.

Polypeptides are composed of long chains of amino acids joined together by peptide bonds.

The diversity of protein structure and function is achieved by variations in the nature of the side groups.

The side groups fall into one of four classes (Table 26-1):

  I   nonpolar side groups
 II   uncharged polar side groups
III   acidic side groups
 IV   basic side groups

Nonpolar side groups are hydrophobic.

Polar side groups are hydrophilic.

26-4 A protein is uniquely specified by its primary structure.

Three-letter designations for each amino acid are used to write abbreviated structures of peptides (Table 26-1). By convention we start with the free amino end of the peptide when writing the structure of a peptide.

The chain to which the amino acid side groups are attached is called the polypeptide backbone.

Proteins are naturally occurring polypeptides.

The order of the amino acid units in a polypeptide is called the primary structure of the polypeptide.

26-5 Disulfide bonds strongly influence the shape of proteins.

Disulfide bonds (—S—S—) are formed between two cysteine side groups on neighboring sections of polypeptide chains (Figure 26-3).

A disulfide bond in the same polypeptide chain produces a loop in the chain (Figure 26-4).

26-6 The shape of a protein molecule is called tertiary structure.

The α-helix shape of certain proteins results from the formation of hydrogen bonding (Figure 26-5).

The structure within regions of a protein is called secondary structure (for example, α-helical structure).

Nonpolar side groups avoid water and tend to cluster within the protein structure (Figure 26-6).

Polar side groups tend to be on the outside of the protein in contact with water (Figure 26-7).

Tertiary structure denotes the three-dimensional shape of a protein and is determined by X-ray analysis (Figure 26-8).

The shape of a protein depends upon the nature and the order of the amino acid units making up the protein chain.

Tertiary structure plays a major role in protein function.

26-7 Enzymes are protein catalysts.

Cells contain thousands of different enzymes.

Enzymes are extraordinarily specific catalysts.

The lock-and-key theory gives a simple picture of enzyme specificity (Figure 26-9).

A substrate is a reactant that binds to the enzyme in an enzyme-catalyzed reaction.

The particular shape and molecular nature of the binding side determines enzyme specificity.

26-8   Normal hemoglobin and sickle-cell hemoglobin differ by two out of 574 amino acids.

Hemoglobin is the protein that transports oxygen in the bloodstream from the lungs to the tissues.

The shape and function of a protein depends in exacting detail upon its amino acid sequence.

Hemoglobin has two sets of identical chains called α and β.

The amino acids in position 6 of the β chains differ in normal and sickle-cell hemoglobin.

26-9   Starch and cellulose are polymeric carbohydrates.

Carbohydrates serve as an energy source (starch) and as a structural material (cellulose).

Carbohydrates are formed by photosynthesis in green plants:

$$n CO_2(g) + n H_2O(l) \xrightarrow{\text{sunlight}} -(CH_2O)_n + n O_2(g)$$

Carbohydrates are predominantly polyhydroxy ring compounds.

Monosaccharides are carbohydrates that contain just one ring, which is either a 5- or 6-membered ring.

Polysaccharides are composed of monosaccharides linked in α or β linkages.

Sucrose is a disaccharide.

Monosaccharides and disaccharides are usually sweet-tasting and are called sugars.

Starch and cellulose are polymers of glucose.

Starch (which is predominantly amylose) is broken down by the enzyme amylase into the disaccharide, maltose.

Glucose is the source of energy for numerous cellular processes.

Vertebrates do not possess the enzyme that hydrolyzes the β linkages between glucose units in cellulose.

26-10   DNA and RNA are polynucleotides.

DNA stores and passes on genetic information.

DNA is a polynucleotide.

Nucleotides, the monomers of DNA and RNA, consist of a sugar portion, a phosphate group, and a nitrogen-containing ring compound called a base.

Deoxyribose and ribose are the sugars in the nucleotides of DNA and RNA, respectively (page 1050).

DNA contains only the four bases: adenine (A), guanine (G), cytosine (C), and thymine (T) (page 1051).

RNA contains only the four bases, A, G, C, and U (uracil) (page 1051).

Nucleotides are joined by a condensation reaction between the phosphate group of one nucleotide and the 3-hydroxyl group on another nucleotide (page 1052).

26-11 DNA is a double helix.

The DNA double helix consists of two polynucleotide chains intertwined in a helical fashion (Figures 26-12 and 26-14).

The two polynucleotide chains in the DNA double helix are held together by hydrogen bonding between base pairs. A and T bond together and G and C bond together.

A DNA double helix looks like a long cylinder with the bases stacked one upon another perpendicular to the axis of the cylinder (Figure 26-15).

The bases lie in the interior of the double helix; the sugar-phosphate backbone lies on the outside.

26-12 DNA can reproduce itself.

Each strand of the DNA double helix can act as a template for building a complementary strand.

The two new double helices are identical to the original double helix.

26-13 Genetic information is stored in a triplet code.

Each series of three bases along a DNA segment is a code for a particular amino acid.

A gene is a segment along a DNA molecule that codes the synthesis of one polypeptide.

DNA can have a molecular mass of over 10^9.

B   SELF-TEST

1 Amino acids are monomers from which _____ are built.

2 The general formula for an amino acid is

3 Amino acids exist as _____ isomers.

4 Both isomers of an amino acid occur in biological systems. *True/False*

5 The amino acids in a polypeptide are linked by _____ bonds.

6 Two amino acids form a dipeptide when the _____ group of one amino acid reacts with the _____ group of the other amino acid to form a peptide bond.

7 The nonpolar side groups on amino acids are hydrophobic. *True/False*

8 The acidic side groups in amino acids are hydrophobic. *True/False*

9 The polypeptide backbone is the same for all tripeptides. *True/False*

10 The order of attachment of the amino acids to the polypeptide backbone is the same for all tripeptides. *True/False*

11 The primary structure of a protein is unique to that protein. *True/False*

12 Proteins are poly_____.

13 All proteins contain the same number of amino acid units. *True/False*

14 Two polypeptide chains can be linked together by a _____ bond.

15 A disulfide bond can be formed between two _____ side groups.

16 Disulfide bonds affect the shape of a protein molecule. *True/False*

17 A polypeptide may have a helical shape because of _____ bonds between _____.

18 The α-helix is an example of (*primary/secondary*) structure.

19 Hydrophobic side groups tend to be located on the _____ of a protein.

20 Hydrophilic side groups tend to be located on the _____ of a protein.

21 The three-dimensional shape of a protein is its _____ structure.

22 Enzymes are proteins that _____.

23 The shape of an enzyme is such that only its substrate or a closely related molecule fits into the binding site. *True/False*

24 Carbohydrates have the general formula _____.

25 A monosaccharide is a carbohydrate that consists of just one ring. *True/False*

26 Polysaccharides are built up of _____.

27 The disaccharide, sucrose, is composed of _____ and _____.

28 Starch is a polymer of glucose. *True/False*

29 Humans cannot use cellulose as food because cellulose is a polymer of fructose. *True/False*

30 Nucleotides are the monomers from which the polymers ____ and ____ are built up.

31 Nucleotides consist of a _____, _____, and a
_____.

32 The sugar in DNA is _____.

33 The sugar in RNA is _____.

34 The four bases in DNA are _____, _____, _____,
and _____.

35 Uracil is found in RNA but not in DNA. *True/False*

36 Two nucleotides can be joined by a condensation reaction between the
_____ of one nucleotide and the _____ on another
nucleotide.

37 The sugar-phosphate backbone is the same for all polynucleotides. *True/False*

38 The order of the attachment of the bases to the sugar-phosphate backbone is the
same for all polynucleotides. *True/False*

39 The two polynucleotide chains in DNA are arranged as a _____
_____.

40 In DNA, the amount of guanine is equal to the amount of _____.

41 In DNA, adenine on one chain is always paired with _____ on the
other chain.

42 The two chains in DNA are joined together by _____ bonds.

43 Each strand of DNA acts as a template for reproducing itself. *True/False*

44 Genetic information for the production of _____ is stored
in DNA.

45 Each amino acid is coded by a sequence of _____ base pairs on the DNA
segment.

C CALCULATIONS YOU SHOULD KNOW HOW TO DO

There are no calculations in this chapter. You should know how to:

1 Write reactions between amino acids to form peptides. See Example 26-1 and
Problems 26-5 through 26-10.

2 Write protein structures given the amino acid sequence. See Example 26-2 and
Problems 26-11 through 26-16.

3 Write formulas and condensation reactions of polysaccharides. See Example
26-4 and Problems 26-25 through 26-32.

4   Write polynucleotide formulas. See Problems 26-33 through 26-36.

5   Determine base sequences in double helices. See Examples 26-6 and 26-7 and Problems 26-37 through 26-44.

D   ANSWERS TO THE ODD-NUMBERED PROBLEMS

26-1   (a) No (The four substituent must be different.)

(b) No

(c)

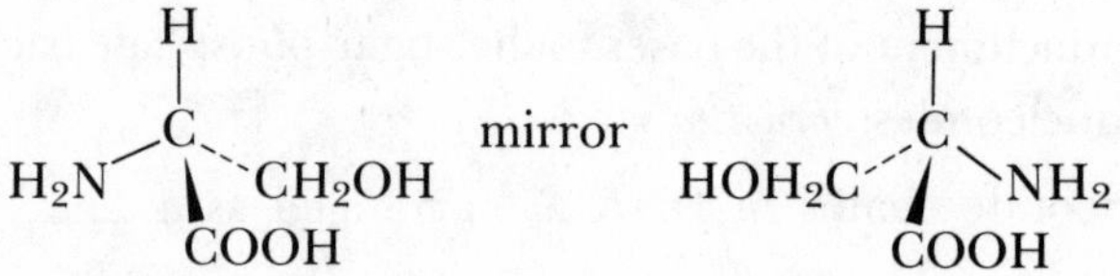

$$H_2N-\overset{\overset{\displaystyle H}{|}}{\underset{\underset{\displaystyle COOH}{|}}{C}}-CH_2OH \qquad mirror \qquad HOH_2C-\overset{\overset{\displaystyle H}{|}}{\underset{\underset{\displaystyle COOH}{|}}{C}}-NH_2$$

(d)

$$Br-\overset{\overset{\displaystyle H}{|}}{\underset{\underset{\displaystyle COOH}{|}}{C}}-Cl \qquad Cl-\overset{\overset{\displaystyle H}{|}}{\underset{\underset{\displaystyle COOH}{|}}{C}}-Br$$

(e)

$$H_3CH_2C-\overset{\overset{\displaystyle CH_3}{|}}{\underset{\underset{\displaystyle Br}{|}}{Si}}-Cl \qquad Cl-\overset{\overset{\displaystyle CH_3}{|}}{\underset{\underset{\displaystyle Br}{|}}{Si}}-CH_2CH_3$$

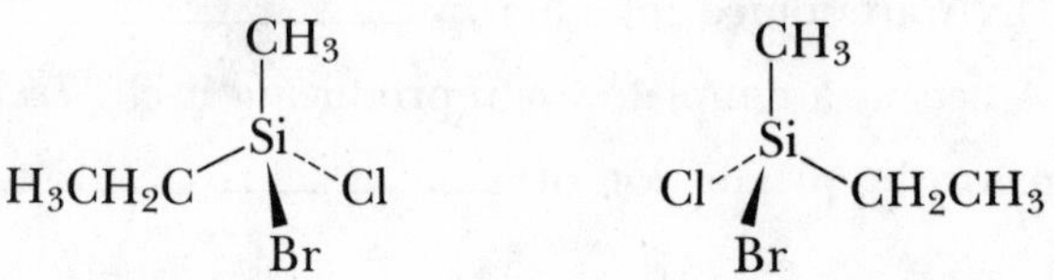

26-3   From Table 26-1 we find that the formula for the side group aspartic acid is

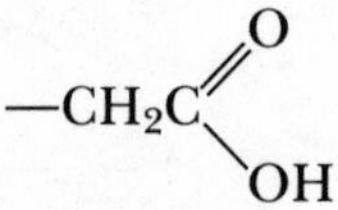

$$-CH_2C\overset{\displaystyle O}{\underset{\displaystyle OH}{\diagup}}$$

Recall that $-C\overset{\displaystyle O}{\underset{\displaystyle OH}{\diagup}}$ or $-COOH$ is the carboxylic acid group. Aspartic acid dissociates in water according to

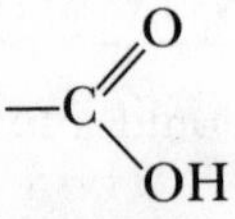

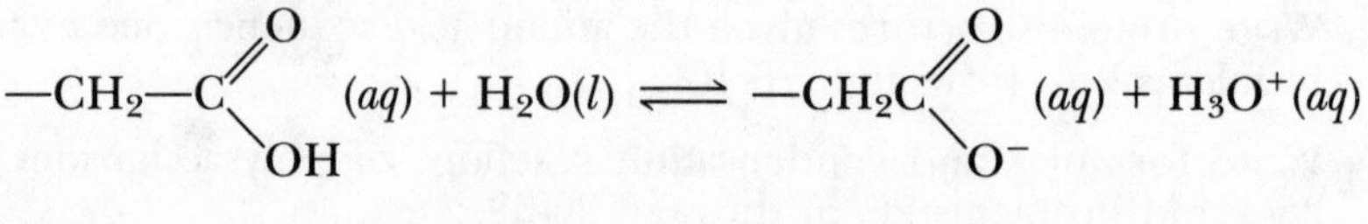

$$-CH_2-C\overset{\displaystyle O}{\underset{\displaystyle OH}{\diagup}}(aq) + H_2O(l) \rightleftharpoons -CH_2C\overset{\displaystyle O}{\underset{\displaystyle O^-}{\diagup}}(aq) + H_3O^+(aq)$$

26-5 We find the formulas for isoleucine and methionine in Table 26-1. One possible reaction is

$$
\begin{array}{c}
\quad\;\; H \quad \overset{..}{\underset{..}{O}} \qquad\qquad\qquad H \\
\quad\;\; | \qquad \| \qquad\qquad\qquad | \\
H_2N\!-\!C\!-\!C\!-\!\boxed{OH + H}\!-\!\overset{..}{N}\!-\!C\!-\!COOH \qquad \longrightarrow \\
\quad\;\; | \qquad\qquad\qquad\qquad | \quad\; | \\
\quad\; CHCH_2CH_3 \qquad\qquad H \;\; CH_2CH_2SCH_3 \\
\quad\;\; | \\
\quad\; CH_3
\end{array}
$$

$$
\begin{array}{c}
\qquad\qquad\qquad\qquad H \quad \overset{..}{\underset{..}{O}} \qquad\qquad H \\
\qquad\qquad\qquad\qquad | \qquad \| \qquad\qquad | \\
\qquad\qquad\qquad H_2N\!-\!C\!-\!C\!-\!\overset{..}{N}\!-\!C\!-\!COOH + H_2O \\
\qquad\qquad\qquad\qquad | \qquad\qquad\; | \quad\; | \\
\qquad\qquad\qquad CH_3CH_2CH \qquad\;\; H \;\; CH_2CH_2SCH_3 \\
\qquad\qquad\qquad\qquad\qquad | \\
\qquad\qquad\qquad\qquad\;\; CH_3
\end{array}
$$

The second possible reaction is

$$
\begin{array}{c}
\quad\;\; H \quad \overset{..}{\underset{..}{O}} \qquad\qquad\qquad H \\
\quad\;\; | \qquad \| \qquad\qquad\qquad | \\
H_2N\!-\!C\!-\!C\!-\!\boxed{OH + H}\!-\!\overset{..}{N}\!-\!C\!-\!COOH \longrightarrow \\
\quad\;\; | \qquad\qquad\qquad\qquad | \quad\; | \\
\quad CH_2CH_2SCH_3 \qquad\;\; H \;\; CHCH_2CH_3 \\
\qquad\qquad\qquad\qquad\qquad\qquad | \\
\qquad\qquad\qquad\qquad\qquad\; CH_3
\end{array}
$$

$$
\begin{array}{c}
\qquad\qquad\qquad\qquad H \quad \overset{..}{\underset{..}{O}} \qquad\qquad H \\
\qquad\qquad\qquad\qquad | \qquad \| \qquad\qquad | \\
\qquad\qquad\qquad H_2N\!-\!C\!-\!C\!-\!\overset{..}{N}\!-\!C\!-\!COOH + H_2O \\
\qquad\qquad\qquad\qquad | \qquad\qquad | \quad\; | \\
\qquad\qquad\; CH_3SCH_2CH_2 \qquad H \;\; CHCH_2CH_3 \\
\qquad\qquad\qquad\qquad\qquad\qquad\qquad | \\
\qquad\qquad\qquad\qquad\qquad\qquad\; CH_3
\end{array}
$$

26-7 Two different dipeptides result because we can form the peptide bond in two ways depending on which carboxyl and amino groups are linked:

$$
\begin{array}{c}
\quad\;\; H \quad \overset{..}{\underset{..}{O}} \qquad\; H \\
\quad\;\; | \qquad \| \qquad\;\; | \\
H_2N\!-\!C\!-\!C\!-\!\overset{..}{N}\!-\!C\!-\!COOH \\
\quad\;\; | \qquad\qquad | \quad | \\
\quad\;\; H \qquad\qquad H \; CH_3 \\
\quad\; \text{gly} \qquad\qquad \text{ala}
\end{array}
$$

or

$$
\begin{array}{c}
\quad\;\; H \quad \overset{..}{\underset{..}{O}} \qquad\; H \\
\quad\;\; | \qquad \| \qquad\;\; | \\
H_2N\!-\!C\!-\!C\!-\!\overset{..}{N}\!-\!C\!-\!COOH \\
\quad\;\; | \qquad\qquad | \quad | \\
\quad CH_3 \qquad\quad H \; H \\
\quad\; \text{ala} \qquad\qquad \text{gly}
\end{array}
$$

26-9 We can form six different tripeptides from two different amino acids. If we represent the side groups of the two amino acids by G_1 and G_2, then the tripeptides are

$$H_2N-\underset{G_1}{\overset{H}{C}}-\overset{O}{C}-\underset{H}{\overset{}{N}}-\underset{G_1}{\overset{H}{C}}-\overset{O}{C}-\underset{H}{\overset{}{N}}-\underset{G_2}{\overset{H}{C}}-COOH$$

$$H_2N-\underset{G_1}{\overset{H}{C}}-\overset{O}{C}-\underset{H}{\overset{}{N}}-\underset{G_2}{\overset{H}{C}}-\overset{O}{C}-\underset{H}{\overset{}{N}}-\underset{G_1}{\overset{H}{C}}-COOH$$

$$H_2N-\underset{G_2}{\overset{H}{C}}-\overset{O}{C}-\underset{H}{\overset{}{N}}-\underset{G_1}{\overset{H}{C}}-\overset{O}{C}-\underset{H}{\overset{}{N}}-\underset{G_1}{\overset{H}{C}}-COOH$$

$$H_2N-\underset{G_2}{\overset{H}{C}}-\overset{O}{C}-\underset{H}{\overset{}{N}}-\underset{G_2}{\overset{H}{C}}-\overset{O}{C}-\underset{H}{\overset{}{N}}-\underset{G_1}{\overset{H}{C}}-COOH$$

$$H_2N-\underset{G_2}{\overset{H}{C}}-\overset{O}{C}-\underset{H}{\overset{}{N}}-\underset{G_1}{\overset{H}{C}}-\overset{O}{C}-\underset{H}{\overset{}{N}}-\underset{G_2}{\overset{H}{C}}-COOH$$

$$H_2N-\underset{G_1}{\overset{H}{C}}-\overset{O}{C}-\underset{H}{\overset{}{N}}-\underset{G_2}{\overset{H}{C}}-\overset{O}{C}-\underset{H}{\overset{}{N}}-\underset{G_2}{\overset{H}{C}}-COOH$$

26-11 Referring to Table 26-1, we find that glu, arg, and trp are the amino acids glutamic acid, arginine and tryptophan. The structural formula for the tripeptide is

$$H_2N-\overset{H}{\underset{\substack{CH_2\\CH_2\\\underset{HO}{C}\underset{O}{}}}{C}}-\overset{O}{C}-\underset{H}{N}-\overset{H}{\underset{\substack{CH_2\\CH_2\\CH_2\\H-N-CNH_2\\\|\\NH}}{C}}-\overset{O}{C}-\underset{H}{N}-\overset{H}{\underset{CH_2}{C}}-COOH$$

glu   arg   trp

26-13 Referring to Table 26-1, we find that tyr, gly, phe, and leu are the amino acids tyrosine, glycine, phenylalanine, and leucine. The structural formula for leu-enkephalin is

26-15 The structural formula for oxytocin is

Notice that the free amino group is on the right in the text. When drawing structural formulas of proteins, we always start with the free amino group on the left. Thus the structural formula for vasopressin is

26-17 Amino acids with polar or charged side groups will occur on the surface of a protein. The amino acids cys, arg, and gln have polar side groups.

26-19 Amino acids with nonpolar side groups cluster in the interior of a protein. Thus the amino acids leu and phe will cluster in the interior of a protein.

26-21 (a) The oxygen can form a hydrogen bond to a hydrogen atom in H_2O.
(b) There are none.
(c) The nitrogen atom can form a hydrogen bond to a hydrogen atom in H_2O.
(d) The two oxygen atoms can form hydrogen bonds to hydrogen atoms in H_2O.
(e) There are none.

26-23 The primary structure of a protein is the order of amino acid units in the protein.
The secondary structure is the structure within sections of the protein.
The tertiary structure is the overall three-dimensional shape of the protein.

26-25 The structural formula for lactose given in the text shows that it is a disaccharide. The reaction between the two monosaccharides that produces lactose is

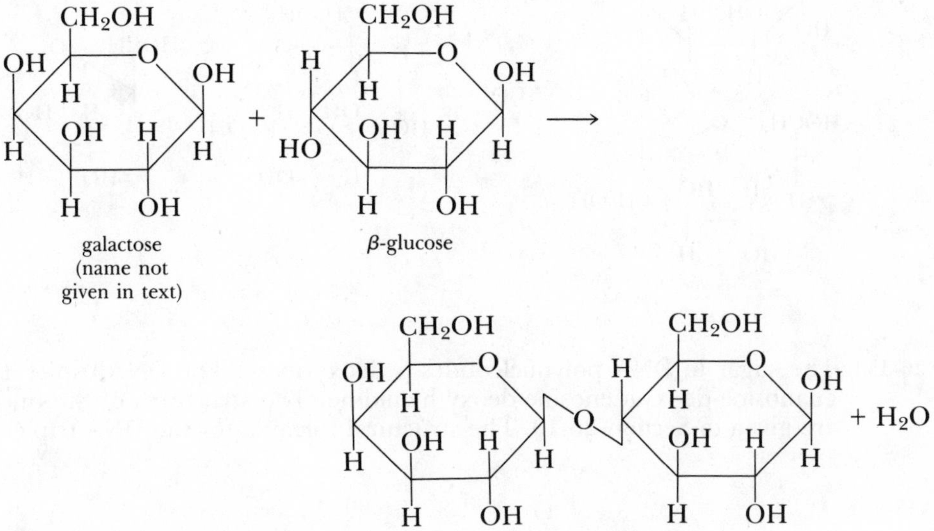

CH$_2$OH

OH
H
OH H
H H
H OH

galactose
(name not
given in text)

+

CH$_2$OH

H
H
HO OH H
H
H OH

β-glucose

$\longrightarrow$

CH$_2$OH

OH
H
OH H
H H
H OH

O

CH$_2$OH

H
H
OH H
H OH
H OH

+ H$_2$O

lactose

26-27 The structural formula for melzitose is (refer to Section 26-9 for the sugar structures)

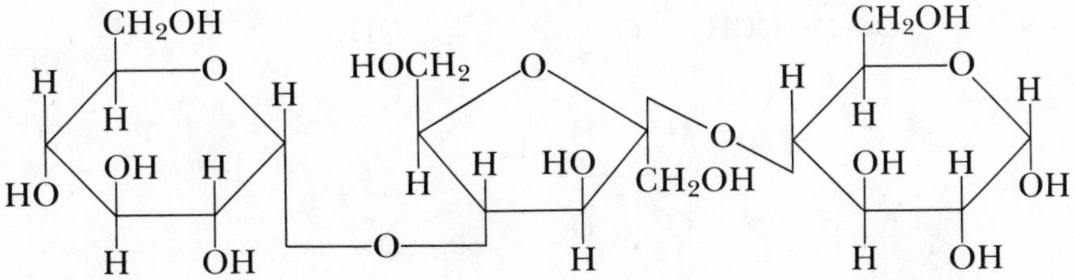

CH$_2$OH

H
H
HO OH H
H OH
H OH

α-glucose

HOCH$_2$ O

H H HO
H CH$_2$OH
H

O

β-fructose

CH$_2$OH

H
H
OH H
H OH
H OH

α-glucose

26-29 The molecular mass of α-glucose ($C_6H_{12}O_6$) is 180. The molecular mass of the amylose polymer is

$$\text{molecular mass} = \text{number of } \alpha\text{-glucose units} \times 180$$

Thus

$$\text{number of } \alpha\text{-glucose units} = \frac{200{,}000}{180} = 1111 \approx 1100$$

26-31

sucrose α-glucose β-fructose

26-33   The sugar in DNA polynucleotides is deoxyribose. The DNA triplet is deoxy-guanosine-deoxyadenosine-deoxythymidine. The structures of the nucleotides are given in Section 26-10. The structural formula for the DNA triplet GAT is

26-35 The sugar in RNA is ribose. The RNA triplet UCU is uridine-cytidine-uridine. The structural formula for the RNA triplet UCU is

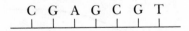

26-37 The two sequences must be complementary to each other: A and T must be opposite to each other, and G and C must be opposite to each other. The other sequence must have the base sequence CAAGGGTTC.

26-39 We must have T and A opposite each other and G and C opposite each other. The complementary base sequence is

$$
\begin{array}{ccccccc}
\text{C} & \text{G} & \text{A} & \text{G} & \text{C} & \text{G} & \text{T}
\end{array}
$$

26-41 The two strands come apart to give

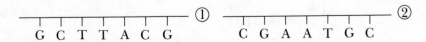

The complements to the two stands are

||||||| ① ||||||| ②
G C T T A C G   C G A A T G C
C G A A T G C   G C T T A C G

26-43   There are two hydrogen bonds for each A–T pair and three hydrogen bonds for each G–C pair. The DNA sequence has four A–T pairs and two G–C pairs. The number of hydrogen bonds in the sequence is

$$\text{number of H bonds} = (4 \times 2) + (2 \times 3) = 14$$

Fourteen hydrogen bonds must be broken to separate the strands.

26-45   The structural formula for the zwitterionic form of alanine is

$$\overset{\displaystyle H}{\underset{\displaystyle CH_3}{H_3\overset{+}{N}-\overset{|}{\underset{|}{C}}-COO^-}}$$

26-47   When [S] is small, the value of $(k_{-1} + k_2)/k_1$ will be much larger than [S]. Thus we can neglect [S] in the denominator. For small [S], the rate law is approximately

$$\text{rate} \simeq \frac{k_2[E_0][S]}{\left(\dfrac{k_{-1} + k_2}{k_1}\right)} = C[S]$$

The rate is proportional to [S]; thus the graph is a straight line. When [S] is large, the value of $(k_{-1} + k_2)/k_1$ will be much smaller than [S]. Thus we can neglect $(k_{-1} + k_2)/k_1$ in the denominator. For large [S], the rate law is approximately

$$\text{rate} \approx \frac{k_2[E_0][S]}{[S]} = k_2[E_0] = \text{constant}$$

The rate is constant for a fixed value of $[E_0]$. We connect the two sections of the plot by a curved line. So the plot looks like

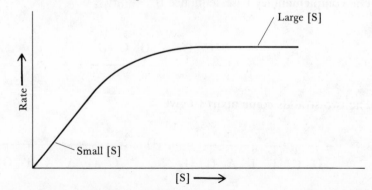

26-49   For large [S]

$$\frac{k_{-1} + k_2}{k_1} + [S] \approx [S]$$

Thus

$$\text{rate} = \frac{k_2[E_0][S]}{\dfrac{k_{-1} + k_2}{k_1} + [S]} \approx \frac{k_2[E_0][S]}{[S]} = k_2[E_0]$$

Reference to Problem 26-47 shows that k_2 is the rate constant for the process

$$ES(aq) \xrightarrow{k_2} E(aq) + P(aq)$$

The units of k_2 are s^{-1}. When all of the enzyme molecules are combined with substrate molecules, the rate is constant and a maximum for the given value of $[E_0]$. Hence

$$k_2 = \frac{\text{rate}}{[E_0]} = \frac{M \cdot s^{-1}}{M} = \frac{\text{molecules of substrate} \cdot s^{-1}}{\text{molecules of enzyme}}$$

Thus the value of k_2 is the number of molecules of substrate that react per second per enzyme molecule.

26-51   The limiting reaction rate is given by

$$\text{rate} = k[E_0]$$

The value of k for acetylcholine esterase is $25,000\ s^{-1}$. Thus we have

$$\text{rate} = \frac{2.5 \times 10^{-5}\ \text{mol} \cdot s^{-1}}{1.0 \times 10^{-3}\ L} = (25,000\ s^{-1})[E_0]$$

$$[E_0] = \frac{2.5 \times 10^{-2}\ \text{mol} \cdot L^{-1} \cdot s^{-1}}{25,000\ s^{-1}}$$

$$= 1.0 \times 10^{-6}\ M$$

26-53   We learned in Chapter 22 that the maximum amount of work that can be obtained from 1.0 g of glucose under standard conditions is equal to the value of ΔG°_{rxn}. Thus

$$\text{work} = \Delta G^\circ_{rxn} = (2.87 \times 10^3\ \text{kJ} \cdot \text{mol}^{-1})\left(\frac{1\ \text{mol}}{180.16\ \text{g}}\right)(1.0\ \text{g})$$

$$= 15.9\ \text{kJ}$$

26-55 We can obtain the equation for the combustion of sucrose from the three equations given:

$$\text{sucrose}(aq) + H_2O(l) \longrightarrow \text{glucose}(aq) + \text{fructose}(aq)$$
$$\Delta G^\circ_{rxn} = -29.3 \text{ kJ}$$

$$\text{fructose}(aq) \longrightarrow \text{glucose}(aq)$$
$$\Delta G^\circ_{rxn} = -1.6 \text{ kJ}$$

$$2 \text{ glucose}(aq) + 12O_2(g) \longrightarrow 12CO_2(g) + 12H_2O(l)$$
$$\Delta G^\circ_{rxn} = (2)(-2.87 \times 10^3 \text{ kJ}) = -5.74 \times 10^3 \text{ kJ}$$

If we add these three equations, then we have

$$\text{sucrose}(aq) + 12O_2(g) \longrightarrow 12CO_2(g) + 11H_2O(l)$$
$$\Delta G^\circ_{rxn} = -29.3 \text{ kJ} - 1.6 \text{ kJ} - 5.74 \times 10^3 \text{ kJ}$$
$$= -5.77 \times 10^3 \text{ kJ}$$

The value of ΔG°_{rxn} for one mole of sucrose is -5.77×10^3 kJ.

The value of ΔG°_{rxn} for 1.0 g of sucrose is

$$\Delta G^\circ_{rxn} = (-5.77 \times 10^3 \text{ kJ} \cdot \text{mol}^{-1})\left(\frac{1 \text{ mol}}{342.3 \text{ g}}\right) = -16.9 \text{ kJ} \cdot \text{g}^{-1}$$

E   ANSWERS TO THE EVEN-NUMBERED PROBLEMS

26-2 (a), (c), (e)

26-4 $RNH_2(aq) + H_2O(l) \rightleftharpoons RNH_3^+(aq) + OH^-(aq)$

26-6 One possible reaction between the two amino acids is

The second possible reaction is

$$H_2N-\underset{\underset{CH_2CH_2CH_2CH_2NH_2}{|}}{\overset{\overset{H}{|}}{C}}-\underset{}{\overset{\overset{\cdot\cdot\overset{\cdot\cdot}{O}}{\|}}{C}}-\boxed{OH} \quad + \quad H-\underset{\underset{H}{|}}{\overset{\overset{H}{|}}{N}}-\underset{\underset{\underset{OH}{|}}{CHCH_3}}{\overset{|}{C}}-COOH \longrightarrow$$

$$H_2N-\underset{\underset{\underset{\underset{\underset{NH_2}{|}}{CH_2}}{|}}{\overset{\underset{CH_2}{|}}{\underset{CH_2}{|}}}}{\overset{\overset{H}{|}}{C}}-\overset{\overset{\cdot\cdot\overset{\cdot\cdot}{O}}{\|}}{C}-\underset{\underset{H}{|}}{\overset{\cdot\cdot}{N}}-\underset{\underset{\underset{OH}{|}}{CHCH_3}}{\overset{\overset{H}{|}}{C}}-COOH + H_2O$$

26-8

$$H_2N-\underset{\underset{\underset{CH_3}{|}}{CHCH_3}}{\overset{\overset{H}{|}}{C}}-\overset{\overset{\cdot\cdot\overset{\cdot\cdot}{O}}{\|}}{C}-\underset{\underset{H}{|}}{\overset{\cdot\cdot}{N}}-\underset{\underset{\underset{O}{\|}}{CH_2-C-NH_2}}{\overset{\overset{H}{|}}{C}}-COOH$$

$$\underset{\text{val}}{} \qquad\qquad \underset{\text{asn}}{}$$

$$H_2N-\underset{\underset{\underset{O}{\|}}{CH_2C-NH_2}}{\overset{\overset{H}{|}}{C}}-\overset{\overset{\cdot\cdot\overset{\cdot\cdot}{O}}{\|}}{C}-\underset{\underset{H}{|}}{\overset{\cdot\cdot}{N}}-\underset{\underset{\underset{CH_3}{|}}{CHCH_3}}{\overset{\overset{H}{|}}{C}}-COOH$$

$$\underset{\text{asn}}{} \qquad\qquad \underset{\text{val}}{}$$

26-10 We can form six tripeptides from three different amino acids. If we represent the side groups of the three amino acids by G_1, G_2, and G_3, then the tripeptides are

$$H_2N-\underset{\underset{G_1.}{|}}{\overset{\overset{H}{|}}{C}}-\overset{\overset{\cdot\cdot\overset{\cdot\cdot}{O}}{\|}}{C}-\underset{\underset{H}{|}}{\overset{\cdot\cdot}{N}}-\underset{\underset{G_2}{|}}{\overset{\overset{H}{|}}{C}}-\overset{\overset{\cdot\cdot\overset{\cdot\cdot}{O}}{\|}}{C}-\underset{\underset{H}{|}}{\overset{\cdot\cdot}{N}}-\underset{\underset{G_3}{|}}{\overset{\overset{H}{|}}{C}}-COOH$$

$$H_2N-\underset{\underset{G_1}{|}}{\overset{\overset{H}{|}}{C}}-\overset{\overset{\cdot\cdot\overset{\cdot\cdot}{O}}{\|}}{C}-\underset{\underset{H}{|}}{\overset{\cdot\cdot}{N}}-\underset{\underset{G_3}{|}}{\overset{\overset{H}{|}}{C}}-\overset{\overset{\cdot\cdot\overset{\cdot\cdot}{O}}{\|}}{C}-\underset{\underset{H}{|}}{\overset{\cdot\cdot}{N}}-\underset{\underset{G_2}{|}}{\overset{\overset{H}{|}}{C}}-COOH$$

$$H_2N-\underset{\underset{G_2}{|}}{\overset{\overset{H}{|}}{C}}-\overset{\overset{\cdot\cdot\overset{\cdot\cdot}{O}}{\|}}{C}-\underset{\underset{H}{|}}{\overset{\cdot\cdot}{N}}-\underset{\underset{G_1}{|}}{\overset{\overset{H}{|}}{C}}-\overset{\overset{\cdot\cdot\overset{\cdot\cdot}{O}}{\|}}{C}-\underset{\underset{H}{|}}{\overset{\cdot\cdot}{N}}-\underset{\underset{G_3}{|}}{\overset{\overset{H}{|}}{C}}-COOH$$

$$\text{H}_2\text{N}-\overset{\overset{\displaystyle H}{|}}{\underset{\underset{\displaystyle G_2}{|}}{C}}-\overset{\overset{\displaystyle \ddot{O}}{\|}}{C}-\overset{\overset{\displaystyle H}{|}}{\underset{\underset{\displaystyle H}{|}}{N}}-\overset{\overset{\displaystyle H}{|}}{\underset{\underset{\displaystyle G_3}{|}}{C}}-\overset{\overset{\displaystyle \ddot{O}}{\|}}{C}-\overset{\overset{\displaystyle H}{|}}{\underset{\underset{\displaystyle H}{|}}{N}}-\overset{\overset{\displaystyle H}{|}}{\underset{\underset{\displaystyle G_1}{|}}{C}}-\text{COOH}$$

$$\text{H}_2\text{N}-\overset{\overset{\displaystyle H}{|}}{\underset{\underset{\displaystyle G_3}{|}}{C}}-\overset{\overset{\displaystyle \ddot{O}}{\|}}{C}-\overset{\overset{\displaystyle H}{|}}{\underset{\underset{\displaystyle H}{|}}{N}}-\overset{\overset{\displaystyle H}{|}}{\underset{\underset{\displaystyle G_1}{|}}{C}}-\overset{\overset{\displaystyle \ddot{O}}{\|}}{C}-\overset{\overset{\displaystyle H}{|}}{\underset{\underset{\displaystyle H}{|}}{N}}-\overset{\overset{\displaystyle H}{|}}{\underset{\underset{\displaystyle G_2}{|}}{C}}-\text{COOH}$$

$$\text{H}_2\text{N}-\overset{\overset{\displaystyle H}{|}}{\underset{\underset{\displaystyle G_3}{|}}{C}}-\overset{\overset{\displaystyle \ddot{O}}{\|}}{C}-\overset{\overset{\displaystyle H}{|}}{\underset{\underset{\displaystyle H}{|}}{N}}-\overset{\overset{\displaystyle H}{|}}{\underset{\underset{\displaystyle G_2}{|}}{C}}-\overset{\overset{\displaystyle \ddot{O}}{\|}}{C}-\overset{\overset{\displaystyle H}{|}}{\underset{\underset{\displaystyle H}{|}}{N}}-\overset{\overset{\displaystyle H}{|}}{\underset{\underset{\displaystyle G_1}{|}}{C}}-\text{COOH}$$

26-12

Structure 26-12: Peptide with side chains CH₂—C(=O)—NH₂ (Asn), CHCH₃/CH₃ (Ile), and CH₂SH (Cys).

26-14

Structure 26-14: Pentapeptide with side chains CH₂—C₆H₄—OH (Tyr), H, H, CH₂—C₆H₅ (Phe), and CH₂CH₂SCH₃ (Met).

26-16

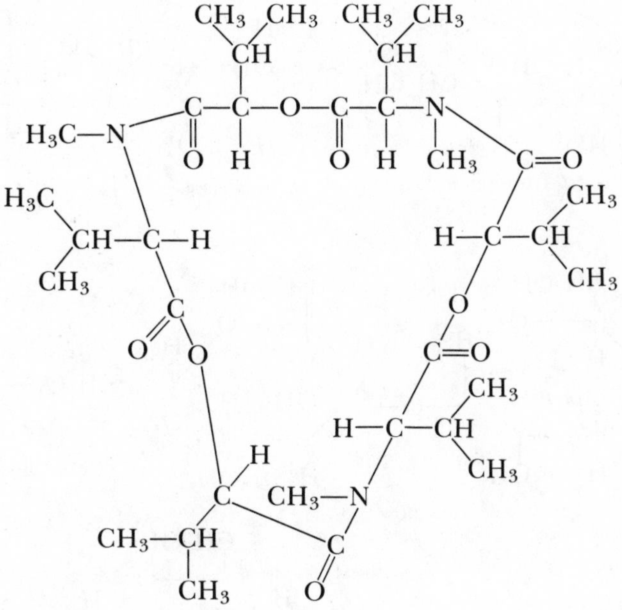

26-18   lys, asn

26-20   val, pro

26-22   (a) The oxygen atom
  (b) The oxygen atom
  (c) The oxygen atom and the nitrogen atom
  (d) The two oxygen atoms
  (e) None

26-24   Factors that govern the secondary and tertiary structures of proteins are
  (1) the presence of disulfide bonds
  (2) hydrogen bonds within the peptide backbone
  (3) interactions between the amino acid side groups and the solvent, water

26-26

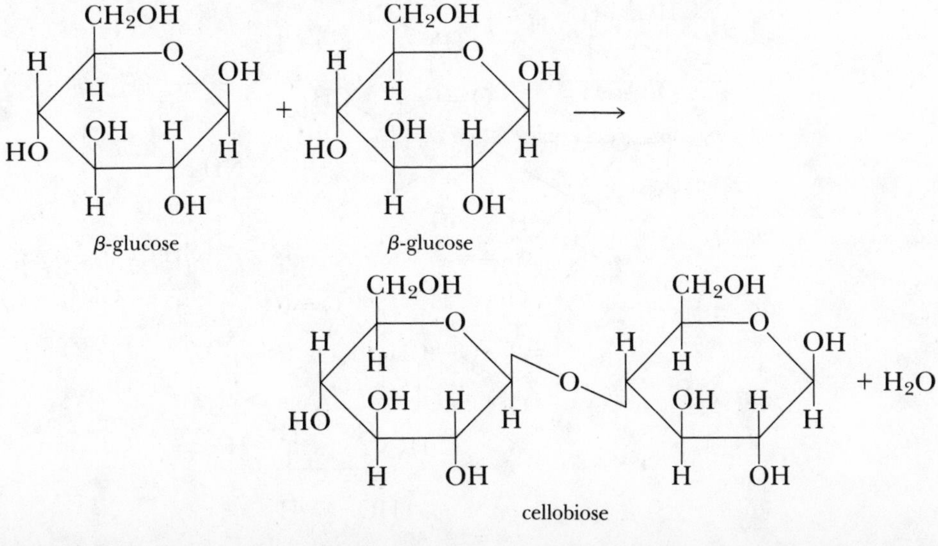

β-glucose   β-glucose

cellobiose

26-28

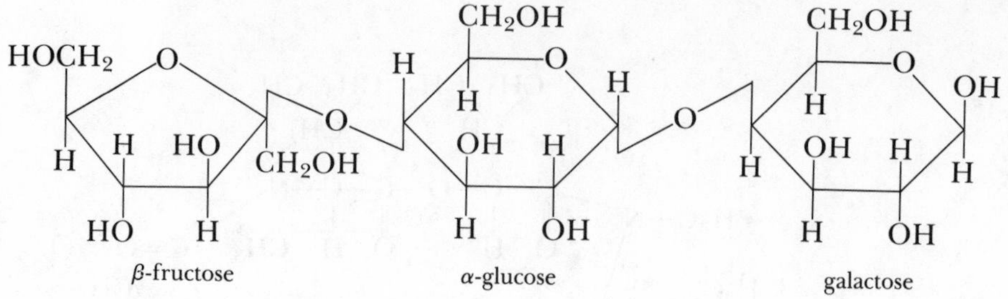

β-fructose   α-glucose   galactose

26-30   3100

26-32

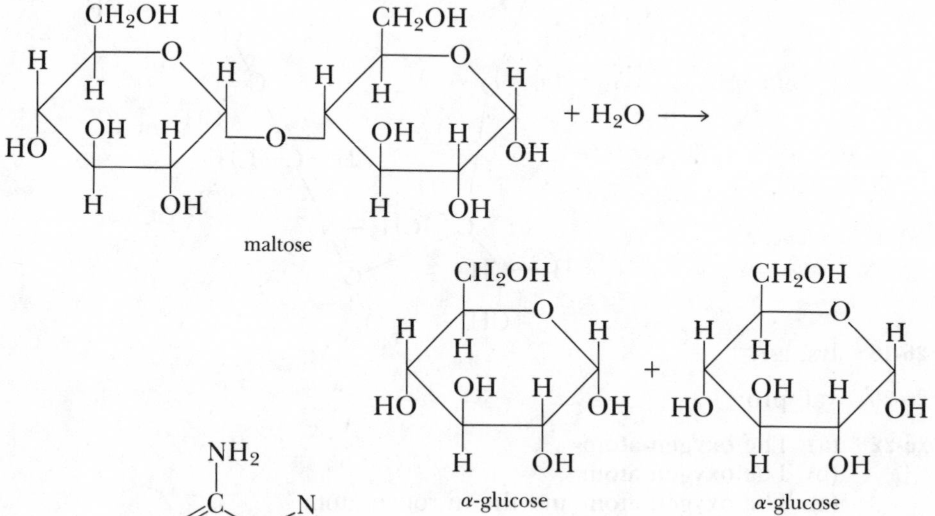

maltose

+ H₂O ⟶

α-glucose   α-glucose

26-34

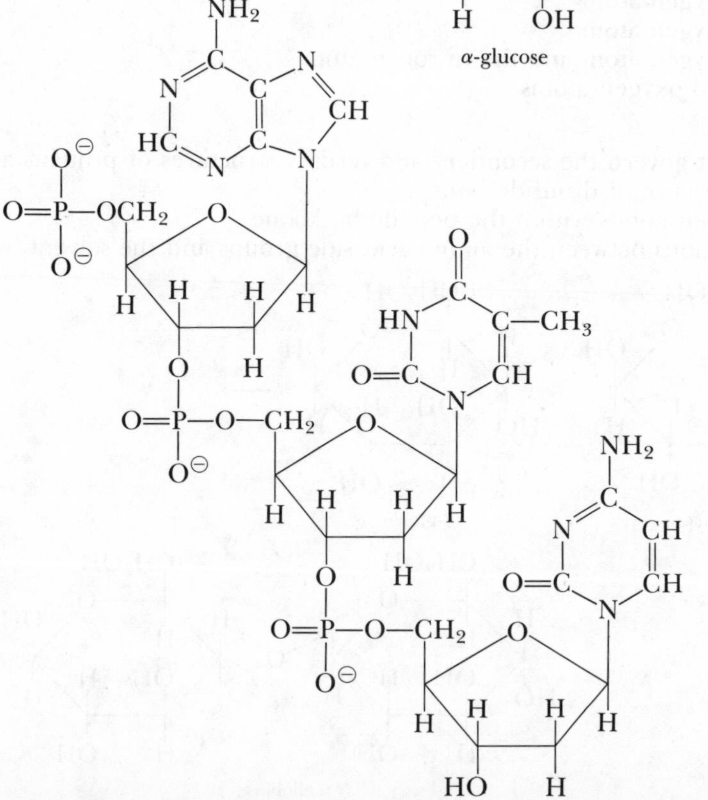

26-36

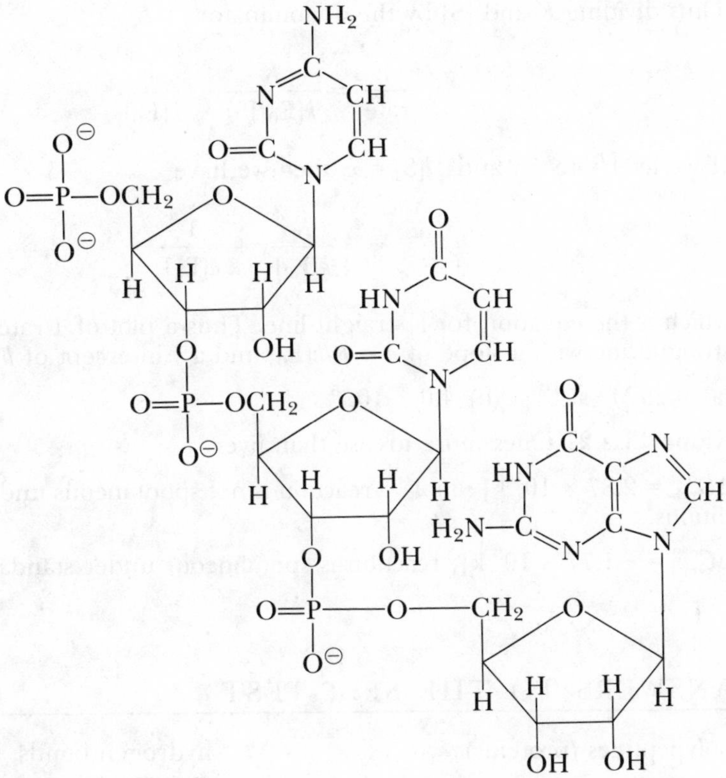

26-38 GTACCGATT

26-40 TTCGCAT

26-42

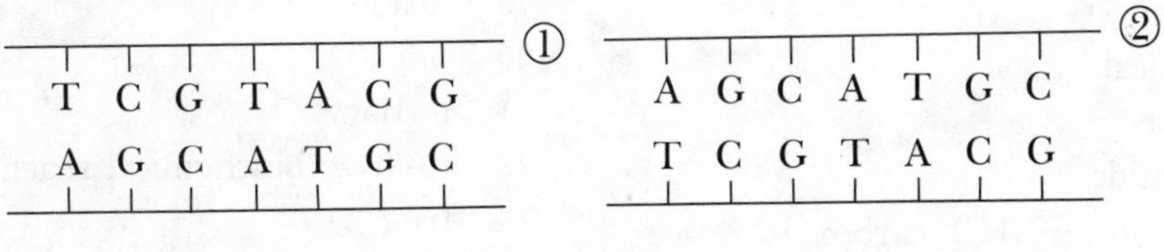

26-44 18

26-46

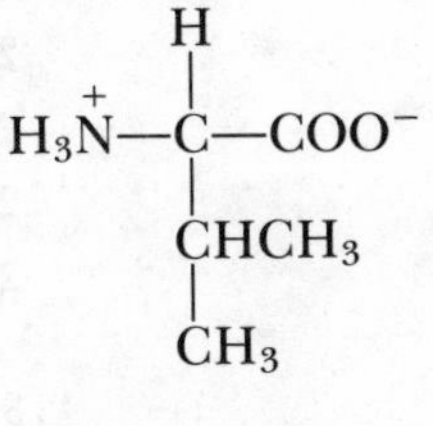

26-48 The rate law in terms of 1/rate is given by

$$\frac{1}{\text{rate}} = \frac{K + [S]}{k[E_0][S]}$$

Thus dividing K and [S] by the denominator

$$\frac{1}{\text{rate}} = \frac{K}{k[E_0][S]} + \frac{1}{k[E_0]}$$

If we let $1/\text{rate} = y$ and $1/[S] = x$, then we have

$$y = \frac{K}{k[E_0]}x + \frac{1}{k[E_0]}$$

which is the equation for a straight line. Thus a plot of $1/\text{rate}$ versus $1/[S]$ is a straight line with a slope of $a = K/k[E_0]$ and a y intercept of $b = 1/k[E_0]$.

26-50   (a) $0.25 \text{ M} \cdot \text{s}^{-1}$ (b) 4.0×10^{-5} s

26-52   Kidney has 21 times more urease than liver.

26-54 $\Delta G_{rxn}^{\circ} = 2.87 \times 10^3 \text{ kJ} \cdot \text{mol}^{-1}$; reaction is not spontaneous under standard conditions.

26-56 $\Delta G_{rxn}^{\circ} = -1.77 \times 10^3 \text{ kJ}$; reaction is spontaneous under standard conditions.

F   ANSWERS TO THE SELF-TEST

1 polypeptides (proteins)

2 $H_2N-\overset{\overset{\displaystyle H}{|}}{\underset{\underset{\displaystyle G}{|}}{C}}-COOH$

3 optical

4 false

5 peptide

6 amino ($-NH_2$), carboxyl ($-COOH$)

7 true

8 false

9 true

10 false

11 true

12 peptides

13 false

14 disulfide

15 cysteine

16 true

17 hydrogen bonds, hydrogen and oxygen atoms in the peptide bonds

18 secondary

19 inside

20 outside

21 tertiary

22 catalyze biochemical reactions

23 true

24 $-(CH_2O)_n-$

25 true

26 monosaccharides

27 glucose and fructose

28 true

29 false (Cellulose is a polymer of glucose.)

30 RNA and DNA

31 sugar, phosphate group, and a base

32 deoxyribose

33 ribose

34 guanine, cytosine, adenine, thymine

35 true

36 phosphate group, 3-hydroxyl group

37 false (The sugar-phosphate backbone is the same in all DNA and the sugar-phosphate backbone is the same in all RNA. The sugars are not the same in DNA and RNA.)

38 false

39 double helix

40 cytosine

41 thymine

42 hydrogen

43 true

44 proteins

45 three

Glossary

A

absolute temperature scale (164): the fundamental temperature scale. The absolute temperature scale is related to the more familiar Celsius scale. The temperature on the absolute temperature scale is found by adding 273.15°C to the temperature on the Celsius scale. The unit of absolute temperature is the kelvin, K. The absolute temperature scale is also called the Kelvin scale.

absorption spectrum (270): the spectrum obtained when atoms or molecules absorb electromagnetic radiation and are raised to excited states.

acid (130): a compound that yields hydrogen ions when it is dissolved in water.

acid dissociation constant, K_a (658): the equilibrium constant for the proton-transfer reaction between an acid and water. For the general reaction

$$HB(aq) + H_2O(l) \rightleftharpoons B^-(aq) + H_3O^+(aq)$$

$$K_a = \frac{[B^-][H_3O^+]}{[HB]}$$

acid dissociation reaction (657): the proton-transfer reaction between an acid and water. The general reaction is

$$HB(aq) + H_2O(l) \rightleftharpoons B^-(aq) + H_3O^+(aq)$$

acidic anhydride (130): an oxide that yields an acid when it is dissolved in water.

acidic anion (672): an anion that reacts with water to produce $H_3O^+(aq)$ in aqueous solution.

acidic cation (672): a cation that reacts with water to form $H_3O^+(aq)$ in aqueous solution.

acidic hydrogen atom (148): a hydrogen atom in a species that dissociates in solution to become a proton.

acidic proton (130): a dissociable hydrogen atom in a species.

acidic solution (649): an aqueous solution in which $[H_3O^+] > [OH^-]$.

acidity (652): a measure of the concentration of $H_3O^+(aq)$ in an aqueous solution.

actinide series (57, 60, 306): the inner transition series that is headed by actinium. The actinide series contains the elements actinium $(Z = 89)$ through nobelium $(Z = 102)$.

actinides (60): the 14-member series of elements that starts with actinium $(Z = 89)$ and ends with nobelium $(Z = 102)$.

activation energy, E_a (624): the minimum energy necessary to cause a reaction between the colliding reactant molecules.

addition of reactions (590): the process of obtaining a reaction by adding together two other reactions. The equilibrium constant of the resulting reaction is the product of the equilibrium constants of the two reactions that are added together.

addition polymerization reaction (1022): a reaction that involves a direct addition of monomer molecules to form a polymer chain.

addition reaction (996): a reaction in which atoms or molecules are added to a molecule.

alcohol (998): an organic compound that contains an —OH group attached to a hydrocarbon chain.

aldehyde (1004): a class of organic compounds that has the general formula RCHO.

aldehyde group (1004): the —CHO group.

alkali metal (49): any of the elements (lithium, sodium, potassium, rubidium, cesium, and francium) that constitute Group 1 of the periodic table.

alkaline earth metals (49): any of the elements (beryllium, magnesium, calcium, strontium, barium, and radium) that make up Group 2 of the periodic table.

alkaline manganese cell (829): a primary battery using the cell

$$\ominus Zn(s)\,|\,Na_2ZnO_2(aq),\ NaOH(aq)\,|\,MnO_2(s),$$
$$Mn_2O_3 \cdot H_2O(s)\,|\,steel^{\oplus}$$

alkane (981): a hydrocarbon that contains only single carbon-carbon bonds. (See saturated hydrocarbon.)

alkene (994): a hydrocarbon that contains one or more carbon-carbon double bonds.

alkyl group (991): a group that is derived from an alkane by removing a hydrogen atom.

alkyl halide (988): a substance that is derived from an alkane by removing one or more hydrogen atoms and replacing them by halogen atoms. (See haloalkane.)

alkynes (1000): the class of hydrocarbons that contain one or more carbon-carbon triple bonds.

allotrope (242): a substance that can exist in different modifications in the same physical state; for example, graphite and diamond are allotropes of solid carbon.

alpha emitter (944): a radioisotope that decays by emitting α-particles.

α-helix (1040): the helical shape of a polypeptide that results from the formation of hydrogen bonds between oxygen and hydrogen atoms in peptide bonds that are separated by three peptide units along the chain.

α-particle (18, 944): a helium-4 nucleus emitted in certain types of nuclear decay.

amalgam (836): a solution of a metal in mercury.

amino acid (1032): monomer from which proteins are built. The general formula for an amino acid is

$$H_2N - \underset{\underset{G}{|}}{\overset{\overset{H}{|}}{C}} - COOH$$

amino acid side group (1032): the organic group —G that is attached to amino acids:

$$H_2N - \underset{\underset{G}{|}}{\overset{\overset{H}{|}}{C}} - COOH$$

amorphous (686): characteristic of a solid that does not have a definite crystal structure (e.g., glass).

ampere (832): the SI unit of current. One ampere is a flow of one coulomb of charge per second.

amphoteric metal hydroxide (761): a metal hydroxide that is soluble in both acidic and basic solutions, but insoluble in neutral solutions.

anion (334): a negatively charged ion.

anode (831): the electrode at which the oxidation occurs. Anions in solution move toward the anode.

antibonding orbital (451): a molecular orbital that has one or more nodes in the region between two nuclei.

antifreeze (536): a substance that is used to lower the freezing point of water.

aromatic hydrocarbon (1003): a class of hydrocarbons that have rings that are stabilized by π-electron delocalization.

Arrhenius acid (648): a substance that produces $H^+(aq)$ in aqueous solution.

Arrhenius base (648): a substance that produces $OH^-(aq)$ in aqueous solution.

Arrhenius equation (625): the equation that describes the temperature dependence of a rate constant. The Arrhenius equation is

$$\log\left(\frac{k_2}{k_1}\right) = \frac{E_a}{2.30R}\left(\frac{T_2 - T_1}{T_1 T_2}\right)$$

where k_1 and k_2 are the rate constants at

the absolute temperatures T_1 and T_2, respectively; E_a is the activation energy; and R is the gas constant.

artificial radioisotopes (951): radioactive isotopes that are produced by nuclear reactions in the laboratory and that are not found in nature.

atom (5, 7): a basic component of matter.

atomic mass (8): the mass of an atom relative to the mass of an atom of carbon-12, which is assigned an atomic mass of exactly 12.

atomic mass unit (8): a unit based on the mass of carbon-12, which contains exactly 12 atomic mass units. The symbol for atomic mass unit is amu.

atomic number (20): the number of protons in the nucleus of an atom. The atomic number of an atom is designated by the symbol Z. Each element has a different atomic number.

atomic radius (306): the distance from the nucleus of an atom to the point where the electronic charge density is very small. Atoms do not have well-defined radii.

atomic spectroscopy (260): the study of the spectra of atoms.

atomic spectrum (258): a line spectrum due to the radiation emitted by gaseous, excited atoms or the radiation absorbed by gaseous atoms.

atomic substance (86): a substance that is composed of single atoms.

atomic theory (7): a theory that postulates that (1) matter is composed of small, indivisible particles called atoms; (2) the atoms of a given element all have the same mass and are identical in all respects, including chemical behavior; (3) the atoms of different elements differ in mass and in chemical behavior; (4) chemical compounds are composed of two or more different types of atoms joined together in simple fixed ratios. The particle that results when two or more atoms join together is called a molecule; (5) in a chemical reaction, the atoms involved are rearranged to form different molecules; no atoms are created or destroyed.

average kinetic energy (179): the average kinetic energy of one mole of a gas, $\bar{E}_{av}$, is given by $\bar{E}_{av} = \frac{3}{2}RT$, where T is the Kelvin temperature and R is the gas constant.

average speed (179): the average speed of a molecule in a gas of like molecules is defined by the relationship $\bar{E}_{av} = \frac{1}{2}M_{kg}v_{av}^2$, where $\bar{E}_{av}$ is the average kinetic energy per mole and M_{kg} is the mass in kilograms of one mole.

Avogadro's law (167): states that equal volumes of gases at the same pressure and temperature contain equal numbers of molecules.

Avogadro's number (88): the number of formula units contained in one mole of any substance. One mole of any substance contains 6.022×10^{23} formula units.

AX_mE_n (407): a general representation of a molecule or ion where A represents the central atom, X_m represents m ligands bonded to the central atom, and E_n represents n lone electron pairs (denoted by E) on the central atom.

axial vertex (403): one of the two vertices that lie above or below the equilateral-triangle base of a trigonal bipyramid. The two axial vertices are equivalent.

azide (200): a compound that contains the azide ion, N_3^-.

azimuthal quantum number (274): the quantum number, l, that specifies the shape of an atomic orbital. The allowed values of l are $0, 1, 2, \ldots, n-1$.

B

balanced chemical equation (45): a chemical reaction, written in terms of chemical symbols, that has the same number of each type of atom on the reactant and the product sides of the equation.

balancing coefficient (45): the number placed in front of the chemical formula of a reactant or product in a chemical equation so that the chemical equation is balanced.

ball-and-stick molecular model (398): a model of a molecule that is constructed to display the angles between the bonds in the molecule.

Balmer series (269): the series of lines in the hydrogen atomic spectrum due to transitions from higher states $(n > 2)$ to the $n = 2$ state.

band of stability (948): the region of stable nuclei in a plot of the number of protons versus the number of neutrons of all known stable nuclei.

barometer (159): a device used to measure the pressure of the atmosphere.

barometric pressure (187): the pressure exerted by the atmosphere.

base (129): a compound that yields hydroxide ions, $OH^-(aq)$, when it is dissolved in water. A base is a proton acceptor.

base (1050): a nitrogen-containing ring compound that comprises a nucleotide. The five bases found in DNA or RNA are adenine, guanine, cytosine, uracil, and thymine.

base protonation constant, K_b (665): the equilibrium constant for the proton-transfer reaction between a base and water. For the general reaction

$$B^-(aq) + H_2O(l) \rightleftharpoons BH(aq) + OH^-(aq)$$

$$K_b = \frac{[BH][OH^-]}{[B^-]}$$

basic anhydride (129): an oxide that yields a base when it is dissolved in water.

basic anion (672): an anion that reacts with water to produce $OH^-(aq)$ in aqueous solution.

basic solution (649): an aqueous solution in which $[OH^-] > [H_3O^+]$.

battery (826): an electrochemical cell or group of cells designed for use as a power source.

β-particle (18, 945): an electron emitted in certain types of nuclear decay.

bidentate (920): a chelating liquid that attaches to two metal coordination positions.

binary acid (131): an acid that consists of hydrogen and one other element.

binary compound (11, 125): a compound that consists of two different elements.

binding energy (454): the energy with which an electron is bound in a molecule.

binding energy (nuclear) (963): the energy required to separate the nucleons in a nucleus.

binding energy curve (965): a plot of the binding energy per nucleon versus the mass number of a nucleus.

blackbody (261): an ideal substance that absorbs and emits electromagnetic radiation of all frequencies.

blackbody radiation (261): the radiation emitted by a blackbody, an ideal substance that absorbs and emits electromagnetic radiation of all frequencies.

bleach (797): an oxidizing agent, such as sodium hypochlorite, used to remove stains or decolorize a sample.

bleaching agent (853): an oxidizing agent used to remove color by oxidizing colored organic compounds to colorless substances.

bleaching powder (797): a bleach that contains calcium hypochlorite, $Ca(OCl)_2$.

body-centered cubic (489): describes the unit cell in which the components of the crystal are located at the corners and in the center of a cube.

boiling-point elevation (531): the increase in the boiling point of a solution containing nonvolatile solutes over the boiling point of the pure solvent. The boiling-point elevation is given by the equation $T_b - T_b^\circ = K_b m_c$, where T_b is the boiling point of the solution, T_b° is the boiling point of the pure solvent, m_c is the colligative molality of the solution, and K_b is the proportionality constant, called the boiling-point elevation constant, for the solvent.

boiling-point elevation constant (534): the proportionality constant between the boiling-point elevation and the colligative molality of a solution. The value depends only on the solvent. The symbol is K_b and the units are $K \cdot m_c^{-1}$.

bomb calorimeter (224): a sealed reaction vessel that is used to measure the heat of combustion of a substance.

bond enthalpy (217): the energy as heat required to break the bond between atom X and atom Y. The symbol for bond enthalpy is $H(X—Y)$.

bond length (368): the average distance between the nuclei of the two atoms that are joined by a covalent bond.

bond order (452): one half of the net number of bonding electrons in a diatomic molecule (see Equation 12-1).

bonding orbital (451): a molecular orbital that is concentrated in a region between two nuclei.

Born-Haber cycle (352): a closed sequence of thermodynamic steps used in calculating lattice energies of ionic compounds.

Boyle's law (162): states that the volume of a fixed mass of gas at constant temperature is inversely proportional to the pressure of the gas.

breeder reactor (969): a nuclear reactor that produces more fissionable material than is consumed.

Brønsted-Lowry acid (648): a proton donor.

Brønsted-Lowry base (648): a proton acceptor.

buffer (710): a solution that is resistant to changes in pH upon the addition of an acid or base.

buret (144): a precision-made piece of glassware that is used to measure accurately the volume of a solution that is added to another container.

C

calorie (228): the amount of energy as heat required to raise the temperature of one gram of water by one Celsius degree; 1 calorie = 4.184 J.

calorimeter (221): a device used to measure the amount of heat evolved or absorbed in a process.

capillary action (487): the rise of a liquid in a thin tube.

carbohydrate (1045): a compound composed of carbon, hydrogen, and oxygen with the general formula $C_x(H_2O)_y$.

carbon-14 dating (954): the determination of the age of formerly living materials from the rate of disintegration of carbon-14 in the sample.

carboxyl group (1008): the —COOH group.

carboxylate ion (1009): the anion that results from the dissociation or neutralization of a carboxylic acid. A carboxylate ion has the general formula $RCOO^-$ or

$$\left[R-C \begin{matrix} \ddot{O}: \\ \\ \ddot{O}: \end{matrix} \right]^-$$

carboxylic acid (1008): a class of organic compounds that contain the —COOH group.

carrier gas (118): the inert gas used to carry a mixture of species through a gas chromatography apparatus.

catalyst (76, 100, 624): a substance that increases the reaction rate but that is not a reactant. A catalyst acts by providing a different and faster reaction pathway (mechanism) than the reaction mechanism that would prevail in the absence of the catalyst.

catalyst poisoning (631): deposition on the surface of a contact catalyst of a noncatalytic substance that renders the surface noncatalytic.

catalytic converter (631): a contact catalyst used to remove various pollutants from the combustion products of a fuel.

cathode (831): the electrode at which reduction occurs. Cations in solution move toward the cathode.

cation (334): a positively charged ion.

cell diagram (809): a notation used to represent an electrochemical cell. By convention, oxidation occurs at the left electrode and reduction occurs at the right electrode.

cell voltage (813): the voltage of an electrochemical cell.

centrifuge (767): an instrument that hastens the settling of a precipitate by centrifugation.

chain reaction (966): a self-sustaining reaction in which the products initiate further reaction; commonly applied to certain nuclear fission reactions in which neutrons that are produced by the fission process cause additional nuclei to fission, hence propagating the reaction.

charge delocalization (448): the distribution of the electronic charge over more than one atom in a polyatomic species.

Charles' law (164): states that the volume of a fixed mass of gas at constant pressure is directly proportional to the absolute temperature of the gas.

chelate (920): a complex that contains a metal ion and at least one chelating ligand.

chelating ligand (920): a ligand that attaches to a metal ion at more than one coordination position.

chemical equilibrium (566): chemical equilibrium is attained when the rate of the forward reaction is equal to the rate of the reverse reaction. A true chemical equilibrium is approachable from either the reactant or the product side of the reaction. At equilibrium the reactant and product concentrations do not change with time.

chemical formula (11): the chemical notation for a compound. The relative numbers of atoms of each element in the compound are indicated by subscripts.

chemical nomenclature (11): the system of naming chemical compounds.

chemical reaction (44): the formation of new substances from other substances by a rearrangement of the constituent atoms.

chemical symbol (3): the abbreviation that is used to designate an element.

chlor-alkali process (835): a method of preparing chlorine, Cl_2, and sodium hydroxide by the electrolysis of an aqueous sodium chloride, $NaCl(aq)$, solution.

chloroalkane (988): a substance derived from an alkane in which one or more hydrogen atoms of the alkane are replaced by chlorine atoms.

chloroplast (77): one of the compartments in cells that contain the chlorophyll pigments.

chromatogram (119): a physical display of the results of a chromatographic separation.

chromatography (118): separation of the components of a solution by the different tendency of adsorption on a condensed phase. The solution phase flows over the condensed (stationary) phase.

cis-trans **isomerism (443, 918):** a form of geometric isomerism. The designation *cis* indicates that two identical ligands are adjacent to each other in some sense. The designation *trans* indicates that two identical ligands are directly opposite each other in some sense.

colligative molality (532): a concentration scale for solute particles in a solution. The colligative molality, m_c, is defined as

$$m_c = \frac{\text{moles of solute particles}}{\text{kilograms of solvent}}$$

The units of colligative molality are $mol \cdot kg^{-1}$.

colligative molarity (540): a concentration scale for solute particles in a solution. The colligative molarity, M_c, is defined as

$$M_c = \frac{\text{moles of solute particles}}{\text{liters of solution}}$$

The units of colligative molarity are $mol \cdot L^{-1}$.

colligative properties (531): the properties of a solution that depend on the ratio of the number of solute particles to the number of solvent particles. The major colligative properties are vapor-pressure lowering, boiling-point elevation, freezing-point depression, and osmotic pressure.

collision frequency, z (181): the number of collisions that a molecule experiences in one second. The number of collisions per second can be estimated by using the relationship

$$z = \frac{v_{av}}{l}$$

where l is the mean free path and v_{av} is the average speed of the molecules.

collision theory (623): the postulate that two molecules must collide with sufficient energy in order to react.

combination reaction (123): a reaction between two different substances in which a single product is formed.

combustion (205): the burning of a substance in oxygen.

combustion reaction (80, 124): a reaction in which a substance is burned in oxygen.

common-ion effect (751): the decrease in the solubility of an ionic solid caused by the presence in the solution of one of the constituent ions of the solid.

complementary base pairs (1055): the base pairs adenine and thymine (A–T) and guanine and cytosine (G–C), which are always opposite each other on the two polynucleotide chains in a DNA double helix.

complex ion (911): a charged chemical species containing a metal ion with one or more attached ligands.

components (524): the species of a solution.

compound (2): a pure substance that can be broken down into simpler substances. A compound is composed of two or more different kinds of atoms.

compound unit (30): a unit of measurement that is expressed in terms of two or more units. For example, density is defined as mass per unit volume, and thus the units of density are mass divided by volume (e.g., g/cm^3), or $g \cdot cm^{-3}$.

compressibility (156): the extent to which a substance changes its volume with increasing pressure.

concentration (105): the quantity of solute dissolved in a given quantity of solvent or solution.

condensation polymerization reaction (1022): the formation of a polymer from two different monomer molecules by splitting out a small molecule such as water.

condenser (117): a component of a distillation apparatus in which the vapors are cooled and thereby converted to liquid.

conduction band (512): a densely-packed set of orbitals that extend throughout a crystal and that are analogous to antibonding orbitals in a molecule. Electrons move through the crystal by means of the conduction band.

conjugate acid (668): an acid that is formed from a species that has accepted a proton from another species.

conjugate acid-base pair (668): two species that are coupled by means of a proton-transfer reaction.

conjugate base (668): a base that is formed from a species that has transferred a proton to another species.

conservation of energy (203): the law describing the concept that the total energy of a system never changes. Energy cannot be created or destroyed.

contact catalysis (631): catalysis in which the reactant molecules come in contact with a solid catalyst.

contact process (244): a method for the production of sulfuric acid, H_2SO_4, in which sulfur is oxidized to sulfur trioxide, which is then combined with water.

continuous spectrum (258): electromagnetic radiation that contains radiation of all the wavelengths in some region.

contour diagram (274): diagram in which lines indicate the region within which there is a certain probability of finding an electron.

control rod (968): one of the cadmium or boron rods used to control the rate of the reaction in a nuclear reactor by absorbing neutrons.

coordinate covalent bond (383): a covalent bond that is formed when one species contributes both electrons to the bond.

Coulomb's law (347): gives the energy change involved when two ions are brought to a separation distance, d, as

$$E = (2.31 \times 10^{-16} \text{ J} \cdot \text{pm}) \frac{Z_1 Z_2}{d}$$

where Z_1 and Z_2 are the ionic charges of the two ions. When d is expressed in picometers, the energy is given in joules.

covalent bond (366): the bond formed between two atoms by a shared electron pair.

critical mass (966): the minimum mass that will support a nuclear chain reaction.

critical point (498): the point in the phase diagram of a substance at which the liquid-gas curve abruptly terminates.

critical temperature (498): the temperature above which a gas cannot be liquefied, no matter what its pressure; the temperature at the critical point.

crystallographic radius (306): an atomic radius that has been determined from X-ray analysis of a crystal containing the atoms of interest.

cubic closest-packed structure (489): the face-centered cubic arrangement that represents the closest possible packing of layers of identical spheres.

curie (971): a measure of the radioactivity of a sample, 1 Ci = 3.7×10^{10} disintegrations per second.

cylindrically symmetric (276): characteristic of a function that depends only on the distance from an axis. A cylindrically symmetric function has a circular cross section.

D

d orbital (275, 907): an orbital for which $l = 2$. There are five d orbitals for each value of $n \geq 3$.

d transition metal series (907): the d transition metal series are as follows:

$3d$ series: $Z = 21$ to $Z = 30$ (Sc to Zn)

$4d$ series: $Z = 39$ to $Z = 48$ (Y to Cd)

$5d$ series: $Z = 71$ to $Z = 80$ (Lu to Hg)

d^x ion (910): a transition metal ion that has x electrons in its outer d orbitals.

$d_{xy}, d_{xz}, d_{yz}, d_{x^2-y^2}, d_{z^2}$ orbitals (909): the set of five d orbitals.

Dalton's law of partial pressures (176): states that the total pressure exerted by a mixture of gases is the sum of the partial pressures of each of the gases. For a mixture of two gases

$$P_{total} = P_1 + P_2$$

Each gaseous component exerts a pressure independent of the other gases.

d-electron configuration (302, 907): the electron configuration of the outer d electrons in a transition metal.

d-orbital-splitting pattern (922, 933): the five d orbitals of a transition metal ion in a complex are split into groups of orbitals of differing energies by the ligands in the complex.

de Broglie wavelength (264): the wavelength associated with a moving particle. The wavelength is given by $\lambda = h/mv$, where h is Planck's constant, m is the mass of the particle, and v is the speed of the particle.

decant (767): to pour off a solution from which a substance was precipitated while leaving the precipitate behind.

decomposition reaction (132): a reaction in which a substance is broken up into two or more simpler substances.

decomposition voltage (831): the minimum voltage that is necessary to decompose a substance electrochemically.

deionize (736): to remove the ions in water by means of ion-exchange resins.

delocalized orbitals (448): π-orbitals in a molecule that are not associated with a particular pair of atoms.

Δ_o (922): the magnitude of the splitting of the two sets of d orbitals, t_{2g} and e_g, on a metal ion in an octahedral complex.

Δ_{sp} (933): the magnitude of the splitting of the two highest-energy d orbitals, d_{xz} and $d_{x^2-y^2}$, on a metal ion in a square-planar complex.

Δ_t (933): the magnitude of the splitting of the two sets of d orbitals, e and t_2, on a metal ion in a tetrahedral complex.

$\Delta \bar{G}_f^\circ$ (879): the standard molar Gibbs free energy of formation of a substance.

ΔG_{rxn} (871): the Gibbs free energy change of a reaction. The value of ΔG_{rxn} for a reaction run at a constant temperature is given by $\Delta G_{rxn} = \Delta H_{rxn} - T\Delta S_{rxn}$, where ΔH_{rxn} is the enthalpy change of the reaction, ΔS_{rxn} is the entropy change of the

reaction, and T is the temperature in kelvins. The value of ΔG_{rxn} is the maximum amount of work that can be obtained from the reaction under the stated conditions.

ΔG_{rxn}° (873): the standard Gibbs free energy change for a reaction, which is the Gibbs free energy change for the reaction run under standard conditions.

$\Delta \bar{H}_f^\circ$ (207): the standard molar enthalpy of formation of a compound. The units of $\Delta \bar{H}_f^\circ$ are kilojoules per mole, $kJ \cdot mol^{-1}$.

ΔH_{rxn} (205): the heat, q_P, absorbed or evolved by a reaction when the reaction occurs at constant pressure.

$\Delta \bar{S}_{fus}^\circ$ (861): the standard molar entropy change upon fusion. The value of $\Delta \bar{S}_{fus}^\circ$ is given by $\Delta \bar{S}_{fus}^\circ = \Delta \bar{H}_{fus}^\circ/T_m$, where $\Delta \bar{H}_{fus}^\circ$ is the molar enthalpy of fusion and T_m is the melting point in kelvins at one atmosphere.

ΔS_{rxn} (868): the entropy change of a reaction at conditions other than standard conditions.

ΔS_{rxn}° (868): the entropy change of a reaction when the reactants and products are at standard conditions. The value of ΔS_{rxn}° is given by $\Delta S_{rxn}^\circ = S_{products}^\circ - S_{reactants}^\circ$, where $S_{products}^\circ$ is the total molar entropy of all the product species and $S_{reactants}^\circ$ is the total molar entropy of all the reactant species.

$\Delta \bar{S}_{vap}^\circ$ (862): the standard molar entropy change upon vaporization. The value of $\Delta \bar{S}_{vap}^\circ$ is given by $\Delta \bar{S}_{vap}^\circ = \Delta \bar{H}_{vap}^\circ/T_b$, where $\Delta \bar{H}_{vap}^\circ$ is the standard molar enthalpy of vaporization and T_b is the boiling point in kelvins at one atmosphere.

ΔU_{rxn} (203): the heat, q_V, absorbed or evolved during a reaction that occurs at constant volume.

density (30): the mass per unit volume of a substance.

desalination (734): the process of removing dissolved solids from seawater.

desiccator (689): a heavy-walled glass or metal container used to dry substances by placing a dehydrating agent in the container along with the substance to be dried.

deuterium (20): the isotope of hydrogen that has a mass number of 2.

deviations from ideality (183): the behavior of a gas such that for one mole of the gas, the ratio PV/RT is not equal to 1.

dew point (485): the air temperature at which the relative humidity is 100 percent; depends on the partial pressure of water vapor in the air.

Dewar flask (222): an insulated vessel that heat cannot readily leave or enter. A thermos bottle is an example of Dewar flask.

diamagnetic (934): not magnetized by an external magnetic field. Diamagnetic molecules contain no unpaired electrons.

diatomic molecule (5): a molecule that is composed of two atoms.

dimer (532): a pair of identical molecules bonded together into a single unit.

dipeptide (1035): a molecule composed of two amino acids joined by a peptide bond.

dipole-dipole attraction (474): the attraction between polar molecules.

dipole moment (387): a measure of the polarity of a bond. The dipole moment has both magnitude and direction. The direction of the dipole moment is represented as an arrow ($\leftrightarrow$) pointing from the positive charge to the negative charge.

direction of reaction spontaneity (586): the direction (left to right or right to left) in which a reaction proceeds toward equilibrium.

disaccharide (1046): a molecule composed of two monosaccharides joined together.

discharge (807): the production of an electric current from an electrochemical cell.

disinfectant (797): an oxidizing agent that is used to destroy microorganisms.

distillation (117): a process by which a substance is separated from a liquid phase by volatilization upon heating. The vapor is then condensed to liquid by cooling.

distribution diagram (720): a plot that gives the fraction of each species in a solution of an acid or a base as a function of the pH of the solution.

disulfide bond (1039): the bond formed between two cysteine side groups on the same or neighboring polypeptide chains. The disulfide bond is of the type $—CH_2—S—S—CH_2—$.

DNA (1050): deoxyribonucleic acid, the substance that contains the genetic information in cells. DNA is a polynucleotide composed of the sugar deoxyribose, the phosphate group, and the four bases adenine, thymine, guanine, and cytosine.

donor-acceptor complex (383): the product of the formation of a coordinate covalent bond between two species.

double bond (373): the bond formed between two atoms by two shared electron pairs.

double helix (1052): the shape of DNA—two polynucleotide chains intertwined in a helical fashion.

double-replacement reaction (139): a reaction of the type $AB + CD \rightarrow AD + BC$ in which the cations in each compound exchange anionic partners.

dry cell (824): a primary battery utilizing the cell

$$\ominus Zn(s)|ZnCl_2 \cdot 2NH_3(s)|NH_4Cl(aq)|MnO_2(s),$$
$$Mn_2O_3 \cdot H_2O(s)|C(s)\oplus$$

dynamic equilibrium (481, 525, 567): a state of balance between forward and reverse processes such that no net change in the system takes place.

dynamite (230): a mixture of nitroglycerin and diatomaceous earth.

E

e_g (922): the set of d orbitals of higher energy on a metal ion in an octahedral complex.

e orbitals (933): the set of d orbitals of lower energy on a metal ion in a tetrahedral complex. The e orbitals consist of the $d_{x^2-y^2}$ and d_{z^2} orbitals.

effusion (182): the process whereby a gas exits through a very small hole in a container.

elastomer (1026): a polymeric substance that can be stretched and that returns to its original shape when the stretching force is released.

electrochemical cell (806): an experimental setup by which an electric current can be obtained from a chemical reaction.

electrode (806): a metal conductor used to establish electrical contact with an electrolyte solution. The electron transfers occur across the metal-electrolyte interface.

electrolysis (79, 830): a chemical reaction that occurs as a result of the passage of an electric current through a solution.

electrolyte (342): a substance that dissolves in water to produce solutions that conduct an electric current.

electromagnetic spectrum (258): the range

of wavelengths or frequencies of electro-magnetic radiation.

electron (16): a subatomic particle that has a negative charge and a mass that is $\frac{1}{1837}$ that of a hydrogen atom.

electron acceptor (788): the reactant that gains electrons in an electron-transfer reaction. The electron acceptor is reduced in an oxidation-reduction reaction.

electron affinity, EA (346): the energy released in the process of adding an electron to an atom. The equation for this process is

$$\text{atom}(g) + \text{electron} \longrightarrow \text{ion}(g) + \text{EA}$$

electron capture (946): a nuclear transformation in which one of the innermost electrons of an atom is absorbed by the nucleus, converting a proton into a neutron.

electron configuration (294): the assignment of electrons to orbitals according to the Pauli exclusion principle.

electron deficiency or **electron-deficient compound (382):** a condition or a compound in which one or more of the atoms other than hydrogen have less than eight valence electrons; such a compound violates the octet rule.

electron diffraction (265): the scattering of a beam of electrons in a definite manner by a substance.

electron donor (788): the reactant that loses electrons in an electron-transfer reaction. An electron donor is oxidized in an oxidation-reduction reaction.

electron microscope (265): an instrument that uses the wavelike property of electrons to investigate subcellular and molecular structures.

electron-pair acceptor (676): an electron-deficient species that can act as a Lewis acid.

electron-pair donor (676): a species with a lone pair of electrons that can act as a Lewis base.

electron pairing energy (927): the energy required to pair up two electrons in the d orbitals of a metal in a complex.

electron-transfer reaction (788): a reaction in which one species is oxidized and another species is reduced.

electronegativity (385): a measure of the force with which an atom attracts the electrons that it is sharing in a covalent bond.

electroneutrality (718): the condition that requires that the sum of all the cationic charges must equal the sum of all the anionic charges in a dry substance.

electronic structure (251): the arrangement of the electrons within an atom.

electrostatic attraction (332): the Coulombic attraction between oppositely charged ions.

element (2): a substance that contains only one kind of atom. There are 107 known elements.

elementary process (619): a chemical reaction that occurs in a single step—the reactants go directly to the products without the involvement of intermediates.

emf series (822): electromotive force series; an arrangement of half-reactions in the order of their $E°$ values.

emission spectrum (270): spectrum obtained when gaseous excited atoms or molecules return to the ground state with the emission of light of characteristic wavelengths.

empirical formula (93): the simplest chemical formula of a substance. (See simplest formula.)

end point (145, 701): the point in a titration at which the indicator changes color.

endothermic reaction (205): a reaction that absorbs energy as heat ($\Delta H_{rxn} > 0$).

energy change (203): difference in energy of a system before and after a process has occurred. The change in energy of a reaction is given the symbol ΔU_{rxn}, where $\Delta U_{rxn} = U_{products} - U_{reactants}$ denotes the change in energy of a reaction.

energy-favored reaction (870): a reaction for which $\Delta U_{rxn} < 0$.

energy state (267): one of the discrete set of energies that an atom or molecule can have.

enthalpy, H (204): a defined quantity given by the equation $H = U + PV$, where U is the energy, P is the pressure, and V is the volume of a system.

enthalpy change, ΔH_{rxn} (205, 858): the energy evolved or absorbed as heat during a reaction when the reaction takes place at constant pressure. The enthalpy change is given as

$$\Delta H_{rxn} = H_{products} - H_{reactants}$$

for a reaction.

enthalpy of formation (207): the enthalpy change for the reaction in which one mole of a compound is formed from its elements.

entropy (859): a quantitative measure of the amount of disorder in a substance. The symbol for entropy is S. The SI unit of entropy is joules per kelvin, $J \cdot K^{-1}$.

entropy change, ΔS_{rxn} (868): the difference in the entropy of the reaction products and the reactants.

entropy-driven reaction (870): a spontaneous reaction for which $\Delta S_{rxn} > 0$ and $\Delta H_{rxn} \geqslant 0$.

entropy-favored reaction (870): a reaction for which $\Delta S_{rxn} > 0$.

enzyme (1043): a protein that catalyzes a chemical reaction in biological systems.

equatorial vertex (403): one of the three vertices of the equilateral triangle that forms the shared base of a trigonal bipyramid. The three equatorial vertices are equivalent.

equilibrium (481): a state characterized by the equality of forward and reverse rates for a process.

equilibrium concentration (568): the value of the concentration of a reactant or of a product when the reaction has attained equilibrium.

equilibrium constant (571): the algebraic relationship between reactant and product concentrations that exists at equilibrium. The form of the equilibrium constant expression for a chemical reaction is obtained by applying the law of concentration action to the balanced chemical equation.

equilibrium constant expression (571): the expression for the equilibrium constant for a chemical reaction that is given by the law of concentration action. For the balanced chemical equation

$$aA(g) + bB(soln) + cC(s) \rightleftharpoons$$
$$xX(g) + yY(soln) + zZ(l)$$

the equilibrium constant expression is given by

$$K_c = \frac{[X]^x[Y]^y}{[A]^a[B]^b}$$

equilibrium shift (580): the response of an equilibrium chemical reaction to a displacement from equilibrium produced by a change in conditions that affect the reaction equilibrium.

equilibrium vapor pressure (481): the pressure of a vapor in equilibrium with its liquid.

equivalence point (701): the pH or point in a titration at which all the acid or base initially present is just neutralized.

escaping tendency (539): the tendency of a substance to leave a solution. The higher the vapor pressure of a substance, the higher the escaping tendency. The lower the colligative molality of the solute, the higher the escaping tendency of the solvent.

ester (1010): a class of organic compounds that result from the reaction between a carboxylic acid and an alcohol.

eutrophication (691): depletion of the oxygen in a body of water by decaying organisms such as algae.

excess reactant (102): the reactant that is present in larger quantity than is necessary to react with the other reactants in a reaction.

excited state (298): an energy state that is higher than the ground state.

exothermic reaction (205): a reaction that evolves energy as heat ($\Delta H_{rxn} < 0$).

expanded valence shell (384): the idea that elements beyond the second row of the periodic table can accommodate more than eight electrons by using d orbitals. Such elements (P, S, Cl) need not obey the octet rule.

external circuit (808): the part of an electrical circuit involving an electrochemical cell that does not include the electrochemical cell.

F

f orbital (275): an orbital for which $l = 3$. There are seven f orbitals for each value of $n \geqslant 4$.

face-centered cubic unit cell (489): the unit cell in which the components of the crystal are located at the corners of the cube and in the centers of the six faces of the cube.

Faraday's constant (814): the charge on one mole of electrons. Faraday's constant, F, is equal to $96,500 \ C \cdot mol^{-1}$.

Faraday's law (835): states that the mass deposited in an electrolysis is given by mass deposited

$$= \frac{\text{current} \times \text{time} \times \text{atomic mass}}{\text{Faraday constant} \times \text{ionic charge}}$$

filtration (115): the process of separating a liquid phase from a solid phase by the use of a material, such as special papers, through which the liquid phase can pass.

first excited state (267): the next higher energy state above the ground state.

first ionization energy (252): the minimum energy required to remove an electron from a neutral atom, A, to produce the A^+ ion.

first law of thermodynamics (203): the law of conservation of energy.

first-order rate law (607): a rate law in which the reaction rate is proportional to the first power of the concentration of a reactant. The rate law is of the form rate = $k[A]$.

fission (965): a nuclear reaction in which a nucleus splits into two smaller, roughly equal-sized fragments.

flocculent (739): a flocculent precipitate is one that does not settle readily.

formal charge (377): the assignment of a charge to an atom in a molecule or ion by a set of rules. The formal charge of an atom is found by the relationship

$$\begin{aligned}\text{formal} \atop \text{charge} &= \begin{pmatrix}\text{number of valence} \\ \text{electrons in the atom}\end{pmatrix} \\ &- \begin{pmatrix}\text{total number of} \\ \text{lone pair electrons}\end{pmatrix} \\ &- \tfrac{1}{2}\begin{pmatrix}\text{total number of} \\ \text{shared electrons}\end{pmatrix}\end{aligned}$$

formula mass (86): the relative mass of a formula unit. The formula mass is the sum of the atomic masses of all the atoms that make up the formula unit.

formula unit (66, 86): the simplest component of a substance. The formula unit may be an atom, a molecule, or a group of ions. A formula unit is defined by the chemical formula. Thus NaCl (one Na^+ and one Cl^-) is the formula unit of sodium chloride.

forward rate (566): the rate of the forward reaction.

forward reaction (631): the formation of the reaction products from the reactants, or the reaction that proceeds left to right for the reaction as written.

fractional distillation (118): a distillation that involves a long distillation column in which the vapor is continuously condensed and revaporized at progressively decreasing temperatures.

Frasch process (238): a process for extracting sulfur from underground deposits by using hot (180°C) high-pressure water to melt the sulfur.

free radical (382): a species in which it is not possible to pair up all the electrons. A free radical contains at least one unpaired electron. All species with an odd number of electrons are free radicals.

free radical reaction (988): a reaction involving free radicals, which are species with unpaired electrons.

freezing-point depression (531): the decrease in the freezing point of a solution below the freezing point of the pure solvent. The freezing-point depression is given by the equation $T_f^\circ - T_f = K_f m_c$, where T_f° is the freezing point of the pure solvent, T_f is the freezing point of the solution, m_c is the colligative molality of the solution, and K_f is a proportionality constant, called the freezing-point depression constant, of the solvent.

freezing-point depression constant (535): the proportionality constant between the freezing-point depression and the colligative molality of a solution. The value depends only on the solvent. The symbol is K_f and the units are $K \cdot m_c^{-1}$.

frequency, ν (257): the number of maxima or minima of a wave that pass a given point per second. The symbol of frequency is ν and the units of frequency are cycles per second, s^{-1}, or hertz, Hz ($1 Hz = 1 \text{ cycle} \cdot s^{-1}$).

fuel (80, 205): a substance that can be used in a chemical reaction to provide energy for the performance of tasks.

fuel rod (968): one of the rods in a nuclear reactor that contain the isotope that undergoes fission.

fusion (970): the process by which a nucleus is produced from smaller nuclei.

G

γ-ray (18): a high-energy electromagnetic wave emitted in certain types of nuclear decay.

gas (155): the physical state of matter having the properties of occupying the entire volume and assuming the shape of its container and having a large compressibility.

gas constant (170): the constant, R, in the ideal-gas equation. Its value depends on the units of P, V, and T:

$$R = 0.0821 \text{ L} \cdot \text{atm} \cdot \text{mol}^{-1} \cdot \text{K}^{-1}$$
$$= 8.31 \text{ J} \cdot \text{mol}^{-1} \cdot \text{K}^{-1}$$

gas electrode (810): an electrode involving a gaseous species.

gas solubility (544): the amount of gas dissolved in a solvent. The solubility of a gas is proportional to the partial pressure of that gas over the solution, and decreases with increasing temperature.

gas thermometer (164): a thermometer that uses the volume of a fixed mass of a gas to measure the temperature.

Gay-Lussac's law of combining volumes (167): the volumes of gases that combine to form reaction products are in the ratio of small whole numbers. The volumes must be measured at the same temperature and pressure.

gene (1058): a segment along a DNA molecule that codes the synthesis of a particular polypeptide.

geometric isomers (918): molecules that have the same chemical formula but different geometric arrangements of the atoms. Geometric isomers have different chemical and physical properties.

Gibbs criteria (of reaction spontaneity) (871): criteria used to predict whether a process is spontaneous or not. The Gibbs criteria are

1. $\Delta G_{rxn} < 0$; the reaction is spontaneous;
2. $\Delta G_{rxn} > 0$; the reaction is not spontaneous—product formation requires energy input;
3. $\Delta G_{rxn} = 0$; the reaction is at equilibrium.

Gibbs free energy (871): a quantity that serves as a compromise function between enthalpy and entropy. For a reaction run at constant temperature, the Gibbs free energy change is given by $\Delta G_{rxn} = \Delta H_{rxn} - T\Delta S_{rxn}$.

Gibbs free energy change, ΔG_{rxn} (871): the change in Gibbs free energy for a reaction. ΔG_{rxn} is given by

$$\Delta G_{rxn} = G(\text{products}) - G(\text{reactants})$$

The value of ΔG_{rxn} determines the reaction spontaneity.

GLC (118): gas-liquid chromatography.

Graham's law of effusion (182): the relation between the rates of effusion of two gases, which is given by

$$\frac{\text{rate}_A}{\text{rate}_B} = \left(\frac{M_B}{M_A}\right)^{1/2}$$

where M_A and M_B are the molecular masses of gas A and of gas B, respectively.

greenhouse effect (318): the increase in temperature of the troposphere resulting from absorption of infrared radiation by increased levels of carbon dioxide.

ground electronic state (267): the state of lowest energy. The ground electronic state is obtained by filling up the atomic orbitals of lowest energy according to the Pauli exclusion principle and Hund's rule.

ground state (267): the lowest possible energy state of an atom or molecule.

ground-state wave function (434): the wave function for the lowest energy state of a species.

group (58): the collection of elements that are in the same column in the periodic table. A group of elements is also called a family of elements.

Group 1 metals (55): the elements that appear in the first column of the periodic table. The Group 1 metals are called the alkali metals.

Group 2 metals (55): the elements that appear in the second column of the periodic table. The Group 2 metals are called the alkaline earth metals.

H

Haber process (195, 590): the method by which ammonia is produced commercially from nitrogen and hydrogen. The reaction

$$N_2(g) + 3H_2(g) \rightleftharpoons 2NH_3(g)$$

is carried out on a commercial scale at 500°C and 300 atm, with the aid of a catalyst.

half-life (614, 950): the time it takes for one half of a sample to undergo reaction; denoted by $t_{1/2}$.

half-reaction (789): one part of an electron-transfer reaction representing either the loss of electrons by a reactant or the gain of electrons by a reactant.

halide (51): a crystalline solid salt produced when a halogen reacts with a metal.

Hall process (836): the industrial method of preparing aluminum by the electrolysis of a solution of aluminum oxide, Al_2O_3, dissolved in molten cryolite, $Na_3AlF_6(l)$.

haloalkane (988): a substance derived from an alkane in which one or more hydrogen atoms of the alkane are replaced by halogen atoms (also called alkyl halide).

halogen (51): a member of the group of elements fluorine, chlorine, bromine, iodine, and astatine, which are the Group 7 elements in the periodic table.

hard water (735): water that contains appreciable amounts of divalent cations, such as Ca^{2+}, Mg^{2+}, and Fe^{2+}, together with the anions HCO_3^- and SO_4^{2-}.

heat, q (204): a mode of energy transfer that occurs as a result of a temperature difference.

heat capacity, C_P (219): the heat required to raise the temperature of a substance by one degree kelvin. The SI unit of heat capacity is joules per kelvin, $J \cdot K^{-1}$.

heat of reaction (204): the amount of energy evolved or absorbed as heat when a chemical reaction occurs.

heating curve (467): a plot of how the temperature of a substance varies with time if it is heated at a constant rate.

heavy water (20): water that is composed of deuterium and oxygen, D_2O.

Henderson-Hasselbach equation (712): an equation that relates the pH of a buffer solution to the stoichiometric concentrations of a conjugate acid-base pair.

Henry's law (544): states that the solubility of a gas in a liquid is directly proportional to the equilibrium partial pressure of the gas over the solution. The equation is $P_{gas} = k_h M_{gas}$, where P_{gas} is the equilibrium gas pressure over the solution, M_{gas} is the concentration of the gas in the solution, and k_h is the proportionality constant, called Henry's law constant, for the gas.

Henry's law constant (544): the proportion-ality constant between the solubility of a gas in a liquid and the equilibrium pressure of the gas over the solution. The symbol is k_h and the units are $atm \cdot M^{-1}$.

hertz, Hz (258): the SI unit of frequency; equal to one cycle per second.

Hess's law (212): states that if two or more chemical equations are added together, then the value of ΔH_{rxn} for the resulting equation is equal to the sum of the ΔH_{rxn} values for the separate equations.

heterogeneous (114): not uniform in chemical composition, for example, a mixture of salt and sugar.

heterogeneous catalysis (631): catalysis in which the catalyst is in a different phase from the reactants.

heterogeneous catalyst (631): a solid catalyst that catalyzes a gas- or solution-phase reaction.

heteronuclear diatomic molecule (457): a molecule that consists of two different nuclei.

high-spin configuration (926): a d-electron configuration of a complex in which the d electrons occupy a higher-energy set of d orbitals before they pair up in the lower-energy set of d orbitals.

homogeneous (104, 523): having uniform properties throughout.

homonuclear diatomic molecule (449): a molecule that consists of two similar nuclei.

Hund's rule (297, 455): states that for any set of orbitals of the same energy, the ground-state electron configuration is obtained by placing the electrons in different orbitals of this set with parallel spins until each of the orbitals has one electron, before pairing up any of the electrons.

hybrid atomic orbital (436): an orbital on an atom that is the result of combining different atomic orbitals on the same atom according to a procedure of quantum mechanics.

hydrocarbon (80, 96, 981): a class of organic compounds that consist of only hydrogen and carbon.

hydrogen bonding (475): a special type of dipole-dipole attraction that involves the electrostatic interaction of a hydrogen atom in one species with an electronegative atom in another species.

hydrogen glass electrode (825): an electrode

used to measure the pH of aqueous solutions. The hydrogen glass electrode responds to the concentration of $H^+(aq)$ in the same manner as a hydrogen gas electrode.

hydrogen ion, $H^+(aq)$ (130): a proton that occurs when a hydrogen atom has lost its electron. In aqueous solution the hydrogen ion, designated by $H^+(aq)$, exists primarily as the $H_3O^+(aq)$ ion.

hydrogen molecular ion (449): the species H_2^+, that consists of two protons and one electron.

hydrogenation (996): addition of hydrogen to a molecule.

hydrolyze (1049): a reaction in which the addition of a water molecule breaks a molecule into two other molecules.

hydronium ion (130, 648): the species, $H_3O^+(aq)$, that is the dominant form of the hydrogen ion in aqueous solution.

hydrophilic (1036): tending to be surrounded by water molecules and to orient toward water ("water loving").

hydrophobic (1036): tending to cluster together and to orient away from water ("water fearing").

I

ideal gas (170): a gas that obeys the ideal-gas law.

ideal-gas equation (170): the equation $PV = nRT$, where P is the pressure, V is the volume, T is the temperature, and n is the number of moles of the gas; R is the gas constant.

ideal-gas law (170): the combination of Charles' law, Boyle's law, and Avogadro's law. The ideal-gas law equation is $PV = nRT$.

ideal solution (528): a solution in which the solute molecules and the solvent molecules are randomly distributed throughout the solution.

indicator (145, 697): a substance that is used to signal, by a color change, the end point in a titration.

inert complex (931): a complex that exchanges its ligands slowly with other available ligands.

infrared spectrum (422): a plot of the infrared radiation energy absorbed versus the wavelength of the energy for a species.

inner transition metals (60, 305): the two 14-member series of transition metals that are usually placed at the bottom of the periodic table. These series are called the lanthanides and the actinides, respectively.

interhalogen compound (412): a compound in which a central halogen atom is bonded to one or more atoms of a more electronegative halogen.

intermediate (621): a species that is formed from the reactants and is involved in the conversion of reactants to products but that does not appear as a reactant or product in the overall reaction.

intrinsic electron spin (280): a characteristic property of an electron due to the spin of the electron around its axis in one of two directions.

ion (23): a species that has either a deficiency of electrons (in which case the ion is positively charged) or an excess of electron(s) (in which case the ion is negatively charged).

ion-exchange resin (738): an organic polymer containing acidic and/or basic groups that can remove cations (via the acid groups) or anions (via the basic groups) by means of an ion-exchange reaction.

ion pair (347): a positive and negative ion held together by electrostatic attraction.

ion-product constant of water (649): the equilibrium constant for the reaction

$$H_2O(l) + H_2O(l) \rightleftharpoons H_3O^+(aq) + OH^-(aq)$$

The ion-product constant is given by $K_w = [H_3O^+][OH^-]$. The value of K_w is $1.00 \times 10^{-14} M^2$ at 25°C.

ionic bond (332): the electrostatic attraction that holds oppositely charged ions together.

ionic charge (67): the positive or negative charge on an ion.

ionic compound (66, 332): a compound that is composed of positive and negative ions. An ionic compound has no net charge.

ionic crystal (345): an ordered array of negatively and positively charged ions.

ionic equation (140): a chemical equation that shows explicitly the ions involved in a reaction.

ionic radius (339): the radius of an ion that is obtained from X-ray crystallographic measurements.

ionic reaction (140): a reaction that takes place between the constituent ions of two ionic compounds in aqueous solution.

ionization energy (251): the minimum energy that is required to remove an electron completely from a gaseous atom or ion.

ionosphere (317): the outermost region of the atmosphere that contains ions and electrons produced by solar radiation.

isoelectronic (25): possessing the same number of electrons as another species (iso- means the same).

isomer (214): compounds with the same molecular formula but different arrangements of atoms are said to be isomers.

isotope (20): an atom of an element that has a particular mass number. Isotopes of an element have the same number of protons but different numbers of neutrons.

IUPAC nomenclature (990): the system of naming organic compounds that has been recommended by the International Union of Pure and Applied Chemistry.

J

joule (178): the SI unit of energy: $1 \, J = 1 \, kg \cdot m^2 \cdot s^{-2}$.

K

karat (896): a unit for expressing the amount of gold in alloys. Pure gold is 24 karat.

ketone (1007): a class of organic compounds that has the general formula $\underset{\underset{O}{\parallel}}{RCR'}$.

kinetic energy (178): the energy of a body due to its motion. The SI unit of kinetic energy is the joule, J. The formula relating the kinetic energy to the speed of the body is $E = \frac{1}{2}mv^2$, where m is the mass of the body and v is its speed.

kinetic theory of gases (178): a molecular theory of gases. A gas is considered as mostly empty space. The gas molecules are viewed as tiny spheres in constant motion. The molecules are traveling about at high speeds and are continually colliding with each other and with the walls of the container. The pressure of a gas is due to the collisions of the molecules of the gas with the walls of the container.

K_p (573): an equilibrium constant expressed in terms of equilibrium partial pressures of products and/or reactants.

L

labile complex (931): a complex that exchanges its ligands rapidly with other available ligands.

lanthanide series (57, 60, 304): the inner transition metal series that is headed by lanthanum. The lanthanide series contains the elements lanthanum ($Z = 57$) through ytterbium ($Z = 70$).

lattice energy (351): the energy released when isolated negative ions and isolated positive ions combine to form an ionic crystal.

law of concentration action (571): states that the equilibrium constant expression for a reaction is given by the ratio of product equilibrium concentrations to reactant equilibrium concentrations, with each concentration factor raised to a power equal to the stoichiometric coefficient of that species in the balanced equation. Pure liquids and solids, whose concentrations cannot be varied, do not appear in the equilibrium constant expression.

law of conservation of mass (5): states that in an ordinary chemical reaction, the total mass of the reacting substances is equal to the total mass of the products formed.

law of constant composition (6): states that the mass percentage of each element in a compound is always the same, regardless of the source of the compound or of how the compound is prepared.

law of multiple proportions (14): states that if two elements combine in more than one way, then the mass of one element that combines with a fixed mass of the other element will always be in the ratio of small whole numbers.

Le Châtelier's principle (580): if a chemical reaction at equilibrium is subjected to a change in conditions that displaces the reaction from equilibrium, then the direction in which the reaction proceeds toward a new equilibrium state will be such as to at least partially offset the change in conditions.

lead storage battery (827): a group of the following cells arranged in series:

$$\ominus Pb(s) \,|\, PbSO_4(s) \,|\, H_2SO_4(aq) \,|\, PbO_2(s),$$

$$PbSO_4(s) \,|\, Pb(s) \oplus$$

The 12-V lead storage battery has six of these cells in series.

Lewis acid (676): an electron-pair acceptor.

Lewis base (676): an electron-pair donor.

Lewis electron-dot formula (256): a pictorial representation of an atom. The nucleus and inner-core electrons are indicated by the chemical symbol of the atom and the outer electrons are indicated by dots placed around the chemical symbol.

Lewis formula (366): the electron-dot formula for a molecule or other species. Covalent bonds are indicated by lines or by electron-dot pairs.

ligand (407, 912): an anion or a neutral molecule that binds to metal ions to form a complex ion. Also, an atom that is bonded to a central atom in a molecule or ion.

ligand-substitution reaction (912): a reaction involving a change in ligands attached to the central metal ion in a complex.

limiting reactant (102): the reactant that is consumed completely in a reaction in which nonstoichiometric amounts of reactants are allowed to react.

line spectrum (258): the resolution of the components of electromagnetic radiation that contains radiation of only a few discrete wavelengths. The spectrum consists of a few lines corresponding to these wavelengths.

liquid (155): the physical state of matter having the properties of fixed volume, assumption of the shape of its container, and very small compressibility.

litmus paper (143, 699): a paper impregnated with litmus, a vegetable substance that is red in acidic solutions and blue in basic solutions.

localized bond orbital (435): the orbital that describes the bonding electrons in a covalent bond between two atoms. The bonding electrons are concentrated primarily in the region between the two atoms joined by the covalent bond.

lock-and-key theory (1043): the postulate that an enzyme acts as a specific template to one of the reactants to catalyze the chemical reaction.

logarithm (652): the power to which 10 must be raised to attain a number. The logarithm of a number a is $\log a = x$ such that $a = 10^x$.

London force (477): the attractive force between nonpolar molecules and atoms arising from the correlation of the electron distributions.

lone electron pair or lone pair (366): a pair of electrons that are not shared between two atoms in a molecule.

low-spin configuration (926): a d-electron configuration in a complex in which the d electrons pair up in the lower-energy d orbitals before they occupy the higher-energy set of d orbitals.

Lyman series (269): the series of lines in the hydrogen atomic spectrum due to transitions from higher states $(n > 1)$ to the ground state $(n = 1)$.

M

macromolecules (1020): molecules that contain thousands of atoms and usually have lengths in the range 100 to 100,000 nm. Most polymers are macromolecules.

magic numbers (948): the numbers 2, 8, 20, 28, 50, 82, and 126. Nuclei that contain a magic number of protons or neutrons are particularly stable and abundant in nature.

magnetic quantum number (278): the quantum number, m_l, that determines the spatial orientation of an orbital. The allowed values of m_l are $-l, \ldots, -1, 0, +1, \ldots, +l$ or $-l \leqslant m_l \leqslant l$.

main-group elements (60): the elements in groups headed by the numbers 1 through 8 in the periodic table.

malleable (18): able to be rolled into thin sheets.

manometer (157): a device used to measure the pressure of a gas. It consists of a U-shaped tube partially filled with mercury. One end of the tube is evacuated and sealed. The other end is attached to the vessel containing the gas. (See Figure 5-2 in the text.)

Markovnikov's rule (997): states that when HX adds to an unsaturated hydrocarbon, the hydrogen atom becomes bonded to the carbon atom in the double or triple bond already bearing the larger number of hydrogen atoms.

mass balance (718): the sum of the concentrations of all species that contain a particular atom must equal the total concentration of that atom. For example, for a 0.10 M $HNO_2(aq)$ solution the mass balance is

$$0.10 \text{ M} = [HNO_2] + [NO_2^-]$$

mass number (20): the total number of protons and neutrons in an atom. The mass number is designated by the symbol A.

mass spectrometer (23): an instrument used to measure the relative masses and amounts of atoms and molecules present in a sample.

mass spectrometry (428): the study of the fragmentation patterns of molecular ions produced in a mass spectrometer. Mass spectra often are used to identify compounds.

mass spectrum (428): a plot of the relative numbers of ions of various masses versus the mass of the ions; obtained from a mass spectrometer.

mean free path, l (181): the average distance a gas molecule travels between collisions. The mean free path depends on the pressure and the temperature. (See Equation 5-15.)

melting-point curve (498): a plot of the pressure at which the solid and liquid phases of a substance are in equilibrium versus the temperature.

mercaptans (248): organic compounds that contain the —SH group.

mercury battery (828): a battery using the cell

$$^{\ominus}\text{steel}\,|\,Zn(s)\,|\,ZnO(s)\,|\,KOH(aq, 40\%)$$
$$|\,HgO(s)\,|\,Hg(l)\,|\,\text{steel}^{\oplus}$$

mesosphere (316): the region above the stratosphere wherein the temperature decreases with altitude.

meta **(1003):** designation for disubstituted benzenes with substituents at the 1 and 3 positions.

metal (3): a substance that has the following properties: it has a characteristic luster; it can be rolled into sheets; it can be drawn into wires; it can be melted and cast into various shapes; and it is a good conductor of electricity and heat. About three fourths of the elements are metals. All the metals except mercury are solids at 20°C.

method of half-reactions (790): a system of balancing oxidation-reduction equations in which the oxidation half-reaction and the reduction half-reaction are balanced separately.

method of initial rates (610): a means of obtaining the rate law from a determination of the reaction rate at the start of the reaction during which time the concentrations of the reactants do not change appreciably.

metric system (28): a system of scientific units of measurement based on the meter, the kilogram, and the second as the base units of length, mass, and time, respectively.

metric ton (100): a mass of 1000 kg or 2205 lb.

micelles (738): small, spherical grease-soap droplets that are soluble in water as a result of the polar groups on the surface.

midpoint (707): the point on the titration curve that is halfway between the starting point and the equivalence point.

mol (87): the symbol for the unit mole.

molality (531): a concentration scale for a solute in a solution. The molality, m, is defined as

$$m = \frac{\text{moles of solute}}{\text{kilograms of solvent}}$$

The units of molality are $mol \cdot kg^{-1}$.

molar bond enthalpy, $\bar{H}$(bond) (216): the enthalpy change associated with the dissociation of one mole of a given type of bond. The units are joules per mole, $J \cdot mol^{-1}$, or kilojoules per mole, $kJ \cdot mol^{-1}$.

molar enthalpy of fusion (467): the energy that is required to melt one mole of a substance. It is denoted by $\Delta \bar{H}_{fus}$. The SI units are $kJ \cdot mol^{-1}$.

molar enthalpy of sublimation (478): the energy that is required to sublime one mole of a substance. It is denoted by $\Delta \bar{H}_{sub}$. The SI units are $kJ \cdot mol^{-1}$.

molar enthalpy of vaporization (468): the energy that is required to vaporize one mole of a substance. It is denoted by $\Delta \bar{H}_{vap}$. The SI units are $kJ \cdot mol^{-1}$.

molar entropy of fusion, $\Delta \bar{S}_{fus}$ (861): $\Delta \bar{S}_{fus}$ is the entropy change that occurs upon melting. The value of $\Delta\bar{S}_{fus}$ is given by

$$\Delta\bar{S}_{fus} = \frac{\Delta\bar{H}_{fus}}{T_m}$$

where $\Delta\bar{H}_{fus}$ is the molar enthalpy of fusion and T_m is the melting point in kelvins.

molar entropy of vaporization, $\Delta\bar{S}_{vap}$ (862): is the entropy change upon vaporization. The value of $\Delta\bar{S}_{vap}$ is given by

$$\Delta\bar{S}_{vap} = \frac{\Delta\bar{H}_{vap}}{T_b}$$

where $\Delta\bar{H}_{vap}$ is the molar enthalpy of vaporization and T_b is the boiling point in kelvins.

molar heat capacity, $\bar{C}_p$ (219): the heat capacity per mole of a substance. The SI unit of molar heat capacity is $J \cdot K^{-1} \cdot mol^{-1}$.

molar heat of formation, $\Delta\bar{H}_f^\circ$ (207): the enthalpy change for the reaction in which one mole of a substance at 1 atm is formed from the elements at 1 atm.

molar mass (173): the mass in grams of one mole of a substance. The units of molar mass are $g \cdot mol^{-1}$.

molar quantity (173): the amount of a substance that contains one mole of the substance.

molar volume (170): the volume occupied by one mole of a substance. At 0°C and 1.00 atm the molar volume of an ideal gas is equal to 22.4 L.

molarity (105): the concentration of a solution expressed as the number of moles of solute per liter of solution. The units of molarity are $mol \cdot L^{-1}$ and the symbol of molarity is M.

mole (87): the quantity of a substance that is equal to its formula mass in grams. The official SI definition of the mole is the amount of substance of a system that contains as many elementary entities as there are atoms in exactly 0.012 kg of carbon-12. The symbol for the unit mole is mol.

mole fraction (528): an expression for the concentration of a solution. In a solution containing n_1 moles of solvent and n_2 moles of solute, the mole fraction of the solvent is defined as

$$X_1 = \frac{n_1}{n_1 + n_2}$$

The mole fraction is a unitless quantity.

molecular compound (124): a compound composed of molecules (as opposed to ions); such compounds generally have low melting and low boiling points.

molecular crystal (366): a three-dimensional ordered array of molecules.

molecular diameter, σ (181): the experimentally determined diameter of a molecule.

molecular formula (95): the chemical formula of a molecular compound; gives the number of atoms of each element that make up one formula unit of the compound.

molecular ion (427): an ion produced by the loss or gain of an electron by a molecule.

molecular mass (13): the mass of a molecule relative to the atomic mass of carbon-12. The molecular mass is the sum of the atomic masses of the atoms that make up the molecule.

molecular orbital (434): a wave function that describes an electron in a molecule.

molecular orbital theory (449): a theory of bonding based on orbitals that extend over two or more atoms.

molecular sieves (518): synthetic zeolites with channels and cavities of various sizes; used to separate molecules of different sizes.

molecular substance (86): a substance that is composed of more than one atom.

molecular vibrations (422): vibrational (back and forth) motions of the atoms in a molecule.

molecule (5, 7): an entity in which two or more atoms are joined together.

monomers (1020): small molecules that are joined together to form a polymer.

monosaccharide (1046): a carbohydrate that contains just one ring.

N

natural abundance (22): the percentage of an isotope of an element that is present in the naturally occurring element.

natural law (5): a concise summary of experimental observations regarding some aspects of the behavior of matter in nature.

Nernst equation (814): the quantitative relationship between the cell voltage E and the value of Q. At 25°C the Nernst equation is given by

$$E = E^\circ - \left(\frac{0.0592\text{ V}}{n}\right)\log Q$$

where $E°$ is the standard cell voltage and n is the number of moles of electrons transferred in the cell reaction as written.

net ionic equation (140): an ionic equation written with the omission of the spectator ions.

net reaction rate (631): the difference between the forward reaction rate and the reverse reaction rate.

neutral anion (672): an anion that does not react with water in aqueous solution to produce either $H_3O^+(aq)$ or $OH^-(aq)$.

neutral cation (672): a cation that does not react with water in aqueous solution to produce either $H_3O^+(aq)$ or $OH^-(aq)$.

neutral solution (649): an aqueous solution in which $[H_3O^+] = [OH^-]$.

neutralization reaction (142): a reaction between an acid and a base.

neutron (19): a subatomic particle that has almost the same mass as a proton and has no charge.

neutron activation analysis (957): an analytical method to measure trace quantities of elements. The sample is irradiated by a beam of neutrons; the nuclear products emit γ-rays of energies that are characteristic of each isotope.

nickel-cadmium battery (828): a battery utilizing the cell

$$^\ominus\text{steel}\,|\,\text{Cd}(s)\,|\,\text{Cd(OH)}_2(s)\,|\,\text{LiOH}(aq)\,|\,\text{NiOOH}(s),$$
$$\text{Ni(OH)}_2(s)\,|\,\text{steel}^\oplus$$

nitride (200): a compound that contains the nitride ion, N^{3-}.

nitrogen fixation (194): a process whereby $N_2(g)$ is converted into nitrogen-containing compounds.

noble-gas outer electron configuration (335): the outer electron configuration ns^2np^6. Metal atoms may attain a noble-gas outer electron configuration by losing electrons. Nonmetal atoms attain a noble-gas outer electron configuration by gaining electrons.

noble gases (55): the elements that appear in the extreme right-hand column of the periodic table. The noble gases are helium, neon, argon, krypton, xenon, and radon. The noble gases are relatively unreactive and were once called the inert gases.

nodal surface (276): a surface over which the value of an orbital is zero.

nonelectrolyte (343): a substance that dissolves in water to produce solutions that do not conduct an electric current.

nonmetal (3): a substance that does not have the properties of a metal. The nonmetals are not uniform in their physical appearance or chemical properties.

nonpolar bond (386): a pure covalent bond.

normal boiling point (483): the temperature at which the equilibrium vapor pressure of a liquid equals exactly 1 atm.

n-type semiconductor (513): a semiconductor produced when atoms with five valence electrons are added in minute amounts to silicon or germanium; n stands for negative.

nuclear equation (944): an equation representing a nuclear reaction.

nuclear magnetic resonance (NMR) (425): absorption of radio wave region electromagnetic energy by a sample in a magnetic field.

nuclear reactor (968): a device using a controlled chain reaction to produce thermal energy to power a heat engine.

nucleon (943): a proton or a neutron in a nucleus.

nucleotide (1050): a monomer of DNA or RNA that consists of a sugar, a phosphate group, and a nitrogen-containing ring compound called a base.

nucleus (19): that (central) part of an atom in which is concentrated essentially all the mass and all the positive charge of the atom.

O

octahedron (403): a regular solid body that has six vertices and eight faces, each of which is an identical equilateral triangle. All six vertices are equivalent.

octet rule (368): states that many elements form covalent bonds so as to end up with eight electrons in their outer shells. The octet rule is particularly useful for compounds that contain carbon, nitrogen, oxygen, and fluorine.

open structure (477): a crystal structure determined primarily by hydrogen bonding.

opposite spins (292): spins in opposite directions. Two electrons that have opposite spins have different values of m_s.

optical diffraction pattern (488): the array of light spots produced when light from a point source passes through an array of small holes.

optical isomer (1034): nonsuperimposable isomers that are mirror images of each other.

orbital (272): a one-electron wave function.

organic acid (1008): an organic compound that contains dissociable protons.

organic compound (981): a compound that contains carbon atoms.

ortho **(1003):** designation for disubstituted benzenes with substituents at the 1 and 2 positions.

osmosis (539): the spontaneous passage of a solvent (usually water) from a dilute solution to a more concentrated solution through a semipermeable membrane.

osmotic pressure (539): the hydrostatic pressure produced in the process of the passage of a solvent through a rigid semipermeable membrane from a dilute solution to a more concentrated solution. The osmotic pressure, π, is given approximately by the equation $\pi = RTM_c$, where R is the gas constant, T is the absolute temperature, and M_c is the colligative molarity of the solution.

Ostwald process (197): the conversion of ammonia to nitric acid involving the oxidation of NH_3 to NO_2 and the dissolution of NO_2 in water.

outer electron (254): an electron in the shell with the highest value of the principle quantum number n.

oxidation (69): a process that involves an increase in the oxidation state of an atom. Oxidation involves a loss of electrons.

oxidation half-reaction (789): the half-reaction in which electrons appear on the right-hand side.

oxidation state (782): a number assigned to an atom in a chemical species by a set of rules based on the number of electrons and on the electronegativities of the various atoms in the species.

oxidation-reduction reaction (69, 781): a chemical reaction involving a transfer of electrons from one species to another.

oxidizing agent (788): the reactant that contains the atom that is reduced in an electron-transfer reaction.

oxyacid (131, 852): an inorganic acid that contains oxygen atoms.

ozone layer (325): the region between 15 and 30 km in altitude in the atmosphere that contains ozone, O_3, produced photochemically by the action of solar ultraviolet light on oxygen.

P

p **orbital (275):** an orbital for which $l = 1$. All *p* orbitals are cylindrically symmetric. There are three *p* orbitals for each value of $n \geqslant 2$.

para **(1003):** designation for disubstituted benzenes with substituents at the 1 and 4 positions.

parallel spins (297): spins in the same direction. Electrons that have parallel spins have the same value of m_s.

paramagnetic (455): magnetized by an external magnetic field and consequently attracted to the region between the poles of a magnet. Paramagnetic molecules contain at least one unpaired electron.

partial pressure (176): the pressure exerted by one component in a mixture of gases.

particle accelerator (960): an instrument that is capable of producing high-velocity particles.

pascal (160): the SI unit of pressure. A pascal, Pa, is equal to 1 newton per square meter, $1 \text{ N} \cdot \text{m}^{-2}$; 1 kilopascal, kPa, corresponds to about $\frac{1}{100}$ of an atmosphere.

Pauli exclusion principle (291): the principle that no two electrons in the same atom can have the same set of four quantum numbers.

peptide bond (1035): the bond formed when the amino group on one amino acid reacts with the carboxylic acid group on another amino acid. The peptide bond is the carbon-nitrogen bond in

$$\begin{array}{c} \quad\quad | \quad\quad\quad | \\ -\text{C}-\text{N}- \\ \quad\; \| \quad\quad | \\ \quad\;\text{O} \quad\;\; \text{H} \end{array}$$

percent dissociation (656): the percentage of an acid in aqueous solution that has transferred a proton to water.

period (58): a horizontal row of the periodic table.

periodic table of the elements (54): an arrangement of the elements according to increasing atomic number such that elements that have similar properties appear in the same column of the table.

peroxide (81): a compound with an oxygen-oxygen single bond (—O—O—). The peroxide ion is O_2^{2-}.

petroleum plantation (986): a farm to grow plants from which hydrocarbons can be extracted.

pH (652): a measure of the acidity of an aqueous solution. The pH is defined as $pH \equiv -\log [H_3O^+]$.

pH meter (655): an instrument used to determine pH by means of electrochemical measurements.

pH transition range of an indicator (697–698): the pH region in which the acid form and the base form of an indicator are present simultaneously in similar amounts. The pH range is equal to $pK_{ai} \pm 1$, where K_{ai} is the acid dissociation constant of the indicator.

phase diagram (498): a simultaneous plot of the equilibrium vapor pressure curve, the equilibrium sublimation pressure curve, and the solid-liquid equilibrium curve (melting-point curve) of a substance.

photochemical smog (324): an especially irritating smog produced by the action of sunlight on a mixture of oxides of nitrogen, oxygen, and hydrocarbons in the atmosphere.

photodissociation (324): the dissociation of a molecule produced by light absorption.

photoelectron spectroscopy (454): the measurement of the photon energies required to eject electrons from gaseous molecules.

photoelectron spectrum (454): a plot of the photon energies required to eject electrons from a gaseous molecule.

photoionization (327): ionization of atoms and molecules produced by light.

photon (263): packet of energy that constitutes electromagnetic energy. The energy of one photon is given by $E = h\nu$.

photosynthesis (77): the conversion of CO_2 and H_2O into carbohydrates and O_2 in plants, a process that is driven by the energy of absorbed sunlight.

π-bond (442): the result of two electrons occupying a π-orbital.

π-orbital (442): a localized bond orbital that is the result of combining p atomic orbitals from different atoms. The cross section of a π-orbital is similar to that of an atomic p orbital.

π^*-orbital (451): designation for an antibonding π-orbital.

pig iron (900): iron obtained directly from a blast furnace.

PIXE (particle-induced X-ray emission) (959): an analytical method that is used to measure quantities of elements in very small samples. A sample that is irradiated with a beam of protons yields nuclear products that emit X-rays of energies that are characteristic of each isotope.

pK_a (666): a measure of the strength of an acid. The value of pK_a is given by $pK_a \equiv -\log K_a$.

pK_b (666): a measure of the strength of a base. The value of pK_b is given by $pK_b \equiv -\log K_b$.

planar (398): two-dimensional; flat.

Planck's constant (262): the proportionality constant, h, that relates the energy, E, and frequency, ν, of electromagnetic radiation. The equation is $E = h\nu$, where $h = 6.626 \times 10^{-34}$ J·s.

polar bond (386): a covalent bond in which the electron pair is not shared equally by each atom. The electron pair is more likely to be found near one atom than near the other atom.

polyatomic ion (126): an ion that consists of more than one atom.

polyatomic molecule (434): a molecule composed of three or more atoms.

polydentate ligand (920): a ligand that attaches to a metal ion at more than one coordination position.

polymer (1020): a long chainlike molecule that is formed by joining together many small molecules called monomers.

polymerization (1021): a reaction in which monomers combine to form a polymer.

polynucleotide (1050): a polymer made up of nucleotides.

polypeptide (1036): a molecule composed of a chain of amino acids joined together by peptide bonds.

polypeptide backbone (1036): the chain in a polypeptide to which the amino acid side groups are attached.

polyprotic acid (717): an acid that can donate more than one proton per acid molecule.

polysaccharide (1046): a polymer composed of monosaccharides.

positional disorder (859): the distribution of the particles of a substance over positions in space.

positron (945): a particle that has the same mass as an electron but a positive charge.

precipitate (148): an insoluble product of a reaction that occurs in solution.

pressure (157): force per unit area. Gas pressure is the force exerted by a gas per unit area on the wall of its container. Common units of pressure are the torr and the standard atmosphere, atm. The SI unit of pressure is the pascal, Pa (1 atm = 760 torr = 101.3 kPa = 14.7 psi).

primary alcohol (1006): an alcohol in which the —OH group is attached to a carbon that is attached to only one other carbon atom, as in RCH_2OH.

primary battery (827): a nonrechargeable battery.

primary structure (1037): the order of the amino acid units in a polypeptide.

primary water treatment (739): the use of physical processes such as filtration, sedimentation, and coprecipitation to remove solid matter from impure water. Bacteria are destroyed by bubbling chlorine through the water.

principal energy level (272): the energy level or shell designated by the principal quantum number, n.

principal quantum number (272): the integer, n, that specifies the energy of the electron in the hydrogen atom. The principal quantum number can take on the values 1, 2, 3, ...

probability density (272): the probability that an electron will be found in a small volume, ΔV, surrounding the point (x, y, z). The probability density is given by $\psi^2 \Delta V$, where ψ^2 is the square of the wave function.

product (45): a substance that is formed in a chemical reaction.

protein (1032): a naturally occurring polypeptide.

proton (47): a subatomic particle that has a positive charge equal in magnitude but opposite in sign to that of an electron, and a mass almost equal to that of a hydrogen atom.

proton acceptor (648): a species capable of accepting a proton from an acid.

proton donor (648): a species capable of donating a proton to a base.

proton-transfer reaction (648): a reaction in which a proton is transmitted from one species to another. It is also called a protonation reaction.

protonation reaction (648): a reaction involving the transfer of a proton from one species to another. It is also called a proton-transfer reaction.

pseudo-noble-gas outer electron configuration (335): the outer electron configuration $ns^2np^6nd^{10}$ where $n = 3, 4, 5, ...$

p-type semiconductor (514): a semiconductor produced when atoms with three valence electrons are added in minute amounts to silicon or germanium; p stands for positive.

pure covalent bond (386): a bond in which the electron pair is shared equally by each atom joined by the covalent bond.

pure ionic bond (386): an electrostatic bond formed when one electron from one atom is transferred completely to another atom.

Q

Q/K (586): the value of the ratio of the reaction quotient to the equilibrium constant of a chemical reaction. The numerical value of Q/K indicates the direction in which a nonequilibrium reaction system spontaneously proceeds toward equilibrium.

quadratic equation (577): an algebraic equation that can put in the form $ax^2 + bx + c = 0$, where a, b, and c are known and x is unknown.

quadratic formula (577): the solution to a quadratic equation. The two roots of a quadratic equation are given by

$$x = \frac{-b \pm \sqrt{b^2 - 4ac}}{2a}$$

qualitative analysis (764): the determination of the species present in a sample.

qualitative observation (5): expression of the result of an observation or experiment as general (nonnumerical) characteristics.

quanta (262): discrete units of electromagnetic energy.

quantitative analysis (764): the determination of the amount of each species in a sample.

quantitative measurement (5): expression of the result of an observation or experiment as a number.

quantized (266): restricted to certain fixed values.

quantum number (272): an integer or half-integer that, in sets of four, characterizes the energy states of atoms.

quantum theory (266): the theory that predicts the quantized energies of particles.

R

radioactive (17, 944): decompose spontaneously by the emission of a small particle such as an alpha or a beta particle.

radioactive decay (946): the process in which a radioactive nucleus emits a particle and transforms to another nucleus.

radioactivity (17, 944): property of certain nuclei that spontaneously emit small particles such as alpha particles or beta particles.

radiocarbon dating (954): carbon-14 dating.

radioisotope (944): a radioactive isotope.

Raoult's law (530): states that the equilibrium vapor pressure of a solvent over a solution is proportional to the mole fraction of the solvent. The equation is $P_1 = X_1 P_1^\circ$, where P_1 is the equilibrium vapor pressure of the solution, P_1° is the equilibrium vapor pressure of the pure solvent, and X_1 is the mole fraction of the solvent.

rare-earth element (60): any member of the lanthanides, or the series of elements lanthanum ($Z = 57$) through ytterbium ($Z = 70$). The rare earths occur because of the sequential filling of the $4f$ orbitals.

Raschig synthesis (199): the formation of hydrazine, N_2H_4, via the reaction of ammonia with sodium hypochlorite.

rate (601): a measure of how fast a quantity is changing with time.

rate constant (607): the proportionality constant between the reaction rate and the concentrations of the reactants that appear in the rate law.

rate-determining step (620): the step in a reaction mechanism that controls the overall reaction rate. The rate-determining step is much slower than any other step in the reaction mechanism.

rate law (605): the rate of a reaction expressed in terms of the concentration of the species that affect the reaction rate.

rate of crystallization (525): the number of moles of solute that crystallize from a solution per second.

rate of solution (525): the number of moles of solute that dissolve per second.

reactant (45): a substance consumed in a chemical reaction; it appears on the left side of the chemical equation.

reaction mechanism (620): the sequence of elementary processes by which reactants are converted to products.

reaction quotient, Q (584): the ratio of arbitrary or initial product concentrations to arbitrary or initial reactant concentrations, with each concentration factor raised to a power equal to the stoichiometric coefficient of that species in the balanced equation. Pure liquids and solids do not appear in the reaction quotient expression. For the balanced chemical equation

$$aA(g) + bB(soln) + cC(s) \rightleftharpoons$$
$$xX(g) + yY(soln) + zZ(l)$$

the reaction quotient is given by

$$Q = \frac{[X]_0^x [Y]_0^y}{[A]_0^a [B]_0^b}$$

reaction rate (602): the rate at which a reactant, A, is consumed or a product, P, is produced. The rate is defined as

$$\text{rate} = \frac{-\Delta[A]}{\Delta t} = \frac{\Delta[P]}{\Delta t}$$

Units of the reaction rate are $M \cdot s^{-1}$ (moles per liter per second).

reactivity series (136): an ordering of the metals according to their chemical reactivity.

redox reaction (781): an oxidation-reduction or electron-transfer reaction.

reducing agent (788): the reactant that contains the atom that is oxidized in an electron-transfer reaction.

reduction (69, 787): a process that involves a decrease in the oxidation state of an atom. Reduction involves a gain of electrons.

reduction half-reaction (789): the half-reaction in which electrons appear on the left-hand side.

relative humidity (484): the ratio of the partial pressure of the water vapor in the atmosphere to the equilibrium vapor pressure of water at the same temperature times 100:

$$\text{relative humidity} = \frac{P_{H_2O}}{P_{H_2O}^\circ} \times 100$$

resonance (379): the procedure of superimposing each of the possible Lewis formulas for a molecule or ion to obtain a more accurate picture of the electron distribution.

resonance form (379): one of the possible Lewis formulas that can be written for a molecule or an ion without altering the positions of the nuclei.

reverse osmosis (540): the process in which the solvent (usually water) passes through a rigid semipermeable membrane from a solution to the pure solvent as a result of applying to the solution a pressure in excess of the osmotic pressure.

reverse rate (566): the rate of the reverse (right to left) reaction.

reverse reaction (631): the formation of the reactants from the reaction products, or the reaction that proceeds right to left for the equation as written.

rhizobium (198): a bacterium that invades the roots of leguminous plants and fixes nitrogen, which is then used by the plants.

RNA (1050): ribonucleic acid. RNA is a polynucleotide composed of the sugar ribose, the phosphate group, and the four bases adenine, uracil, guanine, and cytosine.

rotational motion (466): the rotation of a molecule in space.

S

s orbital (275): an orbital for which $l = 0$. All s orbitals are spherically symmetric.

sacrificial anode (904): a reactive piece of metal that is electrically connected to a less active metal and that is preferentially oxidized, thereby protecting the less active metal against corrosion.

salt (142): an ionic compound formed in a neutralization reaction or in the reaction of a metal and a nonmetal.

salt bridge (806): a concentrated electrolyte solution suspended in a gel that is used to make electrical contact between two different electrolyte solutions that are part of an electrochemical cell.

saturated hydrocarbon (984): a hydrocarbon in which the bonding about each carbon atom is tetrahedral. No more hydrogen atoms can be added to any carbon atom. (See alkane.)

saturated solution (526): a solution in which no more solute can be dissolved.

Schrödinger equation (266): the central equation of quantum theory; it takes into account the wave nature of electrons and yields the discrete energy levels of atoms and molecules.

second excited state (267): the second available energy state above the ground state.

second ionization energy (252): the minimum energy required to remove an electron from an A^+ ion to produce the A^{2+} ion.

second-order rate law (608): a rate law in which the reaction rate is proportional to the second power of the concentration of a reactant. The rate law is of the form rate $= k[A]^2$ or rate $= k[A][B]$.

secondary alcohol (1006): an alcohol in which the —OH group is attached to a carbon that is attached to two other carbon atoms, as in

$$RCH_2\underset{\underset{\textstyle OH}{|}}{C}HCH_3$$

secondary battery (827): a battery that is rechargeable.

secondary structure (1040): the coiled helical portion in different regions of a protein chain.

secondary water treatment (740): the use of aerobic bacteria and oxygen to oxidize soluble organic compounds to CO_2 and H_2O.

semiconductor (60): a semimetal. A semimetal conducts electricity and heat less well than metals but better than nonmetals.

semimetal (59): an element that has properties intermediate to metals and nonmetals.

semipermeable membrane (539): a membrane that allows the passage of only certain species, for example, water molecules.

shell (254, 292): the energy level designated by the principal quantum number, n. The $n = 1$ shell is called the K shell; the $n = 2$ shell, the L shell; the $n = 3$ shell, the M shell; and so forth.

shell structure (292): the arrangement of a group of electrons with similar energies around a nucleus.

side group (1032): the group —G in the amino acid

$$H_2N—\underset{\underset{G}{|}}{\overset{\overset{H}{|}}{C}}—COOH$$

σ-bond (437): a bond that occurs when a σ-orbital is occupied by two electrons of opposite spin.

σ-bond framework (442): all the σ-bonds that are formed by using sp^3, sp^2, sp, p, or s orbitals in a molecule or ion.

σ-orbital (437): a bonding molecular orbital that is cylindrically symmetric when viewed along a line drawn between the two nuclei joined by the covalent bond.

σ*-orbital (451): designation for an antibonding σ-orbital.

significant figures (25): the precision of a measured quantity as indicated by the number of digits used to express the result.

simple cubic unit cell (489): the unit cell in which the components of the crystal are located at the corners of a cube.

simplest formula (92): the formula of a substance derived from an analysis of the composition of the compound. It gives the relative number of atoms in the formula unit. (See molecular formula.)

single-replacement reaction (134): a reaction in which one element in a compound is replaced by another element.

slope (613): the ratio of the change in the vertical coordinate to the change in the horizontal coordinate, $\Delta y/\Delta x$.

solid (155): the physical state of matter having the properties of fixed volume, fixed shape, and very small compressibility.

solubility (526, 744): the maximum quantity of solute that can be dissolved in a given quantity of solvent in ordinary circumstances.

solubility product constant (745): the equilibrium-constant expression obtained by applying the law of concentration action to the equilibrium between an ionic solid and its constituent ions in solution. The symbol is K_{sp}.

solubility rules (744): a set of guidelines that can be used to predict whether an ionic compound is soluble or insoluble in water.

solute (105, 524): a substance that is dissolved in another substance to form a solution.

solution (104, 523): a mixture of two or more substances that is uniform and homogeneous at the molecular level.

solvated electrons (362): a species that results when, for example, sodium metal is dissolved in liquid ammonia:

$$Na(s) \xrightarrow[NH_3(l)]{} Na^+(NH_3) + e^-(NH_3)$$

Solvay process (362): the commercial process used to manufacture $NaHCO_3(s)$ and $Na_2CO_3(s)$.

solvent (524): the substance in which a solute is dissolved to form a solution. The solvent is generally present in greater quantity than the solute.

sp orbital (445): one of the two equivalent hybrid orbitals obtained by the combination of an ns orbital and one np orbital on the same atom. The two sp orbitals point 180° from each other.

sp^2 orbital (441): one of the three equivalent hybrid orbitals obtained by the combination of an ns orbital and two np orbitals on the same atom. The three sp^2 orbitals point to the vertices of an equilateral triangle.

sp^3 orbital (436): one of the four equivalent hybrid atomic orbitals obtained by the combination of an ns orbital and the three np orbitals on the same atom. The four sp^3 orbitals point to the vertices of a tetrahedron.

space-filling molecular model (398): a model of a molecule that is constructed to represent the relative sizes of the atoms in the molecule and the angles between bonds.

specific activity (971): a measure of the activity of a radioactive substance; the number of nuclei that disintegrate per second per gram of radioactive isotope. (See Equation 24-8.)

specific heat, c_{sp} (219): the heat capacity per gram of substance. The SI unit of specific heat is joules per kelvin per gram, $J \cdot K^{-1} \cdot g^{-1}$.

spectator ion (140): an ion present in a solution that does not participate directly in a reaction.

spectrochemical series (929): an arrangement of ligands in order of increasing ability of the ligands to split the metal d orbitals: $Cl^- < F^- < H_2O < NH_3 < NO_2^- < CN^- < CO$.

spectroscopic method (422): any of a number of analytical methods that employ spectra to identify or measure the amounts of compounds.

spectrum (422): a plot of the electromagnetic energy absorbed versus the wavelength of the energy for a species.

speed of light (257): light travels with a speed of 3.00×10^8 m $\cdot$ s^{-1}. It is denoted by the symbol c.

spherically symmetric (273): characteristic of a function that depends only on the distance from a center and not on its direction in space.

spin down (292): the state in which the spin quantum number, m_s, is $-1/2$.

spin quantum number (280): the quantum number, m_s, that designates the spin state of an electron. The allowed values of m_s are $+\frac{1}{2}$ or $-\frac{1}{2}$.

spin up (292): the state in which the spin quantum number, m_s, is $+\frac{1}{2}$.

spontaneous (586): proceeding without external input.

standard atmosphere (atm) (160): a unit of pressure. One atmosphere is equal to 760 torr.

standard cell voltage (816): the voltage of an electrochemical cell when Q for the cell reaction is equal to 1. The standard cell voltage, $E°$, is related to the equilibrium constant for the reaction by the equation

$$E° = \left(\frac{0.0592 \text{ V}}{n} \right) \log K \text{ at } 25°C$$

where n is the number of moles of electrons transferred in the reaction as written.

standard enthalpy change, $\Delta H°_{rxn}$ (206, 868): the amount of energy absorbed or evolved as heat when all gases are at 1 atm and all solution species are at 1 M.

standard entropy, $S°$ (863): the entropy of a substance at 1 atm. If the substance is a solute, then its concentration is 1 M.

standard entropy change, $\Delta S°_{rxn}$ (868): the value of the entropy change for a reaction when all gases, solids, and liquids are at 1 atm and all solutes are at 1 M.

standard Gibbs free energy change, $\Delta G°_{rxn}$ (873): the value of ΔG_{rxn} when all gases are at one atm and all solution species are at one molar.

standard molar enthalpy of formation, $\Delta \bar{H}°_f$ (207, 868): the enthalpy change for the reaction in which one mole of substance at 1 atm is formed from the elements at 1 atm.

standard molar Gibbs free energy of formation (879): the Gibbs free energy change for the formation of a substance at standard conditions from its constituent elements. The standard molar Gibbs free energy of formation is denoted by $\Delta \bar{G}°_f$.

standard reduction voltage (818): the standard voltage, E^0, for a half-reaction based on the assignment of $E^0 \equiv 0$ for the electrode reaction

$$2H^+(aq, 1 \text{ M}) + 2e^- \longrightarrow H_2(g, 1 \text{ atm})$$

The standard cell voltage, $E°_{cell}$, is given by

$$E^0_{cell} = E^0_{right} - E^0_{left}$$

where E^0_{right} is the standard reduction voltage of the right electrode in an electrochemical cell and E^0_{left} is the standard reduction voltage of the left electrode in an electrochemical cell.

stationary state (267): one of the allowed energy states of an atom or a molecule.

steel (902): an alloy composed primarily of iron with variable amounts of carbon and other substances added to produce special properties.

stereoisomers (443): molecules with the same atom-to-atom bonding but different spatial arrangements of the atoms.

stereospecific reaction (1035): a reaction in which the relative orientations of the groups attached to a specific atom are unchanged.

stoichiometric coefficient (96): a numerical coefficient of a reactant or product species in a balanced chemical equation; a balancing coefficient.

stoichiometrically equivalent to, $\Leftrightarrow$ (92): a symbol that denotes a stoichiometric correspondence between two quantities.

stoichiometry (92): the procedures for the calculations of the quantities of elements or compounds involved in chemical reactions.

stratosphere (316): the region from 10 to 50 km in altitude that lies above the troposphere.

strong acid (650): an acid that is completely dissociated in aqueous solution.

strong base (650): a base that produces the greatest stoichiometric concentration of $OH^-(aq)$ possible in aqueous solution.

strong electrolyte (342): an electrolyte that is 100 percent or near 100 percent dissociated into ions in solutions.

structural chemistry (399): the area of chemistry in which the shapes and sizes of molecules are studied.

structural formula (982): a formula that indicates the various attachments of the atoms in a molecule.

structural isomers (984): compounds that have the same molecular formula but different arrangements of the atoms.

subatomic particle (16): one of the particles of which atoms are composed; a proton, neutron, or electron.

subcritical mass (967): a mass of a spontaneously fissionable substance that is insufficient to sustain a nuclear chain reaction.

sublimation (479): the process whereby a solid is converted directly to a gas.

sublimation pressure curve (498): a plot of the pressure of a vapor in equilibrium with its solid versus the temperature.

subshell (256, 292): the group of orbitals designated by a particular l value within a shell.

substitution reaction (134, 987): a single-replacement reaction.

substrate (1043): the reactant that binds to the enzyme in an enzyme-catalyzed reaction.

sugar (1047): a general name for monosaccharides and disaccharides.

sugar-phosphate backbone (1052): the chain in a polynucleotide to which the bases are attached. The nucleotides are joined by bonds with the oxygen atom at the five-carbon position on one nucleotide through a phosphate group to the three-carbon position on a second nucleotide.

supercooled (498): cooled below the triple point without the liquid freezing.

supercritical mass (967): a mass of a spontaneously fissionable substance that exceeds the mass necessary to sustain a nuclear chain reaction.

supernatant (767): the solution from which a substance is precipitated.

superoxide (81): a substance that contains the ion O_2^-, which is called the superoxide ion.

surface tension (486): the inward force that molecules at the surface of a liquid experience. The units are energy per unit area, $J \cdot m^{-2}$.

surfactant (487): a substance that lowers the surface tension of a liquid.

T

t_2 orbitals (933): the set of d orbitals of higher energy on a metal ion in a tetrahedral complex. The t_2 orbitals consist of d_{xy}, d_{xz}, and d_{yz}.

t_{2g} (922): the set of d orbitals of lower energy on a metal ion in an octahedral complex.

termination reaction (1022): a reaction that stops the growth of a polymer chain.

tertiary alcohol (1007): an alcohol in which the —OH group is attached to a carbon that is attached to three other carbon atoms, as in

$$\begin{array}{c} CH_3 \\ | \\ CH_3CCH_3 \\ | \\ OH \end{array}$$

tertiary structure (1040): the three-dimensional shape of a protein.

tertiary water treatment (740): use of specific chemical processes to remove specific chemical pollutants.

tetrahedral bond angle (399): the angle between two bonds formed by an atom whose bonds are directed toward the vertices of a tetrahedron. The tetrahedral bond angle is 109.5°.

tetrahedron (398): a regular solid body that has four equivalent vertices and four equivalent faces, each of which is an equilateral triangle.

tetravalent (399): bonded to four other atoms.

thermal decomposition (133): a decomposition reaction that occurs when the temperature of a substance is increased.

thermal disorder (859): the distribution of the available energy among the particles of a substance.

thermite reaction (136): a reaction between aluminum metal and a metal oxide that yields Al_2O_3 and the free metal.

thermochemistry (204): the study of the heat evolved or absorbed in chemical reactions.

thermodynamics (203): the study of energy transfers.

3d transition metal series (302): the series of 10 elements with atomic numbers 21 through 30.

titrant (701): the solution of acid (base) that is added to a solution of base (acid) during a titration.

titration (144, 701): the neutralization of a given volume of a basic (acidic) solution by slowly adding an acidic (basic) solution of known concentration until the base (acid) has been completely neutralized.

titration curve (701): a plot of the pH of the solution that results when an acid solution is titrated with a base solution (or when a base solution is titrated with an acid solution) as a function of the volume of the added solution.

torr (158): a convenient unit of pressure. The pressure of a gas is expressed as the height of a column of mercury that is supported by the pressure of the gas. One torr is one millimeter of mercury.

transition metal (60, 907): an element in the groups that are not headed by a number in the periodic table. They serve as a transition between the reactive Group 1 and Group 2 metals and the nonmetals.

translational motion (466): the movement of an entire molecule through space.

transuranium element (306, 960): an element of atomic number greater than that of uranium ($Z > 92$).

tridentate (920): a chelating ligand that attaches to three metal coordination positions.

trigonal bipyramid (402): a solid body that has five vertices and six equilateral triangular faces. A trigonal bipyramid has the shape of two triangular pyramids that share an equilateral triangular base.

trigonal planar (401): the shape of a molecule in which the three atoms bonded to a central atom lie at the vertices of an equilateral triangle with the central atom in the center of the triangle. All four atoms lie in the same two-dimensional surface.

trigonal pyramid (405): a solid body that has four vertices and four triangular faces. Three of the four faces are identical. The unique face serves as a triangular base for the pyramid.

triple bond (373): the bond formed between two atoms by three shared electron pairs.

triple point (498): a point on a phase diagram at which three phases of a substance coexist in equilibrium.

triplet code (1058): the sequence of three bases or nucleotides along a DNA segment that codes for a particular amino acid.

troposphere (316): the lowest region of the atmosphere, from 0 to 10 km above sea level. Accounts for 80 percent of the mass and contains essentially all of the earth's weather.

U

unit cell (489): the smallest subunit of a crystal lattice that contains all the structural information about the crystal.

unit conversion factor (29): an expression that is used to convert a physical quantity from one unit to another. It has the value of unity.

unsaturated hydrocarbon (994): a hydrocarbon that contains carbon atoms that are not bonded to four other atoms. Hydrogen atoms may be added to unsaturated hydrocarbons. Unsaturated hydrocarbons contain double and/or triple bonds.

unsaturated solution (526): a solution in which more solute can be dissolved.

uranium-lead dating (953): the determination of the age of a rock sample from the masses of uranium-238 and lead-206 in the sample.

V

valence band (512): the set of bonding orbitals that extend throughout a crystal and that are analogous to bonding orbitals in a molecule.

valence shell electron-pair repulsion (VSEPR) theory (400): the theory that the shape of a molecule is determined by the mutual repulsion of the electron pairs in the valence shell of the central atom.

valence shell electrons (301): the electrons that are located in the outermost occupied shell of an atom.

van der Waals constants (185): the two constants, a and b, that appear in the van der Waals equation. The values of a and b depend on the particular gas.

van der Waals equation (185): an equation that describes the behavior of a nonideal gas. The equation is

$$\left(P + \frac{n^2a}{V^2}\right)(V - nb) = nRT$$

where a and b are van der Waals constants, whose values depend on the particular gas.

van der Waals force (479): a general term for the attractive forces between molecules; van der Waals forces include dipole-dipole forces and London forces.

vapor pressure curve (482): a plot of the equilibrium vapor pressure of a liquid versus temperature.

vapor pressure lowering (530): the amount by which the equilibrium vapor pressure of a solution is less than the equilibrium vapor pressure of the pure solvent.

vector (387): a quantity that has both magnitude and direction.

vibrational motion (466): the back and forth movement of atoms about fixed relative positions in a molecule, or a solid.

visible region (258): the region of the electromagnetic spectrum from 400 to 700 nm.

volatile (118): readily converted from a liquid to a gas; a substance with a relatively high equilibrium vapor pressure.

volumetric flask (106): a precision-made piece of glassware that can be used to prepare a precise liquid volume.

W

water-gas reaction (206): the reaction in which steam is passed over hot carbon to produce a mixture of carbon monoxide and hydrogen:

$$C(s) + H_2O(g) \longrightarrow CO(g) + H_2(g)$$

wave function (272): a function that describes the positions of the electrons in an atom or a molecule. Wave function is denoted by ψ, and has the physical interpretation that $\psi^2 \Delta V$ is the probability that an electron is to be located in the little volume ΔV.

wave-particle duality (264): the concept that both light and matter appear to be particle-like under certain conditions and to be wavelike under other conditions.

wavelength, λ (257): the distance between successive maxima or minima of a wave. The symbol for wavelength is λ and a unit of wavelength is meters.

weak acid (651): an acid that is incompletely dissociated in aqueous solution or that reacts only partially with water.

weak base (651, 656): a base that reacts only partially with water.

weak electrolyte (343): a substance that dissolves in water to produce solutions that conduct an electric current poorly.

work, w (204): energy transferred when a force acts to cause a displacement of a system.

X

X-ray diffraction (265): the scattering of X-rays in a definite pattern by a crystalline substance.

X-ray diffraction pattern (488): the array of spots on an X-ray film that results when X-rays pass through a crystal.

X-ray fluorescence (XRF) spectroscopy (430): the use of X-rays to knock electrons out of atoms, which in turn leads to emission of X-rays with wavelengths characteristic of the particular atoms. XRF is used in chemical analysis.

Y

yield (590): the percent conversion of reactants to products in a chemical reaction.

Z

zeolite (518): an open-framework mineral composed of SiO_4^{4-} and AlO_4^{5-} tetrahedra in which each oxygen is shared by two tetrahedra. Small molecules can enter the cavities and channels in the open structure.

zone refining (511): a recrystallization method involving a moving melted zone that is used to prepare very high-purity crystals.

Physical Constants

Constant	Symbol	Value
atomic mass unit	amu	1.66056×10^{-27} kg
Avogadro's number	N	6.02205×10^{23} mol^{-1}
Bohr radius	a_0	5.292×10^{-11} m
Boltzmann constant	k	1.38066×10^{-23} J$\cdot$K^{-1}
charge of a proton	e	1.60219×10^{-19} C
Faraday constant	F	$96{,}485$ C$\cdot$mol^{-1}
gas constant	R	8.31441 J$\cdot$K$^{-1}\cdot$mol^{-1}
		0.08206 L$\cdot$atm$\cdot$K$^{-1}\cdot$mol$^-$
mass of an electron	m_e	9.10953×10^{-31} kg
		5.48580×10^{-4} amu
mass of a neutron	m_n	1.67495×10^{-27} kg
		1.00866 amu
mass of a proton	m_p	1.67265×10^{-27} kg
		1.00728 amu
Planck's constant	h	6.62618×10^{-34} J$\cdot$s
speed of light	c	2.997925×10^{8} m$\cdot$s^{-1}

SI Prefixes

Prefix	Multiple	Symbol	Prefix	Multiple	Symbol
tera	10^{12}	T	deci	10^{-1}	d
giga	10^{9}	G	centi	10^{-2}	c
mega	10^{6}	M	milli	10^{-3}	m
kilo	10^{3}	k	micro	10^{-6}	μ
			nano	10^{-9}	n
			pico	10^{-12}	p
			femto	10^{-15}	f
			atto	10^{-18}	a